# ARTS & IDEAS

# ARTS & IDEAS

### New and Brief Edition

## William Fleming
*Syracuse University*

**HOLT, RINEHART AND WINSTON, INC.**
New York   Chicago   San Francisco   Atlanta   Dallas
Montreal   Toronto   London   Sydney

*Editor* Dan W. Wheeler
*Picture editor* Joan Curtis
*Designer* Marlene Rothkin Vine
*Editorial assistant* Patricia Kearney

*Composition* New England Typographical Service, Inc., Bloomfield, Conn.
*Black-and-white photolithography* Concord Graphics, New York
*Black-and-white printing* Capital City Press, Montpelier, Vt.
*Color separations* Solzer and Hail, Inc., San Francisco
*Color printing* Lehigh Press, Pennsauken, N.J.
*Binding* Capital City Press, Montpelier, Vt.
9    138    10 9 8

# Preface

An age, like ours, whose existentialist society never ceases to question the meaning of human existence or attempt a description of the ineffable experience of being alive must be seen as ripe and mature in its ultimate susceptibility to humanism. In this its new edition *Arts & Ideas* remains passionately committed to the ever-renewing tradition of the humanities in the Western world — to the implications of those masterpieces of cultural self-realization found in the arts of painting, sculpture, architecture, literature, philosophy, and music. *Arts & Ideas* is a history of the principal styles of Western art as these crystallized in major centers of civilization at moments of high cultural achievement. Thus, specific works of art occupy foreground positions in the review given them, but they are also examined in their relationships to one another and against the background of ideas and issues that animated the life of their times. In the new edition, modern art — especially in its extension into the continuing present — has received a much-increased proportion of the book's space and the author's attention, relative to former editions. This occurs in acknowledgment of the powerful effect that contemporary communications have had in causing the past to belong so thoroughly to the present that even the most reductive abstractions and conceptually advanced works enjoy their radical forms by virtue of a modern sensibility whose vision is saturated with an awareness, often unconscious but certainly pervasive, of the entire tradition that produced it. The present has indeed become a continuing historical now, and the abundance of material found for the new chapter on the humanities since 1945, with its focus on the New York scene, gives testimony to the richness that surrounds us and to the validity of the vast cultural stores that supply our feast.

The history of man is much more than the sum of his military, political, and economic triumphs and failures. Long ago, Aristotle placed poetic truth above mere historical accuracy. To understand the spirit and inner life of a people — the joys, values, and drives that caused it to find life tolerable and meaningful—one must examine its art, literature, philosophy, dances, and music, because these are the instruments by which humankind takes its own measure, the expressions that provide the real record of man's experience as he lived it through perceptions and sensations both rational and irrational. Examined within the context of the times and places of their occurrence and the ideas that generated them, the humanities become the symbolic language in which creative artists addressed themselves to their fellow-men and in which they convey yet—with astonishing invention and conviction — their thoughts, fantasies, social commentary, satirical observations, self-revelations, and images of order. Monuments, cathedrals, mosaics, epics, dramas, sonatas, and songs all register the degree to which man — in his climaxes and eclipses — has attained civilization. A study of the arts in relation to the life and times that produced them provides not only a broader and deeper understanding of human behavior in the past but a truer, more resonant perception of the present, along with some sense of the future that awaits each new generation.

*Arts & Ideas* is a history in that its organization is based on the chronology within the evolution of Western culture, from Egypt and classical antiquity through the Middle Ages and the Renaissance to the modern world. Within the total chronological sweep of Western history, however, the book's content has been made selective so that there may be the kind of intensive concentration on the coincidence of time, place, and idea, on the complex of many interrelated factors that make a period in history culturally significant — that, in brief, have created what now, in retrospect, we can view as *style*.

To make the breadth of the analysis historically coherent, tabular chronologies have been prepared and placed at the beginning of chapters. They are like theater programs, giving times, events, and sites of action as well as casts of characters before the curtain rises on the dramas of the various style periods. Chapter introductions set the scenes for the creative activity to be described. Finally, the sections on ideas attempt to come to grips with the complexities of motivation, interpretation, and meaning.

The new edition now offered draws from what we have assumed to be the best features of *Arts & Ideas*, third edition (1968), and the briefer version entitled, for the simple sake of making a distinction, *Art, Music & Ideas* (1970). That is, the book has been considerably expanded beyond the spareness of the smaller volume while it retains something of the lean concision that seemed to be an improvement over the great heft of the larger and less selective volume.

The present version, for instance, is illustrated by 82 full-color plates, some 18 more than in the big 1968 edition, and a sequence of 439 black-and-white reproductions, representing an increase of well over 100 relative to the "essentials" volume published as *Art, Music & Ideas.* At the same time, the concept of selectivity has been carried forward and applied to the book's illustration program to the extent that only those works of visual art actually discussed in the text have been reproduced, but all monuments analyzed do indeed appear among the present grand total of 521 illustrations.

More significant, however, are the several ways that *Arts & Ideas* has been reworked and extended so as to make its particular approach still more persuasive in behalf of the validity of man's humane accomplishments for life in our own time. The most striking and substantial new feature, of course, is Chapter 22, now the largest in the book and the first devoted to the American scene, New York in the great cultural flowering that burst there during the period after the close of World War II. But enrichments, refinements, and corrections can be found in passages throughout the book. For instance, Rhys Carpenter's recent synthesis of archaeological data now informs the analysis of the Parthenon; in the chapter on ancient Rome, the explanation of the arch and its structural and aesthetic implications has been made more graphic; the same occurs for Gothic vault systems; in the Renaissance chapters Leonardo receives greater emphasis, and an example of his scientific drawing has been reproduced; later, there is deeper penetration of the emotional and psychological depth in the art of Antoine Watteau; included in the treatment of Beethoven's work is a fresh analysis of sonata form; in the 19th century more attention has been paid to English painting and its effect on later Continental developments; some of the sources of 20th-century abstraction are now cited in the art of Paul Gauguin and the Nabis; and throughout the book plans have been added to the illustrations for architecture. Finally, for the first time, a glossary — and quite a full one, with pronunciation guides where these seemed worthwhile — appears as a study aid in support of the text.

During the preparation of the first edition of *Arts & Ideas,* continuously since its publication in 1955, and throughout subsequent revisions and adaptations, I have incurred very heavy debts to the many teachers, colleagues, students, and friends whose contributions to the realization of this project have proved invaluable. This well-wishing host includes Professors Robert Branner, Kenneth J. Conant, Mario del Chiaro, Homer F. Edwards, Colin Eisler, Hardin Goodman, Evelyn Helmick, Anne Hoene Hoy, John Knowlton, Don Murray, Sidney Thomas, Cornelius Vermeule, and Audrey V. Wilson. Abraham Veinus, my distinguished associate at Syracuse University, made numerous suggestions for the text on contemporary music. From David Tatham and Frank Macomber I have received perceptive comments at numerous points along the way. Ronald Komrowski and Jean K. Wolf worked hard to make the new glossary the substantial thing it is. At Holt, Rinehart and Winston I am happy to acknowledge the staff for the devoted effort they made in behalf of the present volume. Editor Dan Wheeler bore a monumental burden at all stages of the book's preparation, during which he was supported by the able performance of Patricia Kearney, his editorial assistant, and Marlene Rothkin Vine, creator of the book's beautiful and appropriate design. Picture editor Joan Curtis collected the illustrations and negotiated the many attendant permissions. To all these I express my heartfelt gratitude.

*Syracuse, N.Y.*                                                         WF
*March 1974*

# Contents

# ARTS & IDEAS

# 1 Genesis of the Arts

## THE CREATIVE DRIVE

The human being is a creative animal. The fountainhead of creativity lies in the imagination, which manifests itself in the projection of images. This the author of Genesis knew full well when he described the creation of man. "And God said, Let us make man in our own image, after our likeness . . ." (Gen. 1:26). The key words are *create* and *image.* The divine principle, then, is creativity. And if God is conceived as the creative force, and man is created in His image, it follows that man also possesses creative powers in his own right, and in turn creates his gods, his ideas, his ideals, his arts, in his own human image. From the void the man-artist conceives an image, from nothingness he gives birth to being, out of chaos he brings order, by selection he makes relationships. Art, then, is the language in images by which man communicates his ideas, his conceptions of himself, his fellowmen, and his universe.

Many and varied are the visages of art, and together they reveal the basic urges and aspirations of mankind. The search for sights and sounds that delight the senses is only one of these many faces. Caveman may have drawn his animals to sharpen his eye before the chase. African tribal man donned the masks of his ancestors to invoke their strength in his struggle for life. Aboriginal man fashioned idols and fetishes to protect him from evil spirits. Medicine men sang magic incantations to restore health. In times of drought the American Indian performed rain dances. Egyptian rulers built and embellished their tombs to provide for their needs beyond the grave.

Through monuments, statues, paintings, dance rhythms, and the sounds of music, man reveals the divinity of his gods, the might of his rulers, the force of nature. For art begins in myth and magic, in imagery and image making, in tombs and temples, in war whoops and anguished outcries, in mating calls and work songs. And the artistic search leads to dark caverns and sunny shores, to sanctuaries and castles, to the abodes of the quick and the dead. Whether carving out a shelter in a cave, laying out sites for religious rites, or burying the dead, human beings—through art—concern themselves with the natural and supernatural, the real and unreal, the seen and unseen, the past and future, the transitory and eternal.

"The thing that hath been, it is that which shall be; and that which is done is that which shall be done: and there is nothing new under the sun." So said the wise writer of Ecclesiastes (1:9), for history holds up the mirror to man, to his present and future as well as to his past, to his achievements as well as to his potential. The search for beginnings is really the quest for continuations, since it is by knowing where he has been that man knows where he is going. The past is never really discarded, only encompassed and eventually transcended. For the story of mankind is like the French philosopher Henri Bergson's concept of duration—a continuous progress of the past, which gnaws into the future and which swells as it advances.

Man's first expressions in the arts are beclouded by the mists of prehistory. Whether he sought safety in the confines of caves or built mud huts, primitive man was involved with architecture. Man constructs to house his body and provide refuge for his spirit, to secure dwelling places for his family and sanctuaries for his gods. Ever since man caught sight of himself or saw a scene reflected in a still pool, he has been seized by the desire to create a human image or an imitation of nature. The bone whistles, reed flutes, and drumsticks found in caves and graves tell of the power of sound to evoke moods and echo the footsteps of man and beast in mysterious rites.

## STONE AGE BEGINNINGS

Antedating all other surviving forms of art are the rock drawings made by paleolithic man in the caves of southwestern France and the northern Spanish

# CHRONOLOGY / Prehistory, Egypt, and the Ancient Near East (all dates are approximate)

## Prehistory B.C.

| | |
|---|---|
| 33,000–10,000 | Paleolithic period (Old Stone Age) |
| 15,000–10,000 | Cave paintings and carvings in southwestern France and northern Spain |
| 10,000– 4,000 | Neolithic period (New Stone Age) Geometric art |

## Egypt B.C.

| | |
|---|---|
| 4000 | Egypt united into one country |
| 3100–2686 | Early Dynastic period |
| 2686–2181 | Old Kingdom (3rd–6th Dynasties) |
| 2650 | Imhotep, architect and physician, built step pyramid of Saqqara for King Zoser (3rd Dynasty) |
| 2590–2568 | Pyramid of Khufu (Cheops) |
| 2540–2514 | Pyramid of Khafre (Chephren), Great Sphinx |
| 2133–1991 | Middle Kingdom (11th–12th Dynasties) Golden age of arts and crafts |
| 1567–1085 | New Kingdom, or Empire (18th–20th Dynasties) |
| 1503–1482 | Reign of Queen Hatshepsut. Temple of Amon, Karnak |
| 1379–1362 | Reign of Akhenaton (Amenhotep IV). Bust of Queen Nefertiti |
| 1361–1352 | Reign of Tutankhamen |
| 1290–1225 | Colossi of Rameses II |
| 672 | Assyrian conquest |
| 525 | Persian conquest |
| 332 | Conquest by Alexander the Great |
| 332– 30 | Macedonian and Greek dynasties |
| 51– 30 | Reigns of Ptolemy XIII and Cleopatra |
| 30 | Egypt became Roman province |

## Near East B.C.

| | |
|---|---|
| 4000–3000 | Sumerian art began |
| 3000 | Foundation of Troy I. Metal working developed |
| 3000–1750 | Babylonians |
| 1792–1750 | King Hammurabi's law code |
| 1400–1200 | Hittite Empire |
| 1350–1000 | Assyrian art began |
| 1250–1200 | Moses flourished |
| 1025– 922 | United Kingdom of Israel |
| 1025–1000 | Saul reigned |
| 1000– 968 | David reigned |
| 968– 937 | Solomon reigned |
| 922– 783 | Two Kingdoms Israel to 783 Judah to 597 |
| 884– 612 | Assyrian Empire |
| 612– 539 | Neobabylonian period |
| 605– 562 | Nebuchadnezzar II, king of Babylon |
| 575 | Ishtar Gate, Babylon |
| 539– 333 | Persian Empire of Cyrus, Darius, and Xerxes |
| 333 | Conquest of Near East by Alexander the Great |

**1.** Paleolithic cave painting. c. 15,000–10,000 B.C. Approximately life-size. Lascaux (Dordogne), France.

coast. Though oral expression, magic incantations, warriors' tales, and love songs undoubtedly flourished in pristine times, poetry and music, in order for it to survive, had to await the advent of the alphabet and notation. Wall paintings and carved stone figures, however, still exist in caves that were occupied in the Old Stone Age some 20,000 years ago.

Through the magic of imagery, early man dealt with hunting and being hunted, with life and death, with existence and extinction (Fig. 1). The cave artist represented what he actually saw with such an acute eye and immediacy of sensation that later literate societies have never excelled the sheer strength of the pictorial record left from prehistory. The herds of beasts and spirited specimens he painted and carved on cave walls and ceilings tell of his precarious place in a world dominated by brutish forces. He made these startlingly lifelike animals by outlining and shading them with charcoal, then adding colors in reddish-brown and yellow-ochre clays. Though horses and antelopes appear in herds, the art of grouping figures or organizing images into complete compositions seems to have been of little or no import. Nor are these paintings and reliefs conceived as decoration or ornament. Their placement in inaccessible subterranean grottoes suggests sanctuaries where magic rituals were enacted. Evidence that

**below: 4.** *Horse.* Greek "geometric" style, c. 750 B.C. Bronze, height 6¼". State Museums, West Berlin.

**right: 5.** *Idol,* from Amorgos, Cyclades Islands. c. 3000 B.C. Marble, height 30". Ashmolean Museum, Oxford.

**above: 2.** *Venus of Willendorf.* c.30,000–10,000 B.C. Limestone, height 4⅜". Natural History Museum, Vienna.

**right:** **3.** *Mask,* from Itumba, Republic of Congo. Wood, height 14". Museum of Modern Art, New York.

lances were hurled at the paintings also points to primitive hunting rites. For caveman, art served life, art and reality were one, and the image was the animal. By imitating his prey exactly, he gained power over it. His idea was to create a double and then assault it, which would enable him to bring his true quarry to bay. As important as the food supply was the propagation of the race, but in cave art the human image appears far less frequently than does that of animals. However, some carvings of the human female form survive from this time. The featureless face of the figure known as the *Venus of Willendorf* (Fig. 2), a possible fertility symbol, exudes pride and contentment as she bends over large breasts and clasps them with tiny arms. Because female animals seem almost always to have been depicted as pregnant and these women, with their fleshy hips, voluminous bosoms, and exaggerated sex characteristics, are shown holding bisons' horns of plenty, the carvings probably are evidence of a cult devoted to fecundity.

Naturalistic animal and human images did not serve the purposes of later, more complex societies. For them, signs and symbols served better than reality to depict the unseen forces of wind and weather, the spirits of good and evil, the souls of the dead. The mask reproduced in Figure 3 was designed to be worn by an African tribesman as he danced by firelight to the accompaniment of drums. After looking at cave art, it seems to be a distortion of reality. The small, round, protruding mouth, the enlarged eyes, the long triangular nose, however, are not intended to represent a living person, but to conjure up the presence of an invisible spirit. By impersonating the unseen presence, by enacting ritual steps and gestures, tribal peoples could come in contact with the vital rhythms and controlling influences of their world. To the tribe, the masked dancer was an ancestral hero, a god to be propitiated, or a demon to be placated. Through such fetishes and idols, divine beings and mythical heroes resided among the living and enabled the tribe to assume their powers and prowess, win victories at arms, or ensure a good harvest.

As seen in a bronze horse from the very early period of Greek art called "geometric" (Fig. 4), the artist was not so much concerned with reproducing the living likeness as he was with grasping the essence, the concept of the horse. Such objects are found in temple precincts where they were brought as *votive offerings* by worshippers who petitioned or thanked the deities for divine favors—for victory in a race, fertility of a farm, restoration to good health.

Similarly, the female form as revealed in Figure 5 is simplified, abbreviated, and abstracted into a compact, flattened shape. The intent of these "island

Genesis of the Arts    3

**left: 6.** Sphinx (c. 2540–2514 B.C.) and Great Pyramid of Khufu (c. 2590–2568 B.C.), at Giza, Egypt. Great Pyramid, height 449' (originally 482'), 755' square at base.

**right: 7.** Hypostyle Hall of Amenhotep III (c. 1390 B.C.) seen from Great Court with Colossi of Rameses II (c. 1280 B.C.), Temple of Amon, Luxor, Egypt.

idols" is not known. Since they cannot stand upright they are not statuettes. Found in tombs, where they were placed beside the body, these carved figures may be goddesses, fertility forms, guides to the underworld, or spirits of the dead. The artist has stamped a preconceived geometrical outline on his material, which is the fine-grained white crystalline marble found in the Cyclades Islands near Crete. The smooth surface treatment is broken by the sharp angular arrangement of the arms, the long straight noses, and the conventional flat-topped heads.

The *conventions* of a period are the inherited, invented, and prescribed formulas that the people who formed its culture generally understood. The traditional arrangement of areas and rooms in a temple or dwelling, the larger-than-life representations and rigid postures of gods and kings, the appearance of a masked deity or hero to pronounce the prologue and epilogue of a Greek drama, the stipulated 14 lines of a sonnet, the repeated rhythmic patterns of dances, the choice of melodic intervals dictated by musical modes and scales—all are conveniences that became conventions through the fact of their acceptance by a representative number of people whose commonly held values and attitudes constituted a culture.

The work of a period or particular artist is often criticized because it seems cliché-ridden or conventional. But all art is based on the observations of some rules. When everything is too much as expected, it tends to be repetitious and boring, but if all is completely unanticipated, it becomes bewildering. Competent craftsmen of any time can be counted upon to master the basic media, the necessary techniques, the accepted conventions of their era. Only the true artist knows how to depart from the rules meaningfully and how to break them brilliantly. Conventions are a body of habits, but a significant work is a stroke of genius. Conventions are perspiration, art inspiration. Conventions are predictable; greatness is unpredictable. Conventions are the heritage of tradition; invention and innovation are the mark of change.

The shift in prehistory from a nomadic to a communal life, from a food-hunting to a food-gathering society, from an animal-chasing to a cattle-breeding economy is reflected in the arts by the shift from naturalistic or direct imitation of nature to a more geometric art based on formal principles and traditional conventions. Such departures from nature replace things that can be seen and touched with invisible and intangible essences. Concrete images yield to abstract forms, naturalism to stylization, imitation to idealization, the actual to the metaphorical. In short, the rendering of reality is replaced by accepted conventions. These are the polar extremes toward which the art of all subsequent periods tended to express itself—the faithful delineation of the natural appearance and "speaking" likeness on the one hand, and the conceptual, geometric, stylized conventions of the established formulas on the other.

# ANCIENT EGYPTIAN ARTS

A judicious mixture of accepted formulas and accurate observation of life is found in the art of ancient Egypt. Through impressive temples and spacious palaces, magnificent statuary and murals, representations of priestly ceremonies and royal processions, the artist could give flesh and blood to the concepts of godhood, kingship, and priestly authority. Originality and innovation were discouraged, which caused artists, for the most part, to concentrate on technique and skill of execution. Yet the paintings on the walls of Egyptian tombs show a keen eye for informal activities and a wealth of naturalistic detail.

Egyptian society was like a pyramid with the Pharaoh as its apex. As a descendant of the sun he ruled with absolute authority and was responsible only to his gods and ancestors. The Pyramid of Khufu (or in Greek, Cheops) is the largest and grandest of funerary monuments, meant to last forever (Fig. 6). The statistics are staggering. Combining the basic geometrical forms of the square and triangle, it was built of 2,300,000 blocks of stone, each weighing about 2½ tons. The stupendous structure covers more than 13 acres, encloses a volume of 85 million cubic feet, and is completely solid except for two small burial chambers. To line it up with the four corners of the world, it was surveyed so accurately that each of its 755-foot sides faces one of the cardinal points of the compass. So skillfully is the stone cut that joinings are scarcely visible. For centuries the pyramids

have been convenient quarries, so that now the original smooth sheath of varicolored sandstone and granite remains in only a few places. For sheer simplicity and endless durability, these masterly solids bid fair to outlast anything mankind has produced.

The companions of this mighty monument are the pyramids of Khufu's dynastic successors and lesser members of the royal line. The guardian of this city of the dead is the inscrutable Sphinx (Fig. 6), which combines the recumbent body of a lion with a human head. It is placed beside the tomb of King Khafre (Chefren in Greek) whose pyramid is second in size only to that of his father. Facing the rising sun, the Sphinx's body symbolizes immortality (Pharaohs were often buried in lion skins), while the face is considered to be a portrait of the deified King Khafre.

The priestly caste made its architectural mark in Egypt's temples. From its origins in the practice of occult magic, this group gradually gained in scientific knowledge and social influence. Cloaked in veils of secrecy, the priests became adepts at geometry and mathematics, knew the heavens and the movements of stars, and could predict the time when the Nile would overflow and bring renewed life to fields and gardens. At first, the priests carved their temples out of the living rock, but gradually they caused them to assume stylized architectural forms. Approaching by broad avenues, worshipers entered through massive pylons into a forecourt beyond which lay mysterious hypostyle halls (Fig. 7) and inner sanctums with forests of columns, each carved with strange hieroglyphic inscriptions.

The colossal statue of Rameses II (Fig. 7) typifies the aloof, rigid, immutable images of the Pharaohs. Serenely above it all, this sculptured form provides no suggestion of movement to disturb its majestic calm. Strict convention dictated the stance, with its severe frontality, stylized ceremonial beard, and hands placed upon the knees. As the direct descendant of Horus, lord of the skies, Rameses appears uncompromisingly as the absolute ruler and judge of his people.

The sole exception to these hieratic representations of Pharaohs occurs during the reign of Amenhotep IV, who rejected the complex of gods and ritual observed by his ancestors, adopted monotheism, and changed his name to Akhenaton ("Beneficial of the Aton," the universal and sole god of the sun). The unfinished bust of his beauteous Queen Nefertiti was found at Amarna in the workshop of the sculptor Tuthmosis (Fig. 8). Despite the royal headdress, regal dignity, conventional elongated neck, and bright paint, the living likeness of a real personality with genuine human warmth shows through. On close examination, the queen can be seen as a woman well past the bloom of youth but not yet prey to the ravages of age. Breaking with formal conventions, as well as with past precedents, Akhenaton

**8.** Tuthmosis. *Queen Nefertiti.* c. 1370 b.c. Painted limestone with inlaid glass eye, height 20". State Museums, West Berlin.

**9.** *Offering Bearers,* from Tomb of Sebekhotep, Thebes. c. 1500–1300 B.C. Tempera on mud plaster, width c. 30". Metropolitan Museum of Art, New York (Rogers Fund, 1930).

allowed himself to be portrayed informally as he offered his queen a flower and fondled his baby daughter, with Nefertiti holding two infant princesses on her lap. Despite the restoration of polytheism, this carried over briefly into the reign of his successor King Tutankhamon, famed because his is the only Pharaonic tomb found in modern times totally intact and unplundered. On the back of Tutankhamon's throne (Pl. 1, p. 7), the King is shown in a relaxed attitude conversing with his consort as the Sun God bestows his divine blessing with many raylike hands.

The dominant fact of Egyptian life was death. And the art forms assume the shapes of mummy cases, stone sarcophagi, death masks, sculptured portraits, pyramids, tombs—all associated with death. The purpose was not to gladden the eye of the living, but to provide for the needs of the deceased in the afterlife. Death for the Egyptian of consequence did not mean extinction but rather a continuity of life beyond the grave. To achieve immortality the body had to be preserved and the tomb elaborately furnished. The inner walls, floors, and ceilings were covered with hieroglyphic inscriptions that identified the deceased, recounted his titles and honors, depicted him surrounded by family and friends, and occupied with his favorite pursuits. The tomb's occupant was shown supervising work in the fields, making offerings to the gods, sailing a boat, hunting or fishing, watching the dance, listening to music, or playing games. In wall paintings and reliefs, fruit and game were provided for his table and handmaidens and manservants for the ministrations of his needs. Everything was introduced to make the deceased feel completely at home.

As seen in tomb paintings (Pl. 2, p. 7; Fig. 9), the Egyptian artist was concerned only with the picture plane, not with creating illusions of depth, modelling his figures in three dimensions, or showing them against a background. According to the usual conventions, the heads are always drawn in profile, but the eyes (several millennia before Picasso) are represented front face. The torsos are frontal, but the arms and legs offer a side view. And though the figures are shown from the right side, they have two left feet so that both big toes are toward the front. If a pool or river is included in a landscape, the view of it is from above, but fish, ducks, plants, and trees in and around it are shown sideways. Important personages always appear larger than their families, retinues, or servants. Yet once these conventions are taken for granted, the scenes appear remarkably lifelike. Naturalistic detail is rendered so accurately that botanists and zoologists can recognize each separate species of plant and animal life. The Egyptian artist also knew how to delineate the fur and feathers of animals and birds by breaking up his color surfaces with minute brushstrokes of various hues. Egyptian tomb art is thus a recreation of life as it was experienced in the flesh, and these still-vital, colorful murals provide an amazingly complete and comprehensive picture of the behavior patterns in an ancient civilization.

## DYNAMICS OF HISTORY

Art history, like philosophy and science, is concerned with causes and effects. Thus, in reviewing the major styles of Western culture, one should keep in mind

**right: Plate 1.** Back of Tutankha-mon's Throne, from Thebes. c. 1365 B.C. Wood covered with gold leaf and colored inlays of faience, glass, and stone; back width 21". Egyptian Museum, Cairo. (See p. 6.)

**below: Plate 2.** *Musicians with Double Aulos, Lute, and Harp,* Tomb of Nakht, Thebes. c. 1420 B.C. (See p. 6.)

Plate 3. *Charioteer*, from Sanctuary of Apollo, Delphi. c. 470 B.C. Bronze, height 6'11". Museum, Delphi. (See p. 28.)

Plate 4. *Orpheus Among the Thracians.* c. 440 B.C. Attic red-figured vase. State Museums, West Berlin. (See p. 34.)

the mainstreams of influence. The dynamics of contact and conquest affect the formative conditioning of art. But conquest is a double-edged sword. On one side the conquerors stamp their image on the conquered, but on the other the overlords absorb many of the forms and expressions characteristic of the subjugated peoples.

Egypt and Mesopotamia developed as landlocked powers and closed societies that, with little dependence on outside forces, were nurtured from inner reserves. But the Greeks were a seafaring folk, and, like the Romans after them, they had to look beyond their shores for the maritime trade, commercial ventures, and colonization essential to their survival. The Greeks came in contact with Egyptian and Mesopotamian scientific and artistic traditions and then appropriated, absorbed, refined, and transmuted them into their unparalleled achievements. Rome, as the cultural melting pot of antiquity, realized a valid and viable merging of the ideas, building methods, ornamental motifs, plastic and pictorial traditions, literary and musical expressions of the Greek, Near Eastern, Egyptian, North African, and Etruscan cultures, together with significant contributions of their own.

It would be perfectly logical to begin the study of the cultural heritage of Europe and America with the Romans. For, until the advent of the Industrial Revolution, Western art, for all practical purposes, was a continuation and a constant variation of the Roman Mediterranean synthesis as it spread northward. Paleolithic art was completely unknown until 1879, when the cave paintings were discovered, virtually by accident. This Cro-Magnon art was so far removed from the cultural mainstream that it had no influence on subsequent periods in antiquity. And, except as a historical curiosity, its effect on modern art has been negligible. Until the late 18th century, pure Greek art forms, as distinguished from Roman adaptations, had no direct influence on Western thought. Only then—when the historian J. J. Winckelmann drew a distinction between the two styles, when Stuart and Revett surveyed and published drawings of the Athenian antiquities, and when Lord Elgin brought many of the surviving Parthenon marbles to London—was a Greek revival style possible (see Chap. 18). Egyptian art, along with Chinese and Indian decorative motifs, first came into modern currency in 18th-century rococo exotic fancies. Egypt later made a greater impact through Napoleon's Egyptian campaign. Egyptology as a science, however, dates only from the last century. Sumerian and Babylonian art came to light in late 19th-century archaeological excavations. Except through Greco-Roman eyes, it has had little or no influence on the arts of the West, save for occasional borrowings by eclectic architects.

Since an artist must represent his world, his society, and his place in the universe as he himself sees them, his work becomes a reflection of his time from a particular point of view. His temple, statue, picture, poem, or piece of music is an indication of how a sensitive member of that society imagines, dreams, thinks, feels, communicates. In this light a building is not a mere pile of sticks and stones, steel and glass, no matter how interesting the shapes these materials may assume, but a created environment, a form of action for some social activity. Masses and voids, solids and hollows, create spatial rhythms. It could be said that the architect is the ballet master who writes the figure of a dance that all who enter must perform. From architectural engineering, it is possible to tell how much man knew about his environment, how advanced his scientific knowledge, whether he was a hunter or farmer, a king or commoner. The Ishtar Gate of ancient Babylon (Fig. 10), for instance,

**10.** Ishtar Gate (restored), from Babylon. c. 575 B.C. State Museums, East Berlin.

shows that the Assyrians knew the principle of the arch and vault long before the Romans came on the scene. Dating from the time of King Nebuchadnezzar II, the gate was part of a proud wall that the King had built to enclose his legendary Tower of Babel. Made of glazed brick, the gate's monumental decorations depict a stately procession of lions and dragons, stylized horses and graceful gazelles.

Sculpture finds its natural ally in architecture as embellishment that relieves the strict functionalism of a structure. Sculpture can provide focal points of interest and endow a building with meaning. In ancient times reliefs and freestanding statues were a visual reflection of the activity the architectural setting was designed to house. In a more exalted sense a statue becomes the image of the heroic or godlike ideal toward which a people is striving. Paintings, frescoes, and mosaics supply the pictorial dimension. In them is represented the visage of an age, as well as man's hopes and fears expressed in the forms of symbols and images. Poetry and music crystallize the rhythms of human activity in songs and dances that reflect work and play, joy and sorrow, as well as the deepest longings and highest aspirations of the human heart. The artist begins the creative process with the vanishing point of the void—empty space and undefined time—then *composes* in the literal sense of selecting materials, placing them together, building them up. The procedure is from the singular toward the plural, from unrelatedness to relatedness, as he reaches out toward the order and unity of a style.

The search for unity within historical style periods, or at least for a coherent grouping of diversities, is crucial for both style definition and art criticism. Cultural expressions, in the manner of the classical unities of Greek drama, usually occur within definite limits of time, place, and action. The search for the underlying ideas that motivate human activities can often reduce to basic simplicity what appears on the surface as a confusing multiplicity of directions. And because the arts are usually experienced simultaneously, not separately, it is often wiser to seek understanding from many directions rather than from one. If a common configuration of ideas can be found, then aspects that previously proved baffling may suddenly fall into place and acquire meaning.

Such ideas may be initiated by artists themselves, either individually or as a group, or by single or collective patrons endowed with sufficient discernment, means, and energy to pursue complicated projects to completion. Such a patron might be a ruler with the vision of Pericles, who presided over the cultural climax of ancient Athens; an enterprising medieval abbot or bishop who envisaged a great monastery or cathedral complex; a family of merchant princes, such as the Medici, who brought Renaissance Florence to its creative peak; or a religious order like the Jesuits, who spread the Counter-Reformation baroque style

in the wake of their missionary endeavors. The 20th century has witnessed the Commonwealth of India commissioning the Swiss-born architect Le Corbusier to design and construct Chandigarh, an entirely new capital city for the East Punjab, complete with every public and private facility. In New York, the heirs of a modern industrialist have sponsored an architectural complex in Rockefeller Center that compares in grandeur with the imperial forums of ancient Rome. And many public agencies and private contributors have joined forces to erect in New York the Lincoln Center "acropolis" that embraces a group of opera houses, concert halls, repertory theaters, libraries, museums, and educational centers.

Whenever a center has attained a degree of civilization, has developed a prosperous economy, has given birth to a number of promising individuals, has fostered an adequate educational system, has in its midst groups of artists and master craftsmen, a significant cultural expression may occur. When this happens, it is usually because some personality of powerful convictions has reacted so strongly to the challenge of his time that he is catapulted into a dominating position. Various explanations have been advanced, such as the "great-man theory," which holds that outstanding persons stamp their image upon an age, and that genius is the primary causal influence on history. Social realists, however, contend that environmental forces shape the characters and actions of the individuals involved. The truth probably lies somewhere between these extremes of nature and nurture, and the interplay between powerful personalities and the stimulus of their times brings about the explosion commonly described as genius.

Techniques of production are the private problems of particular craftsmen. Composition, however, is common to them all. An architect puts building materials together, a poet words, a musician tones. But contrary to the views of some purists, they do not do so in a vacuum of self-expression but in order to communicate thoughts, fantasies, social comments, satirical observations, self-revelations, images of order, and the like. Their works—temples, statues, murals, odes, sonatas, symphonies—are addressed not to themselves but to their fellowmen.

The artist's choice of medium, his way of handling materials, the language with which he expresses his thoughts, his personal idioms and idiosyncrasies, his mode of vision, his manner of representing his world, all add up to a vocabulary of symbols and images that define his individual *style.* In a broader sense, however, a style must include similar expressions in many media, whether in visual, verbal, or tonal forms. Artists, working within a given time and place, share a common sociocultural heritage; therefore, it follows that each has a common point of departure. In the arts, as in politics, there are conservatives who try to preserve traditional values, liberals who are concerned with current trends, and progressives who point to coming developments. The individual artist may accept or reject, endorse or protest, conform or reform, construct or destroy, dream of the past or prophesy the future, but his taking-off point must be his own time. The accents with which he and his contemporaries speak, the vocabularies they choose, the passion with which they champion ideas, all add up to the larger synthesis of a style.

A positive approach, then, can be established on the coincidence of *time, place,* and *idea.* Artists, while working in separate fields, are an integral part of a society, living within a certain geographical and temporal center, and collaborating in varying degrees with each other and with the larger social group. The closer the coincidence, the closer the relationship will be. Composite works of art—forums, monasteries, cathedrals, operas—are always collaborative in nature and must be made to express the several interests they are designed to serve. Liturgical needs, for instance, have to be taken into account in the designs of a cathedral, and the sculptural and pictorial embellishments must fit into an iconography, or symbolic program, and the overall architectonic plan. Hence in one *time* and in one *place,* the arts of architecture, sculpture, painting, music, and liturgy share a common constellation of *ideas* in relation to the contemporary social order and its spiritual aspirations.

True history is no mere record of dates, treaties, battles, kings, and generals. Aristotle long ago recognized this vital fact when he placed poetic truth higher than historical truth. The political experience of a nation is but one phase of its whole life. If one desires to know the spirit and inner life of a people, one must look at its art, literature, dances, and music, where the spirit of the whole people is reflected. While kings, dynasties, and dictators rise and fall, and political revolutions and battles seem abruptly to settle the affairs of men, the arts, as the expression of the living unity and being of man, do not die—though they may have their periods of rise and decline— but go on to reveal the continuity of life. Ultimately what matters in art, as Lionel Venturi pointed out in the case of painting, "is not the canvas, the hue of oil or tempera, the anatomical structure, and all the other measurable items, but its contributions to our life, its suggestions to our sensations, feeling, and imagination." Romain

Rolland has rightly observed: "Art, like life, is inexhaustible; and nothing makes us feel the truth of this better than music's ever-welling spring, which has flowed through the centuries until it has become an ocean."

Through the study of the arts in relation to the life and time out of which they spring, a richer, broader, deeper humanistic understanding can be achieved. The past, as reflected in the arts, exists as a continuous process, and any arbitrary separation from the present and future disappears in the presence of a living work. True critical appraisal of art, or indeed any other human activity, can never be a catalogue of minutiae, a record of isolated moments. Understanding can come only when one event is related to another, and when their sum total is absorbed into the growing stream of universal life from which each particular moment derives its significance. In their natural relationship, the arts become the study of people reflected in the ever-changing images of man as he journeys across historical time, as he searches restlessly for reality, and as he ceaselessly strives to achieve the ideals that create meaning for life.

All creative activity begins in the mind's eye and ear of the artist. A work of art that does not communicate meaning is still born. Art, then, is a two-way process involving both creator and re-creator. The intensity of the observer's activity, to be sure, may be less than that of the artist, but the experience nevertheless consists of the dynamic activity of responding when the viewer, reader, and listener conjure up corresponding sets of perceptions, images, and impressions on their own. To play his part in the creative act, the re-creator must learn the visual, verbal, and auditory vocabularies that make communication possible and that distinguish the finer nuances of sight and sound. Imagination and knowledge must be summoned to supply the frame of reference and the aura that once surrounded the work of art in its original context. Hence it is necessary to know the period and style, the social and religious circumstances, the type of patronage and social position realized by the artist. These pages, then, have been written to guide the viewer, reader, and listener as he sets forth on the quest for enjoyment, knowledge, and understanding of the humanistic experience.

# 2 The Hellenic Style

## ATHENS, 5TH CENTURY B.C.

In the land of Hellas, a small city-state dedicated to Athena, goddess of wisdom, saw the birth of a new spirit—a spirit destined to quicken the human heart and mind then, now, and for ages yet to come. Here in Athens for a brief span of time were concentrated the creative energies of many geniuses—leaders capable of securing Athens' victory in the struggle for supremacy over the Mediterranean world; statesmen with the insight and acumen to make Athens the first democracy in an era of tyrants; philosophers committed to search for an understanding of the physical, social, and spiritual nature of the environment they lived in; and artists who conceived daring expressions—in stone, word, and tone. In 480 B.C. the Athenians had turned the tide against the powerful Persians, but only after their city had been reduced to rubble. Without hereditary rulers, government rested on the shoulders of the citizen class, and the rule of the *demos,* the "people," became the order of the day. Here the statesman Pericles and the philosopher Socrates heard the wisdom of Anaxagoras, who taught

that the universe was governed by a supreme mind that brought form out of the chaos of nature; and that man, by thinking for himself could likewise bring order into human affairs. After the destruction of their city, the Athenians, boldly facing the future, instead of reconstructing their old temples and statuary, launched a new building program that surpassed anything the world had ever seen and that would serve as a classical model and paradigm for all generations to come.

Like many other ancient cities, Athens had developed around an *acra,* or "hill," originally found suitable as a military vantage point. As in other cities, a long-ago victory on this fortified hilltop, known as the *acropolis* (Fig. 11), had been attributed to divine intervention, causing the popular mind to regard the acra as a sacred place, one to be crowned with an appropriate monument—just as the brow of a warrior responsible for a heroic deed would have been adorned with the kingly diadem. Civic buildings, palaces, and temples were erected, and the people in the city below looked up with pride toward the acropolis that recorded their history, represented their aspirations, and had become the center of their religious and civic ceremonies. From the beginning, the Athenian acropolis was never static, and its successive buildings reflected the city's changing fortunes. Once it had been the site of a palace for the legendary king, Erechtheus. Its shift from a military citadel and royal residence to a religious shrine, especially sacred to Athena as the city's protectress, is described by Homer when he notes in the *Odyssey:* "Therewith grey-eyed Athene departed over the unharvested seas, left pleasant Scheria, and came to Marathon and wide-wayed Athens, and entered the house of Erechtheus."

Spreading out from the base of the acropolis was the *agora* (Fig. 12), a meeting and a market place, with its colonnades, public buildings, market stalls, gardens, and shade trees. This ten-acre square was the center of the city's bustling business, social, and political life. Here could be found country folk selling their wares, citizens discussing the news, foreign visitors exchanging stories, and magistrates conducting routine city affairs. On a typical day, Socrates could be heard arguing with the sophists, whom he called "retailers of knowledge," for, as his pupil Plato was to point out, the merchandising in the agora was "partly concerned with food for the use of the body, and partly with food of the soul which is bartered and received in exchange for money." The sophists were concerned primarily with the art of persuasive speech, but some professed to teach wisdom as well. As manipulators of public opinion, they often became intellectual opportunists who would use any line of

reasoning so long as it turned their trick. In his disputations, Socrates showed that sophistry was more a matter and technique of quibbling on the surface over words than of penetrating profoundly into the deeper world of ideas. By pricking some of the sophists' pomposities with the sting of his wit, Socrates gained his immortal reputation as the "gadfly" of Athens.

On the southern slope of the acropolis was the theater of Dionysus (Fig. 13), the sanctuary dedicated to the god of wine and frenzy and patron of the drama, and where the ancient poetic festivals were held. Here, more than 2,000 years before Shakespeare, the people of Athens gathered to marvel at the plays that mirrored their world in dramatic form and, annually, through their applause to pick the winner of the coveted poetry prize that had been won no less than 13 times by Aeschylus, the founder of heroic tragedy. Sophocles, his successor and principal poet of the Periclean period, quickened the pace of Greek drama by adding more actors and actions; Euripides, last of the great tragic poets, ran the gamut of emotions, endowing his plays with such passion and pathos that they plumbed the depths of the human spirit. After the great Periclean age was past, the comedies of Aristophanes proved that the Athenians still were able to see the humorous side of life.

Above the theater, on the rocky plateau of the acropolis, was a leveled site, about 1,000 feet long and 445 feet wide, where the temples were constructed (Fig. 14). Under Cimon and his successor Pericles, this was a place of ceaseless activity by builders, sculptors,

**opposite: 11.** Acropolis, Athens (view from southwest).

**right: 12.** Agora, Athens. (Left, reconstruction of Stoa of Attalus II of Pergamon, c. 150 B.C.)

# CHRONOLOGY / The Hellenic Period

## General History B.C.

c.1600–c.1100 Mycenaean Period
c.1184 Fall of Troy to Achaeans
c.1100 Dorians and Ionians invaded Greek peninsula, conquered Achaeans. End of Mycenaean Period, beginning of Hellenic civilization
c.950– c.800 Proto-Geometric Period; Homeric epics (?)
c.800– c.650 Geometric Period; Homer; Eastern contacts
776 First Olympic games; beginning of Greek calendar
c.700 Hesiod wrote *Theogony* (basis of Greek mythology)
c.650– c.500 Archaic Period
534 Playwriting competitions began at Athens
c.494 Persians under Darius invaded Greece
c.490 Athenians defeated Persians at Marathon
480 Persians under Xerxes defeated Spartans at Thermopylae. Athens sacked and burned. Athenians defeated Persian fleet at Salamis
477 Delian League founded under Athenian leadership
468– 450 Cimon (c.505–450), general, leader of conservative aristocratic party, dominated Athenian politics
454 Delian League Treasury moved to Athens
449– 429 Pericles (c.490–429), leader of popular party, ruled Athens
437– 404 Peloponnesian Wars between Athens and Sparta
413 Athenians defeated at Syracuse, Sicily
404 Athens fell to Sparta. End of Athenian empire

387 Plato founded Academy
359– 336 Philip of Macedonia gained control of Greek peninsula
336 Alexander the Great succeeded Philip as king of Greece
335 Aristotle founded Lyceum
335– 323 Alexander the Great conquered Near East, Asia Minor, Persia, India
146 Corinth destroyed by Romans
86 Athens sacked by Romans under Sulla

### A.D.

c.100 Plutarch (c.46–c.125) wrote *Parallel Lives*
c.140– 150 Pausanius visited Athens. Later wrote description of Greece
529 Athenian schools of philosophy closed by Emperor Justinian

## Architecture and Sculpture B.C.

c.650 Ionic temple of Artemis built at Ephesus
c.600 Kouros from Sounion carved
c.550 Korai of Samos carved
c.530 Archaic Doric temples built at Athens, Delphi, Corinth, Olympia
c.489 Doric temple (Treasury of Athenians) built at Delphi, by Callicrates (?)
c.470 *Charioteer of Delphi* cast
c.470– c.450 *Zeus (Poseidon ?)* cast
467– 449 New temple to Athena on Acropolis (predecessor to Parthenon) being built by Callicrates. Work halted in 449 on accession of Pericles
c.465– 457 Temple of Zeus built at Olympia
450 Phidias appointed overseer of works on Athenian acropolis

448– 440 Temple of Hephaestus (Theseum) built, by Callicrates (?)
447– 432 Parthenon built by Ictinus Parthenon sculptures carved under Phidias
437– 432 Propylaea built by Mnesicles
427– 424 Temple of Athena Nike built by Callicrates
421– 409 Erechtheum built by Mnesicles
334 Choragic monument of Lysicrates built

### A.D.

c.117 Temple of Olympian Zeus completed

## Philosophers B.C.

c.582– c.507 Pythagoras
500 428 Anaxagoras
485 411 Protagoras
469 399 Socrates
427 347 Plato
384 322 Aristotle

## Historians B.C.

c.495– 425 Herodotus
c.460– 395 Thucydides
c.434– c.355 Xenophon

## Sculptors B.C.

c.490– c.432 Phidias
c.460– c.450 Myron active
c.460– c.440 Polyclitus active
c.390– c.330 Praxiteles
c.350– c.300 Lysippus active

## Painters B.C.

c.480– c.430 Polygnotus (noted for perspective drawing)
c.440 Apollodorus, the "shadow painter," flourished (modeled figures in light and shade)

## Dramatists and Musicians B.C.

525– 456 Aeschylus
496 406 Sophocles
480 406 Euripides
c.444– 380 Aristophanes

painters, and other craftsmen. The necessary materials were available in abundance: Paros and other Aegean islands yielded good stone; from nearby Mt. Pentelicus came the fine-grained, cream-colored marble ideal for building and carving; Mt. Hymettus in Athens itself had a blue-white rock, excellent for embellishments; while the dark-gray limestone of Eleusis could be used for contrasting effects. As the buildings rose stately in size and fair in form, the craftsmen, declares Plutarch in his biography of Pericles, were "striving to outvie the material and the design with the beauty of their workmanship, yet the most wonderful thing of all was the rapidity of their execution. Undertakings, any one of which singly might have required, . . . for their completion, several successions and ages of men, were every one of them accomplished in the height and prime of one man's political service."

Pericles had the daring and wisdom to foresee that the unity of a people could rest on philosophical idealism and artistic leadership as well as on military might and material prosperity. A seafaring people, the Athenians had always looked beyond the horizon for ideas as well as goods to add luster to their way of life. In the Delian confederation, once the Persian threats were ended, they joined with the broader community of Greek-speaking peoples of the mainland, the Aegean islands, and the coast of Asia Minor

left: 13. Acropolis, Athens. Reconstruction drawing as of end of 2nd century A.D. (Theater of Dionysus, 4th century B.C., upper right; Odeion of Herodes Atticus, 2nd century A.D., lower left.) Reconstruction by Al. N. Oikonomides.

right: 14. Plan of Athenian acropolis. a. Propylaea; b. Temple of Athena Nike; c. Parthenon; d. Erechtheum.

not only to defend themselves but also to achieve a cultural unity. With the Delian treasury brought to Athens and its ample funds available for her building program, the city was assured leadership in the arts as well as in other practical and idealistic enterprises. Thus, Athens became a city whose acknowledged wealth was in its dramatists Aeschylus, Sophocles, and Euripides; its architects Ictinus, Callicrates, and Mnesicles; its sculptors Myron, Polyclitus, and Phidias; and such painters and craftsmen as Polygnotus, Apollodorus, and Callimachus.

The acropolis was, then, both the material and spiritual treasury of the Athenian people, the place which held both their worldly gold reserves and their religious and artistic monuments. Work continued with unabated enthusiasm until by the end of the 5th century B.C. the acropolis had become a sublime setting, worthy of the goddess of wisdom and beauty, and the pedestal that proudly bore the shining temples dedicated to her.

The Hellenic Style  **15**

# ARCHITECTURE

**The Acropolis and the Propylaea**   On festive occasions, the Athenians would leave their modest homes to walk along the Panathenaic Way (Fig. 15), the main avenue of their city, toward the acropolis. Towering above them, was the supreme shrine—the acropolis where they worshiped their gods, commemorated their heroes, and recreated themselves. Accessible only by a single zigzag path up the western slope, the ascent was never easy. In Aristophanes' *Lysistrata,* a chorus of old men bearing olive branches to kindle the sacred fires chant as they mount the hill: "But look, to finish this toilsome climb only this last steep bit is left to mount. Truly, it's no easy job without beasts of burden and how these logs do bruise my shoulder!"

As the procession neared the summit, the exquisite little Temple of Athena Nike appeared on a parapet to the right (Fig. 25), and ahead was the mighty Propylaea, the imposing frontispiece to the Acropolis (Fig. 16). This project, undertaken shortly after the completion of the Parthenon, was entrusted by Pericles to Mnesicles, who had been chief assistant to Ictinus, the principal architect of the Parthenon. Ictinus himself probably had a hand in planning the Propylaea, whose further relationship to the Parthenon can be found in the proportions of its forms, in the presence of certain features of the Ionic order in a dominantly Doric structure, and in the main axis that the Propylaea shares with the larger monument. Built entirely of Pentelic marble except for some dark contrasting Eleusinian stone in the frieze, the Propylaea was a spacious gateway with wings extending on either side to an overall width of about 156 feet. An enclosure on the left was a picture gallery, and an open room on the right contained statuary. In the center was the portico consisting of six Doric columns with the middle two spaced more widely apart as if to invite entrance. Between the columns facing the city and the corresponding ones on the opposite side facing the acropolis plateau was an open vestibule with columns of the more slender Ionic order, which permitted greater height and space for exhibitions and the waiting crowds (Fig. 17).

Through the portals of the Propylaea the procession entered the sacred area. Amid the revered monuments to the gods and heroes and looming above them was the colossal statue of Athena Promachus, said to have been fashioned by Phidias from the bronze shields of defeated Persian enemies, the tip of her spear gleaming brightly enough to guide homecoming sailors over the seas toward Athens. On the right was the majestic Parthenon; on the left the graceful Ionic Erechtheum.

**The Parthenon**   At first glance, the Parthenon seems to be a typical Doric temple (Fig. 18). Such a shrine was originally conceived as an idealized dwelling to house the image of the deity to whom it was

**above: 15.** Athenian Agora (with Panathenaic Way). Reconstruction. Royal Ontario Museum, Toronto.

**left: 16.** Mnesicles. Propylaea (view from east), Acropolis, Athens. 437–432 B.C.

**below: 17.** Propylaea. Cross section (after H. D'Espouy).

dedicated. Under a low-pitched gabled roof, the interior was a windowless rectangular room called the *cella*, which sheltered the cult statue. The *portal*, or door, to the cella was on one of the short ends, which extended outward in a *portico*, or porch, faced with columns to form the *façade*. Sometimes columns were erected around the building in a series known as a *colonnade*. The construction was simple: a platform of three steps, the top one known as the *stylobate*, from which rose the upright *posts* that supported the *lintels*, or horizontal beams. When these columns and lintels were made of marble, the weight and size of the

superstructure could be increased and the *intercolumniation,* or span between the supporting posts, widened. The history of Greek temple architecture was largely the refining of this *post-and-lintel* system of construction, which permitted the architects a steadily increasing freedom.

The capital of the Doric column is in three parts: the necking, the echinus, and the abacus (Fig. 19). The purpose of any capital is to mediate between the vertical shaft of the column and the horizontal entablature above. The *necking* is the first break in the upward lines of the shafts, though the fluting continues up to the outward flare of the round, cushionlike *echinus*. This, in turn, leads to the *abacus*, a block of stone that squares the circle, so to speak, and smoothly effects the transition between the round lower and rectangular upper members. Above the columns and below the roof is the *entablature*. Directly above the abacus is the *architrave*, a series of plain rectangular blocks stretching from the center of one column to that of its neighbor to constitute the lintels of the construction and to support the upper parts of the entablature—frieze, cornices, and pediment. At this point, sculpture is called into play for decorative purposes, beginning with a carved band known as a *frieze*. In the Doric order, the frieze is made up of alternating triglyphs and metopes. The rectangular *triglyphs* are so named because of their three grooves (glyphs), two in the center and a half groove on either side. They are the weight-bearing members, and, by rule, one is placed above each column and another in the interval between. The sameness of the triglyphs contrasts with the differently carved relief panels of the *metopes*. This alternation creates an interesting visual rhythm, which illustrates the classical principle of harmonizing the opposites of unity and variety. The frieze is protected by the overhanging *cornice* (and enhanced by its shadow), and the *raking cornice* rises gablelike from the side angles to the apex in the center. The triangular space enclosed by the cornices is called the *pediment,* which is recessed to create an indented area or shelf on which free-standing sculpture can be placed to climax the decorative scheme.

On closer inspection, the Parthenon is not so much a typical Greek temple as it is the culmination of the long evolution of the Doric order with variations adapting it to the needs of its time and place. Since the Parthenon was to serve both as a shrine to Athena and as the treasury of the Delian League, the plan called for a double cella (Fig. 14). The larger room on the east was to house Phidias' magnificent gold-and-ivory cult statue of Athena and that on the west was to be the treasury. It was this western cella that technically was the *parthenon,* or chamber of the virgin goddess; later the name was given to the whole building. The outer four walls of the cella were embellished by a continuous frieze, a decorative device borrowed from the Ionic order. A *peristyle,* or colonnade, of free-standing columns completely surrounded the temple, the columns being placed far enough outward from the cella walls to permit an *ambulatory,* or passageway. On each side, along its 228 feet of length, were 17 columns, and along the 104-foot width in front and back were 8 columns—hence the Parthenon is called *octastyle.* (The number of columns used on the portico of a Greek temple was determined by the size of the building rather than by any rigid rule, 6 being the usual number, although some temples had as few as 2, others as many as 10 and 12.) On both the east and west ends of the Parthenon, between the outer colonnade and the entrance portals to the cella, were 6 additional columns that formed the inner porticos.

The outer surfaces of the columns have 20 grooves, or *flutes,* which form concave vertical chan-nels from the bottom to the top of the shaft. *Fluting* serves several purposes, the first being to correct an optical illusion. When seen in bright sunlight, a series of ungrooved round columns appear flattened. In addition to maintaining the round appearance, the fluting makes a constant play of light and shadow and creates a number of graceful curves to please the eye. Through the increased number of vertical lines, the visual rhythm is quickened, and the eye is led upward toward the sculpture of the entablature.

Except for such details as the timbered roof beneath the marble tiles and the wooden doors with their frames, the entire Parthenon was built of Pentelic marble. When freshly quarried, this fine-grained stone was cream colored, but as it has weathered through the centuries its minute veins of iron have oxidized, so that today the color varies from light beige to darker golden tones, depending on the light. In the original design, bright colors played an important part. The triglyphs were tinted dark blue and parts of the molding were red, as is known from ancient sources. The sculptured parts of the metopes were left cream colored, but the backgrounds were painted. In the frieze along the cella walls, the reins of horses were bronze additions, and the draperies of figures here and on the pediments were painted. Such facial features as eyes, lips, and hair were done in natural tints.

For sheer technical skill, the workmanship of the Parthenon is astonishing. No mortar was used anywhere; the stones were cut so exactly that when fitted together they form a single smooth surface. The columns, which appear to be monoliths of marble, actually are constructed of sections called *drums,* so fitted and held tight by square plugs in the center that the joinings are scarcely visible.

The harmonious proportions of the Parthenon have long been attributed to the application of some subtle system of mathematical ratios. But despite close study and analysis by many eminent minds, no geometrical formula has been found that fits all the evidence. However, there is a recurrence in several instances of the proportion of nine to four (9:4), as in the length of the building (228 feet) relative to its width (101½ feet) when measured on the stylobate or top step; in the width of the cornice contrasted to the height of the raking cornice at the center; in the distance between the axial center of one column and the next (about 14 feet) as compared to the diameter of the column at its base; and in the bottom diameter of the columns relative to the width of the triglyphs.

At the same time, many irregularities defy mathematical logic. Any visitor to the Parthenon can observe that the columns stand somewhat closer together at the corners. Also apparent is the gentle arching of the stylobate from corner to corner—the center point on the short ends being about 2¾ inches higher than the corners and the long sides rising about 4 inches higher. Above the columns the architrave supporting the entablature echoes this curve. Noticeable too are the slight outward swelling of the column shafts as they rise (about 11/16 of an inch) and a tapering off toward the top, making inflections known as *entasis*. Entasis creates the impression of elasticity as if, by analogy, the "muscles" of the columns bulged a bit in the act of bearing the load imposed upon them by the building's superstructure. Though somewhat less than true, it has often been stated that not a single straight line is to be found in the Parthenon. If exaggerated and compressed, the lines of the façade would resemble the drawing reproduced in Figure 20, which suggests that Ictinus intended the Parthenon to be more graceful and visually gratifying by virtue of the dominance of curved lines over straight ones.

Deviations from regularity exist elsewhere in the Parthenon. The thickness of the corner columns, for instance, is about 2 inches greater than that of neighboring columns. This increased sturdiness and stability provides optical compensation for the corner columns' being seen against light-filled, open space, rather than against the solid, opaque mass of the cella wall, and for their serving as terminal members of both lateral and longitudinal colonnades. In the spacing between columns, exact measurement reveals variations as great as 1½ inches. The inward lean of the columns is such that the columns are some 3 inches off plumb. The deliberateness of this departure from exactitude is confirmed by the cella walls, which on the outside also tilt inward, while inside their posture is strictly perpendicular to the ground. It has been estimated that if continued upward, the lines of the Parthenon's columns would converge to meet at a point approximately one mile above.

In Doric temples, triglyphs rest, like the ends of cross beams, on the architrave in positions halfway between and just over the tops of columns, leaving the spaces between them to be filled with metopes, which on the Parthenon are marble plaques bearing scenes carved in relief. In contradiction of this rule and its functional origin, triglyphs and metopes gradually squeeze one another slightly out of position toward the extremities of the colonnades so that the corners can be closed by two triglyphs joined at right angles.

Such discrepancies can be attributed to a variety of historical, social, and aesthetic factors, rather than to inept workmanship or to a structural system whose logic has been lost. Like many great works of architecture, the Parthenon reflects the rivalry of political factions, the rising ambitions of rulers, and in general, the changing fortunes of the people who produced it.

And here—as it so often occurs—what seems an imperishable masterpiece, in which every detail accords with the intentions of a master plan, actually emerges as the product of a master builder, Ictinus, in whom genius combined faculties for theoretical calculation and creative invention with a capacity for imaginative adaptation and creative improvisation. The evidence is that Ictinus labored to avoid the rigidities and repetitiousness of the strict Doric order and to make the Parthenon more than the realization of mere mechanical consistency. The analogy to human anatomy can be carried further so that the building appears as a sculpture, compact and firmly structured but resilient and elastic in the relationships among its component parts, which invests the whole with an organic, vital quality like that of life itself. Seen in this way, the Parthenon becomes more visual than logical, more concretely the work of inspired stone masons than the ratiocination of mathematicians. In short, the Parthenon is a work of art, not a cold abstraction.

In its time, the Parthenon stood out as a proud monument to Athena and her people and the attainment of Pericles' ideal of "beauty in simplicity." Begun in 447 B.C. as the first edifice in that great statesman's building program, it was dedicated during the Panathenaic festival ten short years later at a time when the star of Athens was still in ascendancy. It, as well as its companion buildings on the acropolis, would be standing today with only the usual deteriorations owing to the passage of time were it not for a disaster in the year 1687. At that time, a Turkish garrison was using the Parthenon as an ammunition dump, and during a siege by the Venetians a random bomb ignited the stored gunpowder, blowing out the central section. From that time on, the Parthenon has been a noble ruin. Today, after numerous partial restorations, its outline is still clear, and in its incomparable proportions and reserved poise it remains one of the imperishable achievements of the mind of man.

**The Erechtheum**    After Phidias' gold-and-ivory statue was so handsomely housed in the Parthenon, the city fathers wished to provide a place for the older wooden statue of Athena that was thought to have fallen miraculously from the sky. They also wished to venerate the other heroes and deities that formerly shared the acropolis with her. Hence a new building of the Ionic order (Fig. 21) was undertaken. The city records described it as "the temple in the acropolis for the ancient statue."

The site chosen was that where Erechtheus, legendary founder of the city, had once dwelled. As recounted by Homer: "And they that possessed the goodly citadel of Athens, domain of Erechtheus the high-hearted, whom erst Athene daughter of Zeus fostered when Earth, the grain giver, brought him to birth;—and she gave him a resting place in Athens in her own rich sanctuary; and there the sons of the Athenians worship him with bulls and rams as the years turn in their courses. . . ." It was also the spot where Athena and the sea god Poseidon were supposed to have held their contest for the patronage of the land of Attica and the honors of Athens, and which is depicted in the sculptures on the west pediment of the Parthenon. As they asserted their claims, Poseidon brought down his trident on a rock, whereupon a horse, his gift to man, sprang out. A spring of salt water also gushed forth to commemorate the event. When Athena's turn came, she brought forth the olive tree, and the gods awarded her the victory. Later, Erechtheus, whom she protected, tamed the horse and cultivated the olive that gave the Athenians oil for their cooking, butter for their bread, ointment for their bodies, and fuel for their lamps.

Since the sacred olive tree, the salt spring, the mark of Poseidon's trident on the rock, and the tomb of Erechtheus were all in the same sacred precinct, the architect Mnesicles had to design the temple around them, a fact that makes the plan of the Erechtheum (Fig. 14) as complex as that of the Parthenon is simple. The rectangular interior, some 31½ feet wide and 61¼ feet long, had four rooms for the various shrines on two different levels, one 10¾ feet higher than the other. Projecting outward from three of the sides were porticoes, each of different dimensions and design. That on the east has a row of six Ionic columns almost 22 feet high. The north porch (Fig. 22) has a like number but with four in front and two on the sides; while the smaller porch on the south (Fig. 23) is famous for its six sculptured maidens, the caryatids, who replace the customary columns.

Unlike those of the Doric order, Ionic columns (Fig. 19) are more slender and have their greatest diameter at the bottom. Their shafts rest on a molded base instead of directly on the stylobate, and they have 24 instead of 20 flutings. Most striking, however, is the Ionic capital with its scroll-like volutes. The fine columns of the north porch (Fig. 22) rest on molded bases carved with a delicate design. The necking has a band decorated with a leaf pattern; above this comes a smaller band with the egg-and-dart motif, and after the volutes a thin abacus carved with eggs and darts. The columns support an architrave divided horizontally into three bands stepping slightly inward, a continuous frieze rather than the alternating Doric triglyphs and metopes; and above rises a shallow pediment without sculpture. An admired and much-imitated doorway leads into the cella of the Erechtheum. Framed with a series of receding planes, the lintel above combines the decorative motifs that appear elsewhere in the building. As seen in the band that runs around the cella (Fig. 24), these include (from lower to upper) the honeysuckle, bead-and-reel, egg-and-dart, bead-and-reel, and leaf-and-tongue.

Facing the Parthenon, the south porch of the Erechtheum, with its caryatids (Fig. 23), is smaller than the others, measuring only some 10 by 15 feet. Above three steps rises a 6-foot parapet on which the six maidens, about one and a half times larger than life, are standing. In order to preserve the proportions of the building and not appear to overburden the figures, the frieze and pediment were omitted. Grouped as if in a procession, the figures infer a stately forward motion, with three on one side lifting their right legs and those on the other, their left. The folds of their draperies suggest the fluting of columns; and, while the maidens seem solid enough to carry their loads, there is no stiffness in their stances. And just as the cella frieze of the Parthenon reenacts the Panathenaic festival, so these maidens may relate to the ritual of the Erechtheum. A sculptural fragment from an older temple on the acropolis shows a priestess leading a procession in which four maidens balance a long chest on their heads. Since the temple bears the name of their warrior king, the caryatids seem to suggest a ceremony honoring the heroic dead.

On their acropolis, the Athenians brought to the highest point of development two distinct Greek building traditions—the Doric with the Parthenon, and the Ionic with the Erechtheum and the Temple of Athena Nike (Fig. 25). By combining the two architectural orders in the Propylaea and enshrining them separately in the Parthenon and the Erechtheum, the Athenians symbolized that their city was the place where the Dorian people of the western Greek mainland and the Ionians of the coast of Asia Minor across the Aegean Sea had for centuries lived

**below: 24.** Decorative band from the Erechtheum showing honeysuckle, bead-and-reel, egg-and-dart, bead-and-reel, and leaf-and-tongue motifs. Glyptothek, Munich.

**right: 25.** CALLICRATES. Temple of Athena Nike. Athens. c. 427–423 B.C. Pentelic marble, 17′9″ × 26′10″.

together in peace and harmony and through the generations had become one people. In the following century, another order was added: the Corinthian. Taller and more treelike than the Ionic, the columns of the Corinthian order are distinguished by their ornate capitals with double rows of acanthus leaves and fernlike fronds rising from each corner and terminating in miniature volutes. Too ornate for the generally restrained Hellenic taste, the Corinthian had to wait for Hellenistic and Roman times to reach its full development, as seen in the ruins of the Temple of Olympian Zeus (Fig. 26).

## SCULPTURE

**The Parthenon Marbles**    The Parthenon sculptures have a special significance, because they rank high among the surviving originals of the 5th century B.C. The extant Parthenon statuary falls into three groups: the high-relief metopes of the Doric frieze, the free-standing pediment figures, and the low-relief cella frieze. Phidias' celebrated gold-and-ivory cult statue of Athena has long since disappeared, and inferior later copies convey little of the splendor attributed to it by the ancients. As architectural sculpture, the friezes and pediments should not be judged apart from the building they embellish. By providing diagonal lines and irregular masses as well as figures in motion, they offset the more static vertical and horizontal balances of the structural parts. The original location of these sculptures must also be kept in mind by the modern viewer: they were intended to be seen outdoors in the intense Greek sunlight and from the ground some 35 feet below (not out of context in the artificial light of a museum and at eye level).

The craftsmanship of the Parthenon marbles reveals the unevenness common to all group projects. Some sculptures are obviously from the hand of a master; others seem the routine products of artisans. The metopes were completed first, and some may even have been designed for Callicrates' earlier temple left unfinished. That these were in turn surpassed by the finer quality of the pedimental figures and the cella frieze indicates that the Parthenon sculptures derived not from methods of stan-

dardization but rather from a continuous, progressive approach to the ideal of excellence in craftsmanship.

The metopes of the Doric frieze play an important part in the architectural design of the Parthenon by providing a welcome variety of figures to relieve the structural unity, and their diagonal lines contrast well with the alternating verticals of the triglyphs and the long horizontals of the architrave and cornice just below and above. In order to take full advantage of the bright sunlight, these metopes were done in *high relief,* a technique by which the figures are deeply carved so as to project boldly outward from the background plane. The subject of those in the south frieze is the battle of the Lapiths and centaurs after a centaur has kidnapped a Lapith bride at a wedding feast. In one of the most skillfully executed (Fig. 27), the rich spreading folds of the mantle form a fine unifying framework for the human figure, and, in turn, both make a striking contrast with the awkward angularity of the grotesque centaur.

The inner frieze (Figs. 28–30) that ran along the outer walls of the cella was a continuous band about 3¾ feet high, over 500 feet in length, and included some 600 figures. Since this frieze was placed behind the colonnade and directly below roof level, where it had to be viewed close by at a steep upward angle, some sculptural adjustments were called for. The technique, of necessity, was *low relief,* in which the figures are shallowly carved. Because shadows in this indirect light are cast upward, the frieze had to be tilted slightly and cut so that the lower parts of the figures project only 1¼ inches from the background plane, with the relief gradually becoming bolder toward the top where the figures extend outward about 2¼ inches. The handling of space, however, is so deft that as many as half a dozen horsemen are depicted riding abreast without confusing the separate spatial planes. The horses, when seen at eye level, are too small in comparison with their riders. When viewed from below and in indirect light, however, they would not seem out of proportion. The use of color and metal attachments for such details as reins and bridles also helped accent parts and protected the clarity of the design. All the heads, whether the figures are afoot or on horseback, have been kept on the same level in order to preserve the unity of the design as well as to provide a parallel with the architectural line. (This principle, known as *isocephaly,* will also be encountered in later Byzantine art [Pl. 10, p. 91; Fig. 104].)

The cella frieze, unlike the traditional mythological subjects elsewhere in the Parthenon sculptures, depicts the Athenians themselves participating in the festival of their goddess. The scene is the Greater

**below: 27.** *Lapith and Centaur,* metope from Parthenon, frieze. 447–441 B.C. Marble, 3'11" × 4'2". British Museum, London.

**top: 28.** Parthenon. Frieze of west cella. c. 440 B.C. Marble.

**above right: 29.** *Horsemen,* detail of Parthenon west cella frieze. c. 440 B.C. Marble, height 3'7".

**right: 30.** *Poseidon and Apollo,* detail of Parthenon east cella frieze. c. 440 B.C. Marble, height 3'7". Acropolis Museum, Athens.

**31.** *Birth of Athena.* Reconstruction of Parthenon east pediment. Acropolis Museum, Athens.

above: **32.** *Dionysus,* from Parthenon east pediment. c. 438–432 B.C. Marble, over life-size. British Museum, London.

**33.** *Demeter, Persephone, and Iris,* from Parthenon east pediment. c. 438–432 B.C. Marble, over life-size. British Museum, London.

Panathenaea that took place every four years. Larger than the annual local procession because it included delegations from other Greek cities, the Greater Panathenaea was also the prelude to more elaborate poetical and oratorical contests, dramatic presentations, and games. On the western side (Figs. 28, 29), which is still in place, last-minute preparations for the parade are in progress as the riders ready their mounts. The action, appropriately enough, starts just at the point where the live procession, after passing through the Propylaea, would have paused to regroup. The parade then splits in two, one file proceeding along the north and the other along the south side. After the bareback riders come the charioteers; and, as the procession approaches the eastern corners, the marshals slacken the tempo to a more dignified pace. Here are musicians playing lyres and flutes, youths bearing wine jugs for libations, and maidens walking with stately tread. The two files then converge on the east side, where magistrates are waiting to begin the ceremonies. Even the immortal gods, as seen in the panel depicting Poseidon and Apollo (Fig. 30), are present to bestow their Olympian approval on the proceedings. The high point of the ritual comes in the center of the east side with the presentation of the *peplos*, the saffron and purple-tinted mantle woven and embroidered by chosen maidens to drape the ancient wooden image of Athena.

The pedimental sculptures, in contrast to the friezes, are free-standing figures, carved in the round. The themes of both pediments have to do with Athena, that on the west, facing the city, depicting her triumph over Poseidon (see p. 20) and that on the east pediment (Fig. 31) recounting the story of her miraculous birth, the event that was celebrated each summer at the Panathenaea. While but a few fragments of the western pediment remain, enough survives of its eastern counterpart to convey a good idea of its original state.

From various sources it is known that the eastern scene is Mt. Olympus, and Zeus, father of the gods, was seated in the center. On one side stood Hephaestus, cleaving open the head of Zeus to let Athena spring forth in full battle array. The sudden appearance of the goddess of wisdom, like a brilliant idea from the mind of its creator, disturbs the Olympian calm. As the news spreads from the center to the sides, each figure is in some way affected by the presence of divine wisdom in their midst. Iris, the messenger of the gods (Fig. 33), rushes toward the left with a rapid motion as revealed by her windswept drapery. Seated on a chest, Demeter and Persephone are turning toward her, and the rich folds of their costumes bespeak their attitudes and interest. The reclining Dionysus, with his panther skin and mantle spread over a rock (Fig. 32), is awakening and looking toward the sun god Helios, the horses of whose chariot are just rising from the foaming sea at break of day. Three goddesses (Fig. 34) on the opposite

**34.** *Three Goddesses*, from Parthenon east pediment. c. 438–432 B.C. Marble, over life-size. British Museum, London.

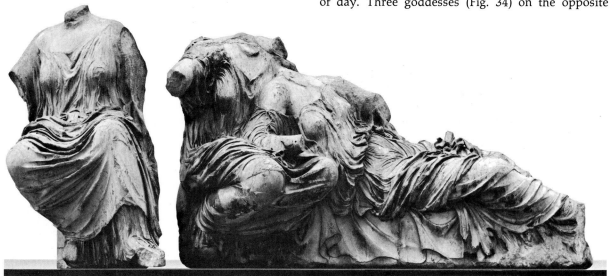

side have postures that bring out their relationship to the composition. The one nearest the center of the pediment, aware of what has happened, is about to rise, while the middle figure is starting to turn toward her. The reclining figure at the right, still in repose, is as unaware of the event as is her counterpart Dionysus on the far left. Like the feminine group on the left, these figures constitute a unified episode in the composition, and their relation to the whole is made clear in the lush lines of their flowing robes. This undulating linear pattern, and the manner in which it transparently reveals the anatomy of the splendid bodies beneath, mark a high point in the art of sculpture. At the far right, the chariot of the moon goddess Selene was seen descending (Fig. 35). Now only the expressive downward-declining horse's head remains to show by his spent energies that it is the end of the day.

Perhaps the most admirable aspect of the whole composition is the ease and grace with which each piece fulfills its assigned space. Fitting suitable figures into a low isosceles triangle and at the same time maintaining an uncrowded yet unified appearance was a problem that long occupied Greek designers. One over-life-size figure, such as Apollo, usually dominated the center, with seated or crouching figures on either side and reclining ones in the acute side angles. The pediment space of the Parthenon stretched about 90 feet and rose over 11 feet in the center. The rising and setting sun and moon chariots defined the time span as that of a single day, while the setting of Mt. Olympus and the single event supplied the identity of time, place, and action in keeping with the classical unities (a principle that will be treated more fully in the section on drama). The ascending and descending chariots gave a contrasting upward and downward movement on the extreme ends, while the reclining and seated figures led the eye to the apex where the climax took place. The subsequent action dispersed the middle figures centrifugally once more toward the sides. The varied postures, rich plastic modeling, and flowing lines connect all the figures with such a unified motion that, even though the center ones are now missing, the meaning is quite clear.

Taken as a whole, the Parthenon marbles present a picture of the Greek past and present plus aspirations for the future. The attempt to interpret the dark ancient myths of a people into more enlightened contemporary terms is to be found here in the sculptures as well as in Greek philosophy, poetry, and drama. The metopes on the east portray the primeval battle of the gods and giants for control of the world, and the triumph of the Olympians hailed the coming of cosmic order out of chaos. The metopes on the south show the Lapiths, oldest inhabitants of the Greek peninsula, subduing the half-human centaurs with the aid of the Athenian hero Theseus. This victory signals the ascendancy of human ideals over the bestial side of human nature. In the north group, the Homeric epic of the defeat of the Trojans is told, while in the west metopes the Greeks are seen overcoming the Amazons, those ferocious women warriors who symbolized the Asiatic enemies and, in this case, allude to the Athenian defeat of the Persians at Marathon. In the east pediment, the birth of the city's patroness Athena is seen; while the west pediment tells the story of the rivalry of Athena as goddess of the intellect and Poseidon, patron of maritime trade, suggesting the conflict of two ways of life—the pursuit of enlightenment and of material wealth. The Panathenaic procession of the cella walls brings history up to date by depicting a contemporary subject. Here the proud Athenians could look upward and see their own images carved on a sacred temple, an echo of the living procession that marched along the sides of the temple on feast days. The climax came after they had gathered at the east portico and the portals of the temple were opened to the rays of the rising sun, revealing the image of the goddess herself. Shining forth in all her gold-and-ivory glory, Athena was the personification of the eternal truth, goodness, and beauty for which her faithful followers were striving. With her help, Greek civilization had overcome the ignorance of the barbarians. The bonds between the goddess and the citizens of her city were thus periodically renewed, and the Parthenon as a whole glorified not only Athena but the Athenians as well.

**The Course of Hellenic Sculpture**    The tremendous distance traversed by the art of sculpture from the archaic, or preclassical, phase prior to the 5th century B.C. to the end of the Hellenic style period in the mid-4th century can be seen clearly when examples are compared. The *Kouros* (Fig. 36) represents the archaic sculptural type of youthful athlete, victor in the games, moving toward the temple to dedicate himself. The advancing left foot provides the only suggestion of movement in the otherwise rigid posture. The anatomy of the torso is severely formal and close to the block of stone from which it was carved. The wide shoulders and long arms attached to the sides provide a quadrangular framework; the long vertical line from the neck to the navel divides the chest; while the diamond-shaped abdomen is defined by four almost straight lines, a heritage of the formalized geometrical conventions of the archaic period.

The *Doryphorus,* or *"Spear Bearer,"* by Polyclitus (Fig. 37), in contrast, moves with greater poise and freedom. Originally in bronze, it is now known only through routine marble copies. The sculptor was renowned in ancient times for his attempts to formulate a canon, or rational theory of proportions, for the human figure. The exact way Polyclitus' theory operated is not known, but the Roman architect Vitruvius mentions that beauty consists "in the proporabove: **35.** *Moon Goddess' Horse,* from Parthenon east pediment. c. 438–432 B.C. Marble, life-size. British Museum, London.

below left: **36.** *Kouros,* from Sounion. c. 615–590 B.C. Marble, height 11″. National Museum, Athens.

below center: **37.** Polyclitus. *Doryphorus ("Spear Bearer").* Roman copy of original of c. 450–440 B.C. Marble, height 6′6″. National Museum, Naples.

below right: **38.** Praxiteles. *Hermes and the Infant Dionysus.* c. 340 B.C. Marble, height 7′1″. Museum, Olympia.

tions, not of the elements, but of the parts, that is to say, of finger to finger, and of all the fingers to the palm and wrist, and of these to the forearm, and of the forearm to the upper arm, and of all the parts to each other, as they are set forth in the Canon of Polyclitus." Whether the module was the head, the forearm, or the hand apparently varied from statue to statue. Once adopted, however, the whole and all its parts were expressible in multiples or fractions of the module. As Vitruvius illustrated the canon, the head would be one-eighth of the total height; the face one-tenth, subdivided, in turn, into three parts: forehead, nose, and mouth and chin. The forearm would be one-quarter the height, and the width of the chest equal to this length of forearm. Like the optical refinements of the Parthenon, however, Polyclitus' canon was not a mechanical formula but one that allowed for some flexibility, so that the dimensions could be adjusted for a figure in movement or for one designed to be seen from a certain angle.

Praxiteles' *Hermes and the Infant Dionysus* (Fig. 38), coming at the close of the Hellenic period, is the epitome of poise and polish. Unlike the rather studied *Doryphorus,* Hermes rests his weight easily on one foot, and the relaxed stance throws the body into the familiar **S**-curve, a Praxitelean pose widely copied in later Hellenistic and Roman statuary. From the stiffness of the stolid archaic *Kouros* and the strength of the stocky *Doryphorus,* the sculptor Praxiteles has arrived at complete plastic mastery of his material. Through the soft modeling and suave surface treatment, Praxiteles suggests the blood, bone, and sinews beneath the skin and gives his cold marble material the vibrancy and warmth of living flesh.

The *Charioteer of Delphi* (Pl. 3, p. 8) and the *Zeus* found at Artemision (Fig. 39)—two of the rare Hellenic bronze originals—and the Roman marble copy of Myron's lost bronze *Discobolus,* or *"Discus Thrower"* (Fig. 40), reveal a transition in style from quiet monumentality to energetic action within a 20-year time span in the mid-5th century. The splendid *Charioteer* once was part of a larger group that included several horses, and, although in action, the figure is given something of the monumentality and equilibrium of a fluted column by the vertical folds of its lower garment. The commanding figure of *Zeus,* poised to throw a thunderbolt, reveals in its powerful musculature the massive reserves of strength of a truly godlike physique. In Myron's *Discobolus,* the taut yet resilient muscles of the athlete are poised momentarily between a backward movement and forward thrust. The vigorous motion is admirably contained by the curved arms that enclose the composition and confine the activity to a single plane.

The archaic *Kore* from Samos (Fig. 41) is one of a file of maidens, originally in a temple courtyard, carrying small animals as votive offerings. Her se-verely cylindrical figure is quite abstract in that everything extraneous has been eliminated and only the essential formal and linear elements retained. The rhythmically repeated vertical lines of the skirt contrast with the ingenious curves of the upper drapery to create a pleasing linear design. The *Athena Lemnia* (Fig. 42) is a superior marble copy of Phidias' original bronze statue that stood on the Athenian acropolis. Phidias here created a mood that is more lyrical than epical, and in ancient sources the statue was referred to regularly as "the beautiful." The serene profile, softened by the subtle modeling, surely approaches the ideal of chaste classical beauty. Praxiteles' *Aphrodite of Cnidos* was proclaimed by Greco-Roman critics as the finest statue in existence. Now known only through such an inferior copy as Figure 43, the "smile playing gently over her parted lips" and the "soft melting gaze of the eyes with their bright and joyous expression" that the Roman writer Lucian so admired in the original can now only be imagined. Praxiteles, however, departed from the draped goddesses of the previous century by boldly portraying the goddess of

**right: 39.** *Zeus (Poseidon?).* c. 460–450 B.C. Bronze, height 6'10". National Museum, Athens.

**left: 40.** MYRON. *Discobolus ("Discus Thrower").* Roman copy after bronze original of c. 460 B.C. Marble, life-size. National Museum, Rome.

love in the nude. By so doing, he created a prototype that influenced all subsequent treatment of the undraped female figure.

## DRAMA

Greek drama was a distillation of life in poetic form, represented (or imitated, to use the ancient term) on the stage. In these vivid presentations, members of the audience through their representatives in the chorus became vicarious participants in events happening to a group of people at another time and in another place. Like all great works of art, Greek drama can be approached on many different levels. At one, it can be a thrilling story of violent actions and bloody revenge. At another, it is a struggle between human ambition and divine retribution, or a conflict of free will and predestined fate. At still another level, it becomes a moving experience that ennobles through lofty language and inspired poetry. Plots were always taken from mythology, heroic legends, or stories of royal houses. Since these age-old themes were forms of popular history known in advance, the dramatist could concern himself with more

**left: 41.** *Kore,* from Samos. c. 550 B.C. Marble, height c. 5′3″. State Museums, East Berlin.

**center: 42.** PHIDIAS. *Athena Lemnia.* Roman copy after original of c. 450 B.C. Marble, height c. 6′6″. Body, Albertinum, Dresden; head, Civic Museum, Bologna.

**right: 43.** PRAXITELES. *Aphrodite of Cnidos.* Roman copy after original of c. 320 B.C. Marble, height 6′8″. Vatican Museums, Rome.

purely poetic functions than plot development. He could provide dramatic commentaries on old tales, reinterpreting them in the light of recent events. He could thus inspire by conjuring up the heroic past, as did Aeschylus in *The Persians;* express individual sentiments in the light of universal experience, as did Sophocles in *Antigone;* invite reexamination of ancient superstitions, as did Euripides in *The Bacchants;* or remind that present difficulties had parallels in time past and, by showing that it has ever been thus, place current problems in broader historical perspective.

The origins of the Greek dramatic form were rooted in the religious rites associated with the wor-

**44.** SCHOOL OF SCOPAS(?). *Dionysian Procession.* 4th century B.C. Marble. National Museum, Athens.

ship of Dionysus (the Bacchus of Roman mythology), the god of wine and revelry, whose cult festivals coincided with spring planting and fall harvesting seasons (Fig. 44). From primitive magical practices, the rituals gradually grew in refinement until they became a vehicle for powerful creative expression. When theaters came to be built, they were located in a precinct sacred to Dionysus. His altar occupied the center of the circular *orchestra* where the chorus sang and danced, and the audience which gathered paid their tribute to him by their presence.

In the beginning, Greek drama had only a chorus, whose function, according to the philosopher Nietzsche, was to conjure up the divine vision in which it "beholds its lord and master Dionysus ... [and] sees how he, the god, suffers and glorifies himself." The vision beheld by the chorus eventually came to be acted out, and the alternation between group *choruses* and individually declaimed *episodes* became the basis of the dramatic form. Put another way, the choral songs were at first a group narration of great deeds. Later, the words attributed to the hero were sung and mimed by the leader of the chorus. Then a second and a third actor were added, and the dialogue of the enacted episodes achieved parity with the alternating choruses. Hellenistic and Roman drama were to upset this classic balance by emphasizing the action and roles of individual performers, but in Hellenic times the collective voice of the chorus and that of the principal actors were equal in importance. As the group chanted its *strophes* and *antistrophes* ("turns" and "counterturns"), it effected transition from scenes, reminded of the past and foretold the future, reflected public opinion, voiced the dramatist's own commentary, and, above all, by acting as its proxy, made the audience feel a part of the play.

The Theater of Dionysus at Athens (Fig. 13), like the better-preserved one at Epidaurus (Fig. 45), had an *auditorium* hollowed out of a hillside to accommodate approximately 18,000 spectators. The semicircular tiers of seats half surrounded the orchestra and faced the *skene,* a scene building or raised platform, on which the actors played their roles. The skene had a permanent architectural façade with three doors for the actors, while the chorus entered and exited at the corners below. The stylized face of the skene, suggesting a temple or palace, was suitable for most dramatic situations, since the action almost always took place in the open. The chorus, for example, usually represented worshipers at a shrine, townspeople or petitioners before a palace, a mob, or a group of prisoners, while the actors moving in and out of the portals above took the parts of priests, heroes, or members of royal families. When the situation demanded another setting, the chorus or an actor would "paint" the scene with a few words so that other sets were unnecessary.

A typical Greek play opens with a *prologue,* spoken by one of the actors. The prologue sets the scene, outlines the plot, and provides a taking-off point for the action that is to follow. The substance of the drama then unfolds in a sequence of alternating choruses and episodes (usually five episodes enclosed by six choruses) and concludes with the *exodus* of the chorus and an *epilogue.* Actors wore masks of general types that could be recognized instantly by the audience. The size and outdoor location of the theaters made facial expressions ineffective, and the swift pace of Greek drama requires the player of a king or peasant to establish immediately a type and character. The masks were equipped with megaphones that helped project the voices, though the acoustics of the bowl-shaped theaters are generally excellent. Masks also proved useful when an actor took more than one part, bringing him immediate acceptance in either role.

Restraint and simplicity were the rule in Greek staging. As with the later Elizabethan theater, scenery was conspicuous by its absence. The only visual illusion seems to have been the *mechane,* a crane that lowered to the stage those actors portraying gods. This *deus ex machina,* or "god from the machine," in later times became a convenient way of solving dramatic problems that were too complex to be worked out by normal means. Direct action, moreover, never occurred on stage. Any violent deed took place elsewhere and was reported by a messenger or another character. The plays proceeded by narration, commentary, speculation, dialogue, and discussion. All these devices—plot known in advance, permanent stage setting, use of masks, offstage action—served two principal purposes: to accent the poetry of the play and to give the freest possible scope to the spectator's imagination. But while Greek drama is a complex of choral song, group dances, mimed action, and dialogue coordinated into a dramatic whole, poetry always is the central dramatic agent. It should also be noted that the Athenians experienced their plays and poetry only in oral presentations. While manuscript copies of literary and philosophical works were available to scholars, books in the modern sense did not exist. Much of the beauty and power of the plays was derived from the heightened experience of poetic declamation as well as from the Greek tongue itself. Not an accentual language, Greek admits of a wide variety of metrical patterns capable of expressing every nuance of action and mood. In experiencing a Greek drama in translation, therefore, the modern reader must let his imagination supply the melody, color, and flowing rhythms of the original language as well as the missing factors associated with a live theatrical production.

The scope of Greek drama was tremendous, extending from majestic tragedy of heroic proportions, through the pathos of *melodrama* (in its proper meaning of "drama with melody") and subtle *satires* (or "satyr plays"), all the way to the riotous *comedies* of Aristophanes. Conflict is always the basis for dramatic action, and the playwrights set up tensions between such forces as murder and revenge, crime and retribution, cowardice and courage, protest and resignation, human pride and humility. When, for instance, a hero is confronted with his destiny, the obstacles he encounters are at once insurmountable and necessary to surmount. In the conflict that follows, the play runs a gamut of emotions and explores the heights to which human life can soar and the depths to which it can sink. In Sophocles' *Oedipus Rex,* the hero starts at the peak of his kingly powers and ends in the abyss of human degradation. Each character in a true drama, moreover, is drawn three-dimensionally

**45.** Polyclitus the Younger. Theater, Epidaurus. c. 350 B.C. Diameter 373', orchestra 66' across.

so as to reveal a typically human mixture of attractive and repulsive, good and bad, traits. The *protagonist*, or central character, can fulfill the necessary conditions of tragedy only when he portrays some noble figure—one "highly renowned or prosperous," as Aristotle puts it—who is eventually brought to grief through some flaw in his own psychological makeup and by some inevitable stroke of fate. The reasons for this must be made apparent to the audience gradually through the process of "causal necessity." A common man's woes might bring about a pathetic situation but not a tragic one in the classical sense. When a virtuous hero is rewarded or the evil designs of a villain receive their just deserts, obviously there is no tragic situation. When a blameless man is brought from a fortunate to an unfortunate condition or when an evil person rises from misery to good fortune, there is likewise no tragedy because the moral sense is outraged.

Under Aeschylus, its founder, Greek tragedy sought to comprehend the mystery of the divine will, often so inscrutable to man—as in his *Agamemnon*. By establishing a working relationship between man and his gods, Aeschylus tried to reconcile the conflict between the human and the divine and find a basis for personal as well as social justice. The implications of the early Aeschylean tragedy were thus strongly ethical, showing clearly that the drama was still identified in his mind with theological thought. The forms of Sophocles' plays were distinguished by their impeccable craftsmanship, while their lofty content was based on the course of human destiny as seen in the light of the moral law of the universe.

Euripides, said the philosopher Aristotle, sought to show men as they are, while Sophocles had depicted men as they ought to be. In some ways, the works of Euripides may not be so typical of the Hellenic style as those of Aeschylus or Sophocles, but his influence on the subseqùent development of the drama, both in Hellenistic and later times, was incalculably greater. *The Bacchants,* the last of his ninety-odd plays, was written at a time when the darkness of disillusionment was descending on Athenian intellectuals toward the end of the disastrous Peloponnesian war, and in it he gives voice to some of the doubts and uncertainties of his time. Like most masterpieces, it is in some respects atypical, while in others it seems to stem from the deepest traditional roots of the theater's origin. Despite some inner inconsistencies and a certain elusiveness of meaning, *The Bacchants* has all the formal perfection and grandeur of utterance of the loftiest tragedies. The strange wild beauty of the choruses, the magic of its poetry, and the complex interplay between the human and divine wills endow it with all the necessary ingredients of the theater at its best.

After the great days of Aeschylus, Sophocles, and Euripides were over, Aristotle, with knowledge of their complete works instead of the relatively few extant examples known today, wrote a perceptive analysis of tragedy and more broadly of art in general in his treatise *Poetics.* According to him, true drama, as indeed all other works of art, must have form in the sense of a beginning, a middle, and an end. Unity of time, place, and action is also desirable. Sophocles' *Oedipus Rex,* for example, takes place in a single day (albeit a busy one); all the scenes are set in front of the palace at Thebes; and the action is direct and continuous without subplots. Other Greek plays encompass a longer span of time and have several settings. But, as Aristotle pointed out, these unities were useful but by no means hard and fast rules. In the episodes, convention held that three actors on stage at one time was the maximum. If the play required six parts, the roles were usually apportioned among three actors. As the action proceeds, the conflict between *protagonist* and *antagonist* emerges, and the play should rise to its climax in the middle episode. Through the proper tragic necessity, the hero's downfall comes because he carried the seeds of his own destruction within his breast. After this turning point, the well-planned anticlimax resolves the action once more into a state of equilibrium. Tragedy, according to Aristotle, had to be composed of six necessary elements which he ranked as follows: Plot, "the arrangement of the incidents"; Character, "that which reveals moral purpose"; Thought, "where something is proved to be or not to be"; Diction, "the metrical arrangements of the words"; Song, "melody holds the chief place among the embellishments"; and Spectacle. Finally, Aristotle summed up his definition of tragedy as "an imitation of an action that is serious, complete, and of a certain magnitude; in language embellished with each kind of ornament, the several kinds being found in separate sections of the play; in the form of action, not of narrative; with incidents arousing pity and fear, wherewith to accomplish its *katharsis* ['purgation'] of the emotions."

## MUSIC

The word *music* today carries with it the connotation of a fully mature and independent art. It must be borne in mind, however, that symphonies, chamber music, and solo instrumental compositions, where the focus is almost entirely on abstract sound, are relatively modern forms. The word *music* is still used to cover the union of sound with many other elements, as in the case of popular songs, dance music, military marches, and church music. It also describes the combination with lyric and narrative poetry, as in songs and ballads; with bodily movements, as in the dance and ballet; and with drama, as in opera.

In ancient Greece, *music* in its broadest sense meant any of the arts and sciences that came under the patronage of the muses, those imaginary maidens

**46.** Douris. *Instruction in Music and Grammar in an Attic School.* Red-figured painting on the exterior of a kylix. c. 470 B.C. State Museums, West Berlin.

who were the daughters of the heavenly Zeus and the more earthly Mnemosyne. Since Zeus was the creator and Mnemosyne, as her name implies, the symbol of memory, the muses and their arts were considered to be the results of the union of the creative urge and memory, half divine, half human. This was simply a fanciful way of saying that music was recorded inspiration. As Greek civilization progressed, the muses, under the patronage of Apollo, god of prophecy and enlightenment, gradually increased to nine, and the arts and sciences over which they presided came to include all the intellectual and inspirational disciplines that sprang from the fertile minds of this highly creative people—lyric poetry, tragic and comic drama, choral dancing, and song. Astronomy and history were also included. The visual arts and crafts, on the other hand, were protected by Athena and Hephaestus—intelligence tempered by fire. Plato and others placed music in opposition to gymnastic or physical pursuits, and its meaning in this sense was as broad as our use of the words *liberal arts* or *culture.*

The Greeks also used *music* more narrowly in the sense of the tonal art. But music was always intimately bound up with poetry, drama, and the dance and was usually found in their company. At one place in the *Republic,* Socrates asks: "And when you speak of music, do you include literature or not?" And the answer is in the affirmative. Thus, while it is known that the Greeks did have independent instrumental music apart from its combination with words, evidence points to the fact that the vast body of their music was connected with literary forms. This does

not imply, of course, that music lacked a distinct identity or that it was swallowed up by poetry, but rather that it had an important and honored part in poetry. Plato, for example, inquires: "And I think that you must have observed again and again what a poor appearance the tales of the poets make when stripped of the colours which music puts upon them, and recited in simple prose. . . . They are like faces which were never really beautiful, but only blooming; and now the bloom of youth has passed away from them?"

Greek music must therefore be considered primarily in its union with literature, as illustrated in the vase painting *Instruction in Music and Grammar in an Attic School* by Douris (Fig. 46). The clearest statement of this again is found in the *Republic,* where it is pointed out that "melody is composed of three things, the words, the harmony [by which is meant the sequence of melodic intervals], and the rhythm." In discussing the relative importance of each, Plato states that "harmony and rhythm must follow the words." The two arts thus are united in the single one of *prosody*—that is, the melodic and rhythmic setting of a poetic text. The Greek melodies and rhythms are known to have been associated with specific moods, or *modes*—scales constructed by adjusting the pitch of tones within the octave as with the more modern major and minor modes. The great variety of Greek modes allowed poets and dramatists to elicit a gamut of emotional responses from their audiences. And while ethical and emotional orientations have changed over the centuries, the basic modal and metrical system of the Greeks has, in effect, continued through all subsequent periods of Western music and poetry.

Music, in both its broad and narrow senses, was closely woven into the fabric of the emotional, intellectual, and social life of the ancient Greeks, and the art was considered by them to have a fundamental connection with the well-being of individuals personally as well as with their social and physical environment. There is no more eloquent tribute to the power of art in public affairs than that made by Socrates who said "when modes of music change, the fundamental laws of the State always change with them." Education for young people in Greece consisted of a balanced curriculum of music for the soul and gymnastic for the body. The broad principle of building a sound body is still one of the ideals of education. Even the welfare of the soul after death had musical overtones, since immortality to many Greeks meant being somehow in tune with the cosmic forces, and being at last able to hear the "music of the spheres." All these notions had to do with the idea of the physical nature being some way in harmony with the metaphysical, and the soul being an attunement of the body. According to the Greek myth of Orpheus, who is depicted in a fine red-figured vase of the early 5th century B.C. (Pl. 4, p. 8), music even had the miraculous power to overcome death. This thought found an enduring place in Western literature, and no writer has expressed it more sensitively than Shakespeare in *The Merchant of Venice* (Act V, Scene 1):

> ...look, how the floor of heaven
> Is thick inlaid with patines of bright gold:
> There's not the smallest orb which thou behold'st
> But in his motion like an angel sings,
> Still quiring to the young-eyed cherubins;
> Such harmony is in immortal souls;
> But, whilst this muddy vesture of decay
> Doth grossly close it in, we cannot hear it.

The most important Greek contribution to music is without doubt a theoretical one—that of coordinating the mathematical ratios of melodic intervals with their scale system. The discovery, attributed to Pythagoras, showed that such intervals as the octave, fifth, and fourth had a mathematical relationship. This can easily be heard when a tuned string is stopped off exactly in the middle. The musical interval between the tone of the unstopped string and the one which is divided into two equal parts will then be the octave, and the mathematical ratio will be $1 : 2$. Then if a segment of the string divided in two parts is compared with one of a string divided into three parts, the resulting interval will be the fifth, and the ratio $2 : 3$. If one compares the tone of the triply divided string with one divided into four parts, the interval will be the fourth and, the ratio $3 : 4$. Hence, mathe-

matically $1 : 2$ equals the octave; $2 : 3$, the fifth; $3 : 4$, the fourth; $8 : 9$, the whole tone; and so on. Music to Pythagoras and his followers thus was synonymous with order and proportion and rested on a demonstrably rational basis. This tremendous discovery seemed to be a key that might unlock the secrets of the universe, which, they reasoned, might likewise be reduced to numbers and be constructed according to the principles of a musical scale. This idea found its way into all aspects of Greek intellectual life, and even Plato built up a conception of the cosmic harmony of the world on these musical principles in his *Timaeus.* It is possible that the architects also incorporated these laws into the proportions and designs of their buildings. The Roman architect Vitruvius, for instance, was thoroughly familiar with Greek musical theory.

Knowledge of Greek music must be gleaned from a variety of sources, such as occasional literary references, poetry and drama, visual representations of musical instruments and music making in sculpture and painting, theoretical treatises, and some very fragmentary surviving examples of the music itself. When all the separate sources are combined, a faint notion of what Greek music actually was like can be gleaned. From them, it is apparent that music's highest development undoubtedly was found in its union with the drama. The Athenian dramatist was by tradition responsible for the music, the training of the chorus, and the staging of his play as well as for the writing of the book. In addition to all this, he often played one of the roles. The great dramatists, therefore, were composers as well as poets, actors, playwrights, and producers.

In reconstructing the Greek drama, one must imagine a Greek audience to whom the drama was a lively aural and visual experience of choral singing and dancing, of vocal and instrumental music, as well as of dialogue and dramatic sequence. Today, with all the choruses and dances missing, such a play as *The Suppliants* of Aeschylus is like the libretto of an opera without the musical score. It is so clearly a lyric drama that the music itself must have been the principal means by which the poet conveyed his meaning. Euripides' *The Bacchants,* on the other hand, has far greater intrinsic dramatic substance, but even here the emotional intensity of the individual scenes often rises to such a pitch that music had to take over where the words left off—just as when a person is so overcome with feeling that words fail and he resorts to inarticulate sounds and gestures.

The weight of the musical expression fell primarily on the chorus, which was the original basis of the dramatic form and from which all the other elements of the drama evolved. We have at last realized, said Nietzsche in his analysis of Greek drama, "that the scene, together with the action, was fundamentally and originally conceived only as a *vision*, that the only reality is just the chorus, which of itself generates the vision and speaks thereof with the entire symbolism of dancing, tone, and word." The chorus performed both in stationary positions and in motion, accompanied by mimetic gestures as it circulated about the orchestra where the choral songs, dances, and group recitatives took place around the altar of Dionysus. The forms of the choruses were metrically and musically very elaborate and were written with such variety and invention that repetitions either within a single play or in other plays by the same poet were very rare.

Interestingly enough, the sole surviving relic of Greek music from the 5th century B.C. is a fragment of a choral *stasimon*, or "stationary chorus," from Euripides' *Orestes*. All ancient Greek manuscripts come down through the ages from the hands of medieval scribes who omitted the musical notation of the earlier copies because it was no longer comprehensible to them. In this instance, the musical notation was included, but all that is left is a single sheet of papyrus now perforated with age. From ancient accounts, however, it is known that the music of Euripides differed considerably from that of his predecessor Aeschylus and his contemporary Sophocles. Euripides was educated in the "new" music by Timotheus, while Sophocles received his instruction from the more conservative rival Lampros. The new music was considered more ornate and was criticized because it was so complex that the words were unintelligible. The text was thus on its way to becoming of as little consequence as that of an opera chorus of today, while traditionally it had dominated the music. Evidence to support this development is found in the literary content of Euripidean choruses, which sometimes have little or no direct connection with the action.

Fragmentary though this scrap of evidence is, these few notes from Euripides' *Orestes* are enough to tell their own story. Since the intervals called for are in half and quarter tones, it means that Euripidean choruses were musically complex enough to demand highly skilled singers. The mode is mixolydian, which is described by Aristotle in his *Politics* as being "mournful and restrained." The words that accompany the fragment perfectly express this sentiment, and, when properly performed, it still conveys this mood. Other than this single relic of choral recitative, the music of the 5th century must remain mute to our ears, and we can only echo the words of Keats in his "Ode on a Grecian Urn": "Heard melodies are sweet, but those unheard are sweeter."

## IDEAS

Each of the arts—architecture, sculpture, painting, poetry, drama, and music—is, of course, a distinct medium of expression. Each has its materials, whether of stone, bronze, pigments, words, or tones. Each has its skilled craftsmen who have disciplined themselves through years of study so they can mold their materials into meaningful forms. But every artist, be he architect, sculptor, painter, poet, dramatist, or musician, is also a child of his time, who in youthful years is influenced by the social, political, philosophical, and religious ideas of his period and who, in turn, during his maturity contributes creative leadership in his special field. No art exists apart from its fellows, and it is no accident that the Greeks thought of the arts as a family of sister muses. Architecture, to complete itself, must rely on sculpture and painting for embellishments; sculpture and painting, for their parts, must search for congenial architectural surroundings. Drama embraces poetry, song, and the dance in the setting of a theater. This was all quite clear in ancient times, as Plutarch quotes Simonides as saying, "Painting is silent poetry; poetry is painting that speaks." When the philosophers Plato and Aristotle discoursed on the arts, they looked for common elements applicable to all. And they were just as keen in their search for unity amid the multiplicities of art as they were for unity among all the other aspects of human experience.

Certain recurring themes appear in each of the arts of the Hellenic period as artists sought to bring their ideals to expression. Out of these themes emerges a trio of ideas—humanism, idealism, and rationalism—that recur continually in Athenian thought and action. These three ideas, then, provide the framework that surrounds the arts and encloses them in such a way that they come together into a significant unity.

**Humanism**     "Man," said Protagoras, "is the measure of all things." And, as Sophocles observed, "Many are the wonders of the world, and none so wonderful as man." This, in essence, is humanism. With himself as yardstick, Hellenic man conceived his gods as perfect beings, immortal and free from physical infirmities but, like himself, subject to very human passions and ambitions. The gods likewise were personifications of human ideals: Zeus stood for masculine creative power, Hera for maternal womanliness, Athena for wisdom, Apollo for youthful brilliance, Aphrodite for feminine desirability, and so on down the list. And because of his resemblance to the gods, Hellenic man gained greatly in self-esteem. When gods were more human, as the saying goes, men were more divine.

The principal concern of the Greeks was with human beings—their social relationships, their place in the natural environment, and their stake in the universal scheme of things. In such a small city-state as Athens, civic duties devolved on each individual. Every responsible person had to concern himself with politics, which Aristotle considered to be the highest social ethics. Participation in public affairs was based on the need to subordinate personal aspirations to the good of the whole state. A man endowed with great qualities of mind and body was honor-bound to exercise his gifts in the service of his fellowmen. Aeschylus, Socrates, and Sophocles were men of action who served Athens on the battlefield as well as in public forums and theaters. One responsibility of a citizen was to foster the arts, and under Athenian democracy the state itself, meaning the people as a whole, became the principal patrons of the arts.

Politically and socially, the Athenian's life was balanced between an aristocratic conservatism and a liberal individualism, which were maintained in equilibrium by the democratic institutions of his society. His art reflects a gravitational pull between this aristocratic tradition, which resisted change and emphasized austerity, restraint, and stylization in the arts, and the new dynamic liberalism, which opposed conservatism with greater emphasis on emotion, the desire to cultivate ornateness, and a taste for naturalism. The genius of Phidias lay in his ability to achieve a golden mean between these opposites, and the incomparable Parthenon and its sculptures were the result.

Humanism also expressed itself in kinship with nature. By personifying all things, animate and inanimate, the Greeks tried to come to terms with unpredictable natural phenomena and to explain the inexplicable. With their forests populated with elusive nymphs and satyrs, their seas with energetic tritons, and their skies with capricious zephyrs, they found an imaginative way of explaining some of the forces beyond their control. These personifications, as well as the conception of the gods as idealized human beings, created a happy condition for the arts. By increasing his understanding of nature in all its aspects, Hellenic man also enhanced his own humanity. Even when the scientific philosophers sought to reduce the universe to basic matter—earth, air, fire, water—man's body and soul were still identified with the basic stuff of the natural world. To create an imaginary world that is also a poetic image of the real world will always be one of the pursuits of the artist. And the Greeks thought of art as a *mimêsis*—that is, an imitation or representation of nature. Since this also included human nature, it implied a re-creation of life in the various mediums of art.

Particularly congenial to this humanistic mode of thought was the art of sculpture. With the human body as the point of departure, such divinities as Athena and Apollo appeared as idealized images of perfect feminine and masculine beauty. Equally imaginative were such deviations from the human norm as the goat-footed Pan, the half-human half-horse centaurs, and the myriads of fanciful creatures and monsters that symbolized the forces of nature. The Greeks were more thoroughly at home in the

physical world than the later Christian peoples who believed in a separation of flesh and spirit. The Greeks greatly admired the beauty and agility of the human body at the peak of its development. In addition to studies in literature and music, Greek youth was trained from childhood for competition in the Athenian and Olympic games. Since it was through the perfection of their bodies that men most resembled the gods, the culture of the body was a spiritual as well as a physical activity. The nude body in action at gymnasiums was a fact of daily experience, and sculptors had ample opportunity to observe its proportions and musculature. The result is embodied in such well-known examples as the statues of athletes attributed to Polyclitus, such as the *Doryphorus* (Fig. 37) and the *Discobolus* by Myron (Fig. 40). As an instrument of expression, the male nude reached a high point in the 5th century B.C., but the female form had to wait for similar treatment until the succeeding century.

Any humanistic point of view assumes that life here and now is good and meant to be enjoyed. This attitude is the opposite of medieval asceticism, which denied the joys of this life as snares of the devil, believing that true good could be attained only in the unseen world beyond the grave. While the Greeks had no single belief about life after death, the usual one is found in the underworld scene of Homer's *Odyssey* when the shade of the hero's mother explains that "when first the breath departs from the white bones, flutters the spirit away, and like to a dream it goes drifting." And the ghost of Achilles tells Odysseus that he would rather be the slave of the poorest living man than reign as king over the underworld. Greek *steles,* or gravestones, usually depicted the deceased in some characteristic worldly attitude— a warrior in battle, a hunter with his favorite horse or dog, or a lady choosing her jewelry (Fig. 47).

The spiritual kingdom of the Greeks was definitely of this world. They produced no major religious prophets, had no divinely imposed creeds, no sacred scriptures as final authority on religious matters, no organized priesthood. Such mottoes inscribed on the sacred stones of Delphi as "Know thyself" and "Nothing in excess" were suggestions that bore no resemblance to the thunderous "Thou Shalt Nots" of the earlier Ten Commandments. Knowledge of their gods came from Homer's epics and Hesiod's book of myths. The character and action of these gods, however, were subject to a wide variety of interpretations, as is clear from the commentaries of the 5th-century drama. This nonconformity bespoke a broad tolerance that allowed free speculation on the nature of the universe. Indeed, the Greeks had to work hard to penetrate the divine mind and interpret its meaning in human affairs. Ultimately, their ethical principles were embodied in four virtues—courage, meaning physical and moral bravery; temperance, in the sense of nothing too much or, as Pericles put it, "our love of what is beautiful does not lead us to extravagance"; justice, which meant rendering to each man his due; and wisdom, the pursuit of truth.

Just as the Greek religious outlook sought to capture the godlike image in human form, so also did the arts try to bring the experience of space and time within human grasp. Indefinite space and infinite time meant little to the Greeks. The modern concept of a nation as a territorial or spatial unit, for instance, did not exist for them. Expansion of their city-state was not concerned with lines on a map but with a cultural unity of independent peoples sharing common ideals. The continuous flow of time also seemed unreal, and their unconcern with a precise historical past is evidenced in the imperfection of their calendar and in the fact that their historians Herodotus and Thucydides were really chroniclers of almost-contemporary events. Their geometry was designed to measure static rather than moving bodies, and their visual arts emphasized the abiding qualities of poise and calm. Greek architecture humanized the experience of space by organizing it so that it was neither too complex nor too grand to be fully comprehended. The Parthenon's success rests on its power to humanize the experience of space. Through its geometry, such visual facts as repeated patterns, spatial progressions, and intervallic distances are brought within easy optical and intellectual grasp. The simplicity and clarity of Greek construction were always evident to the eye, and by defining the indefinite and imposing a sense of order on the chaos of space, the architects of Greece made their spaces clearly intelligible.

Just as architecture humanized the perception of space, so the arts of the dance, music, poetry, and drama humanized the experience of time. These arts fell within the broad meaning of *music*, and their humanistic connection was emphasized in the education of youth, because, as Plato says, "rhythm and harmony find their way into the inward places of the soul, on which they mightily fasten, imparting grace, and making the soul of him who is rightly educated graceful." The triple unities of time, place, and action observed by the dramatists brought the temporal flow within definite limits and are in striking contrast to the shifting scenes and continuous narrative styles of later periods. The essential humanism of Greek drama is found in its creation of distinctive human types; in its making of the chorus a collective human commentary on individual actions of gods and heroes; in its treatment of human actions in such a way that they rise above individual imitations to the level of universal principles; and, above all, the creation of tragedy, in which the great individual is shown rising

to the highest estate then plunging to the lowest depths, thereby spanning the ultimate limits of human experience. In sum, all the arts of Greece became the generating force by which Athenian man consciously or unconsciously felt himself identified with his fellow citizens and with the entire rhythm of life about him. Through the arts, human experience is raised to its highest level; refined by their fires, the individual is able to see his world more clearly in the light of universal values.

**Idealism**    When an artist faces the practical problems of representation, he has two main courses open to him: he can choose to represent objects either as they appear to the physical eye or as they appear to the mind's eye. In one case, he emphasizes nature, in the other, imagination; the world of appearances

47. *Grave Stele of Hegeso.* c. 410–400 B.C. Marble, height 4'11". National Museum, Athens.

as opposed to the world of essences; reality as contrasted with ideality. The avowed realist is more concerned with *concretion*—that is, with rendering the actual, tangible object that he sees with all its particular and peculiar characteristics. The idealist, on the other hand, accents *abstraction,* which is to say he eliminates all extraneous accessories and concentrates on the inner core, the essential qualities of things. A realist, in other words, tends to represent things as they are; an idealist, as they might or should be. Idealism as a creative viewpoint gives precedence to the idea or mental image, tries to transcend physical limitations, aspires toward a fulfillment that goes beyond actual observation, and seeks a concept closer to perfection.

Both courses were followed in the Hellenic style. One of Myron's most celebrated works was a bronze cow said to be so natural that it caused amorous reactions in bulls, and calves tried to suckle her. Such a work would certainly have been in line, in the literal sense at least, with the Greek definition of art as the imitation of nature. In contrast, the painter Parrhasius agreed with Socrates that, since it was impossible to find perfection in a single human model, it was necessary to "combine the most beautiful details of several, and thus contrive to make the whole figure look beautiful."

The case for idealism is argued in Plato's dialogues. He assumes a world of eternal verities and transcendental truths but recognizes that perfect truth, beauty, and goodness can exist only in the mental world of forms and ideas. Phenomena observed in the visible world are but reflections of these invisible forms. By way of illustration, parallelism is a concept, and two exactly parallel lines will, in theory, never meet. It is impossible, however, to find anything approaching true parallelism in nature, and, no matter how carefully a draftsman draws them, two lines will always be unparallel to a slight degree and, hence, will meet somewhere this side of infinity. But this does not destroy the concept of parallelism, which still exists in the mental image or idea of it. Plato's *Republic,* to cite another example, is an intellectual exercise in projecting an ideal state. No one knew better than the author that such a society did not exist in fact and probably never would. But this did not lessen the value of the activity, and the important thing was to set up goals that would approach his utopian ideal more closely than did any existing situation. "Would a painter be any the worse," he asks, "because, after having delineated with consummate art an ideal of a perfectly beautiful man, he was unable to show that any such man could ever have existed? . . . And is our theory a worse theory because we are unable to prove the possibility of a city being ordered in the manner described?" His idealistic theory, however, leads Plato into a rather strange position regarding the activities of artists. When, for instance, they fashion a building, a statue, or a paint-

ing, they are imitating, or representing, specific things that, in turn, are imitations of the ideal forms, and hence their products are thrice removed from the truth. The clear implication is, of course, that art should try to get away from the accidental and accent the essential, to shun the transitory and seek the permanent.

Aristotle, for his part, distinguished between various approaches in art. In his *Poetics,* he observes that "it follows that we must represent men either as better than in real life, or as worse, or as they are. It is the same in painting. Polygnotus depicted men as nobler than they are, Pauson as less noble, Dionysius drew them true to life. . . . So again in language, whether prose or verse unaccompanied by music. Homer, for example, makes men better than they are; Cleophon as they are; Hegemon the Thasian, the inventor of parodies, . . . worse than they are." Aristotle also applied the same standard to drama, pointing out that "Comedy aims at representing men as worse, Tragedy as better than in actual life." In the visual arts, the distinction, then, is between making an idealized image, a realistic image, or a caricature. And it is clearly implied that the true artist should be concerned only with the ideal.

At its high point in the latter half of the 5th century b.c., the Hellenic style was dominated by the idealistic theory. The Greek temple was designed as an idealized dwelling place for a perfect being, and by its logical interrelationship of lines, planes, and masses, it achieves something of permanence and stability in the face of the ephemeral and haphazard state of nature. In portraying an athlete, a statesman, or a god, the Hellenic sculptor concentrated on typical or general qualities rather than on the unique or particular. This was in line with the Greek idea of personality, which it was felt was better expressed in the dominating traits and characteristics than in individual oddities or peculiarities. In sculpture, as well as in all the other arts, the object was to rise above transitory sensations to capture the permanent, the essential, the complete. Thus the sculptor avoided representing the human being in infancy or old age, since these extremes of immaturity and post-maturity implied incompleteness or imperfection and hence were incompatible with the projection of ideal types. The range of representations extends from athletes in their late teens through images of Hermes, Apollo, and Athena, who are conceived in their early maturity, to Zeus, father of the gods, who appears as the fully developed patriarch in all the power of mature manhood. It must also be remembered that few of the Hellenic sculptor's subjects were intended to represent human beings as such. The majority were fashioned to represent gods, who, if cast in human form, must have bodies of transcendent beauty.

In some way, even the intangible tones of music participated also in the ideal world by reason of the mathematical relationships on which they are based. A melody, then, might have something more permanent than its fleeting nature would indicate. One of the main functions of the drama was to create ideal types, and, while the typical was always opposed to the particular, somehow the one arose from the other. The interpretation of this interplay was assigned to the chorus, and the drama as a whole shared with the other arts the power of revealing how the permanent could be derived from the impermanent; how the formula could be extracted from the process of forming; how an abiding quality could be distilled from the state of universal flux; how the type could be found in the many specific cases; and how the archetype could arise from the types.

In the extreme sense, the real and ideal worlds represent blind chaos and perfect order. Since the one was intolerable and the other unattainable, it was necessary to find a middle ground somewhere along the line. Glimpses of truth, beauty, and goodness could be caught occasionally, and these intimations should help man to steer a course from the actual to the ideal. By exercising the faculties of reason, judgment, and moral sense, man can subdue the chaotic conditions of his existence and bring closer into view the seemingly far-off perfection.

The Socratic theory of education, expressed in the balance between gymnastic for the body and music for the soul, was designed as a curriculum leading toward this end. The Greek temple, the nobly proportioned sculptural figures, the hero of epic and tragedy, and the orderly relationships of the melodic intervals in music are one and all the embodiments of this ideal. Politician, priest, philosopher, poet, artist, and teacher all shared a common responsibility in trying to bring it closer to realization. As Socrates said: "Let our artists rather be those who are gifted to discern the true nature of the beautiful and graceful; then will our youth dwell in a land of health, amid fair sights and sounds, and receive the good in everything; and beauty, the effluence of fair works, shall flow into the eye and ear, like a health-giving breeze from a purer region, and insensibly draw the soul from earliest years into likeness and sympathy with the beauty of reason."

**Rationalism**    Rational and irrational forces exist within every society as well as every person. The question remains whether the state or individual tries to solve problems by reason or emotion. "Things are numbers," Pythagoras is supposed to have said, and by this statement to have affirmed that something solid and permanent underlies the shifting appearances of things. A few generations later, Anaxagoras went a step farther by stating that "mind has power over all things that have life." His disciple Socrates continued the argument and kindled in his followers a burning love of truth, not because truth was useful

for worldly success but because truth is an ideal to be pursued for its own sake. The good life in the heyday of Greek civilization embraced not only the ethical principles of courage, temperance, and justice but also wisdom, a virtue achieved by the free exercise of man's rational faculties.

In the Hebraic and Christian traditions, mortal error lay in transgressions of the moral law, but to the Greeks, original sin was a lack of knowledge. The tragedy of Oedipus in Sophocles' drama *Oedipus the King* is his ignorance that does not permit him to know when he is murdering his father, marrying his mother, and begetting children who are also his own brothers. His downfall therefore comes through his ignorance, and his fate is the price he has to pay. In *The Bacchants,* the general theme is the conflict between the known and the unknown. Agave is led to murder her own son because she voluntarily surrenders her reason to an irrational cult. Her son Pentheus' downfall comes because his reason was not strong enough to comprehend the emotional and irrational forces that motivated the lives of the members of his family and his subjects. In order to bring these factors under control, they had first to be understood, and therefore Pentheus lacked the wisdom and tolerance necessary in a successful ruler. The entire Greek philosophical tradition concurred in the assumption that, without the knowledge and the free exercise of the faculty of reason, there is no ultimate happiness for mankind.

By thinking for themselves in the spirit of free intellectual inquiry, the Greeks in considerable measure succeeded in formulating reasonable rules for the conduct of life and its creative forces. This faith in reason also imparted to the arts an inner logic of their own, since when a craftsman's hands are guided by an alert mind, his work can penetrate the surface play of sense impressions and plunge to deeper levels of experience. For all later periods, this balance between the opposites of reason and emotion, form and content, reality and appearance becomes the basis for any classical style. For such subsequent classical movements as the Renaissance and 19th-century neoclassicism, the guiding principle is symmetry, proportion, and unity based on the interrelationship of parts with one another and with the whole.

The qualities of balance, clarity, and simplicity that the Greeks set up as standards of excellence in all the arts depended upon the selective faculty of a well-ordered mind. As Plato put it, "beauty of style and harmony and grace and good rhythm depend on simplicity—I mean the true simplicity of a rightly and nobly ordered mind and character." Plato's attitude toward the arts that did not meet these specifications was highly critical. And since aspiration as well as rule is a necessary condition of creativity, Plato was afraid that some works of art tended to be more the product of divine madness than of reason. Aristotle, without compromising his rational position, was able to distinguish between historical and poetic truth, fact and fancy. But poetic license was severely criticized by Plato. He was disturbed, for instance, by such architectural refinements as the entasis of columns and the tilting of walls for purposes of creating the appearance of perfection by carefully calculated distortions. Since only the world of mathematics seemed fixed and logical, the world of appearances was deceptive, as proved by such illusions as a straight stick appearing bent when thrust into water. The artist, to Plato, was one who sometimes seemed to minister to the deficiencies rather than the strengths of human nature. "Thus," he writes, "every sort of confusion is revealed within us; and this is that weakness of the human mind on which the art of conjuring and of deceiving by light and shadow and other ingenious devices imposes, having an effect like magic." The philosopher also pointed out that "in works either of sculpture or painting, which are of any magnitude, there is a certain degree of deception; for if artists were to give the true proportions of their fair works, the upper part, which is farther off, would appear to be out of proportion in comparison with the lower, which is nearer; and so they give up the truth in their images and make only proportions which appear to be beautiful, disregarding the real ones." Furthermore, that which is true of the deviations of visual lines applies also to the variations in the rhythms of recited poetry and performed music. If mathematical regularity prevails, the result is dull and mechanical. In music, pitch must also waver slightly in order to approximate the human voice and sound natural and interesting. This Plato also considered irrational, and he felt that the only hope was for "the arts of measuring and numbering and weighing [to] come to the rescue of human understanding." It follows that the excellence or inferiority of the several arts then depends upon the manner in which they make use of mathematical principles.

In spite of the suspicions of the philosophers, the Hellenic artists were no less concerned than Plato with the pursuit of an ideal order, which they felt could be grasped by the mind through the medium of the senses. Greek architecture, in retrospect, turns out to be a high point in the rational solution to building problems. The post-and-lintel system of construction, as far as it goes, is eminently reasonable and completely comprehensible. All structural members fulfill their logical purpose, and nothing is hidden or mysterious. The orderly principle of repetition on which Greek temple designs are based is as logical in its way as one of Euclid's geometry propositions or Plato's dialogues. It accomplishes for the eye what Plato was trying to achieve for the mind. The tight unity of the Greek temple met the Greek requirement that a work of art be complete in itself. Its carefully controlled but flexible relationships of verticals and horizontals, solids and voids, structural principles and decorative embellishments give it an inexorable internal consistency. And the harmonic proportions of the Parthenon reflect the Greek image of a harmoniously proportioned universe quite as much as a logical system.

Sculpture likewise avoided the pitfalls of rigid mathematics and succeeded in working out principles adapted to its specific needs. When Polyclitus said "the beautiful comes about, little by little, through many numbers," he was stating a rational theory of art in which the parts and whole of a work could be expressed in mathematical proportions. But he also allowed for flexible application of the rule, depending on the pose or line of vision. By such a reconciliation of the opposites of order and freedom, he reveals the sculptor's kinship with his philosophical and political colleagues who were trying to do the same for other aspects of Athenian life.

Rational and irrational elements were present in both the form and content of Greek drama, just as they were in the architecture of the time. In the Parthenon, the structurally regular triglyphs were interspersed with panels showing centaurs and other mythological creatures. The theme of these sculptures was the struggle between the Greeks as champions of enlightenment and the forces of darkness and barbarism. In the drama, the rational Apollonian dialogue existed alongside the inspired Dionysian chorus. However, even in the latter, the composition of intricate metrical schemes and the orderly and complex arrangements of the parts partake of rationalism and convey the dramatic content in highly ordered form. In the dialogue, the action of the episodes must by rule lead inevitably and inexorably toward the predestined end, just as the lines and groupings of the figures must do in a composition like that on the east pediment of the Parthenon. In the union of mythological and rational elements, tragedy could mediate between intuition and rule, the irrational and rational, the Dionysian and Apollonian principles. Above all, it achieves a coherence that meets Aristotle's critical standard of "a single action, one that is a complete whole in itself with a beginning, middle, and end, so as to enable the work to produce its proper pleasure with all the organic unity of a living creature."

Just as the harmony of the Parthenon depended on the module taken from the Doric columns, so Polyclitus derived his proportions for the human body from the mathematical relationship of its parts. In similar fashion, melodic lines in music were based on the subdivisions of the perfect intervals derived from the mathematical ratios of the fourth, fifth, and octave. So also the choral sections of the Greek drama were constructed of intricate metrical units that added up to the larger parts on which the unity of the drama depended. In none of these cases, however, was a cold

**right: Plate 5.** *Hercules Finding His Infant Son Telephus.* A.D. c. 70. Fresco from Herculaneum, probably a copy after a Pergamene original of 2nd century B.C. National Museum, Naples. (See p. 52.)

**below: Plate 6.** *The Battle of Alexander,* from House of the Faun, Pompeii. 3rd–2nd centuries B.C. Mosaic, c. 8'10" × 16'9". National Museum, Naples. (See p. 53.)

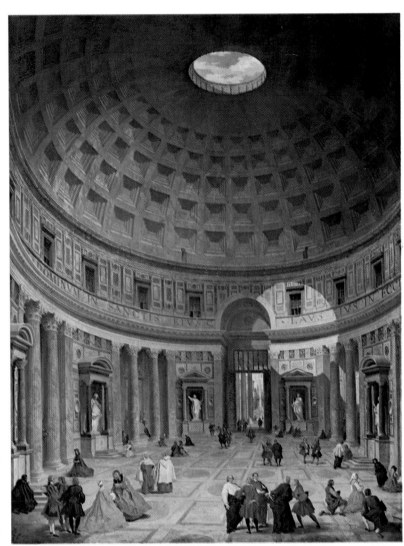

**right: Plate 7.** Giovanni Paolo Pannini. *Interior of the Pantheon, Rome.* c. 1750. Oil on canvas, 4′2½″ × 3′ 3″. National Gallery of Art, Washington, D.C. (Samuel H. Kress Collection). (See p. 70.)

**below: Plate 8.** *View of a Garden.* c. 20 B.C. Wall painting from Villa of Livia at Prima Porta. National Museum, Rome. (See p. 75.)

crystallization the desired effect. In the architecture of the Hellenic style, in the statues of Polyclitus, in the dramas of Aeschylus, Sophocles, and Euripides, and in the dialogues of Plato, the rational approach was used principally as a dynamic process to suggest ways for solving a variety of human and aesthetic problems.

It was also the Greeks who first realized that music, like the drama and other arts, was a mean between the divine madness of an inspired musician, such as Orpheus, and the solid mathematical basis on which the art rested acoustically. The element of inspiration had to be tempered by an orderly theoretical system that could demonstrate mathematically the arrangement of its melodic intervals and metrical proportions. Finally, it should always be remembered that the chief deity of the city was Athena, goddess of knowledge and wisdom. Even such a cult religion as that of Dionysus, through the Orphic and Pythagorean reforms, tended constantly toward increased rationalism and abstract thought. While Athena, Dionysus, and Apollo were all born out of a myth, their destinies found a common culmination in the supreme rationalism of Socrates and Plato, who eventually concluded that philosophy was the highest music.

"We are all Greeks." So said Shelley in the preface to his play *Hellas.* "Our laws, our literature, our religion, our arts, have their roots in Greece." Merely the mention of such key words as *mythology, philosophy, democracy* points immediately to their Greek source. So also do the familiar forms of architecture, sculpture, painting, poetry, drama, and music have their taproots in the age-old soil of Hellas, the land where the Hellenic style was nurtured and brought to fruition.

As the Athenians looked into the mirror of their arts, they well could have reflected on the long road they had traveled from the dark past of prehistory, with all its primitive practices and mythological superstitions. In the light of their radiant present, they confidently shared the direction of their world with their gods who, to be sure, were immortal but not all-powerful. Since even deities had limitations, man's help was urgently needed. The constant search for justice and wisdom was bringing the divine and human worlds closer together into a single universal harmony, and in the process, the gods were humanized and men reached out toward divinity.

The Socratic notion of truth, for example, was not brought down from a mountain or imposed from above by either man or god. It was evolved with practice and effort by the application of rational principles in a dialectical, or give-and-take, process. Since the arts of the Athenians were addressed to reasonable beings, they were more persuasive if they possessed the qualities of balance, order, and proportion than if they attempted to impress by the ponderous mass of a pyramid or the colossal height of a projected tower of Babel. Athenian idealism found expression in a trinity made up of the eternal verities of truth, beauty, and goodness, each in its way a facet of the ideal oneness attainable by the mind of man. The approach to these ideals was not through mystical rites but through the process of dialectics, aesthetics, and ethics. Through these avenues, it was possible to discern on the distant horizon an intellectual, beautiful, and moral living space, broad enough to ensure the expansion of Athenian institutions and arts into a sphere of excellence seldom equalled and never excelled by men before or since.

Such, then, was the remarkable configuration of historical, social, and artistic events that led to this unique flowering of culture. Circumstances, however, conspired to bring about a decline of political power, although Athens was destined to remain the teacher of Greece, Rome, and all later peoples of Western civilization. And the words of Euripides still sound a ringing note down the corridors of time:

> Happy of old were the sons of Erechtheus,
> Sprung from the blessed gods, and dwelling
> In Athens' holy and untroubled land.
> Their food is glorious wisdom, they work
> With springing step in the crystal air.
> Here, so they say, golden Harmony first
> Saw the light, the child of the Muses nine.

# 3 The Hellenistic Style

## PERGAMON, 2ND CENTURY B.C.

Like the earlier city of Athens, Pergamon (or Pergamum) in Asia Minor developed around its acra, the fortified hilltop that became the residence of its rulers and a sanctuary. The Pergamene acropolis was a geographical site with even greater natural advantages than that of Athens, and it played a significant role in the growth of the city. Strategically located on a plain near the Aegean Sea, Pergamon developed a prosperous export trade. The fertile plain, formed by the confluence of three rivers, was easily defensible from the hill; and the city itself, surrounded as it was by the wide sea, high mountains, and precipitous ravines, was impregnable except from its southern approach. Here, in a situation of unusual beauty, grew the city that was to play such an important role in the Hellenistic period.

After Athens fell to Sparta in 404 B.C., Greece veered away from the small democratic city-state as the basic political unit toward more autocratic forms of government. Philip of Macedon first succeeded in bringing the mainland of Greece into a single kingdom; then his son Alexander the Great embarked on a course of conquest leading to a short-lived empire. With great centers separated as widely as Syracuse on the island of Sicily, Alexandria on the banks of the Nile, and the cities of Asia Minor on the east coast of the Aegean, Greek thought and attitudes became more varied and international in scope. The Hellenistic period proper covers the two centuries between the death of Alexander in 323 B.C. and the Roman conquest of Greece in 146 B.C., but in effect it continued through a transitional Greco-Roman era down to 27 B.C., the beginning of the Augustan Age in Rome. Throughout these two centuries, cultural leadership remained in the hands of the Greeks, but as they came in contact with such a variety of native influences, their culture became progressively more cosmopolitan. Hence, the distinction is drawn between the earlier and purer Hellenic and the later more diffused Hellenistic styles.

In Asia Minor, significant art centers developed at Halicarnassus, Ephesus, Rhodes, and especially at Pergamon. The unique position of the latter was owing largely to the energy and political sagacity of the Attalid kings, whose early recognition of the rising power of Rome led to an advantageous alliance with that city of the future. Pergamon was thus both an important center of civilization in its own right and one of the principal bridges over which the Greek tradition passed into the Roman Empire.

The planning of Greek cities apparently goes back no further than the middle of the 5th century B.C. The fame of "wide-wayed Athens" rested on its Panathenaic Way, a street about twelve feet broad. Just wide enough for five or six men to walk abreast, it facilitated the processions to the acropolis, theaters, and market place. Otherwise, the streets of Athens were narrow alleys barely broad enough to permit the passage of a man with a donkey cart. Unpaved in any way, they must have been as dry and dusty in summer as they were damp and muddy in winter and spring. The Athenian residential section was only a mass of mud-brick houses in which rich and poor lived side by side in relative squalor. Only in the agora and on the acropolis did spaciousness develop. But even here buildings were planned with full attention to their individual logic and little or none to their relationship as a group. Each building thus existed independently rather than communally.

Greek city plans, while a vast improvement on their haphazard predecessors, were based on the application of an inflexible geometrical pattern that paid little or no attention to the irregularities of the natural site. When a hill was within the city limits, the streets sometimes became so steep that they could be negotiated only by precipitous stairways. While the residential sections of the ancient city of Pergamon have only now begun to be excavated, it is known that they followed such a regular system. Under Eumenes II, the city reached its largest extent, and the thick wall he built around it enclosed over 200 acres of ground —more than four times the territory included by his predecessor. Ducts brought in ample water from nearby mountain springs to supply a population of 120,000, and the system was the greatest of its kind prior to the Roman aqueducts.

The main entrance to Pergamon was from the south through an impressive arched gateway topped by a pediment with a triglyph frieze. Traffic was diverted through several vaulted portals that led into a square, where a fountain refreshed travelers. From here, the road led past the humbler dwelling places toward the large lower marketplace, which bustled with the activities of peddlers and hucksters of all sorts. This market was a large open square surrounded on three sides by a two-story colonnade behind which were rows of rooms that served for shops. Moving onward, the road went past buildings that housed the workshops and mills for pottery, tiles, and textiles. Homes of the wealthier citizens were located on promontories off the main streets overlooking the rest of the city. At the foot of the acropolis another square opened up, which could boast of a large city fountain and a fine view.

On a dramatic site almost 1,000 feet above the surrounding countryside rose the Pergamene acropolis (Fig. 48), a citadel that ranked among the most imposing in the Greek world. Up the slopes of the hill, on rising terraces supported by massive retaining walls and fortifications, were the buildings and artifacts that gave the city its reputation as a second Athens. By ingenious use of natural contours, the Pergamenes had developed settings for a number of buildings, which not only were outstanding as individual edifices but which, by means of connecting roadways, ramps, and open courtyards, were grouped into a harmonious whole. Here on a succession of rising levels were gymnasiums, athletic fields, temples, assembly places, public squares, wooded groves, and an amphitheater. Above them all, flanked by watch towers, barracks, arsenals, storage houses, and gardens, stood the residence of the kings of Pergamon.

## ARCHITECTURE

On the three lowest of the artificially created terraces of the Pergamene acropolis were a series of open grounds, enclosed by colonnades and buildings, which comprised a triple gymnasium—one for each general age group. The spacious outdoor areas included a playground for boys, an athletic field, and a race course. Provision was also made for dressing rooms, baths, and indoor sports. And, as the education center of the city, the gymnasium also included classrooms and lecture halls. It is significant that such gymnasiums provided mental as well as physical exercise. Their pleasant locations in groves and gardens, in fact, were responsible for the names of such famous schools of philosophy as Plato's Academy and Aristotle's Lyceum, just as the *stoa*, or shady colonnade facing a public building, became the name of the Stoic school of thought. At the Pergamon gymnasium, statues have been found of such mythological figures as Asclepius, son of Apollo and physician of the gods, and Hygeia, daughter of Asclepius and guardian of the health of growing youths, as well as sculptured representations of athletes at their games. A small adjacent temple was dedicated to one of the patron deities of sports, possibly Hermes, the fleet-footed messenger of the gods, or Heracles, mythological paragon of strength; and nearby were statues of Nike, goddess of victory, altars for votive offerings, and busts of prominent athletes who won the Olympic and other Greek games.

Above the gymnasium was the upper agora (Fig. 48, lower left), an open square that served both as an assembly place and as a market for such quality merchandise as the renowned Pergamene pottery and textiles. Above the agora spread the broad marble-paved terrace on which stood the Altar of Zeus, with its famous frieze depicting in marble slabs the battle of the gods as personifications of light and order against the giants as representatives of darkness and chaos. Dating from about 180 B.C., this artistic triumph of the Eumenian period was proclaimed by many contemporary authorities as one of the seven wonders of the ancient world. Since both its structure and sculptures are of major importance, this edifice will be discussed in the following section.

On the next higher level, above the Altar of Zeus, was the precinct dedicated to Athena Polias, or Athena protectress of cities and guardian of laws and city life. Her shrine (Fig. 48, center) was a graceful Doric temple, smaller than the Parthenon, with six-columned porticoes on either end and ten columns on each side. This level was framed by an **L**-shaped, two-storied colonnade that formed an open courtyard in which stood the bronze monument that celebrated the victory of Attalus I, father of Eumenes, over the Gauls (Figs. 49, 50). This colonnade served also as the façade of the great library of Pergamon, which appropriately was placed here in the precinct of Athena, goddess of reason, contemplation, and wisdom. The most precious part of the library was housed in four rooms on the second-story level stretching about 145 feet in length and 47 in width. On their stone shelves, some of which are still extant, rested the ancient scrolls, estimated to have numbered about 200,000 at

**48.** Acropolis, Pergamon. Reconstruction by H. Schlief.

## General Events B.C.

| | | |
|---|---|---|
| 359– | 336 | Philip of Macedon in control of Greece |
| | 336 | Philip assassinated; succeeded by son, Alexander the Great |
| 334– | 323 | Alexander's conquests in Near East, Asia Minor, Persia, India |
| | 331 | City of Alexandria, Egypt, founded |
| | 323 | Alexander the Great died |
| 323– | 275 | Alexander's generals divided empire: Ptolemies in Egypt, Seleucids in Syria and Palestine, Attalids in Pergamon |
| 241– | 197 | Attalus I ruled as king of Pergamon. Defeated Gauls in Galatia. Allied kingdom with Rome. Erected monument commemorating victory over Gauls. Patron of First School of Pergamene sculpture |
| 197– | 159 | Eumenes II, king of Pergamon. Defeated Gauls. Power of kingdom at zenith. Founded Pergamene library. Commissioned Altar of Zeus. Patron of Second School of Pergamene sculpture |
| 159– | 138 | Attalus II, king of Pergamon. Patron of painting |
| | 146 | Roman conquest of Greece |
| 138– | 133 | Attalus III, king of Pergamon. Willed kingdom to Rome |
| | 129 | Pergamon became a Roman province |

## Architecture and Sculpture

| | | |
|---|---|---|
| 359– | 351 | Mausoleum at Halicarnassus built; frieze by Scopas and School |
| 323– | 146 | Hellenistic Period proper; 146–27 transitional Greco-Roman period; great centers of culture at Alexandria, Pergamon, Antioch, and Rhodes |
| c.306 | | *Winged Victory of Samothrace* |
| c.250 | | *Venus de Milo (Aphrodite of Melos)* |
| c.228 | | First School of Pergamon. Attalus I's monument celebrating victory over Gauls |
| 183– | 174 | Second School of Pergamon. Eumenes II's Great Altar of Zeus |
| c.100 | | *Laocoön Group* done at Rhodes |

## Philosophers and Scientists

| | | |
|---|---|---|
| c.341– | c.270 | Epicurus, founder of Epicureanism |
| c.336– | c.264 | Zeno of Citium, founder of Stoicism |
| | c.321 | Aristoxenus of Tarentum, musical theorist, flourished |
| | c.300 | Euclid flourished |
| c.287– | 213 | Archimedes |

## Painters and Sculptors

| | | |
|---|---|---|
| c.359– | c.351 | Scopas active |
| | c.330 | Apelles, court painter to Alexander, flourished |
| | c.200 | Boethos active |

the time of the Attalids. The Pergamon library ranked with that of Alexandria as one of the two greatest libraries of antiquity. Later, after the major portion of the Alexandrine collection of half a million volumes had been burned in an uprising against Caesar, Mark Anthony made a gift to Cleopatra of the entire library of Pergamon.

Below the Athena precinct was the theater (Fig. 48, center left), constructed under Eumenes II about 170 B.C. The auditorium, with its 78 semicircular tiers of stone seats that could accommodate 10,000 spectators, was carved out of the hillside. Below was the circular section of the orchestra, where the chorus performed around a small altar dedicated to Dionysus, and the rectangular scene building for the actors.

Just as the Attalid kings dominated the life of their city and constituted the apex of the social pyramid of their kingdom, so the royal residence crowned the highest point in their capital city. Later, after the realm came under the domination of Rome, part of the palace was demolished to make way for the large Corinthian temple honoring Emperor Trajan that is shown in the top foreground of Figure 48. From their hilltop summit the kings of Pergamon could survey much of their rich domain. From the mountains to the north came the silver and copper that furnished the metal for their coins—so necessary in promoting trade and paying soldiers. From the same region came also supplies of pitch, tar, and timber—greatly in demand for the building of ships—as well as marble for their buildings and sculptures. A panorama thus unfolded around them, starting with the heights of Mt. Ida and the surrounding range (down whose slopes flowed the streams that watered the fertile valleys and broad plains), all the way to the bright waters of the shining Aegean Sea, beyond which lay the shores of the Greek motherland.

Like Croesus, the Attalids of Pergamon were famed for their fabulous wealth, and "rich as an Attalid" was a phrase used by Horace and other Roman writers. But by later standards, the Attalids lived in relative modesty, and the residence generally referred to as the "royal palace" was actually a loose constellation of small buildings, set amid wooded groves and gardens, that shifted from time to time with the changing fortunes and dignities of the kings. Included in the group were living rooms opening out into columned courtyards, chambers devoted to the dynastic

**above: 49.** *Dying Gaul.* Roman copy after bronze original of c. 225 B.C. Marble, height 3′, length 6′3″. Capitoline Museum, Rome.

**right: 50.** *Gaul and His Wife.* Roman copy after bronze original of c. 225 B.C. Marble, height 6′11″. National Museum, Rome.

cult, a barracks for the royal guard, a treasury, and various storerooms for goods, grain, and arms.

The love of display, however, was less in evidence in royal residences than in the great public buildings the Attalids erected and in the ostentatious gifts they made to such cities as Athens and Rome. More important to the Attalid kings than the size and luxury of their dwelling was the close link with the temples of the gods that its location afforded. Both symbolically and practically, their residence was located here in order to dominate the city that spread out below them. From there all eyes would be attracted to the magnificent group of edifices, thus causing the populace to look upward psychologically as well as actually toward the place of the kings and gods who ruled over their lives.

The planning of Pergamon thus cleverly promoted the idea of the monarchy towering above it. There, topographically as well as politically, stood the king, aloof from his people and associated by them with the gods. Even while living, he was accorded such divine prerogatives as a cult statue, with perfumed grain burning on an altar before it, and an annual celebration in his honor. This semidivine status, connected with the king's right to rule, served the practical social purposes of commanding obedience to his laws, facilitating the collection of taxes (often under the guise of offerings to the deities), and uniting the peoples and factions who lived under him. Assisting in this deification were the intellectuals and artists the king attracted to his court, whose works were regarded with awe by the multitude. Native and foreigner alike were overwhelmed by the vast impressiveness of the architecture and sculpture.

The pomp and display that marked Hellenistic life was a distinct departure from the simplicity and no-

bility of the more austere 5th century B.C. Grandeur became the grandiose, and many monuments were erected not to revere the gods but to honor kings who, even in their own lifetimes, assumed semidivine status. The accent was no longer on the abstract idealism and universality of the earlier period but on the glorification of individuals. With the changing times, however, definite advancements in the art of building were taking place. Domestic architecture was emphasized, and Pergamene architects went beyond the simple post-and-lintel method of the Hellenic period by employing the arch and vault in city gates and in underground water and sewer systems. Architecturally as well as culturally, Pergamon forged the link between the Greek and Roman periods. Such was the picture of the brilliant city with thousands of statues, sculptured reliefs, painted murals, and books; and peopled with philosophers, scholars, writers, artisans, and pursuers of luxury and pleasure.

## SCULPTURE

While sculptural works of all kinds are known to have existed in profusion throughout the city of Pergamon, the examples that claim the attention of posterity were located on two of the terraces of the acropolis. In the Athena precinct just below the royal residence, bounded by the temple on one side and the L-shaped colonnades of the library on two others, was a spacious courtyard in which Attalus I erected the sculptural monuments commemorating his victories. The groups he commissioned were in place during the last quarter of the 3rd century B.C. On the terrace below, in the first quarter of the 2nd century B.C., his son and successor Eumenes II built the Altar of Zeus (Fig. 51) with its famous frieze. Historically, the two periods have been distinguished as the First and Second schools of Pergamon, but since they were separated by less than half a century, some sculptors possibly worked on both projects, and if not, they must have had a hand in training their successors. All the bronze originals of the First School have disappeared and can be studied only in the marble copies made by later Hellenistic or Roman artists. Most of the sculptures from the Second School survive, because of the fortunate results of the late 19th-century German excavations, and may be seen today in the Pergamon Museum in East Berlin.

The principal works of the First School were two large monuments in bronze, each of which was composed of many figures. One commemorated the victories of Attalus over the neighboring Seleucid kingdom, but only a few details of this group survive. The other honored his earlier and greater victory over the nomadic tribes of Gauls, which swept down from Europe across the Hellespont into the region north of Pergamon. From this province, called Galatia after them, the Gauls were a constant threat to the Greek cities lying to the south. While his predecessor had

bought them off by paying tribute, Attalus I refused this expedient. He met their subsequent invasion with an army, and the outcome of the battle, fought about thirty miles to the east of Pergamon, was decisive enough to repel the Gauls for a generation. Its consequences were felt far and wide, and all the cities and kingdoms of the Greek world breathed a little easier.

The fierce Gauls had inspired such general terror that their defeat was associated in the popular mind with something of a supernatural character. The name of Attalus was everywhere acclaimed as *Soter* ("Savior," the victor), and after incorporating the lands he had gained, he assumed the title of king. Thereafter, as King Attalus the Savior, he continued to capitalize on his fortunes by embarking on a program of beautifying his city with the services of the best available Greek artists. Sharing the same patroness, Pergamon began to acquire the status of a second Athens, and its ruler that of a political and cultural champion of Hellenism.

Parts of the monument that Attalus erected to the memory of his victory over the Gauls can be seen in numerous museums. The *Dying Gaul* (Fig. 49) and the *Gaul and His Wife* (Fig. 50) are the most famous of the individual elements to survive from antiquity. It was a large collective group that rested on a circular platform some 10 feet in diameter. In the center rose a cylindrical base, about 7 feet high, on which were placed the victorious Pergamenes, while their opponents were found below on three descending steps.

The *Dying Gaul* (Fig. 49) is a fine example of Hellenistic pathos. He is the trumpeter who sounded the call for relief, and the mortally wounded warrior has agonizingly dragged himself out of the thick of the battle to struggle alone against death. His eyes are fixed on the ground where his sword, the trumpet, and other pieces of his equipment are lying. He supports himself weakly with one arm, proud and defiant to the end, while his life's blood flows slowly out of the gaping wound in his side. The anguished expression in the face is portrayed with an intensity not hitherto encountered in Greek art. The strong but rude musculature of his powerful body, so different from that of the supple Greek athletes, marks him as a barbarian. Further contrast is found in his hair, which is greased so heavily that it is almost as thick as a horse's mane, in the moustache (never worn by the Greeks or Romans), and in the collar of twisted gold worn around his neck. All these carefully recorded details show the interest of the period in individuals as such, in the features that distinguished one people from another, and, above all, in the artist's desire to awaken the sympathies of the observer. Thus, by the process of empathy, the sculptor invites the involvement of the observer in the situation. The contemporary audience would have felt both attraction and repulsion toward such a subject and hence would have experienced a strong emotional reaction. The litter of the battlefield beside the Gaul, as well as other realistic details, is not used so much for its own sake as to convey a sense of immediacy in the experience of the beholder. At the same time, the viewer was invited to look beyond the physical wounds and behold the spiritual anguish of the proud but defeated warrior, so reluctant to accept his fate.

The expressive impact of the *Gaul and His Wife* is no less powerful (Fig. 50). The custom of the Gauls was to take their women and children with them on their campaigns. Realizing his defeat, and too proud to be taken a slave, this Gaul has just killed his wife and looks apprehensively over his shoulder at the approaching enemy as he plunges his sword into his own neck. The mood of despair is heightened by the sweeping lines of the woman's drapery, which droops downward in deep folds, casting dark shadows. In both these surviving representations, strong feeling is aroused in the observer by the noble figures who stare death so courageously in the face.

To the Second School of Pergamon are assigned all the works that fall within the reign of Eumenes II, the patron under whom Pergamon achieved the highest point of its power and glory. Like his father before him, Eumenes II had his victories over the Gauls, and in the Altar of Zeus (Fig. 51) he continued the tradition of erecting votive works. It was at once the greatest single monument of the city and one of the few top-ranking architectural and sculptural works of the Hellenistic period. It, too, was intended to glorify the position of the king and to impress the entire Greek world with Eumenes' contribution to the cause of Hellenism in the struggle against the barbarians. Because of the assiduous efforts of the German excavators, it is possible to appraise the Altar of Zeus

almost as an original. Beginning in 1878, piece by piece each fragment was painstakingly unearthed, and after a half-century of study, the entire monument was reconstructed in the Pergamon Museum in Berlin. Famed throughout the ancient world, the altar was described in the early years of the Christian era by St. John as "Satan's seat" (Rev. 2:13). The reference seems to have been prompted by the resemblance of the structure to an immense throne and by the pagan gods and demons depicted in the frieze. While the principal interest is focused on the sculpture, the building also commands architectural attention.

The actual altar on which animal sacrifices and other offerings were burned was a large stone podium standing in the inner courtyard. The altar was surrounded by a U-shaped enclosure known as a *temenos* (Fig. 52). The building rested on a *podium,* or platform, with five steps, above which was the great frieze more than 7 feet in height and 450 feet in length, running continuously around the entire podium, bending inward on either side of the stairway, and diminishing in size as the steps rose. Below, the frieze was framed by a molding and, above, by a *dentil range.* These bricklike blocks served also to support an Ionic colonnade that surrounded the structure and paralleled the frieze. Above the colonnade appeared a friezeless entablature with a second dentil range supporting the roof, and crowning the whole was a series of freestanding statues of gods and mythological animals placed at various points along the outer edges of the roof.

The concept of space that underlies the Altar of Zeus differs from that of the 5th century. In the earlier period, the altar was placed outside the temple, and rituals took place against the exterior colonnades. In the Hellenistic period, the concept of space included an interest in depth. Thus, in the case of the Altar of Zeus, the spectator looked into the interior of a courtyard that enclosed the altar, and not toward a background plane. The wider space between the columns also invited the eye toward the interior, whereas the closer intercolumniation of the 5th century promoted the continuity of the plane. Since the Hellenistic concept embraces the same structural members as the previous Greek style, the Altar of Zeus is more a variation on 5th-century forms than a radical departure from them. The columns, entablatures, and interior walls, consistent with the Greek tradition, clearly define the spatial limits, and there is as yet no hint of the unbounded or infinite.

The general effect produced by the Altar of Zeus as a whole is that of a traditional Greek temple—the Parthenon, for example—turned upside down. The simple dignity of the older Doric temple depended upon its structural integrity. The columns served the logical purpose of supporting the upper members, and the sculptured sections were high above where they embellished but did not dominate the design. At

**53.** *Zeus Hurling Thunderbolts,* detail of Altar of Zeus frieze. c. 180 B.C. Marble, height 7'6".

giants representing such calamities as earthquakes, hurricanes, and floods.

The narrative commences on the inner part of the podium, facing the stairs and, moving parallel with the stairs, proceeds along the south and around the corner to the east. Along the way are introduced the principal characters in the drama—Zeus and his fellow gods whose mortal combat is with Chronus, the father of Zeus and his supporters, the wicked titans and giants. There are also Helios, the sun god, Hemera, the winged goddess of day, her brother Aether, the spirit of air, the moon goddess, and such others as Hecate, goddess of the underworld, Artemis, the heavenly huntress, and Heracles, father of Telephus, the legendary founder of Pergamon. The struggle is between the forces of darkness—the giants—and the spirits of light. In the four panels reproduced in Figure 53, Zeus is seen, appropriately, in combat with no less than three titans simultaneously. Here, the god's powerful figure, wrapped in a swirling mantle, is rearing back to smite the giants with his spear and thunderbolts. While most of Zeus' arm is missing, his hand is seen in the upper left corner of the panel. The titan in the lower left has already been overcome by a thunderbolt, which is depicted as a pointed spear with a handle of acanthus leaves. The second giant is on the other side, his body tense with terror before the blow falls. In the slab to the right, Porphyrion, king of the titans, is shown from the back. From his animal ears to his serpent legs, he is a fearsome, terrible sight as he shields himself with a lion skin from both Zeus' eagle above and the thunderbolts that the mighty god is about to hurl.

Next comes the fine group depicting the part played by Athena, protectress of the city (Fig. 54). Her figure is shown in the second slab, with a shield on her left arm as she grasps a winged giant by the hair with her right and forces him to earth where her sacred serpent can inflict the mortal wound. A moment of pathos is provided by the giant's mother, the earth goddess Gaea, who is seen as a torso rising from the ground. Though she is on the side of the gods, the earth mother implores Athena with her eyes to spare the life of her rebellious son. Gaea's attributes are seen in the horn of plenty she carries in her left hand, a cornucopia filled with the rich fruits of the earth—apples, pomegranates, and grapes with vine leaves and a pine cone. Over her hovers the goddess Nike, symbolizing the victory of Athena.

From this climax in the sky, the action on the shadowy north side gradually descends into the realm of the water spirits, who drive the fleeing giants around the other corner of the stairway into the sea

Pergamon, the traditional order was inverted. Considered more important, the frieze was put below, to be seen more easily at almost eye level. For the sake of tradition, the colonnade was included, but placed above the frieze where it had no structural purpose. Structurality as a guiding principle had yielded to decoration for its own sake, and the art of architecture, in effect, had given way to the art of sculpture. In the case of the Parthenon, the decorative frieze was included to give some variety to what might otherwise have been a monotonous unity. The Altar of Zeus, on the other hand, with the overwhelming variety of the frieze, has the regularity of a colonnade to preserve the unity. The quiet Greek architectural drama, in other words, has now become an architectonic melodrama.

The subject of the frieze is the familiar battle of the gods and giants. In the typical depiction of this scene, it was customary to include the twelve Olympians and an equal number of opponents, but here the unprecedented length of available space demanded a much larger array of participants. Almost certainly scholars of the library were called upon to compile a catalogue of divinities, together with their attendants and attributes, in order to have enough figures to go around. This mythological proliferation, however, apparently taxed the knowledge of the average Greek, because visual footnotes were provided by carved names beside the unfamiliar figures. Further intellectual influence is found in the allegorical treatment of the ancient battle theme. Literal belief in the gods as such was largely a thing of the past, and the local scholars interpreted them as personifications of the forces of nature, the gods representing orderly and benign phenomena and the

**54.** *Athena Slaying Giant,* detail of Altar of Zeus frieze. c. 180 B.C. Marble, height 7'6".

where they drown. Here are the representations of the rivers of Greece. Around the face of the west side and up the stairs are other creatures of the sea. The tumultuous action thus opens and closes on the terrestrial plane, starting on the other side of the stairway with the divinities of the land and ending here with those of the sea. They are separated by the wide stairs as well as by their placement at the beginning and the end of the dramatic conflict between the forces of good and those of evil.

The frieze as a whole is a technical feat of the first magnitude and was executed by a school of sculptors, many of whose names are inscribed below as signatures for their work. In addition to the figures, such details as swords and belt buckles, saddles and sandals, and the cloth for costumes are carved and polished to simulate the textures of metal, leather, and textiles, respectively. The bold high-relief carving, deep undercutting that allows the figures to stand out almost in the round, and rich modeling effects that make full use of light and shadow reveal complete mastery of material. To sustain such a swirl of struggling forms and violent movement over such a vast space is a minor miracle. The traditional Doric frieze could depend for unity on the momentary action in the metopes regularly interrupted by the static triglyphs. Here the unity relies on the continuity of the motion itself. The slashing diagonal lines and sharp contrasts of movement are grouped into separate episodes by the device of coiling snakes. Winding in and out, they are at once the visual punctuation marks that separate the scenes and the connecting links of the composition, leading the eye from one group to another and promoting a sense of constant writhing motion.

Comparing the great frieze with the *Dying Gaul* and *Gaul and His Wife,* one can note a style trend from the First to the Second school. Both allude to the perennial wars between the Pergamenes and Gauls. But, in contrast to the almost morbid preoccupation with pain in the earlier monument, the gods on the Altar of Zeus slay the giants with something approaching gaiety and abandon. Instead of sympathy for the victims, the viewer's reaction is wonder at the marvelously ingenious ways the gods invent to dispatch their enemies. Both accent pathos, but in the earlier examples the compassion of the observer is elicited simply and directly. While the great frieze deals with the battle of the gods and giants, it is a thinly disguised allegory of the war between the Pergamenes and Gauls. The Pergamenes in the guise of the gods have become superhuman figures, while the giants, whose features bear close resemblance to the

Gallic types of the earlier period, are now monsters. Instead of the frank realism of the previous generation, the tale is told in the language of melodrama accompanied by visual grandiloquence. It is put on the stage, so to speak, and done with theatrical gestures and histrionic postures. The emotional range is enormous, beginning with the stark horror of monsters with enormous wings, animal heads, snaky locks, long tails, and serpentine legs, which recall the grotesque prehistoric creatures who inhabited the primordial world. After being terrorized by the sight of such bestial forms, the contemporary audience must have melted into sympathy for the earth mother pleading mercy for her monstrous offspring, and then gone from tears to laughter at the inept antics of some of the clumsy giants. And after hissing the villains, the viewers must have applauded the gods galloping to the rescue. The simple realism of the First School, however, has become exaggerated. In the case of bodily types, the functional physique of the *Dying Gaul* has become the Herculean power of the professional strong man who finds himself more at home in the arena than on the battlefield.

In the case of the whole structure of the Altar of Zeus, it was pointed out that the perception of depth entered into the architectural composition, with the eye being drawn into an enclosed interior. Likewise with the sculpture, the eye does not move only from side to side, as in a plane, but is constantly led back and forth into spatial depth. Because it was painted blue, the marble background no longer offered a solid boundary but dissolved into atmosphere. To escape the plane, some of the figures of the great frieze project outward in such high relief as to be almost in the round; others even step outward from the frieze and support themselves by kneeling on the edge of the steps. The heavy shadows cast by the high-relief carving further intensify this effect. Thus the two-dimensional plane of the Hellenic style was expanded here to suggest some recession in depth.

A general comparison of Hellenistic with the Athenian art of the 5th century B.C. leaves one with the impression of discord rather than harmony; a magnitude that overwhelms rather than dimensions constrained within limited bounds; a wild emotionalism in the place of a rational presentation; virtuosity triumphing over dignified refinement; melodrama superseding drama; variety in ascendance over unity. The Athenian culture, in short, placed its trust in man; the Hellenistic, in superman. No longer the master of his fate, Hellenistic man was engulfed in the storms and stresses of grim circumstances beyond his control.

## PAINTINGS, MOSAICS, AND THE MINOR ARTS

Owing to the enduring qualities of stone, more ancient sculpture has survived than art works in any other form. Buildings were torn down for their materials and replaced by others. Statues in bronze, precious metals, and ivory were intrinsically too valuable to survive as such. Libraries of antiquity either were burned or had their volumes disintegrate in the course of time, so that their books survive only in imperfect copies made by medieval scribes or as fragmentary quotations in other volumes. The musical notation contained in ancient manuscripts could not be understood by these copyists, who eventually omitted it. Mosaics and pottery have fared better, but they, too, were either broken up or carried off by conquerors and collectors. Of all the major visual arts in antiquity, however, painting has suffered most from the ravages of time, and the number of surviving examples is sufficient to give only a hint of what this art must have been at its best. Because of this situation, the impression is easily gained that sculpture was the most important of all the arts. Literary sources, however, attest to the effectiveness of this art and to the high esteem in which it was held by the ancients. The fame of individual painters and the critical praise for their works make it clear that painting was on a par with architecture and sculpture.

Pausanias, a writer of Roman times, described the works of the legendary 5th-century B.C. Athenian painters Polygnotus and Apollodorus. The former worked out the principles of perspective drawing, and the latter was renowned for his use of light and shade and the finer gradations of color. Pausanias also mentioned many paintings at Pergamon. The excavated fragments at Pergamon reveal that the interior walls of temples and public buildings frequently were painted with pictoral panels and had streaks of color

that realistically imitated the texture of marble. Other scattered fragments of paintings show that the Pergamenes loved bright colors, such as yellows, pinks, and greens that contrasted with deep reds, blues, and browns. The palace paintings used motifs of actual animals, such as lions and charging bulls, and imaginary ones, such as tritons and griffins. Interiors of rooms were often decorated with painted friezes similar to sculptural ones; and walls, especially of small rooms, were painted with panels, columns, and pilasters, which cast realistic shadows in order to create the illusion of spaciousness. The writers of antiquity mention that the subjects of paintings were often drawn from mythology or from literary sources, such as the *Odyssey* and the like. It is also known that Hellenistic painting frequently dealt in *genre scenes*—that is, casual, informal subjects from daily life.

Although the original paintings no longer exist, and only fragments of mosaics and vase painting survive, well-preserved copies of Pergamene work have been found in the Greek cities of southern Italy, notably Herculaneum. This city supposedly was founded by Hercules, whose son Telephus founded Pergamon, and a "family" relationship thus existed between the two centers. Herculaneum, in fact, became a later middle-class edition of the earlier richer and aristocratic Pergamon. Both Herculaneum and nearby Pompeii were suddenly buried in a rain of cinders and a hail of volcanic stone that accompanied the eruption of Mt. Vesuvius in A.D. 79. When rediscovered in the 18th century, the two cities yielded many paintings and mosaics preserved almost intact. The prevailing taste was Hellenistic, and the well-to-do patrons, preferring traditional subjects, usually commissioned copies of famous paintings rather than original works.

*Hercules Finding His Infant Son Telephus* (Pl. 5, p. 41) is an adaptation of a Pergamene original. The winged figure in the upper right is pointing out to Hercules his son Telephus, who is seen in the lower left among wild animals and suckling a doe. The place is Arcadia, personified by the stately seated figure. Beside her are the fruits of the land, and at her back a playful faun is holding a shepherd's crook and blowing the pan-pipes. The coloring for the most part is sepia and reddish brown, relieved by lighter blue, green, and whitish tints. The figures appear against the background plane of the sky that projects them forward in the manner of relief sculpture. The drapery and modeling of the flower-crowned Arcadia recall the carving of a marble relief, while the powerful musculature of Hercules' body is cast in the manner of a bronze statue in the round.

Since ancient sculpture usually was painted in vivid colors, and reliefs sometimes had landscapes painted in the backgrounds, the arts of painting and sculpture obviously were closely identified in the Hellenistic mind, and they should perhaps be thought of more as complementary arts than as independent media. Paintings were more adaptable to interiors, while weather-resistant stone made marble reliefs better for out-of-doors. From the extant evidence, it is clear that the visual intention and expressive effect of both arts were closely associated, and that neither could claim supremacy over the other.

Mosaics, the art of which goes back to remote antiquity, were highly favored at Pergamon for the flooring of interiors and for wall paneling. As with later Roman work, geometrical patterns were preferred for floors, while representations of mythological subjects, landscapes, and genre scenes were used for murals. Such compositions are formed of small cubes or pieces of stone, marble, or ceramic known as *tesserae* that are set in cement. One mosaic by the artist Hephaiston that covered the entire floor of a room has a blank center surrounded first by a colorful geometrical design of black, gray, red, yellow, and white marble tesserae (Fig. 55). Beyond this is a wavelike pattern of black and white. Then enclosing the whole is a border about a yard wide with a foliated design of such rich variety that in its 44-foot expanse there is no repetition. Against a dark background are intertwined colored flowers, exotic lilies, vine leaves, and various fruits, all with delicate shadings. In some places grasshoppers are feeding on acanthus leaves; in others small winged Cupidlike *putti*, or boys symbolizing love, are playing among the vines.

Copies of many Pergamene designs have been found at Herculaneum, Pompeii, Naples, and Rome. The floor mosaic depicting the Persian warrior Darius fleeing from the forces of Alexander the Great after his defeat in the battle of Issus is a Pompeian mosaic version of the 1st century B.C. after an earlier Hellenistic painting of renown (Pl. 6, p. 41). According to Pliny the Elder, the most famous mosaicist of antiquity was Sosus, who worked at Pergamon. Among his most widely copied designs was one of doves drinking from a silver dish, and a favorite for dining-room floors showed vegetables, fruit, fish, a chicken leg, and a mouse gnawing on a nut (Fig. 56).

Pergamon was also noted for its textiles, dyed with special chemical and mineral substances, its metalwork of silver and bronze, and its carved gems, as well as for the ceramics it produced in both practical ware and terracotta figurines.

## MUSIC

Pergamon was identified with the musical tradition of that nearby northern Asia Minor region known as Phrygia, which had its own characteristic idioms, modes, rhythms, scales, and instruments. As early as the 5th century B.C., the Greeks in Athens were divided in their musical views as to the relative merits and propriety of the native Dorian tradition and the increasing influence coming from foreign centers. In

**left: 55.** HEPHAISTON. Mosaic from Palace of Attalus II at Pergamon. c. 150 B.C. Whole, 28' square. State Museums, East Berlin.

**above: 56.** SOSUS. *Unswept Dining Room Floor.* Detail of later Roman copy of 2nd-century B.C. Pergamene original mosaic. Vatican Museums, Rome.

particular, the wild and exciting music of Phrygia was gaining in popular favor. The melodies in the Phrygian mode apparently induced strong emotional reactions, and the introduction of a musical instrument called the Phrygian pipe had a similar effect in inflaming the senses. This pipe was a double-reed instrument with a peculiarly penetrating sound, somewhat like the modern oboe. Properly, the single version of the pipe is known as the *aulos* and the double version (shown in Fig. 57) as the *auloi*. In English translations of ancient Greek words, both are often incorrectly rendered as "flute." The Dorian music, however, was associated with such stringed instruments as the lyre and the cithara, the latter being mistranslated as the harp. Both the lyre and the cithara in the Dorian music and the aulos in the Phrygian were used principally to accompany the songs, melodies, and choruses of the two modes and only to a much lesser extent were played as solo instruments by skilled performers. Lyre playing was especially associated in the Dorian tradition with the Apollo cult, and the Greeks attributed to this body of music the quality of *ethos,* or ethical character; the aulos, as the instrument of Dionysus, was associated with *pathos,* or strong feeling, and had a sensuous quality conducive to enthusiasm. To the Athenians, this meant a division in their aspirations and ideals— one instrument and mode of singing were associated with clarity, restraint, and moderation; the other with emotional excitement and aroused passions.

The resultant division of opinion was expressed in the many sculptural representations of the musical contest between the Olympian Apollo and the Phrygian satyr Marsyas. According to an ancient myth, Athena was the inventor of the aulos. One day as she was playing, however, Athena caught sight of her reflection in a pool of water. So displeased was she with the facial grimaces the aulos caused her to make that she threw it away in disgust. Marsyas, happening along, found it and was so enchanted by its sounds that he challenged Apollo, the immortal patron of the muses, to a contest. The god chose to play on the dignified lyre, won the contest handily, and proved once again that mortals are no match for the gods. As a punishment he had his challenger flayed alive.

A 5th-century B.C. representation of the myth attributed to Myron shows Athena, calm and composed, disdainfully throwing away the instrument which distorted her fine features, while Marsyas raises his hands in surprise. A 4th-century relief from Mantineia of the school of Praxiteles represents the contest in progress (Fig. 57). On one side, calmly awaiting his turn, is the seated Apollo with his lyre; on the other, Marsyas is ecstatically blowing on the aulos. Between them is the judge, or music critic, standing patiently but with knife in hand. The Pergamene versions left out the contest and showed the victorious Apollo on one side, the unfortunate Marsyas in the center strung up by the wrists to a tree (Fig. 58) and, on the other side, the crouching figure of a Scythian slave, whetting a knife with keen anticipation (Fig. 59). The choice of the punishment as the part of the myth to be represented—and the evident enjoyment with which this Hellenistic artist tackled his gruesome subject—obviously was designed to tear the emotions to shreds.

The punishment of Marsyas must have reflected the views of those who disapproved of Phrygian music and wished to preserve the ancient traditions. One measure of their hold on the people is found in the attitude of the philosophers who were concerned with maintaining balance and order in the state. Plato, for one, would not admit aulos players into his ideal state, because he considered the instrument "worse than all the stringed instruments put together." He was most emphatic about his preference for "Apollo and his instruments to Marsyas and his instruments." But even the complex stringed instruments were eliminated in favor of the simple lyre and cithara for use in the city, and the pipe to keep the shepherds happy in the country. But while he rejected the aulos, Plato made a curiously human concession in retaining the Phrygian melodies. The two musical modes allowed in the ideal state were the Dorian, which he called the "strain of necessity," and the Phrygian, which was the "strain of freedom." The first was "warlike, to sound the note or accent that a brave man utters in the hour of danger and stern resolve"; clearly a type of military music is implied. However, main-

57. *Contest of Apollo and Marsyas.* Relief from Mantineia, Greece. c. 350 B.C. Marble, height 38¼". National Museum, Athens.

taining such heroic resolve at all times was apparently too much to expect even of the citizen of his utopia, and Plato therefore allowed the Phrygian music "to be used by him in times of peace and freedom of action, when there is no pressure of necessity."

Aristotle, while for the most part agreeing in his musical views with Socrates and Plato, took exception to this, and said: "The Socrates of the *Republic* is wrong in retaining only the Phrygian mode along with the Dorian, the more so because he rejects the [aulos]; for the Phrygian is to the modes what the [aulos] is to musical instruments—both of them are exciting and emotional. Poetry proves this, for Bacchic frenzy and all similar emotions are more suitably expressed by the [aulos] and are better set to the Phrygian than to any other mode." It must be pointed out that Aristotle did not reject the Phrygian mode altogether, but only in the case of the education of youth. For this he strongly recommended only the Dorian music, since it was the "gravest and manliest." The Phrygian might produce too much enthusiasm, while the Dorian was more likely to result in a "moderate and settled temper."

Despite the philosophers and their dire warnings, the stimulating Phrygian music made rapid headway, and in Hellenistic times it was the dominant musical style. The calm, simple, and dignified Dorian tradition of the past, which Plutarch called the age of "beautiful music," was gone, and the wilder, more frenzied strains of Phrygia had taken its place.

While historical facts about the actual musical life of Pergamon are few, it is known that here, as in other Hellenistic centers, the practice of music was accorded a high place in the arts. Both boys and girls received musical instruction in their educational institutions, and sang hymns as they marched in processions or participated in religious observances. The curriculum included the teaching of musical notation and the chanting of poetry to the accompaniment of the cithara. The chief educator of the city, the gymnasiarch, was also expected, among his other duties, to arrange for the appearances of visiting poets and musicians.

The Hellenistic era was one of increasing professionalism in activities that had previously been performed by free citizens as part of their public duties and honors. Participation in athletic contests and performances of certain dances, which earlier had been done only by those of noble birth, were taken over by specialists who often commanded high fees for their services. Professional associations, known as the Dionysiac *technites,* had a membership made up of stage managers, actors, mimes, dancers, and musicians who participated in theatrical productions. These groups functioned as guilds, or unions, and the master craftsmen accepted talented apprentices who understudied them. The Attalids and other Hellenistic monarchs prompted and protected these technites

right: 58. *Marsyas.* Roman copy after Pergamene original. Marble, life-size. Glyptothek, Munich.

below: 59. *Knife Sharpener.* Roman copy after Pergamene original. Marble, life-size. Uffizi, Florence.

with an eye toward improving and maintaining the quality of their theatrical and musical performances.

Tralles, one of the cities of the Pergamene kingdom, provides some general information and one of the best musical examples of antiquity. Less than 100 miles from Pergamon as the crow flies, Tralles was a subject-city of the Attalids, who maintained there a residence which usually was occupied by the high priest of the city as their representative. This Phrygian town was saved from the threat of defeat and enslavement at the hands of the Gauls by the victory of Eumenes II in 168 B.C. Like many other cities of the region, Tralles was so grateful for its deliverance that it instituted annual gymnastic and musical festivals in honor of the Pergamene kings. One of these was the Panathenaea, which honored Athena as the protectress of Pergamon; another was the Eumenaia, which feted the monarch himself. From inscriptions it appears that the Eumenaia was principally a musical contest.

At Tralles, in the latter part of the 19th century, a tombstone was unearthed that bore an inscription of some four lines of poetry accompanied by clear musical notation. It was an epitaph inscribed on a slab of stone by a man named Seikolos for the grave of his wife Euterpe. On transcription it turned out to be the words and music of a short but presumably intact tune in the Phrygian mode from the 2nd century B.C. After hearing about the wild and orgiastic character of Phrygian music, the reader will find this short song a model of sobriety. The mood, in fact, is more melancholy than intoxicating and, since it was carved on a tombstone, the elegiac character would seem to be altogether appropriate.

This little song (above right), well over 2,000 years old, was of a popular type known as a *skolion*, or drinking song, which was sung after dinner by the guests as the cup was passed around for toasts and libations to the gods. The word *skolion* is derived from the Greek meaning "zigzag" and referred to the manner in which the lyre and cup were passed back and forth, crisscrossing the table as each of the reclining guests sang in his turn. The simplicity of this example marks it as the type of tune expected to be in the social repertory of every acceptable guest rather than as one of the more elaborate ballads intended to be sung by professional entertainers. In spirit and mood it is not unlike the familiar "Auld Lang Syne," and the occasions on which it was sung would parallel those when we sing the venerable Scottish air. The substance of the words is the universal one of eat, drink, and be merry for tomorrow we die, which expresses a convivial philosophy of the Epicurean type. Technically, it is in the Phrygian mode with the upper and lower extremes falling on $e'$ and $e$, thus spanning an octave. The tone most often stressed is $a$, which thus becomes the mean between the higher and lower reaches of the melody and consequently functions as its tonal center.

## IDEAS

Many striking differences have been noted between the Hellenistic and earlier Hellenic styles. As the names indicate, both are Greek; but the Hellenic was a more concentrated development of the small city-states of the Greek mainland, whereas the Hellenistic is a combination of native Greek and such regional influences as those of the Near East, North Africa, Sicily, and Italy. The diffusion of Hellenistic art over several centuries and the entire Mediterranean world makes any quest for stylistic unity difficult. It is remarkable, in fact, that there is any unity at all. The style contrast between Hellenic and Hellenistic, moreover, is never one of polar extremes but rather a tilting of the cultural scale in one direction or an-

*Skolion* of SEIKOLOS (after Kunkel)
(2nd or 1st century B.C.)

other. The universal and social humanism of Athens becomes the particular and personal *individualism* of Pergamon and other centers. The noble Hellenic idealism breaks down into a *realism* that looks at the world more in terms of immediate experience than under the aspect of eternity; the uncompromising rationalism of Socrates, Plato, and Aristotle yields to an *empiricism* of scientists, scholars, and artists interested more in the development of methods and techniques and the application of knowledge to practical affairs than in the adventurous spirit of free inquiry. The tendencies that underly the various art enterprises at Pergamon in particular and the Hellenistic period in general, then, are to be found in a pattern of interrelated ideas, of which individualism, realism, and empiricism are components.

**Individualism**     As one phase of humanism, the individualistic bias of Hellenistic life, thought, and art contrasted strongly with the broader social accent of the Hellenic period. In politics, the rough-and-tumble public discussions of free citizens and decisions arrived at by voice vote were superseded by the rule of an inner circle of oligarchs headed by a king who enjoyed semidivine status. The cult of personal hero worship that started with Alexander the Great and continued with the kings that succeeded him in the various parts of his far-flung empire was reflected in the popular biographies of great men; in the building of lavish temples and monuments glorifying not the ancient gods but monarchs and military heroes, such as the famous Mausoleum (Fig. 60) for King Mausolus of Halicarnassus (Fig. 61); in the sculptor's accent on individual characteristics, diverse personality traits, and racial differences. In the earlier Hellenic centers, poets, playwrights, and musicians were mainly skilled amateurs; even in sports the emphasis was on active participation. In the Hellenistic period, however, a rising spirit of professionalism is noted in the fame of individual writers, actors, virtuosos, and athletes, with the result that people became passive spectators rather than active participants.

The search for truth in Athens was a gregarious activity of argumentation participated in by all comers in public squares or in the shady groves of an academy or lyceum where Plato and Aristotle discoursed with colleagues and students. Truth, it was felt, could not be arrived at individually but only through give and take, question and answer, examination and cross-examination, dialogue or dialectical processes. In Hellenistic times, these strenuous mental gymnastics gave way to the more personal contemplation and self-reflection of the Stoic and Epicurean philosophies. The thought of Epicurus found ready acceptance in the rich and flourishing cities of Asia Minor. Epicurus had taught that the highest good was "freedom from trouble in the mind and from pain in the body" and that the pursuit of pleasure was the goal of life. The austere idealism of Socrates thus gave way to a comfortable hedonism. But since some pleasures exceed others, the mind and critical faculties are needed to distinguish among those that give more lasting satisfaction. Epicurus also held that happiness for the individual lay in the direction of the simple life, self-containment, and withdrawal from public affairs. This, in effect, denied the social responsibilities of citizenship and encouraged escapism and extreme individualism.

Since the state controlled so much of the public weal, Hellenistic man found greater enjoyment in his personal and home life. Poverty had been deemed an honorable estate in ancient Athens, where rich and poor lived as neighbors in modest homes. Hellenistic wealth, however, allowed a more luxurious standard of living for a larger percentage of the population. Hellenistic architects, then, took special interest in domestic dwellings; painters and mosaicists were called upon to embellish the houses of the well-to-do; sculptors created figurines with informal, sometimes humorous, subjects, because they were more adapt-able to the home than monumental formal works; together with potters and other craftsmen, all worked to contribute to the life of luxury and ease of a frankly pleasure-loving people.

The Hellenistic artist was more interested in exceptions than rules, in the abnormal than the normal, in types than archetypes, in diversity than unity. In portraiture, he noted more the physical peculiarities that set an individual apart, not those that united him with others. Even the gods were personalized rather than generalized, and the choice of subjects from daily life showed the artist's increased preoccupation with informal, casual, everyday events. He was also more concerned with environmental influences on man than with man's being able to rise above his limitations. The Hellenistic artist, by recognizing the complexity of life, gave his attention to shades of feeling and to representing the infinite variety of the world of appearances.

**right: 60.** Pythios. Mausoleum at Halicarnassus. 359–351 B.C. c. 86 × 106'. Reconstruction drawing.

**far right: 61.** *Mausolus,* from Mausoleum at Halicarnassus. c. 353 B.C. Marble, height 9'10". British Museum, London.

The Hellenistic Style **57**

Hellenistic thought entered on a new emotional orientation. Instead of looking for the universal aspects of experience that could be shared by all, Hellenistic philosophers held that each man has his own feelings, ideas, and opinions entirely different from those of others. In this every-man-for-himself attitude, each must decide what is good and evil, true and false. Instead of seeking a golden mean between such opposites as harmony and discord as did their Hellenic predecessors, Hellenistic philosophers became psychologists analyzing the self and laying bare the causes of inner conflict. The joy, serenity, and contentment of the Hellenic gods and athletes were social emotions that could be shared by all. The sorrow, anguish, and suffering of Hellenistic wounded warriors and defeated giants were private, subjective feelings that separated a man from his fellows and invited inward reflection. It was an old variation on the theme—laugh and the world laughs with you, weep and you weep alone. Artists turned from the ideal of self-mastery to that of self-expression, from the concealment of inner impulse to outbursts of feeling—in short from ethos to pathos. It was said of Pericles that he was never seen laughing and that even the news of his son's death did not alter his dignified calm. A strong contrast to this Olympian attitude is provided by the late Hellenistic *Laocoön Group* (Fig. 62), where the balance of reason and emotion is replaced by a reveling in feeling for its own sake. What is lacking in self-restraint and regard for the limitations of the sculptural medium, however, is amply made up for by the vigor of treatment and virtuosity of execution.

The preoccupation of Pergamene artists with such painful and agonizing subjects as the defeated Gauls, the punishment of Marsyas, and the battle of gods and giants reveals the deliberate intention to involve the spectator in a kind of emotional orgy. Misfortune becomes something that can be enjoyed by the fortunate who participate in the situation with a kind of morbid satisfaction. La Rochefoucauld said: "We all have the strength to endure the misfortunes of others"; and Aldous Huxley observed that when the belly is full men can afford to grieve, and "sorrow after supper is almost a luxury." In the spirit of Stoic philosophy, life and suffering were to be endured with a grim satisfaction akin to a form of morbid enjoyment. The artists of the frieze of the Altar of Zeus, for instance, were incredibly inventive in the ways they found for the gods to inflict pain and death. The composition approaches an encyclopedic inclusiveness in the various modes of combat by the gods and the capacity for suffering by the giants. Nothing like it appears again in art until the Romanesque Last Judgments (Fig. 125) and Dante's *Inferno*.

**Realism**   The increasing complexity and quicker pulse of Hellenistic life weakened the belief in the underlying unity of knowledge and abiding values that produced the poise of Hellenic figures and the impassive calm of their facial expressions. The world of concrete experience was more real to Hellenistic man than one of remote abstract ideals. In his more relativistic view of things, he looked to variety rather than unity and took into account individual experiences and differences. Hellenistic artists sought to present nature as they saw it, to render minute details and ever finer shades of meaning. The decline of idealism was not necessarily the result of decadence, so much as it was a matter of placing man's activities in a new frame of reference, reexamining his goals and redefining basic human values. Confronted with the variety and multiplicity of this world, the Hellenistic artist made no attempt to reduce its many manifestations to the artificial simplicity of types and archetypes. The Hellenic artist portrays man standing aloof and rising above his environmental limitations, but in Hellenistic art man finds himself in the midst of the natural and social forces that beset him on all sides, and he is inevitably conditioned by them. The writhing forms on the great frieze reveal some of the conflicts and contradictions of Hellenistic man. His gods became projections of his own psychological problems. The earlier Hellenic gods appeared to have the world well under control, and the poised Zeus of the 5th century B.C. shows no sign of stress or strain as he hurls his thunderbolt. The deities of the Altar of Zeus, however, are fighting furiously, and things seem to verge on getting out of hand.

In the Athenian architecture of the 5th century B.C., each building, however well in harmony with its site, was an independent unit, and the architects were little concerned with any precise relationship to nearby buildings. Indeed, to have admitted that one structure was dependent upon another in a group would have diminished its status as a self-contained whole and thus rendered it incomplete by Hellenic standards. On the Athenian acropolis, each temple had its own axis and its independent formal existence—in keeping with the conception that each separate work of art must be a logical whole made up only of the sum of its own parts. Only such concessions to nature as were necessary for structural integrity were made. To man alone belonged the power of creating symmetrical form and balanced proportion, and the perfection of each building had to stand as a monument to the mind of man and, as such, to rise above its material environment rather than be bound by it. Hellenistic architecture moved away from the isolated building in the ideal sense of its being a self-contained unit towards a realistic recognition that nothing is complete in itself but must always exist as part of an interrelated pattern. City planning is therefore in this sense a form of realism, and Hellenistic buildings were considered as part of the community as a whole. In the case of the Pergamene acropolis, right: **62.** AGESANDER, ATHENODORUS, and POLYDORUS OF RHODES. *Laocoön Group.* Late 2nd century B.C. Marble, height 8'. Vatican Museums, Rome.

below: **63.** *Old Market Woman.* 2nd century B.C. Marble, height 4'1½". Metropolitan Museum of Art, New York (Rogers Fund, 1909).

the relationship of each building was carefully calculated not only in regard to its natural surroundings but also to its place in the group.

In sculpture, the members of each group were likewise subject to their environment, and man is portrayed as an integral part of his surroundings. By painting in backgrounds and by using higher relief, Hellenistic sculpture becomes more dependent on changing light and shade for its expressive effect, allows for movement in more than one plane, and suggests greater depth in space. In earlier sculpture, a figure always bore the stamp of a type, and personality was subordinate to the individual's place in society. A warrior, for example, had a well-developed physique, but his face and body bore no resemblance to a specific person. He could be identified by a spear or shield and was more a member of a class than a

person in his own right. The Hellenistic desire to render human beings as unique personalities and not as types necessitated a masterly technique capable of reproducing such particular characteristics as the twist of a mouth, wrinkles of the skin, physical blemishes, and individualized facial expressions. Faces, furthermore, had to appear animated and lifelike, so that the subject of a realistic portrait could be distinguished from all others. Fidelity to nature also meant the accurate rendering of anatomical detail. Like a scientist, the sculptor observed the musculature of the human body with precision so as to render every nuance of the flesh. The *Old Market Woman* (Fig. 63), for example, reveals the body of a person worn down by toil. The bent back, sagging breasts, gnarled limbs are the results of the physical conditions under which she has had to live. In the handling of materials, the older Hellenic sculptors never forgot that stone was stone. But their realistic zeal often led later Hellenistic craftsmen to force stone to simulate the softness and warmth of living flesh. The story of the legendary sculptor Pygmalion who chiseled his marble maiden so realistically that she came to life could have happened only in the Hellenistic period, and the sensuous figure of the *Aphrodite of Cyrene* surely bears this out (Fig. 64). The easy grace and charm with which Praxiteles had rendered his gods and goddesses (Figs. 38, 43) find a culmination in such elegant and pol-

**left: 64.** *Aphrodite of Cyrene.* Roman copy of c.100 B.C. after Praxitelean original, found at Cyrene, North Africa. Marble, height 5'. National Museum, Rome.

**right: 65.** *Apollo Belvedere.* Roman copy after Greek original of the late 4th century B.C. Marble, height 7'4''. Vatican Museums, Rome.

ished figures as this Aphrodite and the famous *Apollo Belvedere* (Fig. 65).

Hellenistic emphasis on realism appealed greatly to the forthright Roman conquerors of Greece, and its appeal to these men of action was largely responsible for the ultimate survival of the Pergamene sculptures now known to us.

**Empiricism** The rationalism of Hellenic thought as developed by Socrates, Plato, and Aristotle had emphasized the spirit of free intellectual inquiry in a quest for universal truth. Epicureanism and Stoicism, by contrast, were practical philosophies for living. The abstract logic of the earlier period yielded to an empiricism that was concerned more with science than wisdom, in bringing together the results of isolated experimentation, and in the application of knowledge to the solution of practical problems. More broadly, Hellenistic empiricism stressed fact-gathering, the cataloguing of source materials in libraries, scholarly research, collecting art works, and developing critical criteria for judging the arts.

Epicurus, by eliminating the notion of divine intervention in human affairs, and by his physical ex-

planations of natural phenomena, laid the philosophical basis for a scientific materialism. Hellenistic mathematics extended as far as conic sections and trigonometry, and such astronomers and physicists as Archimedes and Hero of Alexandria knew the world was round as well as its approximate circumference and diameter. Hellenistic scientists had a solar calendar of 365¼ days, invented a type of steam engine, and worked out the principles of steam power and force pumps. Indeed, the modern mechanical and industrial revolutions might well have taken place in Hellenistic times had not slave labor been so cheap and abundant. The progressiveness of the period is also seen in its commercial developments that led to new sources of wealth.

This scientific attitude found brilliant expression in the musical field by the development of the theoretical basis of that art. While philosophers and mathematicians of the earlier period had made many discoveries and had had brilliant insights into the nature of music, it remained for the Hellenistic mind to systematize them and construct a comprehensive and coherent science of music. Under Aristoxenos of Tarentum, a disciple of Aristotle, and under Euclid, the theory of music reached a formulation so complete and comprehensive that it became the foundation for Western music. While it is impossible to go into the intricacies of the Greek musical system here, one should keep in mind that it was in this theoretical field more than in any other that a lasting musical contribution was made.

After establishing his great library, Eumenes II gathered about him many of the outstanding Greek scholars of his day. They were dedicated to the task of preserving the literary masterpieces of bygone days, making critical editions of the works of ancient poets and dramatists, selecting material for anthologies, cataloguing collections, copying manuscripts, writing grammatical treatises, and compiling dictionaries. In their scholarly endeavors, they upheld the works of the ancients above the writers of their own time, and as a consequence their literary production began to be addressed more to other scholars than to the people at large. Such a restricted audience of cultivated readers could not be supplied by Pergamon alone but had to be sought for all over the scattered Greek world. By mutual consent, the pure and majestic Attic Greek of Pericles, Euripides, and Plato became their "common dialect" and the artificial medium of communication between the cultured classes. With this emphasis on a tongue that was no longer spoken, the living language in which writers could address their fellow citizens began to be regarded as a local dialect.

This was a period of antiquarianism, of scholarly rather than creative writing, of erudition instead of inspiration, and only systematic, exhaustive research could have produced the program of the great frieze girdling the Altar of Zeus, which is a veritable catalogue of Greek mythology, complete with footnotes and annotations. The Attalids not only collected art but actually engaged in archaeological excavations, and for the first time the living sculptor and painter were confronted with a museum filled with noted works from the glorious past. Copying the masterpieces of Myron, Phidias, and others became an industry that thrived throughout antiquity until the advent of official Christianity. The age raised the social position of the artist and, as in literature and music, established the history of art and formulated aesthetic standards, so that now art was worthy of attention in the highest intellectual and social circles.

## THE ROAD TO ROME

A reputation for learning had direct bearing on the political purposes of the Pergamene government. The more renowned their capital became for its intellectual and cultural enterprises, the higher its prestige in the Greek world would be. The career of Eumenes II's brother, who eventually succeeded him as Attalus II, is a case in point. As a skillful general, he was invaluable to the Pergamene regime, yet at the conclusion of a successful war he took five years off to study philosophy at the academy in Athens. Furthermore, the proudest boast of the Attalids after their military victories was that they were the saviors of Hellenism from the barbarians. This claim, of course, had to be fortified by the development of their capital as a center of arts and letters. To advertise the cultural achievements of his realm, Eumenes II chose his librarian, the famed grammarian Crates of Mallos, as his ambassador to Rome. By his championship of humanistic learning, and by stimulating Roman desire for more knowledge about Greek philosophy, literature, and art, Crates made a lasting impression on the future world capital.

With literary talents being diverted into the editing of manuscripts, scholars delving into the history of the past, art collectors digging for buried treasure, and musicians writing theoretical treatises, Pergamon was well on its way toward becoming an archive and a museum. In time, this antiquarianism was bound to lead artistic developments into a stylistic eclecticism and to reduce aesthetic procedures to academic formulas and rules—all of which is symptomatic of a hardening of the artistic arteries and the eventual decline of the creative powers. When, therefore, in 133 B.C. Attalus III willed his kingdom to Rome, he was actually presenting that city with a living museum. The vast art holdings of the Attalids soon were on their way to Italy, where the interest and admiration they commanded, when shown in public exhibitions, were destined to have a powerful effect on the taste of the Romans. With them went the Hellenistic craftsmen who would embellish the new world capital with an imperial wealth of edifices, carvings, murals, and mosaics (Fig. 66).

66. *Imperial Procession,* detail of Ara Pacis Augustae, Rome. c. 13 B.C. Marble, height 5'3".

# 4 The Roman Style

## ROME, 2ND CENTURY A.D.

The Antonine Age was "the period in the history of the world during which the condition of the human race was most happy and prosperous. . . ." So wrote Gibbon in *The Decline and Fall of the Roman Empire.* Under Trajan, Hadrian, and Marcus Aurelius, continues the great historian, "the Empire of Rome comprehended the fairest part of the earth and the most civilized portion of mankind." This benign state of affairs Gibbon attributed to the Romans' genius for law and order, their cultivation of tolerance and justice, and their capacity for wise government.

The Arch of Trajan at Benevento (Fig. 67) recalls some of this vanished grandeur by proclaiming the virtues and accomplishments of the first great emperor of Gibbon's chosen period. Commissioned by the Roman Senate to celebrate the completion of the Via Traiana, a 200-mile highway over the mountains that linked Rome with the large port of Brindisi, the arch honored an outstanding achievement in engineering as well as the chief engineer of the Empire. Such a gateway, marking as it did the start of the long road toward the East, challenged the Romans' imaginations to envisage lands that lay beyond the seas and reminded them that their city was not a self-contained unit. Roman awareness that their individual destinies, as well as those of their city and state, were closely bound up with the surrounding territories found logical expression in just such a monument. Among ancient city-states Rome was unique in its solution of the problem of how to maintain its municipal integrity and at the same time manage a far-flung empire. In evolving the institutions by which this political unity could be made compatible with such wide human diversity, the Romans achieved their greatest social distinction.

Monumental arches usually marked the conclusion of a successful military campaign, by which distant barbarian tribes were subdued or some new civilized people brought into the Roman orbit. In the instance of the Arch of Titus in Rome, the returning conqueror, along with his army, a train of captives, and the trophies of war, passed through the arch with the plaudits of the multitudes ringing in his ears.

Trajan's Arch was modeled architecturally after that of Titus, including such details as the attached *Composite* columns, a Roman combination of the Ionic and Corinthian orders. It differs in spirit from the Arch of Titus, however, in that the sculptures celebrate the arts of peace rather than those of war. The reliefs that so liberally cover its surface were arranged in characteristic Roman fashion so as to inform and instruct as well as to delight the eye. On the side facing the town of Benevento and more-distant Rome (Fig. 67), the panels deal with Trajan's domestic policy. He is seen making land grants in the newly conquered Danube region to veterans of his wars; standing in the midst of prosperous merchants grateful for the new harbor he built for them at Ostia, the port of Rome; and receiving the acclamation of the Senate and the people in the Roman Forum. Across the lintel moves a triumphal procession, and on either side of the keystone hover victories with crown and banners. Above, Jupiter and Juno and Minerva (known in Roman mythology as the Capitoline Triad) are seen extending their welcome to the Emperor. As a gesture of approval, Jupiter is turning over his thunderbolt to Trajan, a recognition of the latter's great power as well as a sign that the adulation of the emperor was supplanting the worship of the Olympian deities. This group is placed next to the inscription, which adds to Trajan's usual string of titles that of *Optimo,*

**67.** Arch of Trajan, Benevento. A.D. 114.

"the best," which is said to have pleased him especially since he shared it only with Jupiter.

On the side toward the seaport are the scenes pertaining to Trajan's foreign policy. Germany is seen taking the oath of allegiance; various Oriental rulers are sending tributes through their envoys; and the Emperor is establishing state-sponsored benefits for the relief of poor children. Above, a figure symbolizing Mesopotamia is paying him homage, and the divinities of the Danube territory are welcoming him. The inside passage of the archway is similarly decorated. Although each panel depicts a separate episode, unity is achieved in the repetition of the imperial personage. Variety is obtained by shifting the human and geographical environment. Changes of place are indicated partly by the activities and partly by the background, which signify a setting in Rome by some familiar buildings, a country place by trees, and a remote locality by exotic river gods. The subject matter is obviously propaganda for imperial rule—even to the extent of often showing the Emperor as a figure of superhuman size—but the restrained manner of presentation keeps this aspect from becoming too blatant. The actual sculpture is technically well handled, though there is a tendency to accent linear detail at the expense of unity and repose.

While monumental arches were nonutilitarian in purpose, their form exemplifies the building principle that underlies the Roman achievements in architecture. With the arch the Romans constructed their vaults and domes that carried architecture forward well into modern times. The fact that Trajan's Arch was built in a provincial town south of Rome on the road to and from the great centers of the East—Athens, Pergamon, Alexandria, Ephesus, and Antioch—is a reminder of the route by which the heritage of the classical Mediterranean world became a part of Western cultural tradition. By military conquest, by annexation, by inheritance, and by voluntary action—one by one the proud old city-states and

kingdoms became a part of greater Rome. Likewise all the ideas, institutions, and art forms of this vast region were sifted through the ingenious Roman mind, and, together with notable contributions of her own, Rome gradually achieved a culmination of culture, expressed in her literature, architecture, and sculpture, that could compare favorably with the political eminence of her great empire.

## ARCHITECTURE

**Forum of Trajan**     Following his accession as Emperor in A.D. 98, Trajan began a grandiose project in Rome: the construction of a new forum (Figs. 68, 69). Just as the Empire had grown in his time to its greatest extent, so the population of Rome had risen to over a million, creating a need for larger and more imposing public buildings. The old Forum Romanum of the Republic had long been inadequate, and several extensions had been undertaken in the early years of the Empire. But Trajan's project was so ambitious that it equaled all previous forums combined, bringing the total area covered by such structures to over 25 acres. Needless to say, its magnificence was in every way comparable to its size. Trajan entrusted the project to Apollodorus, a Greek architect-engineer from Damascus, famous for the construction of a stone bridge over the widest part of the Danube before Trajan's second Dacian campaign. But Apollodorus' Greek origin did not necessarily indicate a Hellenistic bias on the Emperor's part; all other known architects in Rome at this time (including those who collaborated

# CHRONOLOGY / Roman Period—Republic and Empire

| | | |
|---|---|---|
| | 753 | Legendary date of Rome's founding |
| c.616– | c.509 | Etruscan period. Tarquin kings reigned |
| | c.500 | Roman Republic founded; Tarquins dethroned |
| | c.450 | Romans colonized Italy |
| | 390 | Rome sacked by Gauls |
| 280– | 275 | Greek power in Italy weakened |
| 264– | 241 | First Punic War; Rome annexed Sicily, Corsica, Sardinia |
| 218– | 201 | Second Punic War; Hannibal invaded Italy; Carthage ceded Spain to Rome |
| 150– | 146 | Third Punic War; Carthage destroyed; African province created |
| | 133 | Pergamon bequeathed to Rome |
| 100– | 44 | Julius Caesar. Conquered Gaul (58–51); crossed Rubicon, occupied Rome, became dictator (49); Forum of Julius Caesar begun (c.48); campaigned in Egypt, Asia Minor, Africa, Spain (48–45); Julian calendar (45); assassinated (44) |
| c.50– | c.10 | Vitruvius active; wrote treatise De Architectura |
| | 43 | Second Triumvirate formed—Antony, Octavian (Augustus), Lepidus |
| | 31 | Naval battle at Actium; Antony and Cleopatra defeated |
| 27– | A.D.14 | Augustus (Octavian) reigned. As Octavian founded principate, took name of Augustus, beginning of Empire; built Forum and Mausoleum of Augustus, Ara Pacis, Baths of Agrippa, Theater of Marcellus, Basilica Julia |
| | 4 | Birth of Jesus; crucified A.D.c.29 |

A.D.

| | | |
|---|---|---|
| 54– | 68 | Nero reigned. Built Baths of Nero, Domus Aureus |
| | 70 | Titus took Jerusalem; temple destroyed |
| | 79 | Vesuvius erupted; Pompeii, Herculaneum destroyed |
| 79– | 81 | Titus reigned. Colosseum finished; Temple of Vespasian, Arch of Titus built |
| 96– | 180 | "Antonine Age," or "Era of Five Good Emperors" (Nerva, Trajan, Hadrian, Antoninus Pius, Marcus Aurelius). Roman Empire reached pinnacle of power |
| 98– | 117 | Trajan reigned. Dacian campaigns (101–106); harbor at Ostia built (103); Via Traiana between Benevento and Brindisi, and Baths of Trajan built (110); Forum of Trajan and Column erected, Arch of Trajan at Benevento begun (113); conquered Armenia, Parthia, Empire extended to Persian Gulf and Caspian Sea (113–117) |
| c.100– | c.120 | Apollodorus of Damascus, architect, active |
| 104– | 105 | Bridge over Danube built by Apollodorus |
| 117– | 138 | Hadrian reigned. Temple of Olympian Zeus at Athens completed (117); Roman Pantheon built (120–124); Villa of Hadrian at Tivoli built (c.120–127); Hadrian's tomb begun (135) |
| 138– | 161 | Antoninus Pius reigned. "House of Diana" at Ostia built |
| 161– | 180 | Marcus Aurelius reigned. Stoic philosopher, author of Meditations (c.174); died near Vienna |
| 211– | 217 | Baths of Caracalla built |

### B.C. 80–A.D. 14 "Golden Age of Roman Literature"

| | | |
|---|---|---|
| 106– | 43 | Cicero, statesman, orator, essayist |
| c.96– | 55 | Lucretius, poet, philosopher, On Nature of Things |
| 87– | 57 | Catullus, lyric poet |
| 70– | 19 | Vergil, Aeneid, Eclogues |
| 65– | 8 | Horace, Odes |
| 59– | A.D.17 | Livy, History of Rome |
| 43– | A.D.17 | Ovid, Art of Love, Metamorphoses |

### A.D. 14–117 "Silver Age of Roman Literature"

| | | |
|---|---|---|
| 3 B.C.– | A.D.65 | Seneca, philosopher, dramatist |
| c.20– | 66 | Petronius, Satiricon |
| 23– | 79 | Pliny the Elder, naturalist, encyclopedist |
| c.50– | c.90 | Epictetus, Stoic philosopher |
| 35– | 95 | Quintilian, Institutes of Oratory |
| 40– | c.102 | Martial, epigrammatist |
| c.46– | 120 | Plutarch, Parallel Lives |
| 55– | c.117 | Tacitus, historian, Annals, Germania |
| c.60– | c.135 | Juvenal, Satires |
| 62– | 113 | Pliny the Younger, writer, administrator; delivered Panegyric to Trajan before Roman Senate (100) |
| 75– | c.150 | Suetonius, Lives of Twelve Caesars |
| | c.160 | Apulius flourished, philosopher, Golden Ass |
| c.160– | c.230 | Tertullian, Christian apologist |

on the project) were Romans, and Apollodorus was thoroughly familiar with Roman building tradition.

Typically Roman in conception, a forum combined a system of open courtyards and buildings all grouped in a specific relationship (Fig. 69). The reconstruction drawing of the Athenian acropolis (Fig. 13) shows that the Parthenon and Erechtheum had little more in common than the site on which they

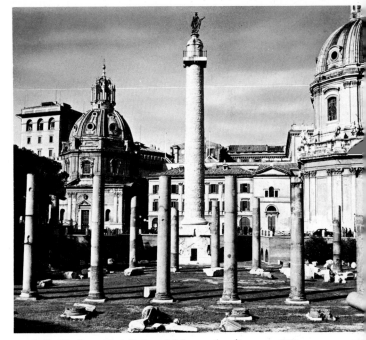

stood. But no part of a forum existed in isolation, and in the case of Trajan's Forum everything was conceived from the beginning on a large scale and with an eye to symmetry. The whole was bisected by a central axis running from the center of the arched gateway, through the middle of the square, through the entrance to the basilica (whose axis is at right angles to the whole forum), to the base of the column, and finally up the steps of the temple to the altar at the back.

Entrance to the forum was made through a majestic triple archway into the large paved quadrangle, enclosed on three sides by a wall and colonnade and on the fourth by the Basilica Ulpia, whose entrances stood opposite those of the archway. Standing in the exact center of the open square was an impressive bronze statue of Trajan on horseback. Though no longer extant, it is known to have resembled the surviving bronze equestrian portrait of Marcus Aurelius (Fig. 70), who sits astride his splendid mount with an equilibrium worthy of the patient Stoic philosopher and the thoughtful mien of the author of the widely read *Meditations*. Flanking the square on the east and west sides were semicircular recesses known as *exedrae* outlined by tall Doric columns. Similar in shape were the series of market stalls rising upward into the two hills. The best preserved are those on the Quirinal side, six stories in height and constructed of brick (Fig. 71). On the forum floor were more than 150 booths—for vegetables, fruits, and flowers; above were large vaulted halls where wine and oil were stored; spices and imported delicacies were sold on

**top left: 70.** *Equestrian Statue of Marcus Aurelius.* A.D. 161–181. Gilt bronze, height 9'10". Piazza del Campidoglio, Rome.

**top right: 71.** APOLLODORUS OF DAMASCUS. Forum of Trajan, Rome. Northeast exedra and market hall. A.D. c. 113–117.

**above: 72.** Column of Trajan and ruins of Basilica Ulpia, Rome. Column of Trajan, A.D. 106–113. Marble; base height 18', column height 97'.

the third and fourth floors; the fifth was used to distribute food and money out of the imperial treasury; and on top were tanks supplied by fresh water from an aqueduct where live fish could be bought.

Adjacent to the open square was the Basilica Ulpia, of which only the rows of broken columns remain (Fig. 72). The term *basilica* was applied rather

The Roman Style  **65**

generally to large public buildings and is approximately equivalent to the modern word *hall* used for meeting places. Since court sessions were also held in a basilica, the term *hall of justice* is likewise related to one of its functions. As an architectural form, the Roman basilica is one link in the long chain of Mediterranean structures that began with domestic dwellings, Egyptian hypostyle halls, and Greek temples and continued with Christian basilicas.

The large rectangular interior of the Basilica Ulpia, named for Trajan's family, was marked by a double colonnade in the Corinthian order that ran completely around the building, supporting a balcony and a second tier of columns that, in turn, supported the beams of the timbered roof (Fig. 73). This large central hall served as a general meeting place as well as a business center. The semicircular interior recesses called *apses,* possibly roofed over with hemispherical vaults and set apart from the central hall by screens or curtains, housed the courts of law.

Beyond the basilica were two libraries, one for Greek and the other for Latin scrolls, separated by a courtyard that enclosed the base of Trajan's Column, the relief sculpture of which will be discussed shortly.

After Trajan's death his adopted son and successor, Hadrian, built at the end of the main axis of the forum the Corinthian temple that climaxed the grand design. Architecturally, it was a large-scale version of the Maison Carrée at Nîmes in southern France (Fig. 74). Like other Roman temples, this one honoring Trajan and the Maison Carrée rested on podiums and had porticoes in the front, which were much more

**73.** APOLLODORUS OF DAMASCUS. Basilica Ulpia, within the complex of the Forum of Trajan, Rome. A.D. 113. Reconstruction drawing of interior.

prominently featured than those in Greek temples. The well-preserved example at Nîmes likewise shows only the columns of the portico standing free, while the rest are attached to the cella, indicating that columns were needed less for structural strength than for embellishment.

The practice of deifying rulers and erecting temples to them was widespread in Hellenistic times, and began in Rome as early as the reign of Augustus. The type of statue that stood in such a temple can be seen in the portrait of Augustus, which was found near Prima Porta (Fig. 75). He stands in the imposing attitude of an *imperator* addressing his troops. Carved on the cuirass, or metal breastplate of his armor, are scenes in low relief recounting the outstanding achievements of his reign and pictures of the gods and goddesses who conferred their favors upon him. At his side is a cupid astride a dolphin, one of the symbols of Venus (Fig. 64, where Aphrodite is the Greek equivalent of the Roman Venus), which alludes to the divine origin of the Julian family. Vergil, the principal poet of his period, traced Augustus' ancestry all the way back to Aeneas, the legendary founder of Rome, whose father was the mortal Anchises but whose mother was none other than the immortal Venus.

Much of Roman religion was a family affair, honoring the living *pater familias* as well as the nearer and more remote ancestors. A room in every household was set aside for this purpose, and the custom was responsible for a whole genre of sculpture, such as the portrait busts entitled *Porcia and Cato* (Fig. 76). In

**74.** "Maison Carrée," Nîmes, France. 16 B.C. Marble; base 59 × 117', podium height 11', column height 30½'.

**below: 75.** *Augustus of Prima Porta.* c. 20 B.C. Marble, height 6'8''. Vatican Museums, Rome.

**right: 76.** *Porcia and Cato*(?), portraits of a Roman couple. c. 1st century B.C. Marble, height 27''. Vatican Museums, Rome.

simple family ceremonies; on the day for honoring the emperor, the rites at his temple were more formal, occasionally including animal sacrifice, a procession, festivities, and amusements. Religion to the Romans was the tradition and continuity of the family and, in the larger sense, the history and destiny of Rome itself.

With the exception of the temple, the Forum of Trajan was completed during his lifetime and was dedicated by him for the use of the people of Rome in A.D. 113. The whole, then, is made up of parts—the triumphal entrance archway, the courtyard and its equestrian statue, the mercantile buildings, the Basilica Ulpia, two libraries, a monumental column, and the temple—all adding up to an architectural composition on a grand scale, designed to accommodate a hierarchy of activities. Beginning with a shopping center and place to transact business, the forum continued with a general meeting place and the halls of justice, moved on to places for quiet contemplation, study in the libraries and the reading of history in visual form on the column, and, finally, came to rest in the precinct for the veneration of the Emperor and the worship of the Roman gods.

**Imperial Baths**   While the forums took care of the more serious pursuits of his people, Trajan never forgot that circuses often were as important as bread in promoting the happiness of his subjects. One of every emperor's duties, in fact, was to provide for public amusement out of his private purse. Only the very wealthy could afford entertainment in their own homes, so the people as a whole had to look for their recreation outside. To this end many baths, theaters, amphitheaters, arenas, and stadiums had been built all over the city. The variety they encompassed has

contrast to the generalized and somewhat idealized image of Augustus as the statesman and imperator, this unpretentious portrait of ordinary citizens is remarkably realistic. Both kinds of sculpture, however, served essentially the same purpose—one as the image of the father of a family in a simple household, the other for the veneration of a great man in a temple. The paternalistic emperors were felt to deserve the universal reverence of the whole Roman family, since they were considered *pater patriae,* or "fathers of their country." Erecting a temple to a distinguished Roman emperor was done in much the same spirit as building the Washington Monument or the Lincoln Memorial in Washington, D.C. Certain days were set aside for the offering of food and drink in

**right: 77.** Tepidarium (heated central hall), Baths of Caracalla. A.D. 211–217. Reconstruction drawing by Spiers.

**below: 78.** Plan of Baths of Caracalla, Rome. 750 × 380'.

never been surpassed, and to this day the highest praise that can be given an elaborate public festival is to call it a "Roman holiday."

Imperial baths provided the people with far more than hot, cold, and tepid swimming pools. They offered such other facilities as dressing rooms, gymnasiums, restaurants, bars, and shady walks. Guests also could attend plays, witness athletic contests, listen to public lectures, read in one of the libraries, or stroll about the galleries where statuary and paintings were exhibited. The baths were, in short, the people's palaces where the sociable citizenry could enjoy together the things that only the rich could afford separately. Favored also as places to show the booty and souvenirs carried off during foreign conquests, the baths are the sites where much ancient statuary has been found, notably the *Laocoön Group* (Fig. 62). These baths also had important hygienic advantages; and with the habit of daily bathing firmly established, the people of Rome probably were cleaner than those of any other city before or since.

Trajan added to the already existing public baths a large establishment also built by Apollodorus. Although the ruins of his *thermae* ("baths") are not so well preserved as the later baths of Caracalla and Diocletian, enough is known to establish a clear picture of what they were like. Only a degree smaller than the later examples, their facilities were on a comparable scale. The large central hall was the earliest known use of concrete *cross vaulting,* the principle of which can be studied in Figure 83 and in the similar central hall of the Baths of Caracalla (Figs. 77, 78), which measured 183 feet in length with an open space

between the walls of 79 feet. From the illustration, it can be seen that the barrel vault that runs lengthwise is three times intersected at right angles by shorter vaults extending across the width of the hall. Besides spanning larger interior spaces without the obstruction of supporting piers and columns, this type of construction had the additional advantage of ample lighting through the clearstory windows, which were provided with thin strips of translucent yellow marble in lieu of glass. Modern architects, when erecting such huge edifices as the Union Station in Washington, D.C., and Grand Central Terminal in New York City, found no better models among large secular structures than these Roman baths.

**Colosseum and Aqueducts**   The Colosseum (Fig. 79), which dates from the late 1st century, was the scene of rather garish forms of mass entertainment, including gory gladiatorial contests between men and wild beasts. The oval form of the Colosseum covers about 6 acres and could seat about 50,000 spectators at one time. Around its circumference run some 80 archways, which served so efficiently as entrances and exits that the entire bowl could be emptied in a matter of minutes. The Roman talent for organization is not only evident here in such practical respects but extends to the structure and decorative design. Three architectural orders are combined in the successive stories of the same building. The attached columns on the lower range are the "home-grown" variation of the Doric, known as the Tuscan; those on the second tier are Ionic; on the third, Corinthian; while on the fourth, which rises to a height of 157 feet, are found shallow, flat Corinthian piers known as *pilasters* between which run a row of sockets for the poles over which a canvas awning was stretched to protect the spectators from sun and rain. The building material

**79.** Colosseum, Rome. A.D. 72–80. Long axis 620', short axis 513', height 160'.

was a concrete made from broken pieces of brick, small rocks, volcanic dust, lime, and water. It could be poured into molds of any desired shape and when dry was as hard as natural stone. The exterior was originally covered with marble facing, and the entire structure would be in good condition today had it not been used later as a quarry for building materials right up to the 18th century. In spite of this, the Colosseum is still one of the most imposing ruins to survive from Roman times, and its popularity as a prototype can be seen in the numerous football stadiums on college campuses.

In order to assure an ample water supply for his thermae, Trajan found it necessary to improve the old system of aqueducts and to add a new one, 35 miles long, that is still in use today. A more beautiful ex-

**80.** Pont du Gard, Nîmes, France. Early 1st century A.D. Length c. 902', height c. 161'.

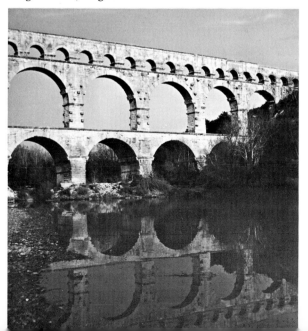

ample of a Roman aqueduct is the Pont du Gard at Nîmes (Fig. 80), which survived from the 1st century A.D. A system of underground and open concrete channels was constructed to bring water from its mountain source to the town 25 miles away. Functioning on the principle of gravity, the ducts were sloped in the desired direction, and in this instance the water was carried almost 300 yards across the valley at a height of more than 160 feet. The graceful lower range of arches support a bridge that is still in use, while the upper series of large and small arches support the water channel.

**The Pantheon** The Roman sense of social organization was also extended into the field of religion with the Pantheon (Fig. 81). While the name might imply a temple to all the gods, in effect the Pantheon became a mirror of the world order, with statues placed in niches to personify the sun, the moon, and the so-called "planetary dieties"—Mercury, Venus, Mars, Jupiter, and Saturn. The Emperor Hadrian himself had a hand in the design of this distinguished edifice, and he occasionally presided over meetings of the Roman senate held in its resplendent and masterly interior (Pl. 7, p. 42).

The Pantheon's geometry is based on the union of a cylinder and a hemisphere over a circular ground plan (Fig. 82), with the interior diameter and the height of the dome both being a little more than 140 feet. The clarity of form achieved by the visible equality of horizontal and vertical dimensions, as well as by the simplicity of design, is evident to the casual eye. The satisfying sense of spatial proportion and the harmonious impression of the interior are based on a union of applied scientific skill and aesthetic feeling. In the Pantheon as well as in the great halls of imperial baths, the Romans advanced architecture to the left: **81.** Pantheon, Rome, A.D. c. 120. Portico height 59'.

below: **82.** Plan of Pantheon.

point where it achieved significant interiors. Unlike other classical temples, the Pantheon invited entrance. The inner surface of the dome is characterized by *coffers,* indented panels which serve the dual purpose of diminishing the weight of the dome and furnishing the basis for its decoration. In the center of each coffer was a gilded bronze star, a motif that related the dome symbolically to the sky. Much of the once-resplendent interior, with its walls sheathed in varicolored marbles of glowing ochre with red, green, and black contrasts, is still visible. Gone, however, are the gilded bronze tiles that once spread across the coffered inner dome like an expansive starry firmament mirroring the heavens. The sole source of light is the single 29-foot round opening in the middle of the dome. This *oculus,* or "eye," as it was called, can be interpreted as an allusion to the all-seeing eye of heaven. Soaring almost 150 feet above the colorful mosaic flooring, it creates a great shaft of illumination that bathes the interior in light of high intensity.

As seen today, the Pantheon exterior is stripped of its former rich and colorful marble covering. The bronze plates of the portico ceiling, the gilded bronze tiles that covered the entire exterior of both the drum and the dome, and the monumental statues of the gods within have all disappeared in the course of time. Despite mutilations, however, the Pantheon is the best-preserved single building that survives from the ancient world and the oldest structure of large proportions with its original roof intact. It holds its own as one of the world's most impressive domed buildings, despite such outstanding competition as Hagia Sophia in Constantinople (Fig. 103), the Cathedral of Florence (Fig. 170), St. Peter's in Rome (Fig. 193), and St. Paul's in London (Fig. 293). Its descendants are legion—the Villa Rotonda (Fig. 215), Thomas Jefferson's home at Monticello, the rotunda he designed for the University of Virginia, the Pantheon in Paris, certain features of the Capitol rotunda in Washington, D.C., and the Low Memorial Library at Columbia University in New York, to name but a few of the buildings inspired by the Pantheon.

**The Roman Architectural Contribution** The Roman contribution to architecture was fourfold: (1) building for use, (2) development of the arch and vault as a structural principle, (3) emphasis on verticality, and (4) design of significant interiors. In the first case, Roman architecture was marked by a shift in emphasis from religious buildings to the civil-engineering projects that had such an important bearing on the solution of the practical problems of the day. This did not mean that the Romans neglected their shrines and temples or that they lacked religious feeling. As in the 19th and 20th centuries, however, the main architectural expression was to be found in secular rather than religious structures. In this category come the basilicas, aqueducts, roads, bridges, even the sewer systems, which so admirably served the utilitarian purposes of the Romans.

Second—and perhaps most important of all—was the Roman exploitation of the possibilities inherent in the arch as a building principle to implement the above objectives. The construction of a true arch by means of the wedge-shaped blocks known as *voussoirs*, as well as some of the implications of the system, can be seen more easily in Figure 83 than explained in words. When such arches are placed side by side in a series, the resulting arcade can be used for such structures as aqueducts and bridges, as seen in the Pont du Gard (Fig. 80). When placed in a series, from front to back, the result is a *barrel vault* (also called a *tunnel vault*), which can be seen in the Arch of Trajan at Benevento (Fig. 67) and which was useful for roofing interiors. When a series of arches span a given space by intersecting each other around a central axis, the result is a dome, as exemplified in the Pantheon (Pl. 7). In greatly oversimplified form, these constitute the technical principles that underlie the Roman architectural achievement.

Third, by their technical advances they were able to increase the height of their buildings in proportion to the growing size of their large structures. The six-story mercantile buildings of Trajan's Forum were an impressive demonstration of the practical advantages of such verticality, which allowed the combination of many small shops into a single structure in a crowded city location. The multifamily apartment houses in Ostia and Rome were also cases in point. The trend was to be seen in the great height that imparted such pleasing spatial proportions to the halls in the Baths of Trajan and Caracalla as well as to the Pantheon—all made possible by cross vaulting and the dome.

Last, the enclosing of large units of interior space was made necessary by the expansion of the city's population. The direction of architectural thought in meeting this need can easily be seen by contrasting a Greek agora with the Forum of Trajan, a Hellenistic theater with the Colosseum, or the Parthenon with the Pantheon. Special attention to space composition and the problems of lighting are in evidence in the planning of such interiors as those of the Basilica Ulpia, the Pantheon, and the halls of the great baths. In all instances, the increasing Roman awareness of the value, tangibility, and reality of the spatial medium is discernible.

## SCULPTURE

**Spiral Frieze of Trajan's Column** To commemorate Trajan's victories in the two campaigns against the Dacian people of the lower Danube region, a monumental column was erected in the Emperor's forum by the Senate and people of Rome. It was placed in the small opening off the Basilica Ulpia between the two libraries (Fig. 72). Its base was originally surrounded by a colonnade that supported an upper gallery from which better views of the sculptures could be obtained. The diameter of the column varies from 12 feet at the base of its shaft to 10 feet at the top. As a whole it rose to a full height of 128 feet, including the 18-foot base, the 97-foot shaft, and a 13-foot colossal statue of Trajan that originally stood at the top. The latter disappeared long ago and has since been replaced by an image of St. Peter. Inside the column is a circular staircase that winds upward to the top and is lighted by small windowlike slits cut into the frieze. According to tradition, Trajan chose the monument as the site of his burial, and his ashes were placed in a chamber located at the base of the column.

The column itself is of the Doric order and is constructed in several sections of white marble. Its surface is entirely covered by a spiral band, carved in low relief, which winds from bottom to top in 23 revolutions. Reading from left to right, the story of the two Dacian campaigns unfolds in a continuous strip about 50 inches wide and 218 yards long in which more than 2,500 human figures make their appearance, in addition to horses, boats, vehicles, and equipment of all kinds.

---

**83.** The *arch* is a curved structural member used to span a space between two vertical elements, such as posts (piers) or walls (A). Wedge-shaped blocks, called *voussoirs* (a), give the arch its form and stability by virtue of their compressed relationship to each other and to the *keystone* (b) at the apex of the semicircle. The curve of the arch rises from the *springing* on either side of the opening (c), and the *compression* of its stones is better able than the *tensile* strength of a *lintel* on posts (B) to resist the downward thrust of the load above. It does this by directing the weight laterally and by transmitting the load to the ground through the line of the arch and the vertical elements supporting it. Placed one after the other, a series of arches make a *tunnel vault* (C). Two tunnel vaults intersecting each other at right angles (D) create a *cross vault*, also known as a *groin vault* (so-called for the groin line [E] along which the vaults join), and the square or rectangular space they define is called a *bay* (d). Intersecting each other around a central axis, a series of arches would form a *dome* (F).

left: **84.** *Trajan's Campaign against the Dacians*, detail of Trajan's Column. A.D. 106–113. Marble, frieze-band height c. 4'2".

below: **85.** *Trajan Addressing Assembly of Troops*, detail of Trajan's Column.

The hero of the story is, of course, the soldierly Trajan, who is shown fulfilling his imperial mission as the defender of Rome against the encroachments of the barbarians. The Empire was always willing to include any people who accepted the values of Mediterranean civilization, but it could tolerate no challenge. When an important kingdom was founded in Dacia, Trajan regarded it as a threat and set out forthwith to bring it under Roman control. While it took two campaigns to do the job, the lasting result of this Romanizing process is reflected in the name of one of the nations of the region—Romania. Trajan's brilliance as a commander was well known, and on this column and other similar monuments his reputation certainly did not suffer for lack of public advertisement. In the frieze, he invariably is present and consistently is portrayed as a resolute figure in complete command of the situation, whatever its nature. Sharing top billing with their general is the Roman army; and their opposite numbers are Trajan's antagonist, the Dacian king Decebalus, and his barbarian hordes.

The beginning of the campaign is placed on the banks of the Danube in a Roman encampment guarded by sentries and supplied by boats (Fig. 84). As the Romans set forth across a pontoon bridge, a river god personifying the Danube rises from a grotto and lends his support by holding up the bridge. From this point onward the action moves with singular directness toward the inevitable climax: the triumph of Roman arms. The ensuing scenes show Trajan holding a council of war; clad in a toga pouring a libation to the gods; and standing on a tribunal as he addresses his troops (Fig. 85). The army is shown pitching a camp on enemy soil; burning a Dacian village; and in the midst of battle. At the psychological moment Jupiter appears in the sky, throwing bolts of lightning at the enemy to disperse them in all directions. The aftermath is then shown with the soldiers crowding around the Emperor and holding up the decapitated heads of the enemy; surgeons are seen caring for the wounded; and Winged Victory makes her appearance.

The scenes are designed to promote the continuous flow of action as smoothly as possible. For reasons of clarity the scenes have to be differentiated, and the artist does this through some ninety separate appearances of Trajan, which always signal a new activity. Other devices employed are an occasional tree, to set off one scene from another, and new backgrounds that are indicated in some places by a mountain, in others by a group of buildings, and so on. The comparison of this type of spiral relief has aptly been made with the form of the unfolding papyrus and parchment scrolls that the educated Romans were accustomed to read. Trajan is known to have written an account of his Dacian campaigns, much as Julius Caesar had done in the case of his Gallic wars, but the document is lost. Since commentaries on this bit of history are so fragmentary, the column has become one of the principal sources of information about it. The impression the viewer receives is so vivid that he feels almost as if he had experienced the campaign with Trajan.

The reliefs have a definite affinity to literature in their manner of telling a story by the process of visual narration. The methods that the Romans used in such cases have been distinguished as "the simultaneous" and "the continuous." The first is the same as that used by the Greeks in the east pediment and frieze of the Parthenon, for example, where all the action takes place at a given moment that is frozen into sculptural form. The simultaneous or isolating method thus observes the classical unities of time, place, and action. The continuous, or cyclic, method was developed by the Romans for just such a series of scenes as Trajan's wars. The unity of action is obtained by the telling of a life story, or it can be broadened to include a couple of military campaigns, as in this instance. The unities of time and place are sacrificed as far as the whole composition is concerned but are preserved in the separate scenes. While the origin of this continuous style is still a matter of scholarly dispute, none has challenged the effective use the Romans made of it. Its spirit is close to their keen interest in historical and current events, and its value for the purposes of state propaganda is obvious.

Despite the direct narrative content, the style is not realistic. For his effects, the artist depended upon a set of symbols as carefully worked out as the words used by writers of epics. The use of a series of undulating lines, for example, indicates the sea; a jagged outline on the horizon stands for a mountain; a giant rising up out of the water represents a river; a wall can mean either a city or a camp; a female figure whose draperies are folded in the shape of a crescent moon informs the observer that it is night. In such symbolism, liberties with perspective inevitably occur, and it is quite usual to find a man taller than a wall and an important figure, such as that of the Emperor, much greater in size than those around him. This technique does not preclude such clearly recognizable things as the banners of certain Roman legions as well as the details of their shields and armor. The Trajan frieze points unmistakably in the direction of the pictorial symbolism employed later by Early Christian and medieval artists, who doubtless were influenced by it.

Much of the work will seem crude if placed beside the sculptures of Hellenistic artists who were still active in Rome. But this relief is clearly and intentionally an example of Roman popular art, and as such it was addressed to that large segment of the populace not accustomed to getting its information and enjoyment from books. Its location between two libraries also indicates a recognition that history could come from pictorial sources as well as from Greek and Latin scrolls. The elegant and placid forms of Greek gods were not apt to arouse the emotions of those Romans who sought amusement in the gladiatorial contests held in the Colosseum. While the educated minority could admire dignity and restraint in their sculpture, the vast majority had to be aroused by just such an energetic direct-action story as this, involving people like themselves. Thus viewed, Trajan's frieze is fresh, original, and astonishingly alive.

The artist who designed the frieze was clearly a master of his medium, who was able to depict with ease in extremely low relief whole armies, pitched battles, and the surrounding landscapes and sky. The care in execution is consistently carried out, and, even though the reliefs at the top were almost completely out of view, the workmanship remains the same. Standing in its prominent location from Trajan's time to the present, this column and the similar one of Marcus Aurelius have had incalculable influence on later art. The continuous mode of visual narration was taken over directly into the catacomb paintings of the Early Christians; was continued in illuminated manuscripts, religious sculptures, and the stained glass of the medieval period; and can still be found going strong in the comic strips of daily newspapers. Even the motion picture owes a certain debt to the technique worked out here in the 2nd century A.D. In this book, examples of the direct influence of this narrative mode include the mosaics relating the story of Christ in the church of Sant'Apollinare Nuovo in Ravenna (Pl. 9, p. 91; Figs. 94–96); the Bayeux Tapestry, which tells the story of the Norman conquest of England (Pl. 13, p. 125; Figs. 130, 131); Giotto's frescoes on the life of St. Francis of Assisi (Figs. 159–161); Michelangelo's Sistine Chapel ceiling murals (Pl. 25, p. 196; Figs. 202–205); and the studious duplication of Trajan's Column made under Napoleon for the Place Vendôme (Fig. 322).

## MUSIC

The practice of poetry and music enjoyed higher favor among the educated Roman amateurs than did dabbling in the visual arts. Suggesting a plan for a building or some of the details of its decorative design was all right for a patrician, but from there on it was the architect's and carpenter's business. With sculpture and painting, a wealthy man could make an imposing impression as a collector, but the actual chiseling and daubing were something for artisans and slaves. When it came to the writing of verse or singing to the accompaniment of the lyre, however, amateurs abounded in the highest ranks of society right up to the emperors themselves. While Trajan's recreations seem to have been as strenuous as some of his military activities, those of his immediate successors included literary and musical pursuits. Hadrian wrote poetry in both Greek and Latin, but it remained for the last of the Antonines, Marcus Aurelius, to make an enduring reputation as a writer and philosopher. Hadrian, Antoninus Pius, and Caracalla were proficient on the cithara and hydraulic organ. Their musical prowess, however, was not destined to put that of their famous predecessor Nero into the shade.

While much is known about Roman literature, no actual examples of Roman music survive. All knowledge of it must be gleaned from occasional literary references, from sculptures, mosaics, and wall paintings that show music-making situations, and from some of the musical instruments themselves. From these sources, it is clear that the Romans heard much music and that no occasion, public or private, was complete without it.

A mosaic showing a small Roman instrumental ensemble performing in an amphitheater during a gladiatorial contest has been found in recent excavations in North Africa (Fig. 86). One musician is shown playing the long, straight brass instrument known as the *tuba,* or "trumpet"; two others are playing the circular *cornu,* or "horn"; while still another is seated at the *hydraulus,* or "water organ." Equipped with a rudimentary keyboard and stops, this highly ingenious instrument produced sounds by forcing air compressed by two water tanks through a set of bronze pipes. Some of these instruments were ten feet high. They were used mainly in open-air arenas where their tone must have resembled that of the calliopes, once so popular in old-fashioned circus parades.

In keeping with the Roman idea of grandeur, the size of their musical instruments was greatly increased. Marcellinus described a performance in which hundreds of players took part, some of whom were said to have performed on "lyres as big as chariots." Owing to their usefulness in warfare, an ever-increasing volume of sound was demanded of wind instruments. Battle signals were relayed by means of trumpet calls, and the more the legions, the bigger and brassier became the sound. This is borne out by Quintilian, who asks a typical rhetorical question, then proceeds to answer it with a characteristic

flourish: "And what else is the function of the horns and trumpets attached to our legion? The louder the concert of their notes, the greater is the glorious supremacy of our arms over all the nations of the earth." The large audiences accustomed to gather in amphitheaters also played a part in the stepping up of the volume of individual instruments and in the development of sizable vocal and instrumental ensembles. Writing in the 1st century A.D., Seneca notes that the size of the vocal and instrumental ensembles was such that sometimes the singers and players in the arena outnumbered the audience. Soloists would be lost in such vast surroundings, and there are descriptions of large groups of singers accompanied by wind instruments of various kinds and the hydraulic organ.

Quintilian also points out some of the practical applications of music to the art of oratory. He particularly emphasizes the development of the voice because "it is by raising, lowering, or inflexion of the voice that the orator stirs the emotions of his hearers." He then cites the example of one of the great speakers of the past who had a musician standing behind him while making his speeches, "whose duty it was to give him the tones in which his voice was to be pitched. Such was the attention which he paid to this point even in the midst of his most turbulent speeches, when he was terrifying the patrician party."

Literary sources point to a high degree of musical activity in Rome during the 2nd century A.D. From the number of Greek-trained singers, instrumentalists, and mimes who were active, clearly the Greek tradition was still very much alive. In its more austere forms, however, Greek art could have appealed only to the aristocratic minority. Hence, like so many other Greek artistic practices, music was adapted to the needs and uses of a large cosmopolitan center that embraced a great variety of tastes. Pliny casually mentions what entertainment was like in a cultivated household, when he chides a friend for not appearing at a dinner to which Pliny had invited him. After describing the menu he had missed, Pliny tells his friend that he was to have been "entertained either with an interlude, the rehearsal of a poem, or a piece of music," whichever he would have preferred.

Music was also a part of every theatrical performance, and, while the Roman drama omitted the chorus that the Greeks had stressed, its dialogue was interspersed with songs accompanied by the tibia. Such musical portions, however, were not composed by the dramatists, as they had been in the Athenian tradition, but were delegated to specialists in this field. The importance of choruses and bands for military morale was not overlooked, and a functional type of military music existed in addition to the trumpet calls to battle. Popular ensembles played music at games and contests, and strolling street musicians were part of the everyday scene.

The fact that not a single note of any of this music exists today testifies that Roman music was primarily a performing art. While the practicing musicians may very well have composed their own songs and pieces or made variations on traditional tunes, none seem to have been concerned with committing them to paper—and if one had done so, the later Church fathers would very likely have seen to it that these pagan melodies were committed to the flames. So, like the folk music that existed only in oral tradition until the advent of modern notation and recording devices, the art died with the people who practiced it.

## IDEAS

As a part of the mainstream of classical culture, Roman civilization shared many of the basic ideas that produced the Hellenic and Hellenistic styles. Significantly, the Romans widened the scope of the arts to include not only works that were aimed at the connoisseur but also those that carried broad mass appeal. The two ideas that differentiate the Roman from earlier aspects of the classical styles and dominate the Roman expression in the arts are the genius for organization and the frank spirit of utilitarianism, evidenced in a conception of the arts as a means to popular enjoyment and the solution of practical problems.

**Organization**    The Roman ability to organize is shown in the building up of a systematic world order, which embraced a unified religion, a unified body of laws, and a unified civilization. Military conquest was, to be sure, one of the means employed, but the allowance of a maximum of self-government to subject peoples, a wide latitude to local customs, even to tribal and cult religions, is proof of the Roman's psychological realism and toleration. Their desire for external unity did not imply internal uniformity, and their frank recognition of this fact was at the root of their success as administrators. With this ability to organize their religious, legal, social, and governmental institutions, their greatest contribution in the arts clearly would lie in the direction of architecture. This organizational spirit, moreover, is revealed most decisively in their undertaking of large public-works projects, such as the building of roads, ports, aqueducts, and the like. It is also seen in their manner of grouping buildings on a common axis, as in the Forum of Trajan, which was so directly in contrast to the Hellenic idea of isolated perfection; in the organization of business activities in common centers, and the various forms of recreation in the baths; in the technical application and development of all the possibilities of construction by means of the arch and vault; in the combination of the Ionic and Corinthian capitals to form the Composite order, their only distinctive contribution to the classical orders; in the combination of three orders on the exterior of the same building, as in the Colosseum where the Tuscan-Doric order is used on the first story, Ionic on the second, and Corinthian on the third and fourth; in the development of the multifamily apartment house; in the attention given to the efficient assembling and dispersing of large numbers of people in such buildings as the Colosseum; in the invention of a supermarket, such as the six-storied example in Trajan's Forum; and finally, in the erection of a supertemple for the principal gods, as in the Pantheon.

The same organizational spirit is reflected in the expansion of interior space, as in the Basilica Ulpia, the Pantheon, and the great halls of the baths, in order to accommodate ever-larger numbers of people. The Greek idea had been to define space in planes, and the exteriors of their temples were designed as backdrops for processions and religious ceremonies. Those who worshiped Athena at the Parthenon were concerned primarily with its external colonnade, not the interior. Space in this sense was defined but not organized, but in the Pantheon, interior space was enveloped and made real (Pl. 7). To the Greeks, space always remained a formless void to be controlled and humanized, but the Romans recognized the possibilities of molding three-dimensional space, enclosing it and endowing it with significant form. Among the many ways they sought to enhance this spatial feeling are a sensitivity to scale; a tendency to design buildings in related structural units; an exploitation of color by the use of polychrome marbles, which enlivened interiors and which added to the perception of depth; a use of illusionistic wall paintings to suggest the third dimension (Pl. 8, p. 42); and an increased attention given to lighting problems. All this the Romans accomplished without sacrificing the classical clarity of form. The same feeling, furthermore, is carried over into sculpture where the tangibility of the spatial environment is reflected in the backgrounds of reliefs by means of buildings and landscapes that suggest depth, whereas the 5th-century B.C. Grecian style consciously omitted any such frame of reference. In addition to this, the organization of time into a temporal continuum, as in the cyclical series presented on the Column of Trajan, shows a new concept of sequential order translated into the pictorial medium.

Still another facet of this Roman organizational ability is found in the allowance for a wide range of taste in the arts. There were styles that appealed to the educated few and those that held the attention of the untutored populace of the middle and lower classes. In one case it was directed to the eye and ear of the connoisseur, and in the other it was frankly popular in its appeal. The conservative tastes of the first group harkened back to the tried-and-true values of Greek art; hence they either collected antique statuary and paintings, or they commissioned new works to be executed in the older style. Exquisite Greek craftsmanship held little interest for the majority, who needed something like a large bronze equestrian statue or a monumental triumphal arch to capture their attention. In Trajan's Forum, due allowance was made for this variety of taste, with the Greek and Latin libraries placed on either side of a court and a column in between, where the story of Trajan's campaigns was related in a carefully worked out popular language of symbols designed to awaken the curiosity of the multitude.

The disdain of the conservative group for popular art was well stated by Athenaeus, a Greek scholar and teacher who resided in Rome A.D. c. 200. He championed the virtues of the older cultural tradition and frequently made unflattering comparisons between the higher standards of the past and those that prevailed in his day. "In early times," he wrote, "popularity with the masses was a sign of bad art; hence, when a certain aulos-player once received loud applause, Asopodorus of Phlius, who was himself still waiting in the wings, said 'What's this? Something awful must have happened!' The player evidently could not have won approval with the crowds otherwise. . . . And yet the musicians of our day set as the goal of their art success with their audiences." Just as in the case of architecture, sculpture, and painting, the Romans were heirs to the Greek musical tradition. The ancient theories survived in philosophical speculation, and Greek music teachers were employed by preference in the homes of the wealthy. The only musical compositions to survive from this period, for instance, are three hymns by Mesomedes, a Greek musician attached to Hadrian's court. Those who cultivated this more austere style felt that music was meant to educate and elevate the mind, but the popular taste lay in quite another direction.

The music making that Athenaeus and his conservative group scorned was obviously the very kind that the majority of Romans enjoyed at their public festivals, military parades, games, sporting contests, races, and to some extent the theater. The modern parallel would be the cleavage that exists between audiences interested in chamber music, symphony concerts, and the opera, and those attracted by bands at football games, Broadway musicals, popular jazz, and hard rock. What the Romans accomplished here was to broaden the base of the appeal of the arts and gear them to a number of different types of audience. They thus succeeded in providing for the entertainment of a large city population, just as their buildings and civil-engineering projects took care of their physical needs.

**Utilitarianism**    In referring to the administrations of the last two Antonine emperors, Gibbon declared that "their united reigns are possibly the only period of history in which the happiness of a great people was the sole object of government." The basis of this claim is to be found in the way the Romans managed to steer a middle course between the Scylla of Greek theoretical abstractions about the nature of an ideal state and the Charybdis of religious speculation on the joys of the world to come, which was to characterize the subsequent Christian phases of the Empire. Speculation on the eternal verities could edify the mind, but the understanding of human behavior was rewarded by more immediate advantages. In the late Antonine Age, Rome had reached an equilibrium based on an acceptance of the Stoic doctrine of "live and let live" and the Epicurean idea of pleasure as an index to the highest good. The transfer of these individualistic doctrines to the forms and policies of a government meant a high degree of tolerance and a recognition that the standard of excellence in either a law or a work of art was the greatest good to the greatest number. The construction of elegantly proportioned temples was therefore not so important as the building of new aqueducts. Maintaining a luxurious private palace was secondary to providing people's palaces, such as the public baths and theaters. A private collection of sculpture was subordinate to public exhibitions in city squares and galleries, where the statues could be seen and enjoyed by many. A play, poem, or piece of music that awakened only the sensibilities of the cultured minority did not rank so high on this scale as those that were applauded by the multitude. In short, the practical arts were favored over the decorative arts; material goods superseded more remote spiritual blessings; and utility was in the ascendance over abstract beauty (though it must be remembered that the two are by no means mutually exclusive).

Since the Romans were little concerned with ideal forms, it was not an accident that their greatest successes occurred in the arts of government rather than in the fine arts. As Vergil said in the *Aeneid:* "Let others melt and mold the breathing bronze to forms more fair . . . or trace with pointed wand the cycled heaven, and hail the constellations as they rise; But thou, Oh Roman, learn with sovereign sway to rule the nations." As was said earlier, the art which proved most congenial to Roman aspirations was that of architecture, especially in its utilitarian aspects as found in the field of civil engineering. Building a 200-mile highway over the mountains, moving part of a hill over 100 feet high to make way for a forum, providing a sewer system for a city of over a million inhabitants, bridging the Danube at its widest point, perfecting such a new building material as concrete—all these were taken in stride.

When it came to sculpture, the Romans saw that subject matter served the purposes of the state by extolling the virtues and deeds of the emperors. Such epic poems as the *Aeneid* performed a similar service in the literary medium; and, as Quintilian said, the loud sounds of the brass instruments proclaimed the glory of Roman arms. Other applications of this utilitarianism are found in the brilliant exploitation of such technical devices as the arch and vault. Their success in solving practical problems is proved by the number of roads, aqueducts, and bridges that are still serving their purpose today (Fig. 87). In sculpture the application of the continuous-narrative method to the telling of a story was progressive, in that it promoted the sense of continuity in the temporal dimension and anticipated later Christian and secular pictorial forms. The development of such a practical form of verbal communication into the art of letter writing, beginning with Cicero and continuing with the younger Pliny, was the literary facet of the same idea. Finally, when Quintilian pointed out how the art of melody could be applied to oratory by the presence of a musician with a pitch pipe to give the speaker a more persuasive tone, the cycle was complete.

Effective as this utilitarianism was, it was purchased at the price of conflict between structure and decoration, extrinsic and intrinsic values, and the purposive and nonpurposive aspects of art. The Romans built and decorated well, but the two activities somehow failed to achieve a harmonious coexistence. This is well illustrated by the somewhat hollow claim of Augustus, who in an earlier period had boasted that he found Rome a city of brick and left it a city of marble. Actually, Rome was still a city of brick and concrete under an Augustan marble veneer. Neither material needs a disguise, or even an apology, as proved by the rhythmical grace of the functional arches of the Pont du Gard. Hence Augustus had no need to imply that Roman structures were solid marble like the Parthenon. As a whole, then, Roman architecture was at its best when it stuck to its frank utilitarianism, undertook vast engineering projects, and successfully solved the practical problems of construction.

Older cultural centers, such as Athens and Pergamon, were so far off the beaten track that their more restrained classical purity did not exert any appreciable influence on the forms of Western art until the

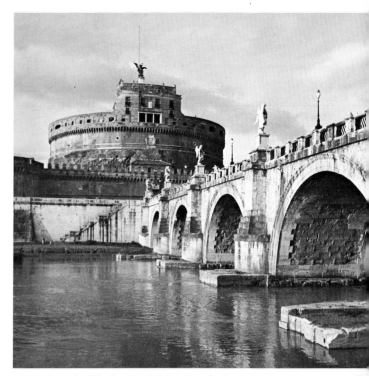

**87.** Hadrian's Tomb (Castel Sant' Angelo), Rome. A.D. 135–139. Bridge (Pons Aelius), A.D. 134.

archaeological discoveries of the 18th and 19th centuries. All intervening phases of classicism were, in effect, revivals of the Roman style. With the establishment of the Roman building methods, Western architecture was firmly set on its course, and it steered in substantially the same direction until the technological discoveries of the 19th and 20th centuries. Consequently, it must be emphasized once more that Rome was the gateway through which all the styles, forms, and ideas of Mediterranean civilization passed in review. After being transformed by the process of selectivity—and with flashes of genuine originality—into a uniquely Roman configuration, they proceeded onward through the arch into medieval culture by way of the new Roman imperial capitals of Byzantium in the East and Ravenna in the West. When Rome declined as the center of world empire, it still remained the capital of Christendom. As the object of pilgrimages, its architectural, sculptural, and literary monuments were bound to exert a massive influence on the rulers, people, and artists who gravitated at one time or another toward the city. Because of this enduring preeminence throughout all subsequent phases of Western culture, no important city exists without a bit of Rome in it. It is therefore with full justification that Rome has been and still continues to be called the Eternal City.

# 5 The Early Roman Christian and Byzantine Styles

## RAVENNA, LATE 5TH AND EARLY 6TH CENTURIES

Many an old Roman coin bears the inscription *Ravenna Felix*—"Happy Ravenna." By a felicitous stroke of fate, this previously unimportant little town on Italy's Adriatic coast became the stage on which the great political, religious, and artistic dramas of a century and a half of world history were enacted. Ravenna was, in turn, the seat of the last Roman emperors of the West, the capital of a barbarian Ostrogothic kingdom, and the western center of the East Roman Empire. A more unprepossessing site could hardly be imagined. To the east lay the Adriatic Sea, to the north and south wide deltas of the River Po, and the only land approach was through marshes and swamps. Yet when the barbarian hordes had Rome under constant harassment, it was this very isolation that led Emperor Honorius to abandon Rome in A.D. 402 and seek in Ravenna a fortress where his hard-

**88.** Mausoleum of Galla Placidia, Ravenna. c. 425.

pressed legions could be supplied by the East Roman Empire through the nearby port of Classe. But with all its natural advantages, Ravenna could hold out against the barbarians only until the year 476, when Odoacer succeeded in entering the all-but-impregnable city and putting an end to the West Roman Empire. The Ostrogothic kingdom of Theodoric, Odoacer's successor, was even more short-lived, and Ravenna fell once more in 540, when Justinian's armies of the East Roman Empire conquered the Italian peninsula and for a brief time reunited the old Empire. Meanwhile a third force, the more enduring power of the Roman papacy, was becoming increasingly influential.

Diverse historical traditions as well as wide geographical distances separated Rome in the west, Byzantium in the east, and the nomadic Ostrogoths in the north. Early in the 4th century, after he had made Christianity an official state religion, Emperor Constantine had moved his court to Byzantium, christening the city the "new Rome." Later, this second capital was called Constantinople in his honor, and soon the East and West Roman empires were going their separate courses. With the encroachments of northern barbarians, a three-way struggle for power began among Justinian, Theodoric, and the pope.

More than the sea stretched between Ravenna and Constantinople, higher mountains than the Alps stood between it and the restive northern barbarians, and greater obstacles than the Apennines separated it from Rome. Metaphysical barriers, in fact, proved more impassable than seas or mountains, because this was the age that was laying the foundations of basic religious beliefs, and in some respects the controversies in Ravenna foreshadowed the later separations of Christianity into Eastern Orthodox and Roman Catholic and Catholic and Protestant denominations. At this time, the main doctrinal battle centered on the nature of the Trinity, and especially on Christ's role

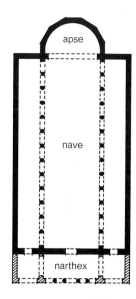

**left: 89.** Interior, Sant' Apollinare Nuovo, Ravenna. c. 493–526.

**right: 90.** Plan of Sant' Apollinare Nuovo.

as the second person in the Trinity. The Ostrogoths, having been converted by Arius of Alexandria (c. 256–336), believed that, since He was created by God the Father, Jesus was subordinate and not of one substance with God. Despite this denial of the Trinity, the Arians revered Christ as the noblest of created beings, but human rather than divine. In Byzantium, it was held that Christ as the Incarnated Word was of one single substance with the Father and hence of divine nature only. The Roman papacy found a middle ground between the two extremes and took the position that, since the Word was made flesh, Christ possessed both divine and human natures and was a full member of the Trinity. Today, such theological controversies seem remote, but in the early centuries of Christianity they were of sufficient intensity to shake empires, depose kings, and cause decades of war.

Paralleling the political and religious controversy, a conflict of art styles took place within Ravenna as successive rulers built and embellished the city. In the 6th century, Ostrogothic Arian heretics, Byzantine patriarchs, and members of the Roman hierarchy, together with the schools of artists each patronized, had different cultural heritages, different aesthetic goals, and different ways of looking at the world. During the days when the Roman Empire was united, cultural influences came from all parts of the Mediterranean world, and, with due allowance for regional diversity, Roman art achieved a recognizable unity. But with the disintegration of Roman power, the adoption of Christianity as an official religion, and the separation of the Empire into eastern and western centers, a reorientation in the arts took place. Though there were many overlapping elements, owing to a common heritage, two distinct styles began to emerge. Hence, when reference is to all the art of this period, the designation will be Early Christian; the term Early

Roman Christian will be used to distinguish the Western style from the declining old pagan Roman arts, on the one hand, and from the subsequent Romanesque and Gothic styles of the later medieval period on the other; and Byzantine will designate the parallel Eastern style.

## ARCHITECTURE AND MOSAICS

Ravenna's replacement of Rome as a capital city demanded a building program that would transform a minor town into a major metropolis. No ruler could afford to be outdone by his predecessors. Hence, the West Roman emperors and Empress Galla Placidia, whose tomb is seen in Figure 88, erected significant secular and religious structures. Then the barbarian king Theodoric, after he came to power, sought to be more Roman than the Romans. As he wrote to an official in Rome, he wished his age to "match the preceding ones in the beauty of its buildings." And the great Justinian, after the Byzantine conquest, made architectural contributions commensurate with his imperial dignity.

**Sant' Apollinare Nuovo—the Rectangular Basilica**
Theodoric included in his building program a church to serve his own Arian sect. Originally dedicated by him to "Our Lord Jesus Christ," this church (Fig. 89) today bears the name of Sant' Apollinare Nuovo, honoring Apollinarus, patron saint of Ravenna and, by tradition, the disciple and friend of St. Peter. The floor plan is a severely simple one (Fig. 90), with a

# CHRONOLOGY / Early Christian Centuries

division of space into a vestibule entrance, known as the *narthex*; a central area for the congregation to assemble, known as the *nave*, separated from the side aisles by two rows of columns; and a semicircular *apse*, which framed the altar and provided seats for the clergy. Older pagan temples, with their small dark interiors, were not suitable models for Christian churches that had to house large congregations. Ancient Greek ceremonies had taken place outdoors around an altar with the temple as a backdrop. The principal architectural and decorative elements of the classic temples—colonnades, frieze, pediments—faced outward. The Christian basilica turned the Greek temple outside in, leaving the exterior quite plain, and concentrated attention on the interior colonnades and the painted or mosaic embellishments of the walls and semidomed apse.

The most complete of these Early Christian basilicas was Old St. Peter's (Figs. 91, 92), so called because it was razed in the 16th century to make way for the present basilica of Bramante, Michelangelo, and Maderno (Fig. 193). Planned from the year 324, when it was dedicated by Constantine, built over the presumed tomb of the Apostle, and as the largest church of the period, Old St. Peter's, until its demolition, ranked as the key monument of Western Christendom. To provide for all Christian activities, it brought together elements of Roman domestic, civic, and temple architecture into a new harmonious composition. Approached by a flight of steps, entrance to the *atrium* was made through an arched gateway. This open courtyard, derived from old Roman country villas, was surrounded by roofed arcades supported by columns; it provided space for congregations to gather, facilities for the instruction of converts, and offices for church officials. In its center was a fountain for the ceremonial washing of hands. The side of the atrium toward the church became the narthex that serves as a frontispiece to the church proper. Through the portals of the narthex, entrance was made to the nave and side aisles (Fig. 93). This spacious, 80-foot-wide nave resembling the rectangular lawcourt halls of Roman public basilicas (Fig. 73), was flanked on either side by two 30-foot-wide aisles and a procession of columns that led the eye along its 295-foot length to the *triumphal arch* (so called because of its derivation from similar Roman imperial structures, such as that in Figure 67). Beyond this was the wide *transept*, the "arms" set at right angles to the nave and an area that functions as a second nave, and the semicircular apse. The ground plan (Fig. 92), then, was roughly **T**-shaped or cruciform, resembling a long Latin cross with short arms. From beginning to end, the design of Old St. Peter's swept along a horizontal axis of 835 feet and opened out at its widest point in the 295-foot transept.

Vertically, a basilica (Fig. 93) rises above the nave colonnades through an intermediate area called the *triforium* that extends to the level of the roofing over the side aisles, above which is the *clearstory* with its rows of windows that light the interior and with its masonry that supports the wooden beams of the shed roof. In keeping with the sheltered and inward orientation of these early basilicas, no windows gave view on the outside world; those at the clearstory were too high and too deeply set to allow even a glimpse of the sky. It was inner radiance of the spirit rather than natural light that was sought.

Sant' Apollinare Nuovo, unlike Old St. Peter's, which had to accommodate a standing congregation of 40,000 or more, was designed as the private chapel of Theodoric's palace. Only the nave remains intact, all other parts being restorations or later additions. As such, its modest architecture would attract only passing attention, but the magnificent mosaics that

**91.** Old St. Peter's Basilica, Rome. c. 333. Grand axis length c. 835', transept width 295'. Restoration study by Kenneth J. Conant.

**92.** Plan of Old St. Peter's.

**93.** Section view of a typical Early Roman Christian basilica.

**94.** *Last Supper.* c. 520. Mosaic. Sant' Apollinare Nuovo, Ravenna.

decorate its nave wall are of major importance in art history. Although they present a harmonious design, the mosaics actually were made in two different periods and styles.

The mosaics of the earlier period were commissioned by Theodoric and are of Early Roman Christian craftsmanship. "Send us from your city," Theodoric had written through his secretary Cassiodorus to an official in Rome, "some of your most skilled marble-workers, who may join together those pieces which have been exquisitely divided, and connecting together their different veins of color, may admirably represent the natural appearance." After Justinian's conquest, the church was rededicated and all references to Arian beliefs and Theodoric's reign were removed. Half a century later, part of the frieze above the nave arcade was replaced by mosaics in the Byzantine style.

Completely covering both walls of the nave, the mosaic work is divided into three bands (Fig. 89). Above the nave arcade and below the clearstory windows, a wide and continuous mosaic strip runs the entire length of the nave in the manner of a frieze. It depicts two long files of saints (the Byzantine part) moving in a majestic procession from representations of Ravenna on one side and Classe on the other (the Early Roman Christian part). The second band fills the space on either side of the clearstory windows with a series of standing toga-clad figures. At the top level, panels depicting incidents in the life of Christ alternate with simulated canopylike niches over the figures standing below. Both the middle and upper

bands are of Roman workmanship, and the scenes in the upper band constitute the most complete representation of the life of Christ in Early Christian art. On one side, the story of the parables and miracles is told, among them the *Good Shepherd Separating the Sheep from the Goats* (Pl. 9, p. 91), an allusion to the Last Judgment. In this and other scenes Christ appears youthful, unbearded, with blue eyes and brown hair. On the opposite side, scenes of the passion and resurrection are presented. In the *Last Supper* (Fig. 94) showing Christ and the disciples reclining in the manner of a Roman banquet, He is seen as a more mature and bearded figure. In all instances He has the cruciform halo with a jewel on each arm of the cross to distinguish Him from the attending saints and angels. His dignified demeanor and purple cloak also tend to show Him in the light of royal majesty. Standing like statues on their pedestals, the figures in the middle band are modeled three-dimensionally in light and shade and cast diagonal shadows. They apparently were once identified by inscriptions over their heads, and the removal of their names suggests they may have been prophets and saints revered by the Arian Christians.

The great mosaic frieze above the nave arcade starts on the left and right of the entrance with representations of the port of Classe and Ravenna, respectively. In the crescent-shaped harbor with three Roman galleys riding at anchor, Classe is seen between two lighthouses. Above the city walls some of the ancient buildings are discernible, and from the gate issues the procession of virgin martyrs. On the opposite side is Ravenna with Theodoric's Palace in the foreground (Fig. 95). Under the word *Palatium* is the central arch where once was an equestrian portrait of Theodoric. Under the other arches, outlines and vestiges of heads and hands indicate that members of his court were also portrayed, and Theodoric was again depicted in the city gate at the right. But when the Ostrogothic kingdom came to its abrupt end, these personages were replaced by simulated Byzantine textile curtains. Above the palace are several of Theodoric's buildings with the Church of Sant' Apollinare Nuovo itself on the left.

As with the cella frieze of the Parthenon, this procession reflects the ritual that regularly took place in the church. According to the early custom, the congregation gathered in the side aisles, with women on one side and men on the other. At the offertory they went forward through the nave to the altar carrying with them their gifts of bread and wine for the consecration. In a stylized way, the procession frieze reenacts this part of the service on a heavenly level. On the left (Fig. 96), 22 virgins are led forward by the Three Wise Men to the throne of the Virgin Mary, who holds the Christ Child on her lap. Arrayed in white tunics with richly bejeweled mantles, the virgins carry their crowns of martyrdom in their hands

**95.** *Theodoric's Palace.* c. 520. Mosaic. Sant' Apollinare Nuovo, Ravenna.

as offerings. In a similar manner, 25 male martyrs on the right are escorted by St. Martin of Tours into the presence of Christ, who is seated on a lyre-backed throne. The eye is led along by the upward folds and curves of their costumes as they tread a flowered path lined with date palms that symbolize both Paradise and their martyrdom. All is ineffably serene and no trace of their earthly suffering is seen. Their heads, though tilted differently to vary the design somewhat, are all on the same level in keeping with the Greco-Byzantine convention of isocephaly. Only St. Agnes is accompanied by her attribute, the lamb; otherwise the faces reveal so little individuality they could not be identified without the inscriptions present in the composition.

A completely different artistic feeling is revealed when these Byzantine figures are compared with the earlier Roman work in the bands above. The unshaded lines of the Byzantine design form a frankly two-dimensional pattern, while the garments of the Roman personages fall in natural folds that model the forms they cover in three-dimensional fashion. All the figures in the upper two bands wear simple unadorned Roman togas, while the saints below are clad in luxurious, ornate Byzantine textiles decorated with rare gems. The Roman figures appear against such natural three-dimensional backgrounds as the green Sea of Galilee, hills, or a blue sky. The Byzantine virgins and martyrs, however, are set against a shimmering gold backdrop with uniformly spaced stylized palms. The candor, directness, and simplicity with which the Roman scenes are depicted likewise contrast strikingly with the impersonal, aloof, and symbolic Byzantine treatment of the nave frieze. Differences of theological as well as stylistic viewpoints are involved, since the Arian-Roman panels accent the Redeemer's worldly life and human suffering, and the Byzantine frieze accents His divinity and remoteness from mundane matters.

The art of mosaic, in general, depends for its effectiveness on directing the flow of light from a myriad of tiny reflectors. After the placement of the panels, the design, and the colors have been determined, the mosaicist must take into account both the natural source of light from windows and artificial sources from lamps or candles. Accordingly, he fits each *tessera*, or small cube made of glass, marble, shell, or ceramic, onto an adhesive surface, tilting some this way, others that, so that a shimmering luminous effect is obtained.

**San Vitale and Central-Type Structures**   Little more than a year's time elapsed between the death of Theodoric and the accession of Justinian as em-

**96.** *Procession of Virgin Martyrs.* c. 560. Mosaic. Sant' Apollinare Nuovo, Ravenna.

peror in Constantinople. Almost immediately at Ravenna, Justinian undertook in absentia the laying of the foundation stone of San Vitale (Fig. 97). In the statecraft of that day, the building of a church that would surpass anything undertaken by Theodoric served as an assertion of Justinian's authority in Italy and evidence of the weakened power of Theodoric's Ostrogothic successors. At first Justinian's position in the capital of the West Roman Empire was anything but certain, and the project languished. Eventually, the use of force was needed to assert his Italian claims, and his armies entered the city in the year 540. Thereafter, construction of San Vitale proceeded apace, and seven years later the church was ready for its dedication by Archbishop Maximian. Its plain redbrick exterior is proof that as little attention was paid to the outside of San Vitale as to that of any other church of the period. But with its rich polychromed marble walls, carved alabaster columns, pierced marble screens, and other delicate details, and, above all, its sanctuary mosaics, the Church of San Vitale is a veritable jewel box.

Architecturally, San Vitale is a highly developed example of the central-type church (Fig. 98), differing radically from Sant' Apollinare Nuovo. Yet it has all the usual features of the basilica, including a narthex entrance, circular nave, surrounding side aisles, and a triumphal arch leading into a sanctuary with an apse and two side chambers. The striking difference, however, between an oblong basilica and a centralized church is the direction of its axis. In the former, the axis runs horizontally through the center of the building dividing the church lengthwise into equal halves, the eye being led toward the apse; in the central-type building the axis is vertical, leading the eye upward from the central floor space to the dome. Were it not for the addition of the oblong narthex on the west and the apse on the east, San Vitale would be a simple octagon. The two side chambers of the apse are usually associated with Eastern Orthodox churches, and their presence here points to the fact that San Vitale was designed as a theater for the Byzantine liturgy. The northern chamber was designated the *prothesis*, to indicate its use as the place where the communion bread and wine were prepared for the altar. In Eastern Orthodox usage, the sacrificial aspect of the mass assumed a dramatic character, and the sacramental bread was "wounded, killed, and buried" on the table of the prothesis before it appeared on the altar, where it symbolized the resurrection of the body. The southern chamber is called the *diakonikon* and served as the vestry and as a place to store the sacred objects used in the orthodox service.

In order to understand San Vitale and central-type churches, one must look at similar buildings at Ravenna and elsewhere. While the ancestors of the rectangular basilica were Roman domestic and public buildings, the centralized church derives from the ancient circular tombs of the *tholos* type. Later examples are seen in Hadrian's colossal sepulchre on the banks of the Tiber (Fig. 87). The ancient prefer-

**left: 97.** San Vitale (exterior of apse), Ravenna. c. 527–547. Diameter 112'.

**above: 98.** Plan of San Vitale.

**99.** *Baptism of Christ and Procession of Twelve Apostles.* c. 520. Dome mosaic. Arian Baptistry, Ravenna.

ence for the circular mausoleum can be explained partly by its symbolism. Immortality was frequently represented by the image of a serpent biting his tail—that is, a living creature whose end was joined to its beginning. Another ancestor is the round classical temple, such as the Temple of Vesta in Rome, and the Pantheon (Figs. 81, 82).

The eight-sided Christian baptistry was taken over directly from the octagonal bathhouses found in ancient Roman villas. There the pool was usually octagonal and the structure around it assumed that shape. Early Christian baptisms involved total immersion, and the transition from bathhouse to baptistry was easy and natural. Since baptism is a personal and family affair, not calling for the presence of a congregation, baptistries usually are small. The Arian Baptistry was built in Theodoric's time in the same style as the earlier "Neonian" Baptistry for the Roman Christians. Both are domed structures with the chief interest centered on the fine interior mosaics. Both have similar representations of the baptism of Christ on the interior surfaces of their cupolas. That of the Arian Baptistry (Fig. 99) shows the ceremony being performed by St. John the Baptist, while the River Jordan is personified as an old man in the manner of the ancient pagan fluvial gods (Fig. 84). Around this central scene are the twelve apostles who move processionally toward the throne of Christ. Just as the

virgins and martyrs reenacted the offertory procession above the nave arcade of Sant' Apollinare Nuovo, so the apostles here mirror the baptismal rites on a more transcendental level. They group themselves around the center above where Christ is being baptized, just as the clergy, family, and sponsors gathered about the font below for the baptism of some Ravenna Christian. Here is yet another example of the *iconography*—the story being told—of the decorative scheme reflecting the liturgical activity that took place within the walls of the building.

The idea of a church built in the same form as a tomb is by no means as somber as it might seem. In the Christian sense, a church symbolized the Easter sepulchre, reminding all of the resurrection of Christ. In His memory, churches were dedicated to martyrs and saints who were believed to be partaking of the heavenly life with Him, just as the faithful hoped that they themselves would one day be doing. The ancient Orphic cult had stressed the idea of the body being the tomb of the spirit. Hence, death and resurrection were aspects of one and the same idea, and the martyr's death was his mystical union with Christ. Indeed, the altar itself was a tomb or repository for the sacred relics of the saint to whom the church was dedicated. Early altars in the catacombs actually were sarcophagi that served also as communion tables. Thus, in the rites of the church, the earthly past of

Christ, His apostles, saints, and martyrs was commemorated, and, at the same time, the glorious heavenly future was anticipated.

Balancing domes over square or octagonal supporting structures was a preoccupation of 6th-century architects. The Romans had found one solution in the case of the Pantheon—resting the dome on supporting cylindrical walls—but in Ravenna later builders found two other solutions. The exquisite little mausoleum of Galla Placidia (Fig. 88), which dates from about A.D. 425, was built in the form of an equal-winged Greek cross. Its dome rests on *pendentives*—that is, on four concave spherical triangles of masonry rising from the square corners and bending inward to form the circular base of the dome (Fig. 100). The role of the pendentives is to encircle the square understructure and make the transition to the domed superstructure. The Ravenna baptistries exemplify the same pendentive solution, but in their cases the domes rest on octagonal understructures. Another solution stemming from the same early period is based upon a system of *squinches*—that is, upon a series of small apselike vaults placed across the angles of the octagonal walls (Fig. 101). This was the method employed for the

**100, 101.** Circular domes can be raised over rectangular buildings by the structural devices of *pendentives* and *squinches*. Pendentives are vaults in the form of spherical triangles that connect arches springing from corner piers and unite at the apex of the arches to form a continuous circular base for the dome to rest upon. Squinches are stone lintels placed diagonally across corners to form a continuous base for the circular dome. Often the squinch is supported from below by masonry built up in wedge or arch formation.

**left: 100.** Pendentives (shaded area) supporting a dome.

**right: 101.** Squinches (shaded area) supporting a dome.

**left. 102.** Interior, San Vitale, Ravenna. 527–547 (clearstory decorations, 18th century). Other octagon 115′; inner octagon 54′9″.

**below: 103.** Interior, Hagia Sophia, Istanbul (Constantinople). 532–537. Dome height 183′.

doming of San Vitale. The eight piers of the arcaded central room below rise upward and culminate in an octagonal drum on which, by means of squinches, the dome rests.

Above the nave arcade and beneath the dome, the builders included a vaulted triforium gallery running around the church and opening into the nave (Fig. 102). This gallery, which was called the *matroneum*, was for the use of women, who were more strictly segregated in the Byzantine than in the Roman rites.

The Eastern parallels of San Vitale are found in Justinian's churches at Constantinople—Sts. Sergius and Bacchus, among others. The great Hagia Sophia ("Sancta Sophia," or "Holy Wisdom"), however, is the foremost monument of the Byzantine style. As a combination of great art and daring engineering, Hagia Sophia has never been surpassed. Externally it is practically square with bulging buttresses and swelling half-domes mounting, by means of pendentives, to a full dome on top. Internally, from the narthex entrance on the west, the space opens into a large nave, and the eye is led horizontally to the apse in the east (Fig. 103). While the most ambitious Gothic cathedral nave never spanned a width of more than 55 feet, the architects of Hagia Sophia achieved an open space 100 feet wide and 200 feet long.

From this discussion it should be obvious that the dome of the central-type structure unifies the separate structural members, and that the eye perceives this unity at a glance. In the interior of San Vitale (Fig. 102) the dome and its supports are clearly visible and the structure is therefore self-explanatory. Psychologically, this equilibrium is important for it produces a restful effect, which is in direct contrast with the restless interiors of later Gothic cathedrals (Fig. 143). There the dynamic surge depends partly on the fact that the exterior buttressing is not apparent. Indeed, the dome of San Vitale is an interior fact only, because on the outside the octagonal base on which it rests has been continued upward and roofed over.

In the apse of San Vitale, facing the altar from opposite sides, are two panels in mosaic that portray the leading figures of the early Byzantine rule in Ravenna. On one, Emperor Justinian appears in the midst of his courtiers (Fig. 104) and on the other, facing him as an equal, is Empress Theodora in all her sovereign splendor (Pl. 10, p. 91). It is significant that the finest extant portrait of the great Emperor should be in mosaic rather than in the form of a sculptured bust, a bronze effigy on horseback, or a colossal statue. It is just this medium that could best capture the unique spirit of his life and times. Concerned with the codification of Roman law, presiding at religious councils, and reconciling divergent political points of view, Justinian based his rule on the manipulation of legal and theological formulas as well as on naked military might. He is then represented as a symbol of unity between the spiritual force of

**104.** *Emperor Justinian and Courtiers.* c. 547. Mosaic. San Vitale, Ravenna.

the Church on one hand and the temporal power of the state on the other.

Preceding Justinian in the procession are the clergymen, among whom only Archbishop Maximian is specifically identified by name. His pectoral cross is held up as an assertion of his power as the spiritual and temporal lord of Ravenna. On the Emperor's other side are his courtiers and honor guard holding their jeweled swords aloft. The shield with its Chrismon insignia points to the status of the soldiers as defenders of the faith. The Chrismon was a widely used monogram of the time, made up of the Greek letters *Chi* (X) and *Rho* (P), which together form the abbreviation of Christ. Somewhat more allegorically, the letters become a combination of the Cross and the shepherd's crook, which symbolize the Savior's death and pastoral mission. In the center stands Justinian, clothed in all his magnificence and crowned with the imperial diadem. The observer knows immediately that he is in the presence of no ordinary royal personage but rather one who could sign his name as the Emperor Caesar Flavius, Justinianus, Alamanicus, Francicus, Germanicus, Anticus, Alanicus, Vandalicus, Africanus, Pious, Happy, Renowned, Conqueror and Triumpher, ever Augustus. But great as Justinian's military exploits were, it is his works of peace that have endured. In addition to a vast building program, the Byzantine Emperor is remembered for his monumental code, the *Digest of Laws,* which prevailed for centuries throughout the Western world.

On her side, the Empress Theodora (Pl. 10), richly bejeweled and clad in the imperial purple, is seen as she is about to make her entry into the church from the narthex. Possibly because of her humble origin as the daughter of the feeder of the bears at the circus of Constantinople, Theodora appears more royal than the King. Her offering recalls another re-

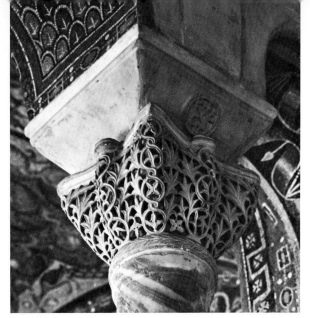

**105.** Byzantine capital, San Vitale, Ravenna. c. 547.

of the scene, emphasizing by their designs the luxury of their Oriental origins.

In addition to the mosaics, the decorative design of San Vitale includes carved alabaster columns, polychrome marble wall panels, perforated marble choir screens, and many other sculptural details. The capitals of the columns are carved with a profusion of intricate patterns, such as that in Figure 105.

The influence of San Vitale on subsequent Western European architecture dates from the time of Charlemagne's conquest. So impressed was Charlemagne with this church that he not only carried off at least half of its original marble and mosaic decorations but also adopted its plan for his imperial chapel at Aachen. When the harmonious proportions of the building as a whole are compounded with the rich optical effects of the mosaics, polychrome marble, and ornamental sculptures, San Vitale, as the counterpart of Hagia Sophia, is the high point of Byzantine art in the West.

## SCULPTURE

From its status as a major art in Greco-Roman times, sculpture declined to a relatively modest place in the hierarchy of Early Christian arts. Instead of constituting a free and independent medium, it became primarily an adjunct to the architectural and liturgical forms of the Church. Even its classical three-dimensionality was in eclipse, and sculpture tended to become increasingly pictorial and symbolic in early Christian usage. When it moved indoors, sculpture underwent a radical change in relation to light and shade. A statue in the round, for instance, was either placed against a wall or stood in a niche, which precluded its being seen from all sides. The close proximity in time and place to the pagan religions also served to channel Christian visual expression in other directions, and with the influence of such dictums as the First Commandment that forbade the making of "graven images," it is remarkable that the art survived as well as it did. A rare extant example of three-dimensional Early Roman Christian sculpture is the *Good Shepherd* (Fig. 106). Figures of peasants carrying calves or sheep to market are frequently found in ancient Greek and Roman genre sculpture. In the Christian interpretation, however, the shepherd is Christ, the sheep the congregation of the faithful, and, when a jug of milk is included, the whole refers to the Eucharist.

Sculpture, in general, proved adaptable to the new demands and purposes. In the new frame of reference, architectural sculpture—capitals of columns, decorative relief panels, carved wooden doors, and, to some extent, statues in niches—continued with appropriate modifications. The principal emphasis, however, shifted toward objects associated with the new form of worship, such as altars, pulpits, pierced

mark by Procopius, who said that she fed the geese of the devil while on the stage and the sheep of Christ when she sat on the throne. On the hem of her robe the offertory motif is carried out by the embroidered figures of the Three Wise Men, the first bearers of gifts to Christ. Since they also were from the East, this may have been a subtle attempt to gain the good graces of Ravenna for its Oriental rulers.

These two mosaic portraits are especially precious because they are among the few surviving visual representations of the vanished glories of Byzantine courtly ceremonials. The regal pair appear as if participating in the offertory procession at the dedication of the church, which took place in the year 547—though neither was actually present on that occasion. Such ceremonial entries were a part of the elaborate Byzantine liturgy, and both the Emperor and Empress are shown as the bearers of gifts. On his side, Justinian is carrying the gold paten, which was used to hold the communion bread at the altar, while Theodora is presenting the chalice that contains the wine. Since their munificence was responsible for the building, decoration, and endowment of San Vitale, the allusion is to gifts of gold as well.

In keeping with the rigid conventions of Byzantine art, all the heads appear in one plane. Those of Justinian and Theodora are distinguished by their halos, which in this case allude not only to their awesome power but to a carry-over of the semidivine status assumed by the earlier Roman emperors. Even though they are moving in a procession, they are portrayed frontally in the manner of imperial personages accustomed to receiving the homage of their subjects. In spite of the stylized medium, the eye can follow the solemn train as it moves in dignified cadence, impelled forward by the linear pattern in the folds of garments. The elegant costumes add to the richness marble screens, and carved ivory reliefs. Smaller items, such as precious metal boxes for relics, lamps, incense pots, communion chalices, jeweled book covers, and patens, all with delicately wrought designs, began to ally the former grand classical art more closely with that of the jeweler.

One of the strongest influences on Early Christian design was the new orientation of thought in the direction of symbolism. As long as the religions of Greece and Rome were anthropomorphic, the sculptor could represent the gods as idealized human forms. But in Christian terms, how could he represent in concrete form such abstractions as the Trinity, the Holy Ghost, the salvation of the soul, or the idea of redemption through participation in the Eucharistic sacrifice? The solution could come only through use of parables and symbols. Thus the Christian idea of immortality could be rendered through Biblical scenes of deliverance—Noah from the flood, Moses from the land of Egypt, Job from his sufferings, Daniel from the lion's den, the men from the fiery furnace, and Lazarus from his tomb.

In Early Chistian relief panels, flora and fauna were included less for naturalistic reasons than to convey symbolic meaning. The dove represented the Holy Spirit, the peacock stood for Paradise, and so on. The Cross is seldom found in Early Christian art, since it recalled a punishment used for the lowest type of criminal. Instead, the Chrismon symbol already seen on the shield of Justinian's soldiers was used. A fish, or the Greek word for it, *Icthys,* is often found as a reference to Jesus making his disciples fishers of men. The letters of the word also constituted an abbreviation for Jesus Christ Son of God, Savior. Such symbols and lettered inscriptions caused sculpture to assume the aspect of engraved designs on stone surfaces, which carried special meaning and mystical significance to the initiated.

One of the chief forms of Early Roman Christian sculpture is the carved stone sarcophagus. The custom of burial above ground was carried over from late Roman times, and a special Christian impetus came from the desire for interment within the sacred precincts of the church. The relics of saints reposed in the altar; tombs of bishops and other dignitaries were housed in the church; while the sarcophagi of laymen were usually placed outside in the atrium. Survivals of this latter custom continue well into modern times with burials taking place in churchyards. A fine example is provided by the sarcophagus of Archbishop Theodore (Fig. 107). The front panel shows the combination of the Chrismon symbol with that of the first and last letters of the Greek alphabet, *Alpha* and *Omega,* another reference to Christ, taken from His statement that He was both the beginning and the end. Their inclusion here on a tomb indicates the end of earthly life and the beginning of the heavenly one. Flanking the symbols are two peacocks symbolizing Paradise and, on either side, a graceful vine pattern in which the small birds feeding on grapes refer symbolically to communion. The inscription reads in

**left: 106.** *Good Shepherd.* c. 350. Marble, height 39''. Vatican Museums, Rome.

**right: 107.** Sarcophagus of Archbishop Theodore. 6th century. Marble, 3'3½'' × 6'9''. Sant' Apollinare in Classe.

translation, "Here rests in peace Archbishop Theodore." On the lid are repetitions of the monogram below, here surrounded by the conventional laurel wreath symbolizing immortality. The end of the sarcophagus that shows in Figure 107 is carved to symbolize the Trinity, with the urn from which springs the tree of life indicating the Father, the cross the Son, and the descending dove the Holy Spirit.

By far the most impressive single example of sculpture of this period is the chair which is thought to be that of Archbishop Maximian (Fig. 108), Justinian's viceroy who is portrayed beside him in the mosaic panel in San Vitale (Fig. 104). Such an episcopal throne is called a *cathedra,* and the church in which it is housed is termed a *cathedral.* When a bishop addresses his congregation from it, he is said to be speaking *ex cathedra.* A cathedra may also be called a *sedes* (the Latin word for "seat"), from which word is derived the term *see,* which once meant the seat of a bishop but now means the territory in the charge of a bishop. Originally *sedes* meant a chair denoting high position. Roman senators used such chairs on public occasions, and modern politicians still campaign for a "seat" in the senate or legislature. Both Jewish rabbis and Greek philosophers taught from a seated position; hence the reference in modern colleges to a "chair" of philosophy or history.

Maximian's cathedra consists of a composition of ivory plaques, carefully joined together and delicately carved. Originally, there were 39 different pictorial panels, some of which told the Old Testament story of Joseph and his brethren, and the others, the story of Jesus. The chair is thought to have been presented to Maximian by Justinian, and the different techniques employed in the various panels indicate collaboration of craftsmen from Anatolia, Syria, and Alexandria. On the front panel, below Maximian's monogram, is a representation of St. John the Baptist flanked on either side by the Evangelists (Fig. 108). The Baptist holds a medallion on which a lamb is carved in relief, while the Evangelists hold their traditional books. The elegant Byzantine craftsmanship of the front panel—with its complex grapevine motif intertwined with birds and animals denoting the tree of eternal life, the peacocks symbolizing heaven, the symmetrically arranged saints, and the luxuriant linear pattern of their classical drapery—lends itself best to just such a static, formal, stylized design. In the Joseph story illustrated in the side panels, however, the overriding concern is with an active narrative as related in a series of episodes. Content and vivid detail then rise above purely formal considerations. While sculpture is not the outstanding Byzantine art, such intricate tracery and arabesque patterns become highly important. Since ivory does not make monumentality either possible or desirable, such details as these, when handled with a jeweler's precision, are perhaps richer and more satisfying than the work as a whole.

At this formative phase, the Western and Eastern styles are not so separate and distinct as they tend to become in the later medieval period. The situation is also complicated by the fact that Roman artists could be summoned to work in Constantinople just as easily as Byzantine artists could be called to Rome or Ravenna. In general, however, one can conclude that the trend in the West was toward the long, rectangular basilica, while the East developed the central-type structure. In mosaics and sculpture, the Early Roman Christian style stays closer to the heritage of classical naturalism, with figures modeled three-dimensionally and appearing against landscape backgrounds, and shows a preference for simpler designs employing recognizable floral and faunal motifs. The Byzantine style, on the other hand, moves more in the direction of flat two-dimensional surfaces, gold backgrounds, nonrepresentational designs, abstract geometrical forms, and luxurious arabesque patterns.

**108.** Cathedra of Maximian (front view). c. 546–556. Ivory panels on wood frame; height 4'11", width 1'11⅝". Archepiscopal Museum, Ravenna.

left: **Plate 9.** *Good Shepherd Separating the Sheep from the Goats.* c. 620. Mosaic. Sant' Apollinare Nuovo, Ravenna. (See p. 82.)

below: **Plate 10.** *Empress Theodora and Retinue.* c. 547. Mosaic. San Vitale, Rome. (See p. 87.)

**left: Plate 11.** *Crucifixion,* cover of *Lindau Gospels.* Rheims or St. Denis, c. 870. Gold and jewels, 13¾ × 10½″. Pierpont Morgan Library, New York. (See p. 106.)

**below: Plate 12.** Page for Initial Q, from *Evangeliary of Abbey at St. Omer.* c. 1000. Illuminated manuscript. Pierpont Morgan Library, New York. (See p. 106.)

# MUSIC

From the writings of Theodoric's learned ministers Boethius and Cassiodorus, some knowledge about the status of musical thought in 6th-century Ravenna can be gained. Like the writings of the Church fathers and other men of letters of the time, however, these reveal much about the theory of the art and little about its practice. Boethius was an indefatigable translator of Greek philosophical and scientific treatises into Latin, among which were no less than thirty books by Aristotle alone. When he fell from favor and was imprisoned, Boethius wrote his *Consolations of Philosophy,* which became one of the most influential medieval books. Called by Gibbon "a golden volume not unworthy of the leisure of Plato or Tully [Cicero]," the *Consolations* later found its way into English via translations by Alfred the Great and Chaucer. Boethius' was a universal mind, capable of discoursing on anything from the mechanical principles of water clocks to astronomy.

Boethius' treatise on music became the common source of most medieval tracts on the subject, and thus, in transmitting the best of ancient Greek musical theory, it became the foundation stone of Western musical thinking. Like the ancients before him, Boethius believed that "all music is reasoning and speculation," and hence more closely allied with mathematics than with the auditory art that music is today. He divided music into three classes, the first of which was the "music of the universe," by which he meant the unheard astronomical "music" of planetary motion. The second was "human music," which referred to the attunement of the mind and body, or the rational and irrational elements of the human constitution, in the manner of a Greek harmony of opposites. The third was instrumental music and song, of which he had the philosopher's usual low opinion, considering only the theoretical aspects of the art as pursuits worthy of a gentleman and scholar. The only true "musician" in his opinion was one "who possesses the faculty of judging, according to speculation or reason, appropriate and suitable to music, of modes and rhythms and of the classes of melodies and their mixtures . . . and of the songs of the poets."

Cassiodorus also wrote in a similarly learned vein after he had retired from public life to the haven of his monastery at Vivarium. But while he was still embroiled in the affairs of Theodoric's kingdom, he was constantly called upon to solve every conceivable administrative problem. Among these was a request from Clovis, king of the Franks, for a *citharoedus*—that is, a singer who accompanied himself on the stringed instrument of the classical lyre type known as the cithara. In his search for such a musician, Cassiodorus turned to his fellow senator Boethius, who was in Rome at the time. His letter first launches into a flow-ery discourse on the nature of music, which he describes as the "Queen of the senses." It continues with interminable discussions about its curative powers, how David cast out the evil spirit from Saul, the nature of the modes, the structure of the Greek scale system, and the history of the art. Then he comes to the lyre, which he calls "the loom of the Muses," and after going off on a few more tangents, he finally gets to the point. "We have indulged ourselves in a pleasant digression," he says, making the understatement of the millennium, "because it is always agreeable to talk of learning with the learned; but be sure to get us that *Citharoedus,* who will go forth like another Orpheus to charm the beast-like hearts of the Barbarians. You will thus obey us and render yourself famous."

Knowledge about the church music of Ravenna at this time is quite conjectural and must be gathered from a variety of sources. From the writings of the Church fathers, great importance evidently was attached to music in connection with divine worship. The problem was how to separate a proper body of church music from the rude folk musical idioms on one hand, and from the highly developed but pagan art music of Rome on the other. From St. Paul and Pliny the Younger, in the 1st and 2nd centuries respectively, it is known that the earliest Christian music sounded very much like the ancient Jewish singing of psalms. A fragment of an Early Christian hymn from the latter part of the 3rd century was recently found at Oxyrhynchos in North Africa. From the Greek text and ancient musical notation, it is possible to establish its stylistic connection with the late Hellenistic musical tradition. Hebrew, Greek, and Latin sources thus provided the basis for Early Christian music, just as they had done in the cases of theology and the visual arts. Out of these diverse elements and with original ideas of their own, the Christians of the Eastern and Western churches over the centuries gradually worked out a synthesis that resulted in a musical art of great power and beauty. The 6th century witnessed the culmination of many early experimental phases; and at its close, the Western form of the art found official codification in the body of music known as Gregorian Chant. In its various transmutations and restorations, as well as in its theoretical aspects, this system has remained the official basis of Roman Church music up to the present time. Closely related forms are still in use throughout Christendom, where free adaptations of its melodies have enriched the hymn books of nearly every denomination.

Knowledge about the Arian liturgy, such as that which was practiced at Sant' Apollinare Nuovo during Theodoric's reign, is very obscure, because all sources were destroyed when the orthodox Christians gained the upper hand and stamped out the Arian heresy. From a few derogatory comments, however,

*Aeterne rerum Conditor* (after Dreves)
(hymn of St. Ambrose)

Ae - ter - ne re - rum Con - di - tor, Noc - tem di - em - que qui_ re - gis,

Et tem - po - rum das tem - po - ra, Ut al - le - ves fa - sti - di - um_

*Alleluia* (Ambrosian chant (after Wellesz)
of Byzantine origin)

Hal - le - lu - - - - jah.

it is known that hymn and psalm singing by the congregation as a whole was among the practices. Arius, the founder of the Arian sect, was accused of insinuating his religious ideas into the minds of his followers by means of hymns that were sung to melodies derived from drinking songs and theatrical tunes. Such hymns were frowned upon in orthodox circles because they were too closely allied with popular music. Furthermore, the Arian way of singing them was described as loud and raucous, indicating that they must have grated on the ears of the more civilized Roman Christians.

The popularity of these musical practices, however, was such that the Arians were making too many converts. So in the spirit of fighting fire with fire, St. Ambrose, bishop of Milan, where the Arians were strong, compromised by introducing hymn and psalm singing into the Milanese church service. A first-hand account of it is contained in a passage from St. Augustine's *Confessions*. In the 4th century, when Bishop Ambrose was engaged in one of his doctrinal disputes with the Byzantine Empress Justina, he and his followers at one point had to barricade themselves in a church for protection. "The pious people kept guard in the church, prepared to die with their bishop," wrote St. Augustine. "At the same time," he continues, "was it here first instituted after the manner of the eastern churches, that hymns and psalms should be sung, lest the people should wax faint through the tediousness of sorrow: which custom being retained from that day to this, is still imitated by divers, yea, almost by all thy congregations throughout other parts of the world." The practice spread widely and was incorporated into the Roman liturgy during the following century. Since Ravenna was the neighboring see to that of Milan, the musical practices there must have been quite similar.

Some half-dozen hymns can be attributed to the authorship of St. Ambrose. Whether he also composed the melodies is not so certain, but they at least date from his time. From the example of *Aeterne rerum Conditor* (above), it can be seen that the extreme simplicity and metrical regularity of these vigorous Ambrosian hymns made them especially suitable for congregational singing. The mosaics of Sant' Apollinare Nuovo show files of male and female saints on opposite sides of the nave arcade (Fig. 89). Below them, the men of the congregation were grouped on one side, while the women and children gathered on the other, thus forming two choirs. The psalms were sung in two ways: antiphonally and responsorially. When the two choruses sing alternate verses, then join together in a refrain on the word *alleluia* after each verse, the practice is referred to as *antiphonal psalmody*. When the celebrant chants one verse as a solo, and the choirs perform the next in union, it is called *responsorial psalmody*. Both were widespread practices in the Western church, including Ravenna.

Since Sant' Apollinare Nuovo and San Vitale were designed for different purposes, it follows that their music must also have differed. As a part of the Byzantine liturgy, the music heard at San Vitale would have been like that of the cathedral in Constantinople. As in the West, congregational singing was included there at first, but, with the abandonment of the offertory procession, congregational singing was gradually replaced by that of a professional choir. Music for congregational singing must always be kept relatively simple, but with a truly professional group all the rich potentialities of the art can be explored and developed.

Since San Vitale, like Hagia Sophia, was under the direct patronage of the emperor, and since both constituted a part of Justinian's grand design, provision for a group capable of performing the music of the Byzantine liturgy could hardly have been overlooked. The principal difference between the music of the Eastern and Western churches is that between a contemplative and an active attitude. The contemplative aspect of the Eastern liturgy is illustrated by a remark of St. John Chrysostom, who said that "one may also sing without voice, the mind resounding inwardly, for we sing not to men, but to God, who can hear our hearts and enter into the silences of the mind." This attitude contrasts strongly with that of St. Ambrose, who said in connection with the participation of the congregation in song: "If you praise the Lord and do not sing, you do not utter a hymn. . . . A hymn, therefore, has these three things: song and praise and the Lord."

In a static form of worship, greater rhythmic freedom is possible, while the chant that accompanies a procession must have more metrical regularity. The singing of a virtuoso professional choir, furthermore, implies an elaborate and highly developed art, while the practice of congregational singing means the avoidance of technical difficulties. The difference, then, is the difference between the sturdy Ambrosian *syllabic* hymn (opposite, left)—that is, with a syllable allotted to each note—and the *melismatic* alleluia of Byzantine origin (opposite, right)—that is, with each single syllable prolonged over many notes in the manner of a cadenza. Such Byzantine music had a distinctive style of its own, comparable in this respect to that of the visual arts. The elaborate melismas of the latter example would have been heard in San Vitale and in other Byzantine churches at the end of the 6th century. It was precisely such excessively florid alleluias that were ruled out by the Gregorian reform which was to occur in the early 7th century.

## IDEAS

Since all the surviving monuments of Early Christian art are religiously oriented, it follows that the various sources of patronage, the geographical locations, and the liturgical purposes are the qualifying factors in the forms of architecture, the iconography of mosaics, the designs of sculpture, and the performing practices of music. The Early Roman Christian and Byzantine styles were both Christian, and all the arts lived, moved, and had their being within the all-embracing arms of Mother Church. But her Western and Eastern arms pointed in different stylistic directions. The disintegrating Roman power in the West led to decentralization of authority and allowed wide latitude in local and regional styles, while the Byzantine emperors kept tight autocratic control of all phases of secular and religious life. Early Roman Christian art was more an expression of the people; it involved all social levels, its craftsmanship varied from crudity to excellence, and it was more simple and direct in its approach. Byzantine art, however, was under the personal patronage of a prosperous emperor who ruled both as a Caesar and a religious patriarch. Only the finest artists were employed; and the arts, like the vertical axis of a centralized church, directed attention to the highest level and tended to become more removed from the people and more purely symbolic. As the arts of both West and East pass by in review, two ideas seem to be the clues to their understanding: authoritarianism and mysticism.

**Authoritarianism**    Ravenna in the 6th century was the scene of a three-way struggle among a barbarian king, who was a champion of Roman culture; a Byzantine emperor, who claimed the prerogatives of the past golden age; and a Roman pontiff, who had little

military might but a powerful influence based on the apostolic succession. As the conflict shaped up, it was among an enlightened secular liberalism, a theocratic traditionalism, and a new spiritual institution with a genius for compromise. In the course of the century, the Ostrogothic kingdom was vanquished by the Byzantine Empire. However, after a brief period of domination, Byzantine power in the West crumbled, and the political and military weakness that followed became the soil which nurtured the growth of the new Rome. By the end of the century, Gregory the Great had succeeded in establishing the papacy as the authority that eventually was to dominate the medieval period in the West, while the Eastern Empire continued in its traditional Byzantine forms of organization.

The principle of authority was by no means foreign to Christianity, which grew to maturity in the later days of the Roman Empire. With Christianity an official state religion under the protection of the emperors, Christian organization more and more reflected the authoritarian character of the imperial government. Roman Christian philosophers, such as Boethius and Cassiodorus, cited the authority of Plato and Aristotle on all matters. Theologians accepted the authority of the Scriptures and the commentaries on them by the early Church fathers. The thought of the period was expressed in constant quotations and requotations, interpretations and reinterpretations of ancient Hebrew, Greek, Latin, and early Christian authors. No one was willing or able to assume complete authority in his own right; on all issues, each had to cite ancient precedents for his position. The intellectual climate produced by this patristic type of thinking paved the way for the mighty struggle for political and spiritual authority. The only remaining question was what form the authority was to assume, and who would exercise it.

Justinian, who claimed the authority and semi-divine status of the old Roman emperors, lived in an atmosphere so static and conservative that the words *originality* and *innovation* were used at his court only as terms of reproach. Despite the high price, Byzantine civilization purchased only a blanket uniformity. The principal creative energies of Byzantine man were channeled into aesthetic expression, largely because he had no other direction in which to move. Only in art was any variety and freedom to be found. Here again the art of both Church and state were under the sole patronage of the emperor. It was then all the more remarkable that such a flowering as that which produced Hagia Sophia in Constantinople and San Vitale in Ravenna could have taken place. In both of these instances, the methods of construction were experimental, and the solution developed in response to the architectural and decorative problems was strikingly uninhibited and daring.

The Byzantine concept of authority was embodied in the architectural and decorative plans of both

Hagia Sophia and San Vitale. The central-plan church, with its sharp hierarchical divisions that set aside places for men and women, clergy and laity, aristocrat and commoner, was admirably suited to convey the principle of imperial authority. The vertical axis culminated in a dome that overwhelmed Byzantine man by reminding him, when he was in the presence of the Supreme Authority, of his humble place in the scheme of things. The august imperial portraits in the sanctuary showed him that, outside the clergy, only the emperor and empress and those who occupied the top rungs of the social ladder might approach the altar of God. He might not even presume to bring forward his gifts to the altar in the offertory procession. Since all material things came within the province of Caesar, the exalted duty of making the offering was his alone. Byzantine man, furthermore, was not even allowed to raise his voice with those of his fellowmen in God's praise, as it was also the emperor's prerogative to provide a chorus of qualified professional musicians whose privilege this was. The attitude of reverence was not only to God alone but also to His viceroys on earth. The imperial portraits left no doubt about that. The majesty of God was felt through the infinite power of government. Through the solemn rituals of sacred and courtly ceremonies, both spiritual and secular authority were imposed on Byzantine man from above. His place in this world was inexorably determined; and his human dignity was in proportion to the blandness of his acceptance of a unified ideal of one Christian empire with one Church, one emperor, and one body of laws.

On the other hand, as typical forms of the basilica, Sant' Apollinare Nuovo and its companion Sant'

109. Apse, Sant' Apollinare in Classe. c. 530.

110. Interior of apse, Sant' Apollinare in Classe. c. 530.

Apollinare in Classe indicated a contrasting conception of both God and man (Figs. 89, 90, 109, 110). As the twin rows of columns on either side of the nave marched forward, they carried the eyes and footsteps of the faithful with them. The approach to the sacred precincts was encouraged rather than forbidden, and even the gift of the widow's mite was acknowledged in one of the mosaic panels above. Just as the congregation had gone forth from the doors of their homes to the house of the Lord, the processions of saints in the mosaics likewise moved out of the gates of the twin cities of Classe and Ravenna. The rites they attended were not so incomprehensible and fearsome that they had, as in the Byzantine liturgy, to be enacted behind curtains and choir screens. In the West they took place in the open, and ordinary men and women enjoyed the privilege of ministering to the Lord. The spatial divisions of the oblong basilica, to be sure, still allowed for differences of status, such as that of men and women, choir and clergy. The allowance for all to participate in the sacred service, however, modified the authoritative concept, so that there was some religious freedom.

**Mysticism** The art of the 6th century in Ravenna, like that of such other important centers as Constantinople and Rome, makes the transition from the classical Greco-Roman to the medieval world. While some of the ancient grandeur remained, the accent on symbolism laid the foundation for the coming medieval styles. The physical was replaced by the psychical, the rational road to knowledge by intuitive revelation. Many of the older art forms were carried over and reinterpreted in a new light. The Roman bathhouse became the Christian baptistry where the soul was cleansed of original sin, and the public basilica was redesigned for church mysteries. Mosaics, which were used for Hellenistic and Roman pavements, became the mural medium for mystical visions. The shepherd of classical genre sculpture became symbolically the Good Shepherd. Classical bird and animal motifs became symbols for the soul and the spiritual realm. Music became a reflection of the divine unity of God and man; and the classical lyre, because of its stretched strings on a wooden frame, was reinterpreted by St. Augustine as a symbol of the crucified flesh of Christ. Orpheus, by means of its sounds, had descended into the underworld and overcome death. Christ is therefore frequently represented as playing on the lyre, and at Sant' Apollinare Nuovo he is seated on a lyre-backed throne.

The concept of space turned from the limited classical three-dimensional representation of the natural world to an infinite Christian two-dimensional symbolic world. Invisible things rose in importance above those that could be seen with the eyes. While classical man had regarded his world objectively from without, Early Christian man contemplated his subjectively from within. Socrates once asked an artist whether he could represent the soul. The reply was: "How can it be imitated, since it has neither shape nor colour . . . and is not visible at all?" St. Augustine also observed that "beauty cannot be beheld in any bodily matter." Such mystical visions could be perceived only through symbolism. While natural science had been the foundation stone of ancient philosophy, symbolic theology became the foundation of Christian philosophy. Whereas Greek drama (which was a form of religious experience) had reached its climax step by step with remorseless logic, the Christian drama (as expressed in the liturgy) kindled the fires of faith and arrived at its mystical climax by intuitive means. The denial of the flesh and the conviction that only the soul can be beautiful doomed classical bodiliness and exalted abstract bodilessness. Instead of capturing and clothing the godlike image with flesh and blood, the new concern was with releasing the spirit from the bondage of the flesh.

The great creation and the all-inclusive medium shaped during this period to convey the otherworldly vision was the liturgy. The thought, action, and sequence of the rites of Constantinople, Ravenna, Rome, and other centers determined to a large extent the architectural plans, the symbolism of the mosaics,

and the forms of the sculpture and music. At this time, the fruits of generations of contemplative and active lives gradually ripened into mature structures. The content of centuries of theoretical speculation united with the practical efforts of countless generations of writers, builders, decorators, and musicians to produce the Byzantine liturgy in the East and the synthesis of Gregory the Great in the West. Removed from its primary religious association and seen in a more detached aesthetic light, the liturgy as a work of art embodies a profound and dramatic insight into the deepest longings and highest aspirations of the human spirit.

During the 6th century the controversy still raged as to whether Christ's nature was essentially human or divine. The more the Eastern view emphasized Christ's divinity, the more remote He became. One of the prayers of St. John Chrysostom begins: "O Lord, our God, Whose power is inconceivable and glory incomprehensible, Whose mercy is immeasurable and tenderness to man unspeakable . . . ." Such a conception makes highly presumptuous any attempt to comprehend the divine essence by reason or by direct representation. Hence the mosaics of San Vitale weave such abstract symbols as that of the Chrismon into a rich arabesque of florid designs. Strict symmetry and other means were employed to raise the representation out of the plane of reality and thus to widen the immeasurable gulf between divinity and humanity. The dim lighting, the golden glow of the mosaics, the mysterious symbols whose meaning it was the privilege of Christians to contemplate—all helped conjure up this unfathomable and invisible divinity. The most sacred rites took place behind carved alabaster screens; the choirs sang softly in back of embroidered curtains. The words addressed from Maximian's carved ivory chair took on a superhuman impressiveness. All these in concert conveyed the mystical idea and awakened the vision of eternity in the minds of the beholders.

The Early Roman Christian and Byzantine styles were the responses to the need for new verbal, visual, and auditory modes of expression. In both cases, there was a shift from the forms designed to represent this world to those capable of conjuring up otherworldly visions. Through the poetry of language, the choreographic patterns of step and gesture, and the exalted melodies of the chant, the gripping drama of humanity embodied in the liturgy was enacted in sublime theaters that were furnished with a full panoply of stage settings, decor, costumes, and props created by the inspired hands of the finest craftsmen and artists of the time. The liturgy is, moreover, a continuous pageant lasting not only for a few hours but unfolding with constant variation during the continuous sequence of solemn and joyful feasts through the weeks, months, and seasons of the calendar year, the decades, centuries, and millennia.

# 6 The Monastic Romanesque Style

## THE MONASTERY AT CLUNY, LATE 11TH AND EARLY 12TH CENTURIES

The most typical expression of the Romanesque period was the monastery. The life of ancient Athens and Pergamon had culminated in the constellations of their acropolis buildings, that of Rome had been realized in its forums and civil-engineering projects, while Constantinople and Ravenna had evolved the basilica and palace as the Church and state sides of a theocratic social order. In the Gothic period that succeeded the Romanesque it was to be the cathedral. As Christianity had spread northward after the fall of the West Roman Empire, southern classical forms had met and merged with those of the northern barbarian peoples. This union of the older settled Roman civilization, with its ideals of reason, restraint, and repose, and the newly awakened spirit of the north, with its restless energy and brooding imagination, resulted in the Romanesque, a style that reached its maturity between the years 1000 and 1150. Lacking the security of strong central governments, without the advantages of flourishing cities and towns, monastic man sought peace of mind in the abbey as a haven from the storm-tossed seas of his anarchic social surroundings. Here in these centers off the beaten path he built a miniature world that contained a cross section of Romanesque life. Besides serving as a religious shrine where pilgrims could gather to revere sacred relics, the monastery was the manufacturing and agricultural center of its region as well as a seat of learning, a source for civilization where the only libraries, schools, and hospitals of the time were to be found.

The largest and grandest of all Romanesque monasteries was the abbey at Cluny, and in Figure 111 Kenneth J. Conant has reconstructed its appearance at the pinnacle of its power and fame. Within these walls, men of contemplation were to be found beside men of action; those who were world-weary dwelled side by side with those who knew little of life beyond the cloister; saints brushed shoulders with criminals who sought refuge from the prosecution of secular authorities. Those who were drawn to the vocation of monk were firm believers in the seeming paradox in Christ's words: "For whosoever will save his life shall lose it: but whosoever will lose his life for my sake, the same shall save it" (Luke 9 : 24). By taking the triple vows of poverty, chastity, and obedience, the monk automatically renounced such worldly pursuits as individual material rewards, the pleasures of the senses, the personal satisfactions of family life, and even the exercise of his own free will. According to the Rule of St. Benedict, the founder of European monasticism, a monk "should have absolutely not anything; neither a book, nor tablets, nor a pen—nothing at all. For indeed it is not allowed to the monks to have their own bodies or wills in their power." Through this renunciation of all worldly desires, the monk sought a higher life in the realm of the spirit, which can be summed up most completely in the words of St. Paul: "I live; yet not I, but Christ liveth in me" (Gal. 2 : 20). In order to realize such other-worldly aims, segregation from the secular world had to be effected, and a special way of life found.

In order to provide such a life, a monastery had to be planned so that the monks would have all that was necessary for both their bodily subsistence and their spiritual sustenance. The objective was to be as independent of Caesar as possible so as to render their all unto God. The Benedictine Rule did not prescribe the exact form that a monastic building should take, and, nominally, each abbey was independent to solve its problems according to its needs, the contours of its site, and the extent of its resources. But tradition often operated as rigidly as rules, and with local variations most monasteries adhered to a common pattern. If one allows for the exceptional size and complexity due to its status as mother house of a great order, the plan of Cluny can be accepted as reasonably typical.

Since the life of a Cluniac monk was one of almost continuous religious observances alternating with periods set aside for contemplation, the soul of the monastery was in its abbey church, and its heart was in its cloister (Fig. 112). The church served primarily as the scene of the constant devotional activities of the monks day and night throughout the year, and only secondarily as a shrine for the streams of pilgrims who arrived from near and far to revere relics of saints.

Next in importance to facilities for the church services was the provision for the contemplative life that centered on the cloister. The cloister is found, typically, in the center of the abbey and south of the nave of the church, with the other monastic buildings clustering around it. The usual cloister was an open quadrangular garden plot enclosed by a covered arcade on all four sides. The somewhat irregular shape of the cloister at Cluny in the 12th century resulted from the ambitious building program necessitated by the rapid growth of the monastery. Since this renowned marble-columned cloister no longer exists, the one of St. Trophîme at Arles will serve as an example (Fig. 112).

Such a complete abbey as Cluny had to provide for many other functions. The daily life of the monks necessitated a refectory where they could eat their meals in common, plus kitchens, bakeries, and storage space; a chapter hall where they could transact their communal business; and a dormitory adjacent to the church, for services were held during the night as well as by day. Three small cloisters were included —one for the education of novices, another for visiting monks and religiously inclined laymen who sought refuge from the world, and a third, near a cemetery, for the aged and infirm brothers. The hospice, or guesthouse, provided accommodations for visitors who flocked in during the pilgrimage season. There were also quarters for such craftsmen as blacksmiths, carpenters, and cobblers, as well as stables for dairy cattle and other domestic animals.

The plan of Cluny was thus a coherent system of adjoining quadrangles that embraced courts and cloisters whose variation in size and importance accommodated the differing activities they were designed to serve. Altogether, it was a highly complex and at the same time logical plan for a complete community, taking into account the ideals, aspirations, practices, and everyday activities of a group that gathered to work physically and spiritually toward a common end.

## ARCHITECTURE

Hugh of Semur, greatest of the Cluniac abbots, succeeded Odilo in the year 1049. Under Hugh, Cluny was destined to attain a period of such resplendence that it could be described by an enthusiastic chronicler as "shining on the earth like a second sun." Taking as his model the accepted feudal organization of society, in which smaller and more dependent

**above: 111.** Abbey of Cluny (bird's-eye view from southeast). c. 1157. Reconstruction by Kenneth J. Conant. a. Third Abbey Church (lantern tower over crossing of nave and major transept); b. Cloister of Pontius (main cloister); c. Refectory; d. Monks' dormitory; e. Novices' cloister; f. Visitors' cloister; g. Cloister of Notre Dame; h. Monks' cemetery; i. Hospice; j. Craftsmen's quarters and stables.

**right: 112.** Cloister, Abbey of St. Trophîme, Arles. c. 1100.

# CHRONOLOGY / Monastic Romanesque Period

| | | |
|---|---|---|
| **480– 543** St. Benedict, founder of European monasticism; c.529 built abbey at Monte Cassino, Italy | **1050** Holy Roman Empire at height; ascendancy of papal power | partially collapsed; 1131 church dedicated by Pope Innocent X) |
| **768– 814** Charlemagne ruled at Aix-la-Chapelle (Aachen); Carolingian Period initiated | **1063** Pisa Cathedral begun | **1095** Urban II preached the First Crusade |
| **c.792– 800** Centula monastery built by Charlemagne | **1066** William, duke of Normandy, conquered England; reigned as king of England, 1066–87 | **1096– 1120** Abbey Church of La Madeleine at Vézelay built (1096 church begun; 1104 original Romanesque choir and transept dedicated; 1110 nave finished; 1120 narthex begun and nave revaulted after fire; c.1130 tympanum over the central portal of narthex; 1132 dedicated) |
| **c.796– 804** Palatine Chapel at Aix-la-Chapelle built | **1071– 1112** Pilgrimage church at Santiago de Compostela, Spain, built | |
| **800** Charlemagne crowned Holy Roman emperor in Rome by pope | **1072** St. Peter Damian died | |
| **c.800** St. Gall (Switzerland) monastery begun | **1073– 1085** Gregory VII (Hildebrande), pope | |
| **910** Abbey of Cluny in Burgundy, France, founded | **1077** Emperor Henry IV bowed to Pope Gregory VII at Canossa; Abbot Hugh of Cluny was intermediary | |
| **927– 942** Odo, abbot of Cluny, reputed author of musical treatises | **c.1080** Church of Sant' Ambrogio begun at Milan | **1098** Cistercian order founded; opposed Cluniac order; St. Bernard of Clairvaux was its principal spokesman |
| **962** Otto the Great (936–973) crowned Holy Roman emperor | **c.1080– 1160** Church of St. Sernin built at Toulouse, France | **1109** Pontius became abbot of Cluny |
| **994– 1049** Odilo, abbot of Cluny | **1088– 1099** Urban II, Cluniac pope | **1122** Peter the Venerable became abbot of Cluny |
| **c.995–c.1050** Guido of Arezzo, author of musical treatises, inventor of staff notation | **1088– 1130** Great Third Church at Cluny built (1088 Cluny III begun under Hugh of Semur by architect Hezelo; 1095 apse dedicated by Pope Urban II; 1120 church finished; 1125 nave vaults | **c.1130– 1135** Gislebertus carved sculptures at St. Lazare, Autun |
| **1000– 1150** Romanesque period at height | | **1168– 1188** Matteo carved Pórtico de la Gloria at Cathedral of Santiago de Compostela, Spain |
| **1049– 1109** Hugh of Semur, abbot of Cluny | | |

landowners swore allegiance to the larger and more powerful landlords in return for protection, Hugh began to bring many of the traditionally independent Benedictine monasteries into the Cluniac orbit. With the express approval of the popes, Hugh gradually concentrated the power of the whole order in his hands and transformed Cluny into a vast monastic empire over which he ruled benignly for sixty years. In the Church hierarchy he was outranked only by the pope, and in the secular world he was the peer of kings. He figured prominently in most of the historical events of his day, even to the extent of acting as intermediary between an emperor and a pope on the famous occasion at Canossa, when Henry IV came on bended knee to beseech Gregory VII for forgiveness. Hugh's greatest moment, however, came when Pope Urban II, who had received training as a monk and prior at Cluny under his personal guidance, was present to dedicate the high altar of his great new abbey church. Honor after honor was bestowed upon the monastery by this Cluniac pope, who was also the preacher of the First Crusade.

Hugh had begun by undertaking many new monastic buildings to accommodate Cluny's ever-growing number of resident monks. Eventually the older second church also proved inadequate for the mother house of a great order, especially when delegations of monks from the priories far and wide assembled there for the chapters general. (Records show that on such an occasion in the year 1132, over 1,200 monks were in the processional line.) The growing importance of Cluny as a center for pilgrimages also added to the need for greater space in the abbey church. For these practical reasons, as well as his desire to crown his many achievements with a monument that would rival the legendary temple of Solomon, Hugh began the great new Third Abbey Church. Even with all his power and influence, however, Hugh did not attempt it before the dominant position of Cluny in the scheme of things was completely consolidated, and before he was certain of generous financial support. The farflung priories of the order, numbering at this time well over 1,000 and extending as far as Scotland in the north, Portugal in the west, and Jerusalem in the east, could all be counted on for contributions. In addition, offerings were received from people of all classes, from bishops to the humblest of the parishioners and from great lords down to the poorest pilgrims, who came to worship at the shrine. Thus, in 1088, when he was past 65 and in his 40th year as abbot, Hugh of Semur, with an architect named Hezelo, began the monumental abbey church that in its magnitude and glory eclipsed all other churches in Western Christendom. Gilon, one of his earliest biographers, said that Hugh "began and erected such a church within twenty years that if an emperor had built it within so short a time, it would have been considered marvelous."

**The Great Third Abbey Church at Cluny**   Hugh's great church was dominated on the exterior by its imposing tower forms. The plan included unusual double transepts and many apsidal chapels radiating outward from the choir (Fig. 113). It was usual for large abbey churches to have an impressive lantern tower over the crossing of the nave and the transept. At Cluny, as with St. Sernin at Toulouse (Fig. 114), the immense size dominated the silhouette of the whole exterior, but Cluny's twin octagonal towers astride the transept wings were less common. The minor transept also had its central tower, thus making four on the east end, which, added to the two on either side of the narthex entrance, brought the total to six. Unlike later Gothic cathedrals, the exterior of the third church was unadorned by sculpture, all such

embellishments being concentrated in the interior. Even the western façade remained bare, since it was designed for an introspective, cloistered community and consequently had no need to extend sculptured invitations to the world outside, as did a city church.

While on everyday occasions the monks entered the church from the cloister, high holidays, such as Easter, Pentecost, and the Feast of Sts. Peter and Paul, to whom the church was dedicated, called for a ceremonial entrance from the west end. Here the double portal between the towers led into a spacious three-aisled narthex, which was called the *minor nave.* The narthex, besides serving as the place where the grand procession could be marshaled, took care of the overflow of laymen who gathered in great numbers at Cluny during the pilgrimage season. When ceremonial entrance was made at Cluny, it occurred through three carved portals, the central one of which was 21 feet in height. Over the lintel and enclosed by the arch was an immense *tympanum,* the semicircular area enclosed by the arch, which contained a sculptured relief representing Christ in Glory surrounded by a heavenly host, the four symbolic evangelical beasts, apostles, and elders.

**below: 113.** Plan of Great Third Abbey Church of Cluny. c. 1120.

**right: 114.** Apse, Church of St. Sernin, Toulouse. c. 1080. Lantern tower height 215'.

On entering the nave (Fig. 115), the mighty proportions of the huge basilica loomed up. From the entrance portal to the end of the apse, it extended a distance of 415 feet, while the entire horizontal axis from front to back, including the narthex, reached an overall length of 615 feet. The nave itself had 11 bays that stretched forward a distance of 260 feet. Each bay was separated by a group of columns clustered around supporting piers, which, as the architectural counterpart of the monks, marched in solemn procession toward the climax of the building at the high altar. In width, the nave spread outward 118 feet and was divided into 5 aisles. This division responded in part to the need to provide extra space for altars, since it was now the custom for each monk to say mass every day. The outside aisles, extending all the way around the church and choir, gave pilgrims access to these numerous altars and, more especially, to the smaller chapels in the choir without disturbing the monastic liturgy. These aisles also provided more room for the grand processionals that distinguished the Cluniac liturgy and that demanded ever more impressive and spacious settings. It can be seen in Figure 115 that a stone screen was placed across the nave to close off the space set aside for the monks' choir. The great height of the church was such that the screen did not break the impression of a unified whole, and the eye was drawn aloft to the tall columns around the high altar and above them, in turn, to the lofty figure of Christ, which, gazing downward as if in a vision, was painted in the fresco technique on the interior of the half-dome of the apse.

Whereas the Early Roman Christian basilicas basically were horizontally directed, the Romanesque examples, because of the northern influence, raised the levels of the nave upward vertically. Gradually, this resulted in more and more accent being placed on the parts of the building above the nave arcade. At Cluny, a double row of windows was found, the lower of which was filled in with masonry, while the upper remained open and served as the clearstory. Though it had numerous windows, the church drew criticism from later Gothic builders as being too dark. Its thick walls and massive proportions allowed little direct sunlight to penetrate into the church itself. This was not of great importance, because so much of the monastic liturgy took place at night when the interior was illuminated by candlelight. Churches designed for city people who worshiped by day naturally had to pay more attention to lighting problems.

The nave at Cluny was spanned by ribbed barrel vaulting, 32 feet in the clear, supported by slightly pointed transverse arches. Rising a full 98 feet above the pavement, the vaults were the highest achieved up to this time. But the emotional exuberance of attaining such height outran the engineering knowledge needed to maintain it, and a part of the Cluny vaulting soon collapsed. Out of this accident came experi-

mentation with external buttressing so that when the vaults were rebuilt, a range of rudimentary supports with open round arches was placed outside on the aisle roofs. Cluny thus achieved the distinction of being the first church to have external buttresses supporting its nave vaults, and, with its pointed arches, and high vaulting, Cluny combined for the first time in one structure three of the features that future builders would employ to make the unified system characteristic of the Gothic style.

The Romanesque basilica was an outgrowth of the Early Christian structure (Figs. 92, 93). But a comparison of the Cluny III plan (Fig. 113) with the plan of Old St. Peter's reveals that in the Romanesque building, transept space has increased, room for the large monastic choirs has been provided, and a *chevet* or sequence of chapels now clustered about the transept wings and the apse. Monastic churches gravitated toward the eastern end where the choir assembled after the procession, and especially toward the high altar where the solemn rites were performed. In a city church, the nave had to provide space for a congregation, but in a monastic church the clergy, including the monks, numbered into the hundreds, and the lay congregation often was nonexistent. Logically, then, the space around the altar had to be extended so that all the monks who formed the choir could be seated. The enlarged apse and double transepts at Cluny were clearly developed to give the monks a sense of surrounding the high altar and to produce a spacious and resonant setting for the almost ceaseless chanting.

The high altar itself was set off from the surrounding ambulatory by eight columns of surpassing slenderness and beauty. Crowning them were skillfully carved capitals (Figs. 120–123), all that remains of the apse today. That these were as impressive in Romanesque times as they are now is attested to by Hildebert, bishop of Le Mans, who after a visit wrote: "If it were possible for those who dwell in heaven to take pleasure in a house made by hands, the ambulatory of Cluny would be a place where angels walked."

The decorative plan of the church was carried out on a scale comparable in quality to the grandeur of its spatial dimensions. More than 1,200 sculptured capitals surmounted the columns of the structure, while carved moldings outlined the graceful pointed arches of the nave arcade. Most of the sculpture was painted in rich colors that gave an added glow to the splendor of the interior, and the whole church was paved with mosaic floors inlaid with images of saints and angels or with abstract designs.

All this magnificence did not go unchallenged. St. Bernard, the redoubtable opponent of the Cluniac order, disapproved violently of such extravagances, and in doing so in writing he unwittingly left a first-hand account of the glory of Hugh's church soon after it was finished. In a letter to one of the Cluniac abbots,

**115.** HEZELO. Nave, Third Abbey Church of Cluny. 1088–1130. Reconstruction by Kenneth J. Conant.

## SCULPTURE

Some of the finest sculpture that dates from the period of Cluny's grandeur is in the abbey church of La Madeleine at Vézelay. The nave and narthex are contemporary with Hugh's church at Cluny, and the intelligent restoration in the 19th century by the French medieval archaeologist Viollet-le-Duc accounts for their present good condition. While its proportions are considerably smaller than those of the great basilica at Cluny, La Madeleine today is the largest Romanesque abbey church in France. Rich in historical associations, it derived its principal fame in medieval times as the repository of the relics of St. Mary Magdalene.

The principal interest at Vézelay, however, is the seemingly inexhaustible wealth of sculptured capitals and, above all, the relief compositions over its three portals leading from the narthex into the nave and side aisles. For the first time since antiquity, monumental sculpture appears. In Romanesque churches it was used in the tympanums over the portals, the largest and most intricate sculpture being used in the tympanum over the central doorway.

The splendid tympanum over the central portal at Vézelay (Fig. 116) stems from the first quarter of the 12th century. In its iconography and workmanship, it is by far the most complex Romanesque tympanum, yet the logical division of space keeps the composition from seeming cluttered or confused. Here, as elsewhere, Romanesque designers and sculptors looked for their subjects and models in the drawings and miniature paintings that illustrated the texts of the Scriptures in monastic libraries. Such illuminated manuscripts provided convenient models that the monks could show to the sculptors who were to carry out the projects. At Vézelay, the robe of Christ, as well as those of the apostles, reveals a pattern of clear, sharp, swirling lines, which stems from pen drawings in manuscripts of the time.

The interpretation of the tympanum scene most often suggested is the commission of the apostles as found in the last chapter of Luke's Gospel, and the description of the Pentecost scene in the second chapter of the Acts of the Apostles. A more likely source, however, is the final vision of St. John from the last part of the Book of Revelation. Whether a single scene is intended or two or even three scenes are combined in a subtle Cluniac synthesis is a subject for scholarly speculation. If it is a single scene, the most convincing source is the first two verses of Chapter 22 of the Book of Revelation: "And he shewed me a pure river of water of life, clear as crystal, pro-

he deplored (with Cluny in mind) "the vast height of your churches, their immoderate length, their superfluous breadth, the costly polishings, the curious carvings and paintings which attract the worshiper's gaze and hinder his attentions." His feeling was that "at the very sight of these costly yet marvelous vanities men are more kindled to offer gifts than to pray. . . . Hence the church is adorned with gemmed crowns of light—nay, with lustres like cart-wheels, girt all round with lamps, but no less brilliant with precious stones that stud them. Moreover we see candelabra standing like trees of massive bronze, fashioned with marvelous subtlety of art, and glistening no less brightly with gems than with the lights they carry. What, think you, is the purpose of all this? The compunction of penitents, or the admiration of beholders?"

Cluny Abbey stood proudly until the Revolutionary year of 1798, when a wave of anticlericalism swept France, causing the abbey to be sacked and burned. All the buildings except a single transept wing were blown up by dynamite, and the rubble was sold as common building stone. Some sculptural fragments survive, and the spirit of the great monastery lives on in the influence it exerted on such related structures as St. Trophîme at Arles (Fig. 112), St. Sernin in Toulouse (Fig. 114), and La Madeleine at Vézelay (Figs. 116–118).

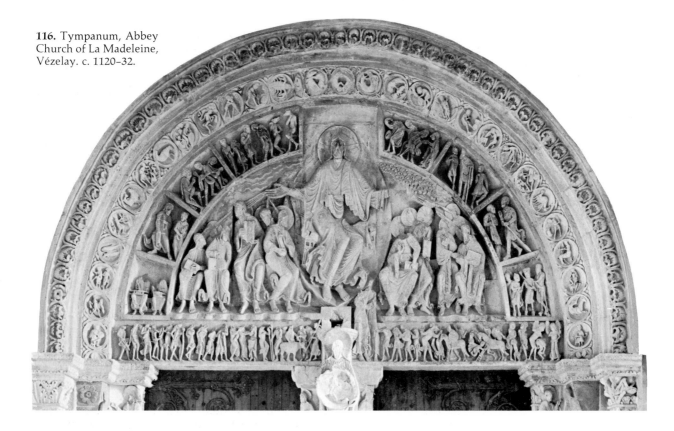

**116.** Tympanum, Abbey Church of La Madeleine, Vézelay. c. 1120–32.

ceeding out of the throne of God and of the Lamb. In the midst of the street of it, and on either side of the river, was there the tree of life, which bare twelve manner of fruits, and yielded her fruit every month: and the leaves of the tree were for the healing of nations."

Here again the figure of Christ dominates the composition, seated, as St. John says, on "a great white throne," but not so much to judge mankind as to redeem it. While the figure is supremely majestic, Christ is not crowned. The streams emanating from his fingers descend upon the barefooted apostles, the archetypes of the clergy, who bring spiritual understanding through the books they hold in their hands and physical healing through the divine mercy which they transmit to mankind. On one side of Christ's head, the water referred to in the quotation flows forth, while on the other are the branches of the tree. The 12 fruits, one for each month, are found among the 29 medallions in the middle band of *archivolts*—the series of arches that frame the tympanum. A figure treading grapes, for example, represents September; October is symbolized by a man gathering acorns for his pigs. The months themselves, besides being connected with these labors, are also symbolized by the signs of the zodiac that, in turn, remind man of the limited time he has in which to attain his salvation. A few of the other medallions picture strange exotic

beasts taken from the *bestiaries,* those curious books of the time that recounted the lore about animals actual and fabulous. A survival from antiquity can be noted in the fourth medallion from the lower right that depicts a centaur.

The inner band of the archivolt is divided into eight irregular compartments that contain figures representing the nations which the leaves of the tree of life are intended to heal. The one on the top left, next to the head of Christ, contains two dog-headed men, called in Isidore's *Etymologies* the "Cynocephaloi," a tribe supposed to have inhabited India. The corresponding compartment on the right side shows the crippled and bent figure of a man and that of a blind woman taking a few halting steps as she is led forward. In the others, the lame supported on crutches are found along with lepers, who gesture toward their sores.

Along the lintel below, a parade of the nations converges toward the center. While the compartments above picture those in physical distress, here are the pagans and heathens of the earth who need spiritual aid. Among these strange peoples who populate the remote regions of the earth are a man and woman (in the far right corner) with enormous ears and feathered bodies. Next to them is a group of dwarfs or pygmies, so small they have to mount a horse by means of a ladder. On the far left, half-naked

On the first of the eight faces of these twin capitals (Fig. 120) is inscribed: "This tone is the first in the order of musical intonations," and the figure is that of a solemn-faced youth playing on a lute. Here the symbolism of the stringed instrument stems from the belief in the power of music to banish evil, as David had cast out Saul's evil spirit when he played to him. The second tone (Fig. 121) is represented by the figure of a young woman dancing and beating a small drum, the inscription reading, "There follows the tone which by number and law is second." Such percussion instruments are known to have been used to accompany medieval processions on joyful feast days in the manner described in the 68th Psalm: "The singers went before, the players on instruments followed after; among them were damsels playing with timbrels." The next inscription (Fig. 122) says: "The third strikes, and represents the resurrection of Christ." The instrument here is of the lyre type with a sounding board added, which is one of the 11th-century forms of the psaltery, the legendary instrument with which David accompanied himself as he sang the psalms. This instrument with its gut strings stretched over the wooden frame roughly resembles a cross and was used as a symbolic reference to Christ stretched on the Cross for the redemption of the world. The fourth figure (Fig. 123) is that of a young man playing a set of chime bells, and the accompanying inscription reads: "The fourth follows representing a lament in song." The Latin word *planctus* denotes a funeral dirge, and the practice of ringing bells at burials is pictured in the contemporary representation of the burial procession of Edward the Confessor from the Bayeux Tapestry (Fig. 131), where the figures accompanying the bier have small bells in their hands.

As a series, the eight inscriptions and symbolic figures reveal much about Cluniac musical practice. For example, in the second, fourth, fifth, and seventh tones, the figures are moving or standing, which seems to point to the processional chants; in the others, they are seated in a manner appropriate to the stationary chants. In those that have to do with action, the instruments are a small hand drum or cymbals, bells, and a horn of some type, while all the seated figures play upon stringed instruments. This symbolism apparently points to some of the rhythmic and melodic differences in the two types of monastic chant—the processional and the stationary—which, in turn, reflect the two aspects of life—the active and the contemplative.

The skillful chorus of Cluny was undoubtedly in the musical vanguard of that day, just as the Third Abbey Church headed architecture and sculpture. Odo's teaching methods clearly indicated that a high degree of vocal culture was expected of his monastic choirs; and, since they sang most of the time, they got plenty of practice. They were thus able to perform

Parallel Organum (10th century) (from *Scholia enrichiriadus*)

chants of considerable complexity, and music was well on its way to becoming a highly developed art. While Gregorian plainsong was a purely melodic style and continued to be practiced as such, during the Romanesque period the choral responses began to show variations in the direction of singing in several parts. The 9th, 10th, and 11th centuries thus saw the tentative beginnings of the *polyphonic,* or "many-voiced," style that was to flourish in the Gothic period and in the Renaissance.

Unfortunately, the polyphonic practice of the pre-Gothic period is known only through theoretical treatises. From the rules they give for the addition of voices to the traditional chant, however, some idea of the early forms of polyphony can be determined. As might be expected, the influence of mathematics and the Pythagorean number theory were found in the musical usages of the time. The perfect intervals of the octave, fifth, and fourth were preferred over all others, since their mathematical ratios indicated a closer correspondence with the divine order of the universe. In a treatise dating from the beginning of the 10th century, some years before Odo's time, the type of choral response known as *parallel organum* is discussed. The original Gregorian melody was maintained intact; and, as a variant in two parts, the principal voice was paralleled by an organum voice at the fifth below, so that there was a strict melodic and rhythmic concordance between the two parts. When sung in three parts, the organum was doubled at the octave above, so that the principal voice was embellished by the movement of parallel voices a fifth below and a fourth above. With the addition of the fourth part, both the principal and organal voices were doubled in octaves, thus making a composite intervallic texture that included the parallel movement of the three perfect intervals: the fourth, fifth, and octave (see above).

Parallel organum, in effect, built a mighty fortress of choral sound around the traditional Gregorian line of plainsong. By thus enclosing it within the stark and gaunt but strong perfect intervals, parallel organum achieved a massive and solid style quite in the spirit of the other Romanesque arts.

The music of this time was yet another expression of the praise of God; and, when related to the great buildings, the richly carved sculpture, the illuminated manuscripts and painted murals, it fits into the picture as a whole. Consequently, when the choir section of a monastic church was being planned, every effort was made to provide resonant setting for the perpetual chant. Hugh's great church was especially renowned for its acoustics. The curved ceiling vaults and the great variety of angles in the wall surfaces of the broad transepts and cavernous nave gave the chant there a characteristic tone color that can be reproduced only in a similar setting. The effect of a monastic choir of several hundred voices performing jubilations with all its heart and soul must have been overwhelmingly impressive.

Cluny's sculptured capitals depicting the tones of plainsong represent an obvious synthesis of the arts of sculpture, music, and literature into an appropriate architectural setting. Their expressive intensity, moreover, bespeaks both the motion and emotion typical of the Romanesque style in general. As such, they are representative products of a people capable of the long and arduous pilgrimages and the fantastic effort associated with the organization of the First Crusade. These sculptures reveal something of that indomitable energy, and especially of a vigorous attitude toward the act of worship, that must have been channeled into a performance style which was emphatic in rhythm. They are, in fact, the embodiment of the spirit expressed by St. Augustine, who admonished the faithful to "Sing with your voices, and with your hearts, and with all your moral convictions, sing the new songs, not only with your tongue but with your life."

## IDEAS

The key to the understanding of the Romanesque as a living and active art is a knowledge of the opposing forces that created it. As the Roman Christian influence spread northward, it encountered the restless surging energies of the former barbarian tribes. In effect, a Church that venerated tradition and encouraged a static order was absorbing peoples with an urge for experimentation and action. The resulting innovations gave ancient forms new twists and turns. When builders combined the horizontal Early Roman Christian basilica, for example, with the northern spire, they took the first step toward Romanesque architecture. The further development of the style was the direct result of this union of southern horizontality and northern verticality, reflecting as it did the broad spirit of the late Roman humanism and the soaring northern aspirations. The musical counterpart is found in the joining together of southern monophony and northern polyphony, which occurred when the Mediterranean tradition of unison melody met the northern custom of singing in parts. The result was the experimentation with primitive forms of counterpoint and harmony that characterized the

music of the Romanesque period. This meeting of southern unity with northern variety, and its slow maturation over the centuries, was thus responsible for the first truly European art style: the Romanesque. The ideas that underlie the monastic aspect of the style are an outgrowth of those motivating the earlier period in Ravenna. The mysticism of the previous period moved into an other-worldly ascetic phase; and Early Christian authoritarianism resulted in the rigid stratification of society into strict hierarchies. The two basic ideas, then, crystallize as asceticism and hierarchism.

**Asceticism**   The monastic way of life demanded the seclusion of the countryside as an escape from the distractions of the world. Since the monk conceived his earthly life to be but a stepping-stone to life beyond, living required only the barest essentials. The very absence of physical luxury led to the development of a rich inner life, and the barren soil of rural isolation almost miraculously produced an important art movement. Poverty, chastity, and humility became virtues as the result of moral rather than aesthetic impulses, but the very severity of monastic life stimulated imaginative experience, and individual self-denial reinforced communal energies.

The attitude of turning away from the world found its architectural expression in the plain exteriors and rich interiors of monastic churches. Thus, the net effect of asceticism was to increase the fervor of the spirit and to express this with great intensity. Two favorite Cluniac saints were the Paul and Anthony who had gone farthest into the forbidding African desert; it was they who had the most fantastic visions and the most horrendous temptations. The diffusion of social centers into widely scattered monastic communities likewise lent a peculiar intensity and a wide variety to the expressive forms of the Romanesque. The arts, consequently, were not intended to mirror the natural world or to decorate the dwelling place of an earthly ruler but, rather, to conjure up other-worldly visions of divine majesty. Hence, all the arts found a common ground in their desire to depict the various aspects of the world beyond.

The monks developed an art of elaborate symbolism addressed to an educated cloistered community versed in sophisticated allegories. Such a symbolic language—whether in architecture, sculpture, painting, or music—could only have been fostered by an abbot like Hugh, whose learning was so universal that he succeeded in adding "philosophy to ornament and a meaning to beauty." By contrast, the later Gothic arts were directed toward the humble of the world and the unlettered people beyond the cloister. While the sculpture and stained glass of the Gothic cathedral were destined to become the Bible in stone and glass for the poor, in a monastic church the comparable forms were always aloof and aristocratic and at times intentionally subtle and enigmatic. This does not mean that Romanesque art was overly intellectualized and remote from the experience of those to whom it was addressed. On the contrary, it was very directly related to the intensity of the inner life and the visionary other-worldly focus of the religious communities that developed it.

Greco-Roman sculpture was successful in its way precisely because classical man had conceived his gods in human form, and as such they could be rendered so well in marble. When godhood was conceived as an abstract principle, a realistic representation of it became essentially impossible. Rational proportions were of no help to Romanesque man, who considered it impossible to understand God intellectually. God had to be felt through faith rather than comprehended by the mind. Only through the intuitive eye of faith could His essence be grasped. Hence He had to be portrayed symbolically, not represented literally, since a symbol could stand for something intangible. Physical substance was secondary, and soul stuff primary; but the latter could be depicted only in the world of the imagination.

A life so metaphysically oriented and one motivated by such deep religious convictions could never have found its models in the natural world. The fantastic proportions of Romanesque architecture, the eccentric treatment and distortions of the human body in its sculpture, the unnecessarily elaborated initials in the manuscript illuminations, and the florid melismas added to the syllables of the chant were all evidence of a rejection of the natural order of things and its replacement by the supernatural. The book of the Bible most admired was Revelation, containing as it did the apocalyptical visions of St. John. The pictorial element in sculpture and painting in both large and small forms reflected Romanesque man's convictions with such intensity that the human figures seem to be consumed by the inner fires of their faith. Calm reason would seek to persuade by placid or serene attitudes, but such animated figures as those of the prophets at Souillac (Fig. 124) and Moissac seem to be performing spiritual dances in which their slender forms stretch to unnatural lengths and their gestures are more convulsive than graceful.

Romanesque man thus dwelt in a dream world where the trees that grew in Paradise, the angels who populated the heavens, and the demons of hell were more real than anything or anybody he beheld in everyday life. Even though he had never seen such creatures, he never doubted their existence. Indeed, the monsters whose fearsome characteristics were described in the bestiaries, and which were represented in the manuscripts and sculptures (Fig. 125), had a moral and symbolic function far more real to him than any animals of mere physical existence. All

**right: 124.** *Isaiah,* on west portal, Church of Notre Dame, Souillac. c. 1110.

**below: 125.** *Last Judgment,* west tympanum, Autun Cathedral. c. 1130–35.

these imaginary creatures existed together in a jungle of the imagination where the abnormal was the normal and the fabulous became the commonplace.

**Hierarchism**    A strict hierarchical structure of society prevailed throughout the Romanesque period, which was as rigid in its way inside the monastery as was the feudalism outside the cloistered walls. The thought of the time was based on the assumption of a divinely established order of the universe, and the authority to interpret it was vested in the Church. The majestic figure of Christ in Glory carved over the entrance portals of the Cluniac abbey churches, and echoed in the mural compositions painted on the interior of their half-domed apses, proclaimed this concept to the world at large. Christ was no longer the Good Shepherd of Early Christian times but a mighty king, crowned and enthroned in the midst of His heavenly courtiers, sitting in judgment on the entire world (Fig. 125). The keys to His heavenly kingdom, as seen in the Vézelay tympanum (Fig. 116) and the apse painting at Berzé-la-Ville (Fig. 119), rest firmly in the grasp of St. Peter, the first of the popes according to the Roman tradition. As if to lend additional emphasis to this doctrine, St. Peter at Berzé-la-Ville is seen receiving a scroll containing the divine statutes from the hands of Christ. The papacy of medieval days always found its most powerful support in the Cluniac order, and through such aid succeeded in establishing an all-powerful theocracy based on this mandate from on high.

The authority of the Church was nowhere better expressed than in these monumental sculptural and mural compositions that from their place of eminence warned those who entered of their position on the road either to salvation or to damnation. The milestones marking the path were placed there by the Church, whose clergy alone could interpret them and assure the suppliant that he was on his way to the streets of gold instead of the caldrons of fire. The frequency with which the apocalyptic vision of St. John was represented, with apostles and elders surrounding the throne of Christ, was evidence of the veneration of the protective-father image in the form of the bearded patriarch.

In such a divine order, nothing could be left to chance; and all life had to be brought into an organizational plan that would conform to this cosmic scheme of things. The stream of authority, descending from Christ through St. Peter to his papal successors, flowed out from Rome in three main directions. The Holy Roman emperor received his crown from the hands of the Roman pontiff, and, in turn, all the kings of the Western world owed him homage, and on downward from the great lords to the humblest serf, all of whom had a preordained place in this great cosmic plan. Next, the archbishops and bishops received their mitres in Rome, and in their bishoprics

they were feudal lords in their own right. Under them, the so-called "secular" clergy, from the parish priest to the deacon, owed their allegiance to the superiors from whom they received their orders. Finally, the monastic communities under their abbots also owed their allegiance to the pope; and through their loyal support of the papacy, the Cluniac order grew so strong that its abbot was, other than the pope, the most powerful churchman in Christendom.

Beginning as a small independent monastery, Cluny was from the first exempted from tribute to any power save that of the pope alone. But instead of remaining an independent unit like other Benedictine abbeys, Cluny adopted the feudal principle by expanding and absorbing other monasteries until it dominated the monastic movement. As the head of a monarchical system, the order was the most powerful unifying force of the time, not only in religious and political affairs but in architectural, artistic, and musical thought as well. Through this adherence to the feudal system, it became a great landowning institution, and in an economy where land was the sole source of wealth, the monasteries became the principal commissioners of works of art. In a world where faith triumphed over reason and where the sole road to salvation was through the Church, the Cluniac order acted as the mainstay of the Roman tradition and helped spread its authority, doctrines, and liturgy all over Christendom.

The ranks of the monks were drawn mainly from the aristocratic class, whose members were among the few free to choose their own way of life. All the higher Church offices were held principally by men from noble families, often by younger sons not eligible under the law of primogeniture to inherit the feudal estates. The vow of poverty applied only to individual ownership, and collectively a monastic community resembled a feudal manor. It was only in later times that the mendicant orders of monks attempted to interpret the vow of poverty literally. Hence, Romanesque art was an aristocratic art, and it remained so throughout the period with the means of patronage concentrated in the hands of its abbots and bishops.

The Romanesque abbey church was organized according to a rigid hierarchical plan that mirrored the strict order of precedence in the processionals of the liturgy for which it was the setting. By its insistence on visible proportions, it bespoke the invisible plan of a divinely ordered world. The regularity of the monastic buildings that surrounded it likewise was designed to enclose those who expressed their willingness to conform to such a cosmic regularity of life, and thus to constitute a human reflection of the divinely established plan for the salvation of mankind. The very spaciousness of the abbey church was far in excess of anything that was needed to accommodate the few hundreds who normally worshiped there. It was, however, the monument that mirrored the unshakable religious convictions of Romanesque man; and, as the house of the Lord and Ruler of the universe, it became a palace surpassing the dreams of glory of any king on the face of the earth. In the insecurity of the feudalistic world, Romanesque man built a fortress for his faith and for his God, which was designed to withstand the onslaughts of heretics and heathens as well as to survive the more elemental forces of wind, weather, and fire. Furthermore, the abbey church was the place where the heavenly Monarch held court, and where His subjects could pay Him their homage in the divine services that went on day and night, year in and year out.

This hierarchical principle, moreover, applied not only to the social and ecclesiastical stratifications but also to the basic thought processes. Authority for all things rested firmly on the Scriptures and the interpretations of them by the early Church fathers. Rightness and fitness were determined by how ancient the tradition was, and scholarship consisted not so much in treading new intellectual paths as in the elucidation of the traditional sources. To the educated, this process took the form of learned commentaries; to the unlettered, it was expressed in the cult of relics. Thousands took to the dusty pilgrimage roads and traveled across France and Spain to touch the legendary tomb of the Apostle James at Compostela. In the arts, this veneration of the past made mandatory the continuance of such traditional forms as the Early Roman Christian basilica and the music of the Gregorian chant.

Yet this traditionalism, curiously enough, never led to stagnation or uniformity. In making learned commentaries on the Scriptures, the writers unconsciously, and sometimes quite consciously, interpreted them in the light of contemporary views. And as the untutored populace traveled about Europe on pilgrimages and later went to the Near East on the Crusades, it absorbed new ideas that eventually were to jar the provincialism of feudal times into a more dynamic social structure.

All the arts, however, exhibited an extraordinary inventiveness and such a rich variety as to make the Romanesque one of the most spontaneous and original periods in history. Diversity rather than unity was the rule of Romanesque architecture. Regional building traditions and the availability of craftsmen and materials contributed to the varied pattern. At St. Mark's in Venice (Fig. 212) there is a combination of the multidomed Byzantine style with Greek-cross ground plans. In Spain, the Moorish influence is felt; in northern Italy, Sant'Ambrogio at Milan (Fig. 126) has the rich red brickwork and square belfry towers typical of Lombardy; while in central Italy, the Romanesque is characterized by zebra-striped exteriors composed of alternating strips of dark-green and cream-colored marbles, as at the Baptistry of Florence (Fig. 170) and the Cathedral of Pisa.

Romanesque structures never became types as Greek temples, Byzantine churches, and the later Gothic cathedrals did. Each building and each region sought its own solutions. Through constant experimentation, the Romanesque architects found the key to new structural principles, such as their vaulting techniques; and, by gradually achieving complete command of their medium, they matured in their building from heavy fortresslike structures into edifices of considerable elegance. Meanwhile, the decorators groped toward the revival of monumental sculpture and mural painting. The need for larger and better choirs likewise led to the invention of notational systems, and the emotional exuberance in worship made many modifications of the traditional chant, which eventually culminated in the art of counterpoint. In all, the creative vitality exhibited in each art medium is a constant source of astonishment.

Within the formal framework provided by the abbey church, architectural detail, sculpture and other decorative arts, music, and liturgy combined as integral parts of the complete architectonic design. The nave and transepts were designed as a resonant hall for the chant, just as the tympanum over the entrance portal and the semidomed interior of the apse were the settings for sculptural and painted mural embellishments. The sculptural representations of plainsong on the ambulatory capitals in the Third Abbey Church at Cluny show a union of music and sculpture, while their inscriptions add a literary dimension. All the arts converge into the unified structure of the liturgy, since all were created in the monastic concept for service in the glorification of God.

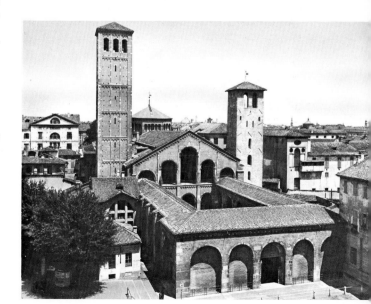

126. Sant' Ambrogio, Milan (view from west). c. 1181. Length, including atrium, 390'; width 92'.

# 7 The Feudal Romanesque Style

## THE NORMAN CONQUEST AND THE BAYEUX TAPESTRY

While a monastery was a haven of peace, a feudal manor was an armed fortress. While the cloistered brothers were laying up treasures in heaven, the feudal lords were garnering theirs on earth. And while the monk was a man of prayer, the landed baron was a man of war.

Surviving examples of secular art from the Romanesque period are so rare that each is practically unique. The treasures of a monastery or cathedral were under the watchful eye of the clergy, and religious restraints against raiding Church property usually were strong enough to prevent wanton destruction. The same cannot be said for secular prop-

urban dwellings remain, such as those at Cluny (Fig. 129). Their arched doorways facing the street sometimes were decorated by sculptured hunting scenes or representations of an artisan's trade—a cobbler bending over his workbench, for example, or a merchant showing cloth to a client. Of interior decorations—mural paintings, wall hangings, furniture, and the like—almost nothing is left. And, since poetry and music were intended to be heard rather than read by these feudal people, little of either was written down.

History, however, is filled with accidents, and by coincidence a single large-scale example of secular pictorial art survives because it was designed for a church instead of a castle. The only French epic poem before the Crusades owes its present existence to the hand of some monastic scribe who happened to write

left: 127. Imperial Palace at Goslar, Lower Saxony, Germany. Begun 1043, rebuilt 1132. Chapel of St. Ulrich (far left), 11th century.

below: 130. *Harold Swearing Oath*, detail of Bayeux Tapestry. c. 1073–88. Wool embroidery on linen, height 20″, whole length 231′. Town Hall, Bayeux.

erty. Feudal castles constantly were subject to siege, and those that survived frequently were remodeled in later centuries with the changing fortunes of their successive owners. Among the best preserved of these Romanesque residences are the Imperial Palace near Goslar, Germany (Fig. 127); the Wartburg Castle, where Tannhäuser's famous songfest took place; and parts of the Palace of the Normans in Sicily, notably the Dining Hall of Roger II, with its emblematic animals and symbols of feudal heraldry (Fig. 128).

Towns did grow up in the protective shadows of a castle, a monastery, or a cathedral, but only a few

114

it down either for some minstrel with a poor memory or because he wanted to preserve it after it had ceased to be sung. The one authentic melody to which such poetry was chanted is extant because it was included as a jest in a 13th-century musical play. And the keep, or fortress, that William the Conqueror constructed in London is still intact partly because of its later usefulness as a royal residence and prison and possibly because it housed an important chapel.

The most complete example of pictorial art is the so-called "Bayeux Tapestry," one of the most eloquent documents of this or any other time. Here, in visual form, is the story of the conquest of England by William the Conqueror recounted from the Norman point of view, in the course of which a vivid picture of the life and attitudes of feudal man unfolds. The term *tapestry* is a misnomer, justified in this case because of its function as a wall hanging. Since the design is applied in woolen yarn to a coarse linen surface rather than woven into the cloth itself, it is more accurately described as an embroidery. Such cloth decorations were used to cover the bare stone walls of castles, but in this case the extraordinary dimen-

sions—20 inches wide and 231 feet long—and possession over the centuries by Bayeux Cathedral indicate that this tapestry or embroidery was intended to cover the plain strip of masonry over the nave arcade of that building. It was probably the product of one of the renowned English embroidery workshops and apparently was completed about 20 years after the great battle it describes. The central figure is, of course, William the Conqueror, who indelibly stamped his powerful personality on the north European scene throughout the latter half of the 11th cen-

# CHRONOLOGY / Feudal Romanesque Period

tury. The span of time is from the closing months of the reign of Edward the Confessor to that fateful day in 1066 when the Conqueror made good his claim to the throne by putting the English forces to rout at the Battle of Hastings.

The Bayeux Tapestry, in its surviving state, is divided into 79 panels, or scenes. The first part (panels 1–34) is concerned with William's reception of Harold, an English duke, whose mission to Normandy ostensibly was to tell William that he would succeed Edward the Confessor as king of England. In one of these scenes, William and Harold are seen at Bayeux (Fig. 130), *where Harold took an oath to Duke William.* (The italics here and later are literal translations of the Latin inscriptions that run along the top of the Tapestry above the scenes they describe.) Placing his hands on the reliquaries that repose on the two altars, Harold apparently swears to uphold William's claim, although the exact nature of the oath is left vague. This is, however, the episode that later became the justification for the English campaign— because Harold, false to his supposed sworn word,

had had himself crowned king. In these early panels, in the upper and lower borders, a running commentary on the action continues a tradition begun in manuscript illuminations. Here the commentary is in the form of animal figures that were familiar to the people of the time from bestiaries and sculpture and the allusion is to certain fables of Aesop. The choice of the fox and crow, the wolf and stork, and the ewe, goat, and cow in the presence of the lion all have to do with treachery and violence and serve to point out the perfidious character of Harold.

William is seated serenely on his ducal throne, foreshadowing his future dignity as king. The scene, furthermore, actually is located in Bayeux Cathedral, the exterior of which is shown in the curious representation to the left of the seated William. Bayeux's bishop was none other than Odo, William's half brother, who in all probability commissioned the tapestry. Odo possibly intended that the tapestry be exhibited each year on the anniversary of William's conquest, and thus forever to commemorate the glory of that occasion—and, of course, the bravery of the bishop and builder of the church.

The main course of the action in the Bayeux Tapestry moves like the words on a painted page—that is, from left to right. At times, however, it was necessary to represent a pertinent episode apart from the principal action, whereupon the pictorial narrator simply reversed the usual order and moved his scene from right to left, thus, in effect, achieving a kind of visual parenthesis and avoiding any confusion with the flow of the main story. Such a reversal is employed in the scene depicting the death and burial of the Confessor (Fig. 131). On the right near the top is *King Edward in his bed* as he *addresses his faithful retainers.* On one side of him is a priest; Harold is on the other; while the queen and her lady-in-waiting are mourning at the foot of the bed. Below, under the words *here he has died,* the body is being prepared for the last rites. Moving toward the left, the funeral procession approaches *the church of St. Peter the Apostle,* the Romanesque predecessor of Westminster Abbey in London, which Edward had built and dedicated but ten years before, while the hand of God descends in blessing. The procession includes monks reading prayers and two acolytes ringing the funeral bells.

**132.** Oseberg Burial Ship. c. 825. Wood. University Museum of Antiquities, Oslo.

When William received word that Harold had been crowned, he immediately determined on invasion, and the second part of the Tapestry (panels 35–53) is concerned with the preparations for his revenge up to the eve of the battle. After all was in readiness, he set sail. The ships seen in the Tapestry are similar to those in which William's restless Viking ancestors invaded the French coast two centuries before (Fig. 132), and it was in just such ships that Leif Eriksen and his fellow mariners apparently reached the eastern coast of North America earlier in the same century.

After the landing, the grand finale begins with the assembling of forces for the great battle (panels 54–79). The Norman side has both archers on foot and knights on horseback, while the English fight in a solid phalanx with immense battleaxes, small spears, and clubs with stone heads. The Normans move in from left to right and the English from the opposite direction. The climax of the battle is reached in a wild scene at a ravine, where men and horses are tumbling about while the *English and French fall together in battle.*

**131.** *Death and Burial of Edward the Confessor,* detail of Bayeux Tapestry.

Shortly after, Harold is killed, and the fighting concludes with the *English turned in flight*. The lower border in these scenes spares none of the horrors of warfare; dismembered limbs are strewn about, scavengers strip coats of mail from the bodies of the fallen, and naked corpses are left on the field.

The design of the Bayeux Tapestry is dominantly linear and, like the illuminated manuscripts of the time, is rendered in two dimensions with no suggestion of spatial depth. The coarseness of the linen and the thickness of the wool, however, create interesting textural contrasts. The eight shades of woolen yarn—three blues, light and dark green, red, buff yellow, and gray—make for a vivid feeling of color, which is not used for natural representation but to enliven the design. Some men have blue hair, others green, and horses often have two blue and two red legs. Faces are merely outlined, though some attempt at portraiture is made in the various likenesses of William (Pl. 13, p. 125). Details, such as costumes, armor, mode of combat, and the deployment of troops in battle, however, are done with great accuracy. For this reason, the Tapestry is a never-ending source of amazement and one of the most important historical documents on the manner of life in the 11th century—so much so that its historical value is often allowed to overshadow its quality as a work of art. Admittedly crude and at times naïve, the Bayeux Tapestry does not elaborate details, for it concentrates on telling its story, and the sweeping effect of the whole takes precedence over any of its parts.

The Bayeux Tapestry is a thing of infinite variety. In the handling of the narration, after a slow beginning with frequent digressions, the designer went on in the middle panels to the rather feverish preparations that culminated in the breathless climax of the battle. In both tempo and organization, the Tapestry can stand comparison with the best works in narrative form, visual or verbal. The details, whether in the main panels or in the upper or lower borders, are handled so imaginatively that they not only embellish the design but add visual accents, comment on the action, and further the flow of the plot. Scenes are separated one from another by buildings that figure in the story and by such devices as the stylized trees that are mere conventions. So skillfully are these arranged that the continuity of the whole is never impeded, and the observer is hardly aware of their presence. All in all, a successful work of art designed for such a long and narrow space is a feat of visual virtuosity of no small order, and it leaves no doubt that it is the product of a master designer.

## SONG OF ROLAND

A *chanson de geste* is a "song of deeds," an action story in poetic form sung by a minstrel to the accompaniment of a viol or lyre, an epic poem in Old French, the medieval vernacular language of France, rather than in Latin. The *Chanson de Roland,* or *"Song of Roland,"* is narrated in an abrupt, direct manner, and transitions between episodes are sudden and unprepared. A martial atmosphere surrounds the characters, including the fighting Archbishop Turpin as well as the Archangels Gabriel and Michael who, like the Valkyries in the German epic *Song of the Nibelungs,* swoop down on the battlefield to bear the souls of fallen warriors to heaven. Though nominally set in an earlier time, the *Song of Roland* is, both in form and spirit, the product of the warlike feudalistic 11th century, and various chroniclers mention it in connection with the Battle of Hastings. Guy of Amiens, one of William and Matilda's courtiers, who died ten years after the battle, was the author of a Latin poem about a jongleur by the name of Taillefer. This "minstrel whom a very brave heart ennobled," Guy relates, led William's forces into the battle throwing his sword in the air, catching it again, and singing a Song of Roland. William of Malmesbury, writing about fifty years after the battle, tells that William began the *Song of Roland,* "in order that the warlike example of that hero might stimulate soldiers."

Taillefer, in the age-old tradition of minstrelsy, was a mime and singing actor, and his rendition of the epic was undoubtedly accompanied by skillful vocal declamation as well as with appropriate gestures and action.

The *Song of Roland* is thus a direct-action story, set in the time of Charlemagne and relating incidents from the campaign in northern Spain where that Emperor had been battling the pagan Saracens for seven long years. Roland, Charlemagne's favorite nephew, and the twelve peers, flower of French knighthood, had been left in charge of the rear guard, while Charles and the main body of the army were crossing the Pyrenees back into France. Betrayed by a false kinsman, strongly paralleling the episode of William and Harold in the Bayeux Tapestry, Roland is attacked near Roncevals by overwhelming pagan forces. The rear guard is cut to pieces, and Roland, before dying a hero's death, sounds his ivory horn summoning his uncle and his army from afar.

The third part of the poem has to do with the vengeance of Charlemagne, just as the corresponding section of the Bayeux Tapestry related that of William. All is action and heroism, with swords flashing, helmets gleaming, drums beating, horns blowing, banners snapping, and steeds prancing. The battle unfolds in what amounts to a blow-by-blow account, echoing frequently with such phrases as "wondrous and fierce is the battle." (Quotations are from Isabel Butler's translation, published by Houghton Mifflin, 1904.) First one hears of the preparations in the camp of Charles. The poet, using a cumulative technique, describes the ten battalions one by one. Knight is added to knight, battle group to battle group, weapon to weapon, in order to build up the full monumentality of the occasion in the listeners' minds and imaginations. All the forces of Western Christendom are eventually drawn up on Charlemagne's side—the French, Normans, Bavarians, Germans, Bretons, and so on. The virtues of the men invariably are those of bravery, valiance, and hardiness; they have no fear of death; never do they flee the battlefield; and their horses are swift and good.

Then quite suddenly and without any transition we are in the midst of the pagan hordes. Ten Saracen battalions are described, and in order to show how the Christians were outnumbered, still another ten is added. The fearsomeness of the enemy, however, is not owed to numbers alone but to their ferocious character. The only admirable quality allowed them is that of being good fighters; otherwise they are hideous to behold, fierce and cruel, and love evil. Yet in spite of this they "ride on like goodly warriors." The physical appearance of the people from these strange parts is fantastically exaggerated. The men of Milciani, for instance, "have huge heads, and along the spine of their backs grow bristles like those of a wild boar." Of the warriors from the desert of Occiant, it is said that "their skins are hard like iron, wherefore they have no need of hauberks or helms [coats of mail and helmets]." Later, during the battle, these same men of Occiant "bray and neigh, and the men of Arguille yelp like dogs." Their religious life is just as much misunderstood as their appearance. The pagans are represented as polytheists who worship as strange an assortment of gods as was ever assembled—Apollo, Tervagant, and Mohamet. When things are not going well from their point of view, they upbraid these gods, take the statue of Apollo and "trod him under their feet"; Tervagant is robbed of his carbuncle; and Mohamet is cast "into a ditch, for the dogs and the pigs to worry and gnaw." Later, when Marsila, the king of Spain, dies, the listener hears that "eager devils seize upon his soul." Such description could not have been written after the Crusades had brought Western warriors into contact with Moslem culture, and so, like the foreigners depicted on the Vézelay tympanum (Fig. 116), the imagery is filled with naïve wonder.

With the lines of battle thus drawn, the setting is described in a single line: "Vast is the plain and wide the fields." Then as the conflict begins, battalion falls on battalion, hewing and hacking, Christian knights hurtle against pagan knights the whole day until the battle is reduced to a personal encounter between Charlemagne and his opposite, Baligant the Amiral (admiral). "He smites the Amiral with the sword of France, shatters the helmet which shines with precious stones, carves through the skull that the brains run out, and through the face even to the white beard, that the Amiral falls dead beyond all help." After this, the pagans flee and the day is won.

The lines of the original Old French proceed according to a rhyming scheme of crude assonance in which the final syllables of each line correspond roughly in sound. The last words of each line of one of the strophes will suffice to illustrate this principle of assonance: *magne, Espaigne, altaigne, remaigne, fraindre, muntaigne, m'enaimet, reclaimet, ataignet.* Much of the direct character and rugged strength of the poem is attributable to rigid avoidance of embellishment. This is observable in such minute details as the forward motion within such single lines as: *So sent Rollanz de tun tens ni ad plus.* Nothing is allowed to impede the progress of these sturdy military monosyllables. So consistently is this carried out all along the line that it even extends to the delineation of the characters themselves. Each is the embodiment of a single ideal and human type: Ganelon is all treachery and hatred; Roland, bravery to the point of rashness; Oliver, reason and caution; and Charles, preeminent in his solitary grandeur, represents the majesty of both Church and state. Through each one of these devices separately and through all of them cumulatively, the poem as a whole rises to the heights of epic art. Its language, style, and form thus well become the brave deeds of the heroic men with whom its narrative is concerned.

## THE ART OF MINSTRELSY

"A verse without music is a mill without water," said Folquet of Marseilles, the troubadour whom Dante immortalized in his *Paradise.* Poetry in medieval times was a popular art form in which verses were chanted by a *jongleur,* or "minstrel," to the accompaniment of a viol or lyre. No festive occasion was complete without a minstrel who sang *chansons de geste,* lays, and romances, told tales and fables, played on a variety of musical instruments, performed dances, and astonished his audience with juggling and sleight-of-hand tricks.

Records of these jongleurs go back many centuries. It is known that jongleurs convened at Fécamp in Normandy in the year 1000 and that they met together regularly during the slack season of Lent, when the Church forbade their public performances, to learn one another's tricks and techniques, and increase their repertories with new tales and songs. A lively account of their place in medieval society is contained in a description of a wedding feast in Provence, which says: "Then the *joglars* stood up, each one anxious to make himself heard; then you could hear instruments resounding in many a key . . . . One played the Lay of the Honeysuckle, another that of Tintagel, another that of the Faithful Lovers, another the lay that Ivan made. . . . Everyone performed at his best and the noise of the instrumentalists and the voices of the narrators made a considerable uproar in the hall."

*Chanson de geste* melody (11th century) — ADAM DE LA HALLE (after Gennrich)

Au - di - gier, dit Raim - ber - ge, bou - se vous di.

*Aucassin et Nicolette,* strophe or *laisse* (13th century) — ADAM DE LA HALLE (after Gennrich)

Qui vau - roit bons vers o - ir _ del de -
de deus biax en - fans pe - tis _ Ni - co -

port du duel cai - tif
le - te Au cas - sins...

The jongleurs of the 11th century were not of noble birth as were most of the later troubadours, *trouvères,* and *minnesingers,* but they were welcomed in every castle and abbey. Under the patronage of the feudal nobility, lyrical music was to bloom in the 12th and 13th centuries into the full-fledged art of the troubadours, trouvères, and minnesingers. Courtly tournaments, brave knights winning fair ladies, and aristocratic poets making music with minstrels enlivened the nobles' entertainments in the Gothic period (Pl. 14, p. 125). The practice of holding songfests also began at this time.

Since the 11th-century secular music forms were just emerging, the models and prototypes undoubtedly were derived from certain formulas for church music. The simple repetitive melodies of the *chansons de geste,* together with the assonated verses and insistent rhythms of the poetry, had much in common with the litany—though, of course, the subject matter differed radically. It is greatly to be regretted that the musical setting of the *Song of Roland* has not been preserved. While jongleurs could refresh their memories of longer epics from the manuscripts they carried in the leather pouches that they wore, these manuscripts included no musical parts. Hence we assume that the melodies were so simple there was no need to write them down.

The music of the *chansons de geste,* according to medieval sources, consisted of a short melody with one note to a syllable, repeated over and over for each verse in the manner of a litany or folk song. At the end of each strophe, or group of lines, was a melodic appendage, which served as a refrain much like the alleluias between the verses of psalms and hymns. In the manuscript of the *Chanson de Roland* the enigmatic letters AOI appear after each of the 321 strophes, while in the songs of troubadours and minnesingers the letters are EUOUAE or some variant. EUOUAE is an abbreviation of the last two words of the lesser Doxology, *sa-e-c-u-lor-u-m a-m-e-n,* and thus is a link between the troubadour's refrain and a Gregorian melody. The AOI in the *Song of Roland* manuscript possibly refers to some similar liturgical cadence formula now lost. If so, either it refers to a repeated vocal cadenza at the end of each strophe, a kind of punctuation mark for the ear to relieve the audience's attention momentarily from the words (as with the "Fa la la's" of Renaissance madrigals), or it indicates a place where a short instrumental interlude was performed on the viol or lyre. Whatever the explanation, the focus of attention in these epics was on the words of the poem, and the musical element was subordinate. In the closing formula, however, the purely musical element could have come to the fore with whatever special effects the jongleur could command.

The single authentic example of a *chanson de geste* melody that survives is found in a little pastoral play from the 13th century by Adam de la Halle, where it is quoted humorously by one of the characters (above left). The two halves of this melody are repeated one for each line of the strophe, following which there would have been a short cadenza or refrain for either the voice or an instrument. The operation of this refrain principle is found in a song from *Aucassin et Nicolette,* a French *chante-fable* (above left). Written about a century later, it is similar in style to that of the *chanson de geste.* The melody of the first eight measures is sung for each line of the strophe, each time to different words. The refrain in the final three bars is then either sung or played between each of the verses and again at the end. The extreme simplicity of these melodies indicates that the music alone would not have held an audience. The dominant interest was epic poetry, and the minstrel's performance of it with appropriate action, gestures, and vocal inflection.

## NORMAN ARCHITECTURE

The architecture of the Normans was sufficiently important to give one aspect of the Romanesque style the name of Norman. The building done in 11th-century Normandy not only had a lasting effect on that region of France but also reached a logical conclusion in the keeps, castles, abbeys, and cathedrals that the Normans later built in England. Since the Romanesque style in England dates from the Conquest, it is still referred to there as the Norman style.

Norman architecture, like many other facets of Norman culture, resulted from the union of the rugged pagan spirit of the Vikings and the Gallic Christian remnants of the disintegrated Carolingian empire. As a representative product of these people, their architecture reflects blunt strength and forthright character. Both the Carolingian and Viking societies were nomadic. Charlemagne and his successors as well as the dukes of Normandy down to William's time frequently shifted their residences, and the insecurity of the times discouraged building in general. But as the feudal system reached its mature stage and a more settled order became possible, the Norman conquerors turned to the assimilation and development of the vast new lands they had acquired instead of seeking further conquests. William's policy thus shifted from offensive to defensive. Earlier he had discouraged the construction of castles and sanctioned only monasteries; now he proposed to impress his new subjects with solid and impregnable fortresses as well as feats of sword on the field of battle.

The Tower of London (Fig. 133), or more specifically the White Tower (Fig. 134), was begun by the Conqueror about 1078 and finished by his successor in order to defend and dominate the town. Its form was that of a Norman keep, and as such it was something new to England. The Tower is simply a massive, square, compact stone building, divided into four stories which rise 92 feet with a turret at each corner. A glance at the plan (Fig. 135) will show some of its many irregularities. Its four sides, for instance, are unequal in length, and its corners are therefore not right angles; three of its turrets are square, while one is round; the one on the west rises 107 feet, while that on the south is 118 feet high; the walls vary from 11 to 15 feet in thickness; and the interior is divided from top to bottom in two unequal parts by a wall running from north to south.

The barrenness of its exterior was well suited to the White Tower's function as a fortress, but the austerity of the interior was a commentary on the bleakness and general lack of physical comforts of medieval life. The tower was divided into four stories by means of wooden floors, and its darkness was relieved only by narrow, slitted, glassless windows, which were more important as launching sites for arrows against an enemy than as sources of light and ventilation. After Norman times, other buildings were added until the whole became a concentric system of fortifications with the old Norman keep as its heart.

above left: **133.** Tower of London (aerial view). 1078–90.

above right: **134.** White Tower, London. c. 1081–90. Height 92'.

left: **135.** Plan of Tower of London.

From William's time to the present, the Tower has been in continuous use as fortress, palace, or prison.

The main floor of the White Tower has three divisions: a large council chamber, which also doubled as a banqueting hall, a smaller presence chamber, and the well-preserved St. John's Chapel (Fig. 136). Like a miniature church, this chapel has a barrel-vaulted nave of four bays, with aisles on either side that command interest because of their early use of cross vaulting. The columns of the nave arcade are thick

**136.** St. John's Chapel, Tower of London. 1078–97.

far left: 137. Façade, St. Étienne (Abbaye-aux-Hommes), Caen. c. 1064–1135. Nave 157½' × 32'10", height of towers, 295'.

left: 138. Interior, St. Étienne, Caen.

and stubby, and the cushionlike capitals have only the most rudimentary scalloped carving by way of decoration. Above is a triforium gallery, which was used by the queen and her ladies, with slitlike windows that serve as a clearstory.

At Caen in Normandy, two buildings were under the personal protection of William and Queen Matilda and designated as their respective burial places —St. Étienne, or Abbaye-aux-Hommes (Fig. 137), and Ste. Trinité, or Abbaye-aux-Dames. Since both were abbey churches, they properly belong in a discussion of the monastic Romanesque style, but here they serve to complete the picture of the Norman style. Begun just prior to the conquest, St. Étienne has a well-proportioned west façade. Four prominent buttresses divide the section below the towers into three parts that correspond to the central nave and two side aisles of the interior. Vertically, the façade rises in three stories, with the portals matching the level of the nave arcade inside, while the two rows of windows above are at the triforium and clearstory levels, respectively. The windows are mere openings and in themselves are quite undistinguished. But the functional honesty in this correspondence of exterior design and interior plan was a Norman innovation that came into general use in the Gothic period.

The twin towers belong to the original design, but their spires are later additions. As with the usual Norman church, the towers are square and in three stories, thus repeating on a higher level the triple division of the façade below. The first story is of solid masonry; the second has alternate blind and open arches; while the greater open space of the third facilitates its function as a belfry and relieves the general heaviness. Otherwise the austerity and ponderous-

ness of the façade in general is a fitting prelude to the gloomy grandeur of the interior (Fig. 138). The church as a whole is as thoroughly rugged and masculine in character as its founder and typifies the spirit of the Norman people and their forceful leader.

When the barren façade of St. Étienne is compared to the exterior of the Tower of London, it becomes apparent that the lack of decoration was a conscious part of the design. One façade impresses by its bold outlines, sturdiness, and straightforward honesty, and the other by its sheer strength and bluntness. Though it was to be replaced soon after the Crusades by Saracenic innovations, the Norman accent on structure rather than embellishment did, however, lead to advances in the art of building. In their churches, the Normans achieved more adequate lighting than in previous Romanesque structures by increasing the space allotted to the clearstory, and more unified interiors by connecting the three levels of the nave arcade, triforium, and clearstory by single vertical shafts between the bays that run from floor to ceiling. Both these features, as well as the harmonious spatial divisions of such a façade as that of St. Étienne, were later incorporated into the Gothic style. Still, when the work of the Normans is placed alongside that of their more skillful Burgundian contemporaries, it seems crude by comparison. The Normans were as blunt and brash as the Cluniacs were ingenious and subtle. The difference, in short, is that between men of action and men of contemplation.

## IDEAS: FEUDALISM

The Bayeux Tapestry, the *Song of Roland*, the abbey churches at Caen, and the White Tower in London are representative examples of the Romanesque style and related in time, place, and content. Each was a high point in the development of Norman culture, falling between the dates of the Battle of Hastings in 1066 and the First Crusade in 1096. The *Song* was sung at the battle; the Tapestry was designed soon after the battle whose tale it tells (and both evidence the same form and spirit); and the building of the abbey churches and tower came with the zenith of William's success and prosperity after the conquest. This relationship coincided with the climax of feudalism, and it is in the terms of this all-embracing concept that the individual works have their unity.

All the separate concepts of the Norman world were contained in the overpowering central idea of feudalism. Like the concentric rings of the inner and outer fortifications of the Tower of London (Fig. 133), individuals in a feudal society were but tiny circles in an expanding cosmic scheme of things that determined their relations to their superiors, their peers, and their inferiors. It was a social system modeled on that of an army; and the ethic that bound the whole together was fealty, a kind of blind loyalty, with right and wrong being fixed by physical force rather than by reason and principle. The feudal system provided a proper place for every man in a strict hierarchy, with barons holding their power from their overlords, ecclesiastical or secular; dukes holding their realms from their king; and the king, emperor, and pope holding the earth as a fief from God.

The feudal virtues were faith, courage, and blind loyalty to peer and superior; any departure from this code was treachery and was dealt with by isolation and defeat. Defection had to be decided on the field of battle, with God awarding victory to the righteous cause. Enemies, however, provided their lineage was in order and their family trees properly pruned, were accorded the distinctions of honor and bravery; otherwise it would have been socially impossible to do battle with them. In the *Song of Roland* and in the Bayeux Tapestry, no one below the rank of baron figures with any degree of prominence; similarly, the abbeys of William and Matilda were intended primarily for persons of rank, and by their foundation the royal pair pledged their feudal oath to God.

In their subject matter, the *Song of Roland* and the Bayeux Tapestry have many points in common. As the song opens: "Charles the King . . . has conquered all the high land down to the sea; not a castle holds out against him, not a wall or city is left unshattered, save Saragossa, which stands on a high mountain. King Marsila holds it, who loves not God, but serves Mahound, and worships Apollon; ill hap must in sooth befall him." If the simple substitution of William for Charles, England for Saragossa in Spain, the barrier of the sea for that of the mountain, and Harold for Marsila is made, the situation becomes the contemporary one that the Tapestry so vividly portrays.

Later at the battle of Roncevals the dominant trio is Roland, Oliver, and the fighting Archbishop Turpin, in whom it is not difficult to recognize their parallels at Hastings: William and his half brothers Robert of Mortain and the irrepressible Bishop Odo.

In both *Song* and Tapestry, the cause for war ostensibly was religious. In one, it was Christianity versus paganism; in the other, the breaking of a sacred oath when Harold became king—and both causes were sanctioned by the pope. Again, in both, the enemy in the best feudal tradition was a worthy adversary, noble and brave but religiously misguided. In the *Song of Roland,* Marsila was crafty but at all times observed the rules of feudal warfare. The glory of Charlemagne's major pagan adversary, with his silks from Alexandria, gold of Arabia, carbuncle-studded sword, and bright gonfalons, is described in poetic language, just as Harold's knightly qualities are pictured repeatedly in visual form. In both, religious symbols figure prominently. Durendal, Roland's sword, is his most sacred possession, having within it a tooth of St. Peter, blood of St. Basil, hair of St. Denis, and a fragment of the Virgin's robe—all souvenirs of his pilgrimage to the Holy Land. At this time, relics had overwhelming importance. In the Tapestry, Harold's seizure of the kingly power was treacherous mainly because the oath had been sworn on the reliquaries in Bayeux Cathedral. Harold's perjury and breaking of a vow sworn under such sacrosanct conditions was sufficient cause for invasion.

Religious conviction is absolute in both *Song* and Tapestry. Such a sweeping statement as "Wrong the pagans, right the Christians are" leaves no room for lingering philosophical or theological doubts on the validity of the cause. In each, the importance and glorification of sheer strength and prowess at arms are apparent from the descriptive details of costume, armor, and weapons, which are dwelt upon with obvious pride. Both Tapestry and poem are set in a man's world on clear-cut loyalties and moral and physical certainties. The chivalry in each is based on the ways of fighting men. The code of Roland and Oliver, and of William and Odo, was clearly that of "My soul to God, my life to the king, and honor for myself." It remained for the Gothic period to add: "My heart to the ladies." Roland's dying thoughts, for instance, are occupied with his family and lineage; his king, the great Charles; his country, the fair land of France; and his sword, Durendal. Significantly, he makes no mention of his betrothed, the Lady Aude. Earlier, the exasperated Oliver had reproached Roland for his rashness in not summoning aid sooner, and at that time he swore: "By this my beard, and I again see my sister, Aude the Fair, never shalt thou lie in her arms." No true or courtly love is this, only the feudal baron bestowing his female relatives like his goods and chattels on those whose faith and courage he has cause to admire. Later, after Charles returns to France, the poor Lady Aude inquires about the fate of her fiancé. The King tells her of his death and as a consolation prize offers her the hand of his son Louis, whereupon the lady expires at his feet. Whether she dies of grief for Roland or from the indelicacy of Charlemagne's suggestion is left open to conjecture. Since scarcely more than a dozen of the 4,000-odd lines of the poem are devoted to her, Henry Adams was well justified in his observation: "Never after the first crusade did any great poem rise to such heroism as to sustain itself without a heroine." Curiously enough, on the Saracen side Marsila's queen takes an important part in the affairs of state after her husband is incapacitated, while nowhere on the Christian side is a woman accorded anything like a similar status. And in the Bayeux Tapestry, the only place where a woman is mentioned by name is the enigmatic inscription *Where a cleric and Aelfgyva,* apparently introduced to give a motive for the minor episode describing an invasion of Brittany. While a few female figures are found in the borders and in attendance at the death of the Confessor, none figures with any prominence. Both works are thus as bold and direct as the poetry and art of the coming Gothic period was delicate and subtle. Roland and his counterparts in the Tapestry fought the good fight for king and country, while the knightly heroes of the later period entered the lists for a loving glance from a pair of blue eyes, the fleeting smile on fair lips, or the fragrant roses tossed from a lady's bower.

Formal considerations of the *Song of Roland* and the Bayeux Tapestry are in keeping with their rugged character. The emphasis everywhere is on the concrete rather than the abstract, content rather than form, and narrative sequence over structure. The telling of the tale in both cases is almost completely unencumbered with either literary or visual flourishes. Just as deeds take precedence over poetic form in the *Chanson,* the narrative element in the Bayeux Tapestry is more important than the decorative detail. Every part of the Tapestry has some direct bearing on the story, and the action in the poem is so direct that it contains hardly a single figure of speech. In both, the attributes are fixed. In the Tapestry, the English always have moustaches and the Normans are clean-shaven. In the poem, kings are always mighty no matter what side they may be on, and knights are invariably brave whatever their allegiance may be. Similarly, in the sculpture of the period, kings always wear crowns, even if they are in bed, apostles always have bare feet, and so on.

Symmetry seldom is considered. The lines of the poem, for example, are rough-hewn but heroic pentameters, which group themselves into irregular strophes averaging fourteen lines in length. Similarly, the space given to individual scenes in the Bayeux Tapestry, like the size of the compartments in the archivolt of the Vézelay tympanum (Fig. 116) and the unequal height of the arches in a Romanesque cathedral wall, is disproportionate and asymmetrical.

Details in the *Chanson,* the Tapestry, St. Étienne, and the Tower of London thus remain crude and unpolished. The Romanesque in general and the Norman period in particular were an era of forming, building, experimenting, and reaching out toward new modes of expression rather than a time of crystallization, polished expression, and ultimate arrival. In architecture, the process of building was more important than what was built. The emphasis given in the Tapestry to representations of castles, fortifications, and specific buildings, such as Westminster Abbey and the abbey churches at Caen, suggests the image of a builder's world and a century of architectural activity and progress. The forthright and direct narration of deeds in the *Song* and Tapestry finds its architectural counterpart in the functional honesty of the style of the Tower and William's church at Caen. Just as the direct-action story of the *Chanson* and Tapestry takes precedence over literary form and decorative flourish, so the structural honesty of the building process, as exemplified in the Tower and St. Étienne, becomes the leading characteristic. The process of lengthening balladic poetry into the epic form of the *chanson de geste* capable of sustaining attention through the long Norman winter evenings or of extending a few pictorial panels into the heroic completeness of a tapestry depicting a major historical episode in its entirety was essentially the same as the process of piling up tall towers capable of piercing the gloomy northern skies.

The image of the Norman world as it thus builds up through the various arts is not essentially a complex one. There was little of the mystical about these clearheaded Viking adventurers. They caught on with alacrity to any progressive development of the time, whether it was the discarding of their rather inflexible mother tongue in favor of the more supple French or the adopting of many of the Cluniac moral and architectural reforms. A good example of their forthrightness is seen in the Bayeux Tapestry, where who a figure is and what he is doing are documented exactly with name and place. Whatever the Normans did, they did always with characteristic determination and energy. Thus the rugged man of action in William unites with the military monosyllables of the *Chanson,* the frank, almost comic-strip directness of the Bayeux Tapestry, and the rough-hewn stones of the tower and abbeys to make a single monolithic structure. Each was concerned with forms of action, and whether in picture, word, or stone, the epical spirit is present. Deed on deed, syllable on syllable, stitch on stitch, image on image, stone on stone—each builds up into the great personality, heroic epic, impressive Tapestry or gaunt tower, and in the process reveals a Norman feudal structure of truly monumental proportions.

**above: Plate 13.** *William's Feast,* detail of Bayeux Tapestry. c. 1073–88. Wool embroidery on linen; height 20″, whole length 321′. Town Hall, Bayeux. (See p. 118.)

**left: Plate 14.** *Heinrich Frauenlob Directing Minstrel Performance.* 14th century. Manesse Manuscript of German Minnesingers. Heidelberg Library. (See p. 120.)

left: Plate 15. North clearstory wall of nave, Chartres Cathedral. c. 1194–1260. (See p. 132.)

below: Plate 16. *Blanche of Castile and St. Louis,* from *Moralized Apocalypse.* c. 1226–34. Illuminated manuscript. Pierpont Morgan Library, New York. (See p. 134.)

# 8 The Gothic Style

## ILE-DE-FRANCE, LATE 12TH AND 13TH CENTURIES

In contrast to the shores of the Mediterranean, where such resplendent centers of culture as Athens, Alexandria, Antioch, Constantinople, and Rome flourished for centuries, northern Europe had been little more than a rural region with a few Roman provincial outposts and, later, a scattering of castles, monasteries, and villages. Before the 13th century not one medieval center north of the Alps could properly have been described as a city. Toward the end of the 12th century, however, Philip Augustus as king of France was promoting the destiny of Paris as his capital, enclosing it with walls and paving some of its streets with stone. The work was continued under his successors, and by the end of the 13th century Paris was the capital of a kingdom of growing importance. With its splendid Cathedral of Notre Dame, its university famed for the teaching of Abelard, Albertus Magnus, Thomas Aquinas, and Bonaventura, and with its flourishing mercantile trade capable of supporting about 150,000 inhabitants, Paris could well claim the status of a capital city. When it is remembered, however, that Constantinople was the hub of the rich East Roman Empire and had been a city of over 1,000,000 since Justinian's time, the status of this first transalpine urban center is seen in proper perspective.

The growth of Paris, while more rapid than other northern centers, was far from an isolated instance. For a full century, the town as a social unit had been gaining ascendancy over the manorial estate, and the literature of the time mentions Ghent with its turreted houses, Lille and its cloth, Tours and its grain, and how all were carrying on commerce with distant lands. With the exception of such occasional references, however, the life of medieval French towns would have remained a closed book had it not been for the visual record preserved in the castles of their feudal lords, in the monasteries, and, above all, in the cathedrals.

The prototype of the Gothic cathedral has been recognized in the Abbey Church of St. Denis just outside Paris. This monastery was under the direct patronage of the French kings and was their traditional burial place. Around the middle of the 12th century its abbot was Suger, a man whose talents were as remarkable as his origin was obscure. The

trusted confidant of two kings, he ruled France as regent while Louis VII was away on a Crusade, and when he undertook the rebuilding of his abbey church, his great personal prestige, as well as its importance as the royal monastery, enabled him to call together the most expert craftsmen from all parts of the kingdom. Suger's church thus became a synthesis of all the ideas that had been tried and found successful by the Romanesque builders. Posterity has had reason to rejoice that the abbot's enthusiasm for his project caused him to write extensively about it, and his book is an invaluable source of information about the architectural thought of the time. In 1130, when St. Denis was in the planning stage, as was mentioned, Abbot Suger had made a prolonged visit to Cluny to learn from first-hand observation about its recently completed church. His commentary on the iconography of St. Denis' windows and sculpture suggests that he took a personal hand in this part of the project, but of the architect who carried out the building no mention is made. St. Denis is notable not so much for its innovations as for its successful combining of such late Romanesque devices as the pointed arch and ribbed groin vault.

Many late Cluniac Romanesque churches had used these features separately, but not before Suger's church had they been grouped into a coherent structural system, and the abbot's position at the French court, as well as the proximity of his church to Paris, assured the widest possible currency of his ideas. Hence, St. Denis became the model for many of the Gothic cathedrals that were built in the region shortly afterward.

The Île-de-France, the royal domain with Paris as its center, was the setting in which the Gothic style originated and where, over a period extending approximately from 1150 to 1300, it reached the climax of its development. The name of this region referred to the royal lands under the direct control of the French king, while the rest of what is now France was still under the dominion of various feudal lords. By heredity, marriage, conquest, and purchase, the Ile-de-France gradually had grown over the years into the nucleus of the future French nation, and like a wheel with Paris as its hub, it radiated outward about 100 miles, with spokes extending toward Amiens, Beauvais, Rheims, Bourges, Rouen, and Chartres, cathedral towns all. The loftiest expression of the medieval period is seen in these miracles of soaring stone—the

127

# CHRONOLOGY / Gothic Period in France

## General Events

**1096– 1291** Crusades: European Christians fought Moslems and Saracens; extended Christianity as well as opened up trade routes

**1137** Louis VII began reign as king of France; married Eleanor of Aquitaine

**1140** Abbey Church of St. Denis, prototype of Gothic cathedrals, begun by Abbot Suger

**1142** Abelard, master of School of Notre Dame in Paris, died at Cluny

**c.1150–c.1170** University of Paris founded

**1163– 1235** Cathedral of Notre Dame in Paris built

**c.1163** Oxford University founded; Cambridge University soon thereafter

**1180** Philip Augustus crowned king of France; enclosed Paris with walls; promoted Paris as his capital city

**1194– 1260** Chartres Cathedral begun after fire destroyed earlier structure; 1006 Fulbert appointed bishop of Chartres; 1020–1028 Romanesque cathedral built by Fulbert; 1134 Fulbert's cathedral destroyed by fire; 1145 Romanesque cathedral again rebuilt; 1194 fire destroyed Romanesque cathedral with exception of narthex, west portals, two towers, three stained glass windows; 1260 cathedral dedicated by Louis IX

**1210** Rheims Cathedral rebuilt

**1215** Magna Charta signed in England

**1220** Amiens and Rouen cathedrals begun

**1223** Louis VIII crowned king of France

**1225** Beauvais Cathedral begun; choir finished in 1272

**1226** Louis IX became king of France under regency of his mother, Blanche of Castile

**1233** Chartres added to Crown territory of France

**1236** Regency of Blanche of Castile ended

**1240** Ste. Chapelle, royal chapel of French kings, begun in Paris

**1250** Albertus Magnus taught at University of Paris

**1274** Scholastic philosophy at height. St. Bonaventura and St. Thomas Aquinas died

## Philosophers

**1079– 1142** Abelard
**c.1193– 1280** Albertus Magnus
**1221– 1274** Bonaventura
**c.1225– 1274** Thomas Aquinas

## Musicians

**c.1122– 1192** Adam of St. Victor, joint author of hymns with St. Bernard of Clairvaux

**c.1150** Leonin active at Cathedral of Notre Dame in Paris

**c.1183** Perotin active at Cathedral of Notre Dame in Paris

**c.1237–c.1288** Adam de la Halle, author and composer of *Le Jeu de Robin et Marion,* a pastoral play with music

**c.1240** "Sumer is icumen in," oldest surviving piece of secular polyphony, written

**c.1260** Franco of Cologne, musical theorist, active

---

crystalized expressions of community effort, religious exaltation, and emotional and intellectual forces of the people who created them. Gothic architecture, moreover, is a struggling, striving, dynamic urge that reaches upward to embrace infinity. Though the building process often spanned several centuries, there are no finished Gothic cathedrals. Completion can take place only in the imagination of the observer. The 19th-century French medieval archaeologist Viollet-le-Duc once projected such a complete cathedral with seven spires—one pair on the west façade, another on the north and on the south transept, and a climactic spire over the crossing (Fig. 139).

Unlike an abbey church, a cathedral is located in a populated area where it comes under the jurisdiction of a bishop, whose official seat it is. A cathedral cannot rise from a plain like a monastic church; it needs the setting of a town where it can soar above the roofs and gables of the buildings that cluster around it. The barren exterior of an abbey forbids, while the intricate carving on the outside of a cathedral awakens curiosity and invites entrance. As the center of a cloistered life, a monastic church is richest in its dim interior, while the most elaborate decoration of a cathedral points toward the dwelling of the people. The tall towers of a Gothic cathedral need space from which to spring and room to cast their shadows. Their spires beckon the distant traveler to the shrine beneath and direct the weary steps of the toiling peasant homeward after a day in the fields, and the bells they enclose peal out to regulate the life of a whole town and its surrounding countryside. They tell of weddings and funerals and of the time for work and rest and prayer.

A cathedral is, of course, primarily a religious center, but in a time when spiritual and worldly af-

**below: 139.** Viollet-le-Duc. Drawing of a Gothic cathedral, complete with a full set of seven spires.

**right: 140.** Chartres Cathedral (view from southeast).

fairs were interwoven, the religious and secular functions of a cathedral were intermingled. Its nave was not only the place for religious services but, on occasion, a town hall where the entire populace could gather for a meeting. The rich decorations that clothe the body of the cathedral told not only the story of Christianity but also the history of the town and of the activities of its people. The cathedral was thus a municipal museum on whose walls the living record of the town was carved. The iconography of a cathedral dedicated to Notre Dame ("Our Lady") was concerned solely with religious subjects. Since the Virgin Mary was also the patroness of the liberal arts, her cathedral often constituted a visual encyclopedia whose subjects ranged over the entire field of human knowledge. The pulpit was not only the place from which sermons were preached but also a podium for lectures and instruction. The sanctuary served as a

theater in which the constantly changing sequence of the religious drama was enacted; outside, the deep-set portals provided stage sets for the mystery plays appropriate to the season, and the porches became platforms from which minstrels and jugglers could entertain their audiences. The stone statues and stained glass were useful not only as illustrations for sermons but also as picture galleries to stimulate the imagination. The choir was not only the setting for liturgical song but, in addition, a concert hall or opera house, where intricate polyphonic motets could be performed and the melodies of the religious dramas chanted.

Chartres (Fig. 140), unlike Paris, was never a center of commerce but a small bishopric in the midst of a rural district well off the beaten path. Its greatest distinction came from its shrine of the Virgin Mary where annually thousands congregated from far and wide to celebrate the Feast of the Virgin, which was the grand climax of the usual sequence of Church festivals. Here, as elsewhere, the cathedral was not only the spiritual center of the lives of the townsfolk but the geographical center of the medieval town as well. Towering over all, its great shadow fell upon the clustering church buildings that included the bishop's palace, the cathedral school, a cloister, a hospice, and an almshouse. Its west façade constituted one side of the market place, and from the cathedral square radiated the narrow streets on which were located the houses and shops of the townspeople. As members of guilds, or associations, the townsmen had contributed their labor and products to the cathedral when it was being built, and as guilds they had donated windows and statuary. They also undertook to fill such continuous needs as candles for the altars and bread for the communion service.

The cathedral itself, toward which all eyes and steps were drawn, represented a composite effort of

The Gothic Style  **129**

**141.** West façade, Chartres Cathedral. c. 1194–1260 (portals and lancet windows c. 1145; south tower c. 1180; north spire 1507–13). Façade width 157'; cathedral length 427'; south tower (right) height 344'; north tower (left) height 377'.

The extraordinary religious enthusiasm that prompted the undertaking and construction of these immense projects is well brought out in the accounts of several medieval writers. Allowing for the enthusiasm of a religious zealot, as well as for the probably symbolic participation of the nobles in manual labor, Abbot Haimon's words reflect the extraordinary spirit of these times. "Who has ever heard tell, in times past," he wrote after visiting Chartres, "that powerful princes of the world, that men brought up in honor and wealth, that nobles, men and women, have bent their proud and haughty necks to the harness of carts, and that, like beasts of burden, they have dragged to the abode of Christ these waggons, loaded with wines, grains, oil, stone, wood, and all that is necessary for the wants of life, or for the construction of the church? . . . When they have reached the church, they arrange the waggons about it like a spiritual camp, and during the whole night they celebrate the watch by hymns and canticles. On each waggon they light tapers and lamps; they place there the infirm and sick, and bring them the precious relics of the Saints for their relief."

## ARCHITECTURE OF CHARTRES CATHEDRAL

When the harmonious proportions of the west façade of the Cathedral of Notre Dame at Chartres (Fig. 141) are first observed, everything appears as right as an immutable truth. Yet what seems so certain, so solid, so monumental is actually the end result of fire salvage, a long process of growth, and a goodly amount of improvisation. Four centuries, in fact, separate the earliest parts from the latest, and the interval between saw rapid construction in time of prosperity, lag in time of poverty, work inspired with religious ardor, and cruel destruction by fire.

The triple portal and lancet windows above first stood a full forty feet behind the twin towers; together they constituted all that remained of the previous Romanesque church after the conflagration of 1194. In the rebuilding, they were moved forward flush with the front towers, and a large rose window was designed to fill the intervening space. Above it the arcade of kings and a gable were added to mask the apex of the wooden roof that protects the vaulting of the nave.

The stylistic difference between the two unsymmetrical spires is one of the most striking features of the Chartres façade. The supporting towers, as a part of the previous church, are approximately contem-

the stone cutters, masons, carpenters, and metal-workers, all of whom gave of their time, skill, and treasure to build it. It thus was the greatest single product a town and its craftsmen could produce. As a great civic monument, it constituted the pride of the community, and the ambitions and aspirations of citizens determined its character and contours. In those days, the importance of a town could be measured by the size and height of its cathedral as well as by the significance of the religious relics its cathedral housed. Consequently, civic rivalry was involved when the vaulting of Chartres rose 122 feet above the ground. Next came the cathedral at Amiens, which achieved a height of 140 feet, and finally Beauvais became the loftiest of all with the crowns of its high vaults soaring over 157 feet.

porary. The upper part and the spire of the one on the right, however, date from the time the later parts of the abbey church at Cluny were being finished; their counterparts on the left are contemporary with the laying of the foundations for St. Peter's basilica in Rome in the early 16th century. Close scrutiny will reveal such minor flaws as the discrepancy between the proportions of the portals and the scale of the façade as a whole, the rose window being set slightly off center; and the awkward joining of the gallery and arcade of kings above it with the tower on the right. In spite of these disparities, the façade bears out the initial impression of unity surprisingly well, and its space is so logically divided as to become an external promise of the interior plan (Fig. 142). Horizontally, the three entrance portals lead into the nave while the flanking towers face the aisles. Vertically, the portals correspond to the nave arcade within, the lancets to the triforium gallery, and the rose window to the clearstory level. By this means, its composition maintains an integral relationship between the inner and outer aspects of the structure.

Rising above the twin towers are the tall tapering spires that seem both a logical and necessary continuation of the vertical lines of the supporting buttresses below and a fitting expression of the Gothic spirit of aspiration generally. The façade of Chartres, however, is rare in having a pair of spires. In Paris, Rouen, Amiens, and elsewhere, spires were projected but never completed; and at Strasbourg, one tower has a spire while the other does not. The two at Chartres make an interesting contrast between the attitudes of the early and late architects. In the older one on the south (right), the builder felt that the junction between tower and spire should be made as smoothly as possible and did so by adding a story between the three levels of the tower below and the single shaft of the spire above. Here the eight dormerlike windows are each surmounted by alternating higher and lower miniature spire forms of their own

that, in turn, overlap the base of the larger spire, break the line, and add to the rhythm of the vertical movement. The transition from the square supporting tower to the octagonal form of the spire, and the continuation of the straight lines rising from ground level to the receding sloping lines of the spire, which culminate 350 feet above, is accomplished with finesse. The later Gothic architect, whose task was to replace the old wooden spire that had burned, was more concerned with intricacy of design and with sending his slimmer and more elegant spire 27 feet higher than its neighbor. While both excel in terms of their own stylistic contexts, it is the old south tower, still sound after seven centuries and almost as many fires, that connoisseurs admire.

When one enters Chartres through the central portal, the broad nave (Fig. 143) spreads out to a width of 53 feet, making it one of the most spacious of all Gothic naves. On either side are amply proportioned aisles with their stained-glass windows that

**left: 142.** Plan of Chartres Cathedral.

**right: 143.** Nave and choir, Chartres Cathedral. c. 1194–1260. Nave length c. 130', width 53', height 122'.

The Gothic Style **131**

allow a rich flood of light to enter. The plan (Fig. 142) reveals that, in comparison with the abbey church at Cluny (Fig. 113), the Gothic architect has practically dispensed with walls. Instead of running parallel to the nave, the supporting piers are now at right angles to it, and the area between is bridged over with vaults, thus allowing open space for glass to light the interior at both ground and clearstory levels. The walls, instead of serving to bear the weight of the superstructure, now exist mainly to enclose the interior and as a framework for the glass. Through the language of form and color, the wall space communicates with the worshipers through representations of religious subjects; and on a sunny day the beams of filtered light transform the floor into a constantly changing mosaic of color. Together with the clearstory windows, the shafts of mysterious light serve also to accent the structural system of arches, piers, and vaults in such a way as to contribute to the illusion of infinite size and height. And since the eye is naturally drawn to light, the interior gives the impression of being all windows (Pl. 15, p. 126).

Returning to the center of the nave, one has his attention drawn next to the arcade of seven bays marching majestically toward the crossing of the transept and on to the choir beyond. The immense piers consist of a strong central column with four attached colonnettes of more slender proportions clustered around them. As Figure 143 plainly shows,

**144.** Chartres Cathedral, transverse section of nave (left) and diagram of vaulting (right). Drawing by Goubert.

piers with cylindrical cores and engaged octagonal colonnettes alternate with piers with octagonal cores and attached cylindrical colonnettes. An interesting rhythm of procession and recession is set up, and a further variation is provided by the play of light on the alternating round and angular surfaces.

The space above the graceful pointed arches of the nave arcade is filled by a series of smaller open arches that span the space between the bays. Behind them runs the triforium gallery, a passage utilizing the space above the internal roofing over the aisles and under the slanting external roof that extends outward from the base of the clearstory. Above the triforium runs the clearstory level, which now fully accomplishes its purpose. The triple pattern of two lancet windows below and a circular one above allots a maximum of space to the glass and a minimum to the masonry.

Covering the span of the nave is the triumph of the Gothic builders, the broad quadripartite vaulting (Fig. 143, 144), which at Chartres rises 122 feet above the ground level. It is this principle of vaulting that underlies all Gothic thinking and, in turn, explains all the supporting facts of shafts, colonnettes, clustered columns, piers, and pointed arches—each of which comes into play to direct the descending weight of the intersecting ribs of the vaults towards the ground as efficiently as possible. The heavier transverse ribbing is carried past the clearstory and triforium levels by the large central shaft, while the smaller cross ribs are borne by the groups of slender colonnettes that extend downward and cluster around the massive central piers of the nave arcade below. Chartres is about midway in the cumulative trial-and-error process by which the Gothic system was eventually perfected. The central piers of the nave arcade are still somewhat bulky, as though the architect could not entirely trust his own daring. Greater slenderness was achieved at Rheims and Amiens, and the tendency toward slimness and height continued until its limit was passed at Beauvais.

Externally, there is an opposite number to each of these interior members (Fig. 145). The function of the flying buttress is to carry the thrust of the vaulting at specific points outward over the aisles to the piers that are set at right angles to the length of the nave. The function of flying buttress, pinnacle, and pier is now clarified. From the observer's point of view, just as in the interior the eye is drawn irresistibly upward by the rising vertical lines, so on the outside it follows the rising vertical piers to the pinnacles, along the rhythmic procession of the flying buttresses toward the gabled roof of the transept, and on to the infinitude of space beyond.

The purpose of the pointed arch also becomes clear now. The Romanesque architects of Burgundy had used it at Cluny mainly as a decorative motif to promote a feeling of height and elegance. Gothic arstantly increasing height, which, in turn, led to loftier vaults and more ethereal effects.

When all these various devices—pointed arch, rib vault, flying buttress, triforium gallery, walls maintained by spacious arcades, window spaces maximized at all levels—came together in a working relationship, Gothic architects were able to bring the inert masses of masonry into a resilient equilibrium of weights and balances. Gothic architecture is thus a complex system of opposing thrusts and counterthrusts (Fig. 145) in which all parts exist in a logical relation to the whole. The weight and position of each stone had to be considered in terms of what was above and below it, so that its force could be properly transmitted along the various levels until that force eventually was grounded. If any part should give way, the entire structure would be endangered. It is all the more remarkable when one remembers that Gothic builders used mortar and concrete in the joinings only as reinforcement and as a kind of structural insurance.

This logic of interior and exterior supports could not always take into account the irregularity of a cathedral's site. Over the years the ground might settle at certain points, or some of the piers and buttresses might be undermined by floods, thus putting the whole structure in danger. It also was impossible to make the vaults at high levels heavy enough to withstand wind and weather. At Chartres and elsewhere, the thin-webbed masonry had to be protected by the addition of wooden roofs, which at Chartres actually burned several times without, however, destroying the stone vaults underneath. The builder of Chartres achieved such stability that his structure has

chitects, however, pointed their arches to raise the crowns of the intersecting ribs of the vaulting to a uniform height so as to achieve greater structural stability. The tendency of the round arch is to spread sideways under the gravitational force of the weight it bears; a pointed arch, being steeper, directs the thrust of its load downward and onto the upright supporting members (Fig. 146). By the ever-increasing skill with which they used the device of the pointed arch, Gothic builders were able to achieve a con-

146. The *pointed arch* and *ribbed groin vault* are fundamental to Gothic architecture, making it a light and flexible building system that permits generous openings in walls for large, high windows, the result of which are well-illuminated interior spaces. Being more vertical, pointed arches thrust their load more directly toward the ground (b), whereas the lower round arches spread the load in a lateral direction (a), which makes them less stable than Gothic arches. Too, pointed arches can rise to any height, whereas the height of semicircular arches is governed by the space they span. In (c) and (d) the space, or *bay*, that has been vaulted is rectangular in shape, rather than square. In (c) the round arches create a domical vault whose shapes and openings are irregular and restricted. In (d) the pointed arches rise to a uniform height and form a Gothic vault with ample openings.

a                    b                    c                    d

147. South Porch, Chartres Cathedral. 13th century.

never had to be reinforced, and it stands today substantially as it did seven centuries ago. Rheims Cathedral has fared equally well by surviving the centuries, two fires, and an artillery bombardment in World War I. Gothic cathedrals, in fact, have so far borne out the hopes of people who desired to raise buildings that "have nothing to fear from fire till the day of judgment."

At Chartres, the wings of the transepts terminate in triple portals (Fig. 147) that in size and magnificence surpass those of the western façade, which had survived from the previous church. The portals in the 13th-century style, however, are enframed by row upon row of richly sculptured receding archivolts that bring a maximum of light and shadow into play. The shape of such sections was partly determined by the tastes of individual donors. The north transept with its portals, porch, and stained glass was the gift of the royal family of France, primarily Blanche of Castile and her son St. Louis (Pl. 16, 126), while its southern counterpart was donated by their arch-rival, the Duke of Brittany. When the cathedral was dedicated in the year 1260, Louis IX was present with such an assembly of bishops, canons, princes, and peasants as had rarely been seen.

Beyond the transepts extend the spacious choir and sanctuary, which are surrounded by a double-aisled ambulatory that gives easy access to the apse and its necklace of radiating chapels. The increasingly elaborate Gothic liturgy demanded the participation of more and more clergymen, and the cavernous recesses of the huge structure were needed to accommodate an ever-growing number of choristers. The apsidal chapels are also a distinctive feature of a developed Gothic plan, so that pilgrims could have access to the various altars where the venerated relics of saints were kept. The Cathedral of Notre Dame at Chartres, as well as earlier churches that stood on the same site, was closely associated with the cult of the Virgin Mary. Its most renowned relic was the legendary veil of the Virgin which, by tradition, had been presented to Charlemagne by the Byzantine Empress Irene. Another chapel enshrined the skull of St. Anne, the Virgin's mother, which was brought back by Crusaders and given to the church in 1205. This relic explains the many representations of St. Anne in statuary and stained glass and the pilgrimages in her honor, which were second only to those of the Virgin. The most important chapel in Gothic cathedrals was the *Notre Dame,* or Lady Chapel, devoted to Mary. It was usually placed on the main axis of the nave beyond the center of the apse, with chapels of other saints grouped on either side. All these considerations caused the parts beyond the transepts to expand to unprecedented proportions.

Gothic interiors need little more decorative detail than the vertical lines of the structural members, the variety of representations in stained glass, and above all, the flow of light. At Chartres, the lighting is so organized as to achieve a gradual crescendo from the dark violet and blue lancets and rose window in the west through the brighter tones of the aisle and clearstory windows of the nave, past the flaming reds of the transept rose windows to the high intensity of the five red and orange lancets in the apse, which soar above the altar and capture the rays of the morning sun. Romanesque abbey churches were lighted mainly from within by lamps and candles, while Gothic interiors are illuminated by sunlight transformed through stained glass into a myriad of mysterious prismatic colors. The interior masses and voids become activated and etherealized by the directional flow of light, and material and immaterial elements fuse into a glowing harmonious whole.

# SCULPTURE OF CHARTRES CATHEDRAL

As important to the medieval mind as the structure itself was the choice and location of the sculptural and pictorial representations that were to give the church its significance and meaning. In a Romanesque monastic church, these were found in the carved tympanums over the narthex portals, on the capitals of the columns throughout the interior, and in wall paintings, especially in the apsidal end. Since such representations were designed for those leading cloistered lives, they gravitated toward the interior, and the variety and subtlety of their subjects make it clear they were meant to be pondered upon and carefully studied. Gothic sculpture was more popularly oriented and faced the outside world, where it clustered around and over the porches and entrance portals to form an integral part of the architectural design. Both the proliferation of figures and the quality of their execution testify to the importance of sculpture in the art of the period. The exterior of Chartres has more than 2,000 carved figures, which are about evenly distributed among the west façade and the north and south porches of the transepts. Gothic sculpture, like the Romanesque, was done by journeymen craftsmen who gathered wherever a church was abuilding. From the enormous productivity of the period, it seems clear that the ranks of these craftsmen must have been numerous, and that the strokes of the sculptor's chisel on stone must have been a familiar sound. The Gothic sculptor had the advantage of excellent stone models to follow, where his Romanesque predecessors had had to translate the lines of illuminated manuscripts into the stone medium. While the Romanesque sculptor thought more in linear terms (Figs. 116, 125), his Gothic counterpart was more concerned with carving in depth; and the placement of the Gothic sculpture out of doors also made the play of light and shade more important. While the technique of the Gothic sculptor undoubtedly was superior, the iconography had become standardized in his time and did not allow him quite so much imaginative freedom as his predecessor had enjoyed. Both Romanesque and Gothic sculpture, however, shows the unevenness of workmanship associated with "school sculpture," because some journeymen carvers were more skillful than others.

The profusion of sculpture in a Gothic cathedral might lead to considerable confusion were it not for the close relationship of the sculptured forms to the architectural framework. The Gothic structure was so complete, so overwhelming, that no amount of decorative license would have been able to overshadow it; but the Gothic carvers had no intentions of going their separate ways, and their work was always conceived and executed in terms of the architectural frame of reference. Even so, the enormous number of examples would be bewildering were it not for

some attempt to unify the iconography. Since it is a people's church, the cathedral could not follow so consistent a system as that of an abbey, which was designed for a small group of people following a common ideal of life. Instead of single unified compositions, therefore, the designer of the Gothic cathedral sought to provide something for every level of taste.

A Gothic cathedral, with the all-embracing activities it housed and the all-encompassing subject matter of its sculpture and stained glass, has often been likened to the comprehensive compendiums of law, philosophy, and theology written by medieval scholars. Cathedrals have also been described as the Bible in stone and glass, or the books of the illiterate; but they should not be overlooked as visual encyclopedias for the educated as well.

The key to the iconography of Chartres is the encyclopedic character of medieval thought as found in the *Speculum Majus* of Vincent of Beauvais, who divided all learning into Mirrors of Nature, Instruction, History, and Morality. The Mirror of Nature is seen in the flora and fauna that are represented in comprehensive fashion; Instruction in the personifications of the seven liberal arts and the branches of learning taught in the universities; History in the story of mankind from Adam and Eve to the Last Judgment; and Morality in the figures depicting virtue and vice, the wise and foolish virgins, the saved and the damned in the Last Judgment, and in the hovering saints and angels and fleeing gargoyles and devils. There is also a recognizable sequence of presentation with a beginning on the west façade, where the story of Christ from His ancestors to the Ascension is told; a middle on the north porch, where the history of Mary is traced along Old Testament lines from the creation of man to her death and heavenly coronation; and an end on the south porch, which takes up the drama of redemption from the New Testament, through the work of the Church, its saints, popes, abbots, and bishops, to the climax of the final day of the universe at the Last Judgment. Each of the three porches has some 700 carved figures clustered in the three tympanums over the portals, the archivolts that enframe them, and the columns below and galleries above. In addition to the Scriptural scenes and lives of the saints, the designers found a place for ancient lore and contemporary history, for prophecy and fact, for fabulous animals and beasts of burden, for old wives' tales and the latest scientific knowledge, for portraits of princes and those of tradesmen, for beautiful angels and grotesque gargoyles (some of which function as water spouts to drain the roof, others as decorative motifs symbolizing demons fleeing from the sacred precincts of the church).

The iconography at Chartres stems from three principal sources: the dedication of the cathedral to Our Lady, a church privilege that was shared with right: 148. West portals ("Royal Portals"), Chartres Cathedral. c. 1145–70.

below: 149. *Life of Virgin Mary*, tympanum of "Virgin Portal," west façade, Chartres Cathedral. 1145–70.

such other Notre Dame cathedrals as those at Paris, Rheims, Rouen, and Amiens; the presence of a cathedral school, an important center of learning, for Mary was also the patroness of the liberal arts; and the preferences of such patrons as the royal family, lesser nobility, and local guilds who donated miscellaneous representations.

It must also be borne in mind that sacred and secular elements in a medieval town and manor were so closely interwoven that every spiritual manifestation had a worldly counterpart. So the cathedral, as the court of Mary, Queen of Heaven, had to surpass in magnificence the grandeur that surrounded any mere earthly queen. Gothic chivalry and courtliness were rapidly replacing the might-makes-right code of Romanesque feudalism. And just as the clergy sang the praises of Notre Dame, so the knights of the castles lauded their ladies in particular and Our Lady in general. The high place of womanhood in secular circles is thus the courtly parallel of the religious cult of the Virgin. In poetry of the time, a knight's lady love is always the paragon of feminine virtue and charm. To woo and win her, he who aspired to her favor had to storm the fortress of her heart by techniques far more intricate and subtle than those needed to take a castle. When successful, he became the vassal of his mistress and she his liege lady to command him as she would. The concept of romantic love originated here in the Gothic period and came to full flower in the complex code of chivalry. With its exaltation of the position of women and its concern with the defense of the weak against the strong, chivalry established the Western code of manners that has remained valid well into the 20th century.

The central portal of the west façade at Chartres is called the Royal Portal (Fig. 148), and its tympanum encloses the figure of Christ in Majesty surrounded by the four symbolic beasts of the Evangelists and the twenty-four elders of the Apocalypse. The tympanum over the left portal depicts the close of Christ's days on earth and His ascension, while on the right is the tympanum of the Virgin Portal (Fig. 149), depicting the beginning of the Savior's earthly life. In the simplest terms, the story is told in three rising panels. Starting in the lower left is the Annunciation, with just the figures of the Angel Gabriel and Mary; the next pair shows the Visitation; the Nativity is in the center; and the shepherds in the midst of their sheep are coming from the right for the Adoration, just as their successors came in from the fields near Chartres to worship at Mary's shrine. The middle panel depicts the presentation of the young Jesus in the temple. His position on the altar foreshadows His later sacrifice. Friends approach from both sides bearing gifts. In the top panel, the Virgin sits crowned and enthroned, holding her Divine Son and attended by a pair of archangels. She is shown frontally as a queen accepting the homage of the humble, who bow their heads as they enter her court through the portal below.

Of great interest are the figures in the archivolts that frame the tympanum. These symbolize Mary's attributes. Like Athena of old, the Virgin was the patroness of the arts and sciences. Albertus Magnus in his *Mariale* declared that the Virgin was perfect in the arts; and in his *Summa*, Thomas Aquinas included among his propositions the question of "Whether the Blessed Virgin Mary possessed perfectly the seven liberal arts"—which, of course, was triumphantly affirmed. These representations are also reminders that this was an age which produced great scholars, and that intellectual understanding as well as faith was now one of the paths to salvation. The fact that Chartres was the location of one of the great cathedral schools is also brought out; and before the founding of the University of Paris, it shared with Rheims the distinction of being the best-known center of learning in Europe.

The curriculum of the cathedral school was, of course, the seven Liberal Arts. These were divided into the Trivium, which dealt with the science of words in the three subjects of Grammar, Rhetoric, and Dialectic, and into the higher faculty of the Quadrivium, which was concerned with the science of numbers through the study of Arithmetic, Geometry, Astronomy, and Music.

On the archivolt, these seven arts are symbolized abstractly by female figures somewhat akin to the ancient muses, while below them are found their most renowned human exponents. Beginning with the lower left corner of the outside archivolt, Aristotle is seen dipping his pen into the inkwell. Above him is a thoughtful figure representing Dialectic. In one hand she holds a dragon-headed serpent symbolizing subtlety of thought, and in the other the torch of knowledge. Then comes Cicero as the great orator, and over him the figure of Rhetoric making a characteristic oratorical gesture. The next pair are Euclid and Geometry, both of whom are deep in their calcula-

tions. In the same band, moving now from the top downward are Arithmetic and probably Boethius. Below them is the star-gazing figure of Astronomy, who holds a bushel basket which signifies the relationship of her science to the calendar, so important in a farming district like Chartres. Ptolemy, to whom the medievalists ascribed the invention of the calendar and clock, is her human representative.

The figures on the lowest level are Grammar and Donatus, the ancient Roman grammarian. Grammar (Fig. 150) holds an open book in one hand and the disciplinary switch in the other over the heads of two young pupils, one of whom is laughing and pulling the other's hair. The last pair in the series of seven are adjacent to those in the inner archivolt. Below is Pythagoras, the reputed founder of music theory, who is shown writing in medieval fashion with a desk over his knees. Above him is the figure of Music surrounded by instruments (Fig. 151). At her back is a monochord, used to calculate the intervals and for accuracy of pitch; on her lap is a psaltery; on the wall hangs a three-stringed viol; and she is striking the set of three chime bells, an allusion to the Pythagorean discovery of the mathematical ratios of the perfect intervals—the octave, the fifth, and the fourth. Both Gerbert of Rheims and his pupil Bishop Fulbert of Chartres are known to have taken an active interest not only in the theory of music but in its performance,

**150–151.** Details, Virgin Portal Tympanum, west façade, Chartres Cathedral. 1145–70.

**150.** *Grammar.*       **151.** *Music.*

and the two figures, showing Pythagoras as the thinker and Music as the performer, signify that Chartres was an important center for both the theoretical as well as the practical aspects of music.

Far more elaborate in scope and less restrained in decorative detail than the west façade is the incomparable north porch, which, with its three portals, stretches out to a width of 120 feet, thus spanning the transept completely. A gift of the royal family of France, its construction and decoration extended from the reign of Louis VIII and the regency of his queen, Blanche of Castile, through that of their son St. Louis (Louis IX), or roughly the first three quarters of the 13th century. The north porch is dedicated to the Virgin and expands the theme of the Virgin Portal on the west façade to encyclopedic proportions. Her history from the annunciation and nativity through the childhood of Jesus is found on the left portal, while the scenes of her death and assumption are depicted on the lintel over the central door, and that of her

152. *St. Anne with Virgin,* trumeau of center portal, north porch, Chartres Cathedral. c. 1250.

enthronement and coronation in the tympanum above. Her attributes are revealed in the archivolts through series after series of cyclical representations, such as those of the 14 heavenly beatitudes and 12 feminine personifications of the active and contemplative life. Especially fine is the single figure of her mother, St. Anne, holding the infant Mary in her arms, which adorns the *trumeau* that supports the tympanum of the central portal (Fig. 152). From the harmonious lines of the folds of her drapery to the dignified and matronly face, the work is one of the most satisfying realizations of the mature Gothic sculptural style.

It will be noted from the contours of the south porch (Fig. 147) that the arches of the portals are now more highly pointed, and their enclosure by triangular gables further emphasizes their verticality. The deep recession of the porch allows for a much greater play of light and shade in the statuary that covers every available space from the bases of the columns to the peak of the gable. The figures on both the north and south porches, in comparison with the earlier ones on the west façade, have bodies more naturally proportioned; their postures show greater variety and informality; and their facial expressions have far more mobility. The representations of plants and animals are considerably closer to nature; and in comparison with the impersonality of those on the west front, many of the human figures are so individualized that they seem like portraits of living persons. In the change of style, however, something of the previous symbolic meaning and monumentality has been lost as well as the closer identity with architecture.

## THE STAINED GLASS OF CHARTRES

Time has taken its inevitable toll of Chartres' exterior sculptures. The flow of carved lines remains, and the varied play of light and shade relieves the present browns and grays. But only traces of polychrome and gilt are left to remind the observer that here was once a feast of color with an effect that now has to be imagined. In the interior, however, where the stained glass remains undimmed, the full color of medieval pageantry still exists. The wealth of pure color in the 175 surviving glass panels hypnotizes the senses, and through the medium of polychromatic light something of the emotional exaltation that inspired medieval man to create such a temple to the Queen of Heaven can still be felt.

Here, as elsewhere, the structural and decorative elements are closely tied together, and, just as with the sculpture, the glass does not exist separately but only as an integral part of the whole. The designer was always aware of the size, proportion, and placement of his window in relation to the architectural setting. Glass is not usually thought of as a building material until the 19th and 20th centuries, but in medieval times and later it did have to fill a large architectural void while taking into account the pressure of wind and weather. This the designer accomplished mainly by dividing the space geometrically into smaller parts by use of *mullions,* the vertical posts that divide the windows; by stone tracery to frame smaller glass panels, as in the great rose windows; by parallel iron bars across the open expanse; and, more minutely, by the fine strips of lead that hold the small pieces of glass in place. While Chartres must divide architectural and sculptural honors with its neighboring cities, the town was especially renowned as the center of glass making, and with the highest achievements of its glaziers exemplified in their own cathedral, Chartres is unsurpassed in this respect.

The great variety of jewellike color was achieved chemically by the addition of certain minerals to the glass while it was in a molten state. When cool, the sheets were cut into smaller sections, and the designer fitted these into his previously prepared outline. Pieces of various sizes next were joined together by lead strips. Details, such as the features in the faces, were then applied in the form of metal oxides and made permanent by firing in a kiln. Finally, the individual panels making up the pattern of the whole window were fastened to the iron bars already imbedded in the masonry. When seen against the light the glass appears translucent, while the lead and iron become opaque black lines that outline the figures and separate the colors to prevent blurring when at a distance.

The stained-glass artists shared with mosaicists and manuscript illuminators a distinct preference for two-dimensional designs. The dignified formality of their figures and the abstract patterns of the borders blended their work admirably into the architectural setting. By thus avoiding any hint of naturalistic effects, such as landscape backgrounds, and by concentrating on patterns of pure color and geometrical forms, they helped to promote the illusion of infinite space.

The iconographical plan of the glass at Chartres, like that of the exterior sculptures, is held together mainly by the dedication of the church as a shrine of the Virgin Mary. There is never any doubt on the part of those who enter that they are in the presence of the Queen of Heaven, who sits enthroned in majesty in the central panel of the apse over the high altar. Grouped around her in neighboring panels are the archangels, saints, and prophets, emblems of the noble donors, and symbols of the craftsmen and tradespeople, almost 4,000 figures in all, who honor her and make up her court. Below, on her feast days, were the crowds of living pilgrims who gathered in the nave and chapels, and who aspired to come into her eternal presence one day as they had come into her shrine.

An interesting commentary on the changing social conditions of the 13th century can be read in the records of the donors of the windows. In the lowest part of each one is a "signature" indicating the individual, family, or group who defrayed the great expense of the glass. Only a royal purse was equal to a large rose window, as evidenced by the fleur-de-lys insignia so prominent in the north rose (Fig. 154). Within the means of members of the aristocracy and the Church hierarchy, such as bishops and canons, were the lancet windows of the nave and choir. The status and prosperity of the medieval guilds of craftsmen and merchants, however, was such that the vast majority of the windows were donated by them. While the royal family of France and the Duke of Brittany were content with windows in the transepts, the most prominent windows of all, the 47-foot-high center lancets of the apse, were given by the guilds; and the one over the high altar, toward which all eyes are drawn, was the gift of the bakers. Each guild had a patron saint, and a window under a guild's patronage was concerned with the life and miracles of its special saint. In the case of the nobility, the family coat of arms was sufficient to identify the donor; with a guild, the "signature" took the form of a craftsman engaged in some typical phase of his work. In the windows of Chartres some 19 different confraternities are represented, including the bakers (Fig. 153).

153. *Bakers,* detail, stained-glass window, Chartres Cathedral. c. 1250.

**154.** North rose window, Chartres Cathedral. 1223–26. Diameter 44'.

The great rose window of the west façade dates from the early 13th century and thus is contemporary with the majority of examples in the rest of the church. The three lancets below it, however, like the portals and surrounding masonry on the exterior, originally were part of the previous church. Besides being the earliest of all the windows, they are, possibly, also the best. Their origin has been traced to the school that did the windows for Suger's church at St. Denis, and their work was on the whole much finer-grained and more jewellike, with infinite care lavished on the geometrical and arabesque patterns in the borders. They are dominated by their vibrant blue background, while the figures and abstract patterns have been accomplished in several shades of red, emerald green, yellow, sapphire, and white. Also dating from before the fire of 1194 is the central section of the regal and resplendent panel known as *Notre Dame de Belle Verrière,* or "Our Lady of the Beautiful Window" (Pl. 17, p. 143).

The great rose window of the north transept (Fig. 154), like the sculpture on the porch outside, glorifies the Virgin Mary. Together with its lancets, the composition shares with the other glass of the 13th century a preference for red backgrounds instead of the earlier blue; the individual panes are larger; the borders are more conventionalized; and its greatest effect comes from the large splashes of warm color that contrast with the cool tones of the lancets of the west façade.

In the Gothic period the art of stained glass replaced the mosaics and mural paintings of the early Christian and Romanesque churches, and is the ultimate stage in the etherealization of interior space. (By giving form and meaning to light, the art of the glazier is perhaps better adapted to the expression of transcendental concepts than any other medium.) By the transformation of raw sunlight into a spectrum of brilliant prismatic color, the architect gained complete control over his interior lighting, which he could cause to flow in any manner he willed. This material control over an immaterial medium could then be placed at the disposal of the architects and iconographers to shape light to their structural, pictorial, and expressive needs. Something of the ecstasy felt by medieval man in the contemplation of the precious stones that adorned the altar and the jeweled glass of the windows is expressed in the following passage by Abbot Suger: "Thus, when—out of my delight in the beauty of the house of God—the loveliness of the many-colored gems has called me away from eternal cares, and worthy meditation has induced me to reflect, transferring that which is material to that which is immaterial, on the diversity of the sacred virtues: then it seems to me that I see myself dwelling, as it were, in some strange region of the universe which neither exists entirely in the slime of the earth nor entirely in the purity of Heaven; and that, by the grace of God, I can be transported from this inferior to that higher world in an anagogical manner."

## GOTHIC MUSIC

Massive and magnificent as the Gothic cathedral is, it can be conceived as the highest achievement of Gothic man only if associated with the various activities it was designed to house. Most important, of course, is the liturgy. As the enclosed space increased, the cathedral grew into a vast auditorium that hummed with collective voices at communal prayer, resounded with readings and the spoken word from the pulpit, and reverberated with the chanting of solo and choral song from the choir.

The Île-de-France, site of the most significant developments in architecture of the 12th and 13th centuries, was also the scene of the most important musical innovations of the Gothic period. Specifically, these were the more sophisticated practices of *polyphonic,* or "many-voiced," music and their relation with the still universally practiced monophonic, or unison, art of Gregorian Chant. Singing in parts was of northern origin in contrast to the prevailing Mediterranean style of singing in unison, and part singing in folk music apparently predates by several centuries its incorporation into church music. Just as the Gothic cathedral was the culmination in the long process of reconciling the northern urge for verticality with the southern horizontal basilica form, so Gothic music was the union of the northern tradition of many-voiced singing with the southern one-voice tradition.

The role of Chartres in these developments is obscure. John of Salisbury, the master of the cathedral school when the symbolic figure of Music was done for the west façade (Fig. 151), is known to have approved the theoretical study of music as a part of the Quadrivium as heartily as he disapproved of certain innovations in the music performed by the choir there. Scholarly discussions about the mathematical ratios of musical intervals had been going on ever since antiquity, and such abstract problems as how the music of the spheres or an angelic choir would sound had been on the academic agenda ever since Boethius' time. It is therefore probable that at this time the greater progress was being made in the field of practical music which John so despised. According to William of Malmesbury, who died about 1142, Chartres was celebrated for its "many musical modulations," and one of the greatest 13th-century musical

theorists, Franco of Cologne, is supposed to have been educated at Chartres. Documents and surviving manuscripts, however, indicate that the greatest forward strides were being made in the Cathedral School of Paris, known after 1163 as the School of Notre Dame.

**School of Notre Dame in Paris**     It has already been noted that, in the construction of the first Gothic church, the builder of St. Denis brought together many principles that had been developed separately elsewhere and for the first time used them in a systematic whole. The same was true of music, and Paris as the growing capital of the French kingdom was the logical place for the pieces to be fitted into a whole. The contrapuntal forms and textures developed in such monasteries as Cluny and in such cathedral schools as Rheims and Chartres, as well as the tradition of folk singing in several parts, were organized systematically for the first time at the School of Notre Dame in Paris. Again, as in the case of architecture, the man and the time can be fixed with certainty. The first great monument of Gothic music was the *Magnus Liber Organi* by Leonin, dating from c. 1163, which, as its name implies, was a great book bringing together a collection of music in two parts, arranged cyclically so as to spread over the entire calendar year.

In the traditional rendering of the Gregorian Chant, some parts were sung by a soloist and answered responsorially by a chorus singing in unison. In the Gothic period, the choir still chanted in the way it had done for centuries, but the solo parts began to be performed simultaneously by two or more individual singers. Notre Dame in Paris, for example, employed four such singers. The distinction between solo voice and choir hence was replaced by the opposition of a group of individual singers and a massed chorus. With several skilled soloists available, the way was open for an art of much greater complexity than heretofore. Since the music, however, was still intended for church performance, it was mandatory that one of the traditional sacred melodies be used; and a special part called the *tenor,* a term derived from the Latin *tenere,* meaning "to hold," was reserved for it. This melody was also known as the *cantus firmus,* or "fixed song," implying that it could not be changed. The development of Gothic music was that of taking this *cantus firmus* as an established basis, and adding one by one the voices called in ascending order, the *duplum, triplum,* and *quadruplum.* Since these voices were superimposed one above the other, a definite verticality of concept is implied, which contrasted strongly with the horizontal succession of tones that characterized the older monophonic chant.

The earliest forms of Gothic polyphony are almost as rigid in their way as the old parallel organum of the Romanesque period, but they are based on the new principle of *punctus contra punctum,* literally "note

*Duplum Organum* (c. 1175)   (in Leonin's style)

*Triplum* (13th century)   (in Perotin's style; after Rokseth)

against note," or point counter point. *Mira Lege* (above) illustrates one of the strictest applications of this idea. The Gregorian melody is in the lower part, while the counterpoint above moves as much in opposition to it as possible. While parallel movement is not against the rule, and from time to time does occur, contrary motion is preferred. A treatise written at the beginning of the 12th century declares: "If the main voice is ascending, the accompanying part should descend, and vice versa." The name given to this newly created melodic line was the *discantus*, or "descant," referring to the practice of singing against the established melody, a practice that has continued in religious and secular music ever since.

In addition to such examples, Leonin's *Magnus Liber* contains another type of counterpoint known as *organum duplum* (top right). The Gregorian *cantus firmus* is found in the lower voice, but the individual tones are stretched out to extraordinary lengths. The descanting, or duplum voice, moves now in free counterpoint consisting of florid melismas over what has in effect become a relatively fixed base.

The greater melodic and rhythmic freedom that the descant assumed called for expert solo singers, and much of the descanting of Gothic times is known to have been improvised. The practice of such a freely flowing melodic line over a relatively fixed bass points to a possible origin in one of the old types of folk singing. Survivals are found in the instrumental music of the Scottish bagpipers, where such a tune as "The Campbells Are Coming" is heard over a droning bass note. In performance, the slowly moving tenor, or *cantus firmus*, may have been sung by the choir, while the soloist sang his freely moving duplum part over it; or the tenor may have been played on the organ, as the instrument is known to have been in use at this time. The organ keyboard was a 13th-century Gothic innovation, and the many manuscript illustrations from the period point to the wide usage of organs. The term "organ point," furthermore, continues to be used to refer to a musical passage in which the bass tone remains static, while the other parts move freely over it.

The next most significant development was the addition of a third part above the other two, which was known as the *triplum*, and from which the term "treble" is derived. This step is associated with the name of the first practicing musician in history to have the attribution of greatness attached to his name.

He was Magister Perotinus Magnus, or Perotin the Great, active in Paris in the late 12th and probably in the early 13th century. In his revision of the work of his predecessor Leonin, Perotin moved away from polyphonic improvisational practices toward an art based on stricter melodic control and clearer rhythmic articulation. By thus achieving a surer command of his materials, and evolving a logical technique for manipulating them, he was able to add a third voice to the original two (see above), and in two known instances even a fourth. The three-part motet, like it predecessors, still had its *cantus firmus* in the tenor, which was the lowest part and held the *mot*, or "word," from which the term *motet* is probably derived. Over it the contrapuntal voices wove a web of two different strands, singing their independent melodic lines. In the hands of Perotin the three-part motet became the most favored and characteristic practice of 13th-century Gothic music.

Besides achieving ever-greater melodic independence, the two contrapuntal voices even had their own separate texts. A three-part motet thus had three distinct sets of words—the tenor, with its traditional line, and usually two contemporary hymnlike verses over and above it—which were sung simultaneously. Intended as they were for church performance, the words customarily were in Latin. However, around the middle of the 13th century, it was not uncommon for one of the contrapuntal voices to have its verses in French. With the entrance of the vernacular language came also popular melodies, so that above the stately tenor, it was possible to have a hymn to the Virgin in Latin and a secular love song in French going on at the same time. By the simple expedient of replacing the sacred melodies with secular tunes, a fully

**Plate 17.** *Notre Dame de Belle Verrière.* 12th century. Stained glass window. Chartres Cathedral. (See p. 140.)

left: **Plate 18.** Giotto. *Pietà (Lamentation).* 1305–06. Fresco, 7'7'' × 7'9''. Arena Chapel, Padua. (See p. 152.)

below: **Plate 19.** Simone Martini. *Annunciation.* 1333. Tempera on wood, 8'8'' × 10'. (Saints in side panels by Lippo Memmi.) Uffizi, Florence. (See p. 156.)

developed musical art independent of the Church was not only possible but by the end of the 13th century had become an accomplished fact.

Gothic music exists in such close unity with other manifestations of the Gothic style that it can scarcely be understood as a thing apart. The subjects of the new hymns, especially those with the words of St. Bernard and the melodies of Adam of St. Victor, were mainly devoted to the Virgin, as were most of the cathedrals and the iconography of the sculpture and stained glass. Instead of a monolithic choir chanting in unison or in parallel organum, the Gothic listener now heard a small group of professional singers. In the case of a three-part motet, he could choose, according to his temperament or mood, to follow either the solemn traditional melody, the Latin commentary above it, or the French triplum in his own everyday mode of speech. This allowance for diversity of musical taste is a part of the general shift from the homogeneity of monastic life in the abbey to the heterogeneity of city life, of which the cathedral is the expression. The new melodic, rhythmic, and textual variety implies a congregation made up of people from all walks of life, just as had been the case with the diversified imagery of the sculpture and stained glass.

Since the individual voices were superimposed one above the other, a concept of verticality, similar to the architectural developments, is realized. The ear, like the eye, needs fixed points to measure rises and falls. In the *Mira Lege* example (p. 142), the intervals of the lower part established the point over which the descant moved in contrary motion. In the case of the *organum duplum* (p. 142), it was the long sustained tone in the tenor against which the soaring upward and plunging downward movement of the melody could be heard. In addition to this linear impulse, all types of counterpoint achieve a sense of rhythmical progress by having a relatively static point against which the more rapid mobility of the other voices can be measured. Together with the several opposing melodies, the clash of dissonant intervals, the simultaneous declamation of separate texts, as well as the progress of several independent rhythms, Gothic music was able to build up a sense of mounting tension that set it apart as a distinctive new style.

## IDEAS

In the century between the dedication of the great Romanesque abbey church at Cluny (1095) and the beginning of Chartres cathedral (1194), much more than a change in artistic styles had occurred. A mighty shift in social and political institutions and in basic modes of thought had taken place, and the resulting changes in church, secular, and artistic life brought into the open sharp divisions of opinion. Old conflicts, long damped by the power of the medieval theocracy, now burst into flames, and new ones broke out, fanned by the breaths of new voices clamoring to be heard. Intellectual disputes grew hot and acrid as emotional tensions deepened. In this critical situation, the rational processes of scholasticism were brought to bear on these divisive forces, and the Gothic is best understood as a clashing and dissonant style in which opposite elements were maintained momentarily in a state of uneasy equilibrium. With the eventual dissolution of the scholastic synthesis in the following century, the basic oppositions became so irreconcilable that they led in some cases to the battlefield, in others to schisms within the Church, and generally to growing philosophical and artistic conflicts.

**Gothic Dualism**     Politically, the age-old struggle of Church and state, evidenced in Romanesque times by the interminable quarrels between popes and Holy Roman emperors, now shaped up as the conflict between traditional ecclesiastical authority and the growing power of northern European kingdoms, especially France and England. Simultaneously came the beginning of a split between the internationalism of the Church and Holy Roman Empire and rising nationalism that produced centuries of rivalry between the south and north for the domination of Europe.

The prevailing monastic and feudal organizations of Romanesque times had tended to separate society into widely scattered units of cloister and manor, thereby isolating many of the causes of social strains. But as the towns began to grow into cities, the disparate elements were brought together in a common center where confrontation made problems more immediate. Tensions mounted between the landed aristocrats on the one hand and the volatile urban groups on the other, between the monastic orders and the growing secular clergy. And towns witnessed at close range the bitter rivalries between abbot and bishop, lord and burgher, clergy and laity. For the common people there was always the contrast between the squalor in which they existed and the luxury of their lords, bishops, and abbots; between the poverty of their daily lives and promises of heavenly glory in the beyond; between the strife of their world and the visions of serenity and peace in paradise. The arts were torn between expressing the aspirations of this world and those of the next, and the artist between accepting a relatively anonymous status in the service of God and competing actively with his fellows in search of worldly recognition. Instead of the comparative unity of artistic patronage in the aristocratically oriented Romanesque period, patronage in the city was now divided between the social groups of aristocrats and clergy on the one hand and the increasingly important bourgeoisie and guilds on the other. The rising power of the middle class far left: 155. Gothic half-timbered house, Rouen. 15th century.

left: 156. Courtyard, House of Jacques Coeur, Bourges. 1443–51.

is well illustrated by such dwelling places as one of the surviving Gothic half-timbered houses at Rouen (Fig. 155), and the splendid residence of the banker Jacques Coeur at Bourges (Fig. 156).

In architecture, be it the interior or exterior of the Gothic cathedral, one has an awareness of the opposition between the masses and voids, the interplay of thrust and counterthrust, and of the principle of attraction and repulsion that awaken dead weights into dynamic forces. In sculpture, the conflict of the particular and universal is seen in the remarkable feeling for human individuality in some of the separate figures and the iconographic necessity of molding them into the dignified impersonality required of a row of prophets and saints. In literature, the opposition between Latin and the vernacular languages becomes as evident as the growing distinction between the sacred and secular musical styles. Within the province of the tonal art are found such external disparities as the fruitless academic discussions about the hypothetical nature of the music of the spheres and the increasing importance of the actual sounds heard in the choirs of the churches; the abstract study of theoretical acoustics in the universities and the practical art of writing and making music. In music also there are such internal differences as the singing of monophonic choruses alternately with groups singing polyphonically, the contrast between voices and instruments, the flow of horizontally moving melodic

lines versus their simultaneous vertical aspects, the juxtaposition of consonance and dissonance, the rhythmical opposition between the independent voices within a polyphonic motet, line against line, *cantus* versus *discantus*—in short all the inherent oppositions of an art based on the principle of point counter point.

**The Scholastic Synthesis**   In the face of so many disparities, it seems only a step short of the miraculous that the Gothic style was able to effect a synthesis at all. Such dualities, however, generated the need for some sort of *modus vivendi,* and that this was achieved is yet another proof of the remarkable intellectual ingenuity and creative vitality of the Gothic period. The method for achieving this coexistence was that devised by scholasticism: a kind of pro-and-con dialogue followed by a resolution. Its results shaped up in the form of the Gothic monarchy, university, encyclopedia, *summa,* and cathedral.

On entering Chartres Cathedral through the Virgin Portal, the worshiper was reminded by the personification of the seven liberal arts that faith needed to be enlightened by reason and knowledge. Architecture had to be a kind of logic in stone; sculpture and glass had to be encyclopedic in scope; and music had to be a form of mathematics in sound. All experience, in fact, had to be interpreted intellectually in contrast to the more intuitive and emotional orientation of the Romanesque. To the scholastic philosopher, God, as the Creator of a world based on principles of reason, was approachable through the logical power of the mind. Hence the key to the understanding of the universe was in the exercise of man's rational faculties. Philosophical truth or artistic value was determined by how logically a proposition fitted a rationally ordered system.

Abelard's *Sic et Non* ("Pro and Con") was an early manifesto of Gothic dualistic thinking. With unprecedented audacity, Abelard posed one pertinent question after another, lined up unimpeachable authorities from the Scriptures and Church fathers for and against the propositions. His purpose was to bring out into the open some of the wide cleavages of thought among sanctioned authorities, and he made no attempt at reconciliation. His scholastic successors debated whether ultimate truth was to be found through faith or reason, blind acceptance of hallowed authorities or evidence of the senses, universals or particulars, causes or effects, theses or antitheses, determinism or freedom of the will, intuition or reason. Thomas Aquinas and his fellow scholastics found the answer in the dialectical method; and Aquinas' synthesis, as found in his *Summa Theologiae* ("Summation of Theology"), was a comprehensive attempt to bring together all Christian articles of faith in a rational system. Abelard's pros and cons, and the divergent views of the previous 1,000 years of speculation, were reconciled by a subtlety of intellect that has never been surpassed. Such a *Summa* was as intricately constructed as a Gothic cathedral and had to embrace the totality of a subject, systematically divided into propositions and subpropositions, with inclusions deduced from major and minor premises. Every logical syllogism was fitted exactly into place like each stone in a Gothic vault; and if one of the premises were disproved, the whole structure would fall like an arch without its keystone. Aquinas' *Summa* mounted the heights of philosophical grandeur, just as the vaults and spires of the Gothic architects soared skyward.

From this highly rationalistic viewpoint followed the scholastic definition of beauty, which, according to St. Thomas, rested on the criteria of completeness, proportion, harmony, and clarity—because, he said, the mind needed order and demanded unity above all other considerations. Mathematical calculation and symbolism therefore played an important part in the thought of the time, though it was sometimes more closely allied with the sort of Pythagorean number-magic now associated with numerology than with the modern sense. The number 3 was especially favored because of its association with the Trinity; 4, to a lesser extent because it signified the material elements of fire, air, earth, and water; 7, as the sum of the two, indicated man, since his dual nature was composed of both spirit and matter; and their product pointed to such groups as the 12 apostles, 12 lesser

prophets, and so on. Since the sacred number was 3, it was used by most of the overall formal divisions, with the encyclopedias and the *Summas* each having three divisions; the syllogism, in three parts; the façades of cathedrals, three portals and the sculptural tympanums above, three rising bands. Naves have a main and two side aisles; vertically, they ascend in the triple division of nave arcade, triforium gallery, and clearstory; and in the clearstory, each bay at Chartres had two lancets and one rose window, and so on. The triple rhyming plan of the Latin poetry as in the *Dies Irae* (p. 157) and in the *terza rima* will serve as literary examples. In music, Gothic composers favored the three-part motet and ternary rhythm, which, because of its Trinity symbolism, was called *tempus perfectum*, while they considered binary rhythms too wordly and for this reason ruled them out.

In the cathedral schools and later in the universities, music was studied mainly as a branch of mathematics. Bishop Fulbert of Chartres emphasized theory in the training of singers, saying that without it "the songs are worthless." His view was generally held throughout the Gothic period, and as one theorist put it, a singer who is ignorant of theory is like "a drunkard who, while he is able to find his home, is completely ignorant of the way that took him home." Mathematical considerations, in fact, led composers to emphasize the perfect intervals of the octave, fifth, and fourth for theoretical reasons more than for the agreeableness of sound. The tendency was to suppress sensuous beauty of tone and emphasize the mathematical, theoretical, and symbolic aspects of the art.

The rise of national monarchies in France and England began to limit the international authority of the papacy, as well as to curb the provincial powers of the feudal lords domestically by increasing centralization of civil authority. In England, a political resolution between king and nobles, and between nobles and commoners, was made in the Magna Charta that became the basis for parliamentary government. In France, the establishment of a working relationship between the king and the urban middle class accomplished a similar purpose. King Louis IX of France was adroit enough to strengthen his own kingdom, while maintaining such good relations with the popes that he became a saint. In the cities the guilds brought patrons and craftsmen together; meanwhile, the system of apprenticeships and examinations ensured a high standard of quality and workmanship.

The undertaking of the fantastic crusades was found to be a way of uniting many opposing European factions in a cause against a common enemy. The code of chivalry was an attempt to reconcile the opposition between idealistic love and the gratification of the senses, and, more broadly, to establish a standard of behavior between strong and weak, lord and peasant, rich and poor, oppressor and oppressed.

157. Salisbury Cathedral. 1220–58. 473 × 230', height of spire 404'.

The Gothic universities were set up as institutions to bring together all the diverse disciplines and controversial personalities and to fit all the various intellectual activities into a single universal framework. Scholasticism became the common mode of thought, and its dialectic the common method of solving intellectual problems.

The structural uniformity of Gothic vaulting and buttressing was, in effect, the Gothic builder's answer to Romanesque experimentalism. Ample allowance for urban heterogeneity was made in the iconography of the individual cathedral and in the differences of cathedrals from town to town, and country to country, where each had distinctive character (Fig. 157). Both internally and externally, Gothic architecture tried to synthesize the building with the space surrounding it. Externally, the eye follows the multiplicity of rising vertical lines to the spires and pinnacles and then to the sky. Inside, the experience is similar; the vertical lines rise to the window levels and thence through the glass to the space beyond. In contrast to the monastic church that was based on the notion of excluding the outside world, the Gothic cathedral attempted an architectural union of the inner and outer world as the exterior and interior flowed together through the glass-curtained walls. The thrust and counterthrust of

the interior vaulting was paralleled on the outside by that of pier and flying buttress; the sculptural embellishments of the exterior were repeated in the iconography of the glass in the interior. Through the medium of stained glass, the iconographers endowed light with meaning by transforming physical light into metaphysical illumination.

The various European languages and dialects found a place for themselves in secular literature, but Latin was championed by the Church and universities as the universal language of scholarship. In music, the Latin and vernacular were reconciled in the polytextual motet; and when one language was used, the same form provided a highly ingenious method by which an authoritative text was declaimed, while at the same time one or more running commentaries upon it could be presented. Gothic music also represented a synthesis of theory and practice functioning together as equals. Through all these separate manifestations the Gothic spirit was revealed, whether in the systematic logic of St. Thomas, in the heightened sense of time and movement achieved by the musicians, or the visual aspirations and linear tensions of the builders.

No one of these resolutions was in any sense final, and the Gothic style must, in the last analysis, be viewed as a dynamic process rather than an end result. By contrast, a Greek temple or even a Romanesque abbey is a completed whole, and in both the observer's eye eventually can come to rest. The appeal of the Gothic lies in the very restlessness that prevents this sense of completion. The observer is caught and swept up in the general stream of movement, and from the initial impulse, he gets the desire to continue it. The completion, however, can only be in the imagination. There were, in fact, no finished cathedrals; each lacked something, from a set of spires in some cases to a nave as at Beauvais. Vincent's encyclopedia and Thomas Aquinas' *Summa* were likewise never completed.

Gothic unity is therefore to be found mainly in such methods and procedures as its dialectic in philosophy, structural principles in architecture, and techniques of writing in literature and music. No more effective processes could have been devised to deal with the specific incongruities with which the Gothic mind had to contend. They were, in fact, the only ways to reconcile the seemingly irreconcilable, to arrive at the irrational by ingenious rational arguments, and to achieve the utmost in immateriality through material manifestations. The object of Gothic thought was thus to work out a method for comprehending the incomprehensible, for pondering on the imponderables, for dividing the indivisible. Gothic art as a whole was designed to bridge the impossible gap between matter and spirit, mass and void, natural and supernatural, inspiration and aspiration, the finite and the infinite.

# 9 The Early Italian Renaissance Style

## ITALIAN PANORAMA, 14TH CENTURY

The oppositions that the Gothic 13th century had managed to maintain in a state of uneasy equilibrium by the application of scholastic logic and strict structurality broke out in the 14th century into open conflict. Like a stormy landscape, Italy was alternately chilled by the winds of a waning medieval winter and warmed by the first breaths of a waxing Renaissance spring. Gothic cathedrals were still being built in the north, while the dormant beauty of classical art was being revived in the south. Thunderous threats of fire and brimstone and fear of the Lord were hurled from church pulpits one day, to be followed the next by comforting Franciscan parables and assurance of divine love and mercy. Professors in universities still argued with the icy logic of scholastic philosophy, while the followers of St. Francis were persuading people with simple human truths. Some painters designed images of doomsday filled with warring angels and demons, while others portrayed Biblical stories as seen through the eyes of simple folk. And people wondered whether the world they lived in was a moral trap set by the devil to ensnare the unwary or a pleasant place a benign Creator meant them to enjoy.

For a drama of such sweeping scope, no single city or center could serve as the stage. All Europe, in fact, was the theater for this many-faceted performance in which men and their arts were in a state of creative ferment. The old Ghibelline and Guelph wars, which had started as a struggle between the forces loyal to the Holy Roman Empire and the partisans of the popes, assumed a new shape in the 14th century. People were moving from the country to the towns, where the entrenched landowning aristocrats rallied around the Ghibelline banner, and the growing ranks of merchants and craft guilds raised the Guelph flag.

The new Franciscan and Dominican orders rarely kept to their cloisters but took to the highways and byways as preachers to all who would gather and listen. Internal Church dissensions were such that even the popes had fled their hereditary see in Rome to hold court in widely scattered residences, most notably at Avignon in southern France. Writers, such as Dante and Petrarch, became exiles from their native cities, and their words were written during extended sojourns in half a dozen centers. Like them, the great painters were journeymen, traveling to wherever their commissions called them. Giotto, the leader of the Florentine school, did fresco cycles that occupied him several years each in Rome, Assisi, and Padua as well as in his home city. Simone Martini of Siena was active in Pisa and Naples before he painted a chapel in St. Francis' church at Assisi. Then he spent his last years at the papal court in Avignon. The great sculptors of Pisa worked also in Siena, Florence, Padua, and Arezzo. Musicians, likewise, sought their fortunes at various courts, with French and Flemish influences and musical forms dominating the Italian musical scene. Artistic idioms in general showed wide variation, with local styles springing up in such centers as Venice, Pisa, Siena, and Florence, while an international style took shape in southern France at Avignon, where the papal court attracted the best talents from every country.

In this era of change, the little village of Assisi in the Umbrian hills of central Italy became more representative than a large center like Rome. A town of such small size would, of course, have been too insignificant to support a major art movement, and no important artist could have survived in this provincial location, had Assisi not been the birthplace of one of the most beloved of medieval saints. Consequently, after the completion in the mid-13th century of Assisi's great pilgrimage basilica, many of the outstanding artists of the age gathered there as journeymen to decorate its walls.

The town of Assisi was built upon a rocky hill in the midst of a countryside more austere than lush. A truly mountainous terrain might have nurtured a rugged spirit capable of bringing down some new

## General Events

| | | |
|---|---|---|
| | 1140 | Guelph and Ghilbelline wars began |
| 1182– | 1226 | St. Francis of Assisi; 1210 founded Franciscan order (confirmed by pope, 1223); 1225 wrote *Canticle of the Sun*; 1228 canonized |
| 1198– | 1216 | Innocent III, pope; Church reached pinnacle of power |
| 1228– | 1253 | Basilica of St. Francis built at Assisi |
| | 1229 | Thomas of Celano's first *Life of St. Francis* |
| | 1247 | Thomas of Celano's second *Life of St. Francis* |
| 1252– | 1273 | Great Interregnum |
| | c.1260 | Pulpit in Pisa Baptistry finished by Niccolo Pisano |
| | 1262 | St. Bonaventura's *Life of St. Francis* |
| 1278– | 1283 | Campo Santo at Pisa built by Giovanni di Simone |
| c.1296– | 1300 | Frescoes on life of St. Francis painted at Assisi |
| c.1305– | 1309 | Giotto painted frescoes on history of the Virgin at Padua |
| 1308– | 1311 | Duccio painted Maestà altarpiece, Siena Cathedral |
| 1309– | 1376 | Popes at Avignon |
| | 1310 | First *Compagnie dei Laudesi* founded in Florence |
| 1314– | 1321 | *Divine Comedy* written by Dante Alighieri |
| | 1316 | *Ars Nova*, musical treatise, by Philippe de Vitry |
| | c.1320 | Giotto painted Bardi Chapel frescoes in Santa Croce, Florence |
| | 1322 | *Little Flowers of St. Francis* |
| 1330– | 1339 | Bronze doors of Baptistry at Florence cast by Andrea Pisano |
| | c.1334 | Andrea Pisano and Giotto collaborated on sculpture for Florence Campanile |
| | 1348 | Black Death swept Europe |
| 1348– | 1352 | *Decameron* written by Boccaccio |
| | c.1350 | *Triumph of Death* painted in Campo Santo at Pisa by Traini |
| | c.1354 | *Triumph of Death* written by Petrarch |
| 1378– | 1417 | Great Schism between rival popes |

## Philosophers

| | | |
|---|---|---|
| c.1214– | 1294 | Roger Bacon, Franciscan monk and scientist |
| c.1225– | 1274 | Thomas Aquinas, scholastic philosopher |
| c.1270– | 1347 | William of Occam, Franciscan monk and nominalist philosopher |

## Painters

| | | |
|---|---|---|
| 1240– | c.1302 | Giovanni Cimabue |
| c.1255– | 1319 | Duccio di Buoninsegna |
| c.1266– | c.1336 | Giotto di Bondone |
| c.1285– | 1344 | Simone Martini |
| 1305– | 1348 | Pietro Lorenzetti active |
| 1321– | 1363 | Francesco Traini active |
| 1323– | 1348 | Ambrogio Lorenzetti active |

## Sculptors

| | | |
|---|---|---|
| c.1205– | 1278 | Niccolo (d'Apulia) Pisano |
| c.1250– | c.1317 | Giovanni Pisano |
| c.1270– | 1349 | Andrea Pisano |

## Writers

| | | |
|---|---|---|
| 1265– | 1321 | Dante Alighieri |
| 1304– | 1374 | Petrarch (Francesco Petrarca) |
| 1312– | 1353 | Giovanni Boccaccio |

## Musicians

| | | |
|---|---|---|
| c.1200– | c.1255 | Thomas of Celano |
| | 1306 | Jacopone da Todi died |
| 1291– | 1361 | Philippe de Vitry |
| 1325– | 1397 | Francesco Landini, organist-composer at Florence |

commandments from above, but the gentle rolling green hills instead brought forth the most humble of Christian saints. A large city might have produced a great organizer of men, capable of moving the minds of the many with his clever speech to bring about a new social order. Francis of Assisi, however, recognized the dangers of bombastic oratory and the transient nature of all forms of social organization, and he accomplished his mission with the sweet persuasion of simple parables and the eloquence of his own exemplary life.

While the mature life of St. Francis fell within the 13th century, the collection of tales that made him a living legend, as well as the full development of the Franciscan movement, belongs to the 14th. The clergy who received their training in the universities and the scholarly orders of monks had never reached a broad segment of society. The Franciscans, however, found a way into the hearts and minds of the multitudes by preaching to them in their own vernacular and in the simplest terms, and Franciscan voices were heard more often in village squares than in the pulpits of the churches. The essence of the Franciscan idea is contained in the mystical marriage of the saint to Lady Poverty, the subject of one of the Assisi frescoes. When a young man had approached Christ and asked what he should do in order to have eternal life, the answer came, "... go and sell that thou hast, and give to the poor, and thou shalt have treasure in heaven: and come and follow me" (Matt. 19 : 21). St. Francis took this commandment literally, and in his last will and testament described his early life and that of his first followers. "They contented themselves," he wrote, "with a tunic, patched within and without, with the cord and breeches, and we desired to have nothing more. . . . We loved to live in poor and abandoned churches, and we were ignorant and submissive to all." He then asked his followers to "appropriate nothing to themselves, neither a house, nor a place, nor anything; but as pilgrims and strangers in this world, in poverty and humility serving God, they shall confidently go seeking for alms."

## THE BASILICA OF ST. FRANCIS AT ASSISI

Had St. Francis' precept of complete poverty been followed strictly, no great art movement would have developed at Assisi. A building program involved the accumulation and expenditure of large sums, and immediately after Francis' death this matter created dissension among those who had been closest to him. Brother Elias wanted to build a great church as a fitting monument to his friend and master, while others felt that Francis should be honored by the closest possible adherence to his simple life pattern. The monument Brother Elias had in mind would take a vast treasure to erect, and many of his fellow friars were shocked when Elias set up a porphyry vase to collect offerings from pilgrims who came to Assisi to honor Francis. Yet only two years later, at the very time of his canonization, a great basilica and monastery was begun on the hill where St. Francis had wished to be buried.

Taking advantage of the natural contours of the site, the architects designed a structure that included two churches, a large one above for pilgrims and a smaller one below for the Franciscan monks.

In spite of their comparatively large size, both churches are without side aisles, having just central naves terminating beyond transepts in polygonal apses. The large interior areas are spanned by spacious quadripartite groin vaults in the Lombard manner, which are partially supported by rows of columns set against the walls. Italian Gothic, contrary to the northern style, did not accent well-lighted interiors in which the walls were almost completely replaced with stained-glass windows. The southern sun made shade more welcome, and the interiors took on the character of cool retreats from the burning brightness of the world outside. The absence of a nave arcade and side aisles, and the small number of stained-glass windows, allowed ample wall space in both Assisi churches for the brightly colored fresco paintings that cover them. Lighted principally by the clearstory, the walls of the upper church glow in the dim interior with a mild inner light all their own, illuminated as they are by scenes from the life of St. Francis. More than anything else, it is these murals that bring the

twin churches their most special distinction, and the names of the artists who worked on them read like a roster of the great painters of the period: Cimabue and Giotto of Florence and Simone Martini and Pietro Lorenzetti of the Sienese school.

## THE LIFE OF ST. FRANCIS IN FRESCO

On entering the nave of the upper church at Assisi (Fig. 158), the observer encounters on its walls the series of frescoes on the life of St. Francis that tradition attributes to Giotto. His actual role as principal or part of a school of artists, his activity as designer or painter, are still matters of scholarly conjecture. The date generally assigned to the work is the four-year span just before the jubilee year of 1300. Knowing that pilgrims in unprecedented numbers would be traveling to Rome for the celebrations, the artists at Assisi made every effort to cover the bare walls of the upper church in time. The frescoes for the friars' own lower church had to wait until the mid-14th century for completion.

Giotto, like other master artists of his period, had learned to work in a variety of techniques. In addition to frescoes, he did mosaics, painted altarpieces in tempera on wood, and was a sculptor. Several years before his death, he was named the chief architect of Florence, and in this capacity he designed the bell tower of the cathedral (Fig. 170), still popularly called "Giotto's Tower." Some of the sculptured reliefs on the ground-floor level of this campanile may have been his, and others were presumably carried out from his designs by Andrea Pisano. Giotto's greatest fame,

**158.** Nave, Upper Church of St. Francis, Assisi. 1228–53.

159. GIOTTO(?). *Miracle of the Spring.* c. 1296–1300. Fresco. Upper Church of St. Francis, Assisi.

municative value, and the masterly execution of Giotto's cycles rank them among the highest achievements in world art.

The first two panels of the series at Assisi are worthy of Giotto himself, but since Giotto worked with a corps of assistants, it is impossible to be completely certain these are actually his work. On the right, after one passes through the entrance portals, is the *Miracle of the Spring* (Fig. 159), while on the left is the well-known *Sermon to the Birds.* The order of the scenes is psychological rather than chronological. The placing of this pair on either side of the entrance seems to have been done to impress pilgrims at the outset with the most popular Franciscan legends—those showing the saint ministering to the poor and humble on one side, and his kinship with all God's creatures, including his brothers the birds, on the other.

The literary source for the *Miracle of the Spring* is in the *Legend of the Three Companions,* which tells of Francis' journey to the monastery of Monte La Verna. A fellow friar, a peasant, and his donkey accompanied him, but the way was steep and the day hot. Overcome by thirst, the peasant cried out for water. Kneeling in prayer, the saint turned to him saying: "Hasten to that rock and thou shalt find a living water which in pity Christ has sent thee from the stone to drink." Pilgrims entering the church were athirst for spiritual refreshment, and the placement of this picture assured them that they had arrived at a spiritual spring.

The composition is as simple as it is masterly. St. Francis is the focal center of two crisscrossing diagonal lines like the letter **X**. The descending light from the rocky peak in the upper right reveals the contours of the mountain in a series of planes and reaches its greatest intensity in its union with St. Francis' halo, diminishing in his shadow where his two companions and the donkey stand. The dark mountain at the upper left moves downward toward the shadowy figure of the drinking peasant at the lower right, as if to say he is still in spiritual darkness. But since St. Francis is also on this diagonal line, the way to enlightenment is suggested. Giotto's inimitable mountains are found in such other of his major compositions as *Joachim Returning to the Sheepfold* (Fig. 169), the *Flight into Egypt,* and the great *Pietà* (Pl. 18, p. 144), all in the Arena Chapel at Padua. Structurally, the mountains advance and recede to form niches for his figures, and their hardness and heaviness are complementary to the compassion and expressiveness of his human beings. The mountains, or architectural backgrounds, do not exist in their own right but be-

however, rests most securely on the three fresco cycles in Assisi, Padua, and Florence.

The fresco medium calls for the rapid and deft strokes of a sure hand and for designs that harmonize with the architectural scheme and awaken walls into a vibrant and colorful life. After first covering the entire wall with a layer of rough plaster and allowing it to dry thoroughly, the artist makes a *cartoon,* a preliminary drawing in charcoal, on the surface. Then, taking an area he can finish in a single day, he smooths on a thin layer of wet plaster and retraces his original drawing. Next, earth pigments are mixed with water, combined with white of egg as a binder, and applied directly to the fresh plaster—hence the term *fresco.* The pigments and wet plaster combine chemically to produce a surface as permanent as that of any medium in painting. Artists sometimes paint over the surface after it is dry, but this repainting usually flakes off in time. If corrections are necessary, the entire section must be knocked out and redone. Fresco, then, is a medium that does not encourage overly subtle types of expression; and it is best adapted to a certain boldness of design and simplicity of composition. The emotional depth, the com-

come volumes and masses in Giotto's pictorial designs as well as inanimate extensions of human nature. Giotto's spatial proportions, furthermore, are psychologically rather than actually correct. Human beings, in keeping with their greater expressive importance, loom large against their mountain backgrounds; and his scattered trees are more spatial accents than natural trees.

Perhaps the most dramatic of the series is *St. Francis Renouncing His Father* (Fig. 160) after a controversy involving worldly goods. In his haste to abandon the material world, Francis casts off his garments and stands naked before the townspeople saying: "Until this hour I have called thee my father upon earth; from henceforth, I may say confidently, my Father who art in Heaven, in whose hands I have laid up all my treasure, all my trust, and all my hope." The bishop covers Francis with his own cloak and receives him into the Church. The expressions of the various figures as revealed in their gestures and facial expressions make this fresco an interesting study of human attitudes. The angry father has to be physically restrained from violence by a fellow townsman, yet his face shows the puzzled concern of a parent who cannot understand his son's actions. His counterpart on the other side is the bishop, who becomes the new father of the saint in the Church. Disliking such a scene, his glance shows both embarrassment and sympathy. These opposing figures are supported respectively by the group of townspeople with the apartment house and the clergymen with church buildings. An interesting pictorial geometry is used to unify the picture and resolve the tension. The two opposing groups, symbolizing material pursuits and spiritual aspirations, become the base of a triangle; between them the hand of St. Francis points upward toward the apex where the hand of God is coming through the clouds.

A notable example of Giotto's late style is found in the *Death of St. Francis* (Fig. 161), the climax of a series of seven he did twenty years later for the Church of Santa Croce in Florence. The static horizontal lines of the recumbent body are relieved by the varied gestures of the surrounding groups, and with one exception all eyes concentrate on the head of St. Francis. The architectural framework echoes the disposition of the figures, with the horizontal line of the wall paralleling the body of St. Francis and the vertical lines, those of the standing figures. Within this setting a sense of depth is conveyed by color. The ermine collar and red robe of the figure kneeling at the saint's right hand project him into the foreground; the neutral grays and browns of the habits of the monks back of the bier place them in the middle ground; and the deep blue sky recedes into the background. Here again Giotto uses a triangular pattern in telling his story. According to St. Bonaventura's biography, at the moment of Francis' death one of the brothers beheld a vision of the saint's "soul under the likeness of a star exceeding bright borne on a dazzling cloudlet over many waters mounting in a straight curve unto Heaven. . . ." In the fresco, the sides of the

left: 160. GIOTTO(?). *St. Francis Renouncing His Father.* c. 1296–1300. Fresco. Upper Church of St. Francis, Assisi.

below: 161. GIOTTO. *Death of St. Francis* (without 19th-century restorations). c. 1318–20. Bardi Chapel, Church of Santa Croce, Florence.

The Early Italian Renaissance Style    153

left: 162. NICCOLO PISANO. *Annunciation and Nativity*. 1259–60. Detail of marble pulpit, Bapistry, Pisa.

below left: 163. GIOVANNI PISANO. *Nativity and Annunciation to the Shepherds*. 1302–10. Detail of marble pulpit, Pisa Cathedral.

the populations of such cities as Florence, Siena, and Pisa perished. A chronicler of Siena, after burying five of his children, said quite simply: "No one wept for the dead, because everyone expected death himself."

An event so cataclysmic, and one that spread over the entire continent, was bound to have a deep effect upon social and cultural trends. Many survivors found themselves suddenly impoverished or, through unexpected inheritances, vastly enriched. Thousands of residents in the relatively immune countryside flocked into the cities to take the place of those who had died. The lives of individuals underwent radical changes that quickened their normal instincts. For some, it was the "eat, drink, and be merry" philosophy, exemplified in Boccaccio's *Decameron*; for others, it was the moral recrimination and repentance, as seen in the purgatorial vision of the same author's later *Corbaccio*. Driven by fear and a sense of guilt, people felt that something had gone disastrously wrong and that the Black Death, like the Biblical plagues of old, must have been sent by an angry God to chastise mankind and turn him from his wicked ways. Both Boccaccio and Petrarch among the literary men turned to this view after their earlier, more worldly writings, and what was true of literature was true also of painting.

Giovanni Pisano and his father Niccolo were the two outstanding sculptors of their time. Niccolo Pisano, also known as Nicola d'Apulia from his southern Italian origin, designed a handsome pulpit with six religious panels for the Baptistry at Pisa, and some years later Giovanni did one for the cathedral. The panels of both depict scenes from the New Testament. The differing attitudes of the father's generation and of the son's are revealed when panels dealing with the same subject are compared; together, their work represents the trend of sculpture before the Black Death.

Niccolo's panel of the *Annunciation and Nativity* (Fig. 162) clearly was influenced by the ancient sarcophagi the sculptor knew from his formative years spent near Rome. The Virgin appears as a dignified Roman matron reclining in a characteristic classical pose, while the angel at the left in the Annunciation section is seen against a classical temple and is dressed in a Roman toga, as are many of the other figures. Niccolo employs the old simultaneous mode of narration, with the Virgin making three appearances on the same panel, and the relief as a whole is permeated by a monumental calm. Giovanni's work, as evidenced by his *Nativity and Annunciation*

triangle are the line carried upward from the saint's head by the gesture of the disciple who sees the vision and the line formed by the inclining crucifix that meet at the apex where the heavenward journey is seen. Giotto thus ties the story content, emotional situation, and dramatic tension into a tight whole in his pictorial structure.

## BEFORE AND AFTER THE BLACK DEATH

All went well in Italy during the first third of the 14th century. Townspeople prospered, life was good, the arts flourished. Beginning in 1340, however, a series of disasters befell the peninsula, starting with local crop failures and continuing with the miseries of famine and pestilence. The climax came in an outbreak of bubonic plague in the catastrophic year of 1348. In this so-called "Black Death," more than half *to the Shepherds* (Fig. 163), moved away from his father's classicism into the French Gothic orbit. His figures are smaller in scale and more naturally proportioned to their surrounding space. Greater animation and agitation of line replace the serene repose of his father's style. The work of both father and son, however, has a sense of human warmth that closely resembles the spirit of Giotto's frescoes.

Nearby Siena, prior to the Black Death, was also enjoying a period of prosperity. Unlike its rival city Florence, which was a Guelph stronghold where power was held by the guilds and rich merchants, Siena was a staunch Ghibelline town dominated by the landed aristocracy. These oppositions led Florence in a progressive direction and kept Siena as a bastion of tradition. Cimabue, the leading Florentine artist of the late 13th century who brought the Gothic style to its apogee in his city, was succeeded by the formidable figure of Giotto whose painting points clearly to the coming Renaissance. In Siena, however, the great Duccio was followed by Simone Martini and the Lorenzetti brothers, who continued in the Byzantine tradition that had been introduced into Italy via such centers as Ravenna and Venice

many centuries earlier. Despite this traditionalism, the Sienese school poured enough late-Gothic wine into the old medieval wine skins to bring about a brilliant, albeit final, flowering of Italo-Byzantine painting.

Three altarpieces for Florentine churches—similar in purpose, theme, and form but different in style—will illustrate this painterly trend. Cimabue's *Madonna Enthroned* (Fig. 164), designed for the high altar of Santa Trinità, has all the feeling of medieval majesty and monumentality. Gothic verticality governs the two-story composition with four solemn prophets below displaying their scrolls and the ascending deployment of the eight angels above. The Madonna sits frontally on a solid architectural throne of complexly inlaid wood. Her dark-blue mantle and rose-red robe are flecked with highlights of gold that combine with the rich folds to create a rhythmic linear pattern. The Christ Child conforms to the theological image of the miniature patriarch born knowing all things. Duccio's so-called *"Rucellai" Madonna* (Fig. 165), from the Church of Santa Maria Novella, is in a lighter, more buoyant and decorative vein. While Duccio undoubtedly knew Cimabue's monumental

**right: 164.** CIMABUE. *Madonna Enthroned*. 1270-85. Tempera on wood, 12'6" × 7'4". Uffizi, Florence.

**far right: 165.** DUCCIO. *"Rucellai" Madonna*. 1285. Tempera on wood, 14'9" × 9'6". Uffizi, Florence.

The Early Italian Renaissance Style **155**

style, his kneeling angels are airier, as if gently set-
tling down after a heavenly flight. The folds of the
background drapery, liberal use of gold, Byzantine
opulence of line, surpassing delicacy of the zigzag
edges of the Madonna's robe, slight off-center angle
of the throne, gauzy drapery of the Child whose
mantle has slipped down—all achieve a maximum of
grace and elegance.

The new direction of the early Renaissance, however, is manifest in Giotto's *Madonna Enthroned* (Fig.
166), painted for the Church of Ognissanti about
twenty years later than those of Cimabue and Duccio.
Two angels kneel in the foreground, while the angels
of the heavenly choir are placed one in front of the
other so as to expand the sense of space and to create
a recession in depth toward the back row where six
grave saints are depicted. The drawing is simplified,
thus parting company with its predecessors, the Madonna's gaze meets that of her beholders, her figure
is heavier, the breasts prominent, the Child in a more
natural posture, and the Madonna's robe is modeled
in light and shadow to delineate the flesh beneath.

In the *Annunciation* (Pl. 19, 144) by Duccio's
Sienese disciple and Giotto's contemporary, Simone
Martini, aristocratic aloofness prevails. The Gothic
setting is courtly with the elegant vase of lilies and
the regal Madonna draped in a French-style blue
gown rendered in powdered lapis lazuli. Disturbed in
her reading by the sudden appearance of the Archan-
gel Gabriel, his robes and wings aflutter, the startled
Virgin recoils in fear and astonishment as she hears
the words that appear in relief: "Hail Mary . . . the
Lord is with thee." The composition is a masterly
combination of color and curvilinear design.

As a result of the Black Death of 1348, Sienese
art declined. The reaction to the great plague is well
illustrated in the series of frescoes on the inner walls
of the Campo Santo at Pisa. The theme is the Last
Judgment, and Traini's *Triumph of Death* (Fig. 167)
took its name from a poem by Petrarch. While no
cause and effect relationship between picture and
poem can be proved, both were reactions to the
plague, both shared common attitudes of the time,
and both were based on a similar theme.

*Triumph of Death* is a grandiose utterance, with so
much detail crowded into every square inch of space
that something in it was bound to appeal to everybody. Like the sermons of the time, each part warned
of the imminence of death, the terrors of hell if the
soul were claimed by the devil, or the bliss of being
carried off by the angels.

In Figure 167 a group of mounted nobles are
shown equipped for the chase, but instead of the
quarry they are pursuing, they find only the prey of
death. Inside the three open coffins serpents are consuming the corpses of the onetime great of the earth.
Petrarch also speaks of death as the great leveler
when he asks "the Popes, Emperors, nor Kings, no

**166.** GIOTTO. *Madonna Enthroned.* c. 1310. Tempera on
wood, 10'8" × 6'8". Uffizi, Florence.

**opposite: 167.** FRANCESCO TRAINI. *Triumph of Death* (detail).
c. 1350 (partially destroyed 1944). Fresco. Campo Santo,
Pisa.

enseigns wore of their past hight but naked show'd
and poor. Where be their riches, where their precious
gems? Their miters, scepters, robes and diadems?"
Hard by is a bearded Anchorite monk unfolding a
prophetic scroll that warns them to repent before it
is too late. The only relief from this scene of horror
and desolation is found in the upper left where some
monks are gathered around a chapel busying themselves with the usual monastic duties. Apparently
only those who renounce the world can find respite
from its general turmoil and terror of death.

## MUSIC AND LITERATURE

**The Dies Irae and the Canticle of the Sun**    The
contrast between the dour, threatening medieval

world view and the benign, joyful Franciscan spirit is illustrated by two 13th-century hymns. The facts of their composition alone are sufficient to point out the ideational cleavage of the period. The *Dies Irae*, which so admirably reflects the prevailing medieval spirit, was written by the great Latin stylist Thomas of Celano a few years before he met St. Francis and became one of his friars. The second, the *Canticle of the Sun*, is by St. Francis himself. Thomas of Celano entered the Franciscan order about the year 1215, enjoyed the friendship of St. Francis for several years, and was entrusted by Pope Gregory IX with the official biography that was written shortly after Francis' canonization in 1228.

In the triple stanzas and 57 lines of the *Dies Irae*, the medieval Latin poetic style reaches a high point. Its content invokes the vision of the final dissolution of the universe, the sounding of the angelic trumpets calling the dead forth from their tombs, and the overwhelming majesty of the coming of Christ as king to judge the quick and the dead. The grandeur of its language and the perfection of its poetic form are in every way equal to this solemn and awesome theme. The images and moods run a gamut from anger and terror to hope and bliss before coming to a close with a final supplication for eternal rest. A sampling of its 19 vivid verses can be gained from the following quartet of 3-line stanzas:

Day of Wrath! O day of mourning!
See fulfilled the prophets' warning,
Heaven and earth in ashes burning!

*Dies Irae*
(sequence, early 13th century)

Di - es i - rae, di - es il - la Sol - vet saec - lum
Quan-tus tre-mor est fu - tu - rus, Quan-do ju - dex

in fa - vil - la, Te - ste Da - vid cum Si - byl - la.
est ven - tu - rus, Cunc - ta stri - cte dis - cus - su - rus.

Wondrous sound the trumpet flingeth;
Through earth's sepulchres it ringeth;
All before the Throne it bringeth.

Guilty, now I pour my moaning,
All my shame with anguish owning;
Spare, O God, Thy suppliant groaning!

While the wicked are confounded,
Doomed to flames of woe unbounded,
Call me, with Thy saints surrounded.

Although the colorful alliterations and verbal rhythms of the Latin original have a music all their own, the *Dies Irae* is inseparable from a melodic setting in the mixed Dorian mode (above). While the melody cannot with certainty be attributed to Thomas of Celano, the close correspondence of tone and word makes it definite that they were at least from the same time. Both the poem and its melody found their way into the liturgy as a sequence that is still an indispensable part of the requiem mass for the dead. Se-

O Chri-sto' ni-po - ten- te, Do-ve sie-te_ in-vi - a - to, Che

si po-ve - ra-men - te_____ Gi - te_ pel-le - gri-na-to?

quences are so named because they follow the gradual and alleluia in the part of the mass between the reading of the epistle and the gospel. They attained wide popularity during this period and usually were sung by both congregation and choir.

The most characteristic Franciscan contribution to poetry and music is found in a body of informal spontaneous hymns called *laudi spirituali*—songs of praise or, simply, "lauds"—traceable directly to St. Francis and his immediate circle. The practice of spontaneous hymn singing continued from his time onward and in the 14th century was firmly established as the most popular form of religious music. Singing societies known as *Compagnie dei Laudesi*, "companies of laudists," have existed up to the present time, mainly in Italy. Besides Provençal French, Francis had learned the songs of Provence from his mother, who was of an old family of that region, and the biography known as the *Legend of the Three Companions* recounts how he sang aloud the lauds and canticles while praying and how during his travels "the holy man sang praises in French with a voice loud and clear." Since this was the great period of the troubadours, when many of the best known of these lyric poets visited Italy, St. Francis certainly was well acquainted with their lyrics and music. By his knowledge of the forms of these Provençal poets and by his practice of bursting into rhapsodic verse in his own vernacular Umbrian Italian, he played a leading role in the new poetic movement. Significantly, he called himself and his companions who sang the lauds with him *jongleurs de Dieu*, "minstrels of God." St. Francis thus identified himself with the musicians of the people rather than with the troubadours or aristocratic writers of amorous verse.

In music, as in his religious work, St. Francis drew together the sacred, courtly, and popular traditions. The lauds were thus a poetic bridge between the traditional music of the Church, the music of the castle, and the music of the streets. The words always had a religious theme; often they were mere paraphrases of psalms and litanies sung to popular airs but, above all, they were music and poetry that the people could both sing and feel with their hearts. Contrapuntal choral music, whether it was in the form of a church motet or a secular madrigal, was a sophisticated musical medium that needed the voices of skilled professionals. By contrast, the lauds were folklike in spirit, simple and direct in their appeal, and sung either as solos or jointly with others in unison. Just as the highly trained monastic choir was characteristic of the Cluniac movement and the contrapuntal chorus the musical counterpart of the northern Gothic spirit, the lauds became the special and characteristic expression of the Franciscans.

The *Canticle of the Sun*, known definitely to be by St. Francis, is at once the most sublime of all the lauds as well as the most original. The legend goes that when St. Francis was recovering from an illness in a hut outside the convent of St. Clare, the nuns heard from his lips this rapturous new song. The informality, even casualness, of its composition and its rambling rhythms and rhymes make it as simple and unaffected in its form as the Umbrian dialect in which it is written. It is thus characteristically opposed to the canons of scholarly Latin on one hand and to the erotic courtly utterances of the troubadours on the other. Sincerity and deep human feeling dominate the unequal strophes of St. Francis' songs of praise, rather than any attempt at learned communication or poetic elegance.

> O most high, almighty, good Lord God, to Thee belong praise, glory, honor, and all blessing!
>
> Praised be my Lord God with all his creatures, and especially our brother the sun, who brings us the day and who brings us the light; fair is he and shines with very great splendor; O Lord, he signifies to us Thee!
>
> Praised be my Lord for our sister the moon, and for the stars, the which He has set clear and lovely in heaven.
>
> Praised be my Lord for our sister water, who is very serviceable unto us and humble and precious and clean.
>
> Praised be my Lord for our brother fire, through whom thou givest us light in the darkness; and he is bright and pleasant and very mighty and strong.

The Assisi manuscript that contains the words of the *Canticle of the Sun* in its purest form also provided space for musical notation, which is, alas, blank. While the original melody seems to have been lost forever, countless lauds do survive, some of which date back to shortly after St. Francis' time. A Franciscan monk by the name of Jacopone da Todi, who died in 1306, was one of the most prolific producers of lauds. His most famous hymn is the *Stabat Mater Dolorosa*, which was officially incorporated in the liturgy in the 18th century to be sung for the Feast of the Seven Dolours. This remarkable man, like St. Francis before him, was of Umbrian origin, and, after a succession of such diverse careers as lawyer, hermit, and Franciscan preacher, he turned poet and composer. His hymns readily found their way into the texts of the early miracle plays, and his music became the foundation of the laudistic tradition. The example above is a part of one of his lauds. Its emotional intensity and stylistic character mark it as typical of the early Franciscan movement.

## Dante's Divine Comedy

In the early years of the 14th century, a synthesis of divergent philosophical, political, and religious world views was achieved by Dante Alighieri in his *Divine Comedy*—at once the greatest book of the medieval past and a prophecy of Renaissance things to come. In one stroke, Dante established vernacular Italian as a modern literary language and endowed his country with its most enduring literary masterpiece. The *Divine Comedy* is not only a synthesis of scholastic and Franciscan philosophies but of the whole thought of the medieval period and of Greco-Roman antiquity as its author knew it. Classical figures, such as Aristotle, Vergil, Ovid, and Cicero, rub shoulders across its pages with Boethius, St. Thomas Aquinas, St. Francis, and Giotto who, as tradition has it, portrayed Dante in a *Paradiso* of his own painted in the Chapel of the Bargello at Florence (Fig. 168).

The form of the poem is laden with medieval mathematical symbolism, the mystical number 3 serving as a kind of trinitarian motif. Each stanza has three verses; the rhyming scheme is the melodious *terza rima*—*aba, bcb*, etc.; one time after another, Dante is terrified by three animals; in each case he is saved by the mediation of three holy women; he is piloted on his travels by three guides. The whole poem is divided into three parts—Hell, Purgatory, and Heaven; each section contains 33 cantos, the number of Christ's years on earth; and, finally, the introductory canto, added to the three times 33 others, brings the total to an even 100, that number having the quality of wholeness or completion.

In spite of the heavy burden of number theory and other scholastic baggage—discourses on the laws of planetary motion, civil and canon law, medieval science, dialectical argumentation, and allegorical meanings, such as that of Vergil representing reason and Beatrice inspiration—Dante is far from an orthodox scholastic thinker. If he were, he would have written a treatise in the learned Latin instead of a poem in Tuscan Italian. No scholarly discourse ever began with the announcement: "The style is careless and humble, because it is in the vulgar tongue, in which even housewives hold converse." The revolutionary nature of this linguistic departure is almost impossible for the modern reader to understand, for in Dante's time literature was a possession of the learned few who possessed an adequate knowledge of Latin. All those who read poetry, philosophy, or history in effect had to do so in a foreign language. But even to an Italian, Dante's progress through the Inferno, Purgatory, and Paradise is not an easy one to follow. The path is hard and rough, and its obscurity comes from the doubts and conflicts that clouded the time. Since lecturers in Italian universities offered commentaries on it soon after the poet's death, the *Divine Comedy* must also have been difficult for those close to Dante's own time.

For all its carefully worked out form, and in spite of its inclusion of a cross section of the medieval scientific knowledge, the *Divine Comedy* is neither learned, elegant, nor aristocratic. It is obscure, unpolished, and abrupt. It is also so complex that no key, whether that of theology, metaphysics, philosophy or politics, will open the door to complete understanding. In contrast to the philosophical writings of that day, it mixes its subjects at times to the point of confusion. References to local politics are found side by side with glimpses into the beauty of Paradise; names of unremembered inhabitants of the towns Dante visited are placed beside those of the immortals; crude gossip and old wives' tales keep company with the scientific knowledge of the period. Hell and Heaven, faith and reason, events of the past and present, history and prophecy, paganism and Christianity, and the Greco-Roman and medieval worlds are all present in its pages. The mass of detail is kept from marring the greatness of the poem only by the vast conception of the whole and by the tight formal framework which tend to throw the multiplicity of its parts into proper perspective. Compensation for the confusion is found in the incomparable beauty of its language, so much of which is lost in translation. Dante, like Giotto, possessed the gift of making his characters live by just a few deft strokes. Like St. Francis', his allegories are not mere riddles for the learned doctors but lively tales for the untutored.

**168.** GIOTTO(?). *Portrait of Dante*, detail of fresco from Chapel of Palazzo del Podestà, Bargello, Florence. c.1325.

Dante has a true musician's ear for sound, and his verses have a music all their own. He also has the expert painter's eye for the minute details of appearances, and his images are a feast for the inner eye of the imagination as well. One instance of this imagery is his sensitivity to the medium of light. Primarily it is a spiritual light that concerns him, but he conjures up its vision in familiar everyday impressions filtered through the mind's eye of a great poet. He sings of sunlight, firelight, starlight; the sparkle of precious stones; the gleaming rays of a lamp in the darkness; the translucent effects of light filtered through water, glass, and jewels; rainbows and the colored reflections from clouds; the ruddy glow of infernal flames and the pure unearthly radiance of Paradise; the light of the human eye and that of the halos surrounding the heads of the saints; and finally, soaring toward the firmament, each of the three sections of the poem closes on the word "stars."

In spite of the preponderance of so many medieval elements, Dante achieves much that is associated with the Renaissance viewpoint. For all its mathematical structure, the *Divine Comedy* is full of violent human storms, passionate outbursts on the unnecessary wickedness of those in high places, and a general reassertion of the role of emotion in human affairs. For all his austerity, remoteness, and unapproachability, Dante does not pronounce a stern and final judgment. The very title would preclude this, because in his conception, "Comedy, indeed, beginneth with some adverse circumstances, but its theme hath a happy termination. . . ." Dante further specifically states that the didactic purpose of his poem is "to remove those living in this life from a state of misery and to guide them to a state of happiness." He writes with an unbounded faith in humanity, and when he relates the punishments meted out to those who suffer in his Inferno, he does so with the practical moral purpose of correcting such wordly evils as simony, usury, and avarice that he saw being practiced in the world as he knew it. It is important to point out that Dante did not write only the Inferno—a general impression derived from the romantic 19th-century writers who practically took this part to be the whole. His Purgatory and his Heaven, line for line, are equal in space with his Hell.

While the *Divine Comedy* is subtitled the *Vision of Dante Alighieri,* and the scene is laid in Hell, Purgatory, and Paradise, Dante's vision was not concerned only with life after death. By inference, he is describing the spiritual course of human life from birth in original sin through the purgation process of experience to a knowledge of ideal goodness. This dynamic spiritual journey is full of quite unmedieval emotions. After plunging with Dante into the bowels of the earth, the reader makes an upward ascent through the infernal regions on the back of Satan to the mountain of Purgatory, and, finally, into the metaphysical stratosphere of the various stages of Heaven. Civilization likewise, as Dante saw it, had struggled upward from the pagan world of Greece and Rome to the theocratic foundations of the medieval world, which had rested on an all-powerful Church and its secular counterpart, the Holy Roman Empire. It is a vertical and dynamic concept representing the ascent of humanity from the depths to the heights, from darkness into the light.

## IDEAS

The 14th century in Italy had one foot in the Middle Ages and the other in the Renaissance. The opposing world views are reflected in the great Church schism; the social struggle between the old landed aristocracy and the growing cities; the incompatibility of Gothic architecture and the sunny landscape of Italy; the presence of medieval devils and genuine human types in Giotto's frescoes; the opposing visions of the Inferno and Paradise in Dante's *Divine Comedy;* the attitudes expressed in poetry and painting before and after the Black Death.

The backward and forward directions are illustrated also in the struggle within the minds and consciences of individual men. The life of St. Francis, to cite one example, combined an other-worldly self-denial with an obvious this-worldly love of natural beauty. Fire for him was not created so much for the purpose of roasting the souls of sinners in Hell as to give light in the darkness and warmth on a cold night. The Romanesque St. Peter Damian had said: "The world is so filthy with vices the holy mind is befouled by even thinking of it." In contrast, the Gothic encyclopedist Vincent of Beauvais exclaimed: "How great is even the humblest beauty of this world!" St. Francis in his *Canticle of the Sun* found evidence of God's goodness everywhere—in the radiance of the sun, in the eternal miracle of springtime. He saw all nature as a revelation of divinity and, seeing thus, foreshadowed a departure from the divisive medieval dualism based on opposition of flesh and spirit. After a lifetime of self-mortification, he humbly begged pardon of his brother the body for the suffering he had caused it to endure.

The two great Italian writers of the 14th century—Petrarch and Boccaccio—reveal a similar inner conflict. Boccaccio, in his youth, wrote the worldly and joyous *Decameron* and reveled in the rediscovery of classical Greco-Roman literature. In his old age, however, he disavowed the *Decameron* and disposed of his library because it contained so many pagan books. Petrarch's poetry was a curious blend of Gothic chivalry and revival of ancient Roman forms; he wondered whether it was better to write in classical Latin or in vernacular Italian; and his early sensuous sonnets to Laura contrast with his later *Secret,* a moralistic dialogue with the ghost of St. Augustine.

The 14th century thus straddles the medieval and the Renaissance worlds. Looking backward, it represents a culmination of certain aspects of later medievalism; looking forward, it anticipates many of the ideas of the Renaissance. The breakdown of medieval symbolism is seen in the growth of naturalism in painting, and the shift from an other-worldly focus to one on this world is apparent in the rise of humanitarianism. It is important, however, to distinguish between the 14th-century naturalism, which is largely an outgrowth of late Gothic ideas, and its more scientific equivalent in the 15th century and between Franciscan humanitarianism and the more classically oriented humanism of the later Renaissance.

**Late Medieval Naturalism**     The abstractions of the scholastic mind found a new challenge in the concretions of the philosophers who called themselves "nominalists." Late scholasticism had, in fact, become more and more a strained exercise in logical gymnastics, and its forms all too often disregarded the real world and the facts necessary to give substance to thought. The nominalists simply turned the scholastic processes of thought completely upside down. They insisted that generalities are built up from the grouping of individual objects, whereas scholastics, by beginning with a hypothetical proposition or eternal Platonic idea, derived the facts of the phenomenal world from their proposition. To use the language of the schoolmen themselves, the scholastics reasoned *a priori*, while the nominalists did so *a posteriori*; one started from premises *ante rem*, and the other from propositions *in re*; or, to put it more simply, one reasoned *before* and the other *after* the fact. These systems approximate the difference between deductive and inductive thought, the latter leading to the experimental method of modern science.

The nominalist viewpoint, as it gained a foothold, weakened medieval authoritarianism, in which the word of Aristotle and the Church fathers was accepted without question, and initiated the modern practice of finding facts from firsthand observation. Particular things became more important than universal forms. A plant, now, was a vegetable or flower that grew in a garden rather than the manifestation of an *a priori* universal idea of a plant existing in the mind of God. The result of this new mental orientation was a renewed interest in a tangible reality that would have as important consequences in art as it did in the realm of scientific inquiry. In the next century, it was to lead to the representation of figures amid natural surroundings, the rendering of the body with anatomical accuracy, the modeling of figures three-dimensionally by means of light and shadow, and the working out of laws of linear perspective for foreground and background effects.

While opposing systems of logic were being argued in the universities, the friars of St. Francis were bringing his message to town and country folk. With them, religious devotion became a voluntary, spontaneous relationship between man and God rather than an imposed obligation, an act based on love rather than on fear. The Franciscans also sought to establish a common bond between a man, whatever his station in life, and his fellowmen—an important shift from the vertical feudal organization of society, in which men were related to those above and below them by a hierarchical authority, to a horizontally oriented ethical relationship that bound man to his fellowmen. St. Francis everywhere saw evidence of God's love in everything, from the fruits and flowers of the earth to the winds and the clouds in the sky—a concept that was to have great consequences for the course of art. The birds to which St. Francis preached, for instance, were the birds that were heard chirping and singing every day, not the symbolic dove of the Holy Ghost or the apocalyptical eagle of St. John. While this tendency toward naturalism was already noticeable in the 13th-century sculpture of Chartres and elsewhere, it became widespread in the 14th century. As this view of the natural world gained ascendance over the supernatural, based as it was on concrete observation rather than on metaphysical speculation, it released the visual arts from the perplexing problems of how to represent the unseen. The love of St. Francis for his fellowmen and for such simple things as grass and trees, which could be represented as seen in nature, opened up new vistas for artists to explore.

St. Francis' message was taught in parables and simple images of life that all could understand, and Giotto succeeded in translating these into pictorial form. In this favorable naturalistic climate, he found his balance between the abstract and the concrete, between divine essence and human reality. By refraining from placing his accent on symbolism, Giotto moved away from medieval mysticism and in his pictures portrayed understandable human situations. To him, the saints were not remote transcendental spirits but human beings, who felt all the usual emotions from joy to despair; just as did the people in the Italian towns he knew so well. Now that he no longer had to be concerned mainly with allegories but could reproduce the world of objects and actions as he saw it, a new pathway was opened. Even his contemporaries could see that Giotto was blazing new trails. Yet when they extolled him for his faithfulness to nature, their praise must be measured by the art that had preceded his time rather than by 15th-century or later standards. While Giotto undoubtedly showed a love of nature as such, he never accented it to the point where it might weaken his primary human emphasis. His interest was less in nature for its own sake than in its meaning in the lives of his subjects.

In viewing a picture by Giotto, one does well to begin with his people and be concerned only secondarily with their natural surroundings, because his pictures are in psychological rather than in linear perspective. His subjects seem to create their own environment by their expressive attitudes and dramatic deployment. While his work shows an increasing preoccupation with problems of natural space, this space remains subordinate to his expressive intentions, and his use of color and shading gives his human figures the sense of depth and volume that brings them to life. In this way, both human nature and nature as such attain an intimate and distinctive identity in Giotto's art.

**Franciscan Humanitarianism**    Long before, Cluny had changed the character of monasticism by uniting cloistered life with feudalism. Now the new orientation of the Franciscan order was no less revolutionary. St. Francis did not confine his monks in cloisters but sent them forth as fishers of men. The idea of evangelical poverty, humility, and love for mankind expressed through living and working with simple people resulted in a union with, rather than a withdrawal from, society. The Franciscans did not shun the world so much as they shunned worldly pursuits, and, as G. K. Chesterton has remarked, what St. Benedict had stored, St. Francis scattered. The Cluniacs were, in the proper sense of the word, an order—that is, their discipline required a strict hierarchical organization. The Franciscans by contrast were, in every sense of the word, a movement.

The icy intellectualism of the medieval universities was bound to thaw in the warmth of Franciscan emotionalism. Asceticism and self-denial held little appeal for an increasingly prosperous urban middle class. The mathematical elegance of Gothic structurality began to yield to more informal types of buildings. The logical linear patterns of the surviving Byzantine pictorial style gave way to the expressive warmth of Giotto's figures, and the vacuous stylized faces of Byzantine saints pale in the light of the human tenderness found in a smiling mouth or tearful eye in a Giotto picture. The formal architectural sculpture and abstract patterns of Gothic stained glass were replaced by the colorful informality of mural paintings in fresco. St. Francis in his music, as in his religious work, drew the sacred and popular traditions closer together, and in the lauds he encouraged people to sing; he gave them a music that they could feel in their hearts without having to understand it with their brains.

When Dante declared that Giotto's fame outshone that of Cimabue, and when Boccaccio proclaimed that Giotto revived painting after it had "been in the grave" for centuries, Giotto's contemporaries were recognizing in his art the presence of a new spirit and style. These are also apparent in the *Decameron*, where the ten city dwellers satirize the manners and foibles of Gothic knights, abbots, and monks and the outmoded feudal ideal to which they clung. And they

were also apparent in music. In France, Philippe de Vitry published a musical treatise c. 1316 with the title *Ars Nova*, or "new art," which he opposed to the *ars antiqua*, or "old art," of the Gothic 13th century. The new movement of which he was the spokesman, especially in its ardent championship of the new secular rhythms, was deemed sufficiently important to warrant censure in a vigorous bull issued by Pope John XXII at Avignon in 1325.

A new spirit of freedom was in the air, a freedom from tradition. St. Francis earlier had struck out in a new religious direction, and Giotto, by translating the saint's life into pictures, avoided the traditional Biblical subjects and their traditional stylized treatment. Actually he was working on an almost contemporary subject as well as rendering it in a new manner. Subjects that came within the iconographical tradition, such as *Joachim Returning to the Sheepfold* (Fig. 169) and the *Pietà*, or *Lamentation* (Pl. 18), were done far more dramatically than before. In general, Giotto's figures moved about in the space he created for them with greater suppleness than heretofore. His world was marked by a new and intelligible relationship between man and his fellowmen, between man and nature, and between man and God.

Representations of Christ as an infant in arms began to replace the mature image in divine majesty of the Gothic period, and along with the growing interest in the cycle of Christ's infancy, legends of Mary's life became more and more prominent. The emotional element in the Passion was largely conveyed through compassion for the Virgin as the mother of sorrows. This was as true for Giotto's cycle in Padua as it was for Jacopone da Todi's *Stabat Mater Dolorosa*. The adoption of the vernacular tongue in literature, the informal treatment of fresco painting, and the folk spirit in the music—all make it apparent that the works of art were being addressed to a new group of patrons. Furthermore, one of Giotto's recorded sayings reveals the artist's new conception of himself. Each man, he said, "should save his soul as best he can. As for me, I intend to serve painting in my own way and only so far as it serves me, for the sake of the lovely moments it gives at the price of an agreeable fatigue." Even the Black Death had some beneficial effects for the artists after Giotto's time, because the younger masters could assert their independence and develop new ideas and techniques with fewer restrictions from their conservative guilds.

What appears to be a renewed interest in classical antiquity began to be seen, heard, and read in the works of the artists and writers of the 14th century. The panels of Niccolo Pisano's pulpit show the classical Roman influence of such narrative reliefs as Trajan's Column (Figs. 84, 85). His son Giovanni, in spite of the Gothic orientation of his own work, placed ancient Roman sarcophagi alongside contemporary examples in the arcade of the Campo Santo in Pisa. The Roman poet Vergil appears prominently in Dante's *Divine Comedy*. All these phenomena, however, can be explained much more logically as the continuation of a tradition that had, in fact, never really died out. If Niccolo's sculpture is placed chronologically after a group of French Gothic examples, it certainly seems to be closer to the art of ancient Rome than to the Gothic. But since Roman sculpture was present everywhere in Italy, any Italian sculptor with his eyes open could not miss seeing it. Simple as it may sound, the explanation is a geographical rather than a chronological or psychological one: central Italy is closer to Rome than to northern France. Since Dante was writing an epic poem, the obvious antecedent was the *Aeneid*, which had never ceased to be read. While a growing consciousness of the classical in the works of Dante and his contemporaries is not to be overlooked, it must be seen from the 14th-century point of view as a continuation of a cultural tradition rather than as a rebirth of classicism. The influence of the classic authors and classical art had never been quite so neglected or dead as many historians have supposed. Vergil, Cicero, and certain works of Aristotle were as widely read in medieval times as they were in the 14th and 15th centuries.

This is not to deny the fact that a new spirit of curiosity enlivened the search, instituted by Petrarch and Boccaccio, in monastic libraries for manuscripts by other Greek and Roman authors than those who bore the hallowed approval of Church tradition. This probing also went hand in hand with the discovery in Rome of some long-buried antique sculpture and with the study of Roman building methods. Even though Petrarch amid much classical fanfare was crowned in Rome with the laurel wreath, that ancient token of immortal fame, and even though he wrote his cycle of Triumphs with the Roman triumphal arch form in mind, it is doubtful that he or Dante or Boccaccio did more than bring the ancient world a little closer to their own time. They certainly had no such admiration for pagan antiquity for its own sake as did the 15th-century Florentines. Even though Giotto spent some time in Rome, the joyous humanistic spirit that permeates his work is much closer to the new Franciscan outlook and the continuous tradition of Roman relief sculpture and fresco painting than to any conscious reappraisal of classical culture as such. It is necessary, then, to disassociate the spontaneous 14th-century Franciscan humanitarianism from the more self-conscious revival of antiquity that characterized developments in 15th-century Florentine and early 16th-century Roman humanism.

The 14th-century conflict of opposing ideas and forward-backward trends has variously been designated as the post-Gothic, proto-Renaissance, or pre-Renaissance period. But any period that contains the magic names of St. Francis, Dante, Petrarch, Boccaccio, Giotto, Duccio, and Simone Martini and that exhibits such a high degree of originality and creativity can well stand on its own rather than be a postlude or a prelude to another. In style as well as ideas it is indeed the Early Renaissance.

**169.** GIOTTO. *Joachim Returning to the Sheep-fold.* 1305–06. Fresco. Arena Chapel, Padua.

# 10 The Florentine Renaissance Style

## FLORENCE, 15TH CENTURY

Colorful festivals were the delight of all Florentines, but March 25, 1436, was a special occasion that would linger long in the memory of these prosperous and pleasure-loving people. The dedication of Florence's newly completed cathedral (Fig. 170) brought together an unprecedented number of Church dignitaries, statesmen, and diplomats, and in their entourages were famous artists, men of letters, and musicians. The white-robed pontiff Eugene IV, crowned with the triple tiara, attended by 7 cardinals in bright red and no less than 37 bishops and archbishops in purple vestments, made a triumphal progress through the banner-lined streets, accompanied by city officials and heads of the guilds with their honor guards. Appropriately enough, the cathedral was christened Santa Maria del Fiore ("St. Mary of the Flower"), since Florence (derived from *flora*) was indeed the city of flowers. March 25 was also the Feast of the Annunciation, the beginning of new life nine months before Christ's birth, and both the Annunci-

ation and Nativity were favorite subjects of Florentine painting.

The eyes and thoughts of all Florentines that day were directed upward to the mighty cupola that crowned the crossing of their cathedral and gave their city its characteristic profile. Though initiated in the late 13th century, the building's construction had languished because no architect possessed the necessary knowledge to dome such an enormous, gaping, 140-foot-wide octagonal space (Fig. 171). But Filippo Brunelleschi, after studying the Pantheon and other ancient monuments in Rome, had returned and undertaken the gigantic task now at the point of completion. Starting at a level some 180 feet above ground, he sent eight massive ribs soaring skyward from the angles of the supporting octagon to a point almost 100 feet higher where they converged at the base of a lantern tower. Concealing them from external view, he added two minor radial ribs between each major one, twenty-four in all, to make his inner shell. Reinforcing these by wooden beams and iron clasps at key points, he then had the necessary sup-

left: **170.** Florence Cathedral group. Cathedral begun by ARNOLFO DI CAMBIO, 1296; dome by FILIPPO BRUNELLESCHI, 1420–36; present façade 1875–87. Cathedral length 508′, dome height 367′. Campanile ("Giotto's Tower") begun 1334 by GIOTTO; continued by ANDREA PISANO, 1336–48; height 269′. Bapistry (lower right) 1060–1150.

below: **171.** Plan of Florence Cathedral.

port for the masonry of his inner and outer shells. The structure is, in effect, an eight-sided Gothic vault. But by concealing the functional elements and shaping a smooth external silhouette, Brunelleschi crossed the bridge into Renaissance architecture.

Opposite the façade of the cathedral is the old Romanesque baptistry (Fig. 170, lower right), which was feeling new Renaissance life with Ghiberti's gilded bronze doors. Already in place were the handsome north doors, and the sculptor was well on his way to completing the east doors (Pl. 20, p. 177), which Michelangelo was later to hail as worthy of being the "Gates of Paradise." Helping him cast these doors in his workshop at various times were the architect Michelozzo, the sculptor Donatello, and the painters Paolo Uccello and Benozzo Gozzoli. Donatello, at the same time, was working on a series of statues of prophets for niches on the exterior of both the cathedral and the campanile, traditionally known as "Giotto's Tower."

In Pope Eugene's entourage were some of the leading Florentine humanists, including the artist-scholar Leone Battista Alberti, who had just completed his book *On Painting* and was at work on his influential treatise *On Architecture*. On hand to provide music for the occasion was the papal choir, whose ranks included the foremost musician of his generation, Guillaume Dufay, who composed the commemorative motet for the occasion. Antonio Squarcialupi, regular organist of the cathedral and private master of music in the Medici household, is thought to have composed the solemn high mass. According to an eyewitness, the magnificent pontifical procession was preceded by a great band of wind players, "each carrying his instrument in hand, and arrayed in gorgeous cloth of gold garments." After them came the combined choirs that "sang at times with such mighty harmonies that the songs seemed to the listeners to be coming from the angels themselves."

Lining the streets for the grand procession and crowding their way into the vast nave of the cathedral were the colorfully costumed citizens of this prosperous Tuscan town. In contrast with northern countries, in this region city life had come of age. At a time when many feudal aristocrats still inhabited their dank fortresslike castles, the Florentine patrician families lived in a style that could well have been the envy of kings. The working members of the population belonged to the various guilds and trade organizations, the most important of which were those dealing with the carding, weaving, and dyeing of wool and silk for the famous Florentine textile industry. Metalcrafts and stonework followed in importance, and so on down to the butchers and bakers. The masters of the principal guilds were the influential citizens from whose ranks the members of the Signory, or city council, were chosen and from which the merchant and banking families emerged.

The most renowned of these was the Medici family, whose head at this time was Cosimo. By a combination of political sagacity and financial acumen in manipulating his large fortune, he dominated the government of the city. Knowing his fellow townsmen's passion for equality, Cosimo never assumed a title or other outward sign of authority but, instead, was the benign political boss, ruling from behind the scenes with the support of the guilds, which knew that a stable government and peaceful relations with their neighbors were the best safeguards of their prosperity. The Medicis were also the papal bankers who received on deposit Church funds from England, France, and Flanders; and from their branch offices in London, Lyon, and Antwerp, they lent the money at fantastic rates of interest to foreign heads of state. With the papal revenues, they also bought English wool, had it processed in the Netherlands, shipped it to Florence to be woven into fine fabrics, and exported these at a handsome profit. It was Cosimo who made the florin the soundest currency in Europe. But political power and high finance were not the only pursuits of this ambitious banker.

Cosimo's other accomplishments were unusual for a Renaissance merchant capitalist. As a diligent student of Plato, he became one of the founders of the Neoplatonic Academy, an institution that had enormous intellectual influence. From all the parts of Europe where his financial interests extended, he commissioned works of art, while at home he gathered a library of rare manuscripts for scholars to study and translate. Through his generosity, a group of Dominican monks had just moved into the monastery of San Marco, which was being rebuilt for them by his personal architect Michelozzo. Among the monks was Fra Angelico, whom Cosimo encouraged to decorate the monastery walls with his famous frescoes. Although Masaccio, one of the century's most original painters, had been dead for six years, Filippo Lippi, the future teacher of Botticelli, was active and looking to Cosimo for commissions. Cosimo took Donatello's advice, collected antique statuary, placed it in his gardens, and encouraged young sculptors to work there. Small wonder, then, that the Signory voted him the posthumous title *Pater Patriae*—"Father of His Country."

For such solemn ceremonies as dedications and coronations, it was the custom to perform a motet especially written for the occasion. Dufay, a musician educated in the Burgundian French tradition, had been a member of the papal choir since 1428 and had composed such an occasional motet for the ceremonies at the conclusion of peace between Pope Eugene and the Emperor Sigismund in 1433. The motet, coming as it does outside the normal liturgical music of the mass, lent itself well to the purposes of an occasional piece that could be composed for a specific ceremony to a text which contained topical allusions.

# CHRONOLOGY / 15th-Century Florence

## General Events

| | | |
|---|---|---|
| | 1401 | Competition for Florence Baptistry north doors |
| 1403– | 1424 | Ghiberti worked on Florence Baptistry north doors |
| | 1406 | Pisa under Florentine rule |
| | 1421 | Giovanni de' Medici elected magistrate |
| 1425– | 1452 | Ghiberti worked on Florence Baptistry east doors |
| | c.1429 | Pazzi Chapel begun by Brunelleschi |
| | 1434 | Pro-Medici government elected; Cosimo de' Medici (1389–1464) began rule |
| 1434– | 1444 | Pope Eugene IV resided in Florence |
| | 1436 | Florence Cathedral dedicated (begun 1298; dome by Brunelleschi) |
| 1439– | 1442 | Council of Florence brought nominal union of Eastern and Western Churches |
| 1444– | 1459 | Medici-Riccardi Palace built by Michelozzo |
| | 1447 | Parentucelli, Florentine humanist, elected Pope Nicholas V |
| 1464– | 1469 | Piero de' Medici ruled after Cosimo's death |
| 1469– | 1492 | Lorenzo de' Medici ruled |
| | 1476 | Portinari Altarpiece by van der Goes of Flanders brought to Florence |
| | 1478 | Pazzi family led unsuccessful revolt against Medici; Giuliano de' Medici assassinated; Lorenzo consolidated political power |
| | c.1480 | Heinrich Isaac succeeded Squarcialupi as organist at cathedral; court composer to Lorenzo |
| | 1482 | Marsilio Ficino's translations of Plato's dialogues printed |
| | c.1485 | Alberti's treatise *On Architecture* printed; *On Painting* (1436), *On Sculpture* (1464) also printed c.1485 |
| | 1489 | Savonarola (1452–98) preached moral reform. Michelangelo apprenticed to Ghirlandaio |
| | c.1490 | Aldine Press founded in Venice; began publishing works of Plato and Aristotle |
| | 1492 | Lorenzo de' Medici died |
| | 1494 | Medici exiled from Florence; government dominated by Savonarola |
| | 1497 | Burning of books, pictures, and all "vanities" |
| | 1498 | Savonarola burned at stake |

## Painters

| | | |
|---|---|---|
| 1387– | 1455 | Fra Angelico |
| 1397– | 1475 | Paolo Uccello |
| c.1400– | 1461 | Domenico Veneziano |
| 1401– | 1428 | Masaccio |
| c.1406– | 1469 | Filippo Lippi |
| c.1416– | 1492 | Piero della Francesca |
| 1420– | 1497 | Benozzo Gozzoli |
| 1423– | 1457 | Andrea del Castagno |
| c.1429– | 1498 | Antonio Pollaiuolo |
| 1444– | 1510 | Sandro Botticelli |
| 1449– | 1494 | Domenico Ghirlandaio |
| 1452– | 1519 | Leonardo da Vinci |
| 1458– | 1504 | Filippino Lippi |

## Sculptors

| | | |
|---|---|---|
| 1371– | 1438 | Jacopo della Quercia |
| 1378– | 1455 | Lorenzo Ghiberti |
| 1386– | 1466 | Donatello |
| 1400– | 1482 | Luca della Robbia |
| c.1429– | 1498 | Antonio Pollaiuolo |
| 1435– | 1488 | Andrea del Verrocchio |
| 1475– | 1564 | Michelangelo Buonarroti |

## Musicians

| | | |
|---|---|---|
| 1400– | 1474 | Guillaume Dufay |
| 1430– | 1495 | Jean de Ockeghem |
| 1436– | 1475 | Antonio Squarcialupi |
| c.1450– | 1517 | Heinrich Isaac |
| 1450– | 1505 | Jacob Obrecht |
| c.1460– | 1521 | Josquin des Prez |

## Writers and Philosophers

| | | |
|---|---|---|
| 1304– | 1374 | Petrarch (Francesco Petrarca) |
| 1313– | 1375 | Giovanni Boccaccio |
| 1433– | 1499 | Marsilio Ficino |
| 1449– | 1492 | Lorenzo de' Medici |
| 1454– | 1494 | Angelo Poliziano |
| 1463– | 1494 | Pico della Mirandola |
| 1469– | 1527 | Niccolo Machiavelli |
| 1478– | 1529 | Baldassare Castiglione |

## Architects

| | | |
|---|---|---|
| 1377– | 1446 | Filippo Brunelleschi |
| 1391– | 1473 | Michelozzo di Bartolommeo |
| 1404– | 1472 | Leone Battista Alberti |

The words in this case begin: *Nuper rosarum flores ex dono pontificis*—"Flower of roses, gift of the pontiff." The cathedral is referred to as this "most spacious temple," and Brunelleschi's dome is praised as a "mighty artifice," a "marvel of art." The text appropriately concludes with a supplication to the Virgin Mary on behalf of the people of Florence: "O Virgin, the glory of virgins, thy devoted people of Florence beseech thee that he who prays ... may deserve to receive thy gracious benefits...." Since such motets were composed for official occasions, their style tended toward traditional practices rather than experimentation. Dufay therefore built his formal structure on the severe isorhythmic principles developed by the 14th-century French composers. Such a method is governed by certain rules of musical logic, and the forms are compounded of sections that are unified by an identity of rhythmic relationships but not necessarily of melodic patterns. Such music was never intended primarily to please the ear or stir the emotions but to mirror the hidden harmonies of the universe and thus to constitute a worthy offering to its Creator. In Dufay's conception, however, the universe is no mere structure but is populated with shapely melodies, warm harmonic colors, and a variety of rhythmic forms.

This dedicatory scene of Santa Maria del Fiore has often been cited, both by those who witnessed it and by later historians, as the beginning of a new era. There was, of course, a new spirit in the air, but at the same time it was never clearer that no sharp break with the medieval past was being made. The cathedral itself was late Gothic in style; Brunelleschi's dome was constructed by Gothic vaulting methods; and Dufay's isorhythmic motet was a late Gothic musical form. The Italian Gothic, however, had never had either the dynamic verticality or the aspiring force of its northern counterpart. Brunelleschi's dome was, to be sure, the first of such magnitude to be constructed since antiquity, but smaller domes over the crossing were not unusual in Tuscany. But while the construction of Brunelleschi's dome fell within the scope of the Gothic, the new emphasis was on smoother lines and the shapeliness of the external silhouette. Dufay's motet, for its part, showed an increasing secular feeling in church music, since the composer was apparently much less concerned with making a pious setting of his text than he was with making his mathematical proportions fit smoothly into his musical structure. While such mental gymnastics were late Gothic in conception, the Italian sense of melodic contour, the increased emphasis on secular duple

time, the softening of the dissonant passing tones, and the pliancy of the contrapuntal texture all point in the direction of the Renaissance. Dufay's special contribution was in clothing the austere skeletal structure of such a composition with skillful voice leading and a fluency of sound that made it a joy to the ear as well as to the mind.

## PAZZI CHAPEL AND MEDICI-RICCARDI PALACE

Impressive as is the immense cupola of Florence's cathedral, the new architectural spirit is more readily grasped in Brunelleschi's smaller Pazzi Chapel (Fig. 172). Here, in a building of diminutive proportions, the architect could give his full attention to design without having to be absorbed in complex construction problems (Fig. 173). The fruits of his studies of ancient Roman buildings are more in evidence, and the break with the Gothic tradition is complete. The harmonious spacing of the columns of the portico, the treatment of the walls as flat surfaces, and the just balance of horizontal and vertical elements make Brunelleschi's design the prototype of the Renaissance architectural style. The entablature gives still further evidence of the classical influence. The curved pattern above comes directly from ancient Roman sarcophagi, while the elegant carving of the Corinthian capitals, the Composite pilasters, and other design details reveal Brunelleschi's early training as a silversmith as well as his study of authentic Roman originals.

**left: 172.** FILIPPO BRUNELLESCHI. Façade, Pazzi Chapel, Cloister of Church of Santa Croce, Florence. c. 1429–33. 59'9" × 35'8".

**below: 173.** Plan of Pazzi Chapel.

The interior bears out the promise of the façade and shows a Roman classical concern with the logical molding of interior space (Fig. 174). Devoid of Gothic mystery and indefiniteness, the pilastered walls give a cool, crisp impression. Frames of dark-colored stone divide the surfaces into geometric forms easily assimilated by the eye. Mystery and infinity have yielded to geometrical clarity. The rectangular room is covered by transverse barrel vaults, with a low dome on pendentives rising in the center at the point of intersection. Somewhat hesitantly to be sure, this interior indicated a new concept of space without, however, realizing its full implications. The clear-cut simplicity of its design made the Pazzi Chapel a highly influential model throughout the Renaissance, and the unity of its centralized organization under a dome became the point of departure for the church plans of Alberti, Bramante, and Michelangelo.

When Cosimo de' Medici decided to build himself a new house, he is said to have rejected a palatial plan submitted by Brunelleschi, with the observation that envy was a plant that should not be watered. For the Medici-Riccardi Palace (Fig. 175) he chose instead a less ostentatious design submitted by Brunelleschi's disciple Michelozzo. (The palace has a dual name because it was acquired in the 17th century by the Riccardi family.) As the design materialized, the building turned out to be an appropriately solid structure,

eminently suited to the taste of a man of such considerable substance as Cosimo. As a type, such buildings were actually a continuation, rather than a revival, of the multistoried Roman city apartment house. Here the dominance of solid mass over the space allotted to the windows, plus the heavily rusticated masonry of the first story (many of the stones protrude more than a foot) still has something of the forbidding aspect of a medieval fortress. But as the eye moves upward, the second and third floors present an increasingly urbane appearance. The accent on horizontal lines, seen in the molding strips that separate the three stories and in the boldly projecting cornice at the roof level, are quite unmedieval. A classical allusion can be seen in the semicircular arches that frame the windows (the pediments over those on the lower story are a somewhat later addition). Details, such as the colonnettes of the windows on the second and third floors as well as the egg-and-dart pattern and the dentil range that appear in the cornice frieze, are definitely Renaissance in style.

Cosimo's sense of austerity stopped with the palace's exterior, and inside the doors everything was on a princely scale. With the frescoes of Benozzo Gozzoli and an altarpiece by Filippo Lippi decorating its second-floor chapel, easel paintings by Uccello and Botticelli hanging on salon walls, antique and contemporary bronze and marble statues standing in the

**below: 174.** FILIPPO BRUNELLESCHI. Interior, Pazzi Chapel, Cloister of Church of Santa Croce, Florence. c.1429–33.

**right: 175.** MICHELOZZO. Façade, Medici-Riccardi Palace, Florence. 1444–59. Length 225′, height 80′.

courtyard and gardens, collections of ancient and medieval carved gems and coins in its cabinets, and precious metal vessels and figurines standing on its tables, a library with priceless manuscripts including the works of Dante, Petrarch, and Boccaccio, the Medici-Riccardi Palace was, in fact, one of the first and richest museums in Europe.

## SCULPTURE

In the year 1401, the Signory of Florence together with the Guild of Merchants had held a competition to determine who should be awarded the contract for the projected north doors of the baptistry. Like the earlier pair by Andrea Pisano, the material was to be bronze, and the individual panels were to be enclosed in the quatrefoil pattern. The subject, for the purpose of the contest, was to be the Sacrifice of Isaac. Some half-dozen sculptors were invited to submit models, among them Brunelleschi and Lorenzo Ghiberti. Both men were in their early twenties; both were skilled workers in metal and members in good standing of the Goldsmiths' Guild. A comparison of their panels, however, reveals many significant differences of viewpoint and technique (Figs. 176, 177). Brunelleschi's composition shows the influence of Gothic verticality in the way the design is built in three rising planes; Ghiberti's composition is almost horizontal, and his two scenes are divided diagonally by a Giotto-like mountain. Brunelleschi's panel is crowded, and his figures spill out over their frame; Ghiberti's is uncluttered, and all his figures and details converge toward a center of interest in the upper right formed by the heads of the principal figures. Brunelleschi accents dramatic tension, with Abraham seizing the screaming Isaac by the neck and the angel staying his hand at the last moment; Ghiberti sacrifices intensity for poise and decorative elegance. Brunelleschi shapes Isaac's awkward body with Gothic angularity; Ghiberti models it with the smooth lines and impersonal grace of a Hellenistic statue. (Ghiberti's *Commentaries* mention the discovery near Florence of the torso of an ancient classical statue on which he modeled his Isaac.) Finally, Brunelleschi cast his relief in separate sections, mounting these on the bronze background plate; Ghiberti, with greater technical command, cast his in a single mold. The decision in Ghiberti's favor showed the way the aesthetic winds were blowing in 1401. Ghiberti then set to work on the 20 panels of the north doors, which were to occupy the major part of his time for the next 24 years, while Brunelleschi, accompanied by his friend Donatello, traveled to Rome to study architecture.

Ghiberti's north doors were no sooner in place than he was commissioned, this time without competition, to execute another set. The famous east doors, on which he worked from 1425 to 1452, tell their own tale (Pl. 20). The Gothic quatrefoil frames were now

**176.** Filippo Brunelleschi. *Sacrifice of Isaac.* 1401. Gilt bronze, $21 \times 17\frac{1}{2}''$ (without peripheral molding). National Museum, Florence.

**177.** Lorenzo Ghiberti. *Sacrifice of Isaac.* 1401. Gilt bronze, $12 \times 17\frac{1}{2}''$ (without peripheral molding). National Museum, Florence.

The Florentine Renaissance Style    **169**

a thing of the past, and, while his north doors were conceived in terms of their architectural function, the east doors served largely as a convenient framework for decoration. They even show some disregard for techniques appropriate to the three-dimensional medium of relief sculpture and in effect become pictures painted in gilded bronze. Ghiberti attempts daring perspectives far in advance of the painting of the period; and some figures, such as those in the center panel of the left door, are in such high relief as to be almost completely in the round. In the Adam and Eve panel at the top of the left door (Fig. 178), he uses three receding planes: the high relief in the lower foreground is employed to tell the creation of Adam (left) and Eve (center) and the expulsion (right) in the present tense; the immediate past is seen in the half relief of the middle ground showing the Garden of Eden; and in the low relief of the background God and his accompanying cloud of angels seem to be dissolving into the thin air of the remote past.

On either side of the pictorial panels, Ghiberti included a series of full-length figurines that alternate with heads which recall Roman portrait busts. Hebrew prophets on the outer sides are set opposite pagan sibyls, all of whom were supposed to have foretold the coming of Christ. The figure beside the second panel from the top on the right door is that of the Biblical strong man Samson, but his stance and musculature are those of a Hellenistic Hercules. Ghiberti mentions in his *Commentaries* how he sought to imitate nature in the manner of the ancient Greeks when molding the flora and fauna of these door frames. The care and delicate craftsmanship he lavished on these and other details make the east doors a high point in the metalworker's art. Ghiberti, as was said, belonged to the Goldsmiths' Guild, and its influence is felt in many aspects of Florentine art. It is to be seen not only in such door moldings but in pulpits, wall panels, window brackets, columns, pilasters, cornices—all of which were wrought with a wealth of fine detail lovingly dwelt upon.

Donatello's personality and career contrast strongly with Ghiberti's. A man of fiery temperament and bold imagination, Donatello scorned the fussy details which allied Ghiberti's work with that of the jeweler, and his sculpture has a rugged grandeur that makes Ghiberti's appear precious by comparison. While Ghiberti studied local examples of antique sculpture and read Vitruvius' treatises, Donatello had gone to Rome with Brunelleschi to see the finest surviving classical statuary. While Ghiberti remained a specialist in bronze, Donatello was at home with all materials—marble, wood, painted terracotta, gilded bronze; in all mediums—relief and in the round, small scale and heroic size, architectural embellishment and independent figure; in all subjects—sacred and secular, historical scene and portraiture. While Ghiberti had a single style, Donatello had many. His power of epical expression, enormous energies, vehemence, and impetuosity make him the representative sculptor of his period and the immediate artistic ancestor of Michelangelo.

*Lo Zuccone*, or "Baldpate" (Fig. 179), is one of a series of marble statues that Donatello was commissioned to do for the Florence Cathedral and its campanile in 1424. Designed for a third-story niche of the campanile, it was intended to be seen about 55 feet above ground level. The deep-cut drapery and lines of the face consequently took into account this angle of vision and lighting. By the boniness of the huge frame, the powerful musculature of the arms, the convulsive gesture of the right wrist, the tension of the sinews of the neck, and the intensity of the face, Donatello sought to produce a powerfully expressive rather than a handsome figure. Representing an Old Testament prophet (either Habakkuk or Jeremiah), the figure is full of inner fire and fear of the Lord, a seer capable of fasting in the desert, dwelling alone on a mountaintop, or haranguing an unheeding multitude from his niche and exhorting men to penitence. The classical influence is discernible in the drapery, an adaptation of the toga, and in the rugged features and baldness, which recall realistic Roman portraiture. With *Lo Zuccone*, Donatello created a unique figure of strong individuality, not one of the traditional iconographical types. The nickname the Florentines gave the statue shows that it was accepted as such.

**178.** Lorenzo Ghiberti. *Story of Adam and Eve,* detail of east doors, Baptistry, Florence. c. 1435. Gilt bronze, 31¼" square.

In his bronze *David* (Fig. 180), Donatello works in a more lyrical vein. As a figure meant to be seen from all angles, the *David* is definitely a departure from the Gothic tradition of sculpture in niches and as architectural embellishment; and as the first life-size bronze nude in the round since antiquity, it marks the revival of classical nude statuary. David stands alone in the confident attitude of the victor over the vanquished, a sword in his right hand, a stone in his left. The serenity of the classical profile and the stance and modeling of the youthful body show Hellenistic influence. A local touch is provided by the Tuscan shepherd's hat, which throws the smooth, delicate-featured face into strong shadow and serves to accent the somewhat gawky lines of the adolescent body. The opposite end of Donatello's emotional range is seen in the spectral *Repentant Magdelene* (Pl. 21, p. 177). The emaciated, cadaverous figure stood in the Florence Baptistry as a reminder to the participants in the baptismal ceremony of the original sin that is washed away, and of the universal presence of death among the living.

Quite another attitude is revealed in the work of the succeeding generation, of which Antonio Pollaiuolo and Verrocchio are the leading representatives. The work of Pollaiuolo is dominated by scientific curiosity, especially in regard to human anatomy. (He is known to have dissected cadavers in order to study the muscle and bone structure at first hand.) Trained with his brothers in his father's goldsmith shop, he specialized in such muscular figures as the bronze *Hercules Strangling Antaeus,* of which he made both painted and sculptural versions (Fig. 181). The legends of the strong man of antiquity were excellent subjects that permitted the artist to bring out the musculature of the male figure in action. In this instance, Hercules overcomes his adversary, the Lybian giant, by raising him off the earth that was the source of his strength while Antaeus struggles desperately to release the stranglehold Hercules has upon him. The sinews in Hercules' legs as they bear the weight of both bodies should be noted. Pollaiuolo also painted a series of pictures on the Labors of Hercules. Like his work in bronze, they are studies of muscular tension, full of athletic energy and quite unrelieved by gracefulness.

Verrocchio, a contemporary of Pollaiuolo, was the official sculptor of the Medici. For this powerful and prolific family he designed everything from tournament trophies and parade paraphernalia to portraits and tombs.

Verrocchio, like Antonio Pollaiuolo, was also a painter at a time when sculpture led the field in experiments with perspective, anatomy, and light and shadow. Unlike the classical orientation of Ghiberti and Donatello, Pollaiuolo and Verrocchio were primarily scientifically minded, and it was in Verrocchio's workshop that Leonardo da Vinci got his training. It was Leonardo who carried on the unquenchable scientific curiosity of his master, while it remained for Michelangelo, under the stimulus of Donatello's art, to carry on the humanistic ideal into the next century.

## PAINTING

With Brunelleschi and Donatello, the third member of the triumvirate of early 15th-century innovators was Masaccio, the only one born within the century. The importance of his series of frescoes in the Brancacci Chapel of the Church of Santa Maria del Carmine can hardly be overestimated. In the *Expulsion from the Garden* (Fig. 182), he chose one of the few subjects in the iconographical tradition in which the nude human body could be portrayed in churches without raising ecclesiastical eyebrows. By defining the source of light as coming diagonally from the right

**left: 182.** MASACCIO. *Expulsion from the Garden.* c. 1427. Fresco, 6'6" × 2'9". Brancacci Chapel, Church of Santa Maria del Carmine, Florence.

**below: 183.** MASACCIO. *Tribute Money.* c. 1427. Fresco, 8'4" × 19'8". Brancacci Chapel, Church of Santa Maria del Carmine, Florence.

right: **184.** FRA ANGELICO. *Annunciation.* c. 1445–50. Fresco, 7′6″ × 10′5″. San Marco, Florence.

below right: **185.** BENOZZO GOZZOLI. *Journey of the Magi* (detail). c. 1459–63. Fresco, length 12′4¼″. Chapel, Medici-Riccardi Palace, Florence.

and by having Adam and Eve approach it, Masaccio was able to represent them as casting natural shadows. In addition, by surrounding his figures with light and air, by relating them to the space they occupy, by modeling them in light and shadow like a sculptor would so that they appear as if seen in the round with all the weight and volume of living forms, Masaccio achieved one of the great innovations in painting—*atmospheric perspective.* Masaccio, moreover, was well aware of the drama of the situation. The full force of man's first moral crisis is expressed by the human body alone with almost no reliance on surrounding details. Eve, aware of her nakedness, cries aloud, while Adam, ashamed to face the light, expresses his remorse by covering his face. Even the avenging angel who drives them out of the garden reflects the tragedy of the fall of man by an expression of human concern and solicitude. Adam's right leg was apparently drawn so as to show the motion of the expulsion; but the proportions of his arms, and the drawing of Eve's lower hand, are definitely incorrect. Such flaws, however, are minor in comparison with the momentous step in painting that puts man in an entirely new relationship to his spatial environment.

The *Tribute Money* (Fig. 183), another of the Brancacci Chapel frescoes, illustrates still further the principle of atmospheric perspective. Approached by the tax collector, Jesus tells Peter that the first fish he catches will have a coin in its mouth. The old simultaneous mode of presentation is employed with St. Peter appearing first in the center, then at the left fishing, and finally at the right paying the debt. Masaccio's premature death at the age of twenty-seven prevented a more complete realization of his discoveries, and it remained for Leonardo da Vinci and Michelangelo to work out their full implications.

Spiritually, Fra Angelico was in many respects a late-Gothic artist, who never painted anything but religious subjects. While he dwelt lovingly on the older forms, he did, however, often treat them within the new frame of reference. The *Annunciation* that he painted for the upper corridor of his own monastery of San Marco is a remarkable blend of these old and new elements (Fig. 184). A mystic by temperament, Fra Angelico found angels as real as his fellow human beings. But while he always paints with the deepest religious sentiment, his figures in this case appear within the new conception of space. The perspective and the 15th-century architectural details are so exact that the event could well be taking place in a corner of the San Marco cloister that Michelozzo recently

had rebuilt. Furthermore, the native Tuscan flowers seen in the garden are well enough observed to satisfy a botanical expert. The lighting, however, is far from the natural illumination of Masaccio; Fra Angelico makes it seem that the figure of Gabriel and the ineffable purity of Mary are beheld as if in a vision.

Unlike the eyes of Fra Angelico, those of his favorite pupil Benozzo Gozzoli were focused firmly on this world. With Cosimo's son Piero as his patron, Benozzo painted the *Journey of the Magi,* a favorite subject for pomp and pageantry. Here, his talents were more than equal to their task, a fresco cycle that covers three walls of the chapel in the Medici Palace. In the detail (Fig. 185), a sumptuously attired and

The Florentine Renaissance Style **173**

**186.** PAOLO UCCELLO. *Battle of San Romano.* c. 1455. Tempera on wood, 6′ × 10′5″. Uffizi, Florence.

caparisoned young Wise Man sits astride his splendid steed. At the head of the retinue that follows in his wake Benozzo portrays three generations of the Medici family. From right to left, Piero de' Medici (in profile) appears at the head of the procession. Emblazoned on the lower part of the harness of his white horse is the motto *Semper* ("Forever"), a part of the Medici coat of arms, each letter being in the center of one of the jeweled rings that make a continuous chain. Beside him is the elderly Cosimo (also in profile) on a gray mule with a blackamoor groom at his side. The youthful Giuliano and his older brother, the future Lorenzo the Magnificent, are at the extreme left. Bringing up the rear are various intimates and retainers of the Medici court, with the artist himself in the second row back identified by a cap band that reads *Opus Benotii* ("Work of Benozzo"). Other faces may represent the philosopher Pico della Mirandola, the poet Poliziano, and Fra Angelico.

The procession winds around through the mountains and valleys of the lovely Tuscan landscape punctuated by tall parasol pines and needle cypresses toward the niched altar where Fra Filippo Lippi's *Nativity* (Pl. 22, p. 178) was seen. His Madonnas are lithe and girlish, babies plump and childlike, his saints benign and patriarchal. The linear emphasis of his drawing, softened by his lush palette of pastel hues, had a decisive influence on the art of his pupil Botticelli. In the *Nativity,* the pictorial space is bisected symmetrically by the Trinity with God the Father imparting a blessing on His Son through the descending rays of the Holy Spirit, which find an earthly echo in the rising vertical lines of the tree trunks. Niches are thus created for the figures of the Madonna, St. John, and St. Joseph.

To decorate one of the salons of the Medici Palace, Cosimo called upon Paolo Uccello. As a student of

spatial science, Uccello was trying to solve the problem of *linear perspective*—the formula of arranging lines on a two-dimensional surface so that they converge at a vanishing point on the horizon and promote the illusion of recession in depth. One of his three scenes depicting the *Battle of San Romano* (Fig. 186), a skirmish of 1432 in which the Florentines put the Sienese army to flight, shows his pioneering effort in applying Euclidean geometry to pictorial mechanics. As a scientific experiment, Uccello lays his lances and banners out on the ground as if on a chessboard. He was evidently so absorbed with his lines that his bloodless battle is staged more in the manner of a dress parade than a clashing conflict. He also did not develop the element of light and shade, so that his merry-go-roundlike horses, despite the variety of their postures, remain as flat as cardboard. For all this intellectual effort, the solution of the linear problem eluded him, and in this respect he was always a pupil and never a master.

Present in Florence during the 1440's was Piero della Francesca. As an assistant to Domenico Veneziano, he absorbed the richness of Venetian color; studying Masaccio, he learned about atmospheric perspective and how to model figures in light and shade; and associating with Ghiberti, Brunelleschi, Alberti, and Paolo Uccello, he eventually became a master of linear perspective and later wrote a treatise on the subject. His *Resurrection* (Fig. 187), painted for the chapel of the town hall of his native Umbrian town of Borgo San Sepolchro, is one of his most sophisticated works. His geometrical clarity of design is seen at once in the compact pyramidal composition that builds up from the sleeping soldiers (the second from the left is generally thought to be a self-portrait) and sarcophagus to the figure of Christ modeled like a classical statue and holding the triumphant banner.

Color contrasts, as well as light and shade, play appointed roles both in the pictorial mechanics and in the symbolism. The somber tones of the soldiers' costumes are offset by the diaphanous pink of Christ's robe. Furthermore, the dark-clad soldiers, paralleled by the shadowy earth, set up an alternating rhythm with the glowing figure of Jesus against the Easter dawn. The barren earth on the left yields to the springtime regeneration of the fields on the right; and the effect of the brightening sky above, together with the radiant spirit of Christ with the piercing, almost hypnotic gaze, is reflected in the disturbed soldiers below, who, though still asleep, are yet dimly aware of the dawn.

Painting in the first part of the 15th century had to reckon with many different trends and diverse personalities. Sandro Botticelli, however, rose above the majority of his contemporaries and became the most representative artist of the humanistic thought that dominated the latter half of the century. Botticelli enjoyed the patronage of the Medici family, and his *Adoration of the Magi* (Fig. 188) portrays the clan as had his predecessor Benozzo Gozzoli (Fig. 185). Among the admirably arranged figures, one finds the elderly Cosimo kneeling at the feet of the Christ Child; also kneeling are his two sons Piero and Giovanni; to their right, standing against the ruined wall, is seen the profiled figure of Giuliano, the handsome grandson of Cosimo and the younger brother of Lorenzo the Magnificent, who is to be found in the

above: 187. Piero della Francesca. *Resurrection.* c. 1460. Fresco, 9'6" × 8'4". Gallery, Palazzo del Comune, Borgo San Sepolcro.

left: 188. Sandro Botticelli. *Adoration of the Magi.* c. 1475. Tempera on wood, 3'7½" × 4'4¾". Uffizi, Florence.

The Florentine Renaissance Style    175

extreme left foreground. His opposite number at the right usually is identified as Botticelli himself. Though the coloring is bright—ranging from the cool azure of the Virgin's robe and the dark-green and gold embroidery of Cosimo's costume to the ermine-lined crimson cloak of the kneeling Piero and the bright orange of Botticelli's mantle—it falls into a harmonious pattern. Attention should also be called to the classical touch provided by the Roman ruin in the left background.

Botticelli was not a popular painter of pageants like Benozzo Gozzoli and his contemporary Ghirlandaio but a member of the sophisticated group of humanists who gathered around his Medici patrons. In this circle, which included the poet Angelo Poliziano and the philosophers Marsilio Ficino and Pico della Mirandola, Lorenzo the Magnificent, and his cousin Pierfrancesco di Lorenzo de' Medici, classical myths were constantly discussed and interpreted. The dialogues of Plato, the *Enneads* of Plotinus, and Greek musical theory were all thoroughly explored. With the Florentine interest in the pictorial arts, the ancient references to sculpture and painting were not neglected. This neopagan atmosphere with its Christian concordances is reflected in many of Botticelli's paintings.

*Venus and Mars* (Pl. 23, p. 178) is one of Botticelli's allegorical pictures inspired by the humanistic speculations of the Florentine Neoplatonists. Commissioned apparently for a marriage in the famous Vespucci family, the unusual shape of the panel suggests that its prototype was a classical sarcophagus, and that it was intended either for a wedding chest or a bed board. Venus and Mars were, of course, the

mythological lovers of antiquity; and Marsilio Ficino, in his commentary on Plato's *Symposium,* mentioned that "Mars is outstanding in strength among planets because he makes men stronger, but Venus masters him . . . ." The wealthy Vespucci family, close associates of the Medici, numbered several celebrated members, among them Simonetta Cattaneo, wife of one Marco Vespucci, and Amerigo Vespucci, the Florentine geographer and explorer whose claim that he had discovered an unknown continent gave his name to the new world. The fair Simonetta was elevated into a Platonic personification of ideal beauty and goodness. As such she was enshrined by Poliziano and Lorenzo the Magnificent in a poetic niche, much as Beatrice had been by Dante and Laura by Petrarch. She is also thought to have inspired the ideal Venus type that appears in many of Botticelli's masterpieces.

In the *Birth of Venus* (Fig. 189), a celebrated masterpiece, Botticelli depicts the goddess vividly as she floats across the green sea on a pink shell gently blown by Zephyrs. On the shore ready to clothe her in a flowery mantle is one of the *Horae,* or "Hours." The coloring of the picture is as cool as called for by a classical subject. The fluttering drapery of the side figures imparts a sense of lightness and movement and leads the eye toward the head of Venus, which is surrounded by an aura of golden hair. The incisiveness of outline, the balletlike choreography of lines, the pattern of linear rhythms recall the technique of relief sculpture.

Medici patronage reached out beyond Florence to all the European centers where the family had branch banks—Milan, Venice, Lyon, London, and especially

**189.** SANDRO BOTTICELLI. *Birth of Venus.* c. 1480. Tempera on canvas, 6'7'' × 9'2''. Uffizi, Florence.

above: **Plate 20.** Lorenzo Ghiberti. *Gates of Paradise,* east doors of the Baptistry, Florence. 1425–52. Gilt bronze, height 18′6″. (See pp. 165, 169, 170.)

right: **Plate 21.** Donatello. *Repentant Magdalene.* 1454–55. Wood, height 6′2″. Baptistry, Florence. (See p. 171.)

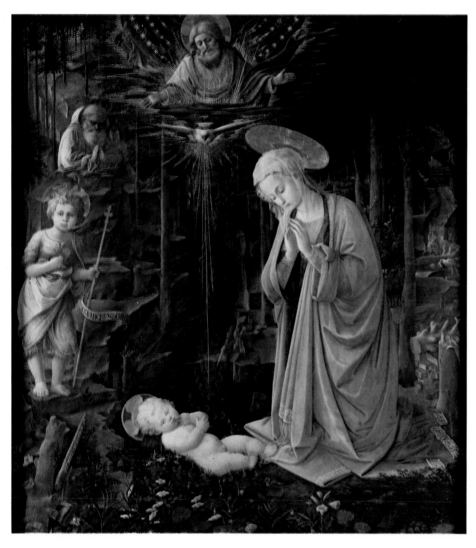

left: **Plate 22.** Fra Filippo Lippi. *Nativity.* c. 1459. Tempera on wood, 4'2" × 3'10". State Museums, Berlin. (See p. 174.)

below: **Plate 23.** Sandro Botticelli. *Venus and Mars.* c. 1485. Oil on wood, 2'2¾" × 5'7¾". National Gallery, London (reproduced by courtesy of the Trustees). (See p. 176.)

Bruges, where two Medici representatives figured prominently in Flemish painting. *Giovanni Arnolfini and His Wife* (Pl. 24, p. 195) by Jan van Eyck is a masterly portrait of the shrewd, calculating Medici banker. Bright light suffuses the entire space and illuminates every object evenly and naturally. Each detail is described with the keenest observation from the more subdued tones and textures of the wooden floor and shoes, the furry dog, and the cloth of costumes and bed to the higher gloss of the metal chandelier and the mirror, itself a picture in miniature containing a wedding certificate and a self-portrait of the artist as witness to the ceremony.

In the latter half of the 15th century, Tommaso Portinari, another Medici representative in Bruges, commissioned an altarpiece for the hospital of Santa Maria Nuova in Florence (Fig. 190). Hugo van der Goes, the artistic heir of van Eyck, painted the donor, his wife and children, and their patron saints, Thomas and Margaret, in the wide folding wings of the triptych. In the central panel, depicting the Adoration of the Shepherds, one sees the same close observation of naturalistic detail as van Eyck's—from the weather-beaten faces of the shepherds to the brocaded cloth of the angels' robes. But van der Goes is also concerned with symbolism—the harp in the tympanum of the background building indicates that Mary and the Child stem from the house of David; the sheaf of wheat signifies Bethlehem; and the flowers, the future sorrows of Mary. The artist also makes use of some spatial distortion to achieve expressive effect—the floor tipping slightly upward to project the figures forward; the relative sizes of the figures in relation to the picture plane, with Joseph, Mary, and the shepherds in the middle ground looming larger than the angels in the foreground.

**190.** Hugo van der Goes. *Portinari Altarpiece.* c. 1476. Oil on wood, $9'2\frac{1}{2}'' \times 21'8\frac{1}{2}''$. Uffizi, Florence.

The arrival of this triptych in Florence in 1476 created a sensation, for it provided the first opportunity local painters had to observe a large-scale product by one of their northern contemporaries. Clearly it influenced Ghirlandaio and Botticelli. Their special interest was in the new *oil medium* perfected by Jan van Eyck. In Italy, such panels traditionally were done with water-soluble pigments in the process known as *tempera.* The Flemish painters, however, were now using oil to suspend pigments. The boards on which they painted were first built up with a fine white cementlike substance called *gesso,* and on this a *cartoon,* or full-scale sketch, of the picture was drawn with ink and modeled in light and shade. After the painting had been made in opaque oil colors, a translucent glaze with varnishlike brightness was then applied. This glaze, also in an oil medium, could be worked with the brush to give irridescent effects, so that the colors seemed to glow from within the picture. Gradually, the deeper colors and brilliant enamellike finish of this oil medium supplanted the brighter-colored but duller surfaces of Italian tempera painting.

## POETRY AND MUSIC

The principal poets of the Florentine Renaissance were Lorenzo de' Medici and Poliziano. Lorenzo's title *Il Magnifico,* in retrospect, seems fitting recognition of his activities as poet, humanist, philosopher, discoverer of genius, patron of the arts and sciences, and adviser to writers, sculptors, painters, and musicians.

The Florentine Renaissance Style    **179**

Under the wise guidance of his grandfather Cosimo, *Pater Patriae,* Lorenzo had been educated by Pico della Mirandola and other Latin and Greek scholars of the highest repute to be the type of philosopher-ruler that Plato had expounded upon in his *Republic.* Social conditions, however, had changed considerably since Cosimo's time, and while his grandfather had been a banker with intellectual and artistic tastes, Lorenzo became a prince whose power rested on philosophical prestige and leadership in matters of taste as well as on his banking fortune. Lorenzo maintained embassies at all the principal courts to which he made loans, but while he was willing to finance foreign conflicts, provided he saw a substantial profit for himself, he preferred to fight his own wars with words. By having the services of the greatest humanists under his command, he never ran out of ammunition in the form of elegantly turned phrases, apt epithets, veiled threats, and invectives. Changes in the status of the arts had also come about as the 15th century progressed. In the early decades Ghiberti had been employed by the Signory, and his work was intended for public view. Later the major commissions came from a few families, and under Lorenzo the arts took on more of a courtly character, and the audiences grew correspondingly more restricted. Some painters were able to remain outside the charmed circle and to make careers depicting social scenes of births and marriages for an upper middle-class clientele. Botticelli's pictures, however, were mainly for the humanistic connoisseurs.

Lorenzo himself, though the leader of this exclusive group, had the instincts of a popular ruler and did not neglect the common touch. He participated actively in the gay Florentine festivals by composing new verses for the traditional folk tunes, by encouraging others in his circle to do the same, and by holding competitions among composers for better musical settings of the songs. Lorenzo thus gave new impetus to popular literature in the vernacular. In a commentary on four of his own sonnets, he went to considerable lengths to defend the expressive possibilities of Tuscan Italian; and, after comparing it with Hebrew, Greek, and Latin, he found that its harmoniousness and sweetness outdid all the others. While he continued to write sophisticated sonnets, Lorenzo also wrote popular verses that have, in addition to their beauty and literary polish, all the spontaneous freshness, humor, and charm of folk poetry. In some of his pastoral poems he even uses the rustic dialogue of true country folk. Few poets could rival the lyricism of his *canti carnascialeschi,* or "carnival songs," one of which contains the oft-quoted lines:

> *Quanto è bella giovinezza,*
> *Che si fugge tuttavia!*
> *Chi vuol esser lieto, sia:*
> *Di doman non c' è certezza.*

> Fair is youth and free of sorrow,
> Yet how soon its joys we bury!
> Let who would be, now be merry:
> Sure is no one of tomorrow.

In order to flourish, popular poetry needed appropriate musical settings. A young man of 18, Lorenzo was in search of a composer to set his lyrics, and a letter he wrote in 1467 requests the "venerable Gugliemo Dufay," who by this time was approaching 70, to compose music for his verses. This was the same Guillaume Dufay who some 30 years earlier had composed the dedicatory motet for the cathedral.

Popular music making in Florence and other Italian cities was as much a part of the good life as any of the other arts. But it was mainly an art of performance, and little music was ever written down. When the time came to appoint a successor to Squarcialupi after his death in 1475, Lorenzo's choice fell on Heinrich Isaac, a native of Flanders and a rapid and prolific composer. Florence immediately became a second home to this truly cosmopolitan figure, and native Italian idioms soon were combined with those of his own background and training.

Isaac's duties included those of organist and choirmaster at the Florence Cathedral as well as at the Medici Palace, where Lorenzo is known to have had no less than five organs. Together with the poet Angelo Poliziano, he was also the teacher of Lorenzo's sons, one of whom was destined to be the music- and art-loving Pope Leo X. But most important, Isaac collaborated with Lorenzo on the songs written for popular festivals. He thus became cocreator of one of the popular genres of secular choral music that eventually led to the madrigal. Dufay's settings of Lorenzo's verses are now lost, but many by Isaac are extant. In one of these, he shows the tendency away from complex counterpoint and toward simple harmonic, or chordal, texture. Its style is that of a Florentine *frottola,* a carnival song for dancing as well as singing, and its lilting rhythm freely shifts its meter.

As the setting stands (opposite above), it could be performed for three-part chorus; as a solo song with the two lower parts taken by the lute or two viols; or as a vocal duet with the soprano and any one of the two other voices. The collaboration of Lorenzo and Isaac thus resulted both in a meeting of minds and a merging of poetic and musical forms. Lorenzo's verses were a union of the courtly *ballata* and popular poetry while Isaac succeeded in Italianizing the Burgundian *chanson,* or "song"—Italianizing in this case means simplifying, omitting all artificiality, and enlivening a rather stiff form with the graceful Florentine folk melodies and rhythms. It can be seen that such a movement worked both ways by raising the level of popular poetry on the one hand, and at the same time rejuvenating the more sophisticated poetic and musical forms by contact with popular idioms.

## IDEAS

The dominating ideas of the Florentine Renaissance cluster around three concepts—classical humanism, scientific naturalism, and Renaissance individualism. In their broadest meaning, humanism, naturalism, and individualism were far from new. Humanism in the humanitarian Franciscan sense was a carryover from the 13th and 14th centuries; naturalism stemmed from late Gothic times; and some form of individualism is always present in any period. The term *Renaissance*, implying as it does a "rebirth," is a source of some confusion. To the early 16th-century historians, it meant an awakening to the values of ancient classical arts and letters after the long medieval night. But just what, if anything, was *reborn* has never been satisfactorily explained. Since all the principal ideas were present in the Gothic period, one might do better to speak of a maturation of certain tendencies present in late medieval times. Yet there was a specific drive that gave an extraordinary impetus and color to the creative life and thought of this small Tuscan city-state in the 15th century. It is important to discover what it was, and what it was not, that gave Florence its special flavor.

Though Florentine humanism evolved from the Franciscan spirit, it did take on a consciously classical coloration. Here again, however, a word of caution is necessary when speaking of a "rebirth" of the spirit of antiquity. In Italy, much more than in northern Europe, the classical tradition had been more or less continuous. Roman remains were everywhere in evidence. Many Roman arches, aqueducts, bridges, and roads were still in use, while fragments of ancient buildings, such as columns, were used and reused as building materials. In the late 13th century, Niccolo Pisano's sculptural models were the Roman remains he saw all around him, and by the 15th century the revival of the classical male nude as an instrument of expression is seen in the work of Ghiberti, Donatello, Pollaiuolo, and Verrocchio. At the beginning of the 16th century Michelangelo had developed such a formidable sculptural technique that his *David* not only rivaled the work of such ancient craftsmen as Praxiteles (Fig. 38), but actually surpassed them (Fig. 191). Aristotle was still the official philosopher of the Church, and ancient musical theory continued to be studied. What was new to Florence was the study of the Greek language, the setting up of Ciceronian rather than medieval Latin as a standard, and a passionate interest in Plato. In spite of a certain antiquarianism, however, the net result was less a revival of things past than a step forward. It was—as such movements usually are—a search for past precedents to justify then-present practices.

Much has been said also about the pagan aspect of this interest in antiquity. Here again it was less anti-Christian than appears on the surface. Florentine Neoplatonism was certainly antischolastic, but it was mainly a substitution of the authority of Plato for that of Aristotle. Marsilio Ficino, as the high priest of the movement, in his interpretation of the *Republic* and *Laws*, speaks of Plato as the Attic "Moses." He is also known to have added "Saint" Socrates to the litany and to have burned a candle before the bust of Plato.

**191.** Michelangelo. *David.* 1501–04. Marble, height 18'. Academy, Florence.

In this light, his thought appears more as a reinterpretation of Christianity in Platonic terms than paganism as such. There was also a certain amount of anticlericalism in Florence, just as it existed elsewhere at this time. Lorenzo, however, as papal banker and a father who chose the Church for his son Giovanni's career, was not so much a religious skeptic as he was a political realist. It is important to keep in mind that the Florentine humanists were a small band of learned men, whose Platonic disputations have made much more noise in the corridors of history than they did in their own time. Actually, they never had, nor did they seek, a large audience. In the first quarter of the following century, however, the humanists had the international forum of Rome. The artistic expression of Neoplatonism came to its climax in the works of Michelangelo, and the full discussion of this elitist movement—which must include the art of Botticelli and Raphael, the patronage of Julius II and the Medici popes Leo X and Clement VII, and the Neoplatonic philosophers—will be discussed in the chapter that follows.

Naturalism, in the sense of fidelity to nature, appears in a well-developed form both in the northern Gothic sculpture and in the poetry of St. Francis, who had died as long before as 1226. By the 14th century, representations of man and nature alike had pretty well lost their value as other-worldly symbols. But rather than remaining a generalized interest in this world, Florentine 15th-century naturalism took a noticeably scientific turn. Careful observation of natural phenomena and the will to reproduce objects as the eye sees them was evidence of an empirical attitude; dissection of cadavers in order to see the structure of the human body revealed a spirit of free inquiry; and the study of mathematics so as to put objects into proper perspective involved a new concept of space. Clearly a new scientific spirit was now afoot.

While individualism as such is practically universal, the distinctive feature of its Florentine expression was that conditions in this small city-state were almost ideal for artists to come into immediate and fruitful contact with their patrons and audience. Competition was keen; desire for personal fame was intense; and a high regard for personality is seen in the portraiture, biographies, and autobiographies.

It should therefore be clear that the Florentine Renaissance was characterized by no sharp cleavage with the past, and that its special savor lies in the quality of its humanism, in the tendency of its naturalism, and in its particular regard for individualism.

**Scientific Naturalism** The two basic directions taken by the naturalism of the 15th century led to a new experimental attitude and a new concept of space. A close partnership between art and science developed, with architects becoming mathematicians, sculptors anatomists, painters geometricians, and musicians acousticians. The spirit of free inquiry was by no means confined to the arts alone. It permeated all the progressive aspects of the life of the time from a reexamination of the forms of secular government to Machiavelli's observations on how men behave in a certain given set of political circumstances. This searching curiosity reached its full fruition in the early years of the next century in Machiavelli's political handbook *The Prince;* in the same author's attempt to apply the Thucydidean method of rational historical analysis in his *History of Florence;* and in the scientific observations in Leonardo's notebooks, which cover everything from astronomy to hydraulics. Well within the 15th century, however, the same spirit manifested itself. Ghiberti's *Commentaries* took up the mathematical proportions of the human body as the basis of its beauty, and he wrote the first treatise in Italian on optics. Brunelleschi, as a diligent student of Vitruvius, was concerned with the mathematical proportions of his buildings. Alberti, in his books on painting, sculpture, and architecture, stressed the study of mathematics as the underlying principle of all the arts.

The sculptors and painters who followed the leadership of Antonio Pollaiuolo and Verrocchio were animated by the desire to express the structural forms of the body beneath its external appearance, and their anatomical studies opened the way to the modeling of the movements and gestures of the human body. The result was the reaffirmation of the expressive power of the nude. In painting, naturalism meant a more faithful representation of the world of appearances and one based on detailed and accurate observation. Even Fra Angelico showed an interest in the exact reproduction of Tuscan botanical specimens in the garden of his *Annunciation;* and Botticelli, under the influence of Pollaiuolo and Verrocchio, combined objective techniques with his highly imaginative subject matter. The culmination of this line of thought was reached in Verrocchio's pupil Leonardo da Vinci, who considered painting a science and sculpture a mechanical art. Leonardo's scientific probing went beyond the physical and anatomical into the metaphysical and psychological aspects of human nature. A detail from his early, unfinished *Adoration of the Magi* (Fig. 192), for instance, reveals through turbulent gesticulations and quizzical facial expressions the bewilderment and emotional turmoil of the Wise Men as they try to comprehend the miraculous meaning of the Messiah's coming.

In music there was a continued interest in Greek theory, coupled, however, with attempts to experiment with acoustical problems. The compositions of Dufay and others of the northern school were characterized by extreme erudition; and mathematical laws were strictly applied to such aspects of composition as rhythmical progressions, formal proportions, and the development of elaborate technical devices.

**192.** Leonardo da Vinci. *Adoration of the Magi* (detail). 1481–82. Tempera on wood, $7'11\frac{5}{8}'' \times 8'\frac{7}{8}''$ (entire work). Uffizi, Florence.

Highly dramatic was the conquest of geographical space that began with the voyages of Columbus, leading to the development of trade routes and commerce and the tapping of new and distant sources of wealth. In architecture, this breakthrough in space is reflected in the raising of Brunelleschi's cupola almost 400 feet into the air. In painting, it is seen in the placing of figures in a more normal relationship to the space they occupy, and in landscape settings; in Masaccio's development of atmospheric perspective, in which figures are modeled in light and shade; in the working out of rules for linear perspective whereby the illusion of depth on a two-dimensional surface is achieved by defining a point at which lines converge; and in *foreshortening*, the diminution in the size of figures and objects in direct ratio to their distance from the picture plane.

Since the subject matter of medieval art was drawn from the other world, it fell outside the scope of naturalistic representation and had to be rendered symbolically. Art now entered a new phase of self-awareness as Renaissance artists began to think less in terms of allegory, symbolism, and moral lessons and more in terms of aesthetic problems, modes of presentation, and pictorial mechanics. In medieval music, the emphasis had been on perfect intervals and mathematical rhythmic ratios in order to please the ear of God. Renaissance musicians now reversed the process by concentrating on sounds that would delight the human ear. The new spirit was also heard in the extension of the range of musical instruments in both higher and lower registers, to broaden the scope of tonal space. Thus, the development of pleasant harmonic textures, the softening of dissonant passing tones, and the writing of singable melodies and danceable rhythms are all related phenomena giving style to the period.

In this trend toward scientific naturalism, the arts of painting and sculpture became firmly allied with geometrical and scientific laws, a union that lasted until 20th-century expressionism. The 15th-century Florentine artists literally reveled in the perspective, optical, and anatomical discoveries of their day. And when all the basic research, experiments, and discoveries had been made, it was left for their successors—Leonardo da Vinci, Michelangelo, and Raphael—to explore their full expressive possibilities.

**Renaissance Individualism**     Whether one considers the Renaissance patrons' reasons for commissioning artists, the forms and techniques employed in the various arts, the regard for human personality

seen in portraiture, the desire for personal prestige through art, or the social status of the artist, one finds evidence everywhere of a special attitude of Renaissance man toward himself, his fellowmen, and his place in the world. The religious nature of the vast majority of the works of art has already been pointed out, but personal patronage was in the ascendancy. Brunelleschi built the Pazzi Chapel, Masolino and Masaccio decorated the Brancacci Chapel, and Benozzo Gozzoli and Filippo Lippi did the paintings for the Medici Chapel on commission from private donors as memorials to themselves and their families. San Lorenzo, the parish church of the Medici, was rebuilt and redecorated by Brunelleschi and Donatello—but the money came from Cosimo and not from the Church. Fra Angelico decorated the corridors of the monastery of San Marco, which was under the protection of the Medici family, and Squarcialupi and Isaac were on the payroll of the Medici when they played the organ in the cathedral, in a church, or in the family palace. Piousness and the desire for spiritual salvation were not the only motives for such munificence; a knowledge that the donor's present and posthumous fame depended on his building of monuments and his choice of artists to decorate them was also present.

In addition to the circumstances of patronage, certain technical considerations within the arts themselves point in the same individualistic direction. The development of perspective drawing, for example, implied that the subject in the picture—whether a Madonna, a saint, or an angel—was definitely placed in this world rather than symbolically in the next, and hence was more on a par with the observer. The unification of space by having all the lines converge at one point on the horizon tended to flatter the spectator. By such clear organization of lines and planes, linear perspective presupposes that everything is seen from a single optical vantage point. While it is actually that of the artist, he makes it seem as if it were also that of the observer. By closing his form, the artist further implies that nothing of importance lies outside, and the whole of the picture can then be taken in at a glance. Since nothing, then, is beyond the grasp of the viewer, and all can be comprehended with relatively little effort, the eye and mind of the onlooker are reassured. The central-type church that Alberti, Bramante, and, later, Michelangelo and Palladio preferred to design, in which the space is unified under a dome, is the architectural expression of the same idea. The Gothic cathedral purposely led the eye and imagination outward into the transcendental beyond, while the central-type church revolves around man himself. Standing under the cupola, the observer is aware that the axis of the building is not objectively outside or transcendentally beyond but subjectively in himself. He is, for the moment, the center of the architectural space. The center of the universe exists not at some remote point beyond the horizon but within man himself.

Human figures, whether rendered as prophets or protraits, tended to become more personal and individual. Each statue by Donatello, be it *Lo Zuccone* or the *David*, was a human individuality who made a powerful and unique impression. Even Fra Angelico's Madonna was a personality more than an abstraction, and his figure of the Angel Gabriel possessed genuine human dignity. Whether the medium was marble, terra-cotta, paint, words, or tones, there was evidence of the new value placed on human individuality. Whether the picture was a disguised family group, as Botticelli's *Adoration of the Magi,* or a personal portrait, as Verrocchio's bust of Lorenzo, the figures were authentic personages rather than stylized abstractions; even though Lorenzo de' Medici was the most powerful political figure of Florence, Verrocchio saw him as a man, not as an institution.

The higher social status accorded Florentine artists was evidenced by the inclusion of self-portraits in such paintings as that of Benozzo Gozzoli in his *Journey of the Magi* and the prominent position Botticelli accorded himself in his *Adoration of the Magi.* Ghiberti's personal reminiscences in his *Commentaries* were probably the first autobiography of an artist in history; his inclusion of the lives and legends of his famous 14th-century predecessors were the first biographies of individual artists. Signatures of artists on their works became the rule, not the exception; and the culmination came when Michelangelo realized that his work was so highly individual that he no longer needed to sign it. The desire for personal fame grew to such an extent that Benvenuto Cellini no longer was content to let his works speak for him but wrote a voluminous autobiography filled with self-praise. The painter Giorgio Vasari likewise took up the pen to record the lives of the artists he knew personally and by reputation. More broadly, such works as Pico della Mirandola's essay on the *Dignity of Man,* Machiavelli's *The Prince,* and Castiglione's *The Courtier* were written to enhance the intellectual, political, and social status of man in general and the scholar, politican, courtier, and artist in particular.

In late medieval and early Renaissance times, artists were content with their status as craftsmen. They were trained as apprentices to grind pigments, carve wooden chests, make engravings, and prepare wall surfaces for frescoes as well as to carve marble reliefs and paint pictures. In the late 15th and early 16th centuries, however, it was not enough for an artist to create works of art. He had to know the theory of art and the place of art in the intellectual atmosphere of his period. The quality most admired in Renaissance man was *virtù* (the word comes closer in the modern sense to "virtuoso" than "virtuous"). *Virtù* revealed itself in the boundless vitality and extraordinary ability that led to the achievements of a Lorenzo the Magnificent or the breathtaking conceptions of a Michelangelo. With *virtù,* the Renaissance artist could no longer confine himself to a single specialty but sought to become the *homo universale,* the "universal man." Brunelleschi was a goldsmith, sculptor, engineer, and mathematician as well as one of the leading lights of Renaissance architecture. Alberti was an athlete, horseman, brilliant wit, Latin stylist, mathematician, architect, musician, playwright, and founder of Renaissance theory of art. For Leonardo it is more difficult to find a field in which he was not proficient than one in which he excelled.

From Lorenzo's time through the early 16th century, the greatest artists were intellectuals. Alberti was a scholar-architect who wrote books on the subject, designed buildings on paper, and left the actual construction to a master mason. Botticelli associated with men of letters and worked elaborate allegories into his pictures. Leonardo da Vinci thought sculpture inferior to painting because of the physical labor involved, and in his later years devoted himself more to science than to painting. Bramante and Raphael were to be artist-scholars as well as architects and painters. Michelangelo hated the workshop, even though the realization of his grandiose designs depended on the work of many hands. He was to become the ideal of the modern individualistic artist, consciously an intellectual, dealing with popes and princes as equals, insisting that he painted with his brains not with his hands, and rejecting all offers of noble titles. When people began calling him "the divine," the cycle was complete.

# 11 The Roman Renaissance Style

## ROME, EARLY 16TH CENTURY

On April 18, 1506, when the foundation stone of the new Basilica of St. Peter was laid (Fig. 193), Rome was well on its way to becoming the undisputed artistic and intellectual capital of the Western world. Pope Julius II was gathering about him the foremost living artists in all fields, and together they continued the transformation of the Eternal City from the darkness of its medieval past into the resplendent Rome of today. Donato Bramante, originally from Umbria but educated in Lombardy, was the architect at work on the plans for the central church of Christendom. Michelangelo Buonarroti from Florence was collecting the marble for a monumental tomb and was about to begin the painting of the Sistine ceiling. Raffaelo Sanzio from Umbria would soon be summoned from Florence to decorate the rooms of the Vatican Palace. The Florentine Andrea Sansovino was carving a cardinal's tomb in one of Julius II's favorite Roman churches, Santa Maria del Popolo, where the Umbrian Pinturicchio was covering its choir vaults with a series of frescoes. The singer-composer Josquin des Prez, already a member of the papal choir for eight years, had left to become choirmaster to the king of France. The papal court under Julius II and his successor Leo X was such a powerful magnet that for three years the three greatest figures of the Renaissance—Leonardo da Vinci, Michelangelo, and Raphael—found themselves at the Vatican. In 1517, however, the aged Leonardo abandoned the artistic field of honor there to become a courtier of Francis I of France.

The flight of the Medici from Florence in 1494 had signaled a general exodus of artists. Many found temporary havens in the ducal courts of Italy, but the magnet of attraction proved to be the papal court at Rome. Hence, during the days of the two great Renaissance popes, Julius II (della Rovere) and Leo X (de' Medici), the cultural capital shifted from Florence to Rome. And, since Leonardo, Andrea Sansovino, Michelangelo, and Pope Leo were from Florence, and since Bramante and Raphael had absorbed the Florentine style and ideas in extended sojourns there, the cultural continuity was unbroken. It was, in fact, like a smooth transplantation from the confines of a nursery to an open field—a move that gave artists the opportunity to branch out from local styles into the

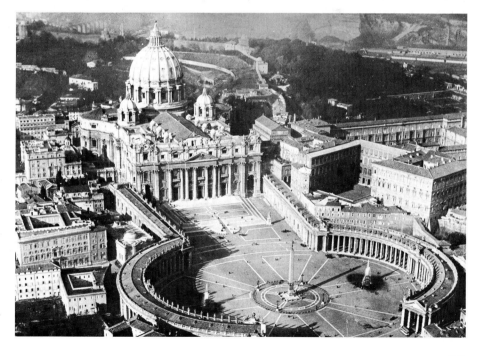

**193.** St. Peter's Basilica and the Vatican, Rome. Apse and dome by MICHELANGELO, 1547–64; dome completed by GIACOMO DELLA PORTA, 1588–92; nave and façade by CARLO MADERNO, 1601–26 (façade height 147', width 374'); colonnades by GIANLORENZO BERNINI, 1656–63.

# CHRONOLOGY / Late 15th- and Early 16th-Century Rome

## General Events

| | | |
|---|---|---|
| 1471– | 1527 | Roman Renaissance art and humanism climaxed |
| 1471– | 1484 | Sixtus IV (della Rovere), pope |
| 1473– | 1480 | Sistine Chapel built |
| 1481– | 1482 | Sistine Chapel sidewall frescoes painted by Rosselli, Ghirlandaio, Botticelli, Perugino, Signorelli, Pinturicchio, Piero di Cosimo |
| 1484– | 1492 | Innocent VIII (Cibò), pope |
| 1486– | 1492 | Josquin des Prez in Sistine Chapel Choir |
| 1492– | 1503 | Alexander VI (Borgia), pope |
| 1493– | 1506 | Excavations uncovered ancient Roman frescoes and statues: *Apollo Belvedere, Laocoön Group* |
| 1496– | 1501 | Michelangelo in Rome, working on *Bacchus* and *Pietà* |
| 1503– | 1513 | Julius II (della Rovere), pope |
| | 1505 | Michelangelo began Julius II's tomb |
| | 1506 | New Basilica of St. Peter begun by Bramante; Old St. Peter's razed |
| 1508– | 1512 | Michelangelo painted Sistine Chapel ceiling. Raphael painted frescoes in Vatican Palace |
| | 1512 | Cappella Giulia Choir founded |
| 1513– | 1516 | Leonardo da Vinci in Rome |
| 1513– | 1521 | Leo X (de' Medici), pope |
| | 1515 | Ariosto wrote *Orlando Furioso* ("Madness of Roland") |
| | 1517 | Protestant Reformation began in Germany with Luther's 95 Theses |
| | 1521 | Luther excommunicated |
| 1523– | 1534 | Clement VII (de' Medici), pope |
| | 1523 | Michelangelo worked on Medici tombs in Florence |
| | 1527 | Rome sacked by Emperor Charles V; Clement VII imprisoned |
| | 1528 | Castiglione's *The Courtier* published |
| | 1532 | Machiavelli's *The Prince* published |
| 1534– | 1549 | Paul III (Farnese), pope |
| | 1534 | Church of England separated from Rome. Reaction to Renaissance humanism began |
| 1535– | 1541 | Michelangelo painted *Last Judgment* in Sistine Chapel |
| | 1542 | Michelangelo painted frescoes in Pauline Chapel |
| | 1547 | Michelangelo named architect of St. Peter's |
| | 1550 | Vasari's *Lives of Most Eminent Painters, Sculptors, and Architects* published |
| c.1550 | | Philippe de Monte in Rome; published first book of madrigals 1554 |
| | 1551 | Orlando di Lasso in Rome |
| | 1564 | Michelangelo died |

## Architects

| | | |
|---|---|---|
| c.1444– | 1514 | Donato Bramante |
| 1475– | 1564 | Michelangelo Buonarroti |
| 1556– | 1629 | Carlo Maderno |

## Sculptors

| | | |
|---|---|---|
| 1460– | 1529 | Andrea Sansovino |
| 1475– | 1564 | Michelangelo Buonarroti |
| 1500– | 1571 | Benvenuto Cellini |
| c.1524– | 1608 | Giovanni da Bologna |

## Painters

| | | |
|---|---|---|
| c.1441– | 1523 | Luca Signorelli |
| c.1450– | 1523 | Perugino |
| 1452– | 1519 | Leonardo da Vinci |
| 1454– | 1513 | Bernardino Pinturicchio |
| 1475– | 1564 | Michelangelo Buonarroti |
| 1483– | 1520 | Raphael Sanzio |

## Writers

| | | |
|---|---|---|
| 1474– | 1533 | Ludovico Ariosto |
| 1478– | 1529 | Baldassare Castiglione |
| 1483– | 1531 | Martin Luther |
| 1511– | 1574 | Giorgio Vasari |
| 1544– | 1595 | Torquato Tasso |
| 1548– | 1600 | Giordano Bruno |

## Musicians

| | | |
|---|---|---|
| c.1445– | 1521 | Josquin des Prez |
| c.1521– | 1603 | Philippe de Monte |
| 1525– | 1594 | Giovanni da Palestrina |
| c.1532– | 1594 | Orlando di Lasso |

universal air of Rome. Such projects as the building of the world's largest church, the construction of Julius II's tomb, the painting of the Sistine ceiling, and the Vatican Palace murals could be found only in Rome. Nowhere else were monuments of such proportions or commissions of such magnitudes possible. In Rome also were the cardinals in residence, who maintained palaces and princely retinues that rivaled the brilliance of the papal court.

The interest in antiquity had animated many other Italian centers, but when the Renaissance got under way in Rome, it was, so to speak, on home soil. When antique statues were excavated elsewhere, they caused a considerable stir. In Rome, however, many of the ancient monuments were still standing, and when the archaeological shovels probed the proper places, a veritable treasure trove was waiting. One by one the *Apollo Belvedere* (Fig. 65), the *Venus of the Vatican,* and the *Laocoön Group* (Fig. 62) came to light to give new impetus to the work of Michelangelo and other sculptors. The frescoes from Nero's Domus Aurea and the Baths of Titus provided the first important specimens of ancient painting. While the art of working in tempera on fresh plaster had never died out, these ancient Roman fragments gave fresco painting a new impetus in the Renaissance vocabulary.

Julius II had received most of his training in diplomacy and statecraft from his uncle Pope Sixtus IV, and, fortunately, a passionate love of the arts was included in this education. It was Sixtus who had built the chapel that has subsequently borne his name, and who had installed there the group of papal singers that have ever since been known as the *Cappella Sistina,* or the "Sistine Chapel Choir." It remained for Julius to establish a chorus to perform in St. Peter's—one that still bears his name, the *Cappella Giulia,* or "Julian Choir." This latter group corresponded to the ancient Schola Cantorum and prepared the singers for the Sistine Choir. Both have always received strong pontifical support, and both continue yet as flourishing institutions.

Essentially a man of action, Julius II was an expert wielder of the sword as well as the crozier. He met his age on its own terms, and the spectacle of *il papa terribile* riding a fiery steed into the smoke of battle had a remarkably demoralizing effect on his enemies. As one of the principal architects of the modern papacy, he also saw the need of a setting commensurate with the magnificence of the apostolic Church and made it a matter of policy to command artists as well as soldiers. At the end of his career, his volcanic energies spent, Julius II became the subject of one of Raphael's most penetrating portraits (Fig. 194).

When Leo X ascended the papal throne, one of the eulogies ran: "Venus has had her day, and Mars his, now comes the turn of Minerva." Venus symbolized the reign of the Borgia pope, Alexander VI; Mars, of course, referred to Julius II; and Minerva, the Roman equivalent of Athena, was Leo who, as the son of Lorenzo the Magnificent, brought with him to Rome the spirit of Florence, that latter-day Athens. Michelangelo, whom Leo had known since his childhood at the Medici palace, was unfortunately bound by the terms of his contract to serve the heirs of Pope Julius, but the suave and worldly Raphael was available—and more congenial to the personal taste of Pope Leo than the gruff titan. Once again Raphael served as papal portraitist in the unusually fine study *Leo X with Two Cardinals* (Fig. 195).

Heinrich Isaac, Leo's old music teacher, wrote the six-part motet that commemorated his accession, and Isaac's pupil became one of the most liberal of all Renaissance patrons of music. Other princes of Europe had difficulty in keeping their musicians, because the Pope's love of the tonal art was so well known. Leo collected lute and viol players, organists, and the finest singers; chamber music was avidly cultivated at the pontifical palace; and a wind ensemble performed at papal dinners. Leo's encouragement of music to the point of putting it on a par with literary pursuits caused considerable murmurings among men of letters. As a competent composer in his own right, he knew the art from the inside as few patrons have ever known it. As a philosopher, writer, connoisseur, and collector, his patronage, like that of his father, was accompanied by an active participation in many of the pursuits that he sponsored. The Renaissance historian Jacob Burkhardt put it well when he wrote that Rome "possessed in the unique court of Leo X a society to which the history of the world offers no parallel."

## SCULPTURE

Despite his many masterpieces in other media, Michelangelo always thought of himself first and foremost as a sculptor. Other projects were undertaken reluctantly, and on the contract for the painting of the Sistine Chapel ceiling he pointedly signed *Michelangelo sculptore*—"Michelangelo the sculptor"—as a protest. His first visit to Rome at the age of 21

coincided with the discovery of some ancient statuary, including the *Apollo Belvedere*, that proved a powerful stimulant to his own productivity. His most important statues from this early period illustrate the conflicting pagan and Christian ideals that were to affect his aesthetic thought throughout a long career.

The *Pietà* (Fig. 196), now in St. Peter's, was commissioned in 1498 by Cardinal Villiers, the French ambassador to the Holy See. Its beauty of execution, delicacy of detail, and poignancy of expression reveal that Michelangelo was still under the spell of the Florentine Renaissance. Its pyramidal composition follows a type worked out by Piero della Francesca (Fig. 187) and by Leonardo da Vinci, as exemplified in his drawing for *Madonna and Child with St. Anne* (Fig. 197). Michelangelo uses the voluminous folds of the Virgin's drapery as the base of the pyramid and her head as the apex. The figure of Christ is cast in the perfect form of a Greek god, while the Madonna, though overwhelmed by grief, maintains a classical composure. No tears, no outcry, no gesture mar this conception of Mary as the matronly mother of sorrows. Yet Michelangelo allows himself many liberties with the proportions of his figures in order to heighten their expressive effect and enhance the harmony of his design. The excessive drapery exists to provide a multiplication of folds and sweeping lines. The horizontal body of Christ is far shorter than the vertical Madonna, but the disproportion serves to make the composition more compact. The triangular shape, as a self-sufficient form, holds the attention within the composition and obviates the need for such external considerations as niches or architectural backgrounds. As such, the *Pietà* is a sculptural declaration of independence, and it bears the unique distinction of being the only work Michelangelo ever signed.

After finishing the *Pietà*, Michelangelo went home to Florence, where he worked on the *Bruges Madonna* and the *David* (Fig. 191). In 1505, however, he was summoned back to Rome by the imperious Julius to discuss a project for a colossal tomb. In the inception of this gigantic composition, the artist's imagination for once met its match in his patron's ambitions. Julius' monument was conceived as a small temple within the great new temple—St. Peter's—that was abuilding. It was to rise pyramidally from a massive quadrangular base visible from all four sides, and it was to include more than forty statues.

When Julius died in 1513, only a few parts of the project had been finished, and a new contract with his heirs had to be negotiated. Further revisions were made later, each reducing the proportions of the project and eliminating more of the unfinished statues. In its final form of 1545, the great temple had shrunk to the relatively modest wall tomb now in the aisle of the Church of San Pietro in Vincoli.

Tombs of the popes, like the triple tiaras with which they are crowned, were traditionally in three rising zones, symbolizing earthly existence, death, and salvation. For the original project, Michelangelo translated these divisions into Neoplatonic terms representing the successive stages of the liberation of the soul from its bodily prison. For the final project, the monument lapsed into more traditional stratifications. In the original scheme, the lowest level was to have figures symbolizing those who are crushed by the burden of life and those who rise above the bonds of matter (Fig. 198). This idea was retained in some of the later revisions, and some six of the so-called "Slaves" or "Captives" and one "Victory" survive in various stages of completion.

On the second level of the original project were to have been placed heroic figures of the leaders of mankind, those individuals who pointed the way toward the divine goal of humanity—reunion with God. Moses and St. Paul were to represent the old

**198.** MICHELANGELO. *Projected Tomb of Julius II.* Drawing. Uffizi, Florence.

and new law, while Rachel and Leah would personify the active and contemplative ways of life. Of these, only the Moses was finished by Michelangelo.

The three figures that date from the years 1513 to 1516, when Leo X was pope, are the two "Slaves" now in the Louvre and the *Moses*. The *"Bound Slave"* (Fig. 199) is the more nearly finished of the two, and it seems to represent a sleeping adolescent tormented by a dream rather than the "dying captive" it is sometimes called. The imprisoned soul, tortured by the memory of its divine origin, has found momentary respite in sleep. The cloth bands by which the figure is bound are only symbolic, since Michelangelo is not concerned with the external aspect of captivity but rather with the internal torment. It is the tragedy of man, limited by time but troubled by the knowledge of eternity; mortal but with a vision of immortality; bound by the weight of his own body yet dreaming of a boundless freedom. This tragedy of the tomb was understood only too well by Michelangelo himself, who had the conception of his great project in mind but was doomed to see only a few fragments of his dream completed. Figures, such as the "Slaves" and "Victory" that Michelangelo envisaged, were associated with the triumphal arches as well as with the mausoleums and sarcophagi of ancient Rome. The similarity between the *"Bound Slave"* (Fig. 199) and the younger son in the 2nd century B.C. *Laocoön Group* (Fig. 62, figure on the left) has aptly been pointed out.

The Platonic idea of man's soul confined in the bonds of the flesh was continued in a later version of the tomb. The imprisonment of the spirit by matter in these "Captives" is all but complete. Unconscious, locked in their stone wombs, they struggle and writhe to be born out of their material medium. Their unfinished state gives an interesting glimpse into Michelangelo's methods, which were similar to that of relief sculpture. The statue to Michelangelo was a potential form hidden in the block of marble awaiting the hand of the master sculptor to be born. "The greatest artist has no single concept which a rough marble block does not contain already in its core . . . ," wrote Michelangelo in a sonnet, and the artist-creator must discover, "concealed in the hard marble of the North, the living figure one has to bring forth. (The less of stone remains, the more that grows)." The Neoplatonic implication is that the soul of man is still entombed in the body and can only be perfected into pure being by the hand of a higher creative power.

*Moses* (Fig. 200) is the only statue completed entirely by Michelangelo's hand to find its place in the finished tomb. Both Julius II and Michelangelo pos-sessed the quality of *terribilità* that is incarnated in this figure. Julius was known as *il papa terribile*, meaning the "forceful" or "powerful pope," imbued with the fear of the Lord. Michelangelo conceived his *Moses* as the personification of a powerful will, and partially as an idealized portrait of the indomitable Julius who, as the codifier of canon law, had something in common with the ancient Hebrew lawgiver. Moses is further portrayed as the personification of the elemental forces—the human volcano about to erupt with righteous wrath, the calm before a storm of moral indignation, the dead center of a hurricane of emotional fury, the author of those thunderous "Thou Shalt Nots" of the Ten Commandments, the man capable of ascending Mt. Sinai to discourse with God and

left: 199. MICHELANGELO. *"Bound Slave."* 1513–16. Marble, height 7'5". Louvre, Paris.

right: 200. MICHELANGELO. *Moses.* 1513–15. Marble, height 8'4". San Pietro in Vincoli, Rome.

coming back down to review all humanity from the seat of judgment. The smoldering agitation revealed through the drapery, the powerful musculature of the arms, the dominating intellectuality of the face, the fiery mood, and the torsions of the body as it twists in the act of rising are characteristic of Michelangelo's style. An interesting detail is the carved irises of the eyes, also done earlier in his *David* (Fig. 191), which Michelangelo did to express a look of fixed determination. When he wanted to convey the qualities of dreaminess, gentleness, and resignation, as in his Madonnas, he left the eyes untouched.

Michelangelo worked at the time when many of the most outstanding examples of antique statuary were being unearthed and admired. Inevitably this led to critical comparisons. Michelangelo, like the Greco-Roman artists, saw man as the lord of creation, but man's natural environment was always a matter of indifference to him. His early art especially was an affirmation of man's supreme place in the universal scheme of things. That world was populated by god-like beings at the peak of their physical power, full of vitality, creatively active, and buoyantly self-confident. As his art matured, his men and women were beset with quite unclassical tensions, doubts, and conflicts. Unlike the statues of antiquity, his figures, when they come to grips with fate, are armed with mental and moral powers that imply the hope of ultimate victory. Having thus surpassed the art of the ancients as well as that of his own time, not only by his technical mastery but by his expressive power, he came to be regarded by his contemporaries with awe. Vasari, his biographer, wrote: "The man who bears the palm of all ages, transcending and eclipsing all the rest, is the divine M. Buonarroti, who is supreme not in one art only but in all three at once." History has had no reason to reverse this judgment.

## THE SISTINE CEILING

When Michelangelo fled from Rome because of accumulated frustrations with plans for Julius II's tomb, the Pope resorted to every means from force to diplomacy to get him to return. Knowing he had a restless genius on his hands, Julius conceived some interim projects to keep Michelangelo busy until all the problems with his tomb were solved. Thinking it soon to be done, he set Michelangelo to painting the Sistine Chapel ceiling.

The building itself, the roof of which can be seen paralleling the nave on the right of St. Peter's in Figure 193, was built by and named for Julius' uncle, Sixtus IV, as the private chapel of the popes. The interior consists of a single rectangular room 44 by 132 feet (Fig. 201). Around the walls were frescoes painted by the foremost 15th-century artists, including the Florentines Ghirlandaio (who was one of Michelangelo's teachers), Botticelli, and Perugino

**201.** Sistine Chapel, view toward Michelangelo's *Last Judgment* (1534–41, fresco) over the altar. Vatican, Rome. 1473–80. Ceiling height 68'.

(teacher of Raphael). Above the frescoes were 6 windows in the side walls, and overhead was a barrel-vaulted ceiling 68 feet above the floor with 700 square yards of surface stretching before Michelangelo.

The entire Sistine ceiling was conceived as an organic composition motivated by a single unifying philosophical as well as artistic design (Fig. 202). The iconography is a fusion of traditional Hebrew-Christian theology and Neoplatonic philosophy that Michelangelo knew from his days in the Medici household. The space is divided into geometrical forms, such as the triangle, circle, and square, which were regarded in Plato's philosophy as the eternal forms that furnish clues to the true nature of the universe. Next is a three-way division into zones in which the varying intensity of the lighting plays a part. The lowest and darkest comprises the eight triangular spandrels and the four corner pendentive-shaped spandrels. The second is the intermediate zone that includes all the space outside the spandrels except that allotted to the nine center panels, which in turn constitute the third and brightest zone.

**202.** MICHELANGELO. Ceiling, Sistine Chapel. 1508–12. Fresco, 44 × 128'. Vatican, Rome. (See also Plate 25.)

Symbolically these divisions correspond to the three Platonic stages—the world of matter, the world of becoming, and the world of being. Analogies to such triple divisions run as an undercurrent through all aspects of Plato's thought. Plato divided society, for instance, into three classes: workers, free men, and philosophers, which he symbolized by the metals brass, silver, and gold. Each stratum had its characteristic goal: the love of gain, the development of ambition, and the pursuit of truth. Learning was similarly broken down into the three stages of ignorance, opinion, and knowledge. Plato's theory of the human soul was also tripartite in nature, consisting of the appetitive, emotional, and rational faculties, located in the abdomen, breast, and head, respectively. Of these only the rational or intellective part could aspire to immortality.

Michelangelo placed uninspired man on the low level of the spandrels. In the intermediate area are the inspired Old Testament prophets and pagan sibyls who have knowledge of the divine and mediate between man and God. In the central section are the panels that tell the story of man in his direct relationship to God, and they are seen through the architectural divisions as if taking place beyond on a more cosmic plane. Instead of starting at the beginning and proceeding chronologically as in the Book of Genesis, Michelangelo conceives the story of creation in reverse order, or as the Platonic ascent of man from his lowest estate back to his divine origin. In this return to God, the soul in its bodily prison gradually becomes aware of God and moves from finiteness to infinity, from material bondage to spiritual freedom. Immortality, in this sense, is not the reward for a passive and pious existence but the ultimate achievement of a tremendous effort of the soul struggling out of the darkness of ignorance into the blinding light of truth.

The eight center spandrels tell the dismal tale of humanity without vision, who, as St. Luke says, "sit in darkness and in the shadow of death," awaiting the light that will come when the Savior is born. In the four corner spandrels are the heroic men and women whose active deeds secured temporal deliverance for their people: David's slaying of Goliath, Judith's decapitation of Holophernes, Haman's punishment through Esther, and Moses and the brazen serpent.

This serves as an introduction to the representations of the seven Hebrew prophets, who alternate with five pagan sibyls like a chorus prophesying salvation. These are the inspired men and women who, through the exercise of their minds and imaginations, become the mediators between the human and divine spheres. They are placed, consequently, outside the confines of the dark spandrels and in a zone where the lighting approaches that of the central panels.

The *Delphic Sibyl* is the first of the series (Fig. 203). In the Greek tradition and in Plato, she was the priestess of Apollo at Delphi. In Vergil's *Aeneid*, Book VI, she is described as a young woman possessed by the spirit of prophecy. In the grip of divine fury, she turns her head toward the voice of her inspiration. Though clothed in Greek garments, her beauty recalls that of Michelangelo's early Madonnas (Fig. 196).

Above each of the prophets and sibyls and enframing the central panels are *ignudi*, or "nude youths," as seen in Figure 205. In the Christian tradition, these figures would have been represented as angels, but in the Platonic theory, they personify the rational faculties of the sibyls and prophets by which man rises to the contemplation of divine truth, and by which he is able to bridge the gap between the physical and spiritual, or earthly and heavenly regions. Thus, all the prophets and sibyls have a single figure below to denote the body, a pair of nudes behind them to signify the will, and a heroic *ignudo* to personify the immortal soul. These three levels correspond to Plato's tripartite conception of the soul—the appetitive, the emotional, and the intellective. These symbolic figures also play an aesthetic part in the softening of the harsh contours of the architectural design. The nude adolescents function ostensibly as the bearers of the garland that runs around the central panels and from which the painted bronze medallions are suspended. By covering the corners of the frames, and by their postures, they contribute a needed diagonal accent and bring a welcome variety to the design as a whole.

The first of the histories in the nine central panels is the *Drunkenness of Noah* (Fig. 204). As in the "Slave" figures of the Julius monument, the picture of Noah shows man in his most abysmal condition as the victim of his own bodily appetites. His servitude is symbolized at the left, where he is seen tilling the parched soil. Though still strong physically, his spirit is overwhelmed by the flesh. His sons, young adolescents in their physical prime, do not seem to be discovering their father's nakedness, as related in the Bible, but the tragic fate of man himself, who must work, grow old, and die. Noah's reclining posture recalls that of the ancient Roman river gods, and in this case the head has sunk forward on his chest in what seems to be a premonition of death. After this picture of Noah as the prisoner of his own baser nature, the next panel represents the *Deluge*, which shows the plight of man when beset by the elemental forces of nature beyond his control. In the third panel, *Noah's Sacrifice*, man's dependence on God is first implied.

The *Fall of Man and Expulsion from Paradise* follows next. Then the last five panels are concerned with various aspects of God's nature. In the *Creation of Eve*, He appears as a patriarchal figure closed within the folds of His mantle. In the *Creation of Adam* (Pl. 25, p. 196), God is seen in the skies, His mantle surrounding Him like a cloud, as He moves toward the earth and the inert body of Adam. The creative force is here the divine fire that flashes like lightning from the cloud to the earth. Adam's body is one with the rock on which he lies, not unlike the unfinished "Slaves" of the Julius tomb. In keeping with the Platonic idea of life as a burden and imprisonment, Adam is awak-

**above: 203.** MICHELANGELO. *Delphic Sibyl,* detail of Sistine Ceiling. 1509. Vatican, Rome.

**left: 204.** MICHELANGELO. *Drunkenness of Noah,* detail of Sistine Ceiling. 1508–09. Vatican, Rome.

193

**205.** MICHELANGELO. *God Dividing the Light from Darkness*, detail of Sistine Ceiling. 1511. Vatican, Rome.

ening to life reluctantly rather than eagerly. With His other arm, God embraces Eve, who again resembles Michelangelo's Madonna types, and who looks with fear and awe on this act of creation; His fingers point to the coming Christ Child, while behind Him are the heads of unborn generations of man.

In the *Creation of the Sun and the Moon*, the representation of God becomes a personification of the creative principle, while in *God Dividing the Light from Darkness* (Fig. 205), the final panel of the series, the climax and the realm of pure being are attained. Here is clarity coming out of chaos, order from the void, existence from nothingness, the idea from unconsciousness. You shall know the truth and the truth shall make you free, according to the Scriptures; or know thyself, as the Delphic oracle told Socrates. The conception of God has progressed from the patriarchal human figure of the *Creation of Eve* to that of a cosmic spirit in the intervening panels, and now He is seen as a swirling abstraction in the realm of pure being. The Neoplatonic objective of the union of the soul with God has been achieved by the gradual progress from the bondage of the spandrels, through the prophetic visions of the seers, and, finally, by ascending the ladder of the histories into the pure light of knowledge, to the point of dissolution into the freedom of infinity. In the words of Pico della Mirandola, man "withdraws into the center of his own oneness, his spirit made one with God."

The weight of expression, story content, and philosophical meaning is carried entirely by Michel-angelo's disposition and treatment of the 300-odd human figures in a seemingly infinite variety of postures. The colors are limited by the medium, and as the work progressed Michelangelo's preference was more and more in the direction of shades of gray, which accented the three-dimensional, sculpturesque quality of the figures. Such large projects are almost always school jobs, but internal evidence of the frescoes and documents suggest that Michelangelo did all the painting himself, with assistants doing the preparatory work only.

Though he later returned to the Sistine Chapel to paint the *Last Judgment* on the altar wall (Fig. 201) and worked on another group for the Pauline Chapel in the Vatican, Michelangelo never recaptured the buoyant optimism and creative force of the earlier series. The impact of the Sistine Chapel ceiling today, as it was on Michelangelo's contemporaries, is like a revelation of one of the eternal verities. Coming as this stupendous work did at the height of the artist's creative powers, the composition as a whole is among the highest peaks in the mountain range of Western art.

At the same time that Michelangelo was painting the Sistine ceiling, Raphael, a younger contemporary, was at work on the murals of the Vatican Palace. In *School of Athens* (Pl. 26, p. 196), Raphael presents such a complete visual philosophy that it places him, along with Michelangelo, in the rarified ranks of artist-scholars. Raphael's fresco is full of intellectual as well as pictorial complexities. Yet by the expanding space of the setting and the skillful deployment of the figures, as well as their relationships to each other and the architecture, it is clear and uncluttered. As members of a philosophical circle intent on reconciling the views of Plato and Aristotle, Raphael and his friends held that any point in Plato could be translated into a proposition of Aristotle and vice versa—the principal difference being that Plato wrote in poetic images, while Aristotle used the language of rational analysis. The two philosophers, "who agree in substance while they disagree in words," are placed on either side of the central axis of the fresco with the vanishing point between them. The book Plato holds in his hands is his *Timaeus*, and he points skyward to indicate his idealistic world view; Aristotle carries his *Ethics* and indicates by his earthward gesture his greater concern with the real and practical world.

In the spacious hall, which recalls the Roman poet Lucretius' remark on "temples raised by philosophy," the various schools of thought argue or ponder on the ideas propounded by the two central figures. On Plato's side a niche contains a statue of Apollo, patron of poetry; on Aristotle's is one of Athena, goddess of reason. This division of the central figures equates the entire picture, with the metaphysical philosophers ranked on Plato's side and the physical scientists

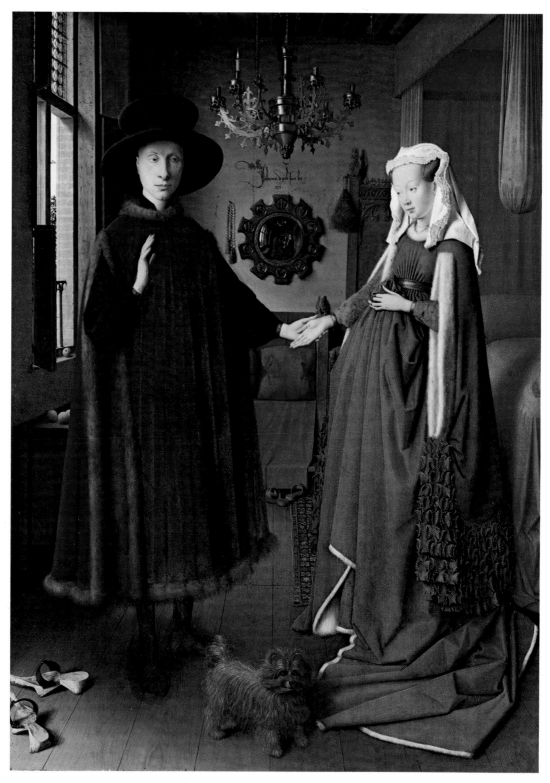

**Plate 24.** JAN VAN EYCK. *Giovanni Arnolfini and His Wife.* 1434. Oil on wood, 33 × 22½″. National Gallery, London (reproduced by courtesy of the Trustees). (See p. 179.)

**Plate 25.** MICHELANGELO. *Creation of Adam*, detail of Sistine Ceiling. 1511. Vatican, Rome. (See p. 193.)

**Plate 26.** RAPHAEL. *School of Athens*. 1510–11. Fresco, c. 26 × 18′. Stanza della Segnatura, Vatican, Rome. (See p. 194.)

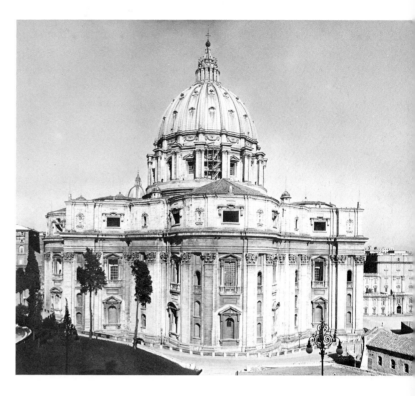

**above: 206.** St. Peter's. Plan of MICHELANGELO.

**above right: 207.** St. Peter's. Plan of present complex.

**right: 208.** MICHELANGELO. Apse and dome, St. Peter's. Begun 1547. Dome height 452'.

pursuing their various researches on Aristotle's. Spreading outward are groups corresponding to the divergent schools of thought within the two major divisions, and which carry the various arguments to their logical conclusion. The figure of Plato is thought to be an idealized portrait of Leonardo da Vinci, and in the group at the lower right Raphael portrayed his architect friend Bramante as Archimedes demonstrating on his slate a geometrical proposition. At the extreme right, Raphael paints a self-portrait in profile next to his friend and collaborator, the painter Sodoma. In *School of Athens* as a whole, Raphael captured the intellectual atmosphere and the zest with which Renaissance ideas were argued. By his grouping and placement of figures, and by their attitudes, attributes, and gestures, he provides a far clearer commentary on the complex thought of his time than did the more tortuous philosophical treatises of the period. To paint such metaphysical abstraction at all, and clothe them with plastic form, is a triumph of clear thinking and logical organization; and posterity is fortunate to have this summation of Renaissance humanism as seen through the eyes of such a profound artist.

## THE DOME OF ST. PETER'S

The foundations of the new St. Peter's (Fig. 193) had been laid as early as 1506, when Michelangelo was starting plans for Pope Julius' tomb. Comparatively

little progress had been made in the tempestuous years that followed, in spite of the succession of brilliant architects. Michelangelo favored the centralized church plans of Brunelleschi and Alberti just as his predecessor Bramante had done. The latter's design, however, was to have culminated in a low dome, modeled after that of the Pantheon but with a peristyle base and a lantern on top. Michelangelo accepted Bramante's Greek-cross ground plan with a few alterations of his own (Fig. 206), but he envisaged a loftier canopy rising over the legendary site of St. Peter's tomb. This dome was to be of such monumental proportions that it would unify not only the interior spaces and exterior masses of the building but would serve also as the climax of the liturgical, religious, and artistic forces of the Catholic world and as a symbol of Christendom.

Michelangelo's first problem was an engineering one—to find out if the masonry was strong enough to support such a dome. It was not, and he had to reinforce the four main piers until each was a massive 60 feet square. Pendentives became the means by which the square understructure was encircled, and then the drum was ready to rise. Meanwhile he made a large model of the dome itself, so that it could be built by others if necessary. All the preparatory work was thus completed, and Michelangelo lived just long enough to see the drum finished. The dome (Fig. 208) was completed after his death by two of his associates without substantial alterations. But for the aftermath of the Council of Trent and the Counter-Reformation, Michelangelo's centralized church might also have been finished. The new spirit of orthodoxy, however, frowned on anything that might be considered a pagan form, and a reactionary wave was started in favor of a return to the traditional Latin-cross plan. In the early 17th century, Carlo Maderno undertook the lengthening of the nave and the design of the façade (Figs. 193, 207). Liturgically, the new nave provided more space for the grandiose processions; practically, it afforded room for larger congregations; historically, it absorbed all the area formerly occupied by Constantine's basilica, demolished to make way for the new structure; but, aesthetically, the proportions suffered, and the climactic effect of the great dome was diminished. The scale of the interior, however, had been set by Michelangelo's huge piers beneath the dome, and Maderno had to continue the same proportions. The vaulting thus rises a little over 150 feet above the pavement, while the enormous interior covers more than 25,000 square yards in area.

The exterior of the church Michelangelo planned can best be seen from the apse, and the interior from beneath the dome where it appears as the compact unified structure he wanted. From the apse of the completed church (Fig. 208), where the lengthened nave does not detract, the effect is still substantially as Michelangelo intended it to be. From this vantage point the building itself appears as a great podium for the support of the vast superstructure; and from the ground level to the base of the dome there is a rise of about 250 feet. The cupola then continues upward to the top of the lantern, where an ultimate height of 452 feet above the ground level is attained. Coming as it did with the spread of the Counter-Reformation and the commercial exploitation and colonization of the New World, St. Peter's and its great dome had enormous influence on future church architecture (Figs. 293–296) and on such secular structures as the Capitol in Washington, D.C., and on a number of the American state capitols.

## JOSQUIN DES PREZ AND THE SISTINE CHAPEL CHOIR

"I am well aware that in his day Ockeghem was as it were the first to rediscover music, then as good as dead, just as Donatello discovered sculpture in his; and that of Josquin, Ockeghem's pupil, one might say that he was a natural prodigy in music, just as our own Michelangelo Buonarroti has been in architecture, painting, and sculpture; for just as Josquin has still to be surpassed in his compositions, so Michelangelo stands alone and without a peer among all who have practiced his arts; and the one and the other have opened the eyes of all who delight in these arts, now and in the future." So wrote a Florentine literary historian in a book on Dante published in

1567. Josquin des Prez, to whom he referred, was thus still regarded almost half a century after his death as a figure comparable to that of Michelangelo. A Florentine could bestow no higher praise. This opinion, moreover, was held by musicians. The distinguished theorist Glareanus wrote that the work of Josquin was "the perfect art to which nothing can be added, after which nothing but decline can be expected."

The so-called *ars perfecta*, or "perfect art," rested on the typical Renaissance historical assumption of the great development of the arts in antiquity, which had been lost in medieval days and subsequently rediscovered in the then-modern times. The quotation above is a critical application of this doctrine of perfection regained to the art of music. Italians, whether at home or abroad, took the greatest pride in the achievements of their own architects, sculptors, and painters, but universally they acknowledged the supremacy of the northern composers. The spread of the northern polyphonic art dated from the time the popes had become acquainted with it at Avignon. Later, it led to the establishment of the *Cappella Sistina* in 1473, which was dominated by Flemish, Burgundian, and French musicians, whose influence from there spread over the entire Christian world. From this time forward, the mastery of these artists in contrapuntal writing became the standard of perfection.

Under Pope Sixtus IV, church music had moved from its status as the modest handmaiden of the liturgy to a position of major importance. The grandeur of the Roman liturgical displays called for music of comparable magnificence. Owing to the prevailing taste of the time, musicians from the great singing centers of Antwerp, Liège, and Cambrai flocked to Rome to seek their fortunes. The highest honor of all was an appointment to the Sistine Choir, whose privilege it was to perform on the occasions when the pope officiated. Membership was highly selective, totaling from 16 to 24 singers except during the time of the musical Leo, who increased it to 36. These singers were divided into four parts: boy sopranos, male altos, tenors, and basses; normally they sang *a cappella*—that is, "in the chapel manner" without instrumental accompaniment—a practice that was exceptional rather than usual at the time. The quality of the choir can be deduced from the roster of distinguished men who made their reputations in its ranks. In the archives are numerous masses, motets, and psalm settings composed by Josquin des Prez during his service there from 1486 to 1494. Palestrina, who learned contrapuntal fluency from Josquin, became a member in 1551 and later brought the organization to a pinnacle of technical perfection.

In Josquin's compositions, the stark barren intervals of Gothic polyphony and all traces of harshness in the voice leading are eliminated. He allows dissonances to occur only on weak beats or as suspensions on the stronger ones. His rhythms and forms are

*Ave Maria* (4-part motet)  JOSQUIN DES PREZ

based on strict symmetry and mathematically regular proportions. His writing is characterized by the usual northern fondness for canonic imitations and other complicated contrapuntal constructions. Such devices, however, are managed with complete mastery, and his tremendous technique in composition never intrudes upon his expressive design. He was at home in all Renaissance musical forms, excelling perhaps in his motets and in his solo and choral chansons. In Rome, where his unique abilities were combined with the warmth and fluidity of Italian lyricism, Josquin mellowed in his music until it achieved a style of incomparable beauty, formal clarity, and the purest expressivity.

Josquin's four-part motet *Ave Maria* will serve as an admirable illustration of his art. Like Michelangelo's early *Pietà*, it is in a perfectly self-contained form, emotionally restrained, and full of luxuriantly flowing lines. Even such a short excerpt as that reproduced above shows his penchant for canonic imitation between the voices and the smoothness of contour that comes with stepwise melodic motion. He treats all four voices with balanced impartiality but prefers to group them in pairs, as in this example, in order to achieve a transparency of texture and an ineffable purity of sound. Darker sides of Josquin's emotional spectrum can be found in his requiem masses and in his setting of the psalm *De Profundis*.

Later periods saw in Michelangelo both a summing up of the Renaissance and the beginning of the baroque style. Josquin's place was more limited; and while he enjoyed universal acclaim as the greatest musical mind of the early 16th century, the very perfection of his art implied that it was on the verge of becoming archaic. Josquin's mantle was inherited by a number of composers in the succeeding generation, who carried his art to its logical conclusion. Palestrina's music is, perhaps, better adapted to religious purposes, though he remains Josquin's inferior in in-

vention, inspiration, and depth of expression. Victoria carried the style to Spain, William Byrd to England; and through Philippe de Monte and Orlando di Lasso, it spread throughout France and Germany. In the 17th century, though the art was still studied, it became known as the "antique style" in contrast to the baroque music, which was called the "modern style." Within its limitations the art has never been surpassed. Even today it is considered the ideal for church music.

## IDEAS: HUMANISM

Florentine humanism and its Roman aftermath were motivated by a reappraisal of the values of Greco-Roman antiquity, by an attempt to reconcile pagan forms with Christian practices, by a desire to reinstate the philosophy of Plato and reinterpret that of Aristotle, and, above all, by a rediscovery of the world and man. The Renaissance humanist was not primarily religious- or scientific-minded. He tended to substitute the authority of respected classical writers for that of the Bible and Church dogma. In looking forward, he found more convenient and convincing precedents in the civilizations of Greece and Rome than in the immediate medieval past. Lorenzo de' Medici, for instance, found a new orientation for secular government in Plato's *Republic;* Machiavelli, a new method for writing history in Thucydides; and Bramante, a new adaptation of the Greco-Roman temple for Christian worship.

Bramante's Tempietto (Fig. 209) was a conscious revival of the rounded commemorative structures of antiquity (Figs. 81, 82). This temple in miniature, coming as it did at the outset of the 16th century, became the architectural manifesto of the Roman Renaissance, just as Brunelleschi's Pazzi Chapel (Figs. 172–174) had been in the 15th-century Florentine Renaissance. Placed in the cloistered courtyard of the Church of San Pietro in Montorio, the little temple, like a sculptured reliquary, rests on the site where St. Peter is supposed to have been crucified. For his architectural order Bramante chose the simple yet monumental Roman Doric. He adhered to the classical principle of the module whereby all parts of the building are either multiples or fractions of the basic unit of measure. He also promoted the feeling of balance and proportion by making the height and width of the lower floor equal to that of the upper story. Spare of ornament, the only formal decorative element is in the Doric frieze with the regular triglyphs alternating with metopes that employ a shell motif. Above all, Bramante wished to demonstrate the cohesiveness and compactness of the centralized plan under the unifying crown of a cupola. Later when Pope Julius entrusted him with the design of the new St. Peter's, Bramante had his chance to build on a monumental scale. Here again he turned to antiquity for inspiration and is reputed to have declared: "I shall place the Pantheon on top of the Basilica of Constantine."

The humanists preferred purer versions of classical art forms to the adaptations that had been made in the thousand-year period between the fall of Rome and their own time. The members of the Florentine humanistic circle learned to read and speak ancient Greek under native tutors. Ficino translated the dialogues of Plato, while Poliziano translated Homer from the original Greek into Italian and wrote treatises in Latin on Greek poetic and musical theory. Other scholars catalogued and edited books for the Medici library, while Squarcialupi compiled the musical compositions of the preceding century. The interest in cataloguing, editing, translating, and commenting was pursued with such enthusiasm that it all but blotted out the production of live literature. The Latin of Renaissance scholars was Ciceronian rather than medieval Latin, which they considered corrupt. The architects read Vitruvius and preferred central-type churches modeled on the Pantheon to the rectangular basilica form that had been evolved over the centuries. They revived the classical orders and ar-

chitectural proportions in a more authentic form. Decorative motifs were derived directly from ancient sarcophagi, reliefs, and carved gems. Sculptors reaffirmed the possibilities of the nude, and with Michelangelo it became the chief expressive vehicle of his art. Painters, lacking tangible survivals, used mythological subjects and the literary descriptions of ancient works.

Musicians reinterpreted Greek musical thought, and some made concrete attempts to put into practice the theories expounded in Euclid's musical treatise. The Greek assertion that art imitates nature was universally acknowledged, but in architecture and music this had to be applied in the general sense of nature as an orderly and regular system conforming to mathematical proportions and laws. Josquin des Prez was hailed as a modern Orpheus who had regained the lost perfect art of the ancients—though the Greeks would have been bewildered by his musical style. Josquin's less enthusiastic admirers pointed out that the trees and stones still showed some reluctance to follow him as they had not in the case of the original Orpheus. His art, however, like that of Michelangelo, was thought by the humanists to be a path back to classical paradise.

Both Botticelli and Michelangelo set out to produce works in the Neoplatonic spirit. The literary ancestry of Botticelli's *Allegory of Spring* (the famous *Primavera*), *Birth of Venus* (Fig. 189), and *Venus and Mars* (Pl. 23, p. 178) has been traced through the poetry of his contemporary Poliziano back to the Roman poets Lucretius and Horace. Their philosophical forebear, however, is the Plato of the *Symposium*, which deals with the nature of love and beauty. Man, according to Plato's theory, has drunk of the waters of oblivion and forgotten his divine origin. Falling in love with a beautiful person reminds him of his natural affinity for beauty. From physical attraction and ephemeral loveliness, he is led to thoughts of the lasting beauty of truth and, finally, to the contemplation of the eternal verities of absolute beauty, truth, and goodness. Venus is, of course, the image of this transcendent beauty, and the way to approach it is through love. The eternal feminine, as Goethe later said in the closing lines of *Faust*, draws us ever onward. Michelangelo's Plato, however, was the Plato of the *Timaeus*, which discourses on the creation of the world by the Demiurge, the metaphysical nature of the human soul, and the return to God. Unlike Botticelli's fragile dream of beauty, Michelangelo had a virile vision of the creative process itself. When Botticelli came under the influence of the fiery Savonarola with his resurgence of medievalism, he repented of his paganism and turned exclusively to

209. Donato Bramante. Tempietto, San Pietro in Montorio, Rome. 1504. Marble; height 46', diameter of colonnade 29'.

religious pictures. Botticelli never tried to combine his paganism and Christianity as did Michelangelo, and for him they remained in separate compartments and on an either/or basis. Michelangelo, however, had the mind to assimilate Platonic abstractions, the overwhelming urge to express his ideas, and the technical equipment to translate them into dramatic visual form. But the voice of Savonarola spoke loudly to him, too, and in his rugged mind Michelangelo was destined to wrestle with the two essentially irreconcilable philosophies for the rest of his life. Leonardo da Vinci, contrariwise, kept the religious themes of his painting (Fig. 210) and his scientific inquiries (Fig. 211) in separate intellectual compartments.

Michelangelo's Madonnas reveal the unity between bodily beauty and eternal beauty; his *Moses* links human moral power with eternal goodness; and his organic compositions connect temporal with eternal truth. His triple divisions symbolizing the stages of the soul as it progresses from its bodily tomb to its liberation and reunion with God are a constantly recurring preoccupation. Even in his abstract architectural forms of St. Peter's, the pilasters are the "slaves" imprisoned by the weight of the material burden they must carry, while overhead soars the lofty dome in the geometrical perfection of the circular form, symbolizing the paradise that man has lost and that he must somehow regain. The whole building is thus conceived as an organic system of upward pressures and tensions, culminating in a cupola that ascends toward the divine realm and finally dissolves into the freedom of infinity.

**210.** LEONARDO DA VINCI. *Last Supper.* 1495–98. Fresco, 14'5″ × 28'¼″. Santa Maria della Grazie, Milan.

**211.** LEONARDO DA VINCI. Drawing for flying apparatus (helicopter), from Manuscript B. c. 1485–90. Bibliothèque de l'Institut de France, Paris.

# 12 Venetian Renaissance, Mannerism, and Early Baroque

**VENICE, 16TH CENTURY**

A glimpse of Venice as it was at the threshold of the 16th century can be seen through the eyes of the painter Gentile Bellini. His faithful reporting in *Procession in St. Mark's Square* (Fig. 212)—so accurate that architectural historians can make reconstructions of buildings long since razed; that researchers can study the mosaics and sculptures of St. Mark's Basilica as they were before later restorations; that historians of liturgy, musical performances, and costume find it prime source material—belongs to Renaissance naturalism. When compared with the forthcoming flights of mannerist and early baroque imaginations, the stateliness and stability of Bellini's painting are all the more striking. Hence, the subject matter of the *Proces-*

*sion in St. Mark's Square*, its story content, mode of representation, formal organization, and the circumstances of its commission reveal much about the life of Venice and the unique developments in the arts during a period of transition.

St. Mark's Basilica at once proclaims Venice the meeting place of Orient and Occident. Begun in the 10th century, it is the product of centuries of community effort. Indeed, an early law required every Venetian ship to bring back materials for the construction or decoration of the church. As a result, fragments from every Mediterranean country can be found somewhere in its fabric—from the four Roman bronze horses of the first century A.D. over the central portal (Fig. 213), the Alexandrian polychrome marble columns and Greek alabaster windows, to the

**212.** GENTILE BELLINI. *Procession in St. Mark's Square.* 1496. Oil on canvas, 12 × 24′. Academy, Venice.

present-day changes. The plan is that of a Greek cross with domes covering each of the wings and a cupola 42 feet in diameter at the center.

Above the narthex entrance, stretching the full width of the façade, is an open gallery on which, in Bellini's picture, several figures can be seen. Above the gallery is a row of five 13th-century Gothic ogee gables that frame the upper tier of mosaics. On the crest of the central gable is the winged lion of St. Mark, one of the four beasts that symbolize the Evangelists, placed here to honor him as the city's patron saint. To the right is a corner of the Doge's Palace where the ruler and his guests are seated on the second-story arcade. This bizarre variation of a Gothic town hall rises in two stories of open pointed arches surmounted by a third story notable for its diamond-shaped design in bright-pink marble tiling. On the left is the old library from which many spectators watch the activities in the square. The building with its castellated roof and curious chimney pots also dates from medieval times.

More remarkable than its architecture, however, is the institution of the library itself. In lieu of outstanding literary figures, Venice treasured the collections of books that had been left her by the poet Petrarch, the Greek scholar Cardinal Bessarion, and other donors, because in this watery city the danger of fire was less than elsewhere. In addition to these collections, the library housed all the specimens of the city's elegant printing and book-making industry, which included fine but inexpensive editions of classics published here for the first time by the famous Aldine Press, and which gave such great momentum to the spread of learning throughout the educated world. In the 16th century, these collections were transferred to the handsome building across the square designed by Sansovino especially to house them (Fig. 214).

In the procession scene, a feeling of open public life and freedom of social movement can be sensed in both the participants and the bystanders. The independence of Venice and the prosperity of her citizenry were owing in many respects to the city's unusual situation. Built on a group of island lagoons at the head of the Adriatic, Venice was truly what a Florentine poet described as "a city in the water without walls." Secure from attack by land and by sea as a result of its possessing the largest navy then in existence, Venice carried on an active commerce between East and West that afforded her citizens a manner of life unrivaled in its time for comfort and luxury. Lacking the ups and downs of other medieval and Renaissance cities, such as Pisa and Siena with their brief periods of florescence, Venice developed slowly and consistently from the glow of its Byzantine dawn, through a Renaissance high noon and a brief thunderstorm of mannerism, to its florid baroque sunset.

**top: 213.** Four horses of Greek origin. 1st century A.D. St. Mark's Basilica, Venice. Life-size, gilt bronze.

**above: 214.** Jacopo Sansovino. Library of St. Mark, Venice. Begun 1536. Length c. 290', height c. 60'.

Here lived no literary giant such as Dante, no magnifico with the vision of a Lorenzo, no political philosopher of the caliber of Machiavelli, no thundering religious reformer like Savonarola. In fact, without great men of letters, without outstanding individual art patrons, without inspired religious leaders—in short, without experiencing the heights and depths of the human spirit known in Florence or Rome—Venice built up in its architecture, painting, and music a culture uniquely its own.

Venetian Renaissance, Mannerism, and Early Baroque **203**

# CHRONOLOGY / 16th-Century Venice

## General Events

| | | |
|---|---|---|
| | 1453 | Fall of Constantinople to Turks; Venetian commerce challenged |
| | 1492 | Geographical discoveries by Spanish and Portuguese navigators weakened Venetian maritime trade |
| | 1495 | Aldine Press began publishing inexpensive editions of Greco-Roman classics |
| | 1501 | *Odhecaton,* anthology of vocal and instrumental works by Josquin des Prez, Obrecht, Isaac, and others printed in Venice by Petrucci |
| | 1517 | Protestant Reformation began |
| 1527– | 1562 | Willaert choirmaster of St. Mark's |
| | 1536 | Library of St. Mark built by J. Sansovino |
| | 1540 | Loggietta at base of Campanile built by Sansovino |
| 1545– | 1563 | Council of Trent initiated Counter-Reformation |
| | 1549 | Basilica at Vicenza built by Palladio |
| | 1550 | Villa Rotonda near Vicenza begun by Palladio |

| | | |
|---|---|---|
| | 1565 | Church of San Giorgio Maggiore, Venice, built by Palladio |
| | 1570 | Palladio published *Four Books of Architecture* |
| | 1571 | Naval Battle of Lepanto; Venice and Spain defeated Turks |
| | 1573 | Veronese called before Inquisition |
| 1576– | 1578 | Church of Il Redentore, Venice, built by Palladio |
| 1579– | 1580 | Olympic Theater, Vicenza, built by Palladio |
| | 1584 | Procuratie Nuove, continuation of Sansovino's Library of St. Mark design, built by Scamozzi |
| 1585– | 1612 | Giovanni Gabrieli choirmaster of St. Mark's |
| | 1589 | Olympic Theater at Vicenza dedicated with performance of Sophocles' *Oedipus* (music by A. Gabrieli) |
| 1613– | 1643 | Monteverdi choirmaster of St. Mark's |
| | 1631 | Santa Maria della Salute begun |

### Architects

| | | |
|---|---|---|
| 1486– | 1570 | Jacopo Sansovino |
| 1508– | 1580 | Andrea Palladio |
| 1552– | 1616 | Vincenzo Scamozzi |
| 1604– | 1675 | Baldassare Longhena |

### Painters

| | | |
|---|---|---|
| 1429– | 1507 | Gentile Bellini |
| c.1430– | 1516 | Giovanni Bellini |
| c.1455–c.1526 | | Vittore Carpaccio |
| c.1490– | 1576 | Titian (Tiziano Vecelli) |
| c.1470– | 1528 | Matthias Grünewald |
| 1471– | 1528 | Albrecht Dürer |
| 1478– | 1510 | Giorgione |
| 1510– | 1592 | Jacopo Bassano |
| 1518– | 1594 | Jacopo Tintoretto |
| 1528– | 1588 | Paolo Veronese |

### Musicians

| | | |
|---|---|---|
| c.1480– | 1562 | Adriano Willaert |
| 1510– | 1586 | Andrea Gabrieli |
| 1516– | 1565 | Cipriano de Rore |
| 1517– | 1590 | Gioseffo Zarlino |
| 1557– | 1612 | Giovanni Gabrieli |
| 1567– | 1643 | Claudio Monteverdi |
| 1602– | 1676 | Francesco Cavalli |

### Italian and International Mannerists

| | | |
|---|---|---|
| c.1492– | 1546 | Giulio Romano |
| 1494– | 1540 | Rosso Fiorentino |
| 1494– | 1556 | Jacopo Pontormo |
| 1500– | 1571 | Benvenuto Cellini |
| 1503– | 1540 | Francesco Parmigianino |
| 1503– | 1572 | Agnolo Bronzino |
| 1511– | 1574 | Giorgio Vasari |
| 1529– | 1600 | Giovanni da Bologna |
| c.1540– | 1609 | Federigo Zuccaro |
| 1555– | 1619 | Ludovico Carracci |
| 1560– | 1609 | Annibale Carracci |

The fall of Constantinople to the Turks and the rising power of the Ottoman Empire spelled competition for Venice's commercial empire, and sporadic warfare had already begun. While Venice had given birth to one great explorer, Marco Polo, the voyages of the 16th-century Spanish, Portuguese, Dutch, and English navigators were being exploited to enrich rival countries, thereby upsetting the traditional economy in which Venice had flourished. Italy was soon to become a battleground in the European power struggle between the Holy Roman Empire and France. Charles V, Titian's great patron, became emperor in 1519, and in addition to Spain his dominions included the Low Countries, Germany, and Austria. Francis I of France, feeling his country caught in a giant pincers, tried to fortify his position by invading Italy. But one by one each Italian kingdom, principality, dukedom, and republic fell to Charles V. Finally, by sacking and pillaging Rome itself with his ruthless mercenaries and imprisoning Pope Clement VII, Charles achieved the surrender of the papacy.

The religious crisis brought on by opposing forces of the Reformation and Counter-Reformation likewise unsettled Venice's trade and cultural relations with northern Europe. Though the Universal Inquisition was felt more mildly in Venice than elsewhere, Roman Catholic censorship of printed matter and assertion of the clergy's control of art proved more than a threat to Venice's publishing industry and artistic freedom. Venetians, to be sure, were no strangers to insecurity as fabulous fortunes were made overnight when their ships came in, while financial ruin and debtor's prison followed shipwrecks, seizure by pirates, or sinkings in naval battles.

This Pandora's box of troubles created a crisis in the literal sense of a split, with East and West divided,

**left: 215.** ANDREA PALLADIO. Villa Rotonda, near Vicenza. Begun 1550. 80 × 80'. Dome height 70'.

**above: 216.** ANDREA PALLADIO. Plan of Villa Rotonda.

the Ottoman Turkish Empire on one side and an alliance of Christian European states on the other; with Christendom itself rent asunder by the Reformation and the Counter-Reformation; with Italy under siege by both the Holy Roman Emperor and the King of France. Such a critical state, with its accompanying inner anxieties and complicated contradictions, was bound to find expression in the arts.

One road out of the crisis was to lead to a freezing of Renaissance convention, formal logic, and balanced symmetry in a conservative academic *mannerism*—art "in the manner" of the great masters of the immediate past, such as Michelangelo and Raphael. The other was to lead to the search for a new style in a free mannerism with its deliberate violations of Renaissance proportions, experimental forms, capricious eccentricities, unresolved tensions, and restless imbalances. A reconciliation of these opposites was eventually to resolve itself into the synthesis of the baroque style, which developed in the 17th century.

## ARCHITECTURE

As did all the other arts, Venetian architecture reached out toward new forms. Although begun as early as 1536 and still within the Renaissance tradition, the Library of St. Mark by Jacopo Sansovino already had enough new ideas to qualify it as a transition to the coming baroque style (Fig. 214). Standing out boldly from the façade are the rich decorative details the Venetians loved. Instead of the solid, flat surfaces of a Renaissance façade with a rusticated ground floor (Fig. 175), Sansovino has an open arcade, paralleled above by the row of deeply indented windows. This projection in depth makes for an effective play of light and shadow, an element hitherto asso-

ciated more with sculpture and painting than with architecture. The dignified arcade of the lower story serves as a base for the increasingly rich adornment of the upper parts. The deeply arched windows of the second floor are unified by the regularity of the Ionic columns, while the poses of the sculptured nudes in the spandrels provide variety. Above runs a frieze of cherubs in high relief holding garlands that alternate with small, deep-set windows. Over this rises a balustrade that goes all the way around the roof and supports a row of statues silhouetted against the skyline, with obelisks at the corners.

Sansovino's designs influenced Andrea Palladio, the greatest architect associated with the Venetian style. As the author of the highly influential *Four Books of Architecture*, first published in Venice in 1570, Palladio has left a detailed exposition of his philosophy. In the preface to this work, Palladio paid eloquent tribute to his ancient Roman mentor Vitruvius, whose writings stimulated his study of the classical buildings in Rome. "Finding that they deserved a much more diligent Observation than I thought at first Sight," he noted, "I began with the utmost Accuracy to measure every minutest part by itself." Palladio's ideas thus were based on a thorough grounding in traditional design. He also saluted his immediate predecessor Sansovino, whose Library he praised as "perhaps the most sumptuous and the most beautiful Edifice that has been erected since the time of the Ancients."

Palladio's architecture can be studied more fully in nearby Vicenza, then a part of the Venetian Republic's holdings on the mainland. Just outside Vicenza is the Villa Rotonda (Fig. 215), a country house in the grand style and the prototype of many later buildings. The plan is a cube enclosing a cylindrical core, topped by a saucer dome (Fig. 216). On four sides grand flights of steps lead to Ionic porticoes that project 14 feet forward and are 40 feet wide. The pediments are those of a classical temple, with statues on either side and above. Each portico provides entrance into the imposing reception room that gives the villa the name *rotonda*. This central salon is as high as the house itself and culminates in the cupola above. Alcoves left over from the parts between the round central hall and the square sides of the building allow space for four winding staircases and for no less than 32 rooms in the adjoining corners—all excellently lighted both from the outside and from the eight round windows at the base of the cupola. At the corners of the main floor are four large reception rooms, each 20 by 30 feet, and four smaller ones—

eight in all on this floor alone. Below, a basement includes storerooms, servants' quarters, and kitchens. Palladio's achievement here is a house that is spacious but simple in plan.

When advancing years curtailed Sansovino's activities, Palladio was called to Venice to construct several buildings, among them the Church of Il Redentore or "the Redeemer" (Fig. 217). Palladio set himself the problem of reconciling the Greco-Roman temple with the traditional oblong Christian basilica plan (Fig. 218). Since a classical temple is of uniform height with a simple shed roof, and a Christian basilica has a Latin-cross ground plan with a central nave rising high above two side aisles, his solution shows great ingenuity. The central part of the façade of Il Redentore becomes the portico of a classical temple complete with columns and pediment to face the high central nave within, while the acute angles of a fragmentary second pediment face the side aisles. The pediment idea is repeated in the small triangle above the entrance and in the side angles at the roof level, to make in all two complete and two incomplete pediments. This broken-pediment motif was later incorporated into the baroque vocabulary. To create the feeling of deep space, Palladio alternated square pilasters with round attached columns and arranged the pediments in a complex intersecting design. The interior is a model of geometrical clarity (Fig. 219); and in order to create the impression of spatial depth, he eliminated the traditional walled apse that usually

left: **217.** ANDREA PALLADIO. Façade, Il Redentore, Venice. 1576–92.

right: **218.** ANDREA PALLADIO. Plan of Il Redentore.

**219.** ANDREA PALLADIO. Interior, Il Redentore, Venice. 1576–92.

220. ANDREA PALLADIO. Interior, Olympic Theater, Vicenza. 1580–84.

below: 221. VINCENZO SCAMOZZI. Façade (detail), Procuratie Nuove, Venice. 1584.

bottom: 222. GIULIO ROMANO. Courtyard (detail), Palazzo del Tè, Mantua. 1525–35.

closes the space around the altar and replaced it by a semicircular open colonnade against clear glass windows, which leads the eye past the altar and on into the distance.

The last building Palladio undertook was the Olympic Theater at Vicenza (Fig. 220). It was begun the year of his death and finished later from his designs by Scamozzi. An ingenious device to create the feeling of deep space is seen through the central arch from which actors made their entrances—a rising ramp flanked by building façades, which recedes only about fifty feet but creates the illusion of a long avenue leading to an open city square in the distance. Clearly inspired by ancient Roman amphitheaters, the Olympic has, in turn, been the inspiration for many later theaters, including one of London's largest, the Palladium.

Scamozzi, the younger collaborator of both Sansovino and Palladio, was commissioned in 1584 to add a wing to Sansovino's Library on the side toward St. Mark's Square (Fig. 221), to house the Procuratie Nuove, the new civic agencies. His design shows the usual Palladian angularity, but he turned to Michelangelo for the alternation of semicircular and angular window brackets. A touch of manneristic caprice is found in the precariously perched nudes atop the third-story window brackets.

Similar mannerist shock techniques are seen in the Palazzo del Tè, or "Tea Palace" (Fig. 222), that Giulio Romano built for the ruling family of the neighboring duchy of Mantua. To enclose this small pleasure garden, he built a wall of heavily rusticated masonry much too massive for its function, and Doric columns far larger than necessary to support the frieze. This dramatic overstatement, however, pales in comparison with the syncopated, and somewhat unnerving, effect of the frieze itself in which every third triglyph slips downward a notch.

It remained for Longhena in the early years of the 17th century to make the break from the brittle recti-

223. BALDASSARE LONGHENA. Santa Maria della Salute, Venice. 1631–56. c. 200 × 155'.

linear style of Palladio and Scamozzi and carry Venetian architecture over into the exuberant baroque spirit with his Church of Santa Maria della Salute (Fig. 223). From the octagonal base, each side of which is treated like a Roman triumphal arch and surmounted by a triangular pediment pierced by a Palladian "porthole," the structure culminates in the high-pitched main dome and the smaller echoing one at the rear. Buttressing the cupola and mediating between it and the octagonal mass below are striking ornamental scrolls. The elaborately decorated exterior is held together by the good composition of the design as a whole. This building was far more to the taste of the Venetians than the restrained and academic Palladian style, and it is one of the finest examples of the early baroque.

Palladio, however, emerges as the most influential architect of his period. His thought as he expressed it in *Four Books of Architecture*, with their sketches and drawings, had an even wider influence in France, England, Ireland, and America than did his buildings. The English translation, published with notes by his disciple Inigo Jones, did much to establish the Georgian tradition both in England (Fig. 291) and in

America, where it was carried on by Thomas Jefferson. The latter's staunch Palladianism is seen in the designs he prepared for his residence at Monticello and the Rotunda of the University of Virginia (Fig. 323), both of which are adaptations of the Villa Rotonda (Fig. 215). Jefferson also wanted to build the White House at Washington, D.C., on the same plan, but his proposal, submitted anonymously, was not the one chosen. However, even in its present form the White House has Palladio's winged design on either side of a classical temple portico.

## PAINTING

Venetian painting in the course of the 16th century ran a gamut of styles—from the Renaissance work of Giorgione, with its partial emancipation from traditional subject matter and story content, to the mannerist and protobaroque paintings of Tintoretto and Veronese, with their illusionism and flights of imagination. Technically, Venetian painting is marked by the refinement and perfection of painting with oil on canvas, since the methods of tempera on wood panels and fresco were unsuited to the damp Venetian climate. Venetian painters also developed rich color palettes and used high intensities of light by which the principal figures are dramatically spotlighted and subordinate ones thrown into various degrees of shadow.

Giorgione's *Concert Champêtre*, or "Pastoral Concert," impresses with its spaciousness and its distribution of interest from foreground to background (Pl. 27, p. 213). The eye first is arrested by the four figures of the picture plane, then is led leisurely toward the middle ground where the shepherd is tending his flock, and finally comes to rest on the gleaming water of the distant horizon. This pastoral idyll is enlivened by such oppositions as the clothed male figures and feminine nudes; the pairing of the urbane courtier and stately lady at the left with the rustic shepherd and shepherdess on the right; the attitudes of the two women—one intent upon her lover, the other turning away; and by the lute symbolizing lyric poetry and the flute, pastoral poetry.

Giorgione's so-called *Tempest* (Fig. 224) is even less concerned with storytelling than *Concert Champêtre* and more with pictorial mechanics. The sunny foreground and human figures define the picture plane, while the eye is led in receding planes to deep space and the threatening sky in the distance. Stability is maintained by judicious balance of vertical (the standing figure, broken columns, trees, and buildings) and horizontal lines (the unfinished parapet and bridge). In both the *Pastoral Concert* and the *Tempest*,

Giorgione creates a mood rather than tells a story, builds a picture rather than communicates concrete meaning. A puzzle to his contemporaries who were accustomed to the usual iconographical subjects, Giorgione is understandable to the modern observer who is used to separating subject matter from pictorial form and to seeing a picture as a composition complete within itself rather than as an illustration of a religious or literary theme.

The dynamic vertical movement of Titian's *Assumption of the Virgin* marks a definite departure from Renaissance calm and static monumentality (Fig. 225). In this dramatic composition, heavenly and earthly spheres converge momentarily. Below in deep shadow are grouped the apostles, their arms raised toward the intermediate zone and the ascending Madonna, whose gesture, in turn, directs the eye to the dazzling brightness above. The upward motion then is arrested by the descending figure of God the Father surrounded by His seraphs. Linear movement and gradations of light, as well as transitions of color from somber shades to light pastel hues, are skillfully adapted by Titian to carry out his theme of the soaring human spirit triumphant over the gravitational pull of material considerations. Titian herewith created a new pictorial type that was to have a profound influence on the mannerist El Greco (Fig. 256), the baroque sculptor Bernini (Fig. 250), and a number of 17th-century painters.

Titian's sumptuous coloring also became the model for such later Venetians as Tintoretto, as well

**left: 224.** GIORGIONE. *Tempest.* c. 1505. Oil on canvas, $32\frac{1}{4} \times 28\frac{3}{4}''$. Academy, Venice.

**above: 225.** TITIAN. *Assumption of the Virgin.* 1516–18. Oil on canvas, $22'6'' \times 11'8''$. Frari Church, Venice.

**226.** TINTORETTO. *Last Supper.* 1592–94. Oil on canvas, 12′ × 18′8″. San Giorgio Maggiore, Venice.

as for such baroque masters as Rubens and Valázquez. The extraordinary brilliance and bright tonality of the master's palette has been startlingly revealed by the recent cleaning and restoration of the *Bacchus and Ariadne* in London's National Gallery (Pl. 28, p. 213). Titian depicts the mythological incident of the god's return from India accompanied by his motley band of revelers. On seeing the deserted and lovelorn Ariadne, he leaps from his panther-drawn chariot, his pink drapery aflutter, to embrace her in wedlock. Titian devises a slashing diagonal direction for the precipitous downward plunge of Bacchus, a device to be emulated often in the baroque period. A subtle touch of visual counterpoint can be seen in the sky where the incident is reenacted by the clouds whose shapes echo the drapery and gestures of the principals, and where the starry crown of immortality awaits Ariadne. In spite of Titian's compositional innovations and great influence on later periods, his art as a whole remains within the scope of the Renaissance. The painting of his younger colleague Tintoretto, however, crosses the stylistic bridge and penetrates deep into the expressive possibilities of Venetian free mannerism.

The drawing of Michelangelo and the color of Titian were the twin ideals of Tintoretto. His violent contrasts of light and dark; his off-center diagonal directions; his interplay of the natural and supernatural, earthly and unearthly light, human and divine figures; and his placement of principal figures on the periphery of the action, whence he created lines that lead the eye in several different directions—all these elements combine to make his art both dynamic and dramatic.

In his *Last Supper* (Fig. 226), Tintoretto represents the miraculous moment when Jesus offers the bread and wine as the sacrificial body and blood of man's redemption. To illuminate this unfathomable mystery of faith, Tintoretto bathes his canvas in a supernatural luminosity that emanates partly from the figure of Christ and partly from the flickering flames of the oil lamp, the smoke of which is transformed into an angelic choir hovering to form a gloriole around the head of Christ. The drastic diagonals of the floor are paralleled by those of the table, but instead of directing the eye to the head of Christ, they lead to an indefinite point in the upper right and to space beyond the picture.

Of all subjects, the most congenial to Veronese's art was festivity. Painted with the primary object of delighting the eye, his canvases nevertheless captured an important aspect of Venetian life—the conviviality of large social gatherings and the love of sumptuous surroundings embellished with fruits, flowers, animals, furniture, draperies, and jesters in bizarre costumes. Veronese seems never to have refused a commission to do a feast, and a note on the back of one of his drawings, believed to be in his own handwriting, bears this out. "If I ever have time," he wrote, "I want to represent a sumptuous banquet in a superb hall, at which will be present the Virgin, the Saviour, and St. Joseph. They will be served by the most brilliant retinue of angels which one can imagine, busied in offering them the daintiest viands and an abundance of splendid fruit in dishes of silver and gold. Other angels will hand them precious wines in transparent crystal glasses and gilded goblets, in order to show with what zeal blessed spirits serve the Lord."

*Marriage at Cana* is truly a complete picture in that Veronese paints a historical-religious subject, includes portraiture, works in genre scenes, delights in still-life detail, and puts everything in an outdoor urban setting in lieu of a landscape (Pl. 29, p. 214). The meaning of the picture, moreover, can be read on many different levels, from the surface to a deep allegorical interpretation. In his consummate rendering of the world of appearances Veronese most completely realizes himself, and in so doing the Verona-born artist succeeds in being more Venetian than the Venetians. The scene, except for the central figures of Jesus and Mary, is that of a rich wedding feast in Venice, drawn from observation and imagination.

The guests are a portrait gallery of the great personages of the 16th century. The black-bearded groom, dressed in purple and gold and seated at the extreme left, is Alfonso d'Avalos, a contemporary Spanish grandee. Next to him as the bride is Eleanor of Austria, sister of Charles V and in real life the second wife of Francis I of France. Other royal portraits include those of Francis I, Charles V, Suleiman I, sultan of Turkey, and Queen Mary of England. Monks, cardinals, and the artist's personal friends are also depicted. The major interest in portraiture is concentrated on the orchestra in the center foreground, which is made up of the leading Venetian painters of the day. To the right, in this large canvas, the figure holding the cup in his left hand is the artist's brother Benedetto Cagliari, who collaborated with him by adding architectural backgrounds to this and other of Veronese's large paintings. Less important figures are everywhere. Above and behind Christ's head a butcher chops meat with a cleaver, while bustling servants prepare food or rush to and fro to serve it on smoking gold and silver platters.

For unity in composition, Veronese's picture relies principally on the horizontal and vertical linear patterns beginning with the table, back through the balustrade and the rich Corinthian columns on either side, to the Sansovinian-Palladian architecture against the bright sky. The rigidity of such a plan is softened by the series of intricate curves that carry the eye to the head of Christ. A fine balance is contained in the opposition of the crowded scene below to the serene architectural order and the spaciousness of the open sky above.

Beyond its sumptuous surface, Veronese's *Marriage at Cana* probes for the deeper philosophical meaning of the miracle. The hourglass and musical score on the table were often used in Renaissance art as symbols of the passage of time. The painter-musicians, moreover, are to be interpreted as representations of the three ages of man, a traditional humanistic theme. In a period when great artists enjoyed the favors of princes—Titian, for instance, was ennobled by Emperor Charles V and highly honored by his son Philip II of Spain—famous painters would never have been depicted as mere public entertainers. The bearded Titian is portrayed as the patriarch of Venetian artists, clothed in a red damask robe and playing the bass viol; Veronese in a brilliant yellow cloak sits opposite, with Tintoretto whispering in his ear. Both are in their middle years and both have violas da braccia. The young flute player in back is thought to be Jacopo Bassano, placed behind the other musicians since wind instruments had been ranked lower by Plato and Aristotle.

In Christian thought, the Marriage at Cana, the first of Christ's miracles in which water was changed to wine, is considered as a prophecy of the Last Supper, in which He transubstantiated the bread and wine into His body and blood to be shed for the remission of sins. The Scriptural passage describing the wedding feast reveals Jesus as being reluctant to comply with Mary's request, answering "... mine hour is not yet come" (John 2 : 4). The picture on this level then becomes an allegory of time, which Plato had so eloquently described as being the moving image of eternity.

Another of Veronese's colossal canvases is the *Feast in the House of Levi*, painted as a Last Supper for a Venetian monastery (Fig. 227). Questions were soon raised, however, about the propriety of its content. By tradition a *Last Supper* portrayed only Christ and the twelve apostles, but Veronese had included some fifty figures, and this departure from tradition brought him before the Inquisition.

In one of the most remarkable documents in the history of painting—a summary of the painter's actual testimony—much about this picture in particular and about Veronese's conception of art in general is revealed. The inquisitors were disturbed not only by the number of figures but by the presence of a dog and cat, which Veronese had painted in the foreground. Even more disquieting was the inclusion of German soldiers sitting on the staircase at the very time when the Roman Catholic Church was experiencing a theological confrontation with the Lutheran Reformation in Germany.

**227.** PAOLO VERONESE. *Feast in the House of Levi.* 1573. Oil on canvas, 18'2" × 42'. Academy, Venice.

*Question.* Did anyone commission you to paint Germans, buffoons, and similar things in that picture?

*Answer.* No, milords, but I received the commission to decorate the picture as I saw fit. It is large and, it seemed to me, it could hold many figures.

*Q.* Are not the decorations which you painters are accustomed to add to paintings or pictures supposed to be suitable and proper to the subject and the principal figures or are they just for pleasure—simply what comes to your imagination without any discretion or judiciousness?

*A.* I paint pictures as I see fit and as well as my talent permits.

*Q.* Does it seem fitting at the Last Supper of the Lord to paint buffoons, drunkards, Germans, dwarfs and similar vulgarities?

*A.* No, milords.

*Q.* Do you not know that in Germany and in other places infected with heresy it is customary with various pictures full of scurrilousness and similar inventions to mock, vituperate, and scorn the things of the Holy Catholic Church in order to teach bad doctrines to foolish and ignorant people?

*A.* Yes, that is wrong; but I return to what I have said, that I am obliged to follow what my superiors have done.

*Q.* What have your superiors done? Have they perhaps done similar things?

*A.* Michelangelo in Rome in the Pontifical Chapel painted Our Lord, Jesus Christ, His Mother, St. John, St. Peter, and the Heavenly Host. These are all represented in the nude—even the Virgin Mary—and in poses with little reverence.*

---

* *Literary Sources of Art History: An Anthology of Texts from Theophilus to Goethe,* ed. Elizabeth G. Holt (copyright 1947 by Princeton U. Press), reprinted by permission of Princeton U. Press.

The figures seated with Jesus at the damask-covered table should be the twelve apostles, but only two could be specifically identified by the artist—St. Peter, on His right, in robes of rose and gray, who according to the painter is "carving the lamb in order to pass it to the other end of the table"; and St. John, on His left. When questioned about the other figures, Veronese was evasive and pled that he could not recall them as he had "painted the picture some months ago." Since but ten months had passed, a faulty memory was his convenient way of avoiding explanation of the portraits of Titian and Michelangelo seated at the table directly under the left and right arches, respectively.

The verdict required Veronese to make certain changes in the picture. Rather than comply, he merely called the painting *Feast in the House of Levi*, thereby placing it outside the iconographical tradition. The altercation with the Inquisition is a landmark in art history. By defending his work, Veronese raised aesthetic and formal values—space, color, form, and composition—above those of subject matter.

## MUSIC

The high peak of Renaissance musical development was the polyphonic style of the Netherland composers. The general admiration for this art at the beginning of the 16th century was summed up by the Venetian ambassador to the court of Burgundy, who, in effect, said that three things were of the highest excellence: first, the finest, most exquisite linen of Holland; second, the tapestries of Brabant, most beautiful in design; and third, the music, which certainly could be said to be perfect. With such sentiments being expressed in official circles, it is not surprising to find that a Netherlander, Adrian Willaert, was appointed

**above: Plate 27.** Giorgione. *Concert Champêtre ("Pastoral Concert").* c. 1510. Oil on canvas, $3'7\frac{1}{4}'' \times 4'6\frac{3}{8}''$. Louvre, Paris. (See p. 208.)

**left: Plate 28.** Titian. *Bacchus and Ariadne.* c. 1520. Oil on canvas, $5'8'' \times 6'7\frac{7}{8}''$. National Gallery, London (reproduced by courtesy of the Trustees). (See p. 210.)

**Plate 29.** Paolo Veronese. *Marriage at Cana.* c. 1560. Oil on canvas, 21'10'' × 32'5''. Louvre, Paris. (See p. 211.)

**Plate 30.** Matthias Grünewald. *Nativity,* center panel of the front opening of the *Isenheim Altarpiece.* Completed 1515. Oil on wood, 8'9$\frac{7}{8}$'' × 10'$\frac{7}{8}$''. Musée d'Unterlinden, Colmar. (See p. 222.)

in the year 1527 to the highest musical position in Venice: that of choirmaster of St. Mark's.

Adoption of the northern musical ideal is but another instance of the cosmopolitanism of the Venetians; and under Willaert, a leading representative of the polyphonic art, and his successors, Venice became a center of musical progress, while Rome remained the bastion of tradition. The measure of its religious freedom also predisposed Venice to new developments, and a number of new musical forms and modifications of older ones were the results. In vocal music, this meant the development of the madrigal, the modification of the church motet, and the development of the polychoral style that made simultaneous use of two, three, and sometimes four choirs. Instrumental music found a new idiom in the organ *intonazione, ricercare,* and *toccata* for keyboard solo, and in the *sinfonia,* and early *concertato* and *concerto* forms for orchestra. Here the Venetian school spoke in a new voice and in tones of individual character. During the late 16th century, as it gradually lost favor, the old *ars perfecta* became known as the *stile antico* in contrast to the *stile moderno,* which was associated with Giovanni Gabrieli in Venice and his organ music, early orchestral writing, and the development of the polychoral style; with Vincenzo Galilei, Peri, and Caccini in Florence and their solo songs and early opera experiments; with Frescobaldi in Rome and his virtuoso organ works; and with Claudio Monteverdi in Mantua and Venice, whose madrigals and operas became the cornerstone of baroque music.

The culmination of the musical development that Willaert began was reached in the work of Giovanni Gabrieli, who held the position of first organist at St. Mark's from the year 1585 until his death. His principal works were published under the title of *Symphoniae Sacrae* in 1597 and 1615. The domed Greek-cross plan of St. Mark's, with its choir lofts placed in the transept wings, seems to have suggested some unusual acoustical possibilities to composers. When a choir is concentrated in the more compact space at the end of a long nave, as in the traditional Latin-cross church, it is more unified. When placed in two or more widely separated groups, as at St. Mark's, the interplay of sound led to experiments that resulted in the so-called "polychoral style." In effect, it dissolved the unified choruses of the Netherland tradition and heralded a new development in the choral art. These *chori spezzati*—literally, "broken choruses"—as they were called, added the element of spatial contrast to Venetian music and new color effects were created. These included the echo nuance, so important in the entire baroque tradition; the alternation of two contrasting bodies of sound, such as chorus against chorus, a single choral line over a full choir, solo voice opposing full choir, instruments versus voices, and contrasting instrumental groups; the alternation of high and low voices; a soft dynamic level alternated

with a loud one; the fragmentary versus the continuous; massive chords on one side with contrapuntal weaving together of many melodies on the other; and blocked chords contrasting with flowing counterpoint. The resultant principle of duality is the basis for the *concertato* or *concerting* style, both words being derived from *concertare,* meaning to compete with or to strive against. The word appears in the title of some works Giovanni published jointly with his uncle Andrea Gabrieli in 1587: *Concerti . . . per voci et stromenti* ("Concertos . . . for voices and instruments"). The term later came to be widely used, with such titles as *Concerti Ecclesiastici* appearing frequently.

The motet *In ecclesiis* (above), written as the second part of the *Symphoniae Sacrae,* is an example of Gabrieli's mature style. Though the specific occasion for which it was intended is unknown, Gabrieli's motet is of the processional type and as such appropriate music for ceremonies similar to that depicted in Bellini's picture (Fig. 212). And the choirs he deployed in groups, as well as a brass ensemble, are similar to Bellini's details (Figs. 228, 229). Since Bellini's setting was in St. Mark's Square, all the Venetian love of civic pomp and splendor are in evidence, and Gabrieli's music was in every respect quite able to fulfill the similar demands of any such later outdoor ceremonial. His art was as typical of its time and place as

**228 and 229.** GENTILE BELLINI. Details of Figure 212. *Brass Ensemble* (above). *Choristers* (below).

that of his colleagues in the other arts—Titian, Veronese, Sansovino, and Palladio.

The Latin text of *In ecclesiis* reads like one of the Psalms of David. Together with a parenthetical English translation, it goes in part:

> *In ecclesiis benedicite Domino*
> (Praise the Lord in the congregation)
> *Alleluia, alleluia, alleluia.*
>
> *In omni loco dominationis benedic, anima mea,*
>     *Dominum.*
> (In every place of worship praise the Lord, O my
>     soul.)
> *Alleluia, alleluia, alleluia.*

> *In Deo, salutari mea et gloria mea.*
> *Deus auxilium meum et spes mea in Deo est.*
> (In God, who is my salvation and glory,
> my help, and my hope is in God.)
> *Alleluia, alleluia, alleluia.*
>
> . . . . . . . . . . . . . . . . . . . . . . . .
>
> *Deus, Deus, adjutor noster aeternam.*
> (O God, my God, our eternal judge.)
> *Alleluia, alleluia, alleluia.*

The structure of Gabrieli's motet is based on the recurring word *alleluia*, which functions as a refrain and acts as a divider between the verses. The alleluias also are set in the static triple meter suggesting a pause in the procession, while the stanzas have the more active beat of march time. The work opens with the sopranos of Chorus I singing the first verse with organ accompaniment. The first *Alleluia* refrain (measures 6–12) is taken by the sopranos of Chorus I, all of Chorus II, and the organ (the numbering of the bars follows the edition published by G. Schirmer, Inc., New York). The tenors of Chorus I then sing the second verse with organ accompaniment (measures 13–31), while the *Alleluia* following this verse is the same as at first. Now come the blazing chords of the instrumental Sinfonia (32–43) with their strange, almost barbaric dissonances. The third verse is sung in two-part counterpoint by the altos and tenors of Chorus I supported now by the six-part instrumental group without organ. The *Alleluia* after this verse (93–99) is taken by the same two voices of Chorus I, with the full Chorus II and organ but without the brass ensemble. The fifth verse is for full double choir, instruments, and organ, making a total of 14 independent parts. The gradual build-up of volume can be heard in the sequence of sopranos and full chorus; tenors and full chorus; the instrumental Sinfonia first alone, then in combination with tenors and altos; and the instrumental color against the chorus with organ support. The cumulative climax is then brought about by the final grandiose union of all vocal and instrumental forces, ending in a solid cadence radiating with color and producing the huge sonority necessary to bring the mighty work to its close. The magnificence of these massive sounds seems to fill the out-of-doors, just as it had filled the vast interior of St. Mark's.

Giovanni Gabrieli's music foreshadows the baroque by setting up such oppositions as chorus against chorus, solo and choir, voices versus instruments, strings alternating with wind ensembles; the interplay of harmonic and contrapuntal textures; diatonic and chromatic harmony; the polarities of soprano and bass lines, loud and soft dynamics; and the distinction of sacred and secular styles.

While Gabrieli's vast tonal murals became the precedent for the later "colossal baroque," it remained for his great successor Claudio Monteverdi to divine the inner spirit of the new style. With Mon-

*Zefiro torna* ("Return, O Zephyr")          MONTEVERDI

l'on - - - - - - - de

e da mon-ti  da mon-ti e da val-li  da val -li  i - me  e pro-fon- de

teverdi in music, as with Longhena in architecture, the transition to the baroque is complete. Appointed master of music of the Most Serene Republic in 1613 after serving as court composer at Mantua for 23 years, Monteverdi achieved a working synthesis of Renaissance counterpoint and all the experimental techniques of his own time. The new emotional orientation is stated in the foreward to his *Eighth Book of Madrigals* (1638): "I have reflected that the principal passions or affections of our mind are three, namely, anger, moderation, and humility or supplication; so the best philosophers declare, and the very nature of our voice indicates this in having high, low, and middle registers. The art of music also points clearly to these three in its terms 'agitated,' 'soft,' and 'moderate' [*concitato, molle,* and *temperato*]." The collection has the significant subtitle, "Madrigals of War and Love," and Monteverdi says he intends to depict anger, warfare, entreaty, and death as well as the accents of brave men engaged in battle. According to Monteverdi, vocal music of this type should be "a simulation of the passions of the words." Descriptive melodies in this *representative* style reflected the imagery of the poetic text. In Monteverdi's madrigal *Zefiro torna* ("Return, O Zephyr"), the word *l' onde* ("waves") is expressed by a rippling melody while *da monti e da valli ime e profonde* ("from mountains and valleys high and deep") is rendered by precipitously rising and falling lines (see above).

A striking instance of Monteverdi's "agitated" style occurs in his short theater piece *The Combat of Tancred and Clorinda,* the text of which comes from the twelfth canto of *Jerusalem Delivered* by the Italian baroque poet Torquato Tasso. In his preface, Monteverdi requests the singers and instrumentalists to play their parts "in imitation of the passions of the words." The score includes a rhythmic figure representing the galloping of horses and a *tremolando* on the strings to simulate trembling or shuddering. At Mantua, Monteverdi had already written his *Orfeo* (1607), the first full-length and complete opera in music history. At Venice, where the first public opera house was established in 1637, he continued with a series of lyrical dramas of which only the last two survive: *Return of Ulysses* (1641) and the *Coronation of Poppea* (1642), both being heard today in concert halls and opera houses with increasing frequency.

## IDEAS: MANNERISM

Venetian architecture, painting, and music—with their recurring themes, attitudes, qualities, shapes, and ideas—transcend a merely local style. All three are sufficiently representative not only to embrace a significant phase of mannerism but also to mark the beginning of baroque art.

Venetian space is never in repose but is restless and teeming with action. Sansovino's and Palladio's buildings with their open loggias, recessed portals and windows, and pierced deep-cut masonry invite entrance; and inside, their capacious interiors allow for freedom of movement. Action is also felt in the lively contrasts of structural elements and decorative details, rectangularity juxtaposed with rotundity, and complete and broken intersecting pediments. Palladio's churches, with their open semicircular colonnades around the altar and windows in the apse, allow the eye to continue into deep space beyond. The reflection of façades in the rippling waters of the canals and the use of mirrored interior walls serve to activate the static masses of masonry and to increase the perception of light and space.

The compositional decentralization of Venetian painting is a similar manifestation in two dimensions. Dynamic space is felt in the winged balance of opposites on the picture plane. The receding planes of a composition in depth that let the eye travel from fore- to middle and background with points of interest in each succeeding plane, as in Giorgione's *Concert Champêtre* (Pl. 27) and *Tempest* (Fig. 224); in the rising planes of a vertical organization, as in Titian's *Assumption* (Fig. 225); in the giddy heights reached by Veronese in his *Triumph of Venice;* and in the wheellike rotary movement Tintoretto sets up in his *Bacchus and Ariadne* (Fig. 230). The diagonal accent is found in the slashing movement from upper right to lower left in Titian's *Bacchus and Ariadne* (Pl. 28). Breaking up the unity of central perspective in the pictures of Tintoretto and Veronese produces a fragmentation that leads the eye simultaneously in several directions.

A similar expression is heard in music. In Gabrieli's "broken" choirs, parts of one group are contrasted with the full sound of a whole chorus, and the sequence of contrasting sonorities progressively builds up ever-larger volumes until the climax is reached in the union of them all. The tossing back and forth of contrasting or unequal sound masses in the concerting style, the alternation of loud and soft dynamic levels of opposing groups as well as in the Venetian echo nuance, and the polarization of high and low parts—all are devices to intensify the motional and emotional effects of music.

While mannerism had its inception in Florence early in the 16th century and subsequently flourished elsewhere, it was the Venetian adaptation of the style that was most readily assimilated into the baroque.

**230.** Tintoretto. *Marriage of Bacchus and Ariadne.* 1577–88. Oil on canvas, 4'9" × 5'5". Doge's Palace, Venice.

Living in the shadow of such universal masters of the immediate past as Leonardo da Vinci, Michelangelo, and Raphael created a dilemma for the younger generation of painters. Quite aware that a golden age had preceded them, and that there was no possibility of improving on the craftsmanship of their illustrious forebears, these young artists found themselves at a crossroads. Following the old paths would mean selecting certain ideas and techniques of their predecessors and reducing them to workable formulas. Striking out in new directions would imply taking for granted such perfected technical achievements as linear and atmospheric perspective, mathematical principles of foreshortening, and correct rendering of anatomy and then deliberately breaking the rules with telling effect.

The first course meant working "in the manner" of the giants of the past, and academies sprang up to transmit the traditional techniques to young artists. The second course led to bold, dramatic departures from past precedents. It was this revolutionary aspect that partisans of the Renaissance saw as the dissolution of an ideal order and the adoption of an "affected manner" by highly individual artists. Either course eventually led in new directions, and some present-day historians separate the period of about 1520 to 1600 from the dying Renaissance and the baroque that was aborning. To encompass and characterize

much of the art of these years, they propose a period and style called *mannerism*. Since mannerism was born of crisis, it is a style facing in two different directions. The more conservative artists linked themselves with tradition and consequently can be classified as *academic mannerists;* the more liberal group can be termed *free mannerists.*

**Academic Mannerism**     When Vasari, the disciple of Michelangelo, used the term *de maniera,* he meant working in the manner of Leonardo, Michelangelo, and Raphael. By reducing their art to a system of rules, he could work fast and efficiently; and his boast was that before his time it took a Michelangelo six years to finish one work, while he had made it possible to do six works in one year. The experimental stage was over; the era of fulfillment was at hand. No more eccentric geniuses and soul-searching prophets, only competent craftsmen. Such was the course taken by Vasari, Palladio, and Veronese. Vasari, in Florence, was instrumental in founding an Academy of Design in 1561. At Bologna in 1585, the Carracci family established an institute with the significant word *academy* in its name, and there courses in the theory and practice of art were offered.

Such academic mannerist artists did not go to nature as Leonardo had done but studied masterpieces with the thought of assimilating systematically the vocabularies of the late Renaissance giants. Art, in other words, did not hold up a mirror to nature but rather to art. At the lowest level, this implied well-schooled craftsmen and a style based on stereotypes; an eclectic borrowing and reassembling without the birth pangs of the original creative synthesis. At its highest, this approach could lead to virtuosity of execution. In no way did it rule out inspiration—that intangible essence that could be caught but not taught.

With Palladio, academic mannerism came to terms with the classical orders of his ancient Roman mentor Vitruvius. By adapting Roman architectural forms to contemporary needs, he contained the Venetian love of lavishness and curbed the excesses of overdecoration. Veronese, by the symmetry of his designs, his closed forms, and the organizing function of his architectural backgrounds, was able to handle large crowds and bustling movement without impairing his pictorial unity. And while Gabrieli's music broke up the unity of the Renaissance choir—encompassing and increasing the scope of musical space—his adherence to the traditional Renaissance polyphonic methods kept his work under strict academic control.

**Free Mannerism** Mannerism also included the "mannered" art of highly individual artists who, in their revolt against Renaissance ideals, cultivated eccentricity and reveled in inner conflicts. This generation of painters could no longer be thrilled by the mathematics of linear perspective or by finding the proper relationship of figures to their surrounding space. Instead, they found excitement in breaking established rules with dash and daring and in violating Renaissance assumptions for the sheer shock effect. Under such capricious conditions, naturalism gave way to the free play of the imagination; classical composure yielded to nervous movement; clear definition of space became a jumble of picture planes crowded with contorted figures; symmetry and focus on the central figure were replaced by off-balance diagonals that made it difficult to find the protagonist of the drama amid the multiplicity of directional lines; backgrounds no longer contained the picture but were nebulous or nonexistent; the canon of body proportion was distorted by the unnatural elongation of figures; chiaroscuro served no more to model figures but to create optical illusions, violent contrasts, and theatrical lighting effects; and strong deep color and rich costumes faded to pastel hues and gauzy fluttering drapery. In short, the Renaissance dream of clarity and order became the mannerist nightmare of haunted space, and art was in danger of becoming artifice.

Some of these tendencies were already present in the High Renaissance. Giorgione's enigmatic pictures that broke with the iconographical tradition puzzled his contemporaries. In Leonardo's *Madonna and Child with St. Anne* (Fig. 197), the figures are uncomfortably superimposed on each other; how St. Anne supports the weight of the Madonna and what they are sitting on is left to the imagination. In the black terror and bleak despair of Michelangelo's *Last Judgment* (Fig. 239), clarity of space no longer exists—there are crowded parts and bare spaces; the size of figures is disproportionate; and one cannot even be sure who are the saved and who the damned.

The exception in the High Renaissance, however, became the rule under mannerism, which quickly, albeit briefly, emerged as an international style. Such Florentine mannerists as Rosso Fiorentino and Benvenuto Cellini (Fig. 231) were summoned to Paris to become court artists of Francis I, and Raphael's pupil Giulio Romano was the official architect of the Duke of Mantua (Fig. 222). In spite of their desire to dazzle and their capriciously contrived tricks, these men had no intention to deceive, since this art was addressed to the sophisticated few. Only those well aware of the rules could enjoy the witty turns and startling twists by which they were broken. This courtly phase of the mannerist style, however, was too much restricted to a single class and too refined and self-conscious in its aestheticism to endure long. In the more cosmopolitan, middle-class atmosphere of Venice, where the group patronage of the *scuole* broadened its base, mannerism gained vitality and virility. It was these aspects that were transmitted almost intact to the baroque.

**231.** Benvenuto Cellini. Saltcellar of Francis I. 1539–43. Gold, $10\frac{1}{4} \times 13''$. Kunsthistorisches Museum, Vienna.

232. GIOVANNI BELLINI. *St. Jerome Reading.* c. 1505. Oil on wood, 19¼ × 15½". National Gallery of Art, Washington, D.C. (Samuel H. Kress Collection).

233. GIOVANNI BELLINI. *Madonna and Child.* 1505. Oil on wood, 19⅝ × 16⅛". Borghese Gallery, Rome.

## VENICE THE CROSSROADS

Venice during the 16th century was the stylistic clearing house for currents of thought flowing from the Italian South, the Mediterranean East, and the European North. Flemish and German merchants had trade connections and resident communities in the city of canals, while prosperous commerce was continuous. Equally active was the traffic in artists. Among others, the two greatest northern painters of their time made extensive visits to this mecca of the arts—Albrecht Dürer at the threshold of the 16th century and Peter Paul Rubens at the onset of the 17th century. The span between them marked the march from the Renaissance through mannerism to the baroque.

Stemming from the German city of Nuremberg, Dürer was destined to effect a fruitful synthesis of northern aesthetic ideas with southern Renaissance theories and practice. Without for a moment sacrificing his own strong individuality, Dürer struck a balance in his art between Germanic pietistic puritanism and Italian hedonistic paganism, between northern severity and mystical introspection and southern freedom and rationality. When the young Dürer first came to Venice in 1495, Gentile Bellini was working on his *Procession in St. Mark's Square* (Fig. 212). His brother Giovanni was doing a series of altarpieces for Venetian churches as well as teaching his pupils, among whom it is believed were Giorgione and Titian. Cumulatively this quartet of painters spoke to northerners in different accents, but for Dürer the most persuasive voice of all was that of Giovanni Bellini. Even on a later visit, the German master referred to Giovanni as "still the greatest painter in Venice."

The root of Giovanni Bellini's art was a harmonious, familial blend of his father Jacopo's Renaissance heritage and the special contributions of his brother Gentile and his brother-in-law Andrea Mantegna of Mantua. But the beautiful branches were Giovanni's own painting that embraced an emotional gamut from the silent suffering of his *Pietà*, through the melancholy meditations of saints and hermits (Fig. 232), to the lyrical grace and joyous maternity of his Madonnas (Fig. 233)—all set in poetic landscapes suffused with the soft, mellow, golden light that brought all of nature into a warmly glowing unity. The fruits of Giovanni's luminous art nurtured the development not only of his pupils and successors but also that of Dürer.

In his *Self-portrait* (Fig. 234) Dürer divides his pictorial space so that the figure is seen against a closed background on one side, while the other suggests deeper space. This northern device was also absorbed into the Venetian vocabulary as seen in the works of Giovanni Bellini, Giorgione, and Titian. Here Dürer reveals himself not as a craftsman and artist, but as a grave, confident young master and an emancipated

Renaissance humanist. The dated inscription of 1498 bears the legend: "I made this according to my appearance when I was 26." The long curly hair and elegant costume are accents of visual enrichment, while the serious, searching expression provides a sombre note. Foreboding also is the landscape with its menacing mountains that loom over the fertile Italian plain in the foreground. For beyond these Alps lay Germany which was facing a tortured century of peasant wars, internal dissents, and religious reformation as it sought to extricate itself from the morass of outmoded medievalism.

*Hercules at the Crossroads* is a highly personal statement that may mirror this young artistic strongman's inner struggle between northern and southern crosscurrents (Fig. 235). This copper engraving exemplifies the graphic arts (woodcuts, etchings, silverpoint) that occupied Dürer's attention throughout his creative career quite as much as did his painting. The traditional mythological legend tells of Hercules' choice between Virtue and Vice, lawful and licentious love. In this case, however, Virtue is no mere placid personification of the good life, but an irate Amazon taking up the cudgel to punish her adversary who, for her part, is actively engaged in amorous pursuits with a horned satyr. Hercules faces Virtue, but his position is quite equivocal as he is looking at Vice while trying to stop the fight and subdue the overzealous efforts of Virtue. The drawing of the Hercules clearly shows the influence of Pollaiuolo whom Dürer greatly admired (Fig. 181). And while Dürer came under Italianate influences, his prints in turn were to have a notable effect on the work of the Florentine and Venetian mannerists.

Dürer's lifelong preoccupation with the accurate rendering of nature is seen in his *Madonna and Child with a Multitude of Animals* (Fig. 236). His beasts show no affinity with medieval bestiaries but are true-to-life animals from field and forest. Dürer's lambs gambol and graze, his foxes stalk their prey, his birds take wing. Such minute and meticulous observations were gained not only from his eager eye but also from assiduous study of treatises on geological formations, the structure of plants, and the anatomy of animals and birds.

The spirit of the North but dimly touched by the rays of the Italian Renaissance sun is marvelously realized in the *Isenheim Altarpiece* (Fig. 237) by Dürer's older contemporary, Matthias Grünewald. This masterpiece was painted for the monks of St. Anthony, an order that maintained hospitals for the poor. The work consists of a cycle of scenes painted on the front and back of two sets of folding panels, with immovable side wings, paired one behind the other. This intricate form shows an affinity for the northern art of the book, opening leaf after leaf to allow the stories of the Christian calendar to pass by in review. Terrestrial, celestial, and infernal beings alike are present to worship, to witness, to horrify, to tempt. The moods run from the ecstatic joy of the music-making angels in the *Nativity* panel (Pl. 30, p. 214) to the abyss of despair in the *Temptation of St. Anthony* (Fig. 238), where the words of the suffering saint are inscribed on a scrap of paper at the lower right: "Where were You, good Jesus, where were You? Why did You not come to heal my wounds?" The details range from the Annunciation and Nativity, through the Passion and Entombment of Jesus, to the fantastic ordeals of St. Anthony, the legendary founder of Christian monasticism.

The unusual and obscure iconography derives from a number of sources including the Scriptures, the mystical writings of St. Bridget of Sweden, and the pictures of Grünewald's contemporaries, not the least of whom was Dürer. The strange *Nativity* (Pl. 30) omits St. Joseph, the crib, the animals and shepherds. The *Crucifixion* scene includes St. John the Baptist, rare in this context (Fig. 237). In this *Nativity* Mary appears twice, on the right as the more familiar Madonna with Child, and on the left kneeling in prayer in a Gothic templelike chapel, her head surrounded by transcendental light. Such a vision is described by St. Bridget in her *Revelations,* and the allusion also suggests the Magnificat in St. Luke (1 : 46–55) where the Virgin prays: "My soul doth magnify the Lord, and my spirit hath rejoiced in God my Saviour." The images of the prophets, musicians, and the Venetian glass pitcher at her feet may point to the Revelation of St. John where the 24 elders of the Apocalypse appear with vials to symbolize their prayers and with musical instruments to signify their praises given to the Lord.

In the *Crucifixion* Grünewald depicts the Baptist on the right side of the cross, St. John the Evangelist on the left, and Sts. Sebastian and Anthony on the side wings (Fig. 237). He thus includes the interceders for the principal maladies treated at the hospital: St. Sebastian for the plague, the two Johns for epilepsy and St. Anthony for St. Anthony's fire (often thought to be the feverish, infectious inflammation of the skin now known as erysipelas). No Italian harmony mollifies the grim agony of the crucified Christ. Festering sores and dried blood cover the ghastly green flesh. Such details are naturalistically descriptive, but the unnatural dimensions of the figures bear no relation to southern Renaissance practice. Is Grünewald following the medieval way of proportioning his figures according to their theological or dramatic importance? Compare the size of the Magdalene's hands with those of the Savior. Or is he emphasizing graphically the inscribed prophecy of the Baptist: "He must increase, but I must decrease" (John 3 : 30)? In either case he is sacrificing "correct" proportions for the sake of his design and expressive intent.

The *Temptation of St. Anthony* (Fig. 238), with its ghoulish and monstrous apparitions, reminded the suffering patients of the horrendous ordeals endured by their patron. With its all-encompassing range of human feeling, Grünewald's altarpiece becomes one of the most moving documents in art history. As such it is comparable in scope and magnitude to Michelangelo's Sistine ceiling (Pl. 25, p. 196; Figs. 201–204), Raphael's frescoes in the Stanza della Segnatura (Pl. 26, p. 196), and Dürer's *Apocalypse* or *Passion* series, all of which were completed in the same decade.

## ROADS TO THE BAROQUE

From Venice, as well as from Rome and the centers where international mannerism flourished, the roads to the baroque fanned out in all directions. The thriving painting industry assured currency for Venetian ideas in every civilized country. The writings of Palladio, as translated into English with commentary by Inigo Jones, led to the architecture of Christopher Wren and the Georgian styles and thence to the colonial and federal styles in America. The printing of musical scores assured Venetian composers of general prominence. Venetian diplomacy, by avoiding commitments to either extreme, paved the way for the acceptance of certain aspects of the Venetian style in both Reformation and Counter-Reformation countries. Venetian innovations in architecture and painting were eagerly adopted in the Church and court circles of Spain and France. Both the Church hierarchy and the aristocracy needed the impressive splendor of the arts to enhance their exalted positions. The more monumental the buildings, the more lavish the decorations, the more grandiose the musical entertainments, the better the arts served their purpose. Hence, it was natural for both to seek out the richest expression of this ideal, which in Venice was to be found in abundance.

El Greco, after studying in Titian's workshop and absorbing Tintoretto's mannerism, found his way to Church and court circles in Spain, where his art left an indelible impression. Rubens spent eight years in Italy, much of the time making copies of Titian's pictures, then took the Venetian techniques with him to the Low Countries and France. Rubens and his pupil van Dyck, in turn, transmitted them to England, and eventually they reached America. In the Counter-Reformation countries, church music remained more constant to the Roman tradition, but Venetian music was readily accepted in secular circles. However, for the Reformation centers—Holland, Scandinavia, and particularly northern Germany—the greater liturgical freedom of Venetian musical forms proved more adaptable to Protestant church purposes precisely because of their deviation from orthodox Roman models. Sweelinck, who studied in Venice with Andrea Gabrieli and Zarlino, carried the Venetian keyboard style to Amsterdam, where his great reputation brought him organ students from Germany who later taught the generation of Pachelbel and Buxtehude, both major influences on the style of Bach and Handel. Cavalli, Monteverdi's successor at the Venetian opera, was called to Paris to write the music for the wedding festivities of Louis XIV. Heinrich Schütz, the greatest German composer before Johann Sebastian Bach and George Frederick Handel and another force in determining their art, was a pupil of both Giovanni Gabrieli and Monteverdi. In sum, the Venetian style became a part of the basic vocabulary of the baroque language.

# 13 The Counter-Reformation Baroque Style

The cataclysmic events that convulsed Rome and all Europe in the course of the 16th century awakened the Eternal City from its Renaissance dream of harmony and confronted it with the stark reality of contradiction and conflict. Subsequently, every aspect of life—religious, scientific, political, social, economic, and aesthetic—was destined to undergo reexamination and radical change. A succession of disturbing visitors proved to be harbingers of developments to come. Martin Luther had been in Rome at the turn of the century, and his observations had added fuel to the fire of his moral indignation. The reform movement he initiated, along with Zwingli and John Calvin, was to sever the unity of the Universal Church and divide Europe into Reformation and Counter-Reformation camps.

The next visitor, the Holy Roman Emperor Charles V, was even less welcome. Previously, the voyages of the great navigators and the exploits of the conquistadors who followed in their wake had brought most of North, Central, and South America under the Spanish crown. With the monopoly of the spice trade of the Orient and with the gold and silver mines of the New World pouring fabulous riches into its treasury, Spain was rapidly becoming the most powerful country in the world. By a combination of heredity, marriage, and high finance, Charles I of Spain had become Charles V of the Holy Roman Empire. With the Low Countries, the Germanies, and Austria firmly in his grasp, the ambitious Emperor turned his attention next to Italy, and, one by one, the formerly independent duchies and city-states came under his domination. Opposition from any quarter was intolerable, and in 1527 His Catholic Majesty's mercenaries marched on Rome, sacking and plundering. Eight days later the great city was a smoking ruin, the Vatican a barracks, St. Peter's a stable, and Pope Clement VII a prisoner at Castel Sant' Angelo. Thereafter, the papacy had no choice but to acquiesce in Spanish policy; a Spanish viceroy ruled in Naples, and a Spanish government was installed in Milan. Through the Gonzagas in Mantua, the Estes in Ferrara, the Medici in Florence, the Spaniards controlled all important centers; and with Spanish rule came Spanish austerity and religiosity, etiquette and courtly elegance.

Another visitor was the astronomer Copernicus, whose book on the *Revolution of the Planets in Their Orbits* was destined to change the conception of the cosmos from an earth-centered to a sun-centered world. A shock reaction followed as Renaissance man began to realize he inhabited a minor planet whirling through space, and that he was no longer at the center of creation. Later, when his observations tended to prove the Copernican theory, Galileo was tried for heresy, sentenced to prison, and released only when he recanted. The cumulative effect of these and other scientific discoveries began to weaken the belief in miracles and divine intervention in human affairs.

Then came the theologians, during the sessions of the Council of Trent that undertook the reform of the Church from within. When the test came, bold humanistic thinking was transformed into violent reaction; Neoplatonic philosophy was succeeded by a reversion to Aristotelian scholasticism; the distant but seductive voices of pagan antiquity were drowned out by the roar of rekindled medieval fire and brimstone; the reveling in sensuous beauty was followed by bitter self-reproach; promises of liberal religious attitudes were inundated by a return to strict orthodoxy; new access to literature and knowledge through the printing press and scientific discoveries was suppressed through the Universal Inquisition and the *Index Expurgatorius;* God appeared not as the Loving Father but as a terrifying Judge, Christ not as the Good Shepherd but as the Great Avenger.

The founders of the new Counter-Reformation religious orders, which were to shape the course of Roman Catholicism in the 17th century, were in Rome at various times. Philip Neri brought together, for informal meetings in his Congregation of the Oratory, laymen of all classes, from aristocrats to street urchins, and encouraged them to pray or preach as the spirit moved them. By dramatizing and setting to music familiar Biblical stories and parables (prototypes of the baroque oratorios), he generated a cheerful devotional spirit that stirred the hearts of the poor and humble. Ignatius Loyola came from Spain to obtain papal sanction for his Society of Jesus, a militant order generally known as the "Jesuits" and dedicated to foreign missionary work, education, and active participation in worldly affairs. There were also the mystics Teresa of Avila and John of the Cross, whose abilities to combine the contemplative and active ways of life resulted in a significant literary expres-

**239.** MICHELANGELO. *Last Judgment,* detail (self-portrait on flayed skin in lower right). 1534–41. Fresco, 48 × 44'. Sistine Chapel, Vatican, Rome.

sion of the period and in the reorganization and redirection of the Carmelite orders; and there was Carlo Borromeo, the young energetic archbishop of Milan, who wrote manuals for artists as well as for the students and teachers in the many seminaries he founded. At a single grand ceremony in the newly completed Basilica of St. Peter on the 22nd of May, 1622, Ignatius Loyola, Francis Xavier, Teresa of Avila, and Philip Neri were canonized and admitted to the honors of the altar. Thereupon, Giacomo Vignola, Giacomo della Porta, Carlo Maderno, Gianlorenzo Bernini, and Francesco Borromini were called upon to build churches and chapels dedicated to them.

In this floodtide of reform, the classical harmony, stability, and poise of Renaissance art were not hardy enough to survive, nor could the overrefined, overly dramatic art of mannerism adapt itself to the new religious climate. Gaiety gave way to sobriety, Venuses reverted to Virgins, Bacchuses and Apollos to bearded Christs. The organic form and unity of Michelangelo's Sistine ceiling was succeeded by the calculated shapelessness of his fearful *Last Judgment* (Figs. 201, 239). Palestrina was conscience-stricken for having written madrigals and henceforth wrote only masses. Under the rulings of the Council of Trent, Church art was firmly realigned with religion, and the clergy had to assume responsibility for the way artists rendered religious subjects.

The lives and attitudes of Counter-Reformation artists were profoundly affected by the new religious climate. Michelangelo's *Last Judgment* received censure because his Apollo-type Christ was unbearded and because such pagan classical details as Charon, the sepulchral boatman rowing souls across the river Styx, had been included. Drapery was ordered to cover his "offending nudes," and only the timely intervention of a group of artists saved the *Last Judgment* from complete obliteration. The great man became a recluse in his last years, gave up figurative art for the abstractions of architecture, and devoted himself to the building of St. Peter's, a project for which he would accept no fee. In the privacy of his own studio, he worked intermittently at sculpture and brooded over his last *Pietàs,* one of them intended for his own tomb. Palestrina was banished from his post as leader of the Sistine Choir because he refused to take the priestly vow of celibacy and give up his wife. Later he was reinstated and entrusted with a reform of Church music.

Gianlorenzo Bernini, busiest and most successful sculptor-architect of the Counter-Reformation baroque, was closely associated with the Jesuits and regularly practiced St. Ignatius' *Spiritual Exercises.* An-

drea Pozzo, who painted the illusionistic ceiling of the Church of Sant'Ignazio, was a member of the Society of Jesus. El Greco, Spain's greatest representative of Counter-Reformation art, was a religious mystic in whose last visionary canvases physical matter practically ceases to exist, his attenuated figures more spirit than flesh, his settings more of the realm of heaven than of earth.

As matters shaped up, the Counter-Reformation baroque style had its inception in Rome where it reached its apogee in the fifty-year period from c. 1620 to 1670; its reverberations were felt simultaneously in Spain, the strong secular arm of the Church militant. Thereafter the impetus spread throughout the Roman Catholic countries of Europe and traveled with the missionary orders to the Americas and everywhere in the far-flung colonies established by Spain and Portugal.

## ROMAN COUNTER-REFORMATION ART

**Architecture**   As the central monument of the Jesuit order, the Church of Il Gesù in Rome became the

## General Events: Rome

**1527** Charles V's mercenaries sacked Rome. Protestant Reformation in progress under Luther in Germany, Zwingli and Calvin in Switzerland. Reaction to Renaissance humanism began

**1534** Counter-Reformation began

**1540** Society of Jesus (Jesuit order) founded by Ignatius Loyola

**1542** Universal Inquisition established

**1543** Copernicus' *De Revolutionibus Orbium Coelestorum* published. Censorship of printed matter began

**1545** Council of Trent (1545–63) undertook reform within Church; reaffirmed dogma

**1547** Michelangelo named architect of St. Peter's

**1555** Volterra ordered to paint drapery on "offending" nudes in Michelangelo's *Last Judgment*

**c.1562** Teresa of Avila and John of the Cross reformed Carmelite orders

**1575** Congregation of the Oratory (founded by Philip Neri) approved

**1616** Galileo enjoined by pope not to "teach or defend" researches confirming Copernican theory; called before Inquisition in 1633

**1622** Canonization of Ignatius Loyola, Teresa of Avila, Philip Neri, Francis Xavier

## General Events: Spain

**1474– 1516** Ferdinand and Isabella reigned; West Indies discovered by Columbus (1492); South America (1498); expulsion of Moors and Jews from Spain

**1516– 1556** Charles I, king of Spain; became Holy Roman Emperor Charles V in 1519

**1556– 1598** Philip II, king of Spain; Spanish empire reached greatest extent

**1561** Madrid chosen as capital

**1563– 1584** Escorial Palace built

**1583** Victoria published *Missarum libri duo,* book of masses dedicated to Philip II

**1588** Spanish Armada sunk by English navy

**1598– 1621** Philip III, king of Spain; decline of Spanish power

**1600** Victoria published collection of masses, motets, psalms, hymns, dedicated to Philip II.

**1604** Cervantes' *Don Quixote,* Part I, published in Madrid (Part II, 1615)

**1621– 1665** Philip IV, king of Spain

**1623** Velázquez appointed court painter

**1648** Treaty of Westphalia; Spanish power in Europe checked

## Architects and Sculptors

| | | |
|---|---|---|
| ? – | 1567 | Juan Bautista de Toledo |
| 1507– | 1573 | Giacomo Vignola |
| 1530– | 1597 | Juan de Herrera |
| 1531– | 1621 | Juan Bautista Monegro |
| c.1540– | 1604 | Giacomo della Porta |
| 1556– | 1629 | Carlo Maderno |
| c.1580– | 1648 | Gomez de Mora |
| 1598– | 1680 | Gianlorenzo Bernini |
| 1599– | 1667 | Francesco Borromini |
| 1665– | 1725 | José de Churriguera |
| c.1683– | 1742 | Pedro de Ribera |

## Painters

| | | |
|---|---|---|
| 1498– | 1578 | Giulio Clovio |
| c.1541– | 1614 | El Greco (Domenicos Theotocopoulos) |
| 1573– | 1610 | Michelangelo Merisi da Caravaggio |
| 1599– | 1660 | Diego Velázquez |
| 1617– | 1682 | Bartolomé Murillo |
| 1642– | 1709 | Fra Andrea Pozzo |

## Musicians

| | | |
|---|---|---|
| c.1500– | 1553 | Cristobal Morales |
| c.1500– | 1566 | Antonio de Cabezón |
| 1524– | 1594 | Giovanni da Palestrina |
| c.1548– | 1611 | Tomás Luis de Victoria |

## Writers

| | | |
|---|---|---|
| 1491– | 1556 | Ignatius Loyola |
| 1515– | 1582 | Teresa of Avila |
| 1538– | 1584 | Charles Borromeo |
| 1542– | 1591 | John of the Cross |
| 1547– | 1616 | Miguel de Cervantes |
| 1562– | 1635 | Lope da Vega |
| 1600– | 1681 | Pedro Calderón |

prototype (Figs. 240–242) for many Counter-Reformation churches (Figs. 243–245). Indeed, so many different versions and variants have since appeared that with justification it has been called the most influential church design of the past four centuries. Commissioned in 1564, Il Gesù combines classical motifs from the Renaissance heritage with some of the new elements that were to identify Counter-Reformation architecture. The nucleus of the structure—the domed crossing of the nave and the short tran-

septs—are derived from Michelangelo's and Palladio's centralized plans, like those reproduced in Figures 206 and 216. But the short longitudinal nave reaching forward from the crossing repeats the compromise reached in St. Peter's when Bramante's and Michelangelo's plans were combined with the appendage of Carlo Maderno's long nave, as seen in Figure 207. Giacomo Vignola's design for the façade, somewhat revised after his death by his successor Giacomo della Porta, recalls a Roman triumphal arch on the ground right: 240 GIACOMO VIGNOLA and GIACOMO DELLA PORTA. Façade, Il Gesù, Rome. c. 1575–84. Height 105', width 115'.

below: 241. Plan of Il Gesù.

bottom left: 242. ANDREA SACCHI and JAN MIEL. *Urban VIII Visiting Il Gesù.* 1639–41. National Gallery, Rome.

below: 243. FRANCESCO BORROMINI. Façade, San Carlo alle Quattro Fontane, Rome. Begun 1635, façade 1667. Church 52 × 34'; façade width 38'.

floor, but the lean-to roofing over the side chapels is masked with graceful scrolls that swirl upward toward the triangular templelike pediment.

Borromini's San Carlo alle Quattro Fontane is one of the most ingenious expressions of the period (Fig. 243). Turning to full advantage the small site at the intersection of two streets with a fountain at each of the four corners, the architect devised a plan that embraced a complex interplay of geometrical shapes. The plan is formed by two equilateral triangles joined

right: 244. FRANCESCO BOR-
ROMINI. Plan of San Carlo
alle Quattro Fontane.

left: 245. FRANCESCO BORRO-
MINI. Interior of dome, San
Carlo alle Quattro Fontane,
Rome. c. 1638.

at the base to make a diamond-shaped rhomboid, which was then softened with curved lines (Fig. 244). Like a rippling stage curtain, the undulating walls rise upward toward an oval dome, the inner surface of which is encrusted with coffering of octagons and elongated hexagons that join to produce Greek crosses in the intervening spaces (Fig. 245). These shapes diminish in size toward the top to suggest greater height. Partially concealed openings allow light to filter in and give the honeycomblike pattern a gleaming brightness. The façade (Fig. 243) is set into swaying motion by the alternating concave and convex walls and the flow of curvilinear forms, which allow a maximum play of light and shade over the irregular surface.

**Painting and Sculpture**    Of all the painters and sculptors active in post-Renaissance Rome, two tower above all others—Caravaggio and Bernini. Taking his name from his native town, Caravaggio brought the northern Italian and Venetian tradition of free mannerism with him to Rome; while the sculptor-architect-designer-painter Bernini synthesized Renaissance, Michelangelesque, mannerist, and baroque elements and brought the baroque to its expressive climax in the Eternal City. Restless and rebellious, Caravaggio was always at odds with society and his patrons. Bernini, despite his passionate temperament,

was nevertheless a suave courtier. "It is your good luck," Bernini was told by the newly elected Pope Urban VIII, "to see Maffeo Barberini pope; but we are even luckier that Cavaliere Bernini lives at the time of our pontificate." Caravaggio's life and career proved brief, solitary, and precocious; Bernini's long, social, and prodigiously productive. Both artists were destined to have far-reaching effects on future developments—Caravaggio with his bold chiaroscuro on later Italian and French baroque painters, as well as on Rubens and Rembrandt; Bernini with his twisted columns and visionary illusionism on baroque sculpture and architecture.

Caravaggio, who painted in Rome from c. 1590 to 1606, scorned Renaissance decorum, dignity, and elegance and set out to depict religious subjects in a vivid, down-to-earth way. His *Calling of St. Matthew* shows the future Evangelist among a group at a public tavern (Pl. 31, p. 231). A significant darkness hovers over the table where tax money is being counted; and as Jesus enters, a shaft of light illuminates the bearded face of St. Matthew and the countenances of the young men in the center. As the light strikes each figure and object with varying degrees of intensity, it becomes the means by which Caravaggio penetrates the surface of events and reveals the inner spirit of the subjects he depicts. The *Calling of St. Matthew* was at first refused by the church for which it had been painted, because it showed the saint in a too-worldly situation, even though the story is told by the Evangelist himself.

In the *Conversion of St. Paul*, Caravaggio creates a blinding, lightninglike flash to highlight the saint's inner illumination (Fig. 246). "And suddenly there shined round about him a light from heaven," reads the New Testament passage, "and he fell to earth, and heard a voice saying unto him, Saul, Saul, why persecutest thou me?" (Acts 9 : 4–5). As the observer beholds St. Paul's prone body from an extremely foreshortened angle, with arms flung out as if to embrace the new light, he is caught up in the event and shares the wonderment and concern of the attendant and the huge horse.

Caravaggio's efforts to create a truly popular religious art as seen through the eyes of the common man met with a mixed reception, and, paradoxically, it was only the sophisticated few who grasped its originality and significance. Both the Roman priests and public preferred more conventional elegance and illusionism, and it was the work of Pozzo and Bernini that this audience found more congenial to its taste.

Andrea Pozzo succeeded in capturing the new spirit in his extraordinary painting on the barrel-vaulted ceiling of the Church of Sant'Ignazio (Fig. 247), a sister church in Rome of Il Gesù (Fig. 242) and dedicated to the founder of the Jesuit order. Above the clearstory windows, the walls of the building seem to soar upward so that the vaulting of the nave becomes that of heaven itself. In a series of remarkable foreshortenings, St. Ignatius is borne aloft by a heavenly host, ascending in ever-winding spirals toward figures symbolizing the Trinity. Here all the lines converge and beams of light radiate outward to illuminate the four corners of the world—personified by allegorical representations of Europe, Asia, Africa, and America—where missionary work of the Society of Jesus was carried on. Pozzo was also the author of a definitive book on perspective, in which he advised artists "to draw all points thereof to that true point, the Glory of God."

left: **246.** CARAVAGGIO. *Conversion of St. Paul.* 1601–02. Oil on canvas, 7'6½" × 5'9". Cerasi Chapel, Santa Maria del Popolo, Rome.

above: **247.** FRA ANDREA POZZO. *St. Ignatius in Glory.* c. 1691. Fresco, nave ceiling. Sant'Ignazio, Rome.

In Gianlorenzo Bernini, the impetuous and versatile architect-sculptor-painter, the Roman Counter-Reformation baroque found its most representative and prolific exponent. Designer of the Piazza of St. Peter's that begins with the trapezoidal *piazza obliqua* in front of the basilica's façade and opens out into the mighty elliptical area enframed by massive fourfold Doric colonnades (Figs. 193, 208); sculptor of many of the basilica's key chapels, notably the one in the apse containing the Chair of St. Peter; designer of such public monuments as the Fountain of Four Rivers in Piazza Navona (Fig. 248)—Bernini, even more than Michelangelo, is responsible for lifting the face of Rome and for giving the city the appearance it has today.

Of all his works, the Cornaro Chapel dedicated to the *Mistica Dottora* St. Teresa, is most typical of

The Counter-Reformation Baroque Style   **229**

248. GIANLORENZO BERNINI. Fountain of Four Rivers, Piazza Navona, Rome. 1648–51.

The polished white-marble group is framed by dark marble columns and set in a niche of varicolored marbles of brown, red, pink, green, and amber hues. Gleaming gilded-bronze rays descend from above, and the whole is lighted magically by a concealed window glazed with yellow glass. On either side are groups in relief portraying members of the Cornaro family, donors of the chapel, who watch the miraculous proceedings as if from stage boxes at the theater.

The chapel begs the question—"Is it architecture, sculpture, painting, stage design? Is it sculpture in the

this phase of the baroque (Fig. 249). In the central sculptured group over the altar (Fig. 250), Bernini portrays the saint in a state of ecstasy, his source being Teresa's visionary writings. She describes the appearance of a bright angel holding a golden spear, which he has plunged into her heart. "The dart wherewith He wounded me / Was all embarbed round with love / And thus my spirit came to be / One with its Maker, God above."

St. Teresa, as revealed by the undulating folds of her deep-cut drapery, seems to be rising and falling in voluptuous rapture, and the angel (closely resembling Cupid with his dart) is about to pierce her heart.

above: 249. *Cornaro Chapel, Santa Maria della Vittoria, Rome.* 18th-century painting. Museum, Schwerin, Germany.

left: 250. GIANLORENZO BERNINI. *St. Teresa in Ecstasy.* 1645–52. Marble and gilt bronze, life-size. Cornaro Chapel, Santa Maria della Vittoria, Rome.

above: **Plate 31.** CARAVAGGIO. *Calling of St. Matthew.* c. 1597–98. Oil on canvas, 11'1" × 11'5". Contarelli Chapel, San Luigi dei Francesi, Rome. (See p. 228.)

left: **Plate 32.** EL GRECO. *Martyrdom of St. Maurice and Theban Legion.* 1581–84. Oil on canvas, 14'6" × 9'10". Escorial Palace. (See p. 236.)

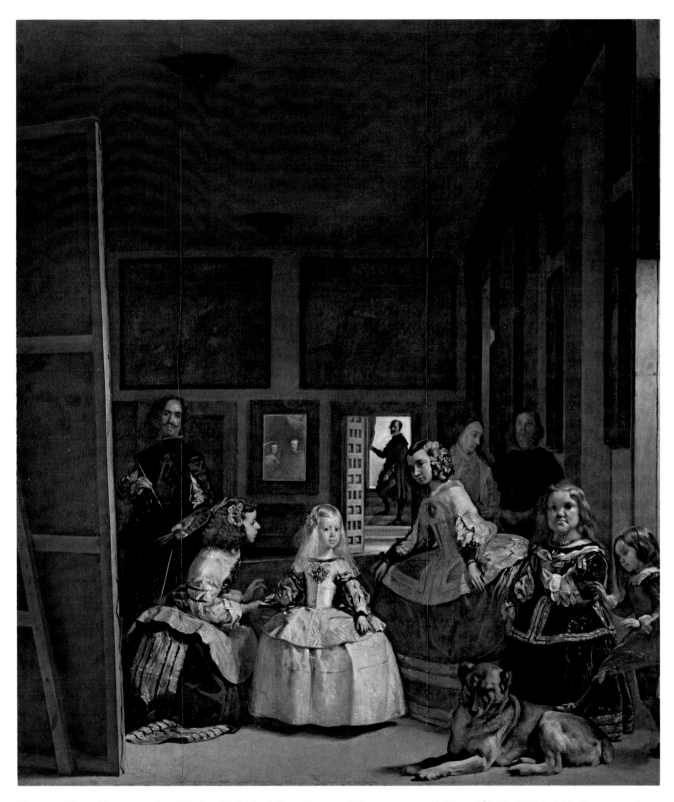

**Plate 33.** Diego Velázquez. *Las Meninas ("Maids of Honor")*. 1656. Oil on canvas, 10′5¼″ × 9′¾″. Prado, Madrid. (See p. 238.)

round, in relief?" The answers in each case must be "yes"—but combined not separated, in fusion not isolation. The sculpture group is surrounded by actual and simulated architecture; the painted sky and the theatrical lighting form part of a single conception in which real and visionary elements blend into one, in which metal, marble, forms, colors, and light harmonize as a multimedia concert of the arts.

## SPANISH COUNTER-REFORMATION ART

The close alliance of Italy and Spain that had begun with the invasion of Charles V continued throughout the baroque period. Politically and economically the Spanish crown controlled all major Italian regions by viceroys and puppet regimes. Papal sanction of the Jesuit order made the influence of its militant missionaries worldwide and brought sainthood to two of its Spanish founding members, Ignatius Loyola and Francis Xavier. And the words of two great Spaniards, St. Teresa of Avila and St. John of the Cross, perhaps most completely captured the Counter-Reformation spirit in literature and became the most widely read in the Roman Catholic world.

The personal tastes of that morose monarch Philip II, who succeeded his father Charles V, were austere to the point of severity. His worldly position and ambitions, however, made it mandatory that he surround himself with the necessary magnificence to command awe and respect. To unify his kingdom, wrest local authority from his feudal lords, and vest himself with all the power of an absolute monarch, Philip selected as his capital the then-obscure but centrally located town of Madrid. There, an enormous building program had to be undertaken to house the court and provide city palaces for the aristocracy.

With the riches of the Old World and the unlimited resources of the New at his command, Philip summoned the leading artists of Europe to help build and embellish his chosen capital, and his ambassadors were under instruction to buy any available masterpiece of painting and sculpture. While they remained in their native cities, Titian and other Italian artists continued to paint for Philip as they had for his father. But Domenicos Theotocopoulos, the Greek-born artist who had been trained in the Venetian mannerist style and had studied the work of Michelangelo and Raphael in Rome, settled in Spain, where he became known as the foreigner El Greco ("the Greek"). The Spanish composer Victoria, though he was fully established in Rome, dedicated a book of masses to Philip in the hope of receiving a court commission. Attracted by the glitter of Span-

ish gold, other artists from all parts of Europe, known and unknown, flocked to Madrid in search of fame and fortune. Thus, while Spain's power and prestige were to decline in the 17th century, the precedent set by Charles V and Philip II as patrons of the arts was continued by Philip III and Philip IV to round out a full century of brilliant artistic activity.

**Architecture**      Bound by the terms of his father's will to build Charles V a tomb, bound by his own solemn oath to found a monastery dedicated to the Spanish martyr St. Lawrence, on whose day he gained his great military victory over the French, and bound also by his intense religious fervor and his consciousness of his royal prerogatives, Philip II envisioned a vast architectural project that would coordinate these diverse objectives and resolve some of his own inner conflicts. As the plan matured in the King's mind, this monument was to be at once a temple to God, a mausoleum for his ancestors and descendants, a national archive of arts and letters, a dwelling place for the Hieronomite monks, a college and seminary, a place of pilgrimage with a hospice for strangers, a royal residence, and, in general, a symbol of the glory of the Spanish monarchy.

A site in the barren foothills of the Guadarrama Mountains about thirty miles from Madrid was chosen for the undertaking, which took its name from the near-by village of Escorial. The original plans were drawn up by Juan Bautista de Toledo, who had studied with Jacopo Sansovino and Palladio and worked on St. Peter's in Rome under the direction of Michelangelo. Subsequently, the work was completed by Juan Bautista's collaborator, Juan de Herrera.

According to Philip's instructions, the monument had to embody the ideals of "nobility without arrogance, majesty without ostentation." As it stands, the Escorial is a vast quadrangle of almost 500,000 square feet, which is subdivided into a symmetrical system of courts and cloisters (Fig. 251). The form symboli-

**251.** J. B. DE TOLEDO and JUAN DE HERRERA. Escorial Palace, near Madrid. 1553–84. Engraving after Herrera.

cally refers to the gridiron of St. Lawrence on which he met his martyrdom. The corner towers can be said to represent the legs of the iron grill, while the palace, which projects from the east end, forms its handle. Elsewhere in the building the grill is widely used as a decorative motif.

The Escorial strikes a note of gloomy grandeur and stark magnificence in keeping at once with the Spanish spirit as well as with the dour personality of Philip II. Each side presents a long expanse of wall, entirely devoid of decoration, its monotony broken only by the endless rows of seriate windows (Fig. 252). The principal entrance (Fig. 251), which is found on the west front, is carried out in the strict Doric order with only the royal coat of arms and a colossal statue of St. Lawrence holding his gridiron to relieve the general austerity. The portal leads into the Patio of the Kings, which takes its name from the statues of David, Solomon, and the other kings of Israel over the entrance to the imposing church located on the central axis.

Much of the Escorial's area is devoted to the monastery and seminary of the Order of St. Jerome. The heart of this section is the handsomely designed, spacious, double-decked cloister known as the Court of the Evangelists (Fig. 253). The walk below is again in the Doric order with its simple frieze punctuated by the rhythmical triglyphs. Still more space for monastic meditations is provided by the Ionic gallery, which, in turn, is surmounted by a balustrade in the Palladian manner. In the center of the garth is a small structure of polychrome marble that functions as an echo of the great dome of the church which soars above it. Statues by Monegro of each of the four Evangelists look outward from their niches toward their respective pools, which are watered from spouts in the forms of the symbolic evangelical beasts.

In the palace section of the Escorial are the reception halls, the impressive galleries, and the state dining rooms that go with the grandeur of the proud

Spanish monarchy. The only departure from the prevailing air of splendor is the monastic severity of Philip's own apartment. Elsewhere there are the quarters of the majordomos, the secretaries of state, the lords of the bedchamber, lodgings for ambassadors, and apartments for members of the royal family. To awe friends and warn foes, pictures of Spain's sea and land victories line the walls of the ambassadorial waiting rooms. Other halls are hung with rich Flemish tapes-

left: 252. Escorial Palace (side view).

above: 253. JUAN DE HERRERA. Court of Evangelists, Escorial Palace. 1563–84. 210 × 207'.

opposite above: 254. GOMEZ DE MORA. Façade, La Clérica (left). 1617. Casa de las Conchas ("House of Shells," right). 1514. Salamanca.

opposite below: 255. JOSÉ DE CHURRIGUERA. Altarpiece, San Esteban, Salamanca. 1693.

tries depicting Biblical, mythological, and literary subjects. The picture galleries contain a vast number of the paintings that were purchased so liberally over the centuries by the Spanish kings. The Escorial still houses many of Philip's own collection of the Venetian masters he so much admired. Other Italian schools, as well as Flemish and native Spanish artists, are represented by outstanding examples.

The Escorial, by reaching out to bring all the functions of an absolute monarch within a single structure, is baroque in the grandeur of its conception. However, the restraint of Philip's taste, as well as the discipline of his architects, kept decorative exuberance well within academic bounds. Exercising the prerogatives of an absolute monarch, Philip insisted on the right to pass on the suitability and style of every public building that was undertaken during his reign. Herrera, as the court architect, was commissioned to inspect all such plans and, as a consequence, became an artistic dictator who enforced the restricted preferences of his royal master on the nation. Not until after Philip's death did Spain have the freedom to develop the richly elaborated style that is now such a prominent feature of its large cities. And some of the florid baroque's emotional exuberance and excesses came as a direct reaction to the

formal severity of Philip's time. Daring designs, fantastic forms, curved lines, the spiral twist of corkscrew columns replaced the austere façades and classical orders enforced by Herrera.

Architectural developments at Salamanca and Madrid will dramatize the situation. The Casa de las Conchas, or "House of the Shells," is a Renaissance structure built in 1514, well before Philip's time (Fig. 254, right). It nevertheless shows the tendency toward applied decoration that was popularly known as the *plateresque style,* a name derived from the Spanish word *platero* ("silversmith"). Across the street is the church of the Jesuit college of La Clérica, which was begun after the period of Philip and Herrera (Fig. 254, left). The lower part dates from the early 17th century and was designed by Juan Gomez de Mora. Even though it still adheres nominally to the classical orders, the decorative urge is seen clearly in the attached Composite columns and in the baroque triglyphs above them, as well as in many of the other details. The towers and gable belong to the latter part of the 17th century and were executed by Churriguera, whose name is associated with the more florid aspects of Spanish baroque, the *Churrigueresque* style.

Churriguera's ornate altarpiece for the Church of San Esteban is an architectural-sculptural-pictorial extravaganza (Fig. 255). More than ninety feet high, it combines the Composite order with gilded and garlanded twisted columns, set at various depths, that writhe upward in rhythmic profusion.

The Counter-Reformation Baroque Style    235

**Painting**    While the Escorial was still abuilding, Philip II commissioned El Greco to paint an altarpiece for the Chapel of St. Maurice. The subject of El Greco's early masterpiece, the *Martyrdom of St. Maurice* (Pl. 32, p. 231), is typical of the Counter-Reformation in that it has to do with the dilemma of the individual who is caught between conflicting loyalties. St. Maurice, the figure in the right foreground, was the commander of the Theban Legion, a unit of Christians serving in the Roman imperial army. An order has just arrived commanding all members of the unit to acknowledge the orthodox Roman deities or be put to death. In the expressive gestures of their hands, St. Maurice and his staff officers reveal their positions. Christ, it is true, has sanctioned by his own example the rendering unto Caesar the material things that are Caesar's, but the worship of false idols is another matter. The line is thus clearly drawn, and a choice has to be made between duty to the state and duty to the Church, between the city of man and the city of God. St. Maurice points upward, indicating his decision.

El Greco's spiral composition is well adapted to convey the tension between the material and spiritual

realms, the natural and supernatural, the terrestrial and celestial. It can be sensed in the twitching muscles, flamelike fingers, taut faces, and swirling upward motion of the composition itself. In serpentine fashion, it winds around to the left middle ground where St. Maurice is seen again, this time giving comfort to the men as they await their turn for decapitation. The tempo is accelerated toward the background where the nude figures of the soldiers seem already to have parted company with corporeality and are drawn into the spiritual vortex that bears them aloft on a Dantesque whirlwind. The eye is led upward by the constantly increasing light and the transition of color from the darker hues below to the vaporous pink and white clouds above. There a visionary vista in the heavens is beheld, where some of the angelic figures hover and hold crowns for those who suffer and die below, while others produce the strains of celestial harmony.

Despite the grimness of the subject, the light, transparent palette that El Greco employs gives the work an almost festive air, with the rose-colored banners, steel-blue and lemon-yellow costumes set against a background of silvery gray. The originality of the work, with its daring color dissonances and the lavish use of costly ultramarine blue, forfeited for El Greco the favor of King Philip, whose tastes ran to the more conservative Italian style. El Greco made only one other attempt to interest the royal patron: a study for a picture later called the *Dream of Philip II.* The commission for its execution, however, never came.

If the doors to the Escorial were closed, the gates to Toledo, see of the archbishop primate, always remained open to El Greco. His reputation there had been securely established by the series of paintings he had done for the Church of San Domingo el Antiguo. Most renowned of these was the *Assumption of the Virgin* for the high altar (Fig. 256). El Greco's model was the picture Titian had painted on the same subject some sixty years earlier (Fig 225). El Greco's version, however, reveals the baroque preference for open space, while Titian contains all action within his picture. By dividing his composition into three planes, Titian starts a vertical ascending motion in the lower two but arrests it by the descending figure of God above. By combining the acute receding diagonal lines of the apostles, El Greco in his *Assumption* forms a conelike base from which the Madonna soars aloft in a spiraling movement that leads the eye upward out of the picture into the open space above.

Also for Toledo, El Greco painted his masterpiece, the *Burial of Count Orgaz,* for his own parish church of San Tomé (Fig. 257). The count, who rebuilt and endowed the church, was legendarily honored in 1323 by the miraculous appearance of Sts. Stephen and

Augustine, who gently lower him into his tomb just below the picture. The vivid terrestrial and visionary celestial spheres are separated by the flickering torches and swirling draperies as the soul of the Count is borne heavenward on angelic wings to be received by the radiant figure of Christ. The row of mourners include portraits of the Toledo clergy and gentry, among them a self-portrait of the artist directly above the head of St. Stephen. A note of subtle humor is struck in the portrait of El Greco's eight-year-old son Jorge Manuel as the acolyte in the lower left. The boy points to the encircled white-and-gold rose embroidered on St. Stephen's vestment—the circle being the symbol of immortality, the rose of love. On his son's pocket handkerchief El Greco signed in Greek: "Domenicos Theotocopoulos made me, 1578." But the date is not that of the picture but of his son's birth.

The driving out of the money changers from the temple is the only incident in the Gospels where Christ assumes an attitude of righteous anger and the only time when He resorted to physical action and corporeal punishment. Consequently, the subject had been rare in Christian iconography, but it was revived during the Counter-Reformation when the Roman Catholic Church was undergoing just such a purgation. El Greco painted no less than six versions of it. In *Expulsion from the Temple* Christ appears in the role of the refining fire as prophesied by Isaiah, and His mood of fiery anger is reflected in El Greco's clashing colors of crimson red, pink, orange, and greenish yellow (Fig. 258). While Christ's gesture bespeaks vio-

**opposite above: 256.** EL GRECO. *Assumption of the Virgin.* c. 1577. Oil on canvas, 13'2" × 7'6". Art Institute, Chicago.

**opposite below: 257.** EL GRECO. Chapel with *Burial of Count Orgaz.* 1586. San Tomé, Toledo, Spain.

**right: 258.** EL GRECO. *Expulsion from the Temple.* c. 1572–74. Oil on canvas, 4'8" × 4'11". Minneapolis Institute of Arts (Dunwoody Fund).

**259.** Diego Velázquez. *The Water Carrier of Seville.* c. 1619–21. Oil on canvas, 41½ × 31½". Wellington Museum, London (Crown copyright reserved).

but as a complete contrast to El Greco and as an equally great contribution to the high Spanish period, it is more appropriately discussed here.

While El Greco concerned himself almost exclusively with religious subjects, Velázquez, with few exceptions, painted scenes of courtly life. In contrast to El Greco's personal involvement in his pictorial content, Velázquez sees his world with cool detachment and an objective eye. His work is admirably summed up in his masterpiece *Las Meninas*, or the *"Maids of Honor"* (Pl. 33, p. 232). With it, the painter combines the formality of a group portrait with the informality of a genre scene in his studio. Attention is about evenly distributed among the various groups. In the foreground, the Infanta Margarita, dressed in a gown of white satin, is standing in the center. On the left, a maid of honor is offering her a drink of water from a red cup on a gold tray. At the right is a group made up of a second maid of honor and two of the court dwarfs, one of whom is poking the sleepy mastiff with his foot. In the middle ground, on the left, is Velázquez himself wearing the cross of the Order of Santiago, which was conferred on him by his friend and patron, the King. He stands before a canvas which, by reason of its large dimensions, seems to be *Las Meninas* itself. He is looking at King Philip IV and Queen Mariana, whose faces are reflected in the mirror at the back of the room. As a balance for his own figure, Velázquez paints the conversing lady-in-waiting and courtier in the right middle ground. In the rear of the room, a court attendant stands in the open doorway pulling back a curtain, possibly to adjust the light.

Velázquez is a virtuoso in the handling of space and light. With the utmost precision, he has organized the picture into a series of receding planes, and by so doing, he gives the figures their spatial relationships. The first plane is in front of the picture itself where the King and Queen and, by inference, the observer are standing. Next comes that in which the principal group stands in the light of the window at the right, which again is outside the picture but which provides the brilliant illumination that falls on the blonde hair of the princess. The light here is balanced by that from the door at the rear, which defines the plane in the background. In between is the intermediate plane with the figures of Velázquez and the attendants, who are shown in more subdued light. Otherwise the space is broken up geometrically into a pattern of rectangles, such as the floor, ceiling, the easel, the pictures hanging on the wall, the mirror, and the door at the back.

In such a precise analytical study of space and light, which lacks both the spiritual mysticism of El Greco and the worldly grandiosity of the Venetian painters, the baroque qualities are not immediately apparent. Velázquez, however, is a virtuoso of external rather than internal vision, and therefore his ba-

lence, His face is serene in the knowledge that what He does is for the good of those whom He chastises. The atmosphere recalls that of a Last Judgment with the figure of Christ separating the two groups. The side toward which His lash is directed is full of turbulence and confusion as the traders cringe under the accusing eye, yet try to save their wares. On the other side, all is calm as the disciples ponder the meaning of the event. The four heads in the lower right acknowledge El Greco's debt to his artistic mentors Titian, Michelangelo, Giulio Clovio, and Raphael.

Spain's other great baroque master, Diego Velázquez, had spent his early years in his native Seville painting genre pictures such as the well-known *Water Carrier of Seville* (Fig. 259). Less than a decade after El Greco's death, the new monarch Philip IV appointed Velázquez his court painter. Velázquez' art, consequently, comes within the category of the aristocratic baroque, which is treated in the next chapter, roque qualities are found in such things as the intricate play of light and shadow, the complex spatial arrangements, the fact that much lies outside the picture space itself, and the subtle relationships of the subjects to each other. Proof of the latter is evidenced by the fact that Velázquez experts still cannot agree on what is actually going on. Is Velázquez painting the King and Queen, and have the Infanta and her ladies wandered in to look around? Or is Velázquez looking into a mirror as he paints the Infanta, and have her parents dropped in to watch the proceedings?

Just as Spanish architecture showed a reaction when the restraints of the earlier period were lifted, Spanish painting moved away from the austerity and intensity of the previous century. No painter could sustain the spiritual insight and emotional power of El Greco. The relaxation into sentimentality is clearly seen in Murillo's *Immaculate Conception* (Fig. 260). The subject was one in particular favor with the Spanish church, and Murillo and his workshop are known to have turned out some twenty versions of it. According to Roman Catholic belief, Mary was conceived miraculously without original sin. Artistically she is rep-

resented as in St. John's vision: "And there appeared a great wonder in heaven; a woman clothed with the sun, and the moon under her feet, and upon her head a crown of twelve stars" (Rev. 12 : 1). In this instance she is borne aloft by cherubs holding the lily, rose, olive branch, and palm leaf—symbols of purity, love, peace, and martyrdom.

**Music**   The Roman zeal for reform predisposed Church music to look more to the past than the future, to traditional rather than experimental forms. "The Antiphoners, Graduals, and Psalters have been filled to overflowing with barbarisms, obscurities, contrarieties, and superfluities as the result of clumsiness or negligence or even wickedness of the composers, scribes, and printers," read the papal brief authorizing Giovanni da Palestrina to undertake the reform of Church music along lines laid down by the Council of Trent. An ardent advocate of the Flemish contrapuntal style of Josquin des Prez and Heinrich Isaac, Palestrina, together with his great contemporaries Orlando di Lasso and Tomás Luis de Victoria, brought that art to its final fruition. Palestrina's prayers in song achieved a fluidity and transparency of texture, a balance of melody and harmony, a spiritual and organic unity worthy of the closing years of the *ars perfecta*, or "perfect art." The music of his younger colleague Victoria, however, has a darker mood, a brooding emotional fervor, and a deeper concern with the dramatic meaning of his texts. After serving thirty years as a chaplain, singer, and composer in the German College in Rome, an institution founded by his fellow Spaniard Ignatius Loyola, Victoria returned to his native country as choirmaster in court circles.

The music at the court of Philip II, like the architecture, painting, and sculpture, was religiously oriented, and the records of the period, as well as the design of the church at the Escorial, testify to the important place accorded the tonal art there. The choir at the Escorial was established even before the whole building was completed and in 1586 numbered in its ranks 150 monks. The choir section of the church is divided into two parts, since Philip's musical preferences were for the Venetian double-choral style he had heard in his youth. Besides the two organs in the choir, there are two others on either side of the nave, both large double-manual concert instruments of Flemish manufacture, 50 feet wide and 40 feet high. The same maker also built three portable organs for processions, which were placed in the galleries, thus making it possible on high feast days to hear 7 organs pealing forth.

Victoria's settings of the *Offices for Holy Week* have become an established tradition for performance in the Sistine Chapel. One of these is the four-part motet *O vos omnes,* the text of which comes from Jeremiah and the mood of which is one of lamentation. The

**260.** Bartolomé Murillo. *Immaculate Conception.* c. 1666–70. Oil on canvas, 6'9'' × 4'8⅝''. Prado, Madrid.

*O vos omnes* (4-part motet)  TOMÁS LUIS DE VICTORIA

Si    est do - lor   do  -  lor    si - mi - lis

passage above shows the characteristic grieving motif in the descending tenor voice in measure 4, as well as the dissonance created by the dip of the minor second by the same voice in measure 5, both of which intensify the word *dolor*, or "sorrow."

Victoria never wrote a single note of secular music. As he stated in one of his dedications, he was led by some inner impulse to devote himself solely to church music. In his motets and masses, he even avoided the secular *cantus firmus* themes that were customarily employed by his contemporaries. Instead, he chose his motifs and melodies from his own religious works or from the traditional plainsong. In later compositions after his return to Spain, Victoria's work took on an even greater fervor and passionate intensity. With its ascetic quality, religious ardor, and devotional spirit, his music rises in its way to the same heights of mystical grandeur as the writings of St. Teresa of Avila, the architecture of Herrera, and the pictures of El Greco.

## IDEAS: MILITANT MYSTICISM

The Counter-Reformation was accompanied by a vigorous reassertion of the mystical world view. In keeping with the spirit of the times, however, it was a practical mysticism of this world as well as the next, a realistic blending of the active as well as contemplative life, a religious experience not limited to future saints but broadened to include all those faithful to the Church as the mystical body of Christ. The new mysticism was socially oriented to enlist laymen as well as clergy, those active in worldly affairs as well as those behind convent walls. It was a rekindling of the fires of faith at a time when the foundations of faith were threatened by new scientific discoveries; a call to arms for all those willing to fight for their convictions in a war to the finish against doctrines the Roman Catholic Church considered heretical; a military mysticism of a Church militant on the march.

The enemy was made up of the various Protestant movements at home; the pagan religions of Africa, Asia, and the Americas abroad; the materialistic world view that went with growing nationalism and colonial expansion; and the forces of rampant rationalism unleashed by free scientific inquiry. The Counter-Reformation was just as much a resurgence of spiritual and moral values in the face of growing

scientific materialism as it was an anti-Protestant movement. The Church plainly saw that if the mechanistic image of the world as "matter in motion" were generally accepted, the belief in miracles would be undermined, the notion of divine intervention in worldly affairs would be destroyed, and the sense of mystery would be drained out of the cosmos.

The new psychology was not so much concerned with abstract theological speculations as with concrete religious experience through vivid imagery. The mysticism of St. Teresa and St. John of the Cross differed from medieval mysticism in its rational control and written documentation of each stage of the soul's ascent from the abyss of sin to the ecstasy of union with the divine.

The most typical expression of the Church militant, however, was the Society of Jesus, founded by that soldier and man of action St. Ignatius Loyola. His Jesuits helped adapt Church doctrine to modern conditions, faced the moral and political realities of the century, and took an active part in education, public affairs, as well as missionary work. Under the director general, a Jesuit enlisted as a "warrior of God under the banner of the Cross" and stood ready to go for the "propagation of the faith to the Turks or other infidels even in India or to heretics, schismatics or some of the faithful." The whole world, for missionary purposes, was divided into Jesuit provinces, and the priestly army of occupation followed in the wake of the navigators and conquistadors.

The spiritual side of the Jesuit military organization is reflected in St. Ignatius' *Spiritual Exercises*, a precise, disciplined exploration of the mysteries of faith through the medium of the senses. As part of the Jesuit system of education, St. Ignatius worked out a four-week series of meditations leading to a purgation and purification of the soul. All faculties are brought into play so that the experience becomes a vividly personal one. Sin is the subject of the first week, and its consequences are felt through each of the senses in turn. In the "Torment of Sight," the student visualizes the terrible words engraved on the gates of Hell—*Ever, Never*—and sees the flames spring up around him. In the "Torment of Sound," he listens to the groans of millions of the damned, the howls of demons, the crackle of flames that devour the victims. With the "Torment of Smell," he is reminded that the bodies of the doomed retain in Hell the corruption of the grave. Their "stink shall come up out of their carcases," prophesied Isaiah (Isa. 34 : 3). For the "Torment of Taste," the condemned shall suffer hunger like dogs; "they shall eat every man the flesh of his own arm" (Isa. 9 : 20), and their wine shall be the "poison of dragons, and the cruel venom of asps" (Deut. 32 : 33). And in the "Torment of Touch," the damned will be enveloped in flames that boil the blood in the veins and the marrow in the bones but do not consume the victim. Both flames and flesh are forever renewed so that pain is eternal. In the final phases, the progress leads up to the suffering, resurrection, and ascension of Christ, and it closes with the contemplation of heavenly bliss. By proclaiming that man could influence his own spiritual destiny, Jesuit optimism held a ready appeal for men of action.

Such a strong accent on sense experience as the means to excite religious feeling was bound to have repercussions in the arts. Through architectural, sculptural, pictorial, literary, and musical illusions, miracles and transcendental ideas could be made to seem real to the senses, and the mystical world view could be reasserted through aesthetic imagery. The increasing complexity of life, the proliferation of new knowledge, the deepening of psychological insights—all shaped the course of baroque art. As religious, social, and economic pressures mounted, people were increasingly inclined to resolve their insecurities by turning to the cults of visionary saints or to the power of the absolute state. Artists were enthusiastically enlisted to enhance the power and glory of both Church and state. Counter-Reformation churches were spacious, light, and cheerful; and visual artists, dramatists, and composers joined forces to make them like theaters where a concert of the arts played a prelude to the delights of future heavenly bliss.

Renaissance clarity of definition and the compartmentalization of space into clearly perceived patterns gave way to an intricate baroque geometry that took fluidity of movement into account. Neat Renaissance lines, circles, triangles, and rectangles became the intertwining spirals, parabolas, ovals, elongated lozenges, rhomboids, and irregular polygons of the baroque. With Borromini, horizontal and vertical surfaces were set into waves of rippling rhythms; balance and symmetry yielded to restless, unsettled movement; walls were molded sculpturally; surfaces treated with a rich play of color, light, and shadow. Pictures escaped from their vertical walls and settled upon spherical triangular pendentives and spandrels, concave and convex moldings, and the inner surfaces of ceilings, vaults, and domes. With Pozzo's paintings, solid walls, vaulted ceilings, and domes dissolved into nebulous, illusionistic vistas of the great beyond. With Bernini, marble saints and angels floated freely in space. With El Greco, corporeal being almost ceased to exist, and his figures are more spirit than flesh, his landscape backgrounds more heavenly than earthly. St. Teresa recorded and published her ecstatic visions in sparkling Spanish prose and poetry so that a wide public could experience them vicariously. Palestrina and Victoria illuminated the hymns of the liturgical year with the clarity of their counterpoint, and their melodies made them glow with new meaning.

By adopting the baroque style as their own and helping shape the artistic vocabulary of the time, the Jesuits not only brought baroque art down from the exclusive aristocratic level but carried the new idioms with them wherever they went, thus broadening the baroque into an international style. Counter-Reformation baroque churches are found as far afield as Mexico (Fig. 261), South America, and the Philippines. The extraordinary vigor of the Church militant thus succeeded in tapping new spiritual sources and invigorating Roman Catholicism to such an extent that it emerged once more as a popular religious movement.

**261.** Mexico City Cathedral. 1656–1791.

# 14 The Aristocratic Baroque Style

## FRANCE IN THE TIME OF LOUIS XIV

Everything about Louis XIV suggested grandeur. His concept of kingship assured him of the designation of *le grand roi;* his code of etiquette created the grand manner; he was in every sense the *grand seigneur;* a splendid avenue in Paris is named *Rue Louis le Grand;* and his reign gave his century the name of *le grand siècle.* At the time his portrait was painted by Hyacinthe Rigaud in 1701 (Fig. 262), Louis had been king in name for well over half a century and a king in fact for a full forty of those years. Dressed in his ermine-lined coronation robes, with the collar of the Grand Master of the Order of the Holy Ghost draped about his regal chest, Louis XIV might actually be uttering the words for which he was so famous: *L'Etat c'est moi*—"I am the state." Since he was in fact the personification of France, his portrait, appropriately, was that of an institution; and his figure was as much a pillar holding up the state as is the column that supports the building in the background. Pompous and pretentious though the portrait may be, it formed part and parcel of the illusionism of a period that strove to make such transcendental abstractions as the divine right of kings, absolutism, and the politically centralized state seem real to the senses.

The success of this system of centralization is seen in the list of positive accomplishments of a reign in which the feudal power of the provincial nobles was broken; the Church became a part of the state instead of the state a part of the Church; Paris became the intellectual and artistic capital of the world; and France attained the dominant position among European nations. For the arts, the alliance with absolutism meant that they were of value as instruments of propaganda, factors in the assertion of national power and prestige and the means of enhancing the glory of the court, impressing visiting dignitaries, and stimulating export trade. All this led, of course, toward the concept of art as an adjunct to the cult of majesty and as the perpetuator of the myth. With the King as principal patron, art inevitably became a department of the government, and Louis was surrounded with a system of cultural satellites each of whom was supreme in his own field. The foundation of the Academy of Language and Literature in 1635, the Royal Academy of Painting and Sculpture in 1648, and the others which followed made it possible for Boileau to dominate the field of letters, Lebrun that of the visual arts, and Lully the art of music. Absolutism

**262.** HYACINTHE RIGAUD. *Louis XIV.* 1701. Oil on canvas, 9′1½″ × 6′2⅝″. Louvre, Paris.

**opposite: 263.** CLAUDE PERRAULT. East front, Louvre, Paris. 1667–70. Length 570′, height 90′.

therefore meant standardization, since no artist could receive commission or employment except through official channels. Louis, however, knew what he was about, and in an address to the Academy he once remarked: "Gentlemen, I entrust to you the most precious thing on earth, my fame." Knowing this, he defended his writers and artists, supported them generously, and above all exercised that most noble attribute any patron can possess—good taste.

The outward and visible sign of this absolutism was to be seen in the dramatization of the personal and social life of this *roi du soleil*, or "Sun King." The adoption of the sun as his symbol was natural enough, and such motifs as the sunburst were widely used in the decor of his palaces. As patron of the arts, Louis could identify himself freely with Apollo, the sun god, who was also the Olympian protector of the muses. In the morning, when it was time for the Sun King to rise and shine, the *lever du roi* was as dazzling in its way as a second sunrise. This special dawn was accompanied by a cloud of attendants who flocked into the royal bedchamber precisely at 8 A.M. in order to hand the King the various parts of his royal apparel. A similarly colorful ceremony accompanied the *coucher du roi*, when the Sun King in a golden glow of candlelight finally set at 10 P.M. Louis' life was one continuous pageant in which each hour had its appropriate activity, costume, cast, and audience. Less frequent events, such as a christening, a wedding, or a coronation, had their special ceremonies. Even the royal births called for an audience so as to assure the country of the legitimacy of any future sovereign. In the present day of prosaic cabinet officers and drab parliamentary bodies, it is difficult to imagine the overwhelming effect of the formal pomp and circumstance surrounding an absolute monarch's court. If his peers and subjects beheld a sufficiently majestic spectacle or grandiose procession, a ruler apparently could get by with anything.

Throughout a reign of 72 years, Louis XIV played the leading role in this incessant court drama with all the effortless technique and consummate self-assurance of an accomplished actor. Such a great actor needed, of course, a great audience; and such a dramatic spectacle demanded an appropriate stage setting. Architects therefore were called upon to plan the endless series of communicating salons as impressive backdrops for the triumphal entries; landscape designers to fashion the grand avenues for the open-air processions; painters to decorate the ceilings with pink clouds and classical deities so that the monarch could descend the long flights of stairs as if from the Olympian skies; and musicians to sound the ruffles and flourishes that accompanied the grand entrances. It was therefore no accident that the Louvre and Versailles palaces resembled vast theaters, that the paintings and tapestries of Lebrun seemed like curtains and backdrops, that Bernini's, Puget's, and Coysevox's sculptural adornments took on the aspect of stage props, that the most important literary expression should be the tragedies of Racine and the comedies of Molière, and that the characteristic musical forms should be Lully's court ballets and operas.

## ARCHITECTURE

In 1665, at the insistence of his minister Colbert, Louis XIV requested the pope to permit his principal architect Gianlorenzo Bernini to come to Paris to supervise the rebuilding of the Louvre Palace. When he arrived on French soil, Bernini was received with all the honor due him as the ranking artist of his day. The design he made for the Louvre was radical in many ways. It would have necessitated the replacement of the existing parts of the building by a grandiose baroque city palace of the Italian type. Colbert conceded that Bernini's palace with its ballrooms and monumental staircases was truly grand in style, but it actually left the King housed no better than before. After a round of festivities, Bernini returned to Rome; his plan was scrapped; and a French architect, Claude Perrault, was appointed to finish the job. This little episode proved to be a turning point in cultural history. It marked the weakening of Italian artistic influence in France; it also indicated that Louis XIV had plans of his own.

Perrault's façade (Fig. 263) incorporated some parts of Bernini's project, such as the flat roof con-

# CHRONOLOGY / 17th-Century France

## General Events

| | | |
|---|---|---|
| 1598– | 1610 | Henry IV, king of France |
| 1610– | 1643 | Louis XIII, king of France with his mother Maria de' Medici (1573–1642) as regent during his minority |
| 1615– | 1624 | Luxembourg Palace built for Queen Mother by Salomon de Brosse |
| 1618– | 1648 | Thirty Years' War. Spain and Austria defeated, France became dominant European nation |
| | 1621 | Rubens commissioned to paint murals in Luxembourg Palace |
| 1624– | 1642 | Cardinal Richelieu (1585–1642), prime minister |
| | 1635 | French Academy of Language and Literature established |
| | 1636 | Mersenne's *Traité de l'Harmonie Universelle* ("*Treatise on Universal Harmony*") published |
| | 1640 | Poussin returned from Rome to decorate the Louvre Palace |
| 1643– | 1661 | Cardinal Mazarin (1602–61), prime minister |
| 1643– | 1715 | Louis XIV, king of France; ruled without prime minister from 1661 |
| | 1648 | Royal Academy of Painting and Sculpture founded |
| 1661– | 1688 | Versailles Palace built by Louis Le Vau and J. Hardouin-Mansart; chapel added 1699–1708 |
| 1665– | 1683 | Colbert (1619–83), minister of finance |
| | 1665 | Bernini came to Paris to rebuild the Louvre Palace. French Academy in Rome established |
| | 1666 | Academy of Sciences established |
| 1667– | 1674 | East façade of the Louvre Palace built by Perrault |
| | 1669 | Royal Academy of Music (Paris Opera) established under Lully |
| | 1671 | Academy of Architecture established |
| | 1674 | *Alceste*, lyrical tragedy by Quinault and Lully, performed at Versailles. Boileau's *L'Art Poétique* ("*Art of Poetry*") published |
| | 1683 | Government and ministries of France installed at Versailles |

## Architects

| | | |
|---|---|---|
| 1552– | 1626 | Salomon de Brosse |
| 1598– | 1680 | Gianlorenzo Bernini |
| 1612– | 1670 | Louis Le Vau |
| 1613– | 1688 | Claude Perrault |
| 1613– | 1700 | André Le Nôtre |
| 1646– | 1708 | J. Hardouin-Mansart |

## Painters

| | | |
|---|---|---|
| 1577– | 1640 | Peter Paul Rubens |
| 1594– | 1665 | Nicolas Poussin |
| 1600– | 1682 | Claude Gelée Lorrain |
| 1619– | 1690 | Charles Lebrun |
| 1659– | 1743 | Hyacinthe Rigaud |

## Writers and Philosophers

| | | |
|---|---|---|
| 1596– | 1650 | René Descartes |
| 1606– | 1684 | Pierre Corneille |
| 1621– | 1695 | Jean de La Fontaine |
| 1622– | 1673 | Molière (J. B. Poquelin) |
| 1623– | 1662 | Blaise Pascal |
| 1635– | 1688 | Philippe Quinault |
| 1636– | 1711 | Nicolas Boileau |
| 1639– | 1699 | Jean Racine |

## Sculptors

| | | |
|---|---|---|
| 1598– | 1680 | Gianlorenzo Bernini |
| 1622– | 1694 | Pierre Puget |
| 1628– | 1715 | François Girardon |
| 1640– | 1720 | Antoine Coysevox |

## Musicians

| | | |
|---|---|---|
| 1602– | 1676 | Francesco Cavalli, Venetian opera composer |
| c.1602– | 1672 | Jacques de Chambonnières, organist and clavecinist |
| 1632– | 1687 | Jean Baptiste Lully |
| 1668– | 1733 | Couperin le Grand, clavecinist |
| 1683– | 1764 | Jean Philippe Rameau |

cealed behind a Palladian balustrade and the long straight front with the wings extending laterally instead of projecting forward to enclose a court in the traditional French manner. Perrault's own contributions can be seen in the solid ground floor, which is relieved only by the seriate windows. This story functions as a platform for the classically proportioned Corinthian colonnade, with its rhythmic row of paired columns marching majestically across the broad expanse of the façade. The space between the colonnade and the wall of the building allows for the rich play of light and shadow that was so much a part of the baroque ideal. The frieze of garlands adds a florid touch, while the central pediment as well as the classical orders of the columns and pilasters act as a restraining influence.

Even before Bernini came to Paris and long before the Louvre was completed, Louis XIV had conceived the idea of a royal residence outside Paris where he could escape from the restrictions of the city, take nature into partnership, and design a new way of life. Colbert, who felt that a king's place was in his capital, advised against it, and Louis allowed the Louvre to be completed as a concession to Paris. But his real

**264.** Versailles Palace (aerial view). 1661–88. Palace width 1,935′.

capital was destined to be Versailles. This project was sufficiently awe-inspiring to serve as a symbol of the supremacy of the young absolute monarch as he asserted his power over rival nations, the landed aristocracy of his own country, the parliament, the provincial governments, the town councils, and the middle-class merchants. Away from Paris there would be a minimum of distraction and a maximum of concentration on his own person. In a wooded site almost half the size of Paris, which belonged entirely to the crown, everything could be planned from the beginning, nothing need be left to random chance, and a completely new manner of living could be organized.

The grand axis of the Versailles Palace starts with the Avenue de Paris (Fig. 264, top right), bisects the palace building itself, and runs along the grand canal toward the horizon where it trails off into infinity. As the avenue enters the palace grounds, the barracks for the honor guard, coach houses, stables, kennels, and orangeries are found on either side. The latter building caused an ambassador from a foreign country to remark that Louis XIV must indeed be the most magnificent of beings since he had a palace for his orange trees more beautiful than the residences of other monarchs. The wide avenue narrows pro-

gressively with the parade grounds toward the marble court of honor (Fig. 275), above which is found the heart of the plan—the state bedroom of Louis XIV. The whole grand design is so logical, so symmetrical, that it becomes a study in absolute space composition and makes Versailles an all-embracing universal structure which encompasses a vast segment of external as well as internal space. No one building or any part of it is a law unto itself, and together they are inconceivable without their natural environment. The gardens, parks, avenues, and radiating pathways are just as much an integral part of the whole as the halls, salons, and communicating corridors of the palace itself.

Jules Hardouin-Mansart was the architect of the two wings that extend the main building to a width of over a quarter of a mile (Fig. 264). His design is noteworthy for the horizontal accent attained by the uniform level of the roof line, broken only by the roof of the chapel, which was added in the early 18th century. The simplicity and elegance of these long, straight lines, in contrast to the irregular profile of a medieval building, proclaim the new feeling for space. From every room vistas of the garden are a part of the interior design and tell of a new awareness of nature. A detail of the garden façade reveals how freely Mansart treated the classical orders (Fig. 265), and how the levels become increasingly ornate from the podiumlike base below to the attic and balustrade with its file of silhouetted statuary. As a whole the building is a commanding example of baroque exuberance and grandeur tempered by Palladian discretion and restraint.

Some of the interior rooms have been preserved or restored in the style of Louis XIV. The grandest room of the palace is the famous Hall of Mirrors stretching across the main axis of the building and looking out toward the spacious gardens (Fig. 266). Designed by Mansart and decorated by Lebrun, it was the scene of the most important state ceremonies and a kind of apotheosis of the absolute monarchy. Corinthian pilasters of green marble support the ornate vault that is covered with paintings by Lebrun and inscriptions by Boileau and Racine—all to the greater glorification of the Sun King.

The gardens, which were laid out by André Le Nôtre, are not just a frame for the buildings but are incorporated into the whole spatial design (Fig. 267). Their formality and geometrical organization symbolized the dominance of man over nature, but with the idea of embracing nature rather than keeping it at arm's length. The square pools across the garden side, so liberally populated with goldfish and swans, reflect the contours of the building like an external echo of the mirrored chambers within. The statues of river gods and nymphs, which are found at the angles, were executed from sketches by Lebrun and personify the rivers and streams of France. The gardens and park form a logical system of terraces, broad avenues, and pathways radiating outward from clearings. They are lavishly embellished by fountains, pools, canals, pavilions, and grottos, all of which are richly decorated with statuary. More than 1,200 fountains were installed by skilled engineers of waterworks, and with their jets spouting water into the air in many patterns, they were marvels of their craft. Each had its name, and each was adorned with an appropriate sculptural group.

The Versailles Palace, therefore, was not so much a monument to the vanity of Louis XIV as it was a symbol of the absolute monarchy and the outstanding example of aristocratic baroque architecture. It represented a movement away from a feudal, decentralized government toward a modern centralized state. As a vast advertising project it was a highly influential factor in the international diplomacy of the time. By urbanizing the country aristocracy and promoting court activities, Versailles built up for the arts a larger and more discriminating audience. It assured the shift of the artistic center of gravity from Italy to France. The court also functioned as a center of style and dress, and as a school for the training of skilled craftsmen, it virtually assured France continuous leadership in fashion and elegance, a preeminence that remains secure today. By combining all the activities of a court in a single structure, Versailles pointed the way toward the concept of architecture as a means of creating a new pattern of life. At Versailles a large housing development the size of a town was constructed so as to encompass rather than escape from nature. Details of Le Nôtre's garden plan, such as the radiating pathways, were the acknowledged basis for the laying out of new sections of Paris; and the city plan of Washington, D.C., for instance, was a direct descendant of the parks of Versailles. Modern city planners and housing developers have hailed Versailles as the prototype of the contemporary ideal of placing large residential units in close contact with nature. Finally, by starting with a grand design, Versailles pointed the way to the planning of whole cities from the start without the vicissitudes of haphazard growth and change. In this light, Versailles is seen as one of the earliest examples of modern urbanism and city planning on a large scale.

## SCULPTURE

While Gianlorenzo Bernini was working on the Louvre plans, he was besieged by requests from would-be patrons to design everything from fountains for their gardens to tombs for their ancestors. The King as usual came first in such matters, and Bernini received a commission from Louis XIV for a portrait bust (Fig. 268). This minor by-product of the artist's Paris sojourn ultimately turned out to be far more successful than his major mission.

Dispensing with the usual formal sittings, Bernini made rapid pencil sketches while Louis was playing

tennis or presiding at cabinet meetings, so that he could observe his subject in action. He was convinced that movement was the medium that best defined the personality and brought out the unique characteristics of his subjects, and the informal sketches were made, as he said, "to steep myself in, and imbue myself with, the King's features." After he had captured the individuality he was to portray, his next step was to decide on the general ideas—nobility, majesty, and the optimistic pride of youth. Here all the accessories, such as the costume, drapery, position of the head, and so on, would play their part. After the preliminaries were over and the particular as well as the general aspects were settled, the King sat thirteen times, while Bernini, working directly on the marble, made finishing touches.

Like most other works of the period, the bust has its allegorical allusions. Bernini noted in his conversations the resemblance of Louis XIV to Alexander the Great, whose countenance he knew from ancient coins. Courtly flattery was partially responsible, of course; but according to the conventions of the time, if the King were to appear as a military hero, it would be as a Roman emperor on horseback; or, if he were to be the *roi soleil*, it would be in the guise of Apollo. Since Bernini's intention here was to convey grandeur

**268.** GIANLORENZO BERNINI. *Louis XIV.* 1665. Marble, height 33⅛". Versailles Palace.

maximum play to light and shadow. The sculptor has carefully delineated the various textures, such as the smooth flesh, flowing drapery, floating hair, the bark, leaves, and branches, in keeping with his objective of painting in marble. But above all Bernini has realized his express intention, which was to achieve emotion and movement at all costs and to make marble seem to float in space.

The Versailles gardens provided French sculptors with an inexhaustible outlet for their wares. Many went to Italy to copy such admired antiques as the *Laocoön Group* (Fig. 62). These replicas were then sent back and placed on pedestals along the various walks at Versailles. Other sculptors, like Girardon, made variants of Bernini's fountains and incorporated the movement of the water into their designs as he had done. Most of the statuary at Versailles, however, is effective mainly as part of the general setting, and only a few works have survived the test of time to emerge as individual masterpieces. Notable among

**left: 269.** Gianlorenzo Bernini. *Apollo and Daphne.* 1622–25. Marble, life-size. Borghese Gallery, Rome.

**right: 270.** Pierre Puget. *Milo of Crotona.* 1671–83. Marble; height 8'10½", width 4'7". Louvre, Paris.

and majesty, Alexander, as the personification of kingly character, was the logical choice.

In addition to such portraits, Bernini's fame as a sculptor rested more broadly on religious statues, such as his *St. Teresa in Ecstasy* (Fig. 250), on the many fountains he designed for Rome, and on mythological groups such as his *Apollo and Daphne* (Fig. 269), to embellish aristocratic residences. This youthful work is full of motion and tense excitement. According to the myth, Apollo, as the patron of the muses, was in pursuit of ideal beauty, symbolized here by the nymph Daphne. The sculptor chose to make permanent the pregnant moment from which the previous and forthcoming action may be inferred. As Daphne flees from Apollo's ardent embrace, she cries aloud to the gods, who hear her plea and change her into a laurel tree. Though root-bound and with bark already enclosing her limbs, she seems to be in quivering motion. The diagonal line from Apollo's hand to Daphne's leafy fingers leads the eye upward and outward. The complex surfaces are handled so as to give

these sculptures were such works of Puget as his *Milo of Crotona* (Fig. 270). This statue shows the ancient Olympic wrestling champion, who had challenged Apollo himself to a match, being accorded the inevitable punishment meted out to any mortal daring enough to compete with an immortal god. Coysevox, who lived and worked at Versailles, likewise was influenced by Bernini.

**Plate 34.** PETER PAUL RUBENS. *Garden of Love.* c. 1632–34. Oil on canvas, 6'6″ × 9'3½″. Prado, Madrid. (See p. 251.)

**Plate 35.** NICOLAS POUSSIN. *Et in Arcadia Ego ("I Too Once Dwelled in Arcady").* 1638–39. Oil on canvas, 2'9½″ × 3'11⅜″. Louvre, Paris. (See p. 253.)

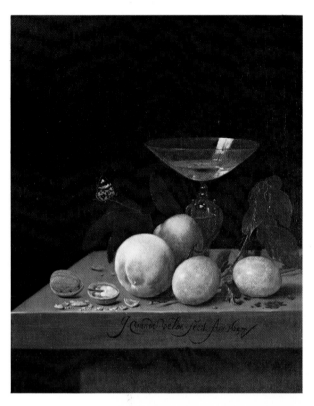

left: **Plate 36.** JAN JANSZ. VAN DE VELDE. *Still Life: Fruit Piece.* 1657. Oil on wood, 15 × 12¾″. Frans Hals Museum, Haarlem. (See p. 259.)

below: **Plate 37.** REMBRANDT. *Sortie of Captain Banning Cocq's Company of the Civic Guard.* 1642. Oil on canvas, 12′2″ × 14′7″. Rijksmuseum, Amsterdam. (See p. 261.)

## PAINTING

Patronage of the arts on a lavish and international scale had been a royal prerogative ever since Francis I's time, and the procession of distinguished figures to the French court, which in the 16th century had included Benvenuto Cellini and Leonardo da Vinci, never ceased. Foremost among the newcomers was that great cosmopolitan Fleming, Peter Paul Rubens. Though loyal to Flanders and Antwerp where he maintained his studio, Rubens had studied the works of Titian and Tintoretto in Venice as well as those of Michelangelo and Raphael in Rome. Never lacking aristocratic favor, he passed long periods in Spain and, particularly, in Italy at Mantua. During Louis XIII's reign, when the Luxembourg Palace was being completed for the Queen Mother Maria de' Medici, her expressed desire was for a painter who could decorate the walls of its Festival Gallery in a manner matching the Italian baroque style of its architecture. Maria's career as Henry IV's queen and as Louis XIII's regent was as lacking in luster as her own mediocre endowments could possibly have made it. Nevertheless, as the direct descendant of Lorenzo the Magnificent, she seemed to sense that the posthumous reputations of princes often depended more on their choice of artists than on their skill in statecraft.

Rubens' cycle of 21 large canvases gave the needed imaginary apotheosis to Maria's unimaginative life, and the success of this visual biography belonged more truly to the man who painted it than to the lady who lived it. The remarkable thing was how Rubens could exercise so much individual freedom within the confines of courtly officialdom and succeed so well in pleasing both himself and his royal mistress. In his grandiose conception, the ancient gods had deserted the rarified regions of Mt. Olympus and taken up their abode in the vastly more exhilarating atmosphere of Paris. Even before Maria's birth, Juno and Jupiter had cajoled the Three Fates into spinning a brilliant web of destiny for her. The governess who taught her to read was none other than Minerva, while her music teacher was Apollo himself. Her mythical eloquence came from the lips of Mercury, and every possible feminine fascination was imparted to her by the Three Graces. When this paragon of brilliance and virtue reached the apex of her grace and beauty, the Capitoline Triad themselves presided over the scene of *Henry IV Receiving the Portrait of Maria de' Medici* (Fig. 271). Minerva, as goddess of peace and war, whispers words of wisdom into the King's ear, while a whimsical touch is provided by the cupids who playfully try to lift the heavy helmet and shield of the monarch's armor. The celestial scene above assures everyone concerned that marriages are indeed made in heaven, where Jupiter with his eagle and Juno with her peacocks are seen bestowing their Olympian blessing.

**271.** Peter Paul Rubens. *Henry IV Receiving the Portrait of Maria de' Medici.* 1622–25. Oil on canvas, 13′ × 9′8″. Louvre, Paris.

The baroque ideal of richness and lavishness is seen once again in a picture from Rubens' later years, the *Garden of Love* (Pl. 34, p. 249). The actual setting for this allegory was the garden of his palatial home at Antwerp, and the ornate doorway in the background still exists. The bacchanalian theme unfolds in a diagonal line beginning with the chubby cherub in the lower left. Rubens himself is seen urging his second wife Helena Fourment, who appeared in so many of his later pictures, to join the others in the garden of love. The rest of the picture unfolds in a series of spirals mounting upward toward the figure of Venus who, as a part of the fountain, presides over the festivities. The use of large areas of strong primary colors—reds, blues, yellows—enlivens the scene and enhances the pictorial structure.

Rubens succeeded in combining the rich color of Titian and the dramatic tension of Tintoretto with an unbounded energy and physical exuberance of his left: 272. PETER PAUL RUBENS. *Rape of Daughters of Leucippus.* c. 1618. Oil on canvas, 7'3" × 6'10". Alte Pinakothek, Munich.

opposite: 273. NICOLAS POUSSIN. *Rape of Sabine Women.* c. 1636–37. Oil on canvas, 5'1" × 6'10½". Metropolitan Museum of Art, New York (Harris Brisbane Dick Fund, 1946).

pursue his classical studies, the independence to work out his own principles and ideals, and the time to paint pictures ranging from mythological and religious subjects to historical canvases and architectural landscapes.

Two truly superb paintings depicting similar violent and passionate themes provide a lively comparison of the temperamental differences between Rubens and his younger French colleague (Figs. 272, 273). Poussin's scene alludes to the legendary foundation of Rome according to the historians Livy and Plutarch. Romulus, having been unsuccessful in negotiating marriages for his warriors, has arranged a religious celebration with games and festivities as a stratagem to bring families from the neighboring town of Sabina to the Roman Forum. For Rubens, the affair is one of robust personal passion with Castor and Pollux who, as Aldous Huxley puts it, "fairly dived into the sea of female flesh that splashed and wildly undulated around them." The more studious Poussin, in his efforts to re-create the classical past, turned to Roman museums for models of many of his figures, and to Vitruvius for his architectural setting. From his position of prominence on the portico of the temple at the left, Romulus is giving the prearranged signal of unfolding his mantle, whereupon every Roman seizes a Sabine girl and makes off with her. Though the subject is one of passion and violence, Poussin manages to temper his picture by a judicious juxtaposition of opposites. The anger of the outraged victims contrasts with the impassive calm of Romulus and his attendants. As a ruler, Romulus knows that the future of his city rests on the foundation of families, and that in this case the end justifies the means. The turbulent human action is counterbalanced also by the ordered repose of the architectural and landscape background. The smooth marblelike flesh of the women contrasts with the bulging musculature beneath the bronzed skins of the Romans, and the contours of the figures generally are clearly defined as if they had been chiseled out of stone. Poussin's constant preoccupation with antique sculpture is readily seen when the group in the right foreground is compared with the Hellenistic *Gaul and His Wife* (Fig. 50). While such direct derivations are comparatively rare, this group is indicative of the close study the artist made of the antique statuary in the Roman museums. The building at the right, a reconstruction Poussin made from a description of a Roman basilica

own. His conceptions have something of the heroic sweep of Michelangelo, though they lack the latter's introspection and restraint. His complex organization of space and freedom of movement recall El Greco, but his figures are as round and robust as the latter's were tall and emaciated. His success in religious pictures, hunting scenes, and landscapes, as well as the mythological paintings that suited his temperament so well, shows the enormous sweep of his pictorial powers. For sheer imaginative invention and bravura with a brush he has rarely, if ever, been equaled.

While Rubens was executing his murals for the Festival Hall, an obscure French painter named Nicolas Poussin, who had been working on minor decorations, left the Luxembourg Palace for the less confining atmosphere of Rome. There he soon built a solid reputation that came to the attention of Cardinal Richelieu, who bought many of Poussin's paintings and became determined to bring the artist back to Paris. In 1640, Poussin did return to decorate the Grand Gallery of the Louvre—and receive from Louis XIII a shower of favors and the coveted title of First Painter to the King. The inevitable courtly intrigues that followed such marked attention made Poussin so miserable that after two years he returned to Rome. There he acted as the artistic ambassador of France and supervised the French painters sent under government subsidies to study and copy Italian masterpieces for the decoration of the Louvre. And there, for the rest of his life, Poussin had the freedom to by Vitruvius, is further evidence of Poussin's desire for accuracy of detail.

*Et in Arcadia Ego* shows Poussin in a quieter and more lyrical mood (Pl. 35, p. 249). The rustic figures of the shepherds might well have stepped out of one of Vergil's pastoral poems, while the shepherdess could be the tragic muse in one of Corneille's dramas. As they trace out the letters of the Latin inscription on the sarcophagus, "I Too Once Dwelled in Arcady," their mood becomes pensive. The thought that the shepherd in the tomb once lived and loved as they casts a spell of gentle melancholy over the group. In this meditative study in spatial composition, the feminine figure parallels the trunk of the tree to define the vertical axis, while the arm of the shepherd on the left rests on the sarcophagus to supply the horizontal balance. Each gesture, each line, follows inevitably from this initial premise with all the cool logic of a geometrical theorem. The subject is obviously a sympathetic one to Poussin, for he had found his own Arcadia in Italy and took a lifelong delight in the monuments of antiquity and the voices from the past that spoke through just such inscriptions. Like the ancients, he tried to conduct his own search for truth and beauty in a stately tempo and with a graceful gesture. Like them, too, he sought for the permanent in the transient, the type in the individual, the universal in the particular, and the one in the many.

Claude Gelée, better known as Claude Lorrain, like his countryman Poussin, also preferred life in Italy to that in his native France. His lifelong interest was landscape, but the convention of the time demanded that pictures contain personages and also have titles for them. Claude solved the problem by painting his landscapes, letting his assistants put in a few incidental figures, and giving the pictures obscure names, such as *Embarkation of the Queen of Sheba*, *Expulsion of Hagar*, or *David at the Cave of Adullam*. With tongue in cheek, he once remarked that he sold his figures and gave away his landscapes. Harbor scenes like the one entitled *Disembarkation of Cleopatra at Tarsus* were his special delight (Fig. 274). In them, he could concentrate on limitless space and the soft atmospheric effect of sunlight on misty air. His usual procedure was to balance his compositions on either side of the foreground with buildings or trees, which are treated in considerable detail. Then the eye is drawn deeper into the intervening space with long vistas over land or sea toward the indefinite horizon. Formal values dominate, and nothing arbitrary or accidental intrudes to mar their stately quality.

The stylistic differences of Rubens and Poussin admirably illustrate the free and academic sides of the baroque coin. Both painters were well versed in the classics, both reflected the spirit of the Counter-Reformation, and both in their way represented the aristocratic tradition. But while Rubens' impetuosity knew no bounds, Poussin remained aloof and reserved; while Rubens cast restraint to the winds and filled his pictures with violent movement, Poussin

274. Claude Lorrain. *Disembarkation of Cleopatra at Tarsus.* c. 1647. Oil on canvas, 3'10¾" × 5'6½". Louvre, Paris.

was austerely pursuing his formal values; while Rubens' figures are soft and fleshy, Poussin's are hard and statuesque; while Rubens sweeps up his spectators in the tidal wave of his volcanic energy, Poussin's pictures are more conducive to quiet meditation. The Academy's championship of Poussin made clear the distinction between academic and free baroque. In the late 17th and 18th centuries, painters were divided into camps labeling themselves either "Poussinist" or "Rubenist," and well into the 19th century echoes were still to be heard in the classic-versus-romantic controversy.

## MUSIC

The musical and dramatic productions at the court of Louis XIV were as lavish in scale as the other arts. Three groups of musicians were maintained, the first of which was the *chambre* group, which included the famous *Vingt-quatre Violons,* or "Twenty-four Viols," the first permanent stringed orchestra in Europe. This was the string ensemble that played for balls, dinners, concerts, and the opera. Lutenists and clavecinists also were found in this group. Next came the *chapelle,* the chorus that sang for religious services, and the organists. The *Grande Écurie* formed the third category, which consisted mainly of the wind ensemble that was available for military processions, outdoor fetes, and hunting parties.

During the years of Louis' minority, the popularity of the court ballet had been challenged by Italian opera, the "spectacle of princes" that Cardinal Mazarin sought to introduce from his native land. In 1660, Cavalli, who had brought the Venetian lyric drama to a high point of development, was invited to Paris to write and produce an opera. It met with a mixed reception, but two years later Cavalli was again on hand to write another, this time for Louis' wedding celebration. Another challenge to the court ballet came from Molière, who united the elements of comedy, music, and the dance into a form he called the *comédie-ballet.* The best known of these is the perennially popular *Le Bourgeois Gentilhomme* ("The Would-be Gentleman"), which was first performed at the court in 1670.

The ever-resourceful Jean-Baptiste Lully, however, was biding his time on the sidelines until he could spring some surprises of his own. A Florentine by birth and French by education, he was fiddling away at the early age of seventeen as a violinist in the *Vingt-quatre Violons.* When Cavalli produced his two operas, it was Lully who wrote the ballet sequences that, incidentally, proved more popular than the operas themselves. It was Lully again who collaborated with Molière by supplying the musical portions of the *comédie-ballets.* And when the propitious moment arrived, it was Lully who came up with a French form of opera that he called *tragédie lyrique,* or "lyrical tragedy." One of the earliest of these was the performance of *Alceste* in the Marble Court at Versailles on July 4, 1674 (Fig. 275). With a genius for organization, Lully used the *Vingt-quatre Violons* as the nucleus of his orchestra, supplementing them with wind instruments from the *Grande Écurie* for fanfares as well as for the hunting, battle, and climactic transformation scenes. The *chapelle* was also drafted into the operatic service, and the generous dance sequences Lully included assured the ballet group plenty of activity. Lully could have had the collaboration of the great dramatist Racine for the texts, but he deliberately chose Quinault, a poet of less distinction, but one who would be more pliable to his demands and who could be counted upon not to claim too much of the credit.

The form of these lyrical tragedies crystallized early and changed relatively little in the following years. Each begins with an instrumental number of the type known as the "French overture." The first part is a ponderous dignified march with dotted notes, massive sonorities, and chains of resolving dissonances as in the ritornel cited above. The second half is livelier in tempo and more contrapuntal in texture. Next came the prologue, and that of *Alceste* is quite typical. The setting is the garden of the Tuileries, the palace in Paris that was still the official royal residence at this time, where the Nymph of the Seine is discovered. Declaiming her lines in recitative style, she makes some topical allusions to the current war, couched in flowery mythological terms. Glory now enters to the the tune of a triumphal march, and a duet and solo air ensue. The two are joined eventually by a chorus of naiads and pastoral divinities, whose songs and dances give assurance that France will be ever victorious under the leadership of a great hero, whose identity is never for a moment in doubt. The overture is then repeated, and the five acts of a classical tragedy follow with much the same formal pattern as that of the prologue.

Two excerpts from Act III, Scene 5, of *Alceste* will illustrate Lully's style. After the death of Alceste, a long instrumental ritornel provides the pompous elegiac strains for the entrance of the mourning chorus.

*Alceste* (ritornel, Act III, Scene 5)  JEAN-BAPTISTE LULLY

*Alceste* (air, Act III, Scene 5)  JEAN-BAPTISTE LULLY

One of the grief-stricken women approaches, indicating sorrow by her gestures and facial expressions. Her "air" (above) is in the recitative style which J. J. Rousseau considered Lully's chief "title to glory." The composer always insisted that the music and all other elements of the opera were the servants of drama and poetry, and he counseled singers to emulate the noble and expansive intonations of the actors trained by Racine. Thus, a Lully air is never so set as an Italian aria but follows the elastic, fluid speech rhythms and the natural declamation of French baroque poetry and prose. The mourning chorus takes up where the air leaves off with a variant of the opening ritornel, and the scene closes with a long cadential passage alternately for orchestra and chorus based on a continuation of the ritornel.

Since the hero was so closely identified with the monarch, a tragic ending was quite impossible. A *deus ex machina*, therefore, invariably appeared in the

**275.** Louis Le Vau. Marble Court, Versailles Palace (during a performance of Lully's *Alceste*, 1674). Engraving by Lepautre. Metropolitan Museum of Art, New York (Harris Brisbane Dick Fund, 1930).

The Aristocratic Baroque Style　**255**

fourth act, just when all seemed darkest, and the fifth act always brought the lyrical tragedy to a triumphant and glorious conclusion.

By exploiting the success of his operas and through clever diplomatic strategy, Lully became by royal warrant the founder and head of the *Académie Royale de Musique.* With the substitution of the word *Nationale* for *Royale,* this is still the official title of the Paris grand opera company. With incredible energy, this musical monopolist of the regime produced an opera every year; and in addition to writing the score, he conducted the orchestra, trained the choir, coached the singers and dancers in their parts, and directed the staging. He ruled his musical and dramatic forces with the iron hand of an absolutist, allowing nothing arbitrary or capricious to creep in anywhere. As a consequence, Lully developed the best-disciplined group of singers, dancers, and instrumentalists in Europe. Their fame spread far and wide, and from contemporary accounts his orchestra was especially noted for the purity of its intonation, uniform bowing of the strings, accuracy of tempo and measure, and the elegance of its trills and melodic ornaments that were compared to the "sparkling of precious stones."

Practically singlehanded, Lully unified the ballet and founded French opera. His standardization of the sequence of dances became known as the "French suite"; his form of the overture, the "French overture"; and his organization of the opera remained standard practice for almost two centuries. Even though Quinault wrote the texts, Lully's operas may be considered the musical reflection of Racine's tragedies. In them are found the same observance of classical proprieties, the same dignified declamation, the same polished correctness. Their limitations were the inevitable outgrowth of the circumstances of their creation. By being addressed so exclusively to a single social group, they neglected to provide the more resonant human sounding board needed for survival in the repertory. Like Poussin, they remained aloof, restrained, and aristocratic. Opera, however, by its combination of grandiloquent language, emotional appeal, sonorous splendor, majestic movement, and visual elegance, emerges as one of the most magnificent creations of the baroque era.

## IDEAS

The many manifestations of the aristocratic baroque style crystallize mainly around two distinct but interrelated ideas—absolutism and academicism.

**Absolutism**    The concept of the modern unified state, which first emerged in the Spain of Philip II, was adapted to French political purposes by Cardinal Richelieu and ultimately reached its triumphant consummation under Louis XIV. "It is the respect which absolute power demands, that none should question when a king commands," was the way Corneille stated the doctrine in 1637 in his heroic drama *The Cid.* As the principal exponent of monarchical absolutism and the centralized state, Louis XIV, the Sun King, assumed the authority to replace natural and human disorderliness with a reasonable facsimile of cosmic law and order. All human and social activities came under his protectorship, and by taking the arts under his paternal wing, he saw that they served as adjuncts to the cult of majesty. Versailles became the symbol of absolutism, the seat of absolute monarchy, and the personal apotheosis of the King.

Just as political absolutism meant the unification of all social and governmental institutions under one head, its aesthetic counterpart implied the bringing together of all the separate arts into a single rational plan. While *le grand siècle* produced some buildings, statuary, paintings, literature, and music that command attention in their own right, they spoke out most impressively in their combined forms. It is impossible to think of Versailles except as a combination of all art forms woven together into a unified pattern and as a reflection of the life and institutions of the absolute monarchy. The parks, gardens, fountains, statuary, buildings, courtyards, halls, murals, tapestries, furnishings, and recreational activities are all parts of a single coordinated design. As such, Versailles accomplished the daring feat of unifying all visible space and all units of time into a spatio-temporal setting for the aristocratic way of life. Indoor and outdoor space are inseparable, even music and the theater went outdoors. Sculpture was an embellishment of the landscape; painting became the handmaiden of interior design; comedy was allied with ballet; and tragedy was absorbed into opera. All the arts, in fact, were mirrored in the operatic form with its literary lyricism, orchestral rhetoric, dramatic declamation, instrumental interludes, statuesque dancing, architectural stage settings, mechanical marvels, and picturesque posturings. In Lully's hands opera became a kind of microcosm of court life, an absolute art form in which all the separate parts related closely to the whole. None was allowed to dominate, nothing was disproportionate.

The spirit of absolutism was also directly revealed in the drama surrounding the life of the monarch. All the arts took the cue, became theatrical, and sought to surprise and astonish. The purely human element was buried under an avalanche of palatial scenery, pompous wigs, props, and protocol. Only in Molière's satires, La Fontaine's fables, and the secret memoirs of the period is it possible to catch glimpses of a more truthful version of the actualities behind the scenes of courtly life. Otherwise the architecture of Versailles, the statuary of Bernini and Coysevox, the triumphal murals of Lebrun, the tragedies of Racine, and the operas of Lully were all designed to promote the illusion that Louis XIV and his courtiers were beings of heroic stature, powerful will, and grandiose utterance.

**Academicism** While the academic movement began formally with the first French academy during the reign of Louis XIII, it was not until later in the century that the implications of academicism were completely realized and its force fully mobilized. Both Louis XIV and his minister Colbert believed that art was much too important to be left exclusively in the hands of artists. The various academies, therefore, became branches of the government and the arts a part of the civil service. An administrative organization was instituted, topped by the King and director through professors, members, and associates, to the students. Approved principles were taught, and theoretical and practical knowledge communicated by lectures, demonstrations, and discussions. Boileau as the head of the Academy of Language and Literature, Lebrun of the Academy of Painting and Sculpture, Mansart of the Academy of Architecture, and Lully of the Academy of Music were subject directly to the King and were absolute dictators in their respective fields. As such, they were the principal advisers to the King and his ministers, and, in turn, they were responsible for carrying out the royal will. Control of patronage was centered in their hands; theirs was the final word in determining who would receive commissions, appointments, titles, licenses, degrees, pensions, prizes, entrance to art schools, and the privilege of exhibiting in the salons.

The academies were thus the means of transmitting the absolute idea to the aesthetic sphere. Academicism invariably implied a patriarchal principle, whereby regularly constituted arbiters of taste placed their stamp of approval on the products in the various art media. These interpreters of the official point of view inevitably tended to become highly conservative. Aristocratic baroque art was the superpersonal expression of a class whose code of behavior was based on etiquette, politeness, and cultivation of good taste. All personal feeling, capriciousness, and eccentricity had to yield to self-discipline, urbanity, correctness, and accepted standards of good form. The academies were therefore charged with the making of aesthetic definitions, artistic codes, and technical formulas valid for their respective fields. They functioned as a kind of board of directors who decided what was best for the stockholders. They had, moreover, the power to enforce their decisions, which meant that academicism could, at best, establish and maintain a high level of creative quality and, at worst, degenerate into conventionalism and downright regimentation, with varying degrees of standardization in between.

One example will show how academicism worked. Under Lebrun, the Academy of Painting and Sculpture favored the restrained style of Poussin over the passionate exuberance of Rubens. It thereby set up an academic subdivision of the baroque style as opposed to the expression of the free baroque. Many reasons for the choice can, of course, be advanced. Poussin's pictorialism, for instance, may—readily and demonstrably—be reduced to a system of formal values based on geometrical principles, while Rubens' style is so personal, impetuous, voluptuous, and violently emotional that it always remains a bit beyond the grasp. Academicism in this case was trying to tame baroque exuberance and reduce it to formulas and rules. Nothing eccentric, nothing unpredictable was allowed to creep in and destroy the general impression of orderliness. The Academy always remained somewhat skeptical of emotion just as it did of color, since neither was subject to scientific laws. The pictorial standards of the Academy were therefore based on formal purity, demonstrable mathematical relationships, logical definition, and rational analysis. These were the qualities that brought academic art the designation of *classic,* a term that was defined at the time as "belonging to the highest class" and hence approved as a model. Since similar standards were generally to be found in Roman antiquity, classic art and Roman art inevitably became associated. The 17th-century adaptation of Greco-Roman models, however, was quite in the spirit of the time, and hence must not be confused with the archaeological exactitude that was set up as the standard for neoclassicism in the late 18th century and the Napoleonic period.

French academicism was from the start an unqualified practical success. Under the academies, the artistic hegemony of Europe passed from Italy to France where it has effectively remained up to recent times. The hundreds of skilled artists and artisans who were trained on the vast projects of Louis XIV became the founders and teachers of a tradition of high technical excellence. French painting alone, to use the most obvious example, continued its unbroken supremacy from the foundation of the Academy to the 20th century. In Spain, by way of contrast, the only successor to El Greco, Velázquez, and Murillo was the lonely figure of Goya; in Flanders there were no outstanding followers of Rubens and van Dyck except Watteau, who to all intents and purposes was French; in Holland there was no one to take up where Rembrandt and Vermeer had left off. In France, however, painting continued on a high level throughout the 18th and 19th centuries; and, by setting high technical standards, academicism was a determining force even in nonacademic circles. The work of Perrault and Mansart in architecture, Boileau in criticism, Molière in comedy, Racine in tragedy, Lully in opera was also absorbed directly into a tradition that succeeded in setting up measuring rods of symmetry, order, regularity, dignity, reserve, and clarity, which to this day still have a certain validity even if only as points of departure.

# 15 The Bourgeois Baroque Style

## AMSTERDAM, 17TH CENTURY

If a visitor to 17th-century Amsterdam—or any of the other sturdy Dutch towns for that matter—looked about the triumphal arches, pretentious palaces, or military monuments, he was doomed to disappointment. In fact, if there was anything grand at all about life in the Low Countries, it was its complete commonplaceness. After they had achieved their cherished independence by wresting their country town by town and province by province from the grasp of the Spanish despots, the people organized themselves and their government with a minimum of unity and a maximum of diversity. The Netherlanders had no intention whatsoever of substituting one brand of tyranny for another, much less a domestic variety; and so the land became the United Provinces under a *stadtholder*, or "governor." Let their English rivals call them the "united bogs"; their muddy swamps and marshlands were poor things, but at least they were their own. Their wars of independence, geographical isolation, constant struggle against the encroachments of the sea, dour climate, seafaring economy, Calvinist Protestantism, and individualistic temperaments conspired with all the other circumstances of Dutch life to focus the center of interest in the home. A Dutchman's home was not even his castle; it was just his solid, comfortable, plain, brick house. Instead of the cult of majesty, his was the cult of the home.

When Jakob van Ruisdael executed the *Quay at Amsterdam* (Fig. 276), he was painting more than just a view of the old fish market at the end of the broad canal known as the Damrak. In this local variant of the international academic style (compare with Fig. 274), he was in fact picturing the bourgeois way of life in a scene where thrifty housewives were gathering up provisions for their dinner tables; where a part of the fishing fleet that gave the Dutch a monopoly of the pickled and salted herring industry was moored; where, lying at anchor in the distance, there were some of the merchant vessels that helped the Dutch create an efficient modern commerce by plying the seven seas, trading their clay pipes, glazed tiles, Delft pottery.

In such a situation, some families inevitably accumulated more than others, and by means of the wealth that was concentrated in their hands, they became a ruling oligarchy. These so-called "regent" families were the ones from whose ranks the members of the town councils and mayors were selected. They were, however, an upper-middle-class group rather than an aristocracy, and there was safety in their numbers. Their power, together with that of the professional and mercantile societies known as "guilds," depended upon the retention of a maximum of local authority. This decentralization favored the growth of universities—those at Leyden and Utrecht became the most distinguished in Europe—and promoted the careers of such eminent native humanists as Constantijn Huygens, friend and patron of Rembrandt, and Hugo Grotius, founder of the new discipline of international law. The freedom to think and work attracted such foreigners as the French philosopher René Descartes, who resided in Holland for almost twenty years, and the parents of Baruch Spinoza—one of the profoundest human intellects of all time—who found refuge in Amsterdam after the persecution of the Jews had made life intolerable for them in their native Portugal.

The architectural expression of this bourgeois way of life is found in the various town halls, in such mercantile structures as warehouses, countinghouses, and the market building, seen on the extreme right in Figure 276, and, above all, in the long rows of gabled brick houses like those seen on either side of the canal in the same picture. Dating from former times were such ecclesiastical buildings as the Oudekerk, or "Old Church," whose Gothic tower is silhouetted against the sky in the right background; originally Roman Catholic, it had been taken over by the Dutch Reformed Church after the Reformation. As organized under the precepts of John Calvin, the Reformed Church held that religious truth was not the monopoly of any individual or any group, and that the word of God was available to all without the mediation of priestly authority. Through the development of the printing press, every family could have its own Bible, and by means of the high degree of literacy that prevailed almost everyone could read it. As in government, the Dutch people were wary of authority in religion; and as confirmed Protestants, they took rather literally the words of Christ to go into their closets and pray. Thus, through family devotions, hymn singing, and Bible reading, much of the important religious activity took place in the home. According to the teaching of Calvin, the reason for going to church was to hear a sermon and sing the praises of the Lord. No architectural embellishments, statuary, paintings, and professional choirs or orchestras should distract the worshipers' attention. Since commissions were no longer forthcoming from Church and aristocratic sources, the artist, more and more, had to conceive his work in terms of the private dwelling.

The prosperous Dutch families fortunately felt the need of an art that would reflect their healthy materialism and reveal their outlook, their institutions, and their country just as they were—solid, matter-of-fact, and without airs. In this happy state of affairs, patronage was spread on a broad-enough basis so that almost every home had at least a small collection of pictures. In spite of the turbulent times, Dutch art avoided heroic battle scenes just as it did grandiose mythological allegories and complex symbolism. Landscape had a strong attraction, since the Dutch had fought for every inch of their soil, and paintings of their fields, mills, and cottages appealed to their sense of proprietorship. Genre scenes were likewise popular, because such casualness and informality harmonized with their domestic surroundings.

The severe simplicity of still-life compositions also found favor, since quiet arrangements of fruit, flowers, oysters, herrings, ceramics, and textiles were visible evidences of the good life (Pl. 36, p. 250). As men of affairs, the Dutch liked corporation pictures where they were depicted among their fellow directors or board members in a group portrait designed to perpetuate their memory on the walls of some guild hall, professional society, officers' club, or char-

itable trust. Above all, the Dutch burgher wanted family portraits for his living room—commemorative pictures of such family festivals as christenings and weddings; paintings of quiet interiors with his wife or daughter dutifully doing some household chore or, if one of them showed special talent, perhaps playing a musical instrument; and for himself, he liked to be portrayed at his work, surrounded by the perquisites of his worldly position (Fig. 277).

Under Calvinistic austerity, the only professional musicians to survive were the church organists, the hired groups of singers and instrumentalists who performed for weddings, banquets, and parades, and the band of music teachers who taught the younger members of the family to sing and to play the lute, viola da gamba, and keyboard instruments, such as the virginals and spinet. Music, therefore, like all the other aspects of Dutch life, was centered largely in the home. During the Renaissance, the Low Countries had dominated European music with the polyphonic glories of their distinguished composers. Only one musical genius of universal stature was left in the Amsterdam of the early 17th century: Jan Pieterszoon Sweelinck, whose career brought to a brilliant

## General Events

**1517** Protestant Reformation began in Germany

**1535** *Institution of Christian Religion* published by John Calvin (1509–64); Dutch Reformed Chruch established later along Calvinist lines

**1566** Revolt of Netherlands against Spain began

**1575** University of Leyden, first of the Dutch universities, founded by William the Silent, prince of Orange

**1602** Dutch East India Company organized

**1618– 1648** Thirty Years' War; 1609 Low Countries given virtual independence in truce with Spain; full independence under Treaty of Westphalia (1648)

**1621** Dutch West India Company founded

**1624** *Tablatura Nova* by Samuel Scheidt

**1629– 1648** René Descartes resided in Holland

**1630– 1687** Limited public art patronage dispensed through Constantijn Huygens

**1631** Rembrandt settled in Amsterdam

**1637** *Discourse on Method* published in Leyden by Descartes

**1642** Dutch explorer Tasman discovered New Zealand

**1644** *Principles of Philosophy* published by Descartes in Amsterdam

**1648** Independence of Netherlands recognized by Treaty of Westphalia

**1652– 1674** Anglo-Dutch commercial wars

**1670** Spinoza published *Tractatus theologica-politicus*

## Painters

**c.1580– 1666** Frans Hals
**1606– 1669** Rembrandt van Rijn
**c.1617– 1681** Gerhardt Terborch
**c.1628– 1682** Jakob van Ruisdael
**c.1629– 1679** Jan Steen
**c.1629– 1683** Pieter de Hooch
**1632– 1675** Jan Vermeer van Delft

## Philosophers and Scientists

**1467– 1536** Desiderius Erasmus
**1583– 1645** Hugo Grotius, founder of international law
**1596– 1650** René Descartes

**1629– 1695** Christian Huygens
**1632– 1677** Baruch Spinoza

## Writers

**1587– 1679** Joost van den Vondel, Dutch dramatist and author of *Lucifer*, poem similar to Milton's *Paradise Lost*
**1596– 1687** Constantijn Huygens, poet, humanist, diplomat

## Musicians

**1562– 1621** Jan Pieterszoon Sweelinck. *English School*
**c.1542– 1623** William Byrd
**c.1562– 1628** John Bull, organist at Antwerp (1617–28), friend of Sweelinck
**c.1562– 1638** Francis Pilkington
**c.1576– 1643** Henry Peacham, author of *Compleat Gentleman*, teacher and composer
**1583– 1625** Orlando Gibbons. *German School*
**1587– 1654** Samuel Scheidt, pupil of Sweelinck
**1596– 1663** Heinrich Scheidemann, pupil of Sweelinck
**1623– 1722** J. A. Reinken, successor of Scheidemann at Hamburg, and influencer of J. S. Bach
**1685– 1750** Johann Sebastian Bach
**1685– 1759** George Frederick Handel

---

close the radiant chapter of Dutch music that had dominated the Renaissance.

All the arts were thus centered in the home. The simple and unpretentious Dutch dwelling with its polished tiled floors, tidy interiors, and window boxes for the tulips was the modest framework for this bourgeois way of life. Unless ceramics are included, there was little sculpture other than a few figurines on the mantelpiece and an occasional statuette. The primary aesthetic indulgences of the Dutch were their pictures and domestic music-making, while such objects as their Delft pottery jugs, tablecloths, laces, and draperies enriched their world of qualities. The reality of daily life was made up of the routine of the business establishment, the market place, and the household. It was a reality of simple truths in which nothing was too small to be overlooked. All things, even the most insignificant, were considered to be gifts of God; and, as such, they were studied in the Holland of the 17th century in the minutest detail.

## PAINTING

Towering above all other Dutch painters, because of the breadth of his vision, the power of his characterizations, and the uncompromising integrity of his ideals, stands the figure of Rembrandt van Rijn in lonely eminence. Like his contemporaries, Rembrandt painted portraits, genre scenes, historical subjects, and landscapes, but unlike them he refused to specialize and succeeded magnificently in all. Furthermore, he brought a new psychological profundity to his portraiture, an unaccustomed animation to his genre scenes, a greater dramatic intensity to his religious pictures, and a broader sweep to his landscapes than had been achieved before in the northern tradi-

**278.** Rembrandt. *Dr. Tulp's Anatomy Lesson.* 1632. Oil on canvas, 5'3⅜" × 7'1¼". Mauritshuis, The Hague.

tion. His discoveries of the power of light, in all its varying degrees, to illuminate character both from without and from within, to define space by the interpenetration of light, and to animate that space by the flowing movement of shadows identify him as a prime mover in the establishment of the northern baroque pictorial style. Rembrandt's art as a whole exhibits a consistent growth from his early to his late years in the capacity to penetrate appearances, to discover and reveal the spiritual forces that lie beneath.

Soon after he settled in Amsterdam, the 26-year-old painter received his first important assignment from the local Guild of Surgeons and Physicians. The result was *Dr. Tulp's Anatomy Lesson* (Fig. 278), a composition that combines group portraiture of the so-called "corporation type" with the anatomy pictures of the medieval and Renaissance tradition. The subjects in this case were the heads of the guild and other prominent citizens, whose names are duly recorded on the sheet of paper held by the figure in the center.

In his painting, Rembrandt's grouping of figures and placement of the heads on different levels impart a certain freedom and informality to the composition. By the use of light, the artist develops the inherent drama of the situation, and by the expression on each of the faces shows reactions that vary from intense concentration to casual indifference. The fullest light is focused on the cadaver and on the hands of Dr. Nicholas Tulp, the professor of anatomy who is giving the lecture. The large open book at the feet of the corpse is quite possibly a recent edition of Vesalius' *Anatomy*. This universally recognized authority was the work of the Dutch scientist Andries van

Wesel (1514–64), who had taught and held just such demonstrations at the University of Padua. Since Dr. Tulp styled himself *Vesalius redivivus* ("Vesalius revived"), the allusion is appropriate. In sum, Rembrandt's dramatization of the spirit of scientific inquiry is a vivid product of a period that has been called the Age of Observation.

Exactly a decade elapsed between the *Anatomy Lesson* and the *Sortie of Captain Banning Cocq's Company* (Pl. 37, p. 250), Rembrandt's masterpiece of the corporation type. Group portraits of such military units that had fought against the Spaniards were common enough at the time to have the designation of "musketeer pictures." Once their original purpose in the struggle for independence was gone, many of these companies continued as parts of the civic guard and as officers' clubs, available as the occasion warranted for anything from emergency duty to a parade. By 1642, most members had become prosperous shopkeepers, who hugely enjoyed dressing up now and then in their dashing uniforms, polishing their shooting irons, and posing as warriors in processions or civic celebrations. In "musketeer pictures," they were usually shown in convivial situations, such as gathered around a banquet table, but in order to get life and movement into his picture, Rembrandt discarded this rather stilted pose and chose to show Captain Cocq's company in action, as if responding to a call to arms. The life-size figures are therefore seen moving out of the city gate before falling into formation.

Popularly known as *The Night Watch*, the painting, thanks to a recent cleaning, has proved to be a "Day Watch" instead. The varnish that had darkened in the an acid solution. When the coating is removed and the plate inked, an etching is made by transferring the inked impression on the metal plate to paper. In this example, the gradations of light and dark run from such inky blackness as that behind the figure of Christ to the whiteness of the untouched paper, like that of the rock in the extreme left. Rembrandt's true artistic stature is revealed in the way his art scales the heights of moral grandeur within severe limitations. The expressive power of this print is as great as the medium is small.

Rembrandt was brought up in a family of Anabaptists who tried to live according to strict Biblical precepts. His religious subjects are seen from a Protestant point of view and, as such, show an intimate personal knowledge of the Scriptures. Since he was not painting for churches, and thus was under no compulsion to conform to the usual iconographical tradition of Madonnas and Child, Crucifixions, and so on, he was free to develop new themes and new points of view. Much of the intimacy and effectiveness of such free works is owed to the fact that they were not conceived as public showpieces. Rembrandt also loved to explore the Amsterdam ghetto and found subjects for his paintings among the descendents of the people who created the Old Testament.

Rembrandt is known to have painted at least 62 self-portraits, surely a record number. The motivation, however, came more from a deep introspective tendency than from personal vanity. Besides, no model was more readily available. Extending from young manhood to his last year, his likenesses of himself read like a pictorial autobiography. After successfully establishing himself in Amsterdam and after his marriage to Saskia van Uylenburch, daughter of a wealthy family, Rembrandt enjoyed a period of material prosperity. In cavalier costume and exuberant mood, he paints himself with his young wife sitting on his knee as he lifts his glass in a toast (Fig. 280).

From 1640 on, Rembrandt sustained a series of tragedies, beginning with his mother's death, which was followed two years later by that of Saskia shortly after the birth of their son Titus. By 1650 artistic tastes had changed, but Rembrandt resolutely followed his own genius, making no concessions to fickle fashions. The penetrating look in the self-image reproduced as Figure 281, glowing with an internal light, peers into the depths of his own character and seems to be asking, "Whither now?" From this time onward, Rembrandt realized more and more that his mission was to explore the world of the imagination and leave the world of appearances to others. Consequently, his countenance bespeaks the serenity of a man who, having chosen his course, knows there is no turning back. Financial troubles increased as debts piled up, and from 1656 to 1660 the artist went through bankruptcy. His fine house with its furnishings, his personal collections of paintings, prints, armor, and

course of time and the original placement near a large fireplace were responsible for the general gloom. Now the free flow of light can be seen moving rhythmically throughout the whole composition, pervading every corner with dynamic gradations ranging from dark to bright. The light is most intense in the center, where Captain Cocq is explaining the plans to his lieutenant, whose uniform catches the rays of the morning sun. As a counterbalance, Rembrandt places the whimsical figure of a young girl in gleaming cream-colored satin at the captain's other side. Strung from her belt are a powder horn and a white cockerel, possibly a Rembrandtian pun on the captain's name. The shadow of Captain Cocq's hand falling across the lieutenant's uniform defines the source of light, that, in turn, blends together and relates all the other figures to the central pair by the intensity of the light illuminating them. Such virtuosity in the handling of light and shadow was one of Rembrandt's unique achievements.

The etching *Christ Healing the Sick* (Fig. 279), familiarly known as the "Hundred Guilder Print," is an example of Rembrandt's several hundred works in what was then a popular medium in the visual arts. Financially, the relatively modest price of an etching assured Rembrandt of some income—and a fairly wide distribution of his work—at those times when his paintings piled up unsold in his studio. (The price in the case of this etching was a record rather than a rule.) Technically, the medium of etching gave Rembrandt the opportunity to explore the qualities of light in simple line patterns independent of pigments and colors. By scratching a coated metal plate with a stylus, an artist makes a linear pattern that is etched, or bitten, into the metal upon immersion in artistic props all were sold to satisfy creditors. At this point (Fig. 282), the searching gaze of the luminous eyes begins to turn inward in self-appraisal as he forthrightly assesses his moral and artistic progress. The last years were saddened by the deaths of his faithful friend and housekeeper Hendrickje Stoeffels (1662) and his son Titus (1668). Still working incessantly, Rembrandt in his last self-portrait shows the familiar face marked by illness and resignation but still full of the deep human compassion that marked his life and art (Fig. 283).

**above: 280.** REMBRANDT. *Self-portrait with Saskia.* c. 1634. Oil on canvas, 5'3½" × 4'3½". Gemäldegalerie, Dresden.

**left: 281.** REMBRANDT. *Self-portrait.* 1650. Oil on canvas, 34¾ × 28". National Gallery of Art, Washington, D.C. (Widener Collection, 1942).

**right: 282.** REMBRANDT. *Self-portrait.* 1656–58. Oil on wood, 20 × 16". Kunsthistorisches Museum, Vienna.

**far right: 283.** REMBRANDT. *Old Self-portrait.* 1669. Oil on canvas, 23¼ × 20¾". Mauritshuis, The Hague.

Between the polar extremes of the introspective Rembrandt and the detached Vermeer is the gamut of subjects and moods projected by their contemporaries. While Rembrandt sought to portray the spirit of the whole man, Frans Hals was content to capture human individuality in a fleeting glance or a casual gesture. In his early work he was more interested in appearances than essences. Later, when he came under the influence of Rembrandt's soul-searching, he gave up his vivid colors and light touch for somber hues and serious subjects. The infectious gaiety of his *Merry Lute Player* is typical of Hals' carefree early period (Fig. 284). With tousled hair and cap cocked at a jaunty angle, the subject might well be an entertainer at a public tavern. The way the glass of sparkling wine is held reveals the source of light, which strikes both face and instrument. In similar pictures the people of Hals' native Haarlem—quarreling fishwives, carousing officers, and tipsy merrymakers—live again with all their animal vitality and capacity for life.

Pieter de Hooch's *Mother and Child* is a quiet study of domestic life in a proper household (Fig. 285). Like his fellow painters, de Hooch knew that light was the magnet which attracted the eye and that its vibrations gave such an interior its share of life and movement.

left: 284. FRANS HALS. *Merry Lute Player.* c. 1627. Oil on canvas, 35½ × 29½". Private collection.

right: 285. PIETER DE HOOCH. *Mother and Child.* c. 1660. Oil on canvas, 20¾ × 24". Rijksmuseum, Amsterdam.

But de Hooch works with a subdued light that matches the tranquility of his subject matter. Sunlight streams inward from the open Dutch door at the back and the window at the upper right. By this means the artist separates his three receding planes without ambiguity; explores the contrasting textures of the tile flooring, transparent glass, varnished wood surfaces, soft textiles, and metallic brilliance of the copper bedwarmer; as well as reveals the figures of mother, daughter, and dog. De Hooch's world is more static than Rembrandt's, his figures less animated than Hals', and his pictorial geometry more casual than Vermeer's. Yet each of his interiors has the timeless tranquility of a still life, with figures and objects blending together in their Dutch domestic surroundings to make a compositional whole.

Jakob van Ruisdael's somber study of a cemetery belongs to the category of the landscapes that meant so much to the Dutch people who had fought persistently for their country against the Spanish oppressors. While his *Quay at Amsterdam* is a forthright cityscape, exact in its descriptive detail (Fig. 276), Ruisdael in *The Jewish Graveyard* seems to be searching for deeper symbolic values (Fig. 286). The setting was the Jewish graveyard at the Oudekerk in Amsterdam, but to heighten the mood of his picture the painter invents many imaginary picturesque details. The abandoned ruins of the old castle and the skeletonlike trunks of two dead trees, which were not in the actual scene, unite with the white stone slabs of the tombs to permeate the picture with thoughts of death. The inscriptions on the headstones—several of which are still there—remind the viewer that the religious toleration of the Netherlands made the country the haven for the Jewish refugees from the Spanish and Portuguese inquisitions. Ruisdael projects a depth of feeling as well as of space into this landscape. With the waterfall and gnarled trees groping toward the threatening sky, he captures something of the sublimity of nature that sweeps both man and all his works before it. His eye for the picturesque anticipates certain aspects of 19th-century romanticism.

In his *View of Delft* Jan Vermeer van Delft painted the profile of his native city (Fig. 287). From the people strolling in the lower left foreground, the artist carries the eye across the canal, along the line of mercantile buildings and houses behind the city wall on the left, past the stone bridge in the center with the steeple of the church rising in the background, to the moored boats and drawbridge on the extreme right. Vermeer's treatment of space is seen in this horizontal sweep, which makes no attempt to draw the eye into deep background space. The effectiveness of the picture is greatly enhanced by the subtle treatment of light and color. As the sunshine filters through the broken clouds, the light falls unevenly over the landscape, varying from the shadowy foreground and the dull red of the brick buildings, through the flame and orange tones in the sunny distance, to the brilliant gleam of the church tower. More than half the area of the picture is allotted to the ever-changing Dutch sky, where patches of blue alternate with the silvery and leaden grays of the clouds, while the waters below reflect the mirror image of the town.

With meticulousness and economy of means, Jan Vermeer also painted a group of interior scenes, such as *Officer and Laughing Girl* (Fig. 288). Here Vermeer's logical organization of rectangles and intersecting surfaces is somewhat softened by the prominence given to the conversing figures. The daring camera-like perspective projects the figure of the officer forward and gives greater size to his large slouch hat and head than to that of the girl. His red coat and

left: 286. JAKOB VAN RUISDAEL. *The Jewish Graveyard.* c. 1660. Oil on canvas, 4'8'' × 6'2¼''. Detroit Institute of Arts.

above: 287. JAN VERMEER. *View of Delft.* c. 1658. Oil on canvas, 38¾ × 46¼''. Mauritshuis, The Hague.

brandt tries to penetrate the world of appearances, Vermeer is content with the visual image. With his warm personal quality, Rembrandt embraces humanity as completely as Vermeer's cool impersonality encompasses space. Rembrandt is concerned at all times with moral beauty, Vermeer with physical perfection. Rembrandt's inner dramas need only the monochromatic crescendo of a single color from deep brown to golden yellow or in an etching from black to white, while Vermeer's absence of drama demands the entire chromatic spectrum. Like a philosopher, Rembrandt lays the soul bare in his moving characterizations, while Vermeer, like a jeweler, delights the eye with his unique perception of the quality and texture of things. Thus, in Holland, as well as in both Spain and France, the 17th century, like a stormy March, had been swept in on the leonine gusts of free baroque flamboyance and had gone out on a gentle lamblike academic breeze.

## MUSIC

The one great musician of 17th-century Holland was Jan Pieterszoon Sweelinck, who succeeded his father and was, in turn, succeeded by his son as organist at the Oudekerk, so that the family rounded out a century of music making there. Under the strict tenets of Calvinism, church music consisted mainly of the congregational singing of psalms and hymns, preferably unaccompanied. As such, the development of music as an art would have been ruled out were it not for the fact that Dutch tradition favored the organ, and the organist was allowed to play preludes and postludes on sacred themes before and after the service. On special occasions, choral settings of the psalms with some degree of elaboration were performed. Sweelinck's viewpoint, like that of the other Dutch composers of the century, was international in scope. He apparently had studied in Venice with Zarlino and Andrea Gabrieli and was a colleague of the famous Giovanni Gabrieli. He had also visited England and was thoroughly familiar with the English keyboard school and choral-composing tradition. His official title was Organist of Amsterdam, and as such his duties included the giving of public concerts. The Oudekerk, according to contemporary accounts, was always crowded on these occasions, and large audiences took delight in his improvisations and variations on sacred and secular themes; the baroque flourishes of his Venetian toccatas; his fantasies "in the manner of an echo," a keyboard adaptation of the Venetian double-choral style; and the choral preludes and fugues that he built on Protestant hymn tunes.

sash also contrast noticeably with the cooler colors of the girl's white cap, black and yellow bodice, and blue apron that allow her figure to recede. The map on the wall is painted with the greatest care in relation to the light and angle of the wall. Its Latin title is quite clear, and reads: "New and Accurate Map of all Holland and West Friesland." The warm, rich, natural light that streams in from the open casement window gives both unity and life to the severe division of planes. It bathes every object and pervades every corner of the room, starting with the maximum intensity of the area adjacent to the source and tapering off by degrees into the cool bluish tones of the shadows in the lower right.

Almost always content to let objects and situations speak for themselves, Vermeer, on rare occasions, ventures into the realm of symbolism. *Artist in His Studio* is, to be sure, a self-portrait, and the studio is his own (Pl. 38, p. 267). The lady, however, personifies Fame, and the artist is starting his picture with her laurel wreath to indicate his pursuit of beauty and immortality. The trumpet, as if to sound a fanfare for a famous person, is one of Fame's attributes; and the book in her arm and the volumes and death mask on the table add a literary and sculptural dimension to this allegory of the arts.

The contrast between Rembrandt's restless searching spirit and Vermeer's sober, objective detachment is fully as great as that between El Greco and Velázquez, or Rubens and Poussin. Rembrandt's light is the glow of the burning human spirit, Vermeer's that from the open casement window. Rem-

**right: Plate 38.** Jan Vermeer. *Artist in His Studio.* c. 1665–70. Oil on canvas, 4'4" × 3'8". Kunsthistorisches Museum, Vienna. (See p. 266.)

**below: Plate 39.** Antoine Watteau. *Gersaint's Signboard.* 1720–21. Oil on canvas, 5'3⅞" × 10'1". State Museums, West Berlin. (See p. 288.)

**left: Plate 40.** Jean Honoré Fragonard. *The Swing.* c. 1766–69. Oil on canvas, 32 × 25½″ Wallace Collection, London. (See p. 288.)

**below: Plate 41.** Jean Baptiste Siméon Chardin. *Still Life: Bowl of Plums.* 1759. Oil on canvas, 17¾ × 22½″. Phillips Collection, Washington, D.C. (See p. 288.)

The other public Dutch music was of the occasional type, given by choral groups and instrumental ensembles that, for a modest price, would furnish anything from the madrigals sung at weddings to the dances played at receptions. All available evidence points to the home as the center of the major part of the musical life of the time. Most of the extant compositions from this period are found in the numerous manuscript copies that were made for home use. Printed scores, however, were obtainable from Venice and London, and early in the 17th century music printing began to flourish in Antwerp, Leyden, and Amsterdam. Holland also became noted as a center for the manufacture of musical instruments. The musical practices of the times can be vividly reconstructed by combining the surviving scores and musical instruments with the rich visual evidence available in the paintings of the period.

Vermeer's *Concert*, for one, shows a typical musical situation in the home (Fig. 289). The trio is made up of a young woman, who reads her song part from the score she holds in her hand; a seated man, who supplies the harmonic background on his theorbo, a species of the lute; and a girl at the spinet, the winged version of the virginals, who plays the keyboard part. On the floor is a viola da gamba, somewhat like the modern 'cello; had it a player, this instrument would serve here to duplicate the bass line of the keyboard part in a combination known as the *continuo*.

**289.** Jan Vermeer. *Concert.* c. 1660. Oil on canvas, 28 × 24$\frac{3}{4}$". Isabella Stewart Gardner Museum, Boston.

*Now Peep, Boe Peep* (1605)   Francis Pilkington

The widespread custom of domestic music-making resulted in a large body of literature that was designed for home rather than public performance. Since such music always had a friendly, sociable basis, it was mainly for two or more participants. Even the solo pieces were written for amateurs and purposely avoided any complexities that might imply showing off. The attitude is well summed up in *The Compleat Gentleman*, published in London in 1622 by the English schoolmaster Henry Peacham. "I desire no more in you," he said, "than to sing your part at first sight; withal to play the same upon your Viol, or the exercise of the Lute, privately to yourself."

An example of the type of music Mr. Peacham's gentlemen were prepared to perform is "Now Peep, Boe Peep," by Francis Pilkington, a number from that composer's *First Booke of Ayres*, published in 1605. The score was arranged and printed so that the participants could be seated comfortably around a table. On the left side, the words and melody of the Canto, in this case the soprano part, appear above the lute tablature. To their right sits the tenor opposite the alto, with the bass in between. A transcription of the beginning of the piece is given above.

One of the interesting things about such a work is the great number of ways it can be performed. In its complete form, it is a vocal quartet with a lute accompaniment that duplicates the three lower parts. It also can be performed as a soprano solo with lute accompaniment; a cappella—that is, for four voices without the lute; as a duet for soprano and any one of the other voices; as a lute solo; as an instrumental piece with viols instead of voices; as a combination of voices and viols; as an instrumental ensemble with doublings of the parts; or with wind instruments substituting for the voices and viols; and so on practically ad infinitum. Such music had to be adaptable to the size, skill, and instrumental capability of any group that might gather together for an evening of musical pleasure in the home.

Keyboard music—for organ, virginals, spinet, clavichord, and harpsichord—was distinctively northern in character. Sweelinck had absorbed both the Venetian and English traditions, and his organ playing attracted to Amsterdam students from all over northern Europe. Through them his influence was widely extended, especially over the Protestant parts of Germany. His most noted pupil here was Samuel Scheidt of Halle, whose *Tablatura Nova*, published in 1624, did much to crystallize the German Protestant organ and choral style. In this book, all the technical procedures he had learned from Sweelinck were brought together and worked out with characteristic Germanic thoroughness. Happily, however, they were coupled with a considerable degree of creative imagination as well as technical invention. In its pages are found compositions intended for home performance, mainly in the form of variations. French and Flemish secular songs as well as dances, like the *allemande, paduan, courant,* and *gaillard,* appear with variants that are full of the complexities which so intrigued the baroque mind. The first two parts of Scheidt's book also contain fugues, echo fantasies, and chorales, while the third is concerned with harmonizations of Lutheran hymns and Protestant chorales with ornamental commentaries in the form of variations. Scheidt's work became a landmark in organ literature, since it assimilated and systematized the ornate Venetian manner, the English keyboard variation style, and Sweelinck's contrapuntal ingenuity. It brought together for the first time a collection of pieces admirably adapted for Protestant church purposes, and a number of musical models for other composers to emulate. A direct line thus extended from Sweelinck, who coordinated the Venetian and English schools, through such pupils as Scheidt, who transmitted the tradition to northern Germany, where Johann Sebastian Bach and George Frederick Handel were born in the year 1685.

## IDEAS: DOMESTICITY

The various aspects of the bourgeois baroque style find a common undercurrent in the idea of domesticity. Many related ideas, such as mercantilism, Protestantism, anti-authoritarianism, nationalism, individualism, the ardent championship of individual rights and liberties, and the practical application of scientific discoveries, converge on this central concept, but the unity lies in the cult of the home. Bourgeois house comforts, for instance, were never so highly cultivated in the warmer, friendlier south, where recreational activity can occur in the open air, while the northern climate was conducive to the concentration of communal pleasures in the home.

The spirit of commerce led to navigational adventure on the high seas and to the exploration of distant lands. The conquests of the Dutch, however, were mainly those of the businessmen; their empire was based on corporate enterprise; and their personal kingdoms were those of the banking houses and holding companies. Hard work and industriousness coupled with frugality led to a widespread accumulation of wealth in the hands of the middle class. No riotous living or public displays of luxury were possible when the church permitted no embellishment in its buildings and no musical elaboration in its services. While both the Anglican and Lutheran reform movements preserved much of the beauty of the traditional Roman Catholic liturgy in a modified form, Calvinistic Protestantism was marked by its extreme austerity. A strict interpretation of Calvinism would lead directly to a gloomy form of asceticism, but the innate good sense and honest enjoyment of material pleasures saved the Dutch from the bleaker aspects of this doctrine. But the principal outlet for their prosperity and desire for aesthetic enjoyment was their homes.

The wealthy burgher, however, did not build a palace—though he certainly had the means to do so. He was content with a comfortable house that was functionally suited to his needs. Fighting the Spanish crown for their independence, and resisting the growing menace of Louis XIV's absolute state, made the Dutch look with disfavor on any form of courtly pomp and ostentation. The Protestant movement also fortified their hostility to authority and intensified their nationalist consciousness. The middle-class merchant particularly resented the draining off of his province's wealth in the direction of Rome, and the resentment was equally strong against the secular arm of the Roman Catholic Church: the Holy Roman Empire. Protestantism thus took root and became identified in the Dutch mind with patriotism. The protection of their national rights, together with their individual freedoms, further focused attention on their homes where they were their own lords and masters.

Philosophy, philology, social theory, and the natural sciences flourished in the Dutch universities. These intellectual pursuits speculated on the existence of an ordered and regulated universe in which everything could be measured and understood. The solid citizen instinctively distrusted the physical and emotional forces that could render his world chaotic and unpredictable. Hence, an ideal universe had considerable appeal for a bourgeoisie whose security and comforts could be perpetuated by it. Descartes' rationalistic cosmology and psychology and Spinoza's mathematically demonstrable ethical system paralleled the concept of art as a form of reasoned organization, but it took a Rembrandt to illuminate this age of reason with an inner glow and to warm this rational world with the fire of human feeling.

Human anatomy was of consuming interest, and with Vesalius' *Anatomy* as a point of departure, dissection was carried over analogously into other fields. Books appeared with such titles as *Anatomy of Melancholy, Anatomy of Wit, Anatomy of Abuses, Anatomy of*

290. Jan Steen. *Merry Family.* 1668. Oil on canvas, $3'7\frac{1}{4}''$ × $4'7\frac{1}{2}''$. Rijksmuseum, Amsterdam.

*the World.* In this Age of Observation, the restless human eye extended by the lens could explore a plurality of worlds, and more things were seen in heaven and earth than were ever dreamed of before. Optical instruments were developed by the skilled lens makers of Holland, whose ranks included Spinoza. An astronomical observatory was constructed at the University of Leyden, where the telescope could scan the skies. Conversely, the microscope opened up a new world in miniature. Though their eyes were on the heavens, Dutch savants did not neglect earthly applications of their discoveries. Astronomical calculations led to the discovery of triangulation and the spiral balance, both of vast value to navigation. The pendulum was applied to the keeping of time, and the pocket watch gave punctuality to daily life.

The circumstances of the Dutch state of mind and material prosperity led to the placement of artistic patronage in the hands of a well-to-do middle class. Outside such necessary public buildings as the town halls, churches, and mercantile structures, Dutch architecture was, for all intents and purposes, domestic architecture. Since the houses were about the same size as middle-class homes today, they provided neither room nor opportunity for monumental sculpture. The major domestic aesthetic expressions occurred, therefore, in painting and music, together with all the minor decorative arts that added to the comfort and beauty of the home. Destined for living-room walls, pictures were correspondingly smaller than those painted for palaces and public halls. Easel pictures rather than murals became the norm for Dutch painting. There was a seemingly insatiable demand for pictures and the output was prodigious. The number of professional artists multiplied with the demand and led to a corresponding degree of specialization. In portraiture there were the painters of the decorous *pater familias* types, of the winebibbers in public tav-

erns, and of corporation pictures. There were landscapists, seascapists, skyscapists, and even those whose specialty was cows. Painters also gravitated to the various social levels, with Jan Steen painting ribald tavern scenes (Fig. 290); Frans Hals finding his subjects among fishwives and fruit peddlers; de Hooch and Vermeer depicting scenes in proper middle-class homes; and Terborch delighting in upper-class manners and elegant society portraiture.

The character of music was likewise molded by bourgeois patronage. In free cities, the organist and other municipal musicians were chosen by committees of the town councils, which supervised the musical life of the community as diligently as any of its other aspects. Auditions were held and competition encouraged. Public employment from the musician's point of view meant freedom from the arbitrary whims of a single aristocratic patron, and this was generally preferred because of the security it implied. When the tastes of the many had to be taken into consideration, however, experimentation tended to be suppressed and standardization often was promoted. This was balanced to a great extent by the opportunities for music making in the home, where musical expression took on a distinct domestic coloration.

The home was thus the factor that determined the art forms and imparted to them such an intimate character and quality. Dutch domestic architecture, painting, and music were all designed to be lived with and enjoyed by middle-class people who frankly took delight in their physical comforts and the arts that enriched their lives. Large canvases designed for altarpieces or to cover palace ceilings, colossal choral compositions for cathedrals, and operatic performances for palaces could produce grandiose oratorical utterances but had no place in the home. The more modest dimensions of a painting or an etching intended for a living-room wall or of a chamber sonata or solo keyboard piece meant to be played in the same room encouraged a more intimate and personal form of communication. The choice of medium is analogous to a composer's selection of the modern symphony orchestra for his epical pronouncements and of a chamber-music group or a piano sonata for his more confidential statements. The home was the dominant architectural form as well as the place where the pictures were hung, the books read, and the music played. In Holland and the northern countries generally, the baroque style was adapted both to Protestantism and to the tastes of the middle class. The bourgeois aspect of baroque art finds it unity in the cult of the home, and domesticity is the key to its understanding.

# 16 The Baroque Synthesis

## LONDON DURING THE RESTORATION

That day in the year of our Lord 1661, as Charles II made his triumphal progress to Westminster Abbey for his coronation, the sounds of Mr. Matthew Locke's march music for the sackbuts and cornets mingled with the cordial cheers of Charles' subjects. They were the cheers of a people wearied by a generation of civil strife and the effort of conforming to the rigors of puritanical idealism. They were the cheers of a people who hoped and prayed that the Restoration would bring them peace and normalcy. They were the cheers of a people who did not know that a few years hence their numbers would be decimated by an outbreak of the dreaded bubonic plague; that their city would be leveled by the Great Fire of London; and that the Restoration, which was supposed to be bringing back the old order, was actually ushering in the new.

The picture of a period embellished by a merry monarch, libertine lords, licentious ladies, and amorous adventurers has been painted all too often. That of a time which vibrated to the thunder of John Milton's poetry, spoke with the polished rhetoric of John Dryden, wondered at the mathematical ingenuity of Isaac Newton's equations, marveled at the majesty of Christopher Wren's architecture, and heard the harmonies of Henry Purcell's music has received much less attention. Even the Merry Monarch had a serious side, developed through the trials and tribulations of a troubled youth (during which his father's stormy reign had led to Charles I's losing his head) and throughout his exile in France where his most formative and impressionable years were spent. Charles II was an amateur astronomer, whose enthusiasm led to the founding of the Greenwich Observatory; a patron of the theater, whose interest played an important role in the development of the Restoration drama; a connoisseur of the arts, whose support of Christopher Wren led to an architectural rebirth in England; and a music lover, who took pride now and then in lifting his voice in song in what has been described politely as a "plump bass." Thus, in 1661, Charles II's years at Louis XIV's court were about to pay off handsomely, because in addition to some questionable absolutistic political ideas and some doubtful French courtly morals, he had brought back with him a goodly measure of Continental enthusiasm for the arts. During his reign, London was to become as much a cultural suburb of Versailles as the common sense of his subjects would bear.

London had caught a brief glimpse of Continental elegance under James I, Charles II's grandfather, who had commissioned Inigo Jones to build the Banqueting House at Whitehall as the first unit of a projected royal palace (Fig. 291). Modeled on Palladian principles, this structure marked a new departure in English architecture. When the great Peter Paul Rubens arrived in England on a diplomatic mission, he was persuaded by Charles I to paint the Banqueting Hall ceiling. Anthony van Dyck, Rubens' most famous pupil, was appointed by Charles to paint a series of family portraits (Fig. 292). Now, on the restoration of the Stuart line and under Charles II, the gates were about to be flung wide open.

Nicholas Laniere was dispatched to Italy to purchase pictures for the royal collections. William Davenant, who had been a guest in Paris of Charles and his mother and had closely observed Lully's musical methods, was summoned to become England's first opera manager. When the French opera composer Robert Cambert was outmaneuvered at home by the wily Lully, he found a ready welcome at the English court. Pelham Humfrey, a promising young composer of 17 and later the teacher of Purcell, was sent to Paris by Charles to see how Lully managed his orchestra and ballet. Since Louis XIV had his *Vingt-quatre Violons,* Charles II would have his Four-and-twenty Fiddles. When the monarch was looking around for a poet laureate, the choice fell to Dryden who was most familiar with Boileau and the French baroque drama. And when Charles heard that King Louis and Colbert were getting ready to remodel the Louvre, he saw to it that Wren was on the spot to study the plans and to meet Bernini and Perrault.

London at the time of the Restoration had a character all its own. The city's population of merchants and clerks was independent of both clergy and monarchy. Living above their shops and countinghouses, this conservative middle class was driven by an "act of God" to change its city, when in 1666 a fire destroyed, according to Samuel Pepys, 13,000 houses, 400 streets, and 90 churches. Before the smoke cleared, Christopher Wren was sketching plans for the city's reconstruction, and even though his ideas were only partially realized, they nonetheless determined the later 17th-century architecture of London and gave the city its superb skyline (Fig. 300).

The collision between the staunch middle-class citizenry and their foreign-bred King brought further tangible proof of the English genius for compromise. The Stuarts from the beginning had tried to impose the Continental concept of absolutism on their reluctant subjects. The extremes of Charles I and his failure to come to terms with the middle-class merchants and their official body, the House of Commons, had brought about the Cromwellian Commonwealth. The uncompromising Oliver Cromwell on his side had alienated the still-powerful aristocracy. Charles II had some success in trying to find a middle ground. His successor James II, however, again overstepped his prerogatives, and it took still another revolution—this time the bloodless Glorious Revolution—to bring about the alliance between the sovereign and the middle class under the formula of a limited monarchy.

Much the same struggle is mirrored in the arts. The French aristocratic baroque, just like the absolute monarchy, was too rich for the English diet. When it came time to build a new cathedral, Charles and his principal architect, Sir Christopher Wren, thought in terms of the richly embellished classical orders, the splendor and spaciousness of the Louvre and Versailles, and the central-church plans of Palladio and Michelangelo. The Church of England clergy and their lay advisors, however, still thought of a cathedral as a tall, imposing Gothic structure. Wren wanted it to be crowned with a dome; the churchmen thought it should have a spire. So Wren built his dome and put a high lantern tower on top of it. Charles wanted the London parish churches to be free of Gothic gauntness and gloom, but the parishioners insisted on belfries with tall-spired steeples. So Wren gave them their steeples, but with classical geometrical flourishes. Charles wanted Lullian opera, but

London theater-goers showed remarkable resistance toward sung recitative. So they got a hybrid form of spoken dialogue interspersed with songs and instrumental interludes.

With political authority divided between the monarch and parliament, literary precedents between the classical and Elizabethan traditions, architectural ideas between the French baroque and English Gothic, and musical expression between the latest Continental developments and native preferences, the British genius for compromise effected a synthesis of aristocratic and middle-class institutions, Roman Catholicism and Protestantism, as well as the Continental and English traditions. Through the efforts and genius of three men—Wren in architecture, Dryden in literature, and Purcell in music—the Continental influences were assimilated with native traditions and synthesized into a distinctive Restoration style.

**above: 291.** INIGO JONES. Banqueting House, Whitehall, London. 1619–22. Length 120', height 75'.

**left: 292.** ANTHONY VAN DYCK. *Five Children of Charles I.* 1637. Oil on canvas, 5'4¼" × 6'6¼". Reproduced by gracious permission of Her Majesty Queen Elizabeth II (copyright reserved).

The Baroque Synthesis    273

## General Events

| | | |
|---|---|---|
| 1603– | 1625 | James I (Stuart) reigned |
| | 1604 | *Advancement of Learning* by Francis Bacon |
| | 1611 | King James' authorized English translation of Bible completed |
| 1619– | 1621 | Banqueting House, Whitehall, built by Inigo Jones |
| | 1620 | *Novum Organum* by Francis Bacon |
| 1625– | 1649 | Charles I reigned; after 1629 ruled without Parliament |
| | 1628 | *Treatise on Terrestrial Magnetism and Electricity* by William Gilbert (1540–1603) published in English edition. Circulation of blood discovered by Harvey (1578–1657) |
| 1642– | 1660 | English Civil Wars |
| | 1643 | Theaters closed by Parliament |
| | 1649 | Charles I executed, England proclaimed Commonwealth |
| | 1651 | *Leviathan; or the Matter, Form, and Power of a Commonwealth, Ecclesiastical and Civil* by Hobbes |
| 1653– | 1658 | Oliver Cromwell (1599–1658) ruled |
| | 1660 | Restoration of monarchy |
| 1660– | 1685 | Charles II reigned |
| | 1661 | *The Sceptical Chymist* by Robert Boyle (1627–91) |
| | 1662 | Royal Society of London for Improving Natural Knowledge founded; Christopher Wren, Robert Boyle, John Dryden, charter members |

| | | |
|---|---|---|
| | 1662 | Christopher Wren appointed deputy surveyor-general to king; 1665 in Paris to observe remodeling of Louvre; met Bernini, Perrault, Hardouin-Mansart |
| 1664– | 1665 | Black Death bubonic plague swept London |
| | 1666 | Great Fire of London |
| | 1667 | *Paradise Lost* by Milton |
| | 1669 | Wren appointed surveyor-general to king |
| | 1670 | John Dryden appointed poet laureate and royal historiographer |
| 1671– | 1680 | St. Mary-le-Bow and other London parish churches built by Wren |
| 1675– | 1710 | St. Paul's Cathedral built |
| | 1678 | *Pilgrim's Progress*, Part I, by Bunyan; Part II, 1684 |
| | 1680 | Purcell appointed organist at Westminster Abbey; named composer-in-ordinary to king (1683) |
| | 1682 | *Venus and Adonis*, chamber opera by John Blow, performed at court |
| | 1685 | *Albion and Albanius*, opera by Dryden and Purcell, performed in London |
| 1685– | 1688 | James II reigned |
| | 1687 | *Philosophiae Naturalis Principia Mathematica* ("Mathematical Principles of Natural Philosophy") by Newton (1642–1727) |
| | 1688 | Glorious Revolution James II deposed; William of Orange and Mary (Stuart) became parliamentary rulers |

| | | |
|---|---|---|
| 1689– | 1702 | William and Mary reigned |
| | c.1689 | *Dido and Aeneas*, opera, composed by Purcell |
| | 1690 | Wing of Hampton Court Palace built by Wren; *Essay Concerning Human Understanding* by John Locke |
| | 1691 | *King Arthur . . . A Dramatick Opera* by Dryden and Purcell performed |
| | 1692 | Nahum Tate appointed poet laureate |
| | 1704 | *Opticks* by Isaac Newton |
| 1722– | 1726 | St. Martin-in-the-Fields built by Gibbs |

## Writers

| | | |
|---|---|---|
| 1561– | 1626 | Francis Bacon |
| 1563– | 1593 | Christopher Marlowe |
| 1564– | 1616 | William Shakespeare |
| 1572– | 1631 | John Donne |
| 1573– | 1637 | Ben Jonson |
| 1588– | 1679 | Thomas Hobbes |
| 1608– | 1674 | John Milton |
| 1628– | 1688 | John Bunyan |
| 1631– | 1700 | John Dryden |
| 1632– | 1704 | John Locke |
| 1633– | 1703 | Samuel Pepys |
| 1652– | 1715 | Nahum Tate |

## Architects

| | | |
|---|---|---|
| 1573– | 1652 | Inigo Jones |
| 1632– | 1723 | Christopher Wren |
| 1682– | 1754 | James Gibbs |

## Painters

| | | |
|---|---|---|
| 1577– | 1640 | Peter Paul Rubens |
| 1599– | 1641 | Anthony van Dyck |

## Composers

| | | |
|---|---|---|
| 1606– | 1668 | William Davenant |
| c.1647– | 1674 | Pelham Humfrey |
| c.1648– | 1708 | John Blow |
| 1658– | 1695 | Henry Purcell |
| 1685– | 1759 | George Frederick Handel |

## ARCHITECTURE

In the crypt beneath St. Paul's Cathedral in London a Latin inscription on a stone slab reads: "Beneath is laid the builder of this church and city, Christopher Wren, who lived more than 90 years, not for himself but for the good of the state. If you seek a monument, look around you." As the observer studies the struc-ture, he will first be struck by the unity of St. Paul's (Fig. 293), for this is the only major cathedral in Europe to be built by one architect, by one master mason, and during the episcopate of one bishop. In contrast, it took 13 architects, 20 popes, and more than a century to build St. Peter's in Rome (Fig. 193). The last stone on the lantern tower above the dome of St. Paul's was put in place in 1710 by one of Wren's sons left: 293. CHRISTOPHER WREN. Façade, St. Paul's Cathedral, London. 1675–1710. 514 × 250', dome height 366'.

below: 294. Plan, as executed, St. Paul's Cathedral.

bottom: 295. St. Paul's Cathedral (view from southeast).

in the presence of the 78-year-old builder, and for another 8 years Wren continued to supervise the completion of the last decorative details.

Even before the Great Fire, Wren was a member of a commission charged with the remodeling of Old St. Paul's. The plan had to be scrapped when a survey after the fire showed the building beyond repair. It was this that gave Wren his great opportunity. Like Bramante and Michelangelo before him (Fig. 206), Wren envisaged a centralized area of great spaciousness surrounded radially by subsidiary spatial units. Like his eminent predecessors, he too preferred a central-church plan based on the Greek cross. In this way, a building of such monumental proportions could have both its exterior mass and interior space dominated by the all-embracing, unifying force of a dome. From a practical point of view, Wren was also aware that he was designing a Protestant cathedral which should permit as many people as possible to be within earshot of the pulpit so as to hear the sermon-centered service of the Anglican Church.

The conservative members of the clergy, with thoughts of the ancient Catholic processional liturgy in mind, wanted a long nave with aisles on either side. Wren, therefore, without sacrificing the heart of his plan, lengthened the edifice by adding an apse in the east and a domed vestibule with an extended porch in the west. His model, however, brought further objections from the clergy, necessitating still other revisions. All Wren's diplomacy, versatility, ingenuity, and, above all, patience were called into play to effect a workable compromise that would satisfy his difficult clients and yet save the essence of his cherished conception. He gave the clergy their aisled nave and

transepts and their deep choir, but these he grouped around the central plan of his original design (Fig. 294). In this way, he could still concentrate great space under the dome. Wren thus was actually building two churches, the clergy's and his own, a procedure that was bound to produce some architectural dissonances but for which he succeeded in finding a satisfactory if somewhat uneasy resolution in the cathedral that was finally completed.

Wren's practical problems with St. Paul's were as numerous as his difficulties with the authorities. Funds for construction were limited; the site demanded engineering ingenuity, for there, as in much of London, solid ground was buried beneath forty feet of clay and sand that could not bear excessive weight. Long before his cathedral was completed, Wren had had to abandon his hopes for an unimpeded view and an axial approach to his façade (Fig. 293) up Ludgate Hill on which St. Paul's rests. In the eagerness to rebuild after the fire, the vicinity had become a clutter of shops and houses, and it took the German air force in World War II to clear the land around the south side and the choir (Fig. 295). And when no quarry

**below: 296.** Christopher Wren. Rotunda, St. Paul's Cathedral. Aquatint by Thomas Malton, 1798.

**right: 297.** Christopher Wren. St. Mary-le-Bow, London. 1671–80. Total height 216'1", steeple 104'6".

**far right: 298.** James Gibbs. St. Martin-in-the-Fields, London. 1721–26.

could supply stone of the necessary lengths for the great columns of his original façade, Wren had had to separate the façade into two separate stories of the Corinthian and Composite orders. His use of paired columns recalls Perrault's colonnade on the east front of the Louvre (Fig. 263). The side turrets were designed after 1700, and it is of more than passing interest that for some time one of them was left hollow except for a circular staircase, so that Wren and his fellow astronomers could use it for an observatory.

The effect of Wren's preferred plan is felt most strongly in the rotunda beneath the dome (Fig. 296). Geometrically, the space is bounded by a gigantic octagon, punctuated at the angles by the eight piers on which the cupola rests. These are bridged over by a ring of contiguous Roman triumphal arches, which, in turn, are crowned by the great dome, the culmination of the entire composition. From this central area, the arches open outward into eight spatial subdivisions that give the interior such constant variety and interest. The centralization under the lofty dome, the complex divisions and subdivisions of space, the imaginative design and Roman detail reveal Wren's affinity for the baroque. The restraining influences of the conservative clergy, the lack of unlimited funds, and Wren's rationalistic viewpoint demonstrate his remarkable feat in making the style palatable to British taste.

Wren's plan for the rebuilding of London met with even stiffer resistance than his project for St.

Paul's. It included the laying out of a series of new streets that radiated outward starlike from central squares and that took the main traffic routes into consideration. Certain public buildings were to be oriented on an axis involving the new cathedral and the Royal Exchange. The spires of the various parish churches were to punctuate the silhouette at certain points and by degrees lead up to the grand climax of St. Paul's dome. The plan, if it had been carried out, would have gone far beyond that of Versailles. But Wren's King was not an absolute monarch with the power to condemn property and the money to buy it. Time also ran against Wren, because the shopkeepers throughout London were in a hurry to rebuild and start their business concerns again. About all he could rescue were the church steeples he was called upon to design.

As London's principal architect, Wren was commissioned to build more than fifty of these new parish churches. Consultations had to be held with the churchwardens on the problems and needs of each church. Owing to the limited funds at the architect's disposal, the churches of necessity had to be rather modest affairs. Wren, in keeping with the spirit of the time, wanted to build them in the restrained baroque style based on the classical orders. His clients and the Gothic tradition still demanded the spires that not only had the force of symbols but the practical purpose of housing the bell tower, which was still a functional unit of a church. Wren's problem, therefore, was to balance the vertical tendency of the steeple with the horizontality of his classical temple façades—once more, the reconciliation of northern and southern building traditions. Wren's solution, among his minor miracles, can only be understood through an actual example.

The steeple of St. Mary-le-Bow (Fig. 297), where the famous Bow Bells once rang out, shows the mathematician's obvious delight in a free play of geometrical forms. From a solid square base it moves through several circular phases and terminates finally in an octagonal pyramid. By the judicious use of baroque scrolls and twists at various points, this is achieved without a hint of abruptness. Knowing that the churches themselves were bound to be hidden by the surrounding buildings, Wren lavished most of his skill on their spires. The continuation of the Wren tradition into the next century is seen in James Gibbs' Church of St. Martin-in-the-Fields (Fig. 298). Wren had always planted his steeples firmly in the ground, so to speak, so that they seemed to grow in an organic relation to the whole composition. Gibbs' spire, by contrast, appears to sprout unexpectedly out of the roof. The memory of these churches and their steeples was carried to the American colonies by the founding fathers; and when they came to build their own churches in new cities, it was to the designs of Wren and Gibbs that they turned for their models.

Despite his many responsibilities, Wren found the time to design some commodious houses for well-to-do middle-class clients. During the reign of William and Mary, he was also commissioned to complete the unfinished Royal Hospital at Greenwich, begun earlier by Inigo Jones, and to add a new wing for Hampton Court Palace. His patron, William of Orange, remembered the good red brick of his native Holland, while Wren recalled the grandeur of the Louvre and Versailles palaces. Another of Wren's famous compromises was effected in his design for the Fountain Court and the garden façade at Hampton Court Palace (Fig. 299).

Thus it was that Wren, the professor of astronomy at London and Oxford, left off probing the mysteries of the heavens with his telescope and equations and became the engineer and architect who penetrated that segment of the sky above London with the majestic spires and domes that gave the city its characteristic profile and skyline (Fig. 300).

## DRAMA AND MUSIC

On the gala occasion of the formal opening of the King's Theatre in 1674, His Majesty and London's most distinguished audience gathered there for the evening's entertainment. John Dryden, that cold, aristocratic but brilliant author, took advantage of the situation afforded by the prologue to express his sentiments in some well-chosen words:

'Twere folly now a stately pile to raise,
To build a playhouse while you throw down plays;
Whilst scenes, machines and empty Operas reign,
And for the Pencil you the Pen disdain;

above: 299. CHRISTOPHER WREN. Garden façade, Hampton Court Palace. c. 1690.

left: 300. CANALETTO. *London.* c. 1750. Oil on canvas, 3'6" × 6'1". Reproduced by gracious permission of Her Majesty Queen Elizabeth II (copyright reserved).

While Troops of famished Frenchmen hither drive,
And laugh at those upon whose Alms they live:
Our English Authors vanish, and give place
To these new Conquerors of the Norman race.

Dryden was thus making the valiant effort of an exasperated man of letters to stem the tide toward the foreign forms of opera, which, in his opinion, threatened to engulf reason with rhyme. The course of events, however, was flowing far too strongly; and, to keep from being inundated, he soon was collaborating with one of those fashionable Frenchmen and writing some fancy "scenes and machines" himself.

With all the adaptability of a thoroughly equipped professional writer, Dryden honestly tried to squeeze some content into those "empty Operas." To help acclimate this exotic form to its new surroundings, he fell back on the tradition of the English court masque, a native equivalent of the French *ballet de cour*, which had set the precedent for the development of opera at the court of Louis XIV. In a performance of Ben Jonson's *Masque of Blackness* at Whitehall in 1605, the dancers included the queen and her ladies, and the designer of the scenic spectacle was none other than the famous architect Inigo Jones (Fig. 301).

When Dryden came to write his *Albion and Albanius,* he had to summon all his tactical skill to balance the opposing elements and try to keep them in proper proportion. In his preface, he was more than a little apologetic about having to write so as "to please the hearing rather than gratify the understanding"; and, he continued, "it appears, indeed, preposterous at first sight, that rhyme, on any consideration, should take the place of reason." His solution was to use spoken dialogue for the ordinary mortals in the play but to include what he called a "songish part" for such supernatural characters as gods and goddesses, spirits and sprites. Their behavior, he observed, "being extended beyond the limits of human nature, admits of that sort of marvelous and surprising conduct, which is rejected in other plays."

Dryden's opera contains many remarkable scenes and machines. In one, "Mercury descends in a chariot drawn by ravens"; in another, "the clouds divide, and Juno appears in a Machine drawn by Peacocks, while a Symphony is playing"; in yet another, Venus and Albanius rise our of the sea in a scallop shell drawn by dolphins to a symphony of "flutes-doux."

In spite of the gaudy machines, Dryden's attempt in this instance was a failure—possibly because it was not sufficiently distinguished from the court masque to be a true opera, but more probably because the music provided by Monsieur Grabu was mediocre. Though Henry Purcell was already 26 years old, England had to wait almost a decade before it was to have the collaboration of a poet and musician comparable in stature to Molière and Lully in France.

While awaiting the invitation from Dryden to collaborate on *King Arthur*, England's greatest composer had to content himself with writing incidental music to dozens of undistinguished plays. The best of them were such Shakespearean adaptations as *The Tempest* and *The Fairy Queen* (from *A Midsummer Night's Dream*), which bear only a remote resemblance to the originals. For his one great opportunity in the operatic field, *Dido and Aeneas,* he had to get along with a book by Nahum Tate, whose stature in English letters is several notches below that of his French counterpart Quinault, who was Lully's chief librettist. But there is not a shred of evidence to show that Purcell was unhappy about the situation. The picture of his career is simply that of a professional composer, diligently active at all times, and technically capable of fulfilling any commission which came his way, whether from church, court, or independent sources.

It was through Josias Priest, a dancing master in one of the London theaters, that Purcell received the invitation to write a short opera to be performed at his boarding school for young gentlewomen at Chelsea. Thus it was that about 1689, Purcell came to write his little operatic masterpiece for a group of schoolgirls. As such it is a true *chamber opera*, designed for a limited space and restricted to a limited cast of characters and a small orchestra. Though small in scale, it is large in emotional scope; and while it falls within the province of amateur performance, it is filled with the utmost musical sophistication. Its immediate antecedent was *Venus and Adonis,* a three-act chamber opera written a few years earlier by Purcell's teacher John Blow. This charming, intimate work had been performed for the entertainment of Charles II and his court shortly before the monarch's death. It was one of the few existing through-composed operas (that is, with the entire text set to music) in English;

*Dido and Aeneas* (recitative excerpts)　　　HENRY PURCELL

*Dido and Aeneas*　　　HENRY PURCELL
("When I Am Laid in Earth")

otherwise, for local precedents there were only the masque tradition and the Dryden-Grabu experiments to guide him. Purcell, however, was conversant with the latest Continental developments in the opera, and it is the piquant blend of these native and foreign elements that gives his work its color and variety.

*Dido and Aeneas* opens with a dignified overture in the Lully style, marked by the halting rhythms and harmonic suspensions of a slow beginning, and the fugal imitations of a lively conclusion. All the orchestral sections seem to have been scored only for strings with the usual keyboard support. For his recitatives and airs, he turns to the models developed by Monteverdi and his successor at the Venetian opera, Cavalli. Purcell makes particularly bold use of the "representative style," a type of word-painting, by which the descriptive imagery of the text is reflected in the shape and turn of the melodic line (above). This prosody of the representative style can be illustrated by the first word in the opera, "Shake" (a), and the menacing movement of the line for "storms" (b). In a comment on Aeneas' parentage, the valor of his father Anchises is characterized by a martial rhythm (c); while immediately afterward a modulation to the minor mode and a caressing chromaticism express the voluptuousness of Venus' charms (d); and when Aeneas' entrance is announced, Belinda's words take on the shape of a trumpet fanfare (e).

The airs show a considerable variety as to type. Dido's opening and closing songs are built over a short repeated bass pattern as in the Italian *ostinato aria*. The melody of "Oft She Visits" is written over a continuously flowing bass line in the manner of an Italian *continuo aria*; while the three-part melodic form of "Pursue Thy Conquest, Love," whose final section repeats the beginning, identifies it as a *da capo aria*.

The emphasis on the choruses and dances is in the English court masque tradition, but both are handled by Purcell with a highly ingenious blend of native and Continental elements. In the palace scenes, the courtiers function as a true Greek chorus by making solemn comments in unison on the action. The final number, "With Drooping Wings," is a typical French mourning chorus straight out of Lullian opera. The witches, however, sing in the English madrigal style with the amusing substitution of some malicious "Ho, ho, ho's" for the jollier "Fa la la's," to signify their sinister purposes. Highly interesting

is Purcell's introduction of a Venetian echo chorus in these solemn surroundings. While the witches sing "In Our Deep Vaulted Cell," an offstage chorus softly echoes "-ed cell." By thus increasing the perception of space, Purcell is able to add the necessary uncanny touch as the witches start to prepare their mysterious charms. The spell is further carried out in the "Echo Dance of Furies," in which an offstage instrumental ensemble echoes the principal orchestra with telling effect. The dances show much of the same stylistic mixture as the choruses. Scene 1 concludes with the courtiers doing a "Triumphing Dance," which is a vigorous version of a Lully *chaconne* treated as a set of instrumental variations over a ground bass. During Act III, when Aeneas is preparing to sail away from Carthage, Purcell paints a typical English seaport scene in which the swinging sailors' dances mingle with the salty comments of a chorus of common people. The angularity of such native rhythms as the hornpipe is a distinct contrast to the more formal *courantes* and *chaconnes* danced by the courtiers.

Purcell's logic and fine dramatic perception do not permit him to soften his opera toward the end by allowing a *deus ex machina* to bring it to a happy ending in the manner of the French court style of Lully. The human will when contending with the gods is always doomed, and the plot must move inexorably onward. The tragedy is therefore carried through to its predestined conclusion with growing eloquence and mounting emotion. As a consequence, "Dido's Farewell" (above) becomes one of the most moving moments in all music, combining as it does the most passionate feeling with the dignified restraint demanded of a tragic heroine out of Vergil's *Aeneid*. It is cast in the form of an *ostinato aria* with an obstinately repetitive bass figure, which descends chromatically to the rhythm of the stately *passacaglia*. Dido's inner struggle is expressed by the tension between the free obbligato melodic line that she sings and the inflexible bass, and she contends with this fixed force as with her tragic fate. Vainly she tries to bend it to her will, as seen in some of the asymmetrical diagonal shifts of her phrases off their center, but in the end she must resign herself to it while the orchestra carries the aria onward to its tragic conclusion.

Within the limitations of this short opera, which takes but little more than an hour to perform, Purcell produced a major work of art. Though it is his only through-composed piece for the lyric stage, it reveals the sure touch of one who knows every aspect of his dramatic business. The extensive emotional range and the variety of technical devices are all the more astonishing in view of the meager resources he had at his disposal. Purcell possesses, first of all, the rare power to delineate and create believable human characters by musical means, a gift he shares with Gluck and Mozart. He is also one of the few composers who know how to convert the dry academic techniques of counterpoint into lively dramatic devices, a characteristic he shares with Bach and Handel. This is apparent, for example, in Dido's first air, "Ah, Belinda." Her melody is like a series of descending sighs over a ground bass that, like destiny, is relentless and unyielding. At the words "Peace and I are strangers grown," the parting of the ways is depicted by a canon at the octave; and on the word "strangers," the predominant four-bar pattern begins to wander and is stretched out into five bars. Again, after Aeneas declares he will defy destiny itself in order to remain with Dido, the chorus makes contrapuntal comments that graphically give expression to their disturbed and conflicting emotions. When Purcell wants to depict the hustle and bustle around the departing ships in the scene at the dockside in Act III, the independent lines of the fugal introduction, with their imitative thematic entries and exits, humorously describe the coming and going of the people. When such skillful means as these are combined with his fanciful orchestration, colorful use of chromaticism, and deep poetic feeling, they are sure to lead to significant ends—as indeed, in this case, they did.

One more opportunity to write an English opera was presented to Purcell when Dryden, the literary arbiter of Restoration drama, invited him to collaborate on *King Arthur* in 1691. Dryden, in this case, was trying to breathe something of the grandiloquence of the French baroque theater into a patriotic English drama. His preface shows that he was still groping for a formula to adapt music and poetry to the English lyric stage, and his sincere misgivings are apparent when he complains: "I have been obliged to cramp my Verses, and make them rugged to the Reader, that they may be harmonious to the Hearer." Like a good rationalist, he was also worried about writing a play "principally designed for the Ear and Eye" rather than for the mind. He still felt that the human characters should speak and that only the superhuman ones should sing. In this parenthetical way, the music could be made to sound more plausible and thus not seem like an intrusion into the course of the main dramatic sequence. Fortunately for Purcell, there were so many superhuman characters that his score assumed very ample proportions. *King Arthur* was a truly distinguished attempt to solve the problem of English opera. In its way, it was another English compromise, since it was neither an opera nor a play but a compound of elements drawn from both. If this collaboration between Dryden and Purcell had continued, it eventually might have led to a distinctive English form of the music drama. As *King Arthur* stands, it remains a noble but inconclusive experiment.

In spite of Purcell's sparing but convincing use of the sung recitative, and his efforts to extract the essence out of Monteverdi's representative style by removing some of the Italian bombast in order to render it palatable to London audiences, recitative simply did not take root. Through-composed opera was destined to remain an exotic plant on English soil. As the *Gentlemen's Journal* of January, 1692, put it, "Experience hath taught us that our English genius will not rellish that perpetual singing."

A judicious comparison between the three great figures of the Restoration style—Wren, Dryden, and Purcell—can be highly illuminating. Each in his way was trying to bring his country up to date on the latest Continental developments, just as each was trying to inject something of the grandeur of the baroque style into an English art form. In order to do so, each was willing to make the necessary compromises to avoid parting company with English audiences. When Wren was designing his preferred models on his drawing board, when Dryden was writing solely for his readers, and when Purcell was composing experimentally for amateurs, each could be as free as he chose. But when it came to building a cathedral, mounting a play, and composing music for the theater, many subtle and even drastic adjustments had to be made. Each man had sufficient mastery in his field and each was sufficiently versatile and inventive to make those adjustments. Each preferred and developed an aristocratic style but never neglected the common touch. Each, in his turn, had an effect on posterity that lasted well into the next century. Wren's buildings became the backbone of the Georgian style; Dryden's works, the background for 18th-century classicism in English letters; and the fact that many of Purcell's works until recently have been thought to be by Bach and Handel is proof enough that they were absorbed directly into the sacred and secular music of the succeeding generation.

## IDEAS

**Baroque Rationalism**    Stimulated by the explorations of navigators of the globe, the scanning of the skies by astronomers, and the ingenuity of inventors, baroque man came to have a new concept of himself and his place in the universe. Galileo's telescope confirmed and popularized Copernicus' theory of a solar system in which the earth revolved around the sun rather than vice versa. The concept of the static Aristotelian universe thus had to yield to one that was full of whirling motion. Since the earth was no longer considered as a fixed point located at the nerve center of the cosmos, man could hardly be regarded any longer as the sole purpose of creation. It was some consolation, however, to know that this strange new moving universe at least was subject to mechanical and mathematical laws, and therefore to a considerable extent predictable. Copernicus and Kepler as well as the other scientists were convinced of its unity, proportion, and harmony; and the fact that man had the privilege of probing into the secrets of nature—if his intellect proved equal to the task—was a highly exhilarating thought. The rationalism of the 17th century, then, was based on the view that the universe could at last be understood in logical, mathematical, and mechanical terms. As a philosophy and semireligion, this world view had far-reaching consequences by preparing for the theories of positivism and materialism, the doctrines of deism and atheism, and the mechanical and industrial revolutions.

While Greek rationalism had been based on the perception and measurement of a static world, baroque rationalism had to come to terms with a dynamic universe. Scientific thought was concerned with movement in space and time. The need for a mathematics capable of comprehending a world of matter in motion led Descartes to his analytical geometry, Pascal to a study of cycloid curves, and both Leibniz and Newton to the simultaneous but independent discovery of integral and differential calculus. Baroque invention led to refinements in navigation, to improvements in the telescope and microscope for the exploration of distant and minute regions of space, the barometer for the measurement of air pressure, the thermometer for the recording of temperature changes, and the anemometer for the calculation of the force of winds. Astronomers were occupied with the study of planetary motion; William Harvey discovered the circulation of the blood in the human body; and physicists were experimenting with thermodynamics and gravitation.

Newton's preoccupation with mass, force, and momentum, his speculations on the principles of attraction and repulsion, and his calculations on terrestrial and celestial mechanics led him to a monumental synthesis that he presented to the British Royal Society in 1686 and published in London a year later. Newton's *Principia* embraced a complete and systematic view of an orderly world based on mechanical principles, capable of mathematical proof, and demonstrable by accurate prediction. His work was, in fact, a scientific *summa* that established the intellectual architecture of the new view of the universe.

Such a changed world view was bound to have important consequences for the arts, which responded in this case with a ringing reassertion of man's supremacy and a joyous acceptance of this new understanding of the universe. The application of rationalistic principles to aesthetic expression is by no means accidental or casual. Before he became an architect, Christopher Wren was a mechanical inventor, an experimental scientist, and a professor of astronomy at London and Oxford. As one of the founders of the Royal Society, he was in close communication with such men as Robert Boyle and Isaac Newton. The fellows of the Royal Society appointed John Dryden to a committee whose purpose was to study the English language with a view toward linguistic reforms. They recommended that English prose should have both purity and brevity, so that verbal communication could be brought as close to mathematical plainness and precision as possible. Dryden's embarrassment in writing an opera that was designed to please the ear rather than gratify the understanding was therefore quite understandable. Purcell's music was based on a system of intricate contrapuntal principles and tonal logic in which given premises, such as sequences or repeated ground basses, are followed by predictable conclusions. Moreover, it is characterized by intellectual discipline, symmetry, clarity, and a sure sense of direction. Purcell's forms are models of brevity in which each part has its place, no loose ends are left dangling, and the cadences bring everything to a positive finish. Together with Wren's architecture and Dryden's poetic drama, Purcell's music reflects a buoyant self-confidence, an inventive spirit that gave birth to new forms, an exploration of novel optical and acoustical ideas, and a conviction that a work of art should be a reflection of an orderly and lawful universe.

## BAROQUE SYNTHESIS AND CONCLUSION

While the baroque period is mainly centered in the 17th century, its extreme temporal limits extend all the way from the mid-16th to the mid-18th centuries, from Michelangelo to Johann Sebastian Bach. During this span of time the concept of the world had moved from a terracentric to a heliocentric universe; philosophical speculation had turned from a supernatural to a natural world view; the fundamental processes of thought had shifted from the acceptance of authority on faith to scientific experimentation; the unity of Christianity symbolized by one universal Church had been opposed by a number of Protestant sects; and the theoretical political unity of the Holy Roman Empire had given way to the practical fact of a balance of power distributed among a family of nations. The baroque period was one in which irresistible modern forces met immovable traditional objects. Out of all the theological disputations, philosophical discussions, scientific arguments, social tensions, political strife, warfare, and artistic creation come both the baroque style and the modern age.

The baroque world was one in which irreconcilable oppositions had to find a way of coexistence. The rise of rationalism was accompanied by the march of militant mysticism; the aristocratic cult of majesty was echoed by the bourgeois cult of domesticity; the internationalism of Roman Catholicism was in conflict with the nationalism of the Protestant sects; religious orthodoxy had to contend with freedom of thought; the Jesuits brought all the arts into their churches, while Calvin did his utmost to exclude the arts as vanities; Philip II built a palatial mausoleum and monastery, while Louis XIV erected a pleasure palace and theater; Charles I tried to force an absolute monarchy on England, and Cromwell's answer was a republican commonwealth; the printing press made books available, while suppression by censorship took them away; the boldest scientific speculation took place alongside a reassertion of the belief in miracles and a renewal of religious fundamentalism; Newton's *Principia* and the final part of Bunyan's *Pilgrim's Progress* appeared in London within two years of each other. In Spain, the emotional involvement of El Greco was succeeded by the optical detachment of Velázquez; in France the spontaneity of Rubens was followed by the academic formalism of Poussin; in Holland, the broad humanity of Rembrandt led to the specialization and precision of Vermeer.

Such oppositions could hardly be expected to resolve themselves into a single uniform style. At best, they could achieve a temporary resolution and a fusion of forms, such as those found in a Counter-Reformation church, the Versailles Palace, Rembrandt's visual dramatization of the Bible, and Purcell's operatic synthesis. In them, forceful striving and restless motion are more characteristic than serenity and repose. Baroque art thus emerges from these tensions and speaks in eloquent accents of the expanding range of human activities, grandiose achievements, and a ceaseless search for more powerful means of expression.

All this took place within the expanse of a tremendously enlarged sense of space. The astronomers told of remote regions populated by an infinite number of stars. Pascal speculated on the mathematical implications of infinity. The gardens and avenues of Versailles were laid out in keeping with this vastly extended conception of space. The vistas led the eye toward the horizon and invited the imagination to continue beyond. The unification of the vast buildings and gardens there placed baroque man wholly within the scope of nature and declared him to be a part of the new measurable universe. Wren's attempt to bring his cathedral, parish churches, and public buildings into one all-embracing scheme was also in keeping with this image of the comprehensive baroque universe. Painters likewise delighted in leading the eye outside their pictures and attempted to convey the impression of infinity through the bold use of light and exaggerated perspective effects. The Dutch landscapists tried to capture atmospheric perspective, and Rembrandt was concerned with the infinite gradations of light. Through use of illusionistic effects, ceilings of Counter-Reformation churches opened the skies and tried to promote the feeling of a world without end.

In music there was a corresponding expansion of tonal space. The organs and other keyboard instruments were built to encompass a wider range from bass to soprano. Both the wind and the stringed instruments were constructed in families, ranging all the way from what Orlando Gibbons called the "Great Dooble Base" to the high soprano register of the violin. Louis XIV and Charles II incorporated this string family into ensembles of twenty-four viols, thus increasing both the resonance and volume of sound through the doubling process. The coming into use of chromatic harmony with all the half-tone divisions of the octave was the internal extension of the same idea. Purcell's opposition of ground basses and soprano melodies emphasized the baroque love of a spacious distribution of sonorities. His adoption of the Venetian double chorus and his dramatic use of the echo effect in *Dido and Aeneas* were still further evidence of the desire to increase the perception of space through sound and to use their aural breadth for expressive purposes.

Above all, the baroque universe was in ceaseless movement. Whether a rationalist thought of it in terms of whirling particles or a mystic as full of swirling spirits, both saw their world as a vortex of spheres and spirals describing infinitely complex patterns of motion. Kepler's planets revolved in elliptical orbits; Counter-Reformation churches were built over undulating floor plans; their walls rippled like stage curtains; the decorative profusion of their façades further activated the static masses and increased their rhythmic pulsation; under their domes terra-cotta angels flew in parabolas; the unyielding stone of the statuary finally rose off the ground and melted into a myriad of fluid forms; paintings escaped from flat wall spaces up to the more congenial concave surfaces of the ceilings, where they could soar skyward and where more daring perspective effects were possible. Baroque music also mirrored a moving universe. Its restless forms took on the color of this dynamic age, and its sound patterns floated freely through their tonal spaces unencumbered by gravitational laws. No longer in bondage to religious ritual, to the dance, or to poetry, its emancipation was now complete. Of such ideas and materials was the image of this brave new baroque world constructed.

# 17 The 18th-Century Styles

## 18TH-CENTURY PANORAMA

The momentum of the baroque style was sufficient to propel it well into the 18th century. New social dynamics, new springs of ideas, new aesthetic currents came together to bring about, in some cases, a confluence of the main baroque streams and, in others, the formation of new ones. With the death of Louis XIV in 1715, the aristocratic baroque style moved into its final rococo phase. The regent for his young successor closed the majestic Versailles Palace and reestablished the royal residence in Paris. Artistic patronage was no longer the monopoly of the court, and the painter Watteau, arriving in Paris the same year the Sun King died, had to look for his patrons among a broad group drawn from the ranks of both the nobility and the middle class. Throughout the century, the operas of Rameau, Gluck, and Mozart were composed for public opera houses where aristocrats rubbed shoulders with the bourgeoisie. The arts, in effect, moved out of the marble halls into the elegant salons, where finesse and charm were considered higher aesthetic virtues than impressiveness and grandeur (Fig. 302).

The rococo, that latter-day manifestation of the aristocratic baroque style, was by no means confined to Paris. All European courts assumed in some degree the character of cultural suburbs of Versailles. French fashions in architecture, painting, furniture, costume, and manners were echoed in such far-off corners as the courts of Catherine the Great of Russia and of Maria Theresa in Vienna. Whether a prince ruled a province in Poland or a duchy in Denmark, French was spoken in his household more naturally than the language of his native country. In Prussia, Frederick the Great built a rococo palace at Potsdam and called it *Sans-souci;* the king of Saxony commissioned the jewellike Zwinger pleasure pavilion in Dresden; and the Prince-Bishop erected a handsome residence in Würzburg. Such French authors as Voltaire and Jean Jacques Rousseau found an international reading public; French dances dominated the balls and French plays the theaters. In southern Germany and Austria, however, Italian influence was still strong. At the court in Vienna an Italian architect finished the Schönbrunn Palace for Maria Theresa; Italian paintings decorated its walls; Metastasio was the poet laureate, playwright, and opera librettist; and only plays and operas in Italian could be performed in the royal theaters. The missionary zeal of the Jesuits working outward from Rome spread and popularized the ecclesiastical counterpart of the aristocratic style throughout the Counter-Reformation countries.

Baroque rationalism had remained restricted to a relatively few eminent minds. In the 18th century, however, as the scientific knowledge of Newton and the social theories of John Locke became the common property of the educated classes, rationalism broadened into the movement known as the *Enlightenment,* a term—like the *rococo*—that generally refers to the period between 1715 and 1789. As the streams of rationalism and academicism converged, the most characteristic expression of the Enlightenment became the 35-volume *Encyclopédie,* edited by Denis Diderot. In this *Classified Dictionary of the Sciences, Arts, and Trades,* some 180 outstanding intellects collected and made available in clear language all the knowledge that had heretofore existed only in difficult scientific tracts.

While the fruits of rationalism became the common property of the middle class, *reason,* in the vocabulary of the 18th century, by no means implied

302. GERMAIN BOFFRAND. Salon de la Princesse, Hôtel de Soubise, Paris. c. 1740. Oval, c. 33 × 26′.

## General Events

| | | |
|---|---|---|
| | 1715 | Louis XIV died |
| 1715– | 1774 | Louis XV, king of France |
| | 1724 | Belvedere Palace, Vienna, finished; Hildebrandt architect |
| | 1726 | *Gulliver's Travels* by Swift |
| | 1728 | *Beggar's Opera* by John Gay (1685–1732) performed in London |
| | 1732 | Hôtel de Soubise, Paris, begun; Boffrand, architect |
| 1740– | 1780 | Maria Theresa, empress of Austria |
| 1740– | 1786 | Frederick the Great, king of Prussia |
| | 1744 | Schönbrunn Palace built in Vienna (begun in 1696 by Fischer von Erlach) |
| | 1748 | *Spirit of Laws* by Condorcet. Excavations at Pompeii begun |
| 1751– | 1772 | *Encyclopédie, or A Classified Dictionary of the Sciences, Arts and Trades* published by Diderot |
| | 1752 | Pergolesi's *Serva Padrona* performed in Paris. *Guerre des Bouffons*, "war" in Paris over serious *versus* comic opera |
| | 1759 | *Candide* by Voltaire |
| | 1762 | *Social Contract* by J. J. Rousseau. Gluck's *Orpheus* performed in Vienna |
| 1762– | 1768 | Petit Trianon, Versailles, built by Louis XV for Mme Dubarry; Gabriel, architect |

| | | |
|---|---|---|
| 1762– | 1796 | Catherine the Great, empress of Russia |
| 1774– | 1792 | Louis XVI, king of France |
| | 1774 | Gluck's *Orpheus* and *Iphigenia in Aulis* performed in Paris |
| | 1775 | Beaumarchais' *Barber of Seville* presented in Paris |
| | 1776 | American Declaration of Independence. *Sturm und Drang* ("Storm and Stress"), play by Maximilian Klinger (1752–1831), gave name to art movement |
| 1780– | 1790 | Joseph II, emperor of Austria |
| | 1781 | Mozart settled in Vienna. *Critique of Pure Reason* by Kant |
| | 1784 | Beaumarchais' play *Marriage of Figaro* presented; 1786 Mozart's *Marriage of Figaro* performed in Vienna |
| | 1787 | Mozart's *Don Giovanni* performed in Prague; in Vienna 1788 |
| | 1789 | French Revolution begun |
| | 1790 | *Faust, A Fragment,* by Goethe published in Leipzig |
| | 1794 | *Progress of the Human Spirit* by Condorcet |
| | 1797 | *Sense and Sensibility* written by Jane Austen; published in 1811 |

## Architects

| | | |
|---|---|---|
| 1650– | 1723 | Johann Fischer von Erlach |
| c.1660– | 1726 | Jakob Prandtauer |
| 1667– | 1754 | Germain Boffrand |
| 1668– | 1745 | Lukas von Hildebrandt |
| 1698– | 1782 | Ange Jacques Gabriel |

## Painters

| | | |
|---|---|---|
| 1684– | 1721 | Antoine Watteau |
| 1697– | 1764 | William Hogarth |
| 1699– | 1779 | J. B. S. Chardin |
| 1703– | 1770 | François Boucher |
| 1725– | 1805 | Jean Baptiste Greuze |
| 1732– | 1806 | Jean Honoré Fragonard |

## Sculptors

| | | |
|---|---|---|
| 1714– | 1785 | Jean Baptiste Pigalle |
| 1716– | 1791 | Étienne Falconet |
| 1738– | 1814 | Clodion (Claude Michel) |
| 1741– | 1828 | Jean Antoine Houdon |

## Composers

| | | |
|---|---|---|
| 1668– | 1733 | François Couperin (Le Grand) |
| 1683– | 1764 | Jean Philippe Rameau |
| 1714– | 1787 | C. W. Gluck |
| 1714– | 1788 | C. P. E. Bach |
| 1732– | 1809 | Joseph Haydn |
| 1756– | 1791 | W. A. Mozart |

## Writers and Philosophers

| | | |
|---|---|---|
| 1667– | 1745 | Jonathan Swift |
| 1689– | 1761 | Samuel Richardson |
| 1694– | 1778 | Voltaire (F. M. Arouet) |
| 1698– | 1782 | Pietro Metastasio |
| 1707– | 1754 | Henry Fielding |
| 1712– | 1778 | J. J. Rousseau |
| 1713– | 1784 | Denis Diderot |
| 1724– | 1804 | Emmanuel Kant |
| 1728– | 1774 | Oliver Goldsmith |
| 1729– | 1781 | G. E. Lessing |
| 1732– | 1799 | Caron de Beaumarchais |
| 1744– | 1803 | J. G. von Herder |
| 1749– | 1832 | Wolfgang Goethe |
| 1749– | 1838 | Lorenzo da Ponte |
| 1759– | 1805 | Friedrich Schiller |
| 1775– | 1817 | Jane Austen |

only cold intellectuality. Reason was considered to be a mental faculty shared by all who chose to cultivate it. Among its implications were common sense, exercise of good judgment, and the development of taste —all of which were accompanied by a healthy involvement in active human pursuits. As applied to the arts, reason meant the search for expressive forms and sentiments of sufficient universality and validity to be accepted by all who subscribed to the principles of good taste and judgment. With the broadening of the bases of wealth and education, the middle class was able to rise and challenge the ancient authority and prerogatives of the aristocracy. Through the power of knowledge released by the Enlightenment,

**303.** Antoine Watteau. Design as engraved by Huquier. $10\frac{1}{4} \times 15''$. Cooper-Hewitt Museum of Design, Smithsonian Institution, New York.

the age-old shackles of superstition, intolerance, and fear began to be thrown off. The ideals of freedom championed by men of reason were eventually written into the American Declaration of Independence and Bill of Rights and became the moving force behind the French Revolution. More and more, it was now the middle class who wrote and read the books, who constructed and lived in the buildings, who painted and bought the pictures, and who composed and listened to the music.

The philosophy of the Enlightenment did not, however, go unchallenged, and undercurrents of irrationalism were found in movements that presaged 19th-century romanticism. Rousseau gave sensibility a deeper emotional tone, and in France generally *sensibilité* meant tugging at the heart strings of readers, observers, and listeners. In Germany, emotionalism burst out in the more violent form of the so-called "Storm-and-Stress" movement that made a rather personal interpretation of Rousseau's initial statement in his *Social Contract:* "Man is born free, and everywhere he is in chains." Goethe's characterizations of Faust and Prometheus and Mozart's Don Giovanni were independent human beings, who defied the gods of convention and demanded a gamut of inner and outer experience, even if they had to pay the penalty of eternal torment. The truth they sought was one of feeling rather than logic, and their curiosity proved insatiable. By bursting the bonds of civilized restraints, they were in full rebellion against hereditary aristocratic privilege as well as stern middle-class morality. Their freedom was far from that of the Enlightenment; it was in fact an antirationalistic, anti-universal, powerfully pro-individualistic freedom that bordered on self-destruction and anarchy.

The 18th century as a whole was marked by a quickening of the pulse of human affairs. The flood of material from the printing presses alone made it all but impossible to keep up with the pace set in philosophy, literature, and music. The spread of wealth led to the development of urban centers and widespread building projects. Writers, painters, and musicians no longer aimed their output exclusively at one social group. While it is often called the Age of Reason, the 18th century gave birth to some of the most bizarre and irrational beings, real or imaginary, ever to populate the mind or imagination. The passionate disputes begun in the 17th century continued, but on the surface at least the divisions did not appear to be so sharp. The irreconcilable oppositions of the baroque were softened in sarcastic satires, gentle ironies, witty repartee, and wistful melancholies. What appeared as a period of comparative quiescence, however, was but the calm before the storm, the prelude to a social explosion that brought the aristocratic rococo to a violent, revolutionary end, and catapulted into the next century the forces of reason and emotion it had generated.

## THE ROCOCO

The word *rococo* apparently was a pun on *barocco,* the Italian word for "baroque," and on *rocailles* and *coquilles,* the French words for "rocks" and "shells," which were so widely used as decorative motifs in the rococo style. As such, the rococo must be considered a modification or variation of the baroque rather than a style in opposition to baroque. Its effect is that of a domesticated baroque, better suited to fashionable town houses than palace halls, though the rococo was used in both.

The rococo suited the intimate salon life of wit and subtle conversation. The style affected both the major art forms and the decorative arts. Typical of the time is an engraved drawing by Watteau that makes the shell a pervasive motif (Fig. 303). Such a design could

**below: 304.** Salon, Hofburg Palace, Vienna. c. 1760–80.

**bottom: 305.** Lukas von Hildebrandt. Façade detail, Belvedere Palace, Vienna. 1724.

**right: 306.** Jakob Prandtauer. Abbey Church, Melk-on-the-Danube. 1702–38.

have been applied to furniture, wall paneling, stage curtains, ceramics, fabrics, and so on. In relation to a Louis XIV interior (Fig. 266), the rococo rooms of Vienna's Hofburg Palace are delicate, light, and charming (Fig. 304). Monumentality, stateliness, and pompous purples are replaced by finesse, elegance, and pastel shades.

At the Belvedere Palace in Vienna, the decorative impulse can be seen as the rococo bursts out-of-doors into a lavish exterior design (Fig. 305). Details that the French architects had for the most part confined to interiors are found here on the garden façade of a summer palace begun in 1713 by Lukas von Hildebrandt for Prince Eugene of Savoy. Palladian academic restraint has been cast to the four winds. On either side of the center windows, highly ornate double Composite pilasters can be found, and over the entrance grotesque caryatid figures are grouped in balletlike formation. Otherwise the architectural orders as points of reference have all but disappeared. The triangular repose of the temple pediments and window brackets of the academic style has dissolved into a pattern of undulating curves and broken rhythms.

The Counter-Reformation fusion of the arts in order to produce mystical-emotional excitement is well exemplified by the Benedictine abbey church at Melk, built in a commanding position on a rocky ledge overlooking the Danube (Fig. 306). In its colorful interior, designed by the Viennese theater architect Jakob Prandtauer, red marble columns and pilasters rise upward toward the flowing lines, undulating curves, and visionary vistas of the heavens that enliven the vaulting. All the other decorative details combine to carry out this sense of heightened motion. A climax is reached in the choir loft and ceiling at the back (Fig. 307), where the tones of the organ mingle with the concealed chorus and float upward past the terra-cotta angels perching precariously on stucco clouds to a point where the eye is lost in the vast atmospheric perspective of the painted vaulting.

The rococo painter par excellence was Antoine Watteau. A quick comparison of the *Music Party* (Fig. 308), an example of his *fêtes galantes* or "elegant entertainment" style, with the sensuous *Garden of Love* by Rubens (Pl. 34, p. 249) will reveal the hallmarks of the new idiom. The dimensions of the pictures alone tell their story, since Watteau did small easel paintings for the drawing room rather than murals for a grand gallery. Watteau, like Rubens, was Flemish, born in the border town of Valenciennes, which Louis XIV had captured for France under the terms of the Treaty of Nijmegen (1679), and he became an ardent admirer of the monumental art produced by the great master of Antwerp. In Watteau's pictures, however, Rubens' massive figures are reduced to lithe and slender proportions. They are animated, but Rubens' bacchanalian furies now dance the graceful minuet. With Watteau the effect is capricious rather than monumental, and the spirit vivacious rather than voluptuous.

In the *Music Party*, a group has gathered on a terrace for a pleasant afternoon of musical instruction. The 'cello has been laid aside, the score is still open, and the lady who has just had her lesson lets her elbow rest on her guitar. The music master is tuning his theorbo before beginning to play, and a soft mood of melancholy anticipation settles over the company.

Beginning as a genre painter specializing in scenes of Flemish village life, Watteau became associated in Paris with decorators and designers of theater scenery and took an interest in the world of elegance as this could be observed in published fashion plates. With extraordinary poetic intuition, he combined these elements to create a new genre in which the fantasy of the stage and the reality of everyday life mixed to play out a comedy of love and desire, of random dalliance giving rise to amorous and unrequited longing. A master draftsman, Watteau devised a methodology based on his drawing from life, continuously, so as to capture in sheet after sheet the nuance and inflection of human pose and gesture, until altogether he had established a considerable range of psychological types. From this stock company, he then cast the

**308.** Antoine Watteau. *Music Party.* c. 1719. Oil on canvas, $25\frac{1}{2}$ × $36\frac{1}{4}$". Wallace Collection, London.

characters of his dramas and composed them in melodious patterns of decorative arabesque.

The generation of Antoine Watteau was the first in over seventy years to experience life without the absolutist rule and the style of grandiloquent public rhetoric espoused by Louis XIV. The averted gazes, turned backs, langorousness, and personal isolation of Watteau's characters—like the theorbo player in *Music Party* struggling alone and somewhat distressed to tune a temperamental instrument—suggest something of the loss of identity and disorientation, of privacy and even anonymity felt by an aristocratic society no longer subjected to the imperious commands of a single, powerfully authoritarian personality.

Sparkling with bravura brushwork, delicious in color (Pl. 39, p. 267), and charming in imagery and conception, Watteau's art evinced a freedom and a fantasy that were entirely new in Western painting. At the same time, a deep poetic sense—of the gentle irony in the preciousness and elusiveness of moments—lifted these scenes of social frivolity to the level of high art. As in *Music Party,* misty, vaporous landscapes are very important in conveying Watteau's ambiguous moods. As in the pastoral novels of the time, ladies and lovers of equal elegance stroll at leisure through lush gardens in fancied emulation of the life of Arcadian shepherds. Watteau handled such scenes with a characteristic lightness of touch and delicacy of sensation that set the tone for the later development of the rococo style.

François Boucher, the favorite painter of Madame de Pompadour, worked in a gayer vein than Watteau. The *Toilet of Venus* shows the 18th-century boudoir ideal of feminine charm in all its artificiality (Fig. 309). Love is no longer the robust passion it was with Rubens but a sophisticated flirtation. Voluptuous, mature womanhood is replaced by slender girlish forms.

Jean Honoré Fragonard was Boucher's successor as the leading exponent of the French rococo. *The Swing* (Pl. 40, p. 268), which was commissioned for the young aristocrat depicted in the lower left, portrays the frivolous, pleasure-seeking pursuits of his class. He has bribed the servant (lower right) to conceal him in the shrubbery while his lady love disports herself. The artist's fine feeling for color and the masterly draftsmanship with which he handles his diagonal composition save it from the twin perils of preciousness and triviality.

Much the same spirit of elegance and charm animates the sculpture of Falconet and Clodion. Terracotta can be modeled quickly, and so it was a fine medium in which to capture the fleeting rhythms of a Bacchic dance, as in Clodion's *Nymph and Satyr* (Fig. 310). These rococo figurines were replete with subtle classical allusions and were even franker in their eroticism than the paintings of the period.

## THE BOURGEOIS INFLUENCE

While the aristocrats were still powerful as leaders of fashion and arbiters of taste, their influence on the arts was on the wane. Not only did wealth put the means of patronage in the pocket of a rising bourgeoisie, but education let the middle class speak more and more in cultured accents. In France, many of Watteau's pictures were painted for bourgeois walls, and in England, the clientele for Hogarth's drawings and engravings came mostly from middle-class ranks. The vast majority of Voltaire's and Rousseau's readers were members of the middle class, while the novels of Richardson, Fielding, and Goldsmith were aimed at this growing reading public. Lessing's *Miss Sara Sampson* (1755) and Diderot's *The Natural Son* (1757) established the German and French bourgeois drama. The collective patronage of the concert hall replaced that of the restricted court circle. Instead of aiming to please one patron, the composer and virtuoso now tried to win the favor of the many. Mozart, for one, felt strong enough to break with his tyrannical archbishop and strike out as an independent composer; and it is far from an accident that his great opera *Don Giovanni* was commissioned for the municipality of Prague rather than for the royal capital of Vienna.

One of Watteau's most significant pictures was painted for a Paris art dealer by the name of Gersaint, proposed by the artist himself who, dying of tuberculosis, wanted for a brief period "to get the stiffness out of my fingers" (Pl. 39). Watteau idealized his sponsor to the extent of showing him as the proprietor of a gallerylike showroom filled with the fashionable elite of Parisian society—though that was not the case at the time. On the right, Gersaint is extolling the virtues of a painting in the manner of Watteau to a lady and gentleman who view it through their lorgnettes; on the left, the picture being packed is the portrait of Louis XIV. This implies farewell to the old regime and a salute both to the new age and style and to the name of Gersaint's shop, *Au Grand Monarque.* The scene (cut in half sometime after 1750) constitutes an urban stage where real characters act out the drama of everyday life in 18th-century Paris.

Genre pictures with casual everyday subjects are to be reckoned among the 18th-century middle-class reactions to aristocratic posturing, similar to those in 17th-century Holland. A master in this category was Chardin, whose sensitive painting revealed visual poetry in the lives of ordinary people going about their daily routines or indulging in quiet pleasures (Fig. 311). His many still-life compositions are veritable glorifications of commonplace things familiar in every household—bottles, cups, jugs, kitchen utensils, fruit and vegetables for the dinner table (Pl. 41, p. 268). But beyond Chardin's modest subject matter and deceptive simplicity, a thoughtful relationship between these objects is discernible. By his careful arrangements, textural contrasts, and subtle coloration, these become symbols of the good life. Chardin's geometrical clarity and pictorial harmony became the model for many modern masters, notably Manet, Cézanne, and Matisse.

The English painter William Hogarth must be reckoned among the distinguished company of 18th-century social satirists. Like Swift's *Gulliver's Travels*, John Gay's *Beggar's Opera,* and Voltaire's *Candide,* Hogarth's series of six pictures entitled *Marriage à-la-Mode* was a merciless exposé of the conditions and customs of his time, tempered by the saving grace of a brilliant wit. As Dickens and Zola, Goya and Daumier were to do in the less-humorous 19th century, Hogarth dramatized the conditions he saw and issued a challenge to society to do something about them. In this case it is the evil of putting human beings on the auction block of marriage. The *Marriage Contract* introduces the characters as in the first scene of a play (Fig. 312). The gouty nobleman points with pride to the family pedigree as he is about to sell his social standing in the person of his son to pay off the mortgage on his ancestral estate. The merchant, who is marrying off his daughter, scrutinizes the settlement through his spectacles just as he would any other hard-driven bargain. The pawns in this game,

the future bride and groom, sit with their backs to each other. The lawyer, Counselor Silvertongue, beginning a flirtation, flatters the future Lady Squanderfield, while her fiancé consoles himself with a pinch of snuff.

The other five scenes show the unhappy consequences of this loveless union as it progresses from

**right: 309.** François Boucher. *Toilet of Venus.* 1746. Oil on canvas, $42\frac{5}{8} \times 33\frac{1}{2}''$. Metropolitan Museum of Art, New York (bequest of William K. Vanderbilt, 1920).

**below left: 310.** Clodion. *The Intoxication of Wine (Nymph and Satyr).* c. 1775. Terra-cotta, height $23\frac{1}{4}''$. Metropolitan Museum of Art, New York (bequest of Benjamin Altman, 1913).

**below right: 311.** Jean Baptiste Siméon Chardin. *Boy Spinning Top.* 1741. Oil on canvas, $26\frac{1}{2} \times 28\frac{3}{4}''$. Louvre, Paris.

boredom and frivolity to infidelities, a duel, and death. In the *Countess' Levee* (Fig. 313), Lady Squanderfield entertains some of her fine-feathered friends as she makes her morning toilet. Counselor Silvertongue, now her lover, shows her tickets for a masked ball that evening, while an Italian barber dresses her hair, a servant passes cups of chocolate, a fencing master snores, a little Moorish slave points gleefully to the horns of a doll (symbolic of a husband whose wife is unfaithful), and a fat singer and his lean flute-playing accompanist add to the general din. The singer may be Carestini, the famous castrato, who sang the feminine leads in Handel's Italian operas.

top: 314. JEAN ANTOINE HOUDON. *Voltaire.* 1781. Marble, height 20″. Victoria & Albert Museum, London (Crown copyright reserved).

above: 315. JEAN ANTOINE HOUDON. *Benjamin Franklin.* 1778. Terra-cotta, $16\frac{1}{8}$″. Louvre, Paris.

This and such other series as the *Harlot's Progress* and the *Rake's Progress* were first made as paintings and then copied in the form of copper engravings. The prints were widely sold by subscription, and this type of group patronage made them financially successful. Every detail in Hogarth's crowded rooms is a commentary on both the action and the taste of his time. Albeit biting satire, his pictures work as art by virtue of their draftsmanship and composition.

As might be expected, bourgeois sculptural expression was at home in the domain of portraiture. Houdon's fine feeling for the delineation of character assures him a place among the foremost portraitists of Western art. His bust of Voltaire is one of several likenesses he did of the famous French philosopher and dramatist (Fig. 314). By the tilt of the head and the humorous gleam of the eye, Houdon captures the bemused look of the philosopher as he ponders and discourses on the foibles and follies of his fellow mortals. To chisel a glance of amiable skepticism in marble is no small feat. By leaving a rough edge in the outline of the pupil of the eye, the artist is able to produce a special glint that gives just the desired effect. By such means Houdon achieved a speaking image in which, during a fleeting moment of animated conversation, the philosopher might just have coined one of his famous epigrams.

Houdon's gallery also embraced many eminent Americans, including Thomas Jefferson, John Paul Jones, Robert Fulton, and Benjamin Franklin (Fig. 315), while he was ambassador to the court of Louis XVI. In 1785, on the invitation of Jefferson, he crossed the Atlantic with Franklin and spent several weeks at Mount Vernon making studies for the statue of George Washington now at the Virginia state capitol at Richmond.

## THE MOZARTIAN SYNTHESIS

Wolfgang Amadeus Mozart's most mature music was written during the last decade of his life as a resident of Vienna. While he continued to compose chamber music for aristocratic salons, an occasional chamber opera for the Schönbrunn Palace, and German *Singspiele* (comic operas) for the popular musical theater, his art attains its most universal expression in the works he created for the public opera houses and concert halls, where noblemen and commoners gathered together for their mutual recreation. It was here that Mozart's musical cosmopolitanism found its widest scope, here that he could explore the endless variety of tragic and comic situations that give his operas their boundless humanity, and here that his dramatic power could make its greatest impact. It is also these qualities that were carried over into the less direct and more abstract form of his symphonies and concertos and that give these compositions their dramatic intensity.

As a highly impressionable child, guided by a wise father, Mozart had been piloted around the important musical centers, met the most eminent composers, and absorbed all the current ideas. In London, he came under the sway of Christian Bach, one of the sons of the prolific Johann Sebastian. Mozart's generation had reacted to that of J. S. Bach and Handel much as the French painters had to Rubens and Lebrun, and their music spoke in the gentler accents of the gallant style rather than in the muscular rhythms and massive sonorities of the baroque. In Paris, Mozart was introduced to the rococo keyboard style, that art of the elegant trifle expressed in tinkling bonbons for the ear. There he also made his first contact with the operas of Gluck, from which he learned his deep regard for dramatic truth and elimination of everything except what was germane to the unfolding of the plot. In Italy, he came to know the full beauty of the human voice and the all-persuasive quality of Latin lyricism. In Mannheim, he heard the finest orchestra in Europe and was struck by the lightning of its dynamic crescendos and diminuendos as well as by the brilliance of its wind instruments. In Vienna, he learned from Joseph Haydn how to divine the soul of the orchestra and to explore the full expressive possibilities of the symphonic form. From firsthand contact he had discovered the idioms of the Neapolitan *opera seria*, Pergolesi's *opera buffa*, Rousseau's pastoral opera, and the German *Singspiel*. The spirit of the Enlightenment can be seen in the logical clarity and constructive unity of his forms; his letters show his enthusiasm for Rousseauian naturalness; and from his knowledge of literature, the explosive energy of the Storm-and-Stress movement finds its way into his music. Everything in his epoch was assayed in the laboratory of his brilliant mind, sifted through his creative consciousness and eventually refined into pure musical gold. In opera, he found the form in which he could combine all these ideas, idioms, and styles into one grand kaleidoscopic pattern, and for him the lyric theater was always his most natural medium of expression.

Mozart's power of characterization is akin to that of Shakespeare, though his dramas are made with musical materials. No composer understood better than Mozart that an opera is not a drama *with* music but a drama *in* music, or knew better that a character has no existence apart from the melody he sings; he *is* the melody. As the supreme musical dramatist, Mozart can awaken a character to life by a phrase or a rhythmical pattern, carry him through living situations by the direction of a melodic line, and develop the most complex interactions with the others in a scene by harmonic modulations and contrapuntal intricacies. His emotional range is enormous. Within but a short span of time, Mozart can be both gay and profound, serene and agitated, cheerful and serious, calm and turbulent, ethical and diabolical, yet all takes place within an ordered framework and nothing ever gets out of hand. His *Marriage of Figaro*, an adaptation of Beaumarchais' play, is one vast human panorama in which all the characters, whether master or servant, nobleman or knave, appear as equal partners in the dance of life. Every possible amorous situation is explored with objectivity, deep psychological insight, good humor, and warm understanding. From Cherubino's adolescent awakening to the fascinations of the opposite sex and the mature love of Figaro and Susanna, he moves on to the Count and Countess as the philandering husband and neglected wife, and finally to a pair of scheming blackmailers. The situations meanwhile run a gamut from intrigue, coquetry, and lust to infidelity, forgiveness, and tender reconciliation. Much of Beaumarchais' political satire is missing, but every nuance of human feeling is explored and exploited to the utmost.

**Don Giovanni**     For *Don Giovanni*, Mozart was fortunate in having the collaboration of Lorenzo da Ponte, a skillful writer and facile adapter with a real theatrical and histrionic flair. On hand at the final rehearsals of this saga of the world's greatest lover, and helping put a few finishing touches on the text, was none other than Giacomo Casanova, a man who had done enough research on the subject to qualify him as an authority. The Don Juan story was far from a novelty, and like the Faust legend, it went all the way back to the medieval morality drama.

Both the subject matter and Mozart's marvelous music led to the adoption and deification of *Don Giovanni* by the following generation, who saw in it the prototype of the romantic opera. In one of his late conversations, Goethe remarked rather wistfully that Mozart should have composed a *Faust*. What the venerable poet overlooked was that Mozart had already done so, since the Faustian concept completely permeates the character of Don Giovanni, who was a Mephistopheles and Faust rolled into one. Stylistically, the opera incorporates the spirit of the Storm-and-Stress drama and led directly to Spohr's opera *Faust*, E. T. A. Hoffmann's *Undine*, and Weber's *Freischütz*. The 19th century unfortunately burdened *Don Giovanni* with all kinds of interpretations. To the partisans of the French Revolution, Don Giovanni was the dissolute nobleman bent like an arch-criminal on bringing about the destruction of the moral law. If so, he was certainly the most beloved villain in all melodrama, with the sympathies of the audience enlisted for once on the side opposite law and order. The philosopher Kierkegaard regarded him as the incarnation of Desire, which by its very nature can never admit of satisfaction. He thus became a Nietzschean superman, or personification of the Dionysian life force. How then is it that in the opera each love affair either ends in frustration or leaves him in some ridiculous situation? To the classical enthusiasts, Don

Giovanni was the mortal who dared to defy the very gods themselves and by so doing brought about his own destruction. To the romantics, he was the towering tragic hero who, like Faust, was the victim of his own insatiable lusts. To others, he was the idealist always in pursuit of perfect beauty.

To find Mozart's real meaning, one must blow off the accumulation of 19th-century moral and philosophical dust and appraise it anew. Is it a tragedy or a comedy? Even today performances tend to emphasize one aspect or the other. Mozart's subtitle *dramma giocosa* suggests a combination of both. In the thematic catalogue of his own works, he also refers to it as an "opera buffa in two acts." Bearing in mind that Mozart was entirely capable of leaving it as a subtle enigma, that his inspired music raises it to the status of a unique masterpiece, and that it was originally composed for a small theater, one may decide that the best approach to it is as a high-spirited 18th-century comedy of manners, in which Molièrian satire is mixed with some Storm-and-Stress demonic elements.

The pace of the opera is breathtaking. In the first scene alone there is an attempted rape, a challenge and duel, the dying gasps of an outraged father, blasphemy, the escape of the culprits, and oaths of vengeance. In all this the absolute dramatic center is Don Giovanni, who bursts the bonds of civilized restraint, defies all social conventions, sweeps aside every barrier in his way, and stands alone against the world. In the *Marriage of Figaro* all the characters interacted with each other; here the figures, like the spokes of a wheel, exist only in their relation to the hub, Don Giovanni. Opposite him are the three feminine leads, each of equal importance—Donna Anna, Donna Elvira, and Zerlina.

Chronologically, Donna Elvira comes first, since she has been seduced and deserted before the curtain rises. Hers is the fury of a woman scorned, joined with the desire to forgive and forget and to save Don Giovanni from perdition. Her character is most clearly revealed in Aria No. 8, *"In qual eccessi,"* where she advises the lightheaded young Zerlina of the pitfalls of life with the dashing Don. Mozart writes it as a typical Handelian baroque rage aria. By so doing, he implies that Elvira's moral preachments are somewhat archaic, and the dignified form makes it an effective contrast to the prevailing frivolity.

The emotional life of Donna Anna, whose screams are heard at the beginning of the opera, is no less complicated. Full of righteous wrath, possibly mixed with some unconscious admiration for Don Giovanni, and tempered with filial affection for her murdered father, she swears vengeance on his assassin. She is joined in this resolve by her gentlemanly fiancé, Don Ottavio, and together they constitute the serious couple usual in Italian opera buffa. Since Don Ottavio is the lonely champion of lawful love versus licentiousness, he is bound to appear somewhat pale in these highly charged surroundings. His two tenor arias, *"Dalla sua pace"* and *"Il mio tesoro"* (Nos. 10B and 21), contain lovely lyricism but are parenthetical rather than part of the main action. Donna Anna, on the contrary, rises to tragic stature in *"Or sai chi l'onore"* (Aria No. 10); where, outraged but attracted to Don Giovanni, she intermingles hatred with passion.

Third in this list is the naïve but flirtatious Zerlina, torn between loyalty to her rustic bridegroom and the flattering attentions of the dashing Don. The duet *"La ci darem la mano"* (No. 7) is a subtle piece of musical characterization in which the division of the melody between the voices and the minute melodic variants point up their respective attitudes. The Don is tender, yet still the imperious aristocrat; Zerlina is feminine and doubtful of his intentions, but enjoying every moment. Later, the aria *"Vedrai carino"* (No. 18) reconciles Zerlina to her young peasant husband and reveals her maternal feelings toward him.

On the male side, Don Giovanni has no romantic competition, only a very substantial shadow in the form of Leporello, the comic manservant who plays Sancho Panza to his Don Quixote. Leporello is a stock opera-buffa character, who expresses his rather earthy cynicism in some chattering patter songs based on a running series of rapidly repeated syllables and notes. He introduces himself in the first aria of the opera; and in the famous "Catalogue Aria" (No. 4), he enumerates his master's amorous conquests in what must surely be the most hilarious set of statistics in history.

The two scenes in which all the characters are on stage are the finales to Acts I and II. In the first, Don Giovanni is entertaining a lively peasant wedding party in the hope of winning the bride Zerlina for himself. Fine dramatic contrast is provided in Don Giovanni's gay drinking song (No. 11) that sparkles like the wine he is ordering, and the sullen resentment of Masetto when he senses that his bride's head is being turned by this glamorous member of the privileged class. The scene reaches its brilliant climax when the dance music strikes up. There are no less than three ensembles on stage in addition to the main orchestra in the pit. Everyone at the time would have recognized this as a typical Viennese public ballroom scene for which Mozart frequently composed music. So that there would be dances that appealed to everybody, minuets were customarily played in one room, waltzes in another, and so on. Here the three groups also play different dances (above right). The first, consisting of two oboes, two horns, and strings, plays the best known of all minuets. On the repetition of the last part, the second stage orchestra, made up of violins and a bass, does a type of square dance known as a *contre-danse;* while a third ensemble, also of stringed instruments, plays an old-fashioned German waltz. An obvious stratification of social levels

*Don Giovanni*    Wolfgang Amadeus Mozart
(dance scene, finale, Act I)

is implied, with the masked figures of Donna Anna and Don Ottavio doing the aristocratic minuet; the peasants stamping out the vigorous, *laendlerlike* meter of the waltz, with strong accentuation on the beats of three and one, while Don Giovanni and Zerlina meet on the middle-class ground of the bourgeois contre-danse. Each social group is thus expressed through a characteristic rhythm. With the stage bands playing against the main orchestra below, all the plots and subplots boiling merrily away, and all the characters conversing and commenting on the action, the resulting rhythmic complexity and dramatic tension make this scene one of the major miracles of musical literature.

In the cemetery scene, which precedes the finale to Act II, Don Giovanni as a fugitive from justice is confronted with the equestrian statue of the Commendatore whom he has murdered at the beginning of the opera. The stentorian tones of the voice from the tomb reproach him for his wickedness; and Don Giovanni, always the courteous host, responds by inviting the statue to a midnight meal. The final scene opens with the preparations for the banquet, while the trumpets and drums sound the proper note of aristocratic hospitality. Like all noblemen of his time, Don Giovanni has his own liveried house orchestra standing by to play dinner music. This wind ensemble plays snatches from two popular Italian operas by Mozart's rivals; and a delightful bit of humor is introduced when they quote the *"Non più andrai"* from his own *Marriage of Figaro,* which happened to be a hit tune of that season, not a classic as now.

Donna Elvira, ever the kill-joy, now enters to play her trump card, which is the announcement that she is returning to her convent where life under the veil will presumably be more peaceful. As she reaches the door, her shriek heralds the arrival of the statue. With ominously heavy footsteps, the monument sings a long melodic line as rigid in its way as rigor mortis itself, reinforced by the sepulchral sounds of the trombones, instruments which were then associated with solemn church festivals and funerals. The contrast between the quick and the dead is brought out by the static pedal point of the statue's melody, around which the other characters react in ways varying from farce to tragedy. When Don Giovanni takes the hand of his marble guest, the horror music that had been foreshadowed in the overture is heard. Strings play spine-tingling scale figures upward and downward, alternately soft and loud. Thunder roars, demons shout, and flames rise upward; and the Don, unrepentant to the last, goes to his doom on a descending D-major scale. Breathlessly, the other characters arrive too late for the excitement but in time to sing a final quintet to these words: "Sinner, pause, and ponder well/ Mark the end of Don Juan!/ Are you going to Heaven or Hell?"

## IDEAS

The 18th-century styles either continued, modified, or departed from the high baroque. The shift of audience from a declining aristocracy to the rising bourgeoisie was accelerated, and the final phase of the aristocratic baroque style was reflected in the rococo; the continuation of 17th-century rationalism was found in the Enlightenment; voices of a classical revival began to be heard; new emotional outbursts were felt in the emphasis on sensibility and in the Storm-and-Stress movement. Besides neoclassicism, discussed in Chapter 18, the ideas that weave the arts of the 18th century into a coherent pattern are the rococo, the Enlightenment, and the emotional reaction to them known as the Storm and Stress.

**The Rococo**    The rococo is the last Western style that can lay claim to universality and the last to adhere strictly to the canons of beauty. The cosmopolitan rococo is a reflection of an aristocracy that still retained dominant control of artistic patronage. This was an international upper class who freely intermarried with the nobility of all parts of Europe, who spoke French and Italian better than the native tongues of their respective countries, who read French philosophers, attended French plays, and collected French art. This was, moreover, an educated group who cultivated wit, charm, social polish, and refinement of taste as a way of life. After the French Revolution and the Napoleonic wars, nationalism grew so strong that the arts appeared more and more in local frames of reference.

Examples of the rococo are found wherever the aristocracy possessed the means to follow the fashionable style (Fig. 316) and where the Counter-Reformationists undertook the building of churches. The hallmarks of the style are found in the paintings of Watteau, Boucher, and Fragonard; the sculptures of

Falconet and Clodion; and in such moments in Mozart as the exquisite aria sung by the Countess at the beginning of Act II of the *Marriage of Figaro.*

**The Enlightenment**    The *Enlightenment* is a blanket term under which it is possible to group such tendencies as the inventive spirit, scientific inquiry, the encyclopedic movement, the optimistic world view, and the belief in progress, turning the light of intelligence on life's problems, substituting reason for custom and tradition, and questioning everything. The impetus that the Enlightenment gave to scientific invention was applied by middle-class manufacturers and businessmen to the production of wealth. Pure science and nature in this case were less important than technology and artifact. The new social order is mirrored almost directly in the shift of artistic patronage in the direction of the middle-class audience. For the first time, it is possible to speak of the bourgeois novel and drama. Watteau painted one of his most important pictures for an art dealer; Chardin, Greuze, and Hogarth found their clientele among the same social segment. And Mozart, by turning the social tables upside down, making the Count the villain and the servant the hero, was certainly bolstering the ego of the bourgeoisie and blasting the aristocracy.

The Enlightenment spirit of free scientific inquiry, which grew out of 17th-century rationalism, was so distinctly anticlerical that it almost developed into a substitute religion. To the deists, God was a kind of cosmic clockmaker who created a mechanical universe, wound it up for all eternity, and let it go. The experimental method of science became the liturgy of this pseudoreligion, the encyclopedia its bible, nature its church, and all men of reason, the congregation. One of the most productive impulses of this aspect of the Enlightenment resulted in the encyclopedic movement. All the important intellects made their contributions to Diderot's *Encyclopédie,* with Voltaire writing the historical parts, Rousseau the sections on music, and so on. The same intellectual spirit, though in different religious circumstances, is observable in the comprehensive musical output of J. S. Bach. In *The Art of the Fugue* he applied the scientific method to musical composition. By keeping his themes constant, he carefully controlled the variables of form and thus systematized all possible fugal types. His extant cantatas add up to four for each Sunday of the year. His keyboard compositions were conceived encyclopedically and comprise examples in every possible form. His 48 preludes and fugues, known as the *Well-Tempered Clavier,* were written as a double cycle, two for each possible tonality; and his Brandenburg concertos explore every possible instrumental combination. His entire works thus emerge as a comprehensive design consciously planned to survey and sum up all the musical practices known to him.

**316.** GIOVANNI BATTISTA TIEPOLO. *Apollo Presenting to Frederick Barbarossa His Bride, Beatrice of Burgundy.* 1751. Ceiling fresco. Kaisersaal, Episcopal Palace, Würzburg.

The Enlightenment image of the cool man of reason inhabiting a world governed by purely rational principles was the object of Voltaire's satirical pen in the novel *Candide.* While maintaining his staunch belief that he lives in the Leibnizian "best of all possible worlds," the hero experiences every disaster known on the planet, including the great earthquake of Lisbon in 1745. The use of satire as a social weapon takes visual form in Hogarth's *Marriage à-la-Mode.* A certain amount of Voltairean skepticism can also be found in the character of Don Giovanni, who fears neither the supernatural nor the hereafter.

The Enlightenment was accompanied by a spirit of optimism and by a belief in progress and the perfectibility of man. Theologically, the Hebraic and Christian viewpoints were based on the fall of man and the doctrine of original sin dating from the expulsion of Adam and Eve from the Garden of Eden. Philosophically, Plato's theory of knowledge was also founded on a doctrine of prenatal perfection and the subsequent acquisition of knowledge by the process of remembrance. Humanists, such as Gibbon and Winckelmann, believed in the intellectual and artistic paradise of ancient Greece and Rome and as a consequence wrote their declines and falls. Without denying the greatness of Greece, the exponents of the Enlightenment were well aware that they had gone far beyond classical science and believed that, if the rational processes could be properly applied, they would eventually surpass the ancients in all fields. Kant, for instance, enthusiastically hailed Rousseau as the Newton of the moral world, and Condorcet in his *Progress of the Human Spirit* enumerated the ten stages by which man had raised himself from savagery to the threshold of perfection. Material progress was certainly an observable fact; and since nature held all the secrets that a man needed to know, and reason could unlock them, eventually man could control his environment. If he therefore would only use his men-

tal and moral powers to their fullest extent, the argument ran, man could go in one direction only, onward and upward.

**"Storm and Stress"**  In the latter half of the 18th century, various irrational tendencies came about as reactions to both the rococo cult of the beautiful and the Enlightenment's emphasis on reason. As early as 1756, Burke's *Essay on the Sublime and the Beautiful* insisted that in literature and art there is an element more important than beauty. This is the Sublime, which transcends mere beauty and can even admit of the ugly. "Whatever is fitted in any sort to excite the ideas of pain and danger," he said, "whatever is in any sort terrible, or conversant about terrible objects, is the source of the Sublime." The free exercise of the emotions and the imagination, even if it meant experiencing the painful, the astonishing, the horrible, was therefore legitimate territory for art to explore. This idea led to a renewed interest in Shakespeare; reveled in Rousseau's descriptions of alpine scenery, accompanied as they were by avalanches and storms; and delighted in the Rousseauian revolt against the restraints of civilization. This line of thought also constituted the background of the Storm-and-Stress movement in Germany. While the Enlightenment was trying to tame nature and bring it under man's control, the *Sturm und Drang* authors were reveling in how nature imposed her obscure and unfathomable will on man. In Goethe's early drama, Faust was the rebel against all accepted forms of wisdom, especially those arrived at through mathematical or scientific formulas. Both Faust and Don Giovanni were engaged in a quest for emotional truth and succeeded in unleashing the infernal forces that eventually consumed them.

Such were the social, ideational, and emotional impulses that defined the horizon before which the panorama of the 18th-century arts unfolded.

# 18 The Neoclassical Style

## PARIS, EARLY 19TH CENTURY

Some books, some archaeological discoveries, and some social upheavals brought to Paris many radical changes in intellectual orientation, in styles of art, and in form of government during the latter part of the 18th and early part of the 19th century. Stuart and Revett, two Englishmen who had visited Greece, published in 1762 *Antiquities of Athens,* which made a clear differentiation between Greek and Roman architecture. Two years later, J. J. Winckelmann's *History of Ancient Art,* the equivalent of a modern best seller, similarly distinguished between sculptures. "The principal and universal characteristic of the masterpieces of Greek art is a noble simplicity and a quiet grandeur," he declared. "As the depth of the sea remains always at rest, however the surface may be agitated, so the expression in the figures of the Greeks reveals in the midst of passion a great and steadfast soul." These words provided the critics of the rococo style with the needed aesthetic ammunition, and verbal volleys were fired at Boucher and Fragonard because of the frivolous content of their paintings (Fig. 309; Pl. 40, p. 268). During revolutionary times, the voice of Diderot, moral philosopher and apostle of the Enlightenment, continued to echo, especially his dictum that the function of art was to make "virtue adorable and vice repugnant."

Ancient Rome now became a symbol for the revolutionary protest. In politics, this at first meant a republican instead of a monarchical form of government. In religion, it was associated with a tolerant paganism as opposed to a dogmatic form of Christianity. (For a brief time, in fact, the Cathedral of Notre Dame in Paris was rededicated to the "Goddess of Reason.") Heroism and self-sacrifice, rugged resolve and Spartan simplicity became manifestations of the revolutionary spirit, and reflections of these qualities were readily found in Roman literature and art. The political writings of Cicero and Seneca were widely read and quoted to confirm the principle that sovereignty resided in the people and that government should be based on a voluntary agreement among citizens. Political pamphlets came to be studded with quotations from Tacitus, Sallust, and Horace, and the oratory of the period was modeled on that of Cicero. The convention hall where the revolutionary legislators met was lined with laurel-crowned statues of Solon, Camillus, and other ancient statesmen, and in debates the speakers relied on apt phrases from Cicero to clinch important points. They referred to their partisans as Brutuses and Catos and to their opponents as Catalines; their postures and gestures were studied imitations of Roman statues, and their oaths sworn on the head of Brutus or by the immortal gods.

Everyone who could read became biography-conscious and spoke like living characters out of Plutarch's *Parallel Lives.* (On the day she murdered Marat, Charlotte Corday had spent her time reading Plutarch.) Never before had public personalities seemed so obviously to have walked straight out of books. Surely Oscar Wilde must have had this revolutionary period in mind when he wittily twisted the old Greek aesthetic doctrine by saying that nature, especially human nature, is the imitation of art.

Many of the symbols of the French Revolution too were borrowed directly from the ancients. The cap of liberty was a copy of the Phrygian cap worn by the liberated slaves in Rome. The *fasces,* or bundle of sticks with the protruding ax tied together with a common bond, was once again the symbol of power.

When Napoleon Bonaparte rose to political power, he too shared the popular enthusiasm for all that was ancient. His chosen models were Alexander the Great and Julius Caesar, especially the latter since Caesar's career and Napoleon's had so many parallels. Napoleon became first a republican consul; later he ruled France through a tribune; and then, after a plebiscite, he emerged as the modern incarnation of a Roman emperor. The *fasces* became his emblem of authority; the eagles of the old Roman legions he made into the insignia of the French battalions, and eventually he was crowned with the laurel wreath, that ancient symbol of immortal fame.

Such a manipulation of the forms and images of ancient glory had a vast appeal to this man of modest birth. Coming to power so soon after the demise of an unpopular monarchy, Napoleon had to emphasize that many of the Roman emperors were of equally plebian backgrounds, and that the imperial toga had not necessarily been hereditary. But his hold on the people was indisputable and his elevation was made with full popular consent. Napoleon's mission was to bring order to what had been political chaos and to consolidate the social gains that had been made. His meteoric career was the success story of the 19th century, embodying as it did the ideal of the emancipated individual rising to leadership through his own efforts rather than by an accident of birth. In it, members of the parvenu society of his time could find substance for their fondest materialistic daydreams. The truth was that now, with the reins of power in their hands, the middle class did not know quite how to manage them. Napoleon did.

Like its Roman prototype, Napoleon's empire was international in scope, and its intellectual and artistic life transcended national boundary lines. What Greece had been to Rome, Italy was now to France. Napoleon brought the Italian sculptor Canova to Paris for various commissions, and his musical preferences were for such composers as Paisiello and Spontini. His proclamation to the Italian people on the eve of his invasion of their country points up this internationalism. "We are the friends of all nations," he protested, perhaps too much, "especially the descendants of Brutus, the Scipios, and of the great men we have chosen for our own model." And he took frequent pains to point out that he was embarking on a cultural as well as a military mission. Here was no barbarian Attila storming the citadel, but a conqueror who came to sack Rome in the company of a group of art experts who were well aware of the value of everything they took. A petition signed by all the important French artists actually had been sent to the Directory in 1796, pointing out how much the Romans had become civilized by confiscating the art of ancient Greece and how France would likewise flourish by bringing original works to Paris to serve as models. While this returning Caesar brought back with him no human captives, his victory celebration was livened by the presence of such distinguished prisoners of war as the *Apollo Belvedere* (Fig. 65), the paintings of Raphael, and the rare treasures he had pilfered from the Vatican and other Italian collections.

## ARCHITECTURE

With the reorganization of the government, the remaking of the constitution, and the recodification of the laws on the model of his reincarnated Roman Empire, Napoleon was determined that Paris should be replanned as a new Rome. He therefore undertook the ordering and commissioning of buildings with the same incredible vigor that marked his activities in other fields. The heart of the new city was still to be the spacious center designed around the old Place Louis XV, which under the Directory had been renamed the Place de la Concorde (Fig. 317). Its axis began on the left bank of the Seine River with the old Palais Bourbon, now the Chamber of Deputies, which was to have its face lifted by a Corinthian Colonnade. It continued across the river, by the bridge that had been begun in early revolutionary days (lower left), to the center of the Place, where some statuary was to cover the spot upon which the guillotine had done its grim work. The termination was to be the unfinished Church of La Madeleine at the end of the Rue Royale, scheduled to be rebuilt in the form of a Roman temple (upper right). To complete his scheme, Napoleon commissioned Percier and Fon-

**317.** Place de la Corcorde, Paris (aerial view).

297

## General Events

| | | |
|---|---|---|
| | 1748 | Excavations begun at Pompeii and Herculaneum |
| | 1762 | *Antiquities of Athens* published by Stuart and Revett |
| | 1764 | *History of Ancient Art* published by Winckelmann (1717–68) |
| | 1766 | *Laocoön* published by Lessing (1729–81) |
| | 1774 | Gluck's *Orfeo* produced at Paris Opera |
| 1785– | 1820 | Federal style in the United States |
| 1788– | 1791 | Brandenburg Gate in Berlin built by Langhans |
| | 1789 | French Revolution began |
| 1792– | 1794 | First French Republic |
| | 1796 | Napoleon's first Italian campaign |
| | 1798 | Napoleon's campaign in Egypt. Battle of the Pyramids |
| | 1799 | Napoleon became First Consul |
| | 1802 | Napoleon made Consul for life |
| | 1803 | Napoleonic Code of Laws issued |
| | 1804 | Napoleon crowned emperor. |
| | | Beethoven finished *Eroica* Symphony |
| | 1806 | Temple of Glory (later La Madeleine) begun by Vignon. Arc du Carrousel begun by Percier and Fontaine. Arc de Triomphe begun by Chalgrin |
| | 1814 | Napoleon abdicated; Bourbons restored to French throne |
| 1814– | 1821 | Louis XVIII, king of France |
| | 1815 | Napoleon defeated in Battle of Waterloo. Elgin Marbles exhibited in London |
| | 1816 | Elgin Marbles purchased by Parliament, placed in British Museum |
| | 1821 | Napoleon died |
| 1824– | 1830 | Charles X, king of France |
| | 1830 | July Revolution |
| 1830– | 1848 | Louis Philippe, king of France; constitutional monarch |

## Painters

| | | |
|---|---|---|
| 1716– | 1809 | Joseph Marie Vien |
| 1746– | 1828 | Francisco Goya |
| 1748– | 1825 | Jacques Louis David |
| 1771– | 1835 | Antoine Jean Gros |
| 1780– | 1867 | J. A. D. Ingres |
| 1791– | 1824 | Théodore Géricault |

## Sculptors

| | | |
|---|---|---|
| 1757– | 1822 | Antonio Canova |
| 1770– | 1844 | Bertel Thorwaldsen |
| 1798– | 1880 | P. J. H. Lemaire |

## Architects

| | | |
|---|---|---|
| 1733– | 1808 | Karl Gotthard Langhans |
| 1739– | 1811 | Jean Francis Chalgrin |
| 1743– | 1826 | Thomas Jefferson |
| 1753– | 1837 | John Soane |
| 1762– | 1820 | Pierre Alexandre Vignon |
| 1762– | 1853 | Pierre F. L. Fontaine |
| 1764– | 1838 | Charles Percier |
| 1784– | 1864 | Leo von Klenze |

## Musicians

| | | |
|---|---|---|
| 1714– | 1787 | Christopher Willibald Gluck |
| 1741– | 1813 | A. E. M. Grétry |
| 1741– | 1816 | Giovanni Paisiello |
| 1760– | 1837 | Jean François Lesueur |
| 1760– | 1842 | Salvador Cherubini |
| 1770– | 1827 | Ludwig van Beethoven |
| 1774– | 1851 | Gasparo Spontini |

taine, his favorite architects, to redesign the Rue de Rivoli, which intersected the axis at right angles and ran parallel to the Seine (middle right). Elsewhere throughout the city, triumphal arches and monumental columns were to proclaim to the world the presence of a new Caesar and Trajan.

Napoleon showed his interest in these projects by frequently conferring with his architects and engineers, by visiting construction sites, and by dreaming up new ideas while on distant battlefields. It was in Poland that he signed the decree for the building of his Temple of Glory, La Madeleine (Fig. 318). According to his express wish, the unfinished church would be transformed and bear a dedicatory inscription: 'From the Emperor to the soldiers of the Grande Armée.' The building was not to look like a church but like such a temple as one would find in Athens or Rome.

For the Temple of Glory, Napoleon personally selected an architectural plan by Pierre Alexandre Vignon, because it fulfilled his conditions by looking sufficiently ancient and pagan. The building is indeed a pagan Corinthian temple, and, except for the sculptural details, it was completed according to Vignon's design (Fig. 319). In the Roman manner, it stands on a podium 23 feet high and is approached by a flight of steps in the front. Running completely around the building is a series of Corinthian columns about 63 feet in height, 18 on each side, 8 on each end, and an additional row of 4 in front that supports the cornice. Since its rededication for religious purposes, this pagan temple of glory has had a large sculptural group by Lemaire on its pediment, representing the Last Judgment. In the center stands the figure of Christ, 17 feet high, with the repentant Mary Magdalene at His feet. To His left are allegorical figures top: **318.** PIERRE ALEXANDRE VIGNON. Façade, La Madeleine, Paris. 1762–1829. Length 350', width 147', podium height 23'.

above: **319.** Plan of La Madeleine.

right: **320.** Interior, La Madeleine, Paris.

representing Envy, Hypocrisy, and Avarice, while on His right are an angel of mercy and personifications of Faith, Hope, Charity, and Innocence.

The interior cella of an ancient temple was never intended as a gathering place and always remained dark and mysterious. Hence, of necessity, Vignon had to depart from precedent and come up with something new. The surprise that awaits the visitor as he passes through the massive bronze doors is complete, for the interior and exterior actually amount to two different buildings. The aisleless nave is divided into three long bays and a choir (Fig. 320), which are not roofed in timber as in a Greek temple or vaulted in the Roman manner but are crowned with three low saucer domes on pendentives. The nave terminates in a semicircular apse that is roofed over by a semidome. Chapels are located in the recesses created by the buttresses that support the domes, and two clas-

sical orders—the Corinthian and Ionic—form the basis of the decorative scheme. Rich use is made of marble paneling, and the domes are coffered in the manner of the Roman Pantheon. What little light there is in this windowless interior comes from skylights at the tops of the domes, an idea derived from the Pantheon's oculus. The best that can be said about this method is that it keeps the exterior roof line intact. The exterior, as a study in classical design, has a certain dignity in its archaeological faithfulness to such older models as the Maison Carrée (Fig. 74), though it excels its prototypes only in its larger proportions. The interior, however, does have a certain originality as an early example of the 19th-century eclectic style.

In 1806, after winning military victories in Germany and Austria, Napoleon entrusted to Percier and Fontaine the building of a triumphal arch. Now known as the Arc de Triomphe du Carrousel, it was designed as a gate of honor to the Tuileries Palace (Fig. 321). It turned out to be a rather slavish imitation of the Arch of Septimus Severus in Rome, though of more modest proportions, but standing on the platform above it was one of Napoleon's proudest battle trophies—the group of four bronze horses taken from St. Mark's in Venice (Fig. 213). Owing to the shifting fortunes of war, Venice later got back the horses as a result of a peace treaty, and a triumphal chariot drawn by horses of a considerably later vintage was installed in their place to celebrate, somewhat ironically, the restoration of the Bourbons in the person of Louis XVIII. The face of the arch is decorated with rather undistinguished bas-reliefs depicting such scenes as the Battle of Austerlitz, the surrender of Ulm, the peace of Tilsit, and Napoleon's triumphal entries into Munich and Vienna.

When finished, the result was too meager to measure up to Napoleon's imperial ambitions, and so another and still grander arch was commissioned for the Place de l'Étoile, now renamed Place Charles de Gaulle. In this familiar Paris landmark, the architect Jean Francis Chalgrin achieved more life and elasticity by freely adapting rather than copying a known model. In it, French baroque precedents, Roman classical inspiration, and academic correctness of execution are combined in a harmonious manner. For his monumental effect, Chalgrin relied on bold proportions and a grand scale. Later, after Napoleonic times, the severity of the general outline was relieved by the skillful placement of high-relief sculptures of Cortot and Rude (Fig. 334), works on a scale comparable to the immense size of the arch itself.

Still not content, Napoleon ordered a monumental Doric column to be erected in the Place Vendôme (Fig. 322). In size and style of ornamentation, it was a conscious copy of Trajan's Column in Rome (Fig. 72), the main difference being that its spiral reliefs are done on a bronze strip made from the guns and cannons captured from the defeated Prussian and Austrian armies. The sculpture recounts the story of the campaign of 1805 in scenes, such as Napoleon's address to his troops, the meeting of the three emperors, and the conquests of Istria and Dalmatia.

The wave of enthusiasm for classical architecture was by no means confined to Paris. Germany, England, and the United States had each experienced classic revivals in the 18th century. During the early 19th century, the Roman revival was strongest in the countries identified with Napoleon's Empire, while the Greek revival was accented in the nations of the anti-Napoleonic coalition, notably England and Germany. In England, such a public building as the British Museum was strongly Greek in character. In Berlin, an early example is the Brandenburg Gate modeled after the Athenian Propylaea. In the United States, the classical revival period corresponded generally to the federal style, which ran its course from c. 1785 to 1820. Buildings that show the Roman influence are the Virginia state capitol, which Thomas Jef-

**far left: 321.** CHARLES PERCIER and PIERRE F. L. FONTAINE. Arc de Triomphe du Carrousel, Paris. 1806. Width 63½', height 48'.

**left: 322.** CHARLES PERCIER and PIERRE F. L. FONTAINE. Vendôme Column, Paris. 1810. Marble with bronze spiral frieze.

**above: Plate 42.** Jacques Louis David. *Le Sacre ("The Coronation").* 1805–08. Oil on canvas, 20′ × 30′6½″. Louvre, Paris. (See p. 305.)

**right: Plate 43.** Francisco Goya. *Executions of the Third of May, 1808.* 1814–15. Oil on canvas, 8′9″ × 13′4″. Prado, Madrid. (See p. 306.)

Plate 44. Eugène Delacroix. *Liberty Leading the People, 1830.* 1830. Oil on canvas, 8'6" × 10'10". Louvre, Paris. (See p. 313.)

Plate 45. Eugène Delacroix. Detail of "spattering of color" on the surface of *Dante and Vergil in Hell.* 1822. Oil on canvas, 6'1½" × 7'10½" (entire work). Louvre, Paris. (Photo: E. Vander Veen, © Time-Life Books.) (See p. 316 and Fig. 333.)

siasm to a pitch of frenzy. It had the requisite Roman setting, and the spectacle of a vestal virgin's struggle between her desire for personal happiness and her vows of service to the state was sufficient to ensure more than 100 performances in its first season in Paris. The libretto stressed glory on the battlefield, and Spontini supplied the necessary triumphal marches. His music is full of the sounding brass and the trumpet's blare, singing in the grand style, and the declamation of massive choruses. One of his contemporaries wrote that "his *forte* was a hurricane, his *piano* a breath, his *sforzando* enough to wake the dead." It was none other than Berlioz who attributed to him the invention of the "colossal crescendo."

Unknown to Napoleon, however, the essence of the heroic ideal had been distilled in musical form in one of the countries he had conquered. Ludwig van Beethoven's *Third Symphony*, which the composer himself called the *Eroica*, or "Heroic," was never heard by the man whose career had suggested it; nor was it played in Paris until 1828, a quarter of a century after it was composed. Yet a French writer of later times, Romain Rolland, could declare with the full weight of history on his side: "Here is an Austerlitz of music, the conquest of an empire. And Beethoven's has endured longer than Napoleon's." The inception of this mighty work apparently took place in 1798 when General Bernadotte, as an emissary of France, visited Vienna. The general was enough interested in music to have the French violinist Rodolphe Kreutzer in his suite, and Beethoven soon came to his attention. It is Bernadotte who is credited with the suggestion that Beethoven write a work honoring Consul Bonaparte, although he probably had in mind little more than a dedication. For four years Beethoven thought about the suggestion, and eventually the *Eroica* bore the desired dedication. But the year that the symphony was completed was the year in which Napoleon accepted the title of Emperor. Beethoven, feeling that the erstwhile apostle of liberty had become both a traitor and a new tyrant, erased the name from the title page and inscribed it instead "to the memory of a great man." This memory indeed had stirred Beethoven deeply, and from the days of his youth he had been a lifelong partisan of the ideals of liberty, equality, and fraternity. It was Napoleon's espousal of these principles, his implacable opposition to hereditary privilege, his will and ability to translate these ideals into action, that had moved Beethoven profoundly as it had so many other artists and writers of the time. The *Third Symphony* is not, and never was, narrowly Napoleonic, but more generally an elaboration of the heroism of one who, for a time at least, rallied the progressive and freedom-loving people of all nations around his standard.

The music Beethoven wrote for the theater was invariably based on themes involving the quest for individual liberty and the cause of popular freedom.

In his only opera, *Fidelio,* he insisted on a libretto that would reflect high moral purpose and steadfast resolve.

In Beethoven's instrumental compositions, these ideals of liberty, equality, and fraternity attained their most abstract and universal expression in his fluid forms. Beethoven used the power of his art to convey the spirit of these great human declarations, and, by so doing, he illuminated the path of man as he works toward his ultimate destiny of progress and perfectibility. His achievement was all the greater because he realized it without programmatic dilutions, thereby strengthening rather than weakening his art. Through the *Eroica*, Beethoven was giving tangible shape to the aspirations of a large segment of mankind during those stirring times. In it, he mirrored the titanic struggle between the opposing attitudes of submission and assertion, between passivity and activity, and between acceptance and challenge. Through it, he gave flesh to the word of the triumph of spirit over matter, will over negation, and the victorious human drive against the forces of suppression. Though the length of the symphony is unprecedented and the orchestra somewhat expanded, Beethoven never fell into the trap that many of the French composers of the revolutionary period did when they equated colossal size with grandeur of utterance. While the revolutionists wrote their choruses for 1,000 voices, accompanied by cannons and three or four combined orchestras, Beethoven added just one horn to his usual brass section. He clothed his ideas in rich folds of lustrous sound that grow out of the poetic idea itself. Furthermore, by raising the level of musical content and making it commensurate with his instrumental forces, he succeeded in producing an organic work of art where the others failed. While the symphony as a whole can be criticized on formal grounds and for a certain lack of unity in the four separate movements, the fiery spirit of creation when Beethoven was at the height of his mature powers has never been surpassed. The *Eroica* was as much a revolution in the musical field as the French Revolution was in that of political thought and action.

The great opening movement is cast in the mold known as *sonata form*, which might be described as a dramatic reconciliation of opposites, or, more technically, as a strategy of thematic and key relationships. Brought to perfection in the late 18th century by Haydn and Mozart, this balanced classical design, with its true Aristotelian beginning, middle, and end, unfolds with an opening section, called an *exposition*, is followed by a central core, the *development,* and then concludes with a *recapitulation.* Optionally a prologue, or *introduction,* and an epilogue, or *coda,* may be added. The exposition presents an abstract dramatic confrontation between a protagonist consisting of related motifs, themes, or subjects within a principal key center (the tonic) and an antagonist comprised of contrasting material in a different key center (the dominant, relative major or minor, etc.). Then ensues the development, or working-out portion, in which the previously presented materials oppose or conflict and interact with one other. The subjects or themes may be broken up by fragmentation or segmentation, new tonal territories explored by modulating to new key centers close or remote, and themes combined in contrapuntal juxtapositions. Finally, the materials are reassembled in the recapitulation that reveals their altered character in a kind of dramatic reconciliation. Beethoven, as his title and situation demand, here projects a first movement on a heroic scale.

Each of the four movements was in its way precedent-shattering. The first is distinguished by its restless surging character and its enormous expansion of first-movement form to encompass a development section of 245 bars. The mobilization of such forces, as well as the transformation of the coda into a terminal development of 140 measures, caused Romain Rolland to call it a "Grand Army of the soul, that will not stop until it has trampled on the whole earth."

A funeral march as the second movement of a symphony was another innovation, though Beethoven had included one in his earlier *Sonata for Piano,* Op. 26, which bears the inscription "on the death of a hero." Its heroic proportions here, as well as its poetic conception as an apotheosis of the hero, link it with the first movement. While such an apotheosis is a fairly common idea for a painting, statue, poem, play, or opera, its incorporation into the more abstract symphonic form is unique. The effect is that of a glowing elegy for the heroic among mankind who give up life itself so that the ideals for which they fought may live. It is, in this case, a collective rather than an individualized expression, though it emphasizes that every great advance of mankind is accompanied by personal tragedy. The stately measured rhythms and muffled sonorities also reminded the listener of Beethoven's time that contemporary heroes, as well as such ancient ones as Socrates and Jesus, often suffered martyrdom at the hands of an uncomprehending society.

The title "Scherzo" over the third movement also appears for the first time in a formal symphony, though again it had been used earlier in piano sonatas and chamber music. Beethoven once more reveals himself a man of the revolutionary period by the substitution of this robust humor for the traditional minuet, but in such a grand design he hardly had any other alternative. Berlioz has referred to its energetic rhythms as a kind of play, "recalling that which the warriors of the *Iliad* celebrated round the tombs of their chiefs."

For his finale, Beethoven writes such a monumental set of variations that it becomes a veritable musical arch of triumph through which the image of a liberated humanity joyfully passes in review. To

*Symphony No. 3*        LUDWIG VAN BEETHOVEN
(finale: *Allegro molto*—bars 76–83)

comprehend its full meaning, one needs to look both backward and forward to other landmarks in Beethoven's work. The theme itself is taken from the last dance of ballet music for *Prometheus.* Its frequent appearance in his notebooks, and its existence in two other versions—a simple country dance and a set of piano variations—show that it figured prominently in his musical thought for several years. For him the theme had definite Promethean associations and a certain buoyant optimism. The figure of Prometheus represented for Beethoven, as for Shelley, "the type of the highest perfection of moral and intellectual nature impelled by the purest and truest motives to the best and noblest of ends." It was Prometheus who first defied the gods in order to bring the divine fire of the arts and sciences from the Olympian hearth to animate the spirits of men and release them from the bondage of ignorance. Prometheus thus became a symbol of creative power through which Beethoven conveyed his conviction of the ultimate perfectibility of mankind. The fiery, precipitous descent of the opening bars had also been heard in the ballet music in a more literal sense. Here it serves as a mighty preparation for the emergence of the skeleton theme.

What is heard at first is simply a structural outline derived from the bass of the Promethean dance, which defines a tonal center together with the upper and lower dominant limits of the tonality. This harmonic vacuum is gradually populated by the addition of a second, third, and fourth voice, while simultaneously the rhythmic divisions are quickened by similar subdivisions. Not until the 76th bar is the Promethean melody joined to its previously heard skeletal bass (see above).

The form of the finale is a series of variations unequal in length and strongly contrasted in style. What had before been but a pleasant little dance tune now assumes the imposing shape of a triumphant melody, which Beethoven, by his additive process, is able to build into the cumulative structure he needs for his victory finale. Here the great idea springs fully grown and fully armed from the brain of its creator. The heroic image is later continued in the finales of the *Fifth* and *Ninth Symphonies,* and the amplification in these later works contributes to a more profound understanding of the earlier *Eroica.*

All three finales envision the emergence of a strong and free human society, and all three start with quasi-popular themes. In the *Eroica,* it is a modest little country dance; in the *Fifth,* a simple marching tune; and in the *Ninth,* an unpretentious hymn. One and all, they are built up to epical proportions. By the use of an immense variety of styles, episodic deviations, a wide range of keys, and shifting orchestral color, they become collective rather than individual expressions. Instead of being restricted to one side of life, they embrace a cross section of musical levels and reach out to encompass the entire human panorama. Some variations are aristocratic in sound, while others are rough and ready. Compare, for example, the elegant sonorities of bars 175–197 in the *Eroica* finale with the boisterous band music heard in bars 211–255. A similar open-air episode to that heard in bars 211–255 occurs in the finale of the *Ninth,* where Beethoven inserts a popular "Turkish" march, scored in a bizarre manner for bassoons, horns, trombones, cymbals, triangle, and drums. Further contrasts in the *Eroica* finale can be heard in the fugal episodes (bars 117–174 and 226–348), which employ sophisticated contrapuntal devices, such as the inversion of the skeleton theme (277–280) and the rather stolid German chorale (249–364) that begins at the point where the tempo is slackened to a *Poco andante.* All this vast variety of forms—dances, songs, fugues, chorales—are arranged sequentially in the manner of a procession that eventually leads up to the rousing triumphant climax heard in bars 381–395. At this point, Beethoven throws in all his orchestral forces, including the brasses and drums, to bring about the image of ultimate achievement of the heroic idea. Afterward there remain only the quieter anticlimax (396–430), in which the whole awesome spectacle is contemplated retrospectively, and the whirlwind *presto* that terminates the movement.

## THE ARCHAEOLOGICAL IDEA

The Napoleonic era was a paradoxical mixture of progressive and retrogressive tendencies. At the very time when the social aspirations of the revolutionary period were about to be realized in democratic forms, Europe was confronted with a militant revival of ancient Roman imperial autocracy. The 18th-century individualism that had led to the struggle for freedom was engulfed in a 19th-century regimentation disguised as a movement to maintain the social gains that had been made. Revolutionary ideals were partially eclipsed by Napoleonic actualities; the desire for freedom collided with the need for order; the rights of man conflicted with the might of man; and spiritual well-being was pitted against material considerations.

New scientific and technological advances competed for attention with revivals of ancient glories. Napoleon boasted of a new culture, yet he clothed it in a Roman toga. But the early 19th century was by no means unique in its revival of a bygone era. Every period in Western art since Greco-Roman days has revived classical ideas and motifs in one manner or another. From the 1,000-year span of Greco-Roman civilization, many choices have been made by succeeding centuries. Dramas and operas have been set in Athens, Sparta, the Alexandrian empire, the Roman republic, and the West and East Roman empires, and their characters have been lofty Olympian deities and rugged Roman heroes. Dramatists have chosen the Roman playwright Seneca as a model, as did Quinault and Racine in the baroque period, and the Athenians Aeschylus and Euripides, as did Shelley and Goethe. Architects in the 17th century, such as Bernini and Perrault, built then-modern palaces that they decorated with classical motifs, while the neoclassicists Vignon, Percier, and Fontaine constructed almost precise models of Greek and Roman temples. Forms of government, likewise, ranged from the democratic republic to the autocratic empire. Aside from the shape and spirit a revival assumes, it is largely a matter of selectivity.

Each period has tended to choose from the past those elements that harmonized with its specific ideals and aspirations. Florentine Renaissance humanists, in their reaction to medieval scholastic thought and the traditional Church interpretation of Aristotle, turned to the pagan beauties of antiquity in general and to the philosophy of Plato in particular. The Renaissance revival of classicism, however, was confined to a few intellectuals and artists. Neoclassicism, on the other hand, was mirrored in forms of government, became the officially approved art style, and rested on a base of broad popular acceptance. Baroque classical interests reflected an aristocratic image of man and were restricted to courtly circles. Louis XIV and his associates identified themselves with the gods of Mt. Olympus, and their moral standards, like those of the ancient deities, were the ethics of a highly privileged class. Napoleonic neoclassicism, by contrast, was oriented toward the comfortable middle class, which saw a congenial hedonistic image in the living standards of ancient Pompeii and Herculaneum but tempered luxury with the stricter moral standards of a revolutionary regime. The new interest in classical sculpture, architecture, and painting was also a bourgeois criticism of the artificiality and extravagance of courtly life as mirrored in the rococo. Without the moral connotations of this revived interest in the ancient world, the choice of conservative classical art forms would have been extremely odd for the revolutionary period.

The principal difference between early 19th-century artists and their predecessors was in the desire for faithfulness to antique models. Archaeological correctness was now possible, owing to a more detailed knowledge of the past. Winckelmann and his generation had made classical archaeology a science, and the excavations at Pompeii and Herculaneum had provided the material and stimulus for authenticity. For neoclassical success, a building had to be archaeologically accurate. The Vendôme Column was planned as a replica of Trajan's Column and the Arc du Carrousel preserved the proportions and shape of the Arch of Septimus Severus, even if reduced somewhat in size. When variations were made, as in the instance of the Arc de Triomphe and La Madeleine in Paris, the results were more interesting. The first two may be likened to a pair of competent academic theses, while the latter pair approximate the livelier style of good historical novels. Archaeological correctness meant lifting an ancient building, which had been designed for a now-antiquated purpose, out of its context, period, and century and putting it down bodily into another period where it had no practical reason for being. This transposition would never have occurred in the rational Enlightenment period. While Palladio, Mansart, and Wren had been concerned with adapting classical principles and motifs to the needs of their times, Vignon, Percier, and Fontaine were busy trying to fit activities of the Napoleonic period into ancient molds.

Likewise, in the neoclassical style, a successful statue had to be accurate. And since such a profusion of antique models existed, the sculptors were limited in their creative freedom. Their desire for exactitude often led them to the point of absurdity (Fig. 330). They omitted carving the irises and pupils of the eyes and left them blank, because they did not know that the Greeks had painted in such details. The prevailing whiteness made their works resemble mortuary monuments, since they had overlooked the fact that the ancients had designed their friezes for the strong light and shadow of the open air and not for the dim interiors of museums. While Praxiteles and Michelangelo had turned marble into flesh, Canova and Thorwaldsen converted the living flesh of their models into cold stone.

Enthusiasm for antiquity sometimes led David into similar predicaments. For the heads of figures in his early pictures he used ancient Roman portrait busts instead of live models. In the baroque period, when Poussin and Claude Lorrain painted Rome, they did so usually in terms of picturesque ruins, but David painted archaeological reconstructions. Madame Récamier was a 19th-century Parisian socialite, but David made her into a fancy-dress reincarnation of a Pompeian matron. David's adherence to lines and planes was often so strict that the effect of his paintings was almost as severe as that of relief sculpture. David was saved, however, from the major pitfalls of his architectural and sculptural colleagues because so few examples of ancient painting were known at the time. As a consequence, he was forced to divert his considerable talent as a painter in the direction of a new style.

In poetry, a similar motivation can be found in the reforms of André Chénier, which were based on his studies of the Latin and Greek originals. For the forms of his odes and elegies, his pastoral idylls and epics, he drew directly on Homer, Pindar, Vergil, and Horace. "Let us upon new thoughts write antique verses," he had declared; and to a considerable degree his enthusiasm helped him to carry out his announced objective.

In this archaeological era, however, the musicians fared the best of all because they had no examples surviving from antiquity to emulate. An opera, to be sure, could get some authenticity into its plot, decor, and costumes; and such productions of 1807 as Persuis and Lesueur's *Triomphe de Trajan,* their *L'Inauguration du Temple de la Victoire,* and Spontini's *La Vestale* tried to make the grade in this respect. All this, however, was on the surface and could hardly be compared with the type of authenticity represented by the Vendôme Column or the Napoleonic arches of triumph. Since the musicians had to evolve their own style, the music of the period has overshadowed the other contemporary arts and its vitality has given it a lasting general appeal. Just as the fussy rococo had brought about a counter-movement in the prerevolutionary neoclassicism, so a reform in music had been carried out in the 18th century under Gluck. By reducing the number of characters in his operas, omitting complicated subplots, strengthening the role of the chorus, transferring much of the lyrical expression to the orchestra, writing simple unadorned melodies, and avoiding Italianate coloratura cadenzas, Gluck had brought about a musical revolution similar to David's in painting and paved the way for a new style. His ideas were based partially on a reinterpretation of Aristotle's *Poetics,* and in his preface to *Alceste* (1767) he had stated that his music was designed to allow the drama to proceed "without interrupting the action or stifling it with a useless superfluity of ornaments." Echoing Winckelmann, he added that the great principles of beauty were "simplicity, truth and naturalness."

These principles found their ultimate expression in the sinewy music of Beethoven, who, by impatiently brushing aside ancient precedents, achieved an expressive style that was genuinely heroic and not merely histrionic. Out of neoclassicism Beethoven emerges as the most truly representative artist, and his art is the outstanding expressive accomplishment of his time.

# 19 The Romantic Style

## PARIS, 1830

Well before the romantic Revolution of July, 1830, new ideas were stirring the minds and imaginations of the intellectuals and artists of Paris. In 1827, as the new movement was gaining momentum, Victor Hugo published his *Chromwell,* a drama with a preface that served as the manifesto of romanticism. Guizot was lecturing at the Sorbonne on the early history of France. François Rude, destined to be the principal sculptor of the period, returned from his Belgian exile. And the painter Delacroix wrote in his journal that when he went to the Odéon Theater to see Shakespeare's *Hamlet,* he met the writers Alexandre Dumas and Victor Hugo. The Ophelia in that production was Harriet Smithson, later to become the wife of the composer Hector Berlioz. Gérard de Nerval's translation of Goethe appeared that autumn and inspired Berlioz to compose *Eight Scenes from Faust,* which later reached popularity in the revision called the *Damnation of Faust.* Delacroix was already at work on his famous *Faust* lithographs to illustrate the edition of Goethe's drama that attained publication in 1828.

All in all, the 1820s were an inspiring time, and when Théophile Gautier later came to write his history of romanticism, he looked back on his youthful years with nostalgia. "What a marvelous time," he wrote, "Walter Scott was then in the flower of his success; one was initiated into the mysteries of Goethe's *Faust,* which as Madame de Staël said, contained everything. One discovered Shakespeare, and the poems of Lord Byron: the *Corsair; Lara; The Gaiour; Manfred; Beppo;* and *Don Juan* took us to the orient, which was not banal then as now. All was young, new, exotically colored, intoxicating, and strongly flavored. It turned our heads; it was as if we had entered into a strange new world." Romanticism was swept in on a wave of political unrest culminating in the July Revolution of 1830, and it was to be the dominant French style until the February Revolution of 1848.

Nowhere is there a better example of the mating of the artistic genius with the spirit of his time than in the life and work of Eugène Delacroix set in the Paris of 1830. His *Liberty Leading the People* brought those glorious July days to incandescent expression (Pl. 44, p. 302). The canvas, in which he distilled the essence of that revolution, is dominated by the fiery allegorical figure of Liberty, here seen as the spirit of the French people whom she leads onward to triumph. No relaxed Mediterranean goddess but a virile, energetic reincarnation of the spirit of 1789, her muscular arms are strong enough to hold with ease both a bayoneted rifle and the tricolored banner of the republic. Though bare-breasted, she betrays no sign of softness or sensuality, and her powerful limbs stride over the street barricades as she leads her followers forward through the oncoming barrage. Though an allegorical figure, she is treated by Delacroix as a living personality. Only the Phyrgian cap and the almost-classic profile, serene in the face of danger, indicate her symbolic significance. She does not hover over the action on wings, as so many other artists depicted her; instead, with her feet on the ground, she is in the midst of the action.

Liberty's motley followers include both impetuous students and battle-scarred soldiers who have heeded her call rather than that of their reactionary king. The boy on the right is recruited from the Paris streets. Too young to understand the significance of the events, he is there, a pistol in each hand, joining in the general excitement. In the background are the remnants of the old guard from revolutionary days still carrying on the struggle. Two main social classes are represented—in the shadows on the extreme left, the man armed with a saber is an obviously proletarian figure, while in front of him toward the center the more prominent figure in the modish frock coat, top hat, and sideburns is a bourgeois gentleman who has grabbed his musket and joined in the general confusion. It was his class that controlled the fighting and derived the benefits from it by stamping its image on the new monarchy represented in the person of Louis Philippe, the "Citizen King." Though the July Revolution was essentially a palace revolt replacing a reactionary Bourbon with his more liberal cousin, no aristocrats are represented as taking part. In the shadow below, the wounded and dying are strewn on the loose cobblestones looking toward Liberty, for she is both their inspiration and their reason for being. Through smoke at the right the towers of Notre Dame are discernible.

Because of the contemporary frame of reference in which one recognizes the familiar shirts, blouses, trousers, rifles, pistols, and other 19th-century paraphernalia, the picture sometimes has been called re-

## General Events

1814  Fall of Napoleon. Restoration of the monarchy under Louis XVIII
1821  Napoleon died
1824  Louis XVIII succeeded by Charles X
1830  July Revolution overthrew old line of Bourbons. Louis Philippe began reign as limited monarch
1837  Commission for the Preservation of Historical Monuments founded by Louis Philippe
1840  Guizot, French historian and statesman, became prime minister
1848  February Revolution overthrew Louis Philippe's government. Second Republic proclaimed; Louis Napoleon, nephew of Napoleon I, elected president
1852  Louis Napoleon elected emperor; reigned as Napoleon III
1870  Napoleon III abdicated after unsuccessful conclusion of Franco-Prussian War. Third Republic proclaimed

## Architects

1726–  1796  William Chambers
1748–  1813  James Wyatt
1752–  1835  John Nash
1790–  1853  François Christian Gau
1795–  1860  Charles Barry
1802–  1878  Richard Upjohn
1814–  1879  Eugène Viollet-le-Duc
1817–  1885  Théodore Ballu
1818–  1895  James Renwick
1824–  1881  George Street

## Sculptors

1784–  1855  François Rude
1787–  1843  Jean Pierre Cortot
1796–  1875  Antoine Louis Barye

## Painters

1771–  1835  Antoine Jean Gros
1775–  1851  J. M. W. Turner
1776–  1837  John Constable
1780–  1867  J. A. D. Ingres
1791–  1824  Théodore Géricault
1796–  1875  Camille Corot
1798–  1863  Eugène Delacroix
1808–  1879  Honoré Daumier
1814–  1875  François Millet

## Writers

1717–  1797  Horace Walpole
1749–  1832  Johann Wolfgang von Goethe
1766–  1817  Germaine de Staël
1768–  1848  Chateaubriand
1771–  1832  Walter Scott
1774–  1843  Robert Southey
1783–  1842  Stendhal (Henry Beyle)
1787–  1874  François Guizot
1788–  1824  Lord Byron
1788–  1860  Arthur Schopenhauer
1792–  1822  Percy B. Shelley
1795–  1821  John Keats
1797–  1856  Heinrich Heine
1799–  1850  Honoré de Balzac
1802–  1870  Alexandre Dumas
1802–  1885  Victor Hugo
1803–  1870  Prosper Mérimée
1804–  1876  George Sand
1811–  1872  Théophile Gautier

## Musicians

1782–  1871  Daniel Auber
1782–  1840  Niccolo Paganini
1784–  1859  Ludwig Spohr
1786–  1826  Carl Maria von Weber
1791–  1864  Giacomo Meyerbeer
1803–  1869  Hector Berlioz
1809–  1849  Frédéric Chopin
1809–  1847  Felix Mendelssohn
1810–  1856  Robert Schumann
1811–  1886  Franz Liszt
1813–  1883  Richard Wagner
1813–  1901  Giuseppe Verdi
1818–  1893  Charles Gounod
1833–  1897  Johannes Brahms
1838–  1875  Georges Bizet

---

alistic. But, because the spirit of the work transcends the event itself, and because the artist has rendered feeling rather than actuality, the picture surely is in the romantic style. By infusing reality with the charge of an electric emotional attitude, Delacroix raises his picture to the level of an idealized though highly personal expression, so that all who see it seem to be experiencing the event for themselves. More eloquent than any page in a history book, the canvas has captured the feeling as well as the facts that make up the incident. It is as if all the noise had awakened the artist from his dreams of the past, and now suddenly wide awake, he has applied his expressive techniques consciously to one of the stirring happenings of his own time.

As always with Delacroix, color plays an important part in the communication of mood. Here, a striking instance of the use of color is seen in the way he takes the red, white, and blue of the banner (the symbol of patriotism) and merges them into the picture as a whole. The white central strip, signifying truth and purity, blends with the purifying smoke of battle; the blue, denoting freedom, matches the parts of the sky visible in the top corners through the smoke; while the red in the flag high above balances the color of the blood of those below who have fallen for the ideal of liberty. Thus, the symbolism of the banner blends into the color scheme, and both combine with the dramatic lighting to define the emotional range. All these, in turn, expand the patriotic theme into a formal pictorial unity of concentrated intensity. With the purchase of this picture in the name of the state by the new bourgeois King at the time of its exposition during the Salon of 1831, the seal of official approval was stamped on the art of Delacroix and the romantic style.

to a friend in Paris, he had commented particularly on its diabolical aspect. The lithographs that eventually resulted show his mastery of illustration and prove Delacroix to have been as adept in works of small dimensions as in compositions executed on an epical scale. Despite his close kinship with Byron and Goethe, Delacroix was not always in sympathy with the work of his romantic Parisian contemporaries. In his diary he spoke of Meyerbeer's opera *Le Prophète* as "frightful" and referred to Berlioz and Hugo as those "so-called reformers." "The noise he makes is distracting," he wrote about Berlioz' music, "it is an heroic mess." Of all musicians he admired Mozart the most, and among his contemporaries only Chopin had the requisite polish and craftsmanship to measure up to his standards.

**above: 331.** Eugène Delacroix. *Mephistopheles Flying* (illustration for Goethe's *Faust*). 1828. Lithograph, 10¾ × 9". Metropolitan Museum of Art, New York (Rogers Fund, 1917).

**right: 332.** Eugène Delacroix. *Faust and Mephistopheles Galloping on Witches' Sabbath* (illustration for Goethe's *Faust*). 1828. Lithograph, 8 × 11". Metropolitan Museum of Art, New York (Rogers Fund, 1917).

## PAINTING

It was characteristic of romantic painting that Delacroix, its leading representative, should look to the fantasy of the literary world for the sources of his pictorial visions rather than to the world of everyday appearances. His choice of subjects as well as his treatment of them makes this immediately apparent. The *Death of Sardanapalus, Mazeppa, Giaour and the Pasha,* and the *Shipwreck of Don Juan* all point to the inception of these French paintings in the poetic writings of the English nobleman Lord Byron. Delacroix's illustrations for Goethe's *Faust* won the complete admiration of none other than this most German of authors, who felt that for clarity and depth of insight they could not be surpassed (Figs. 331, 332).

Delacroix's imagination had been haunted by *Faust* since he first saw it in London, and, in a letter

Delacroix's color technique was a means of conveying a highly emotional and turbulent matter. For him, color was dominant over design, and, as he declared, "gray is the enemy of all painting . . . let us banish from our palette all earth colors . . . the greater the opposition in color, the greater the brilliance." His admitted models in painting were the heroic canvases of Rubens and the dramatic pictures of Rembrandt with their emphasis on the dynamics of light (Pl. 34, p. 249; Pl. 37, p. 250), and among his contemporaries he admired the mellow landscapes and subtle coloring of the English painter Constable (Pl. 46, p. 319). Delacroix's own art was built on an aesthetic of color, light, and emotion rather than on line, drawing, and form. This is nowhere better illustrated than in his early masterpiece *Dante and Vergil in Hell* (Fig. 333), the first of his pictures to attract wide attention when it was exhibited in the Salon of 1822.

Stemming from the predilection for the medieval and macabre, the interest in Dante was one of the main facets of the romantic style. What Homer had been to neoclassicism, the Tuscan poet was to romanticism. Shelley and the Pre-Raphaelites were making England Dante-conscious; and while Schlegel and Schelling were translating and interpreting him for the Germans, Chateaubriand and Sainte-Beuve were performing the same function for the benefit of the French.

In his picture, Delacroix enters the realm of pure pathos. The central figure is that of Vergil in the crimson robe of a Florentine crowned with the laurel wreath, standing with impassive monumentality as a symbol of classic calm. On his left is Dante with a red hood on his head, expressively human in contrast to the serenity of his immortal companion and emotionally involved with his grotesque and gruesome surroundings. He looks with terror on the damned who swirl about him in the water below. The wake of the boat is livid with the writhing forms of the condemned, who hope eternally to reach the opposite shore by trying to attach themselves to the bark. One attempts to clamber aboard, the gnashing teeth of another bite into the edge of the boat, but in vain as they are plunged again into the dark waters. Distress and despair are everywhere. On the right is Phlegyas, the sepulchral boatman, seen from the rear as he strains at the rudder to guide the boat across the River Styx to the flaming shores of the city of Dis, visible in the distant background between the clouds of sulfurous fumes. The lurid coloration creates the illusion that the picture has been painted in blood, phosphorus, and flame.

When Delacroix was at work on it, he had a young friend read Dante's *Divine Comedy* to him and, as he says in his journal: "The best head in my Dante picture was swept in with the greatest speed and spirit while Pierret was reading me a canto from Dante which I knew already but to which he lent, by his accent, an energy that electrified me. That head is the one of the man behind the boat, facing you and trying to climb aboard, after throwing his arm over the gunwale." The particular passage that inflamed the artist's imagination and on which he built the picture is from the eighth book of the *Inferno*.

When first exhibited, the picture brought down storms of protest and vituperation on Delacroix's head, which helped immeasurably to bring the young artist to critical attention. One defender of David's academic tradition called it a "splattering of color" (Pl. 45, p. 302), and another thought he had "combined all the parts of the work in view of one emotion." While its expressive intensity was novel then, the work now easily falls into place as part of the macabre aspect of the romantic style. Even the nude figures, as muscular as those of Michelangelo and Rubens, function here more as color masses than as forms modeled three-dimensionally. As Delacroix once declared, color *is* painting, and his development of a color palette capable of eliciting specific emotional reactions from his viewers was destined to have a far-reaching effect on impressionistic and postimpressionistic painting.

**333.** Eugène Delacroix. *Dante and Vergil in Hell.* 1822. Oil on canvas, 6'1½" × 7'10½". Louvre, Paris.

## SCULPTURE

One of the dominating sculptural works of the romantic style is the *Departure of the Volunteers* by François Rude (Fig. 334). It achieved its stature by its vehement expression and sustained heroic mood, and by its prominent location on one side of the Arc de Triomphe in Paris that assured it the largest possible audience. Sculptured in the boldest high relief, the dimensions of the composition alone—rising to a height of almost 42 feet and spreading laterally 26 feet—make it of truly colossal proportions. Its conception and commission date from the wave of patriotic emotion associated with the Revolution of July, 1830, and the memories that stirred of earlier struggles for freedom. This common source of inspiration was shared by both Delacroix and Rude, whose design certainly owes much to Delacroix's *Liberty Leading the People* reproduced in Plate 44. It took Delacroix but a year to get his painting before the public, but a sculptural work of these proportions took Rude six years to execute.

The scene depicted is that of a band of volunteers rallying to the defense of the newly established French Republic when it was threatened by foreign invasion in 1792. The five resolute figures in the foreground are coming together to meet the common danger and are receiving mutual inspiration from the figure of Bellona, the Roman goddess of war, who hovers over them, inciting them onward with the singing of *La Marseillaise*. A fine rhythmical mood is established by the compact grouping of the figures, reinforced by the repeated motifs of the legs that combine in a neat marchlike manner with the arms of the soldier stooping to tie his sandal. This rhythm serves to weld the composition together as a whole in the manner of a lively yet majestic march. These representatives of the humanity so recently liberated by the French Revolution are self-motivated protectors of their newly won liberty, equality, and fraternity. The full manhood of four of the volunteers is balanced by the potential strength of the finely realized nude figure of the impetuous youth and the waning ability of the old man behind him who can only point out the direction to the others and wave them on. The surging power, directed by the common ideals, impels the volunteers onward with driving force and momentum.

Because Rude designed the *Departure* for a Napoleonic arch of triumph, his motifs are of Roman derivation. The soldiers are outfitted with Roman helmets and shields, though the coats of mail and weapons in the background recall those of the medieval period. The avoidance in the costumes and symbols of any contemporary reference in this representation of an event that had taken place less than a half-century before links the composition with the tendency to draw on the past for inspiration. Popularly, and quite

properly, called the *"Marseillaise* in stone," it represents a most ingenious sculptural use of a musical motif in suggesting the great revolutionary song, which serves to unify the patriotic spirit of the group. The anthem, composed by a young lieutenant in the revolutionary army, Rouget de Lisle, was practically forgotten during the days of Napoleon's Empire, and under the Bourbon restoration was, of course, officially banned. Credit for its rediscovery and revival goes to Berlioz. Stirred to patriotic frenzy by the events of July, 1830, though avoiding direct participation, this erratic genius contented himself with scoring the song for double chorus and orchestra, characteristically asking "all who have voices, a heart, and blood in their veins" to join in. The final stanza begins dramatically with three unaccompanied

**334.** FRANÇOIS RUDE. *Departure of the Volunteers of 1792 (La Marseillaise).* 1833–36. c. 42 × 26′. Right stone relief, Arc de Triomphe de l'Étoile, Paris.

voices; then, as Berlioz gradually marshals his vocal and orchestral forces, a big crescendo leads up to the refrain: "To arms, O citizens." This version received many performances, the most notable being a large benefit with the proceeds going to the families of the victims of the July Revolution. Later, the song was officially adopted as the French national anthem, though not with Berlioz' orchestration, and has become one of the world's best-known tunes.

In a later work, *Joan of Arc Listening to the Voices,* Rude combines emotionalism and medieval subject matter (Fig. 335). Executed originally in 1845 for the gardens of the Luxembourg Palace, it later found its way into the Louvre. Rude represents the Maid of Orleans in peasant costume with a suit of armor at her side, thus indicating both her rural origin and her heroic mission. The mystic element is suggested as she lifts her hand to her ear in order to hear the angelic voices that guide her. By trying to capture the intangible sounds of these heavenly voices as Joan listens quiveringly with upraised head, Rude strains his marble medium to its expressive limits.

Rude, who had grown up in revolutionary times, was always thoroughly in sympathy with the liberal spirit. He accepted exile in Belgium in 1815 rather than live under a Bourbon ruler. Action was his aesthetic watchword. "The great thing for an artist," he once said, "is to *do.*" Some critics find his *Departure of the Volunteers* overcrowded, overloaded, and unbalanced. Others feel that this crowding and imbalance is justified by the subject of a concerted uprising of the masses and that unity is achieved by the direction of its movement. Clearly it shows no will toward classical repose, and its sheer energy makes a clean break with academic tradition. By thus liberating sculpture from many outworn idioms and clichés, Rude revealed himself as a true romanticist.

## ARCHITECTURE

Romantic architecture received its initial impetus from the popularity in the late 18th century of the so-called "Gothic" novels. Romances and plays of this type published in England were variously entitled: *The Haunted Priory; The Horrid Mysteries; Banditti,* or *Love in a Labyrinth; Raymond and Agnes,* or *The Bleeding Nun of Lindenberg;* and *Castle of Otranto,* Horace Walpole's famous novel, subtitled *A Gothic Tale.* The settings for these stories were large baronial halls or decayed abbeys, liberally equipped with mysterious trapdoors, sliding panels, creaking postern gates, animated suits of armor, and sepulchral voices emanating from ancient tombs. Such scenes served as backdrops for the injured innocence of fragile and helpless heroines and the intrepid, if somewhat reckless, courage of dashing heroes. These tales played their part in the redefinition of the word *Gothic*—which Voltaire had called a fantastic compound of rudeness and filigree—into something more mystical, tinged with weirdness and bordering on the fantastic.

These imaginary castles of the novels first took on concrete form in England as the architectural whims of wealthy eccentrics. Walpole, the well-to-do son of a powerful prime minister, had indulged his fancy in a residence that gave its name to one aspect of the romantic style, "Strawberry Hill Gothick." William Beckford, whom Byron called "England's richest son," had the architect James Wyatt construct him a residence he called Fonthill Abbey (Fig. 336). Its huge central tower rose over a spacious interior hall that was approached by a massive staircase (Fig. 337). The rest of the interior was a labyrinth of long drafty corridors that provided the wall space for the proprietor's collections of pictures and tapestries as well as a suitable setting for his melancholy musings. In his frenzy to have it completed, Beckford drove the workers day and night to the point where, in their haste, they neglected to provide an adequate foundation for the tower; and only a few years after its completion, the tower of Beckford's dream castle fell to the ground, taking most of the building with it. Since ruins were greatly admired as residences at the time, this catastrophe only served to enhance the abbey's picturesqueness and make it all the more desirable.

In the early 1820s, Fonthill Abbey became so enormously popular that newspapers wrote of the "Fonthill mania." Visitors numbering up to five left: **Plate 46.** JOHN CONSTABLE. *Hay Wain.* 1821. Oil on canvas, 4'2½" × 6'1". National Gallery, London (reproduced by courtesy of the Trustees). (See p. 332.)

below: **Plate 47.** J. M. W. TURNER. *Rain, Steam, and Speed: The Great Western Railway.* 1844. Oil on canvas, 35½ × 47⅝". National Gallery, London (reproduced by courtesy of the Trustees). (See p. 333.)

**Plate 48.** EDOUARD MANET. *Bar at the Folies-Bergère.* 1881–82. Oil on canvas, 3′1½″ × 4′3″.
Courtauld Institute Galleries, London. (See p. 340.)

hundred a day made the pilgrimage to see it. Beckford's spectacular landscaping, which had involved transplanting over one million trees to create a picturesque setting, commanded the admiration of the painter Constable who lived nearby, as well as that of such poets as Lord Byron and Edgar Allan Poe. To the popular imagination Fonthill Abbey was a Walter Scott novel in stone.

The Gothic novel in literature and the Gothic revival in architecture steadily gained momentum. Jane Austen's *Northanger Abbey*, a delicious satire on the movement, was published just as Sir Walter Scott's historical novels were bringing their author such huge acclaim. Scott's novels were translated into French beginning about 1816, and they, in turn, paved the

way for the popular romances of Hugo and Dumas. Among the surviving English architectural expressions of this literary phase are the Houses of Parliament (Fig. 338), begun by Sir Charles Barry in 1839, and the New Law Courts by George Street, both of which are familiar landmarks in the London of today.

above left: 336. JAMES WYATT. Fonthill Abbey (no longer standing), Wiltshire. 1796–1807. Tower height 278′. Contemporary lithograph.

above right: 337. Interior, Fonthill Abbey. Length c. 25′, width c. 35′. Contemporary lithograph.

left: 338. CHARLES BARRY and A. WELBY PUGIN. Houses of Parliament, London. 1840–60. Length 940′.

In Germany, as early as 1772, the young poet Goethe, under the guidance of his university mentor Gottfried Herder, was writing in praise of the builder of the Strasbourg Cathedral, Erwin von Steinbach. The book significantly was entitled *Von deutscher Baukunst* ("On German Architecture"). Later, Goethe placed his drama on the medieval Faust legend in a Gothic setting. In the 19th century, German literary interest in neomedievalism became the background for Richard Wagner's operas *Tannhäuser, Lohengrin,* and *Parsifal.* Wagner's most enthusiastic patron was King Ludwig II of Bavaria, who helped the composer build his opera house at Bayreuth.

In France, architectural energies at first were diverted toward the preservation of the many medieval monuments still in existence. Less than a year after the July Revolution, Victor Hugo had published his *Notre Dame de Paris* (known to the English-speaking world as *The Hunchback of Notre Dame*). The fact that the real hero of the novel is Paris' Gothic cathedral fanned into flames the popular enthusiasm for the restoration of churches, castles, and abbeys. Support for the reconstruction of Notre Dame was soon forthcoming in official circles from Guizot the historian, who was then prime minister. It was he who founded in 1837 the *Commission pour la Conservation des Monuments Historiques.* In France, as previously in England and Germany, romantic architecture was associated with the resurgence of patriotic and nationalistic sentiment. At last, the Gothic revival had arrived on home soil, channeling French national energies into new flights of the imagination and providing French minds with an escape from recent dreams of Roman imperial glory that had turned into the nightmare of the Napoleonic defeat.

The precise scholarship of the French academic mind found a ready outlet in the establishment of the new science of medieval archaeology, which resulted in the restoration of such buildings as Ste. Chapelle and the Cathedral of Notre Dame in Paris. In his essays on medieval architecture, Eugène Viollet-le-Duc called attention to the engineering logic of medieval builders and demonstrated the organic unity of the Gothic structural system in which each stone played its part, and in the period of Gothic florescence even the decorative details served useful purposes. That everything was necessary and nothing used merely for effect not only revised 19th-century architectural thought but also laid one of the bases for the 20th-century return to functional building.

As comparative latecomers on the medieval revival scene, the French architects were in no hurry to leave their reconstructions and design new buildings. The advantage was theirs when they did so, however, because they could review all the previous experiments and avoid the follies and excesses that characterized the movement elsewhere. Though planned at the same time Victor Hugo, Delacroix, and

**339.** François Christian Gau and Théodore Ballu. Ste. Clotilde, Paris. 1846–57. Width 105', height 216'.

Berlioz were active, it was not until 1846 that ground could be broken for the Church of Ste. Clotilde (Fig. 339). Designed by François Christian Gau, a native of Cologne but a naturalized Frenchman, the project was completed after his death by Théodore Ballu. Although built principally of white stone, Ste. Clotilde received the distinctive technical innovation of cast-iron girders added to the vaulting to assure strength and durability. The girders were disguised by blocks of stone, but the fact that a building of medieval design used materials developed by the 19th-century Industrial Revolution commanded great interest among contemporary architects.

Based on Gothic models of the 14th century, the church has the usual features of a nave with side aisles, transept, choir, and apse with radiating chapels. The space of the richly ornamented façade is divided by four buttresses into three parts, each with an entrance portal. Those on the sides have tympanums showing in sculptured relief the martyrdom of St. Valéry and the baptism of Clovis. The approaches to the portals have niches containing standing figures of the Merovingian saints associated with the earliest history of French nationhood, including Ste. Clotilde, Clovis' queen, and Ste. Geneviève, patroness of Paris.

The interior is lighted by a clearstory with as many as sixty stained glass windows, which carry out the iconographical scheme promised by the sculptures of the façade. The representations tell the legendary stories of Ste. Clotilde and some of her contemporaries, St. Valéry, St. Martin of Tours, and St. Remi, as well as two of her children who were canonized, St. Cloud and Ste. Bathilde. The choir is the setting for a large three-manual organ with a case elaborately carved in the Gothic manner. It was here that the composer César Franck presided from the year 1872 until his death, and here that he made his famous improvisations.

When the Church of Ste. Clotilde is compared with such original Gothic monuments as the cathedrals of Chartres (Fig. 141), Paris, and Rheims, it seems studied, overly symmetrical, and academically frigid. But when viewed in the context of its times and combined with the reflections of medieval fervor of Victor Hugo, the moving craftsmanship of Rude, the chromaticism of Delacroix's painting, and the fantastic imagery of Berlioz' music, it catches some rays of their glowing warmth and becomes at once both their worthy architectural companion and an important incident in the unfolding of the romantic style.

## POETRY

Of the three great literary figures who influenced the writings of Victor Hugo at this time, Dante and Shakespeare were out of the past, and only his elder contemporary Goethe came from his own time. These three writers, as he states in the preface to *Cromwell*, pointed out the sources of the grotesque elements that were to be found everywhere, "in the air, water, earth, fire those myriads of intermediate creatures which we find alive in the popular traditions of the middle ages; it is the grotesque which impels the ghastly antics of the witches' revels, which gives Satan his horns, his cloven feet and his bat's wings. It is the grotesque, still the grotesque, which now casts into the Christian hell the frightful faces which the severe genius of Dante and Milton will evoke . . . ." Needless to say, understanding of his great predecessors involved a high degree of selectivity. It was the *Inferno* section that Hugo extracted out of Dante's *Divine Comedy*. His poem of 1837—*Après une lecture de Dante*—closely parallels Delacroix's picture of Dante: "When the poet paints the image of hell," he wrote, "he paints that of his own life." The substances of the poem continues: "Beset by shades and specters, the poet must grope blindly through mysterious forests as weird forms bestrew his dark voyage. Lost amidst indecisive fogs, with each step he hears lamentations and the faint sounds of the grinding of white teeth in the black night. All the vices such as vengeance, famine, ambition, pride and avarice darken the scene still more. Farther on, the souls of those who have tasted the poison of cowardice, fear and treason are mingled with the grimacing masks of those whom hatred has consumed. The only light amidst this general gloom is the voice of the eternal artist, Vergil, who calls, 'Continue onward.' . . ."

In Petrarch, it was the Triumph of Death that Hugo admired; in Boccaccio, the vivid descriptions of the black plague; in Shakespeare, the macabre scenes from *Hamlet* and the boiling and bubbling of the witches' caldron in *Macbeth;* and in Goethe's *Faust,* the descriptions of the Walpurgis Night. Collectively, these constitute a veritable carnival of the macabre, the horrible, and the lugubriousness of doom and damnation.

Hugo's transition to this new psychology is apparent as early as 1826 when he brought out a new edition of his *Odes* to which he added fifteen *Ballades*, with the fourteenth entitled "Witches' Sabbath." This new orientation he explains in his introduction. The odes, he wrote, included his purely religious inspirations and personal expression, which were cast in classical meters. Those bearing the title of "ballad" have the character of caprice, and include pictorial fantasies, dreams, and legends of superstition. He tells of the latter coming to him under the inspiration of the repertoire of medieval troubadours, especially those Christian rhapsodies of epical nature that were chanted by the minstrels to the accompaniment of their harps as they wandered from one castle to another.

The ballad begins with a description of a Gothic church at midnight; the clock in the belfry tolls twelve, and the witching hour begins. Strange lights flash, the holy water begins to boil in the fonts; shrieks and howls are heard, as from all directions come those who answer Satan's call—specters, dragons, vampires, ghouls, monsters, and the souls of the damned from their fresh-emptied tombs. While Satan sings a black mass, an imp reads the Gospel, and the whole fantastic congregation performs a wild dance.

> All in unison moving with swift-circling feet
> While satan keeps time with his crozier's beat,
> And their steps shake the arches colossal and high,
> Disturbing the dead in their tombs close by.

The last two lines serve as a refrain and are repeated after each of the ten verses, two of which will suffice as samples.

> Come, he-goats profane,
> Come, lizards and snails,

340. Eugène Delacroix. *Margaret in Church* (illustration for Goethe's *Faust,* Part I, lines 3449–82 and 4095–4124). 1828. Lithograph, $10\frac{1}{2} \times 8\frac{3}{4}''$. Metropolitan Museum of Art, New York.

an important part of the requiem mass. The first, fifth, and ninth lines rhyme, while two groups of triple rhyme are placed between them to make a pattern of *a, bbb, a, ccc, a.* The *Dies Irae* had made an earlier appearance in the church scene of Goethe's *Faust,* where Margaret, aware of her forthcoming doom, hears the chorus intone the awesome lines (Fig. 340). Both the technique and imagery of Hugo's ballad are related to the fantastic sections of *Faust,* and both poems, in turn, have a common ancestor in the witches' scene from Shakespeare's *Macbeth.* The similarity of metrical plan and black-magic imagery is unmistakable. One finds the same lilting language that is designed to charm the ear and stimulate the imagination rather than make logical sense, especially in the Walpurgis Night scene from *Faust.* The scene is filled with witches riding he-goats and giant owls; the earth crawls with salamanders and coiling snakes; while bats fly around and glittering fireflies provide the illumination. As Mephistopheles describes the ghostly dance, all manner of gruesome and awesome night creatures—

> . . . crowd and jostle, whirl, and flutter!
> They whisper, babble, twirl, and splutter!
> They glimmer, sparkle, stink, and flare—
> A true witch-element! Beware!

The sources of Hugo's inspiration are thus clear, but while he must be counted among the masters of language and the outstanding literary figures, he was never a prime mover or noted for his originality. Highly skilled as a manipulator of symbols and a master of poetic forms, he was able to give articulate expression to the changing voices of his time. In spite of all this verbal virtuosity and the uniformly high quality of his output, he never succeeded in producing a poetic masterpiece that stood out above all others. In his work all the ideas of his time are mirrored in his unparalleled rhetoric, and his voice is as typical as any within the framework of this period. The brief but pungent reply of a modern critic pretty well sums it up. When asked whom he considered the greatest French poet of the 19th century, he answered, "Unfortunately, Victor Hugo."

Come, serpents with scales,
So fragile and frail.
Burst into the fane!
Let discord take wing,
With melodious swing,
Come, enter the ring,
And repeat the refrain.

And their steps shake the arches colossal and high,
Disturbing the dead in their tombs close by.

From his tomb with sad moans
Each false monk to his stall
Glides, concealed in his pall,
That robe fatal to all,
Which burns into his bones.

Now a black priest draws nigh,
With a flame he doth fly
On the altar on high
He the curst fire enthrones.

The dawn whitens the arches colossal and gray,
And drives all the devilish revellers away;
The dead monks retire to their graves 'neath the halls,
And veil their cold faces behind their dark palls.

For his introduction and refrain Hugo uses a dual rhyming scheme, *aa, bb, cc,* and so on. That of the intervening verses, however, is based on a variant of an old medieval triple-rhyming pattern recalling that of the 13th-century *Dies Irae* (p. 157), which is still

## MUSIC

The salons of Paris during the days of the romantic dawn were populated with poets, playwrights, journalists, critics, architects, painters, sculptors, musicians, and utopian political reformers without number. Heinrich Heine, poet and journalist from

**341.** Gustave Doré. *Berlioz Conducting Massed Choirs.* 19th-century caricature.

north Germany, Chopin from Poland, Liszt from Hungary—all mixed freely with such homegrown artists and intellectuals as Victor Hugo, Théophile Gautier, Lamartine, Chateaubriand, de Musset, Dumas, George Sand, and others. Social philosophers like Lamennais, Proudhon, Auguste Comte, and Saint-Simon, gave a political tinge to the heated aesthetic debates. In this supercharged atmosphere Hector Berlioz must have appeared as an authentic apparition, embodying in the flesh the wildest romantic dreams and nightmares. One contemporary described him as a young man trembling with passion, whose large umbrella of hair projected like a moveable awning over the beak of a bird of prey. The German composer Robert Schumann saw him as a "shaggy monster with ravenous eyes"; his personality as that of a "raging bacchant"; and spoke of his effect on the society of his times as being "the terror of the Philistines." The suave and polished Felix Mendelssohn, on the other hand, found his French colleague completely exasperating, and he continually reproached Berlioz because, with all his strenuous efforts to go stark raving mad, he never once really succeeded.

In one striking personality, Berlioz combined qualities that made him a great composer, the ranking orchestral conductor of his day, a brilliant journalist, and an autobiographer. As a conductor, the painter Gustave Doré caricatured him as the mad musician (Fig. 341). At the first performance of one of his overtures, when the orchestra failed to give him the effect he demanded, he burst into tears, tore his hair, and fell sobbing on the kettledrums. His *Memoirs* are stylistically a literary achievement of the first magnitude and rank with the few top autobiographies of world literature. From this lively source one gathers that Berlioz' development proceeded in a series of emotional shocks which he received from his first contacts with the literature and music of his time. One after the other, the fires of his explosive imagination were ignited by Goethe's *Faust,* which resulted in his oratorio the *Damnation of Faust;* by the poetry of Byron, which became the symphony for viola and orchestra, *Harold in Italy;* and by Dante's *Divine Comedy,* which was sublimated into his great *Requiem.* In music it was first Gluck, then Weber, and he said that he had scarcely recovered from these two when he "beheld Beethoven's giant form looming over the horizon. The shock was almost as great as that I had received from Shakespeare, and a new world of music was revealed to me by the musician, just as a new universe of poetry had been opened to me by the poet." It was, of course, the Beethoven of the *Eroica, Pastoral,* and *Ninth* symphonies. To a milder extent, the literary

figures of Vergil, Walter Scott, and Victor Hugo made up the more distant claps of thunder in his creative brainstorms.

Berlioz even insisted on actually living out his enthusiasms to an alarmingly realistic degree. He fell violently in love with the Irish actress who was playing the feminine leads in the Shakespearean troupe that was so successful in the Paris season of 1827. After a desperate romance leading both to the brink of suicide, he finally married the beautiful feminine package whom he thought of as Juliet and Ophelia wrapped up in one. When his wife turned out to be merely the actress Miss Harriet Smithson, now Madame H. Berlioz, he wrote with acute anguish to a friend: "She's an ordinary woman." The cold dawn of disillusionment brought years of personal misery, compensated for by some happier results on the musical side. For all his external flightiness, his literary, musical, and human loves were completely enduring; and he carried them with him to the end of his life. There one finds him still musing on the "mild, affable, and accessible" figure of Vergil; on Shakespeare, "that mighty indifferent man, impassable as a mirror"; on Beethoven, "contemptuous and uncouth, yet gifted with such profound sensibility"; and on Gluck, "the superb."

Berlioz' autobiographical *Fantastic Symphony,* first performed in the year 1830, contains a complex of many ideas he gathered from the musical and literary

*Fantastic Symphonie*
("fixed idea," or leading melody)

atmosphere that surrounded him. In the detailed programmatic notes he wrote for this work it is clear that he took the idea of poisoning by opium in the first movement from De Quincey's *Confessions of an English Opium Eater,* which had appeared shortly before in a French translation by Alfred de Musset. The musical form of this movement, with its *Largo* introduction and the *Allegro agitato e appassionato assai* continuation, is in the Beethovenian symphonic tradition. Its principal claim to technical originality is the use of an *idée fixe,* or "fixed idea" (above), by which Berlioz conveys the notion of his beloved who is everywhere present and colors his every thought. The metamorphosis of the theme on its appearance in each of the movements fulfills a dual purpose—that of providing a semblance of unity in the sequence of genre pieces, and that of expressing, by its mutations, the necessary dramatic progress. The theme is varied in each of its reappearances and provides the listener with the necessary continuity to build up the image of a dramatic character through the associative process. All evidence, however, points to the fact that this specific programme was written later than most of the music, which apparently was conceived for quite another purpose.

Gérard de Nerval's prose translation of Goethe's *Faust* had appeared late in the year 1827 and was the direct inspiration for Berlioz' *Eight Scenes from Faust.* Since most of the movements of the *Fantastic Symphony* were being written at the same time, this alone would indicate a connection in the creative process. Berlioz was among the earliest to attempt a realization of Goethe's great drama in music. An opera by Spohr had appeared in 1816, but the well-known one by Gounod came many years later. A secular oratorio by Schumann, a *Faust Symphony* by Liszt, and a *Faust Overture* by Wagner are but a few of the many subsequent works on this theme. The subject of Faust was in the wind, and the stages of London, Paris, and other Continental cities rang with the echoes of the many versions of this subject in dramatic and ballet form. The Paris Opera alone had accepted no less than three librettos that were waiting to be commissioned. It is known that Berlioz was angling for one of these, and this fact further fortifies the case for the common source of inspiration for the *Damnation of Faust* and the *Fantastic Symphony.* Since the desired commission was not forthcoming, those parts projected for a Faust

ballet became instead the movements of the *Fantastic Symphony.*

The reveries and passions of the first movement are certainly Faustian in a general, if not specific, sense. Every Faust ballet of the time contained a gay dance sequence for "Auerbach's Cellar" scene, and the second movement of the *Fantastic Symphony,* called the "Scene at the Ball," was probably first written for "Auerbach's Cellar." The external and internal storms of the third movement, the "Scene in the Country," bring out the benign as well as the malignant aspects of the Faustian conception of nature. The closest correspondence, however, comes in the climactic final movements where the relationship is quite unmistakable. The fourth, the grim "March to the Scaffold," was probably composed first as the execution scene where Margaret pays the penalty for the dual crimes of matricide and infanticide. In the *Symphony,* it becomes a musical nightmare of the first order in which the hero (autobiographically Berlioz himself) marches in grotesque rhythms to his own doom. As other writers have pointed out, this scene may well have been suggested to Berlioz by the unfortunate execution of the gifted young poet André Chénier, who met death on the guillotine under Robespierre and thus became the martyred poet of the Revolution. In the final bars of this movement, the fixed melodic idea is sounded in the high piercing register of the clarinet. It is suddenly cut off to suggest the fall of the blade and the decapitation of the hero. After a dull thud and roll of the drums, the grimacing crowds roar their bloodthirsty approval of the execution now accomplished.

The last movements of both the *Eight Scenes from Faust* and the *Fantastic Symphony* have to do with the triumph of the exultant diabolical forces as they claim the souls of their victims. The endings to Berlioz' early works are often the most wild and dissonant parts. No anticlimactic calms after the storms, no carefully planned resolutions, no safe havens after the shipwrecks. The *Symphony* ends with a diabolical "Witches' Sabbath," just as *Harold in Italy* ends with an "Orgy of the Brigands." The grisly scene here is both the climax and the unresolved end, and the movement that most fully justifies the title "Fantastic." It is divided into three distinct sections. The first is introductory and begins with wild shrieks for the piccolo, flute, and oboe, accompanied by the ominous roll of the kettledrums in bars 7 and 8, which is echoed softly by the muted horns in bars 9 and 10 to suggest distance. After a repetition, the tempo changes from *Larghetto* to *Allegro* and the *idée fixe* is heard (21–28). The ghostly appearance of the fixed melodic idea associated with Berlioz' beloved in this final movement undoubtedly was derived from the witches' kitchen scene of Goethe's drama where Faust has gone to have his form changed from that of old age back to young and lusty manhood, and where the

**342.** Francisco Goya. *Witches' Sabbath.* c. 1819–23. Oil on canvas, 4'7⅛" × 14'4½". Prado, Madrid.

conjuring up of the image of Margaret is a part of the process. It is also related to the Walpurgis Night scene where Margaret again puts in a brief appearance. Surely it is a novel notion that the winsome heroine, exemplified in previous mutations as the embodiment of desirability, should now appear at the witches' sabbath. Was she a witch all along and disguised only in his imagination in desirable human form? Or is this merely another manifestation of her "bewitching" power? The entrance at this point of his beloved on her broomstick, accompanied by a pandemonium of sulfurous sounds, is therefore somewhat unexpected. The hero, obviously Berlioz, gives a shriek of horror (29–39) as he listens to her modulate from the previously chaste C major to the more lurid key of E flat. Her instrumental coloration, while still that of the pale clarinet, descends now in pitch to a new low and more sensuous register. After this shocking revelation, she executes a few capers and subsides for the time being as the introduction concludes with bar 101.

The second section is labeled *Lontano* ("in the distance") and begins with the tolling of the chimes recalling the opening lines of Hugo's ballad. After this signal for the unleashing of the infernal forces, the foreboding *Dies Irae* is solemnly intoned, first by the brass instruments in unison octaves. In bars 127–146, it is in dotted half-notes; next, in bars 147–157, the rhythm is quickened into dotted quarters; then it becomes syncopated in triplet eighths (157–162) and ends with an abrupt upward swish of the C scale. With the appearance here in syncopation and in such surroundings of this ancient and honorable Gothic liturgical melody, a solemn part of every Roman Catholic requiem mass, Berlioz fulfills the promise of his programme that he will make a "burlesque parody" on the *Dies Irae*. Besides serving Berlioz as a symbol conjuring up all the fire-and-brimstone aspects of his medieval Christianity, it also introduces

at this point a form of macabre humor. This parody of a sacred melody caused considerable comment at the time. Schumann attributed it to romantic irony, one of the few forms of humor tolerated in a style practiced by artists who took life and themselves with deadly seriousness. Another explanation, however, seems more logical and is to be found by applying a remark that Hugo made in the preface to *Cromwell*. "When Dante had finished his terrible Inferno," he wrote, "and naught remained save to give his work a name, the unerring instinct of his genius showed him that multiform poem was an emanation of the drama, not of the epic; and on the front of that gigantic monument, he wrote with his pen of bronze: Divina Commedia." Thus, if Dante was justified in conceiving his *Inferno* as a comedy, albeit a divine one, then Berlioz could include the *Dies Irae* in this context. Even the devil is conceded to be a clever theologian, and in Goethe's drama he is found in the sacred precincts of the church, whispering in Margaret's ear as she listens to the choir chant the *Dies Irae*.

The title of the final section of Berlioz' *Symphony* which begins with bar 241, is *Ronde du Sabbat,* the neomedieval, blood-curdling, black-mass ballad published by Victor Hugo in 1826. It is also the subject of one of Goya's paintings, *Witches' Sabbath* (Fig. 342). A dance fragment hinted at previously now becomes the "Rondo of the Sabbath" theme and a four-bar phrase forming a fugue subject. The first entrance is for the 'cellos and double basses (241–244); this is followed by the violas (248–251); next, for the first violins fortified by the bassoons (255–258); and the final entrance is scored for the woodwind section and horns. These successive entries, each with a different instrumental combination, mark Berlioz' departure from the academic tradition of the linear fugue. Here he introduces the element of instrumental coloration into the usually austere fugal exposition. Other color combinations follow with melodic and chromatic variants of the subject in a fugal development that has won the composer wide admiration. It must be noted that when Berlioz is writing his wildest and most fantastic images, his mind is always fully in command; and at the climax of such a work as this, he writes a fugue without either violating the rules or sacrificing his expressive intentions. After the fugue on the dance theme has come to its climax with the entire string section playing an extension of the subject (407–413), the *Dies Irae* makes a reappearance, and the two themes are woven together with great skill from bar 414 to the end. Some of Berlioz' enthusiastic admirers have called this contrapuntal section a "double fugue." There is only one fugue, however, with the *Dies Irae* melody running concurrently. With the final blood-curdling shrieks and flying images, a composer, quite probably for the first time in music history, has written a fugue that fulfills its literal meaning—that is, a flight.

After the *Fantastic Symphony*, the use of the *Dies Irae* became a symbol of the macabre, and it has been used countless times since. Liszt's *Totentanz* for piano and orchestra is a set of variations on it, while it appears again in Gustav Mahler's symphonies and in some of Rachmaninoff's variations on a theme of Paganini. With this final movement, Berlioz also established a style that brought the demonic element—and a chain of harmonic and psychological dissonances—into music to stay. Both Moussorgsky's *Night on Bald Mountain* and Saint-Saëns' *Danse Macabre* are cut from the same cloth. One writer has even called this movement of Berlioz' the first piece of Russian music. Some of the wilder moments written by Stravinsky for his *Fire Bird* and *Rite of Spring* would certainly seem to bear this out.

Berlioz was one of the first composers to build up his musical forms by the use of tone color. The only way to understand his music is to hear it in all the full richness of its instrumental sound, because his scores can never be transcribed successfully for piano or any other instrumental medium. In addition to the incomparable richness of his orchestral palette, the sheer quantitative weight he added to the ensembles of his day is nothing short of spectacular. Seldom composing in any but the largest forms, he delighted in the use of orchestral and choral combinations of extraordinary complexity. To assemble all the necessary forces for a Berlioz performance is always a challenge, and the demands his works make on the time and effort of the performers are considerable. In his gigantic *Requiem,* the composer employs an immense principal orchestra, a chorus of 500, a tenor soloist, and 4 huge brass bands. The latter were placed facing the 4 points of the compass, so as to suggest vast space and to enhance the acoustical effect made by the bands when they sound the call for Judgment Day. All this, plus such additional effects as a battery of 16 kettledrums, caused the newspapers to comment the day following the first performance that Paris had not heard such a volume of sound since the fall of the Bastille.

There was always something of the conqueror about Berlioz as he marshaled his orchestral forces in such a composition. Each orchestra had its own conductor, and the choruses were signaled by commanders of lesser rank, with all of them taking their cues from the generalissimo himself, who appeared in the role of a musical Napoleon storming over the battlefield. Berlioz was the first of the great orchestra conductors and the prototype of the great maestros of today. No wonder his contemporaries did not know how to take him and found both his personality and his compositions somewhat difficult to absorb. He always reminded them of something monstrous, and Heinrich Heine characterized him in the following way: "Here is the wingbeat that reveals no ordinary songbird," he wrote, "it is that of a colossal nightingale, a lark the size of an eagle, such as must have existed in the primeval world."

## IDEAS

The dynamics of the revolutionary period, with its social, political, and industrial upheavals, confronted artists with the image of a rapidly changing world. The shift of responsibility and wealth from the aristocracy to the middle class brought about a corresponding change in the patrons for whom the buildings were built, the statues carved, the pictures painted, and the music composed. No longer were the arts produced only for a small sophisticated group of aristocrats; instead, they were addressed to a larger and more anonymous public mainly of the bourgeois class. Finesse, subtlety, and intellectual grasp of complex forms could not be anticipated in audiences. Artists now had to charm, exhort, and astonish. An architect could no longer count on one patron for a single monumental project but had to cater to many clients with smaller buildings involving many different tastes and styles.

The consequences in the arts were profound and far-reaching. Artistic media were brought closer together, and painting and music in particular became allied with literature for poetic allusions and programmatic interpretations. Color in painting, as well as tone color in instrumentation, became important in the vocabulary of romanticism. It was not sufficient, moreover, for an artist to be a fine craftsman. He had now to be a great personality and espouse epic causes. Above all, perhaps, romanticism involved the psychology of escapism from an increasingly industrialized and mechanized world. The mainstream of romantic ideas, then, flowed from the alliance of the arts, colorism, individualism, and nationalism to the various escape mechanisms: revivals of the past, back to nature, and exoticism.

**Alliance of the Arts and Colorism**    Painters and sculptors began to work in a greater variety of forms than before, while poets and musicians likewise revealed the fragmentation of their world view by writing shorter works and generally showing an inability to conceive or present their world as a systematic whole. Even when such a composer as Berlioz did write symphonies, the results were no longer the all-embracing universal structures of Beethoven but sequences of genre pieces strung together by a literary programme or some recurrent motif that give them a semblance of unity.

New also was the idea that an artistic opus was not a self-contained whole but something that shared many relationships internally as well as externally with other works of art. This idea began with the attempts by certain individual artists to overcome many of the arbitrary limitations and technical rules of their separate crafts. The literature of the period was filled with musical allusions, and musicians for their part were drawing on literature with full force for their programme pieces. The architects were called upon to build dream castles out of the novels of Walpole, Scott, and Hugo; and it is difficult to think of Delacroix's painting or Berlioz' music without Vergil, Dante, Shakespeare, Goethe, and Byron coming to mind. The effect on music was a host of new and hybrid forms, such as the programme symphony and the symphonic poem. The tonal art had been associated from its beginning with words, and programme music was by no means an invention of the 19th century. No other period, however, built an entire style on this mixture. There is also a considerable distinction between the setting of words to music, as in a song, or the musical dramatization of a play, as in an opera, and basing a purely instrumental form on the spirit of a poem or the sequential arrangements of episodes taken from a novel. Berlioz wrote overtures not only to operas but to such novels as Scott's *Waverly* and *Rob Roy*. Mendelssohn wrote *Songs Without Words* for the piano leaving the imagination to supply the text, and Berlioz' *Fantastic Symphony* and *Harold in Italy* became operas without words. In such later works as the "dramatic symphony" *Romeo and Juliet* and the "dramatic legend" *Damnation of Faust,* which are scored for soloists and chorus as well as orchestra, he was, in effect, writing concert operas in which the costumes and scenery are left to the listener's imagination. This tendency continued until it reached a climax in Richard Wagner's music dramas, which he conceived as *Gesamtkunstwerke*—that is, complete, consummate, or "total works of art."

Among the important innovations of the time was an increasing emphasis on color in the various artistic media, both for its own sake and for its capacity to convey symbolic meaning. For the architects and sculptors, color was associated with the picturesque and local color. Poetry began to depend on the sounds of words and their appeal to the senses more than to the mind. Hugo's "Witches' Sabbath" with its patterns of repeated sounds and colors would be practically meaningless if this literary tone color were omitted. To Delacroix, more than line or composition, color was the dimension on which he depended for intensity of expression. "When the tones are right," Delacroix wrote in his journal of 1847, "the lines take care of themselves." Berlioz can be understood only when his musical ideas are heard in the original instrumentation. He is a composer who defies transcription. If the English horn solo in the "Scene in the Country," the third movement of the *Fantastic Symphony,* were to be played by a flute or clarinet, Berlioz' expressive intention would vanish instantly. Such an example reveals the extent Berlioz relied on the tone color of specific instruments; and in his hands instrumentation becomes a musical dimension in itself, capable of carrying its own expressive weight independent of melody and rhythm. Both Delacroix and Berlioz based their styles principally on color.

**Romantic Individualism and Nationalism**    The romantic period was also the age of the emancipation of the individual and the era of the great man who attained the heights by his own efforts. Napoleon had stamped his image on his era with his preeminence in the realm of military glory and statecraft, thus giving rise to the idea of similar dominating figures in the smaller worlds of letters, painting, sculpture, architecture, and music. Artists vied with each other for the top rung of the ladder in their respective fields. For sheer virtuosity in letters it would be difficult to surpass Victor Hugo, who could write with mastery in any style. Viollet-le-Duc and other architects could duplicate any building in the history of architecture; and the names of such bravura composer-performers as Paganini and Liszt are legendary. All this was, perhaps, a positive assertion of the diminishing self in the face of growing social collectivization. Each work of art was associated with the personality of a distinctive individual. It was no longer enough for an artist to be a master of his craft, no matter how high the degree of his skill; he had also to be a great man, a prophet, a leader. It was consequently an age of autobiography, confessions, memoirs, portraiture, and showmanship. The will to biography, the necessity of living a "life," often took so much time that it was actually a handicap to artistic production. More than in any other period there was an obligation for the artist to be a personality in the worldly sense in addition to his artistic activities. The place of the artist in society had been a matter of vital concern to such men as David and Beethoven, who combined the moralistic fervor of revolutionary thought with a sense of social responsibility. David's championship of the cause of art in the French legislature, and Beethoven's behavior toward his patrons as their social equal, reveal both men as modern artists who placed the aristocracy of genius on a higher plane than that of birth.

The great individual, however, could not exist in a social or political vacuum. Byron, Delacroix, and others felt compelled to bend their energies and talents to the cause of liberating the oppressed Greek people from the Turkish tyrant's yoke. Whether an artist conceived of himself in classical terms as a Prometheus or in the medieval vocabulary as a knightly champion of the weak against the strong was not too important. He simply needed a geographical sounding board, local color, and a linguistic medium suited to his creative needs. Some could find it in folk tales and ballads of a particular locale; others in collections and variations of Spanish epics, Scottish ballads, German fairy tales; still others in the writing of Italian symphonies, Hungarian rhapsodies, and Polish mazurkas. In this light, nationalism, like the medieval revival, was a northern declaration of cultural independence from the Mediterranean tradition, tied up in the immediate sense in England and Germany with the opposition to Napoleon as a latter-day Caesar. Berlioz' nationalism is expressed in a more subtle way, but his operas without words, concert operas, and music dramas were as distinct a departure from the prevailing Italian operatic tradition as were those of Weber in Germany.

**Escapism**    During the romantic period there was a growing gulf between the realities of the early industrial age and the escapist tendencies in the arts. In recognition of the new technologies an École Polytechnique had been established in 1794 by the revolutionary government. Napoleon, however, yielded to the advice of David and others and allowed the establishment of a separate École des Beaux-Arts in 1806. By thus educating engineers in one school and architects in another, the construction techniques of building tended to be divorced from the stylistic aspects of architecture. When the architects did begin using cast iron, it was to build dream castles and neomedieval cathedrals; and when musicians began to write for the improved horns and trombones, it was to sound the call of Judgment Day and introduce a rain of neomedieval fire and brimstone into their symphonies. In general, then, the full significance of the Industrial Revolution remained for a later age to exploit.

The American and French revolutions, which had held out such high initial hopes and promised the imminent liberation of man, were followed by a reaction bordering on pessimism when the results did not live up to the overly optimistic expectations. Then when the Revolution of July, 1830, had overthrown the last of the old line of Bourbons, the French middle class was finally confronted by a king cast in its own image. As the bourgeoisie beheld Louis Philippe in his frock coat, umbrella in hand, walking down the boulevard to the Bourse, they were somewhat dismayed to find that their monarch was—like themselves—stouter of figure than of heart and—again like themselves—engaged in the pursuit of causes more materialistic than ideal. A bit appalled at what they saw, is it any wonder that they sought psychological compensation in dreams of the more dashing royal personalities of the past, whose recklessness consisted of more hazardous adventures than buying and selling shares on the stock exchange? How could King Louis Philippe, living in a palace replete with the bourgeois comforts of modern plumbing, compare in popular fancy with Joan of Arc's dashing dauphin, living dangerously while being pursued by his remorseless enemies from one dank and drafty castle to another?

The activities of Darwin's earthworms, for instance, were infinitely more useful than the sublime spectacle of one of Delacroix's lions in mortal combat with a stallion. But how could the worms capture the popular imagination as the lions did? A highly productive factory or an ingenious city sewer system made infinitely duller pictures and poetry than the interiors of Oriental harems and the palm-lined shores of the River Ganges. While willing to use the fruits of the Industrial Revolution as aids in the production and dissemination of their artistic wares, the artists of the time were quite convinced that the new technologies were not making their world more beautiful. Thus, the rift between usefulness and beauty widened. Refusing to reconcile themselves to reality, the artists sought ever more fanciful ways and means of avoiding the issue. Certainly they knew what was going on in their world. As intellectuals, they were better educated and better informed than similar groups in other times had ever been.

When employing their escape mechanisms, they were fully aware of what they were escaping from. "Any time but now, and any place but here" became the battle cry of romanticism. The yearning for past periods—whether ancient Greco-Roman or medieval—was expressed in the various revivals. Since the classic and medieval revivals were accepted as official styles, and since they lingered longer than other aspects of romanticism, they have been dwelt upon in these pages at greater length. But the fuller vocabulary of romantic escapism included the "Back to Nature" movement, a longing for the lost paradise of a simple, pastoral life, and exoticism, with its fantasies of life in far-off places.

**Revivals of the Past**    Neoclassicism had been the earliest of the revivals of the past, and the passion for exactitude soon had divided it into separate Greek and Roman revival movements. Through historical novels and romantic imaginations, interest in medieval times was awakened; and as medieval scholars extended their studies, artists delved deeper into the Middle Ages. Revivals of Gothic, Romanesque, and Byzantine styles followed next. The romantic affinity for times past was then expanded into admiration for the Renaissance and baroque periods. The Library of Ste. Geneviève in Paris (Figs. 359, 360) and the Boston Public Library, in their exteriors at least, were revivals of Renaissance architecture, and—shades of the French Revolution—the Paris Opera, begun in 1861, revived Louis XIV's Versailles. Wagner composed the opera *Rienzi* after a novel by Bulwer-Lytton about a ruler of the Roman Renaissance, and Mendelssohn rediscovered the greatness of Bach's oratorios and in 1829 performed the *St. Matthew Passion* for the first time since the composer's death.

In retrospect, the 19th-century antithesis of classic and romantic has been resolved, because both now are seen as component parts of the same broader revival idea. The artists who lived on into the post-Napoleonic period drew their inspiration from Greco-Roman or medieval times with equal facility. John Nash, for example, built himself a neoclassical town house in London and a romantic Gothic castle in the country; Rude made statues of Roman nymphs and of Joan of Arc; Ingres painted the *Apotheosis of Homer* (Fig. 327) and later a picture of the Maid of Orleans; Keats wrote "Ode on a Grecian Urn" and also "St. Agnes' Eve"; Victor Hugo included neoclassical odes in the same volume with his medieval ballads. Berlioz admired Vergil quite as intensively as he did Dante and wrote the *Trojans at Carthage,* an opera founded on the *Aeneid,* as well as the *Requiem,* based on the medieval hymn *Dies Irae.* After neoclassicism and romanticism had run their courses, the revival idea led, in the later 19th century, to a broad eclecticism, whereby a virtuoso architect could build in any past style, a painter could do a portrait or historical canvas à la Titian or Rubens, a poet could employ any form or metrical organization with facility, and a composer could pull out at will a Renaissance or baroque stop on his organ.

England and Germany both claimed the Gothic style as their own, and to them it was a conscious departure from the Greco-Roman ideals of antiquity as well as their rebirth in the Renaissance, baroque, and neoclassical styles. In England especially, the Gothic revival was bound up closely with the wave of prosperity caused by a great industrial expansion, a glowing national pride, and a reaction against the Napoleonic empire that had threatened their own. A reassertion of the separation of the Church of England from Rome took shape in the Oxford movement, which demanded veering away from Greco-Roman architectural forms as essentially pagan, and restoration of medieval liturgies that, in turn, needed appropriate settings.

In Germany, the Gothic revival took the form of a vision of past national glory associated with that country's entrance upon the European scene under Charlemagne, whom the Germans adopted as their national hero *Karl der Grosse.* The relative security and eminence of Germany under the rule of the Holy Roman Empire had continued intermittently up to the reign in the 16th century of the Hapsburg Charles V, the last of the powerful emperors. The past thus played an important role in the 19th-century revival of German power, based as it was on the memory of an empire dominated by the north. Stung into action by its abolition under Napoleon, German nationalism fermented during the 19th century until it matured into the heady wine of Bismarck's statesmanship, the aroma of which reminded Teutonic connoisseurs of the heroic bouquet of such ancient vintages as those of Attila, Alaric, and Frederick Barbarossa.

From the Renaissance on through the aristocratic baroque tradition and the 18th century, French art was closely bound to traditional Greco-Roman forms. During the Revolution of 1789 and its aftermath, a wave of anticlericalism led to the actual destruction of some medieval buildings to protest against Church influence and herald the new freedom. The neoclassicism of the First Empire continued through the early years of the 19th century and, though weakened under the Bourbon restoration, had at least official approval right up to the Revolution of July, 1830. Underneath the political surface, however, the destruction of medieval monuments had indirectly stimulated certain groups to preserve parts of these works in museums. When the glories of their own medieval past were brought to the attention of some Frenchmen, at a time when the popular wave of neo-medieval enthusiasm was gathering such momentum in England and Germany, this was bound to have consequences in France. Unlike Protestant England and Germany, France had broken its ties with Roman Catholicism only briefly during the first wave of revolutionary fervor. Even Napoleon had found it politically expedient to make a concordat with the Vatican and to be crowned in the sacred precincts of Notre Dame in Paris in the presence of the Roman pontiff.

Since the power of the French state was such that it was able to withstand foreign pressure even at the time of the Revolution and, later, to embark on the conquest of the continent under Napoleon, there was no national inferiority complex to be taken into account. Very significantly, it was not until French national power had been thoroughly subdued under the coalition which defeated Napoleon that the romantic style took a firm hold on the French mind and imagination. Even then, it endured officially less than a generation—that is, between the revolutions of 1830 and 1848.

The medieval revival is also found on the American scene. In New York the Gothic spires of Trinity Church rise among lower Broadway's skyscrapers. Two churches by Renwick furnish further examples

**343.** JAMES RENWICK. Grace Church, New York. 1845.

—Grace Church (Fig. 343) and St. Patrick's Cathedral, both dating from the mid-19th century. Many American colleges and universities, in their zeal to be identified with ancient and honorable causes, were also built in the neomedieval style. And scattered throughout the country are half-timbered houses, castle residences, railroad stations, and other public buildings show the wide influence of the medieval revival on 19th-century American architecture.

*Back to Nature*    Rousseau had already sounded the clarion call of "back to nature" in the late 18th century. By so doing, he challenged the urbane, civilized, aristocratic image of man with his projection of the noble savage type whose rustic charm was achieved by shunning society and communing with a nature unspoiled by human hands. For his own part, Rousseau was perfectly willing to be received in courtly circles, and his rustic little opera *Le Devin du Village* ("The Village Soothsayer") was performed for Louis XVI at Versailles with great success. His ideas were partly responsible for the country cottage, complete

with a dairy and mill, that Queen Marie Antoinette had built for herself amid the formal gardens of Versailles (Fig. 344).

The back-to-nature idea took root and became one of the more popular 19th-century escape mechanisms with that segment of the population which lived in cities and dreamed of an idyllic country life they had no intention of living. These people delighted, however, in reading poetry full of nature imagery as well as folk ballads and fairy tales. They hung landscapes by Corot and the now all-too-familiar peasant scenes of Millet on the walls of their apartments and town houses. Beethoven's *Pastoral Symphony* and Wagner's *Forest Murmurs,* as well as dozens of piano pieces and songs, sounded the proper bucolic note in music. Weber's opera *Der Freischütz,* which had been the success of the 1826 season in Paris, brought out some of the darker aspects of nature. In it, much is made of the sinister powers of the night, and the forces over which it rules are effectively presented in the eerie Wolf's Glen scene. Nature, here, as well as in Goethe's *Faust,* included malignant and benign aspects, and both works unleashed terrifying elemental forces as well as powers of a magical and fantastic character.

Outstanding among landscapists was John Constable with his quiet studies of the English countryside, such as *Hay Wain* (Pl. 46, p. 319) and *Salisbury Cathedral from the Bishop's Garden* (Fig. 345). In comparison with the Claude Lorrain landscapes that Constable admired (Fig. 274), the composition of *Salisbury Cathedral* is as relaxed and informal as an English garden when placed beside a formal French one. Constable's major pictorial interests were in rendering mercurial changes of atmosphere; the infinitely varied intensities of light on clear, showery, or foggy days; sunshine filtered through translucent green leaves; and the changing reflections of the varicolored sky and passing clouds on water. To capture these effects Constable made innumerable oil sketches in the open air and later finished his pictures in his studio. When his paintings were exhibited in Paris, their freshness, warmth, and spontaneity created a considerable stir. Delacroix admired Constable's bold use of color, and his descriptive powers and technical innovations had an important influence on the later impressionists.

In contrast to Constable's aim of accurate rendering of natural phenomena, the works of J. M. W. Turner, also English and a contemporary of Constable, were poetic invocations and emotionalized experiences tinged with a haunting romantic melancholy. In his early pictures Turner started with variations on the land- and seascapes of Claude Lorrain, whom he admired above all artists. His style, however, gradually veered away from history painting to more visual effects, while grays and browns yielded to soft, pastel hues and sparkling, rainbowlike yellow and orange tonalities. As the titles of his paintings would imply,

Turner sought to capture on canvas some of the elemental forces of nature—*Snowstorm: Hannibal and His Army Crossing the Alps; Shade and Darkness: The Evening of the Deluge; Wreck of a Transport Ship; Fire at Sea; Keelmen Heaving in Coals at Night.*

In one of Turner's late works, *Rain, Steam, and Speed: The Great Western Railway* (Pl. 47, p. 319), the viewer feels the impact of precipitous movement in the Edinburgh express as it crosses a bridge in a driving storm. The rabbit racing ahead of the crack train symbolizes both speed and the romantic's vision of modern technology as a threat to nature and the organic fundamentals of life. Amid the swirling, spiraling vortex of wind and rain, the engine's firebox glows with hot, flamelike color, which contrasts with the dark blue of the passenger cars and with flecks of light blue in the sky. Constable once chided Turner about his "airy visions painted with tinted steam." But in retrospect, Turner's luminous canvases, varicolored light, and ethereal atmospheric effects proclaim him one of the most daring colorists in the history of painting, his originality deriving in some measure from Goethe's theory of light and color as language for conveying mood and emotion.

above: **344.** RICHARD MIQUE. Marie Antoinette's Cottage *(Le Hameau),* Versailles. 1783–86.

right: **345.** JOHN CONSTABLE. *Salisbury Cathedral from the Bishop's Garden.* 1826. Oil on canvas, $34\frac{1}{4} \times 43\frac{5}{8}''$. Frick Collection, New York (copyright).

The Romantic Style   **333**

**346.** John Nash. Royal Pavilion, Brighton. 1815–21. Lithograph. Metropolitan Museum of Art, New York (Harris Brisbane Dick Fund, 1941).

**347.** John Nash. Dining Hall, Royal Pavilion, Brighton. 1815–21. Lithograph. Metropolitan Museum of Art, New York.

*Exoticism*    The heady perfumes of the Orient also were wafted into the nostrils and thence to the fancies of romantic patrons, intellectuals, and artists. While shrewd businessmen were opening up new foreign markets, and missionaries were going forth from Europe to try to bridge the Christian and pagan worlds, artists busied themselves capturing the popular imagination with scenes of exotic mysteries associated with far-off lands and peoples. As early as 1759, Arthur Murphy in the prologue of a play called *Orphans of China* had proclaimed: "Enough of Greece and Rome: Th'exhausted store of either nation now can charm no more." So the Oriental world was added to the imaginative repertory, and its changing image in one guise or another has been mirrored in the arts up to the present time. Reflections of this early phase can be found in such operas as Gluck's *The Unforeseen Meeting* or *The Pilgrims to Mecca* (1764) and Mozart's *Abduction from the Seraglio* (1785), with

its setting in a Turkish harem, and in William Beckford's Oriental novel *Vathek* (1786). Kew Gardens in London was studded with fanciful structures revealing a wide imaginative range. Some paths led to little rococo pavilions, others to Greek temples or Gothic chapels. Among them were a Moslem mosque, a Moorish palace, and a house of Confucius. A pagoda, built by the conservative Palladian architect William Chambers, is the only one of these bagatelles that has survived.

Only a short time later, Napoleon was fighting his Battle of the Pyramids (1798). In England, a tale entitled *Thalabor the Destroyer* (1799) by Robert Southey included chapters called "The Desert Circle" and "Life in an Arab Tent." Drawing rooms were hung with wallpapers depicting scenes of mandarin China, and fashionable hostesses were pouring tea at Chinese Chippendale tables. The Prince Regent of England, like Kubla Khan in Coleridge's poem, did,

A stately pleasure-dome decree:
Where Alph, the sacred river, ran
Through caverns measureless to man
Down to the sunless sea.

Less poetically though no less fancifully, this was the Oriental pavilion the Prince Regent commissioned his architect to build at his favorite seaside resort of Brighton. John Nash, who had previously built an exotic country house for a gentleman who had lived in India, came up with an Arabian Nights extravaganza in a style that was then referred to as "Indian Gothic." The exterior is an exotic fantasy of minarets and cupolas, pinnacles and pagodas, all constructed over cast-iron frames (Fig. 346). A domed ceiling painted like a spreading palm tree covers the dining hall (Fig. 347). Waterlily chandeliers suspended from the cast-iron claws of scaly dragons, lotus-blossom lamps, Oriental lacquerware, and Chinese Chippendale furniture complete the decor.

Schopenhauer's *World as Will and Idea*, based on the Oriental philosophy of the negation of the will, appeared in 1819. In a revolt against the academic rationalism and scientific naturalism of his time, Schopenhauer turned to Oriental mysticism. He thought man could achieve peace with himself, harmony with his fellow man, and ultimate release into infinity by renouncing personal ambitions and mate-rialistic pursuits. Richard Wagner reflects this idea at the end of *Tristan and Isolde*, when the unhappy heroine, following her lover's death, aspires to the ecstasy of Nirvana by surrendering her tortured spirit to the cosmic rhythms of the universal World-all.

The colorful Japanese prints that found their way to Europe after Admiral Perry's voyage of 1852–54 had an important effect on painting. Gautier published a book called *L'Orient* in 1860, which was based on his travels, and the following year an opera by Auber called *La Circassienne* was performed. At this same time, Delacroix was painting one of his last pictures, *The Lion Hunt*, which vividly portrayed the violent struggle of men and horses against the unbridled ferocity of wild animals. Gounod's opera *The Queen of Sheba* was produced in 1862 at about the same time Ingres was finishing his fleshscape *The Turkish Bath* (Fig. 348). The search for exotic settings eventually culminated in two of the greatest works of the lyrical repertory—Verdi's *Aïda*, written in 1871 for the Cairo Opera in celebration of the opening of the Suez Canal, and Bizet's *Carmen*, which, based on a short story by Mérimée, was first performed in 1875. Toward the end of the century exoticism had begun to pall, and the realistic novelist Zola was making fun of his romantic colleague Gautier because "he needed a camel and four dirty Bedouins to tickle his brains into creative activity."

**348.** Jean Auguste Dominique Ingres. *The Turkish Bath.* c. 1852–63. Oil on canvas, diameter 42½". Louvre, Paris.

# 20 The Realistic and Impressionistic Styles

## PARIS, LATE 19TH CENTURY

While neoclassicism and romanticism were dominated by flights from reality, realism and impressionism tried to come to terms with the contemporary world. One measure of the force of social progress is the rapid rise and overthrow of the various forms of government in France during the period from 1789 to 1852. Between the absolute monarchy of Louis XVI and the Empire of Napoleon III, Paris experienced a revolutionary reign of terror, a republic, the Napoleonic Empire, a royal restoration, a constitutional monarchy, and a socialist commune. While these upheavals were making headlines, even more powerful and radical changes were initiated by the Industrial Revolution. The growth of factories employing the new machine methods of production meant the shift from an agrarian to an urban economy and the migration of large numbers of people from the farms to the cities. While the 18th-century worker had been able to weigh the tangible produce of his farm or take satisfaction in the completion of a handsome, handmade pair of shoes, his 19th-century counterpart exchanged the intangible elements of his time and labor for a precarious and fragmentary living.

The application of modern scientific knowledge to industrial progress opened up many novel possibilities in the arts. Such new materials as cast iron facilitated the rapid construction of buildings and furnished the means whereby complicated decorative devices, hitherto made laboriously by hand, could be produced quickly and cheaply to satisfy the demand for the practical or the picturesque. Painting, likewise, was indebted to modern science for the development of chemical pigments. Synthetic products began to replace the old earth pigments and ground minerals and often resulted in greater brilliancy and intensity than the genuine product. Low-cost reproductions, such as the lithograph and other prints, made it possible for artists to find a wider distribution for their pictures and a new public. The facilities provided by the mechanical printing press brought about the mass distribution of newspapers, novels, and sheet music. Cast-iron instead of wooden frames for pianos meant that pianists could have larger and more durable instruments as well as ones that stayed in tune over longer periods of time. The invention of new valve mechanisms for brass instruments and the comparative standardization of their manufacture gave composers a reasonable assurance of getting the complex instrumental effects they now demanded in their orchestrations.

From the mid-19th century onward, governments were seeking constitutional formulas that would strike a just balance between social rights and material progress; religious denominations were trying to reconcile time-honored Scriptural truths with the new scientific knowledge; social theories were concerned with how political liberalism could evolve side by side with religious orthodoxy; and philosophies were attempting a new resolution between the static absolutes of idealism and the dynamic thought underlying the theories of evolution. Architects were wondering how their work could still remain in the realm of the fine arts and yet make use of the new materials and technological methods they now commanded. Sculptors, such as Rodin, were asking whether the traditional mythological and historical themes could be replaced by more contemporary subjects. The realistic and impressionistic painters were seeking a formula for the incorporation into the accepted framework of pictorial art of the new physical discoveries concerning the nature of light and its perception by the human eye. Novelists, such as Zola, were trying to establish an alliance between scientific and literary methods. Poets and playwrights, such as Mallarmé and Maeterlinck, were looking for a middle ground between the realities of the revolutionary age and the traditional limitations of poetic expression. And composers, such as Debussy, were endeavoring to harmonize the new acoustical discoveries involving the physics of sound with the accepted concepts of tonality and musical form.

Governments and rulers settled down from high-flown heroics and histrionics into the drab but necessary routine of bureaucratic officialdom. The energies of artists were diverted from historical and exotic subjects into everyday life and seemingly trivial occurrences. The novels of Balzac and Dickens were concerned with social comment and criticism, as was the art of Honoré Daumier. The people of Daumier's Paris live on in such genre works as *Third-Class Carriage* (Fig. 349), where the artist's sense of social criticism is muted and his deep understanding and human compassion come to the fore. Ugliness, violence, and shock techniques, however, were intended to arouse but not to insult or offend potential patrons into alienation.

Some artists, though, found life so disillusioning that art became the sole compensation for the miseries of their existence. These painters and poets eventually severed their ties with their potential middle-class patrons altogether and retreated into a private world of art, where the painters painted pictures for a limited audience of other painters of similar persuasion and the poets put down their inspirations principally for the eyes and ears of other poets. They thus led insecure lives of an underprivileged social group and tended to band together in desperate little societies within society.

All these new developments tended to turn artists toward the new world of the great city for their material and inspiration. The artificial replaced the natural, and urban entertainments eclipsed the delights of nature. The usual was dominant over the unusual, and the here-and-now was definitely in ascendance over the there-and-then.

## PAINTING

About the middle of the 19th century, the most important younger painters rejected romantic flights of the imagination and academic glorifications of the heroic past. Gustave Courbet was in the vanguard of those who styled themselves "realists," defined painting as a physical language, and ruled out the metaphysical and invisible. The saints and miracles of the 19th century, according to Courbet, were mines, machines, and railroad stations. With a keen eye and a desire to record accurately what he saw about him, Courbet consciously set out to build an art on the commonplace (Fig. 350). His painting was concerned with the present, not the past; with the momentary, not the permanent; with bodies, not souls; with materiality, not spirituality. His nudes suggested no nymphs or goddesses; they were merely the models who posed in his studio. The villagers

## General Events

| | | |
|---|---|---|
| 1830– | 1848 | Louis Philippe, constitutional king |
| 1837– | 1901 | Victoria, queen of England |
| | 1839 | Daguerre and Niépce published findings on photography; daguerreotype process resulted |
| | 1848 | February Revolution; Louis Philippe overthrown. Second French Republic proclaimed. *Communist Manifesto* issued by Marx and Engels |
| | 1851 | Great Exhibition of All Nations in London; Crystal Palace by Paxton was one of buildings. Louis Napoleon, president of Second Republic, made *coup d'état,* and became dictator |
| 1852– | 1870 | Louis Napoleon reigned as Emperor Napoleon III |
| | 1853 | Admiral Perry opened Japan |
| 1856– | 1866 | *Physiological Optics* published by Helmholtz (1821–94); *On the Sensation of Tone as a Physiological Basis for the Theory of Music* (published 1863) |
| | 1857 | *Les Fleurs du Mal* ("Flowers of Evil") published by Baudelaire |
| 1858– | 1868 | Bibliothèque Nationale built by Labrouste |
| | 1859 | *Origin of Species* published by Darwin |

| | | |
|---|---|---|
| | 1863 | *Life of Jesus* by Renan |
| 1870– | 1871 | Franco-Prussian War; Napoleon III abdicated; Third French Republic established; Germany united as empire |
| | 1871 | *Descent of Man* published by Charles Darwin |
| | 1874 | First impressionist exhibit held |
| | 1889 | *La Grande Exposition Universelle* held in Paris; Eiffel Tower was one of buildings |
| | 1892 | *Pelléas et Mélisande* by Maeterlinck presented in Paris |
| | 1896 | *Matter and Memory* published by Henri Bergson |
| | 1902 | Debussy's opera on Maeterlinck's *Pelléas et Mélisande* produced in Paris |

## Painters

| | | |
|---|---|---|
| 1808– | 1879 | Honoré Daumier |
| 1819– | 1877 | Gustave Courbet |
| 1832– | 1883 | Édouard Manet |
| 1834– | 1903 | James A. McNeill Whistler |
| 1834– | 1917 | Edgar Degas |
| 1839– | 1906 | Paul Cézanne |
| 1840– | 1926 | Claude Monet |
| 1841– | 1919 | Pierre Auguste Renoir |
| 1848– | 1903 | Paul Gauguin |
| 1853– | 1890 | Vincent van Gogh |
| 1859– | 1891 | Georges Seurat |
| 1864– | 1901 | H. M. R. de Toulouse-Lautrec |

## Sculptors

| | | |
|---|---|---|
| 1827– | 1875 | Jean Baptiste Carpeaux |
| 1840– | 1917 | Auguste Rodin |

## Architects

| | | |
|---|---|---|
| 1801– | 1865 | Joseph Paxton |
| 1801– | 1875 | Henri Labrouste |
| 1809– | 1891 | Georges Eugène Haussmann |
| 1832– | 1923 | Gustave Eiffel |

## Musicians

| | | |
|---|---|---|
| 1813– | 1883 | Richard Wagner |
| 1822– | 1890 | César Franck |
| 1833– | 1897 | Johannes Brahms |
| 1835– | 1921 | Camille Saint-Saëns |
| 1838– | 1875 | Georges Bizet |
| 1842– | 1912 | Jules Massenet |
| 1845– | 1924 | Gabriel Fauré |
| 1860– | 1956 | Gustave Charpentier |
| 1862– | 1918 | Claude Debussy |
| 1875– | 1937 | Maurice Ravel |

## Writers and Philosophers

| | | |
|---|---|---|
| 1798– | 1857 | Auguste Comte |
| 1799– | 1850 | Honoré de Balzac |
| 1809– | 1865 | Proudhon (Pierre Joseph) |
| 1812– | 1870 | Charles Dickens |
| 1820– | 1903 | Herbert Spencer |
| 1821– | 1867 | Charles Baudelaire |
| 1821– | 1880 | Gustave Flaubert |
| 1828– | 1906 | Henrik Ibsen |
| 1840– | 1902 | Émile Zola |
| 1842– | 1898 | Stéphane Mallarmé |
| 1844– | 1900 | Friedrich Nietzsche |
| 1850– | 1893 | Guy de Maupassant |
| 1859– | 1941 | Henri Bergson |
| 1862– | 1949 | Maurice Maeterlinck |
| 1870– | 1925 | Pierre Louÿs |
| 1871– | 1922 | Marcel Proust |

attending the *Burial at Ornans* (Fig. 350) are there out of a sense of duty. The priest routinely reads the committal service, and the gravedigger casually waits to complete his job. No one betrays any great grief, and the skull and bone at the grave's edge add a realistic rather than a macabre touch. Courbet, however, sometimes became almost as passionate about the ugly as his predecessors had been about the beautiful. Both Courbet and his younger colleague Édouard Manet, who came under his influence, were sometimes seduced, despite themselves, into a strong emotional interest in their subject matter.

The artists who followed Courbet sought for even greater closeness to nature in order to develop an art based on immediacy of expression. They took their easels out-of-doors and tried to do as much of their

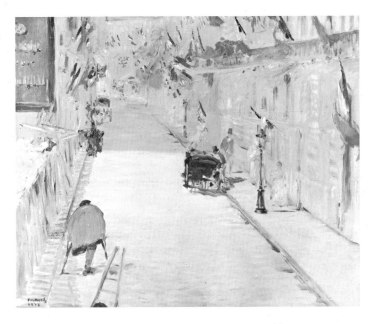

**351.** ÉDOUARD MANET. *Rue Mosnier, Decorated with Flags on June 30.* 1878. Oil on canvas, $25\frac{1}{2} \times 31\frac{1}{2}''$. Collection Mr. and Mrs. Paul Mellon.

painting on the spot as possible rather than to work in their studios from sketches. They were against painting a picture that carried any moral, any message, or any literary associations whatsoever, and they cultivated a calculated indifference toward pictorial content. Optical realism was pursued to the point of separating visual experience from memory and avoiding any associations the mind normally calls into play. In 1874, Claude Monet exhibited a picture called *Impression—Sunrise,* which gave the new movement its name. At first, *impressionism* was picked up as a term of critical derision. The word has remained, and it does have a certain appropriateness, implying the unfinished, the incomplete, an affair of the moment, an act of instantaneous vision, a sensation rather than a cognition.

It is impossible, of course, to substantiate any claim of a direct cause-and-effect relationship between science and art in this period or any formal connection between optical physics and painting. It is equally impossible to state that painters were unaware of or indifferent to such things as the invention of the camera, the scientific discoveries about the nature of light, and the new knowledge about the physiology of the eye. Joint researches of Daguerre and Niépce on the making of photographic images on prepared metal plates, which resulted in the daguerreotype process, had been published as early as 1839. The revelation that visual imagery was primarily dependent on minute gradations of light intensities was bound to have an effect on painting. Physicists, including Helmholtz, made discoveries about the component prismatic parts of white light, and pointed out that the sensation of color has more to do with a retinal reaction in the eye than with objects themselves. The color wheel also demonstrated that two separate hues of a wheel at rest are fused by the eye into a third hue when the wheel is in rapid motion. And when all the colors of the spectrum are rotated, the eye sees them as tending toward white.

Painters also did some speculation of their own on the nature of the visual experience. Form and space, they reasoned, are not actually seen but implied from varying intensities of light and color. Objects are not so much entities in themselves as they are agents for the absorption and refraction of light. Hard outlines, indeed lines themselves, do not exist in nature. Shadows, they maintained, are not black but tend to take on a color complementary to that of the objects that cast them. The concern of the painter, they concluded, should therefore be with light and color more than with objects and substances. A painting should consist of a breakdown of sunlight into its component parts, and brilliance should be achieved by the use of the primary colors that make up the spectrum. Instead of greens mixed by the painter on his palette, separate daubs of yellow and blue should be placed close together and the mixing left to the spectator's eye. What seems confusion at close range is clarified at the proper distance. By thus trying to step up the luminosity of their canvases so as to convey the illusion of sunlight sifted through a prism, they achieved a veritable carnival of color in which the eye seems to join in a dance of vibrating light intensities. As a result of this reexamination of their technical means, the impressionists discovered a new method of visual representation.

Édouard Manet painted *Rue Mosnier* late in his career with the impressionistic theory in mind (Fig. 351). In it, he builds a cityscape out of a configuration

**352.** CLAUDE MONET. *Old St. Lazare Station.* 1877. Oil on canvas, 23½ × 31½". Art Institute of Chicago.

of interrelated planes. By his subtle use of color intensities more than by linear perspective, he achieves the effect of recession and depth. In other versions of this scene, he painted some road menders in the foreground, and his choice of such a casual street scene is in keeping with the general preference for subjects that can be taken in at a glance rather than those that must be studied carefully and in detail. It also exemplifies the conscious cultivation of the accidental—the random scene in which emotional involvement with the subject is impossible.

Manet's last large-scale work, *Bar at the Folies-Bergère,* is a technical tour de force of major magnitude (Pl. 48, p. 320). At first glance the viewer himself would seem to be the customer the barmaid is waiting to serve, but her client apparently is the top-hatted, goateed gentleman who is seen in mirror image behind the girl's reflection at the upper left. For correctness the maid would have to stand almost sidewise to cast such a reflection, but with poetic license Manet lets her face forward. The composition is tightly structured, with the double image of the pensive waitress and the bottles of the stunning still life in the foreground defining the vertical rise, and the marble counter at the picture plane, the table behind, and the mirrored ledge of the balcony taking care of the horizontal balance. The Bohemian scene is bathed in garish gaslight, glints of which are caught by the crystal chandeliers, assorted bottles, the vase and compote dish, and the balcony scene reflected in the shimmering expanse of the mirror. Except for the barmaid, all the figures are suggested rather than defined. With a few bold strokes Manet creates girls with opera glasses, ladies in colorful costumes,

bearded men in stovepipe hats, and above all captures the mood of an evening's diversion.

Renoir, Manet's younger contemporary, had already painted a similar scene set in a popular outdoor Paris café, *Le Moulin de la Galette,* that had been shown in the 1877 impressionist exhibit (Pl. 49, p. 353). The full force of impressionistic color is felt in the rainbow of brilliant hues, especially the variations of blue, and the marvelous quality of filtered sunlight that Renoir had at his command. His obvious intention was to evoke the atmosphere of carefree gaiety and the whirling movement of dance, as well as to revel sensuously in an intangible world of color and light.

More than any other painter, Claude Monet was the central figure of impressionism, and his picture the *Old St. Lazare Station* is among his most typical works (Fig. 352). The rendering of the humid atmosphere, the mixture of steam and smoke, the hazy sunlight filtering in from the open background and the transparent roof, the contrast between the open spaces and the closed forms of the engines and railroad cars are the things that concern him most. There is no hustle and bustle, no drama of arriving or departing people, no crowds or excitement, no interplay of men and machines, such as one might expect in such a setting. Instead, his people merely file from the waiting room toward the train, and the workmen go about their tasks in a matter-of-fact way. The picture therefore becomes an atmospheric study in blues and greens.

The full development of Monet's broken-color technique is even more clearly discernible in the *Garden at Giverny,* his suburban home (Pl. 50, p. 354). In it, he breaks his light up into a spectrum of bright colors that delights the eye by forming shimmering patterns in and around the leaves and lilies. Water imagery repeatedly recurs in impressionistic painting. Its iridescence, its fluidity, its surface reflections, the perpetual play of changing light, make water ideal for conveying the conception of the insubstantial, impermanent, fleeting nature of visual experience. Plate 50 is but one of many versions Monet painted of the same subject (Fig. 402), and his method of work reveals that the objects he painted were of less concern than the light and atmosphere surrounding them. In order to capture the moment he wanted, he would take up in a single day a succession of canvases—one showing the garden at dawn, another in full morning light, and a third in a late afternoon glow. The following morning he would take up the dawn scene where he had left off the day before and, when the light changed, set it aside for the next canvas, and so on. With scientific detachment, he tried to maintain the constancy of his subject matter by painting series of *Haystacks, Rouen Cathedral,* and *Old St. Lazare Station,* so as to focus the interest on the variables of light and atmosphere. Each version varies according to the season, day, or hour. Monet might even be called the "weather man" of painting were it not that, in spite of himself, his genuine involvement with nature usually overcame his objective detachment. As Cézanne once remarked: "Monet, he's only an eye, but my God what an eye!"

Impressionism is clearly an art of the urban man who sees himself in terms of temporal flow, mounting tensions, and sudden change. His volatile life is ruled by impermanent rather than permanent forces, and becoming is more real to him than being. Impressionistic painters purposely chose everyday subjects, such as street scenes, children at play, and life in a night café. When they did go to the country, it was to the suburbs in the manner of city folk on a holiday. As a result, the general effect of impressionist painting is bright, cheerful, and lighthearted rather than heavy or somber. The artists were intoxicated by light rather than life, and they saw the world as a myriad of mirrors that refracted a constantly changing kaleidoscope of color and varying intensities of light. They lived therefore in a visual world of reflections rather than substances, and one in which visual values replaced the tactile. To reproduce the fugitive atmospheric effects the impressionists desired, they had to work directly from nature. This led to a speeding up in the process of painting to a point where working with oils approached the more rapid technique of watercolor. The criticism of hasty work and careless craftsmanship that the impressionists incurred from their contemporaries was sometimes quite justified. But when their intentions are fully taken into account, one finds no lack of technical skill on the part of the style's most important practitioners. They wanted their paintings to seem spontaneous and to have an improvised, fragmentary look. Beauty, like color, they felt was in the eye of the beholder, not in the picture itself. They intended to paint not so much what is seen but how it is seen. Instead of composing, which implies a placing together, they sought to isolate one aspect of experience and explore it to the utmost. Their art therefore becomes one of analysis more than synthesis, sensation more than perception, sight more than insight. As such the cool objectivity of impressionism could be said to represent the triumph of technique over expression.

In their total immersion in the two-dimensional world of appearances, the impressionists consciously neglected the other dimensions of psychological depth and emotional involvement. As a consequence, they soon began to chafe under the arbitrary restrictions of such a limited theory. Nor were their audiences happy with the role of innocent bystander they had been assigned. Both artist and spectator had, in effect, resigned the active role for that of the aloof observer of life who lets the river of experience go by without attempting to divert its flow in any significant direction. In scarcely more than a dozen years after Monet had shown his *Impression—Sunrise,* the movement had lost its momentum. Even though no one painted an *Impression—Sunset* to commemorate the event, impressionism in its pristine form was at an end, to all intents and purposes, with the last impressionist exhibit in 1886. Many of the discoveries that had been made, however, survived in variously modified forms in the work of the postimpressionist painters.

*Sunday Afternoon on the Island of La Grande Jatte* by Georges Seurat shows how the impressionistic theory was carried to a logical, almost mathematical, conclusion (Pl. 51, p. 355). Light, shadow, and color are still the major concerns, and the subject is also that of an urban scene, this time of a relaxed group of middle-class Parisians on a Sunday outing. Instead of informal casual arrangements, however, everything here seems as set as an old-fashioned family portrait. Instead of misty nebulous forms, such details as a bustle, a parasol, or a plug hat are as stylized and geometrical as in a Renaissance fresco. Instead of improvising his pictures out of doors, Seurat carefully composed his large canvas in his studio over a period of years. Instead of hastily painted patches of broken color, Seurat worked out a system called *pointillism* by which thousands of dots of uniform size were applied to the canvas in such a calculated and painstaking way that the most subtle tints were brought under the painter's control. The whole picture, moreover, was subdivided into areas, and a scheme of graduating shades blended tonalities into one another to achieve an overall tonal unity.

Vincent van Gogh's *Starry Night* demonstrates how colors can be used to achieve intensely expressive effects (Pl. 52, p. 356). The deep-purple sky, the yellow light of the stars, the green upward-curling silhouette of the cypress tree all stem from impressionism. Broken color, however, has here become a myriad of dark swirling vertiginous lines used as a means toward revealing an inner ecstatic vision.

Paul Gauguin's *Mahana No Atua*, or *Day of the God*, also shows how the brilliant color of the impressionists can be adapted to make quiet, two-dimensional decorative designs (Pl. 53, p. 357). In 1888 the mature Gauguin articulated his theory of the correspondence between natural form and artistic feeling when, during an outdoor painting session in Brittainy, he interrogated and advised the twenty-five-year-old Paul Sérusier in the following way: "How do you see that tree? . . . Is it quite green? Then put on green, the finest green on your palette;—and that shadow, is it a bit blue? Don't be afraid to paint it as blue as possible." As Gauguin spoke, Sérusier worked through the exercise, using the purest of tube colors to create a brilliant little landscape on the back of a wooden cigar box cover. He called it *The Talisman* (Pl. 54, p. 357). The process Gauguin recommended was that of synthesizing the facts of nature with the artist's own aesthetic—his sense of how and which lines, colors, shapes, and textures should be organized so as to have an intended effect. In an article published in 1890, Maurice Denis—a fellow student of Sérusier and like him a member of a group called the *Nabis* ("the prophets")—formulated Gauguin's ideas into a dictum that became fundamental to all understanding of abstraction in modern art: ". . . a picture—before being a war-horse, a nude woman, or some sort of anecdote—is essentially a surface covered with colors arranged in a certain order." In other words, form and design, much more than actual subject matter, would have the greatest potential for investing a picture with expressive content. Because they were willing to distort the image of nature, Gauguin and his associates called themselves *synthetists;* for the reason that they did it to make each painting just that much more expressive of the artist's feelings and his vision of life, the Gauguin circle considered themselves to be *symbolists.*

In the 1870s, Paul Cézanne was using the prismatic color palette of the impressionists, but he soon discovered the expressive limitations of the theory. His solution for some of the pictorial problems it posed became a turning point in the history of painting. For him, the superficial beauty of impressionism did not provide the firm base on which to build a significant art. The delight in the transitory tended too much to exclude the more permanent values. Instead of severing connections with the past, he said that he wanted "to make of impressionism something solid like the art of the museums." Poussin was the old master he chose to emulate, and his expressed desire was to re-create Poussin in the light of nature. The cultivation of instantaneous vision, according to Cé-

zanne, ruled out the participation of too many other important faculties. His pictures, unlike those of the impressionists, were not meant to be grasped immediately, and their meaning is never obvious. For Cézanne, painting should be not only an act of the eye but also of the mind. If painting aimed only at the senses, any deeper probing of human psychology would be eliminated. Light is important in itself, but it can also be used to achieve inner illumination. Color as such is paramount, but color is also a means of describing masses and volumes, revealing form, creating relationships, separating space into planes, and producing the illusion of projection and recession. Primary colors produce brilliance, but judicious mixtures can run a whole gamut of subtle effects. Cézanne, therefore, retained both light and color as the basis of his art, but not to the extent of eliminating the need for line and geometrical organization. Cézanne's interests are not so much in the specific as in the general. Analysis is necessary for simplification and to reduce a picture to its bare essentials, but for Cézanne composition and synthesis are still the primary processes of the pictorial art. His canvases therefore tend to be more austere than voluptuous, more sinuous than lush. His pictures have order, repose, and a serene color harmony, yet they are capable of rising to high points of tension and grandeur.

The forms Cézanne chose were from his daily experience—apples, mountains, houses, trees—constants by which it is possible to measure the extent of his spiritual growth. "You must paint them to tame them," he once remarked. Mont Ste. Victoire, a rising rocky mass near his home in Aix-en-Provence, was for Cézanne a recurring motif. Just as Goethe wrote his *Faust* throughout his entire creative career, so Cézanne painted his mountain again and again until it became a kind of symbol of his ambitions and aspirations. The contrast of an early and a late version provides an interesting index to his artistic growth. The first *Mont Ste. Victoire,* subtitled *Landscape with Viaduct,* dates between 1885 and 1887 (Fig. 353). Another version with no subtitle was done between 1904 and 1906 (Fig. 354). Both are landscapes organized into a pattern of planes by means of color. Both show his way of achieving perspective not by converging lines but by intersecting and overlapping planes of color. In the first version, there is a complementary balance between the vertical rise of the trees and the horizontal line of the viaduct. In the second, these details are omitted, and a balance is achieved between the dense-green foliage of the lower foreground and the purple and light-green jagged mass of the mountain in the background. In the earlier, the mountain descends in a series of gently sloping lines; in the latter, it plunges precipitously downward. In the former, such details as the road, houses, and shrubs are readily recognizable. In the latter, all is reduced to the barest essentials, and only such formal contours

**right: 353.** Paul Cézanne. *Mont Ste. Victoire.* 1885–87. Oil on canvas, 25¾ × 31⅞″. Metropolitan Museum of Art, New York (bequest of Mrs. H. O. Havemeyer, 1929, the H. O. Havemeyer Collection).

**below: 354.** Paul Cézanne. *Mont Ste. Victoire.* 1904–06. Oil on canvas, 28⅞ × 36¼″. Philadelphia Museum of Art (George W. Elkins Collection).

as the cones, cubes, and slanting surfaces remain. Both pictures, however, are landscapes interpreted by the same sensitive and highly individual temperament. Both show Cézanne's lifelong desire to mold nature into a coherent pattern in order to unite the inanimate world of things and the animate world of the human mind.

In such a still life as *Basket of Apples*, Cézanne works in a more intimate vein (Pl. 55, p. 358). The search for pure formal values, however, still continues. In one of his letters, he remarked that nature reveals itself in the forms of the cylinder, the sphere, and the cone. Here his cylinders are the horizontally arranged biscuits, his spheres the apples, and his cone the vertically rising bottle. They are balanced in this case by the forward-tilting ellipse of the basket and the receding plane of the tabletop. An almost imperceptible feeling of diagonal motion is induced by the distribution of the fruit from the upper left to the lower right, which compositional momentum is brought to an equally imperceptible stop by means of the pear-shaped apple at the extreme right.

Cézanne brought a measure of form and stability into a visual world where everything was change and transition. If he succeeded only at times and failed at others, each result must be equated with the immensity of the task that he set for himself. Like all great masters, he realized in his mature years that he had made only a beginning, and he once remarked that he would forever be the primitive of the method he himself had discovered. His historical position may indeed be just this, but his work may be said to form the bridge between impressionism and modern abstract painting.

## SCULPTURE

Among the sculptural exhibits at the Paris Salon of 1877 was a statue of a nude youth entitled *The Bronze Age* (Fig. 355). Too lifelike, said the academic critics. Too good, thought his fellow sculptors as they started rumors that Auguste Rodin was trying to pass off a statue taken directly from plaster casts of a living model. In official quarters the gossip was given sufficient credence to cause the hasty withdrawal of the work. To refute one and all, Rodin had casts and photographs made of the model who had posed for him, and the following year, with official explanations and apologies *The Bronze Age* was again on exhibition. A short while later it was bought by the state for placement in the Luxembourg Gardens. Such was the gulf, however, between art and life, between a monument and a reality, that in academic circles a statue which looked too real, too lifelike, or natural was considered to be a disgrace.

Like his forward-looking contemporaries in other fields, Rodin had veered away from the heroic toward the natural. Although he admired Gothic sculpture and wrote a book about French cathedrals, his work contains few sermons in stone. Though he admired Dante and drew almost all his later subjects from an early project for the *Gates of Hell* (Fig. 356), his conceptions show little of the escapism that motivated his immediate predecessors. Intended as door panels for a projected building to house the Paris Museum of Decorative Arts, Rodin's gates had as their points of departure the portals of the Florence Baptistry, notably Ghiberti's *Gates of Paradise* (Pl. 20, p. 177), and the writhing nudes of Michelangelo's *Last Judgment* (Figs. 201, 239). The literary source was an odd combination of Dante and Baudelaire. "Dante is not only a visionary but a sculptor," wrote Rodin. "His expression is lapidary in the good sense of the word." Above the actual doors broods the Michelangelesque figure of *The Thinker*—man, not Christ, is here to judge. Rodin's figures are bodies not souls, his damned suffer more from sensuous than spiritual longings. Most details were worked out between 1880 and 1887, except for readjustments that went on until 1917. *The Thinker*, Rodin's best-known work, and *Three Shades* (Fig. 357), *Adam,* and *Eve,* three of Rodin's later large-scale sculptures, were derived from the original germ cell of his inspiration for the *Gates of Hell.*

For Rodin, the process of forming supersedes that of form itself. The *Hand of God* exemplifies this, both in the method of execution and in the subject itself (Fig. 358). Out of an indefinite mass of uncut stone, symbolic of the formless void, the hand of the Creator arises. Divine omnipotence is suggested by the scale of the hand in relation to that of the human figures which are emerging from a lump of uncarved marble. The significance of the work was caught by the philosopher Henri Bergson, author of *Creative Evolution,* who called it "the fleeting moment of creation, which never stops." It is the implication that nothing is ever quite complete, that everything takes place in the flow of time, that matter is the womb which is continuously giving birth, that creation is a never-ending process rather than an accomplished fact—in short, the acceptance of the theory and philosophy of evolution—which gives Rodin's conception its daring.

Not only did Rodin prefer the natural over the heroic, but he always acknowledged his material frankly, seeking neither to disguise it nor to escape from it. In many of his works there is the feeling that his figures are just emerging out of their original stone or clay state, recalling Henri Bergson's phrase, "the fleeting moment of creation, which never stops." It is the implication that nothing is ever quite complete, that everything takes place in the flow of time, that matter is the womb which is continuously giving birth, that creation is a never-ending process rather than an accomplished fact—in short, the acceptance of the theory and philosophy of evolution—which gives Rodin's conception its daring quality. This is not, however, the mighty Michelangelesque struggle of man against his material bonds. Rather it is a sensuous love of material as such, a reveling in the flesh or stone, and a desire to explore all its possibilities and potentialities. If Michelangelo left his figures incomplete and still dominated by their material medium, it was largely because circumstances prevented his finishing them. With Rodin, the incompleteness is a conscious and calculated part of his expressive design. Like the symbolist poets, the novelist Proust, and the dramatist Maeterlinck, Rodin went one step beyond mere description. For Rodin, as for his literary contemporaries, events were nothing in themselves. Only when conjured up later in memory did they acquire the necessary subjective coloration; and only then, paradoxically, could the artist treat them with the needed objective detachment.

Rodin always preferred to work from a memory image rather than directly from a model in the flesh.

**top: 355.** Auguste Rodin. *The Bronze Age.* 1876. Bronze, height 5'11". Minneapolis Institute of Arts (John R. Van Derlip Fund).

**above right: 356.** Auguste Rodin. *Gates of Hell.* 1880–1917. Bronze, height 18', width 12', depth 33". Rodin Museum, Philadelphia.

**above: 357.** Auguste Rodin. *Three Shades.* 1880. Bronze, height 6'3½". Courtesy City and County of San Francisco.

**right: 358.** Auguste Rodin. *Hand of God.* 1898. Marble, height 29". Rodin Museum, Paris.

The Realistic and Impressionistic Styles    **345**

**359.** Henri Labrouste. Library of Ste. Geneviève, University of Paris (the Sorbonne). 1843–50. Length 336'.

When he did work with a model, it was usually to make a quick sketch, a wash drawing, or an impression in wax or soft clay. He could then allow his figures to take plastic shape in this preliminary stage at the moment of inspiration and thus to promote the feeling that they were products of improvisation. The process of transferring his figures into marble or bronze was left until the forms had been refined in memory and had assumed a more subjective and personal quality. Through memory and introspection Rodin was able to give his compositions some three-dimensional plausibility, and by the projection of psychological depth into his work, he gave his art substance and raised it well above the commonplace.

## ARCHITECTURE

Throughout the 19th century there was a sharp division of thought about the work of an architect. Was he primarily an artist or a builder? A designer or engineer? Should he concern himself more with decoration or with structure? Was his place in a studio making drawings or in the field working with his materials? The champions of the pictorial viewpoint achieved such virtuosity that at practically a moment's notice they could produce on their drawing boards a design based on any known building from the past. Late in the century, all the historical styles had been so carefully catalogued and documented that the range of choices was almost unlimited. What had begun as the revival of special periods had now been broadened to include them all. The term for such a freedom of choice is *eclecticism,* and if a name is to be chosen for the architectural style of the period this is the only one possible. The sole limitation on this eclecticism was the generally accepted appropriateness of the styles of certain periods to special situations. The classical was considered best for com-

memorative buildings and monuments, but classicism now could be anything from Mycenaean Greek to late imperial Roman. Medieval was the preference for churches, but this might mean Byzantine, Romanesque, early or late Gothic. For public buildings, Renaissance was thought most suitable, though here again the choice could be from the 15th century on.

The industrial age, however, had produced new methods and materials that opened up novel possibilities. The potentialities of cast iron, for example, had been perceived by engineers and industrialists long before architects began to speculate on the creative applications it could make to their art. The structural use of iron actually dates from the latter part of the 18th century, although at first it was found in bridges, cotton mills, and other utilitarian buildings, where it usually was combined with brick, stone, or timber or else used as a substitute for one or more of them. Nevertheless, the first steps toward a revolution in the art of building had been taken. The century was eventually to see the spanning of broader widths, the enclosure of more cubic space, and projections toward greater heights than had hitherto been thought possible. The new materials and structural principles were both a threat and a challenge to the traditional pictorial designers, and the more they were used in building plans, the more progressive architecture became.

It has already been noted how iron columns and girders had been used quite openly by John Nash in the exotic Brighton Pavilion (Figs. 346, 347), marking one of the first instances of their use in a large residential building. In Paris, François Gau had used iron girders masked with stone facings to reinforce his Gothic-revival Church of Ste. Clotilde (Fig. 339). Now Henri Labrouste, with an even more penetrating insight into the possibilities of the new material at his command, went one step farther in his Library of Ste.

Geneviève. A first glance at its exterior (Fig. 359) reveals simply a well-executed Renaissance-revival building—as such it is indebted to a 15th-century Italian church in Rimini designed by Alberti—with the usual festoons of garlands adorning the space above its seriate windows. A closer inspection, however, shows that the ground floor is conceived as a solid space, while the bold arcade of windows above gives promise of light and air within. Since the building is a library, there is a working relationship between the closed storage space for the books below and the open reading room above. This is as far as the exterior goes toward a unity of means and ends, however, and the stone on the outside gives no hint that the interior is constructed of iron.

By utilizing the strength of metal, Labrouste was able to replace the massive masonry ordinarily required for such a large reading room (Fig. 360) and at the same time provide for a maximum of open space and brilliant illumination. The room is vaulted with two series of arches made of cast iron, supported by tall, thin, fluted cast-iron columns, which form two parallel barrel vaults. An open foliated pattern related to the classical acanthus leaf is used as a decorative motif, and the vaults are supported by tall, thin, fluted Corinthian colonnettes, also made of iron. Labrouste thus managed his material so that he brought out its full structural possibilities. But by allowing his iron colonnettes to assume a form associated with carved stone, he compromised with tradition and let the expressive potentialities lag somewhat behind.

What Labrouste began in the Library of Ste. Geneviève, he brought to a brilliant fulfillment in his later masterwork, the stacks of the Bibliothèque Nationale (Fig. 361). This storage space for books is conceived as the very heart of the library, and it is now brought out into the open alongside the reading room itself. Though closed to the public, a full view of it is possible through a glass-enclosed archway. All superfluous ornamentation is omitted in favor of the function for which it was designed. Except for the bookcases and the glass ceiling, everything is of cast iron. By dividing his space into five stories, four above and one below the ground level, Labrouste provided for the housing of about a million volumes. The floors are of open grillwork, which permits a free flow of light to reach all levels. Frequent stairways provide rapid communication between floors, and the strategically placed bridges allow freedom of access between the two wings. As a composition, they present a pleasing visual pattern of vertical and horizontal intersecting planes. In both these libraries, it is evident that Labrouste has taken a bold stride toward the realization of the potentialities of the modern materials and that his work as a whole represents a positive contribution to the development of a new architecture.

The same year that Labrouste was completing his first library, a new and original structure was going up in London that made no pretensions whatsoever

**362.** JOSEPH PAXTON. Crystal Palace, London. 1851. Cast iron and glass, width 1,851'. Lithograph.

**363.** JOSEPH PAXTON. Foreign Pavilion, Crystal Palace, London. 1851. Lithograph.

of being either a Roman bath or a Renaissance palace. The London *Times* referred to it as Mr. Paxton's "monstrous greenhouse"; and, to be sure, it was conceived and carried out by a landscape gardener skilled in the construction of conservatories and nurseries. The occasion was the Great Exhibition of the Works of Industry of All Nations, where the latest mechanical inventions as well as raw materials were to be brought together with the finished products of industry. Machinery of all sorts was to take its place beside the manufactured arts and crafts that were being turned out by the new factories. The Crystal Palace that Joseph Paxton constructed to house the exposition was destined to eclipse the exhibits them-

selves and to find for itself a unique place in the history of modern architecture (Fig. 362). His light and airy structure was rectangular in shape, 408 feet in width and—with a neat bit of symbolism to coincide with the year of the exhibition—1,851 feet in length. It rose by means of a skeleton of cast-iron girders and wrought-iron trusses and supports, all bolted together with mathematical precision. Its walls and roof enclosed 33 million cubic feet of space in a transparent sheath of glass. The rapidity of its construction was no less remarkable than its form. Previously, the whole structure had been accurately analyzed into a multiplicity of prefabricated parts, and so well planned was it that 18,000 panes of glass were put in place by 80 workmen in one week. Begun the end of September, 1850, it was easily ready for the grand opening, May 1, 1851.

Contrary to expectations, the Crystal Palace turned out to be a thing of surprising beauty and brilliance, as inexpensive in its construction as it was daring in its use of materials. No applied decoration of any sort marred the forthright character of the exterior. And while the iron columns of the interior paid lip service to their classical ancestors, the enormous scale made such details incidental. At the inauguration ceremonies (Fig. 363), Albert, the Prince Consort, stood by a crystal fountain and restated the purpose of the exhibition: to present "a living picture of the point of development at which the whole of mankind had arrived, . . . and a new starting point from which all nations will be able to direct their further exertions." Nothing seemed impossible to the machine age, and the engineers were indeed the prophets of the new order. Everything now seemed set for Victorian man to step out of his self-created pseudo-Gothic gloom into the new shining age of industrial prosperity. Mr. Paxton and his greenhouse, however, had to wait more than half a century before the architects fully caught up with them.

# LITERATURE AND MUSIC

The desire on the part of writers to come to terms with their own world rather than to explore the avenues of escape was responsible for the literary movements known as *realism* and *naturalism.* In some cases, writers cultivated a kinship with the scientific materialism that dominated the thought of the period following the February Revolution of 1848. In others, notably with Zola and Ibsen, they allied themselves with sociology and wrote their novels and plays much as a social worker might handle a case history. Somewhat earlier, Balzac had proved himself far too sophisticated a writer to see much in the medieval period beyond ignorance, poverty, and rustic village life and was able to write glowingly of the beauty of factories and big cities. The subject matter of his novels was drawn from the complex moral and psychological trials of middle-class life in the large urban centers that he knew. This did not imply complete acceptance of the bourgeois image of man; on the contrary, it often meant violent opposition to his accepted values. Attitudes toward their writing varied with the temperaments of individual writers. Flaubert, for one, felt compelled to withdraw from life in order to describe it with the necessary objectivity; and he was convinced that such scientific detachment alone qualified the artist as well as the scientist. Zola, on the other hand, could not write without a passionate self-identification with the oppressed subjects of his novels. In the spirit of a reformer, he found it a necessity to bring social sores out into the sunlight of public exposure to effect a cure. With him, the novelist becomes a social research worker, and the novel a documentary case history.

The art of the symbolist is one of the fleeting moment; everything rushes past in an accelerated panorama. With the metaphor as a starting point, a symbolist prose poem flows by in a sequence of images that sweeps the reader along on a swift current of words with a minimum of slowing down to ponder on their meaning. Like the impressionistic painters, the symbolists reveled in sense data, and, like the realistic novelists, they looked for their material among the seemingly inconsequential occurrences of daily life. But in their endeavor to endow such happenings with profundity, and in their effort to attach to them a deeper symbolic significance, they went one step beyond their colleagues. While the painters had found a new world in the physics of light, and the novelists another new world in the social sciences, the symbolists looked to the new discoveries in psychology. By purposely leaving their poetry in an inconclusive and fragmentary state, they were making use of the psychological mechanism of reasoning from part to whole. Since the poets did not define the whole, the reader's imagination was allowed the full scope of its interpretive power.

Just as the impressionist painters had left the mixing of color to the eye of the observer, and the relationship of the subject matter to the viewer's mind, so Mallarmé and the symbolists left the connection, order, and form of their verbal still lifes to be completed by the reader. They also found a new world to explore in "listening" to colors, "looking" at sounds, "savoring" perfumes, and in all such mixtures of separate sensations known to psychology as *synaesthesia.* By developing a hypersensitive tonal palette, Claude Debussy, like his symbolist colleagues, was able to sound a gamut of images from volatile perfumes *(Sounds and Perfumes on the Evening Air),* fluid architecture *(Engulfed Cathedral),* sparkling seascapes *(La Mer),* exotic festivities *(Iberia, Fêtes)* to gaudy fireworks *(Feux d'Artifice).* The symbolists pushed outward to the threshold limits of perception in order to develop more delicate sensibilities and stimulate the capacities for new and peripheral experiences. They moved about in a twilight zone where sensation ends and ideation begins. The very word *symbolism,* however, implies the images are revelations of something surpassing sense data. And it is here that they parted company with the objectivity of the realists and impressionists, who were largely content with careful description.

Maurice Maeterlinck made an interesting attempt to translate the aims of the symbolist poets into dramatic form. His *Pelléas et Mélisande,* a play first performed in 1892, effects a synthesis of the material world and the world of the imagination. In it, he denies the importance of external events and explores the quiet vibrations of the soul. His symbols function as links between the visible and invisible, the momentary and the eternal. The tangible fragments of common experience, the seemingly trivial everyday occurrences, however, furnish clues to the more decisive stuff of life. "Beneath all human thoughts, volitions, passions, actions," he writes in one of his essays, "there lies the vast ocean of the Unconscious, the unknown source of all that is good, true and beautiful. All that we know, think, feel, see and will are but bubbles on the surface of this vast sea." This sea, then, is the symbol of the absolute toward which all life is reaching, but which can never quite be grasped. What is heard is only the ripples on the surface.

In his drama, the sea, the forest, the fountain, the abyss are the *dramatis personae* in a profounder sense than the human characters, who are but shadowy reflections of real people. In spite of the settings in which they appear, Maeterlinck's characters belong neither to the past nor to the future but hover in an extended now. They seem to have no spatial extension, no volume, but exist more as creatures of duration. So little is externalized that the progress of what plot there is seems to unfold within the characters. One overhears rather than hears the dialogue, and, in the ordinary sense, so little happens that a kind of dramatic vacuum is created which can be filled only by the imaginations of the spectators. Just as the eye must mix the colors in an impressionist painting, so the observer's imagination in a Maeterlinck play must connect the metaphors, must unite the tableaux into a flow of images, must fill each pregnant pause with projections from his own experience, and must supply the emotional depth to its surface play of symbols.

Maeterlinck's good fortune was to find a composer who could fill his silences with the necessary nebulous sounds, who could give voice to the "murmur of eternity on the horizon," and who could write the music that provided the link from dream to dream. It was, indeed, as if the music of Debussy had been created for the very purpose of providing the tonal envelope to enclose Maeterlinck's "ominous silence of the soul." Debussy was able to make the sea sing "the mysterious chant of the infinite." In his score, the references to the ocean on which all the characters are floating toward their unknown destinies are handled with special sensitivity. In one guise or another, its waters are present in practically every scene, either in the fragmentary form of a spring in the forest, a well in a courtyard, a fountain in a park, or the stagnant, fetid pools of underground caverns. This ever-present water imagery is used as the symbol of the flowing, fleeting nature of experience. As an unstable medium without form of its own, it becomes the means of capturing vague atmospheric effects and reflecting subtle changes of mood. The course of Mélisande's life is conveyed by means of these changing waters. She comes from over the sea, is found by a dark pool in the forests, discovers her love for Pelléas at a fountain in the park, and as she dies she asks that the window be opened so that she can once more be with the sea.

Other symbols play their appointed parts. Mélisande weeps in the first scene over the loss of a golden crown, symbolic of her happier state of childhood innocence. Later when she tosses her wedding ring up and down beside the fountain, one knows that she is taking her wedding vows lightly. When it falls into a bottomless well and disappears, it means that her marriage has dissolved. Only the circles on the surface of the water remain, subtly rendered by Debussy in the musical example reproduced here. As the ripples expand they portend of larger developments to come.

Debussy's style first took shape in the songs he wrote on texts by the symbolist poets, but Maeterlinck's drama provided him with the necessary lyric material to ripen it into maturity. Like the poets, his methods were in many ways the opposite of conventional operatic techniques. He followed Wagner in giving the orchestra the main task of carrying on the sequence of the drama; and, as a result, his work became more of a symphonic poem with running

commentary by the singers than a conventional opera. With characteristic insight, Debussy saw that melody, in the sense of a set operatic aria, impeded rather than promoted the dramatic progress. "I wished —intended, in fact—that the action should never be arrested; that it should be continuous, uninterrupted," he commented. "Melody is, if I may say so, almost anti-lyric, and powerless to express the constant change of emotion or life. Melody is suitable only for song [*chanson*], which confirms a fixed sentiment."

In thus considering recitative as the most important element of the lyric drama, Debussy allies himself with his illustrious predecessors Lully and Rameau. But while their characters spoke in the highly inflected accents of baroque theatrical grandiloquence, his speak in cadences more closely approximating modern conversational French. "The characters in this drama endeavor to sing like real persons," the composer wrote; and by bringing their language closer to everyday speech, and allowing the flow of dramatic action to proceed without interruption, his opera assumes a plausibility seldom achieved in such a highly artificial medium. By using modes other than the traditional major and minor, his recitative takes on the flexible character of psalmodic chant. The rhythms are free, and the absence of regular accentuation allows the words to flow with elasticity. Debussy's musical motifs parallel the literary symbols and are often just broken fragments of melody, which suggest rather than define atmospheric effects or are associated with the mood of a character. While used with greater subtlety, they nevertheless are much closer to Wagner's system of leitmotifs than Debussy was willing to admit. His harmonic method likewise was well suited to the rendition of the ambiguities and obscurities of the symbolist poets. His key centers lose their boundaries; progressions move about freely in tonal space; the predominance given to the tritone interval accents the indefinite drift; and everything is in a state of flux, always on its way but never arriving. Debussy's sensitivity to the timbre of sounds borders on the uncanny. He thought of Mélisande's voice as "soft and silky," and the woodwinds dominate the orchestral coloration with their peculiarly poignant and penetrating quality. Above all, performers must know how to make this intangible music live and breathe, how to render its rhythms with the proper elasticity, and how to fill its silences with meaning.

Debussy's evocation of Maeterlinck's pallid world is one of those rare instances of the indissoluble union of literature and music that make it impossible for later generations to think of them as separate entities. Debussy worked on *Pelléas* over a period of ten years and was constantly worrying about the audience reaction to his fragile lyric drama. Maeterlinck's play had not been a success, and in a letter dated August, 1894, Debussy anxiously asks a friend, "How will the world get along with these two poor little beings?" In an obvious reference to the popularity of Zola's writing, he goes on to express his hatred of "crowds, universal suffrage, and tri-colored phrases." Contrary to expectation, however, the opera was a success and was widely performed. His elusive music ultimately proved its capacity to cast a spell over the most indifferent of audiences.

## IDEAS

Any interpretation of the complex interplay of forces that underlies and motivates the divergent tendencies of the latter part of the 19th century faces the usual danger of oversimplification. Two of the most salient ideas, however, are chosen principally because they provide significant insights into the relationship of the several arts. These are: the influence of the scientific method on the arts and the interpretation of experience in terms of time.

**Alliance of Art and Science** Artists in all fields were aware of the extraordinary success of the scientific method. Realism and impressionism brought a new objective attitude into the arts, together with an emphasis on the technical side of the crafts and a tendency for artists to become specialists pursuing a single aspect of their various media. Architects began to look toward engineers for the more advanced developments in building. A painting for an impressionist was a kind of experiment, an adventure in problem solving. Cézanne thought of each of his pictures as a type of visual-research problem. In sculpture, Rodin was seeking for a new synthesis of matter and form. The literary realists were cultivating a scientific detachment in their writing and developing a technique that would enable them to record the details of their minute observations of everyday life with accuracy and precision. Zola, by means of his experimental novel, introduced a modified social-scientific technique to fiction. In addition to his poetic dramas, Maeterlinck wrote popular nature studies, such as *Life of the Bee* and the *Magic of the Stars.* Debussy spoke about some of his compositions as his "latest discoveries in musical chemistry."

Many of the actual discoveries of scientific research opened up new vistas in the various arts. Experiments in optical physics revealed secrets of light and color that painters could explore. New chemical syntheses provided more luminous pigments for their canvases. Increased knowledge of the physiology of the eye and the psychology of perception led to a reexamination of how an observer looks at a picture and what he perceives. New metal alloys and processes of casting were a boon to sculptors. The theories of evolution gave Rodin some poetic ideas on how form emerges from matter, the animate from the inanimate. Helmholtz' *On the Sensation of Tone as a Physiological Basis for the Theory of Music* stirred Debussy and other composers to speculate on the relation of tone to overtone and consonance to dissonance in their harmonic procedures.

The impressionistic painters were convinced that pictures were compounded of light and color, not line and form; the symbolists claimed that poetry was made with words, not ideas; and composers felt that music should be a play of varied sonorities rather than a means of evoking programmatic associations. By pursuing this general line of thought, Monet revealed a new concept of light and color and their interdependence; Rodin, an atmospheric extension of solid three-dimensional form; the symbolists, a new world of poetry; Debussy, a new concept of sound; and Paxton and Eiffel, by incorporating light and air into their designs, achieved a new architectural relationship between inner and outer space. This mechanistic phase, however, could lead just so far, and artists were soon trying to push beyond it into paths that would lead to deeper psychological insights. Each of the postimpressionists in his own way was probing to find how the new discoveries could be used as a means toward new modes of expression. Cézanne's path led into a new concept of pictorial geometry that became an important anticipation of 20th-century art, and the point of departure for cubism. Maeterlinck attempted to humanize science and describe it in poetical terms. In his case, the result was a kind of animism in which stones, fountains, and objects spoke a language and felt a soul life of their own. In an essay on the "Intelligence of Flowers," he tried to establish more sympathetic ties between man and nature. In his stage fantasy *The Bluebird,* Sugar and Bread are among the live characters. Cézanne also felt the living force of the objects he placed in his still lifes, and in a conversation with a friend remarked that there are people who say a sugar bowl has no soul, yet it changes every day. The symbolists also tried to effect a synthesis between the phenomenal world and that of the creative imagination. Their metaphors were material in the sense that they received expression through the senses, but they hinted at the existence of a more profound ideational world and were definitely based on a view that life was something more than the sum of its molecular parts. Debussy also veered away from the exploration of the physical elements of sound toward the deeper psychological implications of tonal symbolism.

**Continuous Flux**    The arts of the late 19th century were also bound together by their common tendency toward the interpretation of experience in terms of time. Progress was an idea that was carried over from the late 18th century. Material progress continued to be an indisputable fact, but what was rapidly becoming apparent was that it did not go hand in hand with moral, spiritual, and aesthetic progress. With industrialization came a specialization in which men were concerned more with fragments than with wholes. Industrial man was rapidly forfeiting to the machine his place as the primary productive unit. With this loss of control came a corresponding shift from a rational world view toward an increasingly irrational one. With industrialization also came a capitalistic economy in which the lives of workers were controlled by intangible forces beyond themselves, such as the fluctuations in foreign markets and on the stock exchange. Two centuries previously, baroque man had been shaken by the Copernican revolution in which the notion of a static earth in the center of the universe was replaced by that of a freely moving satellite around the sun. Late 19th-century man was similarly rocked by the Darwinian and other evolutionary theories, which taught that creation was an ever-continuing process rather than an accomplished fact. As a result of such forces and ideas, the onward-and-upward notion of progress was revised downward to one of continuous flux and change.

The literary and visual realists concentrated on the momentary, the fragmentary, the everyday occurence. Even when they planned their works in more comprehensive schemes, the effect was more that of a broad cross section than a coherent three-dimensional structure. For twenty years, Balzac worked on parts of his *Human Comedy*, Wagner on his Ring Cycle, Rodin on his *Gates of Hell*, and Proust on his *Remembrance of Things Past*. None, however, is a systematic, organic, or logical whole or a single perfected masterpiece. Instead of an all-embracing unity, they are easily broken down into a collection of fragments, motifs, genre scenes, scraps, and pieces. The late 19th

century produced no grandiose metaphysical systems, such as those of Thomas Aquinas, Leibniz, Kant, or Hegel, each of whom tried to encompass all experience in a single universal structure.

The thinker who came the closest to making a coherent picture of this turbulent age was Henri Bergson, a lecturer at the École Normale in Paris. His point of departure was a remark made by the pre-Socratic philosopher Heraclitus, who had said that one cannot step into the same river twice. Bergson cited Heraclitus in support of his theory that time was more real than space, that the many were closer to experience than the one, and becoming was closer to reality than being. Bergson was critical of the intellect because it tended to reduce reality to immobility. He therefore ranked intuition as a higher faculty than reason, because through it the perception of the flow of duration was possible, and through it static quantitative facts were quickened into the dynamic qualitative values of motion and change. Existence is never static but a transition between states and between moments of duration. Experience, he taught, is durational, "a series of qualitative changes, which melt into and permeate one another, without precise outlines . . . ." Art for Bergson is a force that frees man and through which he can grasp "certain rhythms of life and breath," which compel him even against his will "to fall in with it, like passers by who join in a dance. And thus they compel us to set in motion, in the depth of our being, some secret chord which was only waiting to thrill."

Bergson was thus convinced that reality is mobility, tendency, or "incipient change of direction." Looking at or listening to a work of art is perceiving the mobile qualities of the objects or sounds presented. The aesthetic experience is essentially temporal and involves an "anticipation of movement," which permits the spectator or auditor in various ways "to grasp the future in the present." His theory of art is based on what he calls his "spiritualistic materialism" by which finely perceived material activity elicits spiritual echoes. All is based on the "uniqueness of the movement"; and perception of the temporal flow is synonymous with an awareness of the pulsation of life, something that is quite apart from the mechanical or inert matter. Past, present, and future are molded into an organic whole as "when we recall the notes of a tune melting, so to speak, into one another." Time, therefore, is "the continuous progress of the past, which gnaws into the future and which swells as it advances." But Bergson's concept of time is not clock time with its divisions into seconds, minutes, and hours, nor is it concerned with the usual groupings of past, present, and future. These are just arbitrary conveniences, like the points on a clock past which the hands move. Time cannot be spatialized and measured in such a quantitative way; it is a quality, not a substance.

**Plate 49.** PIERRE AUGUSTE RENOIR. *Le Moulin de la Galette.* 1876. Oil on canvas, 4'3½" × 5'9". Louvre, Paris. (See p. 340.)

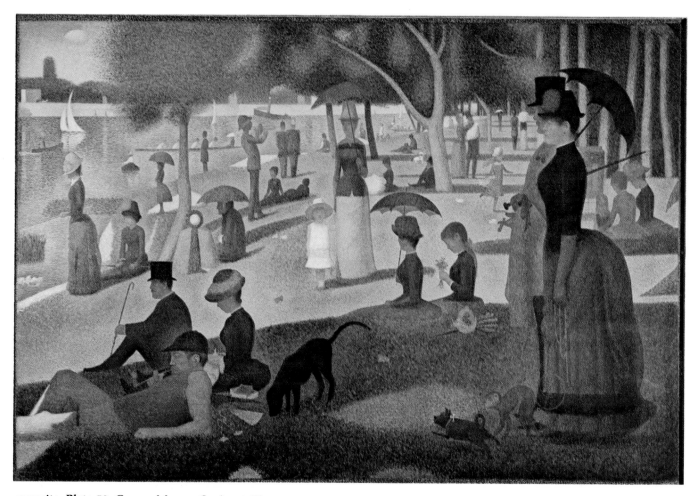

opposite: **Plate 50.** CLAUDE MONET. *Garden at Giverny.* c. 1899. Oil on canvas, 2'11" × 3'3". Art Institute of Chicago. (See p. 340.)

above: **Plate 51.** GEORGES SEURAT. *Sunday Afternoon on the Island of La Grande Jatte.* 1884–86. Oil on canvas, 6'9" × 10'6". Art Institute of Chicago. (See p. 341.)

**above: Plate 53.** PAUL GAUGUIN. *Mahana No Atua* (*"Day of the God"*). 1894. Oil on canvas, 26 × 34½". Art Institute of Chicago. (See p. 342.)

**left: Plate 54.** PAUL SÉRUSIER. *Landscape: The Bois d'Amour* (*"The Talisman"*). 1888. Oil on panel, 10⅝ × 8⅝". Denis Family Collection, St.-Germain-en-Laye, France. (See p. 342.)

**Plate 55.** PAUL CÉZANNE. *Still Life: Basket of Apples.* 1890–94. Oil on canvas, $25\frac{3}{4} \times 32''$. Art Institute of Chicago. (See p. 343.)

no longer seem dedicated to preserving the enduring image of man, and static monumentality has often given way to mobility and machine propulsion. Painters work on Masonite surfaces and in mixed media as well as the traditional oil on canvas, and with palette knife and dripping techniques as well as with the brush. And a new pictorial category of abstract and fantastic pictures has been added to the traditional classifications of history paintings, genre scenes, portraiture, landscape, and still life.

The graphic arts have been expanded to include many new media, among them silk-screen printing and color photography. The arbitrary distinction between the so-called "major and minor arts," fine arts and crafts, beauty and utility has narrowed to the point where architect and engineer, sculptor and furniture designer, a cathedral and a suspension bridge —once thought to be poles apart—have been brought together in the modern unity of form and function. Drama has expanded from the live theater to include the motion picture and television media, and new concepts of language continue to be explored with words used as syllabic sounds in an abstract poetry.

## EXPRESSIONISM AND ABSTRACTIONISM

Pablo Picasso's *Les Demoiselles d' Avignon* incorporated so many of the ideas of the early 20th century that it became a landmark of the modern-art movement (Pl. 57, p. 376). At the turn of the century Paris was alive with young artists, new notions, and stimulating exhibits. Picasso was impressed in turn by the great Cézanne retrospective of 1907; with a showing of pre-Roman Iberian sculpture which, as in most archaic art, represented the human body in angular geometrical patterns; and with expositions of African tribal sculpture. As a result he began to reexamine his pictorial approach, turned away from representational conventions toward tighter geometrical controls, and acquired his first pieces of primitive African sculpture.

*Les Demoiselles d' Avignon* had begun as an allegory. A man seated amidst fruit and women was to have symbolized Vice, while his opposite number entering on the left holding a skull in his hand was to have been Virtue. Under the new influences, however, the original plan was abandoned, and the picture developed in another direction by blending the figures, the background drapery, and the still life below into an abstract design. The girl on the left who is pulling back some curtains became a series of overlapping planes and geometrically arranged contours. The head of the figure in the upper right resembles a mask from Itumba in what remained at this time the colonial territory of the French Congo (Fig. 3), while the head just below and the profile of the figure on the left also show African tribal influence. Picasso's preliminary drawings reveal his fascination with the oval-shaped heads, the long noses, small mouths, and angular bodies that characterize the sculpture of the Ivory Coast. The color, with its spectrumlike shading of bright hues one into another, contributes to the effect of an emotional crescendo, while the formal arrangement of the figures suggests the angular rhythms of a primitive dance.

*Les Demoiselles* is thus a pivotal picture. The heightened postimpressionistic colors combined with the violence and energy of primitive art make it a summary of the avant-garde Paris school of painting at the turn of the century. It also marks Picasso's intuitive invention of *cubism*, that most important step toward abstraction. When Georges Braque, one of the fauve painters, first saw *Les Demoiselles*, he perceived that both he and Picasso had been assimilating Cézanne's geometry of cones, spheres, and cylinders and his principles of construction. Together over the ensuing four years they worked out the rules of cubism.

In sorting out the developments in contemporary art, one has basically but two ways of looking at the world—from within or from without, subjectively or objectively, through emotion or through reason. These outlooks are by no means mutually exclusive, since mind is necessary for emotional awareness, and without emotional drive even the most rational proposition would be empty and devoid of meaning. For purposes of the present study the arts in which emotional considerations are dominant have been grouped under *expressionism;* those in which logical and analytical processes are uppermost are under *abstractionism.* Here a note of caution must be sounded, because all art is expressive to some degree, just as all art is abstract to a certain extent.

*Expressionism* looks within to a world of emotional and psychological states rather than without on a fluid world of fugitive realism, as with impressionism. In their zeal to develop a style with greater emotional force, the expressionist artist turned away from naturalism. With Van Gogh and Gauguin as their point of departure, these painters distorted outlines, applied strong colors, and exaggerated forms to convey their ends (Pl. 52, p. 356; Pl. 53, p. 357). Expressionism in its limited sense applies to the pre-World War I period and to the German art movements known as *Die Brücke* and *Der Blaue Reiter.* A broader definition, however, includes parallel developments in all major centers where artists were concerned primarily with the emotional approach to art and with their passionate involvement in all phases of contemporary life.

The expressionist is fully conscious of the visible world, but, leaving behind the classical idea of art as an imitation of nature, he closes his eyes to explore the mind, spirit, and imagination. He would agree with Goethe's dictum that feeling is all, and he welcomed Freud's delving into the subconscious, which revealed a new world of emotion in the dark drives, hidden terrors, and mysterious motivations underlying human behavior. The expressionist is well aware that he inhabits a number of complex overlapping worlds, and he knows too that there are worlds to be explored which are not seen by the eye and which are not subject to logical interpretation. Expressionistic pictures are in psychological rather than natural focus, describing intangible worlds with new techniques and new symbols, discordant colors and distorted shapes. The clashing dissonances of expressionistic music are intended to arouse rather than soothe the listener, and expressionistic literature intends to startle the reader with subjective revelations of neurotic, psychical, often psychotic, states.

To describe his reactions to physical, psychical, and spiritual events, the expressionist alters, distorts, and colors his images according to the intensity of his feelings. Expressionism, then, may range from quiet nostalgic moods, through sudden shock reactions and hysterical outbursts, to screaming nightmares. The results of such excursions into the subconscious may be quite uneven, but the artists' passport to nether regions is nonetheless valid. In all, expressionism has embraced such movements as neoprimitivism, dadaism, surrealism, and social realism.

*Abstractionism* implies analyzing, deriving, detaching, selecting, simplifying, geometrizing, before distilling the essence from nature and sense experiences. The heat generated by the psychological and political revolutions of the 20th century was felt in expressionism, but the light of the new intellectual points of view is mirrored in the various forms of abstractionism.

In previous centuries, a picture was a reflection, in one way or another, of the outside world. In 20th-century abstractionism, the artist frees himself from the representational convention. Natural appearances play little part in his design that reduces a landscape to a system of geometrical shapes, patterns, lines, angles, and swirls of color and achieves his desired abstract imagery. Choosing his pictorial content from nature, the abstract artist eliminates the unimportant minutiae of the observed world, and refines the haphazardness of nature and ordinary visual experience. His imagination and his invention are concentrated on pictorial mechanics and the arrangement of patterns, shapes, textures, and colors. From the semiabstract cubist art, in which objects are still discernible, abstractionism moves toward nonobjectivism in which a work of art has no representational, literary, or associational meaning outside itself, and the picture becomes its own self-defining referent.

In the early years of the century, physicists were at work formulating a fundamental new view of the universe, which resulted in the concepts of space-time and relativity. In the arts, meanwhile, new ways of seeing and listening were also being worked out. In painting, for example, the cubist canon of multiple-

visual viewpoints was developed, whereby several sides of an object could be presented at the same time. In sculpture, a new theory of volume was worked out, whereby open holes or gaps in the surface suggested the interpenetration of several planes, and the existence of other sides and surfaces not immediately in view. In architecture, the international style, using steel and glass, was able to incorporate in a structure the simultaneous experience of outer and inner space. Literature and music found new ways of presenting materials in the temporal dimension. In literature, the stream-of-consciousness technique merged objective description and subjective flow of images; and in music, the so-called "atonal" method of composition was formulated, by which fixed tonal centers were avoided in favor of a state of continuous flux and constant variation.

Such novel organizations of space and time demanded new ways of thinking about the world, new ways of looking at it, listening to it, and reading about it. Abstractionism thus includes such developments as cubism, futurism, the mechanical style, nonobjectivism, the twelve-tone method of musical composition, and the international style of architecture.

**Neoprimitivism** As the great conflagration of 20th-century expressionism burst into flame, the spark that set fire to that movement called *neoprimitivism* was the 19th-century discovery of the primitive arts of the South Sea Islanders and the wood carvings of African tribes. As the term is used here, neoprimi-

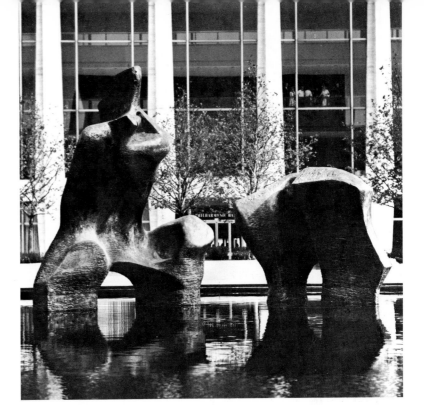

opposite: **367.** AMEDEO MODIGLIANI. *Head.* c. 1913. Stone, height 24¾". Tate Gallery, London (by courtesy of the Trustees).

right: **368.** HENRY MOORE. *Reclining Figure.* 1964. Bronze; length 30', width 17', height 16'. Lincoln Center for the Performing Arts, New York.

tivism is limited to the conscious adaptations by sophisticated artists of authentic specimens of primitive art. The first major artist to employ the exotic patterns and motifs in his woodcuts and paintings had been Gauguin, and such pictures as his *Mahana No Atua,* painted during his extended sojourn in Tahiti, clearly reflect the native influence (Pl. 53, p. 357). Examples of Polynesian craftsmanship, such as oars, arrows, and harpoons, had been collected by traders on their voyages and were shown in the Paris expositions of 1878 and 1889. Later, when expeditions went to the interior of the dark continent, wooden objects carved by Negro tribesmen were brought back for display; and the ethnological museums, founded in Paris and Dresden to house these collections, commanded considerable interest among scholars, artists, and the general public. Books on African sculpture appeared, and in 1890 James Frazer began publishing *The Golden Bough,* a twelve-volume compendium of primitive mores, folklore, magical practices, and taboos.

Primitive art, with its complete negation of the notion of progress, seemed to be the promise of a new beginning. Especially appealing was the animistic attitude of the primitive carvers who divined the spirit of wood and stone and expressed it in the grains, textures, and shapes of their materials. German expressionists were fascinated by the strange weird forms and anti-intellectualism of African images; French artists, among them Matisse, found in their simplified geometrical forms a wealth of decorative motifs and a justification for their abstract designs.

The impact of primitive art also affected the course of 20th-century sculpture. When the young painter Modigliani came to Paris in 1906, he fell so completely under the spell of African Negro sculpture that for a while he traded the brush for the chisel. One of these works, *Head* (Fig. 367), is in the same Ivory Coast style that Picasso had adopted, and, in his paintings, he later used similarly stylized oval faces and elongated forms such as those in *Yellow Sweater* (Pl. 58, p. 377).

The sources of Henry Moore's powerful sculpture are prehistoric primordial forms, Stonehenge, ancient Etruscan tombs, pre-Columbian Mexican carvings, African and Oceanic art, the way wind and water shape trees and erode jutting boulders, and, above all, his own fertility of formal invention. "Truth to material," Moore wrote, "[is] one of the first principles of art so clearly seen in primitive work. . . . The artist shows an instinctive understanding of his material, its right use and possibilities." His recumbent figures are like mother earth or some fertility goddesses of a forgotten cult. The curves and convolutions transcend the human form and become part of the heaving hills and plunging valleys of a rolling landscape. Many of Moore's figures are pierced by holes and hollows so that his sculpture has an interior as well as exterior existence. With the *Reclining Figure* at Lincoln Center, in New York City, Moore expanded his holes by dividing the figure so he could shape, metaphorically, not only his monumental masses but also the space around and between (Fig. 368). The two parts are

**369.** CONSTANTIN BRANCUSI. *Bird in Space.* 1925. Polished bronze, height 4'1¾". Philadelphia Museum of Art (Louise and Walter Arensburg Collection).

**370.** PABLO PICASSO. *Stravinsky* 1920. Pencil drawing, 24½ × 19". Collection the artist's estate.

related but separate with the head and body at one end and the legs at the other. "But between them," Moore remarked, "I am trying to make a kind of mixture of the human figure and of landscape."

The elemental simplicity of Brancusi's sculpture has its formative inspiration in the power of primitive forms and the bold innovations of the fauve painters. Brancusi's objective was to free sculpture from everything extraneous and get down to ultimate essences. One egg-shaped marble piece, for instance, is called *Beginning of the World*. Like the neoprimitives, he accepts his materials for what they are—marble for its smoothness and roughness, metal for its hardness or softness. Whatever the material, he tries to divine its nature and realize its potentialities without forcing

it to simulate something else. "What is real," Brancusi once remarked, "is not the external form, but the essence of things." In his *Bird in Space* he is dealing with a bronze that has such a high copper content it approaches the brilliance of gold (Fig. 369). By molding it into a graceful curvilinear form and giving it a high polish, he releases the metal medium into a form of energy. It is the abstraction of a movement, a feather in flight. Brancusi has sometimes tried to increase the sense of motion in sculpture by placing his figures on slowly rotating turntables. Thus, his glistening surfaces catch the light and his forms seem to float in space.

Knowledge of non-European musical systems had likewise increased rapidly during the late 19th century. The orchestrations of Debussy and Ravel had been influenced by the strange and exotic sounds of the gamelan orchestras from Java, which both composers had heard at the International Exposition of 1889. By far the strongest of these new influences, however, was American jazz music, which had its beginning in New Orleans and Chicago and which was heard in Europe through the traveling Negro bands. In *The Children's Corner* (1908), Debussy included a number called "Golliwog's Cake Walk."

Stravinsky (Fig. 370), whose music reflects many style trends, achieved the neoprimitive musical counterpart of Picasso's *Les Demoiselles d'Avignon* in the ballet *Rite of Spring,* which he wrote for the Diaghileff company in 1913. Subtitled *Scenes from Pagan Russia,* the opening "Dance of the Adolescents" uses repetitive rhythms and syncopated accents similar to those of American jazz. The sharply angular melodies, the complex polyrhythmic textures, the brutal accentuations, and the geometrical movements of the dancers are a masterly realization of the spirit of savagery.

### Wild Beasts, The Bridge, Blue Rider, and Operatic Uproars

The expressionist deals with intensities of feeling rather than intensities of light. For him, the heat of creation supersedes the coldness of imitation, and he presents subjective reactions instead of representing objective realities, reasserting the supremacy of the human imagination over the representation of nature. About the time Picasso was discovering primitive sculpture, other groups were championing expressionism in painting as a reaction to the cool atmospheric effects and objective detachment of impressionism. Van Gogh had pointed the way with his frenzied canvases, passionate pictorial outbursts, saturated colors, and evangelical fervor. Such a painting as *Starry Night* (Pl. 52, p. 356), with the dark-green flames of the cypress trees, rolling rhythms of the hills, and cosmic explosion of the Milky Way, was enough to set imaginations on fire. The barbaric splendor of Gauguin's color harmonies was seized upon as a useful means for producing lively emotional responses, while the expressionists looked more distantly at the luminous colors of medieval stained glass and the imaginative inventiveness of Romanesque sculpture. Primitive arts of Polynesia and Africa played their parts here too.

The violent color clashes and visual distortions of the French painters of expressionistic persuasion earned for them the designation of *les fauves* ("wild beasts"), from a chance remark by a critic at the 1905 Paris Salon d'Automne who thought the room looked like a cage of wild animals. The early work of Matisse, that most civilized of painters, was so classified, though in retrospect it is difficult to understand why. If there was ever anything "wild" about Matisse, it was his reveling in brilliant color for its own sake, a resourcefulness of invention, and a quality of Ori-

ental splendor, which make him a fauve but a fauve devoid of ferocity (Pl. 59, p. 377).

The *Blue Window,* which he painted about 1911, shows his concern with formal aesthetic problems, vibrant color harmonies, and arabesquelike decorative motifs (Pl. 60, p. 378). The picture is composed as an abstract still-life study merging subtly into a stylized landscape. The hatpins in the cushion on the left unite with the empty vase behind them; the flowers in the other vase grow into the foliage and the roof of the painter's studio outside; the Oriental idol in the axial center leads the eye to the vertical division of the casement window; while the lines formed by the contours of the lamp continue with those of the tree trunk in the garden. The bedroom table and its objects are thus united with the trees and sky beyond, and the interior and exterior elements become parts of one design. Depth and recession are suggested only by a slight lessening of the color intensities. In this picture, Matisse approached his dream of an "art of balance, of purity and serenity devoid of depressing subject matter."

For Matisse, expressionism did not apply to the content of his canvases or to the communication of an emotional message but rather to the entire formal management of his pictorial pattern. "Expression to my way of thinking," he once remarked, "does not consist of the passion mirrored upon a human face or betrayed by a violent gesture. The whole arrangement of my picture is expressive. . . ."

German expressionism in the decade before World War I was mainly associated with two groups that developed simultaneously with the fauves: *Die Brücke* ("The Bridge") and *Der Blaue Reiter* ("The Blue Rider"). The Bridge was a loose association of Dresden painters who took this name because they wished to form links with all artists of the expressionistic persuasion, as well as a bridge to the future. They acknowledged their debt to Van Gogh and Gauguin, but most especially to the Norwegian Edvard Munch (Fig. 364).

Emil Nolde was among the most articulate members of Die Brücke, and *Dancing Around the Golden Calf* was one of his many Biblical subjects (Pl. 61, p. 387). Violent color dissonances of blood-red and orange-yellow plus distorted drawing carry his message of the primitive fury and demoniac energies of his tormented dancers. Der Blaue Reiter was the title of a painting by Kandinsky that became the manifesto of the southern German expressionist movement. It was also the name of a book of 1912 edited by Franz Marc and Kandinsky that reproduced paintings shown at a Munich exhibit of the previous year by some of the French fauves and Paul Klee, as well as by Marc and Kandinsky. The book also contained articles on modern art, while the Viennese composer Arnold Schoenberg contributed a chapter on parallel expressionistic developments in music. Marc's art, as seen in his *Tower of Blue Horses* (Fig. 371), is one of vibrating, pulsating rhythms, curvilinear design, and lyrical undulating movement.

Kandinsky was an international figure, who first painted in his native Russia, worked in the postimpressionistic and fauve styles in Paris, and then joined in founding the Blue Rider group in Munich. Works of his Blue Rider period, such as *Improvisation on a Warlike Theme* (Pl. 62, p. 387), still contained natural, human, and animal figures. In this instance, the artist mentions that he painted "subconsciously and in a state of strong tension" during 1913 when rumors of war were rife. This, he added, explains the presence of the two cannons in the lower right and the explosive forms.

By eliminating objects and figures, dissolving material forms, and improvising according to his moods, Kandinsky reached the frontiers of nonobjective art and set the stage for the abstract-expressionists of the 1940s and 1950s, in which painting is "liberated" from nature. His *Picture with White Edge, No. 173* shows what he can express with lines, colors, and shapes (Fig. 372). Commenting on his completely abstract paintings, Kandinsky stated that their content is "what the spectator *lives* or *feels* while under the effect of the *form and color combinations* of the picture"—which may or may not coincide with what the artist had in mind when he painted it.

Kandinsky, who published poetry, plays, and an autobiography, also recognized the affinity of his work to music. By his own account, he strove to reproduce on his canvases the "choir of colors which nature has so painfully thrust into my very soul," and

**above: 371.** FRANZ MARC. *Tower of Blue Horses.* 1912. Oil on canvas, 6'8" × 4'3¼". Formerly State Museums, Berlin (present whereabouts unknown).

**left: 372.** VASILY KANDINSKY. *Picture with White Edge, No. 173.* 1913. Oil on canvas, 4'7¾" × 6'7". Solomon R. Guggenheim Museum, New York.

he believed that a painting should be "an exact replica of some inner emotion." Works that required "an evenly sustained pitch of inner emotional uplift sometimes lasting for days" he called "compositions." Spontaneous shorter works, sketches, and watercolors that "do not last the span of a longer creative period" he designated "improvisations."

Some of the earliest and most violent outbursts of musical expressionism are found in Richard Strauss' operas *Salome* (1905) and *Elektra* (1909), which he wrote in Munich while the Blue Rider movement was developing. Taking off from Richard Wagner's *Tristan und Isolde,* Salome's "love death" is an operatic excursion into the realm of abnormal psychology. In *Salome,* Strauss lures his listeners with sensuous sounds and a rainbow of radiant orchestral colors, and at the same time horrifies them with the gruesome spectacle of Salome's amorous soliloquy to the severed head of John the Baptist. This simultaneous attraction and repulsion is bound to produce emotional excitement and elicit truly expressionistic reactions. The sensational nature of Oscar Wilde's libretto, together with the famous "Dance of the Seven Veils," caused the opera to be banned in New York, Boston, and London. *Elektra* is a dramatically effective version of Sophocles' tragedy (as adapted by Hugo von Hofmannsthal) filled with emotional climaxes, bloodcurdling shrieks, and lurid orchestral sounds.

Arnold Schoenberg's expressionistic song cycle *Pierrot Lunaire* (1912) explores the weird world of Freudian symbolism, and in his monodrama of 1913 *Die Glückliche Hand* ("The Lucky Hand") the dissonances of the musical score are reinforced by crescendos of colored lights. Something of a climax is achieved in Alban Berg's opera *Wozzeck* (1925), a musical dramatization of big-city low life, in which a ballet of beggars, drunkards, and street girls pursue the murderer as he vainly tries to escape from himself. Whereas Wagner had worked up his climaxes over a considerable period of time, generally starting low in pitch and volume and mounting upward in an extended melodic, harmonic, and dynamic crescendo, Schoenberg and Berg telescoped the process. Their music became all climax, with the extremes of low and high, soft and loud following each other suddenly by leaps instead of in a gradual progression. Dissonances with Wagner existed in chains of sequences that eventually resolved. With Schoenberg and Berg, dissonance exists freely for its own sake with little or no relation to consonance.

**Cubism**   Just as the discovery of the rules of linear perspective had revolutionized the expression of the Florentine Renaissance, so *cubism* brought about a new way of looking at things in the 20th century. First worked out in painting, the reverberations of cubism were felt directly in sculpture and architecture, and indirectly in literature and music. A strong shove in the direction of abstraction came from the large retrospective exhibit of Cézanne's painting held in Paris in 1907, where the young painters who saw it were struck by the artist's pictorial architecture. In the catalogue, they noted a quotation from a letter in which Cézanne remarked that natural objects can be reduced to the forms of the cylinder, the sphere, and the cone. Art, they reasoned, is not an imitation of nature in the usual sense but an imposition upon nature of geometrical forms derived from the human mind. As a result, cubist painting became a play of planes and angles on a flat surface. Cézanne's famous sentence, it should be pointed out, never mentioned cubes at all. His cylinders, spheres, and cones are rounded forms, presupposing curvilinear drawing; cubist drawing, on the contrary, is mainly rectilinear.

The Renaissance ideal had been the complete description of a pictorial situation from a single point of view; another vantage point would imply another picture. The cubist theory of vision took into account the breaking up and discontinuity of the contemporary world view in which objects are perceived more hastily in parts rather than more leisurely as wholes. The world, as a consequence, was seen fragmentarily and simultaneously from many points of view rather than entirely from a single viewpoint. In Picasso's *Demoiselles d' Avignon* (Pl. 57), for instance, the faces of the second and third figures from the left are seen frontally, while their noses appear in profile. Picasso and Braque, as the coinventors of cubism, therefore undertook a new definition of pictorial space in which objects were represented simultaneously from many visual angles, in wholes or in parts, opaque and transparent. Just as the Crystal Palace had pointed the way to the interpenetration of the inner and outer aspects of architectural space (Figs. 362, 363), the art of the cubists undertook to move inside as well as outside an object, below and above it, in and around it.

The cubists also were convinced that pictorial space, limited as it is by the two dimensions of the flat canvas, was something quite apart from natural space. From the Renaissance onward, the accepted procedure had been to produce the illusion of three-dimensionality by some form of linear perspective derived from the principles of Euclidean geometry. The cubist painter, however, approached his canvas as an architect in order to construct his picture. Instead of trying to create the illusion of depth, he built his picture on the straight lines of the triangle and T-square by which he defined the planes of his surface. The expression of volume, as achieved by the modeling of objects in light and shade, was also modified, and so was the tactile feeling and structural solidity of Renaissance painting. Instead of representing objects in the round, the cubists analyzed them into their basic geometrical forms, broke them up into a series of planes, then collected, reassembled, tilted them at will into a new but strictly pictorial pattern of interlocking, interpenetrating, and overlapping surfaces and planes. Cubist color at the beginning was purposely confined to the rather neutral tones of gray, green, olive, and ochre. The emphasis was on design and texture, and unity was found in the picture itself rather than in the objects represented. The technique in its earliest stages can be observed in Plate 57 in the way Picasso renders the bodies of the figures on the extreme left and upper right. Braque's *Oval Still Life* (Fig. 373) shows cubism in its more developed form after the rules had been worked out. Typical is its use of natural objects as a point of departure. Such still-life components as the table, violin, and sheet music are then broken up so that they can be reassembled in a design by the artist.

In their early doctrinaire stages, cubist pictures tended to be rather cold, impersonal studies in abstract design (Pl. 63, p. 388), but modifications of this pure state began to appear, such as Picasso's *Three Musicians* (Pl. 64, p. 388). The flat two-dimensional arrangement is retained, but the bright coloration gives the canvas a gaiety not found earlier. The three

masked figures sitting at a table are the same *commedia dell' arte* figures that regularly recur on Picasso's canvases, cubist or otherwise, and that come from his love of circus and theatrical performances in which clowns and other performers dress in gay carnival costumes. The figure on the left playing a violin is a Harlequin, the center one with the clarinet is a Pierrot, while the more solemn monk on the right plays what seems to be an accordion.

Picasso's *Woman's Head* is a translation of cubist principles into the three-dimensional medium of sculpture (Fig. 374). It presents a geometrical analysis of the structure of the human face and emphasizes the most important planes and surfaces. By this process of disintegration, the head can be organized into a number of different facets, each of which can cast its own shadow and thus bring variety and a sense of movement to the composition.

The sculptures of Jacques Lipschitz are three-dimensional adaptations of cubism in its mature phase. The *Man with Mandolin* creates a repetitive pattern of rough stone textures, diagonal lines, tilted planes, irregular rectangles and triangles (Fig. 375). From the side, variants on the main theme appear, and curved shapes are accented to provide contrasts for the dominant rectilinearity of the design (Fig. 376). In other works Lipschitz breaks down the traditional distinction between solids and voids, convex and concave surfaces, wholes and parts in intricately contrived interlocking designs.

The musical counterpart of this new concept of space is found in the breaking up of traditional tonality as well as in the search for new musical resources and mediums of expression. Stravinsky, as a strict adherent of the principles of order, had said that "tonal elements become musical only by virtue of their being organized." The twelve-tone system of musical composition that Schoenberg evolved about 1915 was an answer to the need for a new order and one of the stricter forms of tonal organization. Schoenberg, who preferred to be called a constructor rather than a composer, begins a work by setting forth a basic row of twelve different tones. This row can be played in normal order, upside down by melodic inversion, backward in retrograde motion, and upside down once more in retrograde inversion (see opposite above). Furthermore, it can be presented successively in sequences or simultaneously as in the various species of counterpoint. It can also be played in whole or in part simultaneously as in a chord or tone cluster, or it can be played serially as in a melody.

A row can be used either as an entity or broken up into several shorter themes or motives. It has been

373. GEORGES BRAQUE. *Oval Still Life.* 1914. Oil on canvas, $36\frac{3}{8} \times 24\frac{3}{4}''$. Museum of Modern Art, New York (gift of the Advisory Committee).

estimated that around half a billion different combinations are possible, which certainly is no limitation on its possibilities. The system provides the composer with a wealth of material as well as a certain freedom within an orderly framework. The twelve-tone method has generally been referred to as *atonality* (that is, without tonality), but Schoenberg preferred to call it simply a method of composing with twelve tones that are related only with one another. Tonality is thus relative rather than an absolute, since there is no single tonal center. Tonality in the usual sense, however, is not excluded; rather, it is encompassed and transcended.

One of the most accessible works in the twelve-tone repertory is Alban Berg's *Violin Concerto* of 1935 (above right). The row is a straight ascending vertical series without repetition that can easily be followed by the alert, attentive ear. Ingeniously contrived, the first six tones contain the four triads of tonal music: notes one to three being the minor triad, two to four the augmented, three to five the major, four to six the diminished. A combination of four tones (one to four, two to five, etc.) forms types of seventh chords, while the top four notes make a series of whole tones re-

*Violin Concerto* (1935)  Alban Berg

sembling the scale favored by Debussy and the musical impressionists. Berg's tonal space thus includes traditional and impressionistic melody and harmony as a point of departure into nontonal or atonal music in which tones are relative only to each other rather than to a single tonal center.

**below center: 375.** Jacques Lipschitz. *Man with Mandolin.* 1917. Stone, height 29¾". Yale University Art Gallery, New Haven, Conn. (Collection Société Anonyme).

**below right: 376.** Jacques Lipschitz. *Man with Mandolin* (side view).

**below: 374.** Pablo Picasso. *Woman's Head.* c. 1909. Bronze, height 16¼". Albright-Knox Art Gallery, Buffalo.

**left: 377.** Gino Severini. *Armored Train.* 1915. Oil on canvas, 46 × 34½". Collection Richard S. Zeisler, New York.

**right: 378.** Umberto Boccioni. *Unique Forms of Continuity in Space.* 1913. Bronze, height 3'7½". Museum of Modern Art, New York (acquired through the Lillie P. Bliss Bequest).

## Futurism and Mechanical Style

The movement known as *futurism* was begun in Italy under the leadership of the poet and dramatist Filippo Tommaso Marinetti prior to World War I. Agreeing with Nietzsche, who said that history was the process by which the dead bury the living, Marinetti declared in his *Manifesto* of 1909 that futurism was being founded to "deliver Italy from its plague of professors, archaeologists, tourist guides and antique dealers." The futurists wanted to destroy the museums, libraries, academies, and universities in order to make way for their particular wave of the future. "A roaring motorcar, which runs like a machine gun," they said, "is more beautiful than the Winged Victory of Samothrace." Theirs was a vision of a state ruled by a mechanical superman, in which the people would be reduced to cogs in the gigantic wheel of fully mechanized society.

Above all, the futurists projected an art for a fast-moving, machine-propelled age. They admired the motion, force, velocity, and strength of mechanical forms, and in their pictures they wanted more than anything else to include the dynamic sensation of motion. A galloping horse, they said, has not four legs but twenty. Deriving his inspiration from automobiles, airplanes, trains, and machine guns, Severini painted *Armored Train* with its diagonal lines and plumes of smoke suggesting speed, while the gunfire adds the dimension of action and violence (Fig. 377).

Umberto Boccioni, the most distinguished futurist painter, was also the main sculptor of the group. His *Unique Forms of Continuity in Space* captures the dynamics of motion in the turbulent hurrying stride of a moving figure (Fig. 378). The body itself is felt only in the implied massive muscular tensions. Boccioni's subject is speed as expressed in a continuum of swirling, spiraling lines and the rushing currents of air as the figure cuts his path through space.

Futurism was influential chiefly for its formation of the "mechanical style." By taking ideas from both the cubists and the futurists, Fernand Léger developed a style in which precise and neat parts all fit into an appointed place, as in *The City* (Fig. 379). Léger loved crankshafts, cylinder blocks, and pistons—all painted in gleaming primary colors. Taking Cézanne's statement about cylinders, spheres, and cones more literally than did the cubists, he drew curvilinear forms and modeled them in light and dark. His is a world devoid of sentiment, populated by robots whose parts are pure geometrical shapes. Human forms are introduced only for their "plastic value," and remain "purposely inexpressive." In 1924, Léger made an abstract film called *Ballet Mécanique,* in which machine forms replaced human beings and their activities.

Stravinsky, meanwhile, had composed an *Etude for Pianola* in 1917, and the French composer Arthur Honegger, using the normal symphonic complement, gave voice in 1924 to the triumphant song of the machine in a work called *Pacific 231.* Its name is an allusion to that year's model of an American locomotive, and the piece was designed to evoke the sounds of the railroad, complete with the grinding of the wheels and the shriek of the steam whistle. Perhaps the most successful musical realization of the mechanical style is found in the works of Edgar Varèse. Technically trained in two fields, Varèse was as much a physicist as a musician, and the titles of his works sound as if they came from a laboratory: *Intégrales, Density 2.15* (the specific gravity of the platinum of the flute for which it was composed), and *Ionization.* The last is constructed in a series of interlocking planes of sound that suggest, but are not directly imitative of, rhythms of modern city life. Varèse's expressed aim was to build a music that would face the realities of the industrial world rather than try to escape from it.

**Dadaism and Surrealism**    In their Paris exhibits of 1911 and 1912, the Italian Giorgio de Chirico and the Russian Marc Chagall anticipated the development of *dadaism* and *surrealism.* The latter term, in fact, was coined at that time by the French critic and playwright Guillaume Apollinaire to describe the dream fantasies, memory images, visual paradoxes, and assorted incongruities of their pictures. Chirico's dreamscape *The Disquieting Muses* takes expressionism into an introspective world of free associations (Fig. 380). "Everything," according to this artist, "has two aspects: the current aspect, which we see nearly always and which ordinary men see, and the ghostly and metaphysical aspect, which only rare individuals may see in moments of clairvoyance and metaphysical abstraction." His intention was to break down the barriers of childhood and adulthood, the sleeping and waking states, the unbelievable and the believable, the illogical and the logical, the fantastic and the familiar. *The Disquieting Muses* is filled with an ominous silence and an all-pervading emptiness, made mysterious by deep perspective. Chirico's pictures are informed by Freudian psychology and furnished with sundials casting long shadows, arcaded galleries, empty vans, factories, and strange statues.

**left: 379.** Fernand Léger. *The City.* 1919. Oil on canvas, 7'7″ × 9'8½″. Philadelphia Museum of Art (A. E. Gallatin Collection).

**above: 380.** Giorgio de Chirico. *The Disquieting Muses.* 1917. Oil on canvas, $37\frac{3}{4}$ × $25\frac{7}{8}$″. Private collection.

left: **381.** Marc Chagall. *I and the Village.* 1911. Oil on canvas, $6'3\frac{5}{8}'' \times 4'11\frac{5}{8}''$. Museum of Modern Art, New York (Mrs. Simon Guggenheim Fund).

right. **382.** Marcel Duchamp. *L.H.O.O.Q.* 1919. Rectified readymade, pencil on reproduction of Leonardo's *Mona Lisa;* $7\frac{3}{4} \times 4\frac{7}{8}''$. Private collection.

*I and the Village* grows out of Chagall's memories of Russia (Fig. 381). In one of his childhood reveries he remembered the ceiling of his parents' crowded cottage suddenly becoming transparent. "Clouds and blue stars penetrated along with the smell of the fields, the stable and the roads," he writes, and "my head detaches itself gently from my body and weeps near the kitchen where fish is being prepared." In *I and the Village,* as in a rainbow-hued dream, one image is superimposed on another, the houses are topsy-turvy, the farmer going to the fields is right side up, the peasant woman upside down, and the cow seems to be experiencing a contented reverie about a milkmaid.

Dadaism was the product of the disillusionment, defeatism, and insane butchery of World War I. Anguished artists felt that the civilization that had brought about such horrors should be swept away and a new beginning made. To christen their movement, they chose at random a childish word out of the French dictionary—*dada,* a child's vocalization signifying a hobbyhorse. *Dadaism,* consequently, was a nihilistic movement, particularly distrustful of order and reason, a challenge to polite society, a protest against all prevailing styles in art; it was, in fact, anti-art (Fig. 382). Dada artists worked out an ism to end all isms, painted nonpictures compounded of the contents of wastebaskets, concocted nonsense for the sake of nonsense, wrote manifestoes against manifestoes, and their political expression was anarchy. Their bitter humor and iconoclasm, however, helped to explode hypocritical pomposities and, by reducing the role of art to absurdity, cleared the air for the experiments and innovations of the postwar period. A brief movement, dadaism was absorbed into surrealism, which has aptly been dubbed the "dadaism of the successful."

The surrealist manifesto of 1924 proclaimed that the style was based on "pure psychic automatism by means of which one sets out to express, verbally, in writing or in any other manner, the real functioning of thought without any control by reason or any aesthetic or moral preoccupation." Surrealism, literally "superrealism," implies a greater reality underlying the world of appearances, an illogical, subconscious, metaphysical dream world beyond the logical, conscious, physical one. Members of the group believed in the superior reality of the dream to the waking

**Plate 56.** HENRI DE TOULOUSE-LAUTREC. *At the Moulin Rouge.* 1892. Oil on canvas, $4'3\frac{3}{8}'' \times 4'7\frac{1}{4}''$.
Art Institute of Chicago (Helen Birch Bartlett Collection). (See p. 359.)

**Plate 57.** PABLO PICASSO. *Les Demoiselles d'Avignon.* 1907. Oil on canvas, 8′ × 7′8″.
Museum of Modern Art, New York (acquired through the Lillie P. Bliss Bequest). (See p. 361.)

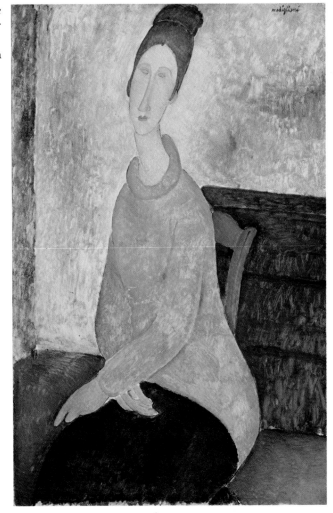

right: **Plate 58.** Amedeo Modigliani. *Yellow Sweater (Portrait of Mme Hébuterne).* 1919. Oil on canvas, $39\frac{3}{8} \times 25\frac{1}{2}$". Solomon R. Guggenheim Museum, New York. (See p. 365.)

below: **Plate 59.** Henri Matisse. *Woman with the Hat.* 1905. Oil on canvas, $32 \times 23\frac{1}{2}$". Private collection. (See p. 367.)

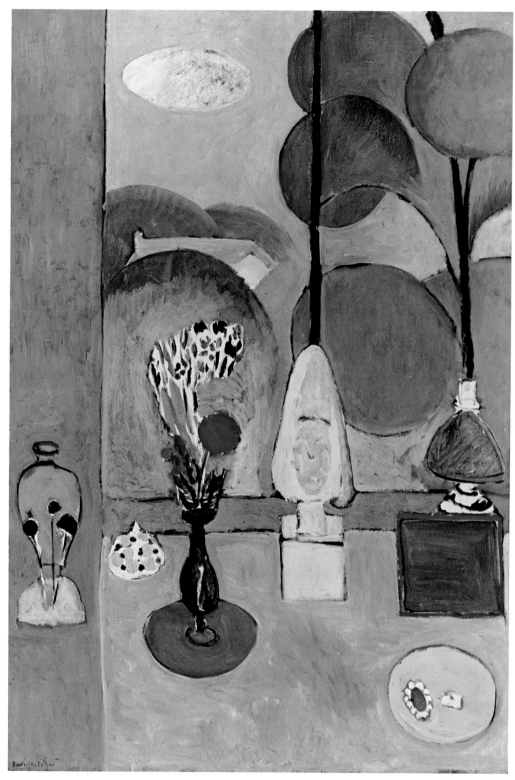

**Plate 60.** HENRI MATISSE. *Blue Window.* Autumn, 1911. Oil on canvas, 4'3½" × 2'11⅝".
Museum of Modern Art, New York (Abby Aldrich Rockefeller Fund). (See p. 367.)

**383.** SALVADOR DALI. *Persistence of Memory.* 1931. Oil on canvas, 9½ × 13". Museum of Modern Art, New York.

state, of fantasy to reason, of the subconscious to the conscious. André Breton, author of the manifesto, also spoke of the "convulsive beauty" of dreams, and Paul Eluard said, "a poem should be the debacle of the intellectual."

The painter Salvador Dali associated himself with the group in 1929 and became one of its leading advocates. He described his pictures as "handpainted dream photographs" and adorned them with symbols of various phobias, delusions, complexes, and other trappings of abnormal psychology. Like Chirico and Chagall, Dali was haunted by the mystery of time, and his *Persistence of Memory* suggests images of evolutionary, geological, and archaeological as well as dream time (Fig. 383).

Today Paul Klee is generally accepted as one of the most significant pictorial talents of the 20th century. Such pictures as *Diana* have caused many to dismiss him with a shrug, a scoff, or a smile (Pl. 65, p. 388). His disarming childlike innocence, however, is a highly deceptive simplicity and usually masks infinitely subtle meaning. His inventiveness outdoes even Picasso. He can delight the eye, tickle the fancy, or repel the observer with images straight out of nightmares. *Apparatus for Magnetic Treatment of Plants, Twittering Machine, A Cookie Picture, Moonplay, Idol for Housecats, Child Consecrated to Suffering, A Phantom Breaks Up*—so the titles run. The symbolism in his *Diana* will show the extraordinary complexity of Klee's art. The title identifies the figure as the mythical goddess of the chase, while the arrow is equipped magically with an eye to ensure unerring accuracy. The broken contours of Diana's body suggest hurried flight through space, and the wheel under the

goddess' foot is derived from Romanesque sculpture where it signified miraculous transportation. The color and surface treatment recall impressionism and Seurat's pointillism (Pl. 51, p. 355).

Klee consciously set out to look at the world through the eyes of a child in order to achieve a spontaneity untroubled by reason. "I want to be as though new-born, knowing nothing," as he put it. With Klee, as with Freud, the child was father of the man. By experimenting with hypnotic suggestion and psychic automatism, he gave his drawings the casual quality of doodles or the impulsiveness of improvisations. His mastery of line was so complete, however, that his work should never be confused with carelessness. By sticking mainly to small forms and to the techniques of watercolor and ink, pencil and crayon, he produced pictures with a refreshing unpretentiousness. He also invested his pictures with an element of genial humor that is notably missing in so much of modern art.

Joan Miró, like Klee, essayed an art of pure imagination existing outside logic or reason. In *Personages with Star* he used the technique of automatic drawing in a trancelike state and produced a painting that shows the influence of Kandinsky (Fig. 384). While much of surrealism is preoccupied with the morbid and the abnormal, Miró lightens his fantasies with whimsy. His pictures have such titles as *Persons Magnetized by the Stars Walking on the Music of a Furrowed Landscape*; they teem with abstract insects that buzz silently and geometrical worms that squirm statically.

Giacometti represents surrealism's sculptural dimension. Giacometti's *Palace at 4 A.M.* uses a geometrical cagelike framework containing spectral and skeright: 384. JOAN MIRÓ. *Personages with Star.* 1933. Oil on canvas, 6'6¼" × 8'1½". Art Institute of Chicago (gift of Mr. and Mrs. Maurice E. Culberg).

below: 385. ALBERTO GIACOMETTI. *Palace at 4 A.M.* 1932–33. Wood, glass, wire, string; height 25". Museum of Modern Art, New York (purchase).

letal forms (Fig. 385). The phantom figures in their interpenetrating open and closed spaces produce a haunting sensation of human isolation and loneliness.

The attempts by the doctrinaire surrealists to work in the arts of sculpture, literature, and music have not been successful, and significant parallels can be found only outside the movement. James Joyce and Gertrude Stein tried to establish a method for subconscious or automatic writing as a way to tap the reservoir of the subconscious mind. The result was the stream-of-consciousness technique, notably ex-

emplified in Joyce's *Ulysses* (1922). The more irreverent iconoclastic tendencies of surrealist painting have their musical parallels in such compositions as Erik Satie's three piano pieces of 1913. Entitled *Desiccated Embryos,* they have semisarcastic expression marks, such as that which calls upon the pianist to play a melody "like a nightingale with a toothache." There is also the biting satire of Prokofiev's brilliant fairy-tale opera *Love of Three Oranges* (1921) and the weird symbolism of Béla Bartók's legendary opera *Bluebeard's Castle* (1922). Paul Klee's world of childhood fantasy finds a charming lyrical counterpart in Maurice Ravel's opera *The Child and the Sorceries (L'Enfant et les Sortilèges)* of 1925. In Colette's libretto, a child breaks some bric-a-brac and toys in a temper tantrum. In a dream sequence, the objects come to life to seek revenge. A Wedgewood teapot and a china cup, appropriately enough, carry on a conversation in broken English while dancing a fox-trot; a little old man pops up out of nowhere and sings multiplication tables and story problems with erroneous answers; two cats sing a hilarious mewing duet; and all that is left of the torn picture of the fairy princess in the story book is "a golden hair and the debris of a dream." Ravel's ingenious orchestration adds whistles, wood blocks, and friction instruments to the usual ones and cheese graters for a range of bizarre effects.

**Neoclassical Interlude**   No century would be complete without its bow before the shrines of Greece and Rome, and just as the Renaissance, the 18th, and the 19th centuries did, the 20th century has it neoclassicism. While works with classical allusions abound in the present century, the neoclassic movement came into sharpest focus in the 1920s. The comparative calm before the storm of World War I had been broken by the emotional extremes of pictorial expressionism and such neoprimitive outbursts as Stravinsky's *Rite of Spring.* In the aftermath of war, order and clarity seemed more important than violent expression, as did the human figure, following the abstractions of cubism and futurism.

In 1917, Picasso had made a trip to Italy where he was impressed by the Pompeian wall paintings and stimulated by meetings in Rome with Stravinsky and Serge Diaghileff, who were there with the latter's Russian ballet company. One direct result was their three-way collaboration on a ballet with song called *Pulcinella,* which was first performed in Paris in 1920. Stravinsky's score was based on the form of the classical dance suite of the early 18th century with music adapted from Pergolesi. Picasso's costumes were designed in the manner of the stylized Pierrot and Harlequin *commedia dell'arte* figures, while his scenery included a backdrop filled with angular distortions showing a street in Naples with a view of the bay and a moonlit Mt. Vesuvius. In 1922, an adaptation of Sophocles' *Antigone* by Jean Cocteau was mounted in Paris. Picasso designed the scenery and masks, while the incidental music for harp and oboe was supplied by Arthur Honegger. An opera called *The Eumenides* by Darius Milhaud, based on Paul Claudel's translation of the tragedy by Aeschylus, was written in the same year. *Mercury* was the title of still another ballet brought out by the Diaghileff company in 1924, with music by Erik Satie and costumes and scenery by Picasso. Three years later, Stravinsky completed his opera-oratorio *Oedipus Rex.* Diaghileff again was the producer, and Jean Cocteau's text, based on Sophocles' tragedy, was translated into Latin so that it would be in a "petrified" language and thus reduced to mere syllabic material. The motionless stance of the actors was intended to make them as static as Greek columns, and the chorus was placed back of a bas relief where only their heads were visible. Such productions continued sporadically throughout the 1930s when Stravinsky was once more found collaborating with André Gide on a work for orchestra, chorus, and tenor called *Persephone* (1934).

Picasso's pictures in the 1920s, such as the *Three Graces* (Fig. 386), also reflect this neoclassicism and are characterized by elegance of line, sculpturesque modeling of bodies, and reduction of pictorial elements to the barest essentials. Others, like *Pipes of Pan* (Fig. 387), are beach scenes in which the figures appear statuesquely against geometrically organized backgrounds and chaste colors of white and blue. While Picasso's painting took another tack after the *Three Graces,* his many book illustrations continued to show classical influences. Picasso had long admired the linear technique of Ingres (Fig. 348), especially the

top: 386. PABLO PICASSO. *Three Graces.* 1924. Oil and charcoal on canvas, 6'6⅞" × 4'11". Collection the artist's estate (courtesy Museum of Modern Art, New York).

above: 387. PABLO PICASSO. *Pipes of Pan.* 1923. Oil on canvas, 6'8½" × 5'8⅝". Collection the artist's estate (courtesy Museum of Modern Art, New York).

pencil drawings. Even in such an austere medium as etching, his illustrations for a new edition of Ovid's *Metamorphoses* (1930) and for Gilbert Seldes' version of Aristophanes' *Lysistrata* (1934) show his capacity for effective expression (Fig. 388).

In the neoclassical interlude, the statues of Maillol and Despiau reassert the expressive importance of the nude figure both in the round and in relief. Maillol's static, stable, calm figures are a welcome relief in a turbulent century (Fig. 389). His neoclassicism is creative not imitative, free not academic. The *Torso of Venus,* with its Praxitelean curve and stance (Fig. 43), its antiquity and modernity, achieves a quiet monumentality that is both universal and timeless.

One of the most consistent patterns of contemporary literature, especially in France, is the reinterpretation of Greek myths in highly sophisticated terms as a subtle device for pointing out modern moralistic or political parallels. This tendency runs regularly through the works of André Gide from his early *Prometheus Drops His Chains* (1899) to his autobiographical story *Theseus* (1946). It can also be found in Franz Werfel's antiwar play *The Trojan Women* (1914) and in Jean Paul Sartre's *The Flies* (1943). The latter was staged in Paris during the Nazi occupation, and the allusion to the plague of flies that sucked Orestes' blood in Aristophanes' bitter comedy could have escaped no one. Poets have sometimes found classical subjects a convenient way of leaving their works in a fragmentary state like antique ruins. Paul Ambroise Valéry's trilogy of 1922, for instance, contains a poem called *Fragments of Narcissus*. T. S. Eliot's *Sweeney Agonistes* (1932), in which the grandeur of the past is contrasted with the banality of the present, likewise is incomplete and bears the subtitle *Fragments of an Aristophanic Melodrama*. Freud's use of the names of characters from Greek literature—Oedipus, Electra, Narcissus—as symbols of recurrent subconscious drives also found its way into literature.

James Joyce's novels *A Portrait of the Artist as a Young Man* (1916) and *Ulysses* (1922) use classical allusions as a frame of reference but avoid the logic and order of Greek forms. The author's admitted inspiration for *Ulysses* was Homer's *Odyssey*. With his adoption of the stream-of-consciousness technique, the classical molds became convenient devices to hold the nebulous, dreamlike sequences in some semblance of unity. They also provide the bewildered reader with a few recognizable straws to grasp when he begins to founder on the sea of such an unfamiliar style of writing. The entire action of *Ulysses* occurs in Dublin in a single twenty-four-hour period to preserve the classical unities of place and time. The plot, concerns a wanderer who voyages through the terrors and temptations of the labyrinth of Dublin's streets while on his way home to his wife and son, which is reminiscent of Odysseus' search for Penelope and Telemachus. In the larger sense, the book is concerned with

**above: 388.** PABLO PICASSO. *The Love of Jupiter and Semele.* Plate 6 for Ovid's *Metamorphoses* (Lausanne: Albert Skira, 1931). Etching, $8\frac{7}{8} \times 6\frac{7}{8}$″. Museum of Modern Art, New York (gift of James Thrall Soby).

**left: 389.** ARISTIDE MAILLOL. *Torso of Venus.* 1925. Bronze, height 3′9″. Courtesy Galerie Dina Vierny, Paris.

man's eternal search for a meaning for life. In Joyce's manuscript, the titles of chapters were based on quotations from the *Odyssey,* but these were omitted when it was printed. Most of the work is obscure and cryptic, but the juxtaposition of the heroic past helps to heighten the squalid picture of the present that the novelist paints.

**Social Realism**    Social realism represents the artist's protest against the intolerable conditions that beset mankind. In the tradition of Goya (Pl. 43, p. 301), Hogarth (Figs. 312, 313), and Daumier (Fig. 349), many contemporary painters have championed the cause of the weak against the strong, the poor against the rich, the oppressed against their oppressors, of righteousness against human folly. In their search they have explored the dregs of society, the urban excrescences of skid row, and the ugliness of the lower depths, thus proving that the paint brush and the pen are often mightier than the sword.

*This Will Be the Last Time, Little Father* is the title of the print by Georges Rouault that describes the heartbreaking farewell of a son as he leaves for war and almost certain death (Fig. 390). Rouault's art is visionary, but his tragic clowns, comical lawyers, static acrobats, and active landscapes reveal his broad compassion for and passionate protests against human exploitation and degradation. His pictures often mirror the grimacing masks of those who presume to sit in judgment on their fellowmen, and the insensitive countenances of people in positions of power who are indifferent to human suffering. His series of 100 etchings and aquatints for two projected portfolios entitled *Miserere* ("Have Mercy on Us") and *Guerre* ("War"), with text by a literary friend, occupied him intermittently in the years following

World War I. Though the portfolios as such were never published, 58 prints have been issued separately. The title page of the war volume in which Figure 390 was to have appeared reads: "They Have Ruined Even the Ruins."

José Clemente Orozco, one of the Mexican muralists deeply involved in his country's revolution, identified himself with the struggle of the illiterate masses as they tried to break the chains of their land-owning and capitalist exploiters. His grim satire also extends to the academic community as pictured in *Gods of the Modern World* (Fig. 391). This macabre comment on the sterility of higher education depicts a skeleton giving birth, while one professor acts as a midwife and others witness the ghastly event.

The New York artist Ben Shahn was an ardent champion of minority groups and the eloquent portrayer of the anonymous city dweller who has lost his sense of community identity. The stark setting and grim countenances of *Miners' Wives* express the anxiety, fear, and desolation of the families of men con-

**above: 390.** Georges Rouault. *This Will Be the Last Time, Little Father.* 1914–27. Copperplate engraving, $28\frac{1}{2} \times 16\frac{7}{8}''$. Museum of Modern Art, New York (gift of the artist).

**left: 391.** José Clemente Orozco. *Gods of the Modern World.* 1932–34. Fresco, 10'6" × 14'8". Dartmouth College, Hanover, N.H. (by permission of the Trustees).

**392.** Ben Shahn. *Miners' Wives.* 1948. Egg tempera on board, 4 × 3'. Philadelphia Museum of Art (given by Wright S. Ludington).

**393.** Pablo Picasso. *Guernica.* 1937. Oil on canvas, 11'6" × 25'8". Collection the artist's estate (on extended loan to the Museum of Modern Art, New York).

nected with a hazardous occupation (Fig. 392). Man's inhumanity to man is the general theme, as Shahn pleads the cause of the victims of social injustice.

In his *Guernica* (Fig. 393), Picasso used a combination of expressionist and abstract techniques as a violent protest against a cruel and inhuman act by modern barbarians. What lighted the fuse that set off this pictorial explosion of carnage and terror was the first saturation air raid of the century—the horrible "experiment" by the German air force carried out against the defenseless Basque town of Guernica, an incident in General Franco's successful rebellion against the legally elected government of the Spanish Republic. Picasso, a loyalist partisan, was in Paris with the commission to paint a mural for the Spanish pavilion of the World's Fair of 1937. Just two days after the news of the bombing reached Paris, he began work. The huge canvas, accomplished in a matter of weeks, took up one wall of the Spanish pavilion, where it made an unforgettable impression on the thousands who saw it. The attention it attracted and the measure of understanding accorded it have been altogether in proportion to *Guernica's* value as one of the century's most important paintings.

*Guernica,* a picture in the great tradition of historical painting, is one of those rare incidents of the right artist painting the right picture at the right time. Its purpose was frankly propagandistic; its intent, to horrify. But besides recalling the apocalyptic visions of Romanesque Last Judgments (Fig. 125), it is a work of social protest in the manner of those 19th-century masters of irony Goya and Daumier. The principal action begins in the lower right where a woman dashes forward, clutching her hands in an attitude of despair. The triangular composition then mounts to its apex at the point where the lamp, horse's head, and the eye of day, with the electric bulb of night as its pupil, converge. From this climax, the eye moves downward to the head of the dismembered warrior in the lower left portion of the painting.

According to Picasso, *Guernica* is allegorical, and he has explained some of the symbolism. The horse with the spear in his back, the inevitable victim of bullfights, signifies victimized humanity succumbing to brute force. The motif of the shrieking mouth is repeated in that of the screaming woman with her dead child at the left, the face of the soldier below, and the victim of the flames at the right. The bull standing for brutality is the only triumphant figure in this symbolic struggle between the forces of darkness and those of light, between barbarism and civilization. Above, an arm reaches forward to hold the lamp of truth over the whole gruesome scene.

*Guernica* appeared at a time when many earlier pictorial experiments could be combined. It employs all the exaggerations, distortions, and shock techniques developed by expressionistic drawing, but it omits lurid coloration in favor of the somber shades of mourning—black, white, and gradations of gray. The abstract design, the overlapping planes on a two-dimensional surface, and the absence of modeling all derive from cubism. So also does the simultaneous principle of the day-and-night symbol; the head of the bull, which is seen both from the front and the side at the same time; and the sensation of inner and outer space by which the observer is at once both inside and outside the burning buildings. The elongation of the heads to express headlong motion coincides with the photography of movement made with stroboscopic light. The screaming, nightmarish subject matter is similar to that of expressionism. Picasso usually painted so rapidly and prolifically that he often had difficulty resisting the temptations of his own facile technique. Consequently, much of his work is uneven. Here, however, after making one hundred sketches, he worked in a disciplined and selective manner that shows the artist in complete command of his medium. Thus, his successful synthesis in *Guernica* of so many of these divergent 20th-century techniques, as well as the vivid dramatization of his subject, has given powerful expression to the chaos and conflicts of this century.

Bitter satires on the junglelike conditions of urban life and the dismal effects of mass media on the popular mind preoccupy the English painter Francis Bacon. In his *Painting,* subtitled *The Butcher,* he speaks with the vocabulary of expressionism and surrealism as he depicts his nightmarish apparition (Pl. 66, p. 389). Less bitter but nonetheless poignantly expressive are Andrew Wyeth's muted evocations of the social decay as well as the unfulfilled aspirations of life on the American scene (Pl. 67, p. 389).

**Nonobjectivism**    Abstractionism was worked out to its logical geometrical conclusion by Piet Mondrian just as expressionism had reached its point of pure abstraction in the work of Kandinsky. The pictures of these two artists are, of course, poles apart. Both artists, however, are *nonobjective* in that they are nonfigurative and nonrepresentational and that the pictorial content of their canvases bears no reference to recognizable objects or to anything outside the actual pictures. All subject matter, all associational meanings, are studiously avoided. The picture with its lines, shapes, and colors is its own referent.

Mondrian's art, like Kandinsky's, evolved gradually from the concrete to the abstract. In his early years, Mondrian painted landscapes and quiet interior scenes in the tradition of his native Holland, and his later style, though completely abstract, owes much to the cool geometrical precision of his great predecessor Vermeer (Pl. 38, p. 267). Mondrian could well be describing his *New York City* (Pl. 68, p. 390) when he wrote: "The new style will spring from the metropolis." He delighted in the criss-cross patterns of city streets, architects' blueprints, gaunt structural steel skeletons of skyscrapers under construction, and simple faces of buildings of the international architectural style (Pl. 69, p. 390). The new art, he continued, would not be individual, but collective, impersonal, and international. All references to the "primitive animal nature of man" should be rigidly excluded in order to reveal "true human nature" through an art of "balance, unity, and stability." This objective he strove to realize by using "only a single neutral form: the rectangular area in varying dimensions." His colors are likewise abstract—black lines of various widths against white backgrounds, relieved occasionally by a primary color "climax"—red, blue, or yellow—in as pure a state as possible. In his opinion, a work of art should be "constructed," and he approached a canvas with all the objectivity of a draftsman making a blueprint. The result of this pictorial engineering is the series of chaste, two-dimensional spatial studies for which he is best known. His visual patterns have a repose that rests on a precise balance of horizontal and vertical elements, and they are clean to the point of being prophylactic. His pictures are far more complex than they may seem to the casual eye; and they have had a great influence on modern design, especially of advertising layouts, posters, rugs, and linoleum.

## ARCHITECTURE

More than any of the other 20th-century arts, architecture has exhibited a greater sense of responsibility, reached a more homogeneous crystallization of style, and achieved a wider popular acceptance. A building, unlike a painting, has to stand up; unlike a sculptural group, it must fulfill some practical purpose. Experi-

**Organic Architecture: Sullivan and Wright**    Louis Sullivan's slogan "form follows function" is subject to a variety of interpretations, but the line of thought it provided led to an important reevaluation of architectural forms in relation to human activities and to a reexamination of basic architectural methods, materials, and purposes. Sullivan's disciple Frank Lloyd Wright, and the architects identified with the international style, accepted the principle that stone should behave like stone, wood like wood, and steel like steel, and that the design should be modified by the materials used. Both also pointed to the absurdity of people catching trains in Roman baths, working in Renaissance office buildings, banking money in Doric temples, living in English Tudor houses, and going on Sunday to Gothic churches. The criterion for a successful building, then, is no longer what it looks like, but how well it fulfills its purpose.

The skyscraper, among the earliest and boldest instances of modern architecture, was made possible by steel-skeleton construction and the elevator. It came out of the American Middle West as an answer to the need for commercial centralization. In the hands of Louis Sullivan, who put up the Wainwright Building in St. Louis in 1891 (Fig. 394), the skyscraper was a "proud and soaring thing," reflecting the pride of the businessman in his work, as well as the drive and power of a technologically oriented people. The principal drawback to skyscrapers, however, is their contribution to congestion in already overcrowded areas. From a human standpoint, their value has thus far been less spectacular than their engineering.

Wright, picking up where Sullivan left off, saw both the advantages and drawbacks of the skyscraper. With characteristic romanticism, he spoke of his buildings in naturalistic terms. His eighteen-story skyscraper in Bartlesville, Oklahoma, has a "taproot" foundation, grows upward like a tree, with its floors and walls cantilevered outward like branches from its central trunk (Fig. 395). Skyscrapers, he was convinced, did not belong in already congested cities but in the open, where they could breathe and have room to cast decent shadows. Wright's philosophy of architecture was that of a liberating force, and his creative freedom allowed for decorative motifs to grow organically out of his basic designs, the relations of masses to voids, the fenestration, the colors and grains of wood, and the textures of stone. Through his masterly articulation, space for living and working comes to life and breathes.

The architect, according to Frank Lloyd Wright, is the poet who imagines the ideal life and fashions the forms, shapes, and spaces that guide men to live

mental architecture is possible, but the discipline of sound engineering has kept architects from some of the wilder flights of fancy seen in painting, sculpture, literature, and music. Today's architect is no mere stone mason—he is an engineer of society, a social philosopher, a poet and idealist, as well as a practical builder.

The needs of a complex, modern, urbanized society and the availability of new materials and structural methods have made a new architecture both possible and necessary. *Ferroconcrete,* or cement reinforced by embedding wire mesh or iron rods in it, leads the procession of new materials. It has the strength of both steel and stone without their weaknesses or expense, it can span broader spaces than marble, and carry the weight of steel. The *cantilever*—the extension of a slab or beam horizontally into space beyond its supporting post—is an ancient principle that had to await its large-scale use until the development of ferroconcrete.

Frank Lloyd Wright on one side and Walter Gropius with Le Corbusier on the other were the leaders of two opposing schools of architectural thought. Wright spoke as a romantic in terms of the union of nature and man that could be realized through his "organic architecture." Gropius and Corbusier were exponents of the international style and its emphasis on building for the machine age.

**right: Plate 61.** Emil Nolde. *Dancing Around the Golden Calf.* 1910. Oil on canvas, $34\frac{3}{4} \times 39\frac{1}{2}''$. Bavarian State Picture Collection, Munich. (See p. 367.)

**below: Plate 62.** Vasily Kandinsky. *Improvisation No. 30 (on a Warlike Theme).* 1913. Oil on canvas, $43\frac{1}{4}''$ square. Art Institute of Chicago. (See p. 368.)

**above left: Plate 63.** Georges Braque. *The Portuguese.* 1911. Oil on canvas, $45\frac{7}{8} \times 32\frac{1}{8}''$. Kunstmuseum, Basel. (See p. 370.)

**left: Plate 64.** Pablo Picasso. *Three Musicians.* 1921. Oil on canvas, $6'7'' \times 7'3\frac{3}{4}''$. Museum of Modern Art, New York (Mrs. Simon Guggenheim Fund). (See p. 370.)

**above: Plate 65.** Paul Klee. *Diana.* 1931. Oil on wood, $37\frac{1}{2} \times 23\frac{5}{8}''$. Collection William Bernoudy, St. Louis. (See p. 379.)

**right: Plate 66.** FRANCIS BACON. *Painting (The Butcher).* 1946. Oil and tempera on canvas, 6'6" × 4'4". Museum of Modern Art, New York (purchase). (See p. 385.)

**below: Plage 67.** ANDREW WYETH. *Mother Archie's Church.* 1945. Tempera on panel, 2'1" × 4'. Addison Gallery of American Art, Phillips Academy, Andover, Mass. (See p. 385.)

above: **Plate 68.** PIET MONDRIAN. *New York City.* 1942. Oil on canvas, 10 × 12'. Courtesy Sidney Janis Gallery, New York. (See p. 385.)

left: **Plate 69.** LE CORBUSIER. L'Unité d'Habitation, Marseilles. 1947–52. Length 550', width 79', height 184'. (See p. 392.)

# 22 Art Styles Since 1945

## REVOLUTIONARY
## AND EVOLUTIONARY ELEMENTS

Since 1945 and the end of World War II, the full force of the revolutionary age continues unabated—in science, industry, and electronics, as well as in the arts. Rapid changes are occurring in religious beliefs, social structures, aesthetic values, mores, and manners. Gradually, social relativity and the pluralistic society have replaced the social absolute, as anthropologists have shown how relative are the behavioral patterns and moral values of today, as psychologists have demonstrated the impossibility of drawing a fine line between the normal and the abnormal, and as existentialists have shaken traditional Western concepts about the meaning and purposes of life and the existence of God.

Highly dramatic are the consequences of electronic communications via radio, television, satellite transmission, laser beam, tape recording, videotape, and color photography. The antennas and tentacles of the electronic media have heightened perceptions and psychologically extended the nervous systems of the new generation. Through electronic eyes people now watch the whole world, and the whole world is watching them. As a result the earth is like a great megalopolis in which each national unit functions merely as an ethnic minority inhabiting a neighborhood within a vast global complex. Thus far, however, the process has produced more diversity than unity, more heat than light, as much conflict as understanding; but the possibilities for better or worse seem boundless. And what has geographically and ethnologically condensed into a planetary city has also contracted in the temporal dimension. Through the accessibility of books and recordings, the art, literature, and music of the past and present are within the reach of everyone. Thus, knowledge and experience of the arts and the human past transform the present into an extended historical now.

In this larger context history shows that all revolutions are really evolutions. Like icebergs, the more sensational aspects of revolutionary change rise only about one-ninth above the surface. The true essence of change is to be found in the invisible, evolutionary portions that lie below. It is here that the continuity of ideas, the ethical and aesthetic concepts are to be found. Past and present are inextricably intertwined on the current scene. History lives on, for instance, in the host of ancient media that are now being rediscovered and adapted to the needs of contemporary expression—mosaics, various fresco techniques, encaustic, painting in tempera, and stained glass. But there are also new modes and methods. Some sculptors use the welding torch to replace the traditional hammer and chisel; laminated woods, sophisticated metal alloys, Plexiglas, and plastics have superseded the older marble and bronze; kinetic devices, powered by motors, electrical currents, and neon tubes, now bring actual motion to sculpture, while formerly, except in the case of fountains, action could be implied only through muscular tension, a bodily stance, or directional orientation; synthetic colors, commercial paints, acrylics, and various textural additives have supplanted the earth pigments and natural oils used for centuries; and canvas is yielding to Masonite, paper, glass, and plastic surfaces.

Contemporary artists show considerable resistance to confinement as specialists working in a single medium, and the integrity of the single medium has been enlarged to permit the inclusion of many processes and materials within a particular work. One might say that artists have become ecumenical and interdenominational as they join hands to participate in multimedia events staged as theater productions, musicals, and films.

Developments in the theater dramatize the themes and attitudes found in all contemporary art expression. The new theater also reflects the multimedia syndrome by mixing elements of text, music, choreographic movement, miming, and motion picture techniques, all brought together in a group effort. Such experimental productions are kaleidoscopic and mercurial, mosaics of impressions, sporadic snatches of emotion and experience. "Action theater," as some of its manifestations are called, is going more and more in the direction of sound, light, pantomime, struggles, shouts, and cries, and doing it at the expense of text. In Julian Beck's *Paradise Now* contemporary characters in faded blue jeans and sweat shirts mix with such historical figures as Queen Elizabeth Tudor, who appears as a rag doll, while Sophocles' Antigone has an altercation with Lady Macbeth as she walks on in a see-through nightgown. For Beck, all theater must grow out of the personal experience of the company. Spasms of kinetic energy are unleashed onstage as the characters grope and writhe. Rational dialogue gives way to inarticulate groans and moans,

# CHRONOLOGY / The Period Since 1945

## General Events

**1926–1927** First motion pictures synchronized with sound

**1939** Commercial television begun

**1942** Nuclear fission, chain reaction, and release of atomic energy achieved experimentally at University of Chicago

**1944** Jean Paul Sartre's *Being and Nothingness* articulated existentialist philosophy

**1945** Atomic bomb developed under J. R. Oppenheimer and tested in New Mexico. United Nations organized in San Francisco. New York City became international art and music center

**1947–1950** United Nations Headquarters built in New York City by Wallace K. Harrison with international team of architects, including Le Corbusier

**1948** LP recordings commercially available

**1950–1953** Korean War

**1951** Experimental Breeder Reaction No. 1 (Argonne National Laboratory) successfully converted nuclear energy into electric power

**1952** Hydrogen-thermonuclear bomb exploded in Pacific testing area

**1957** First earth satellite launched into orbit by USSR; US satellite followed in 1958

**1958** UNESCO (United Nations Educational, Scientific, and Cultural Organization) Building constructed in Paris by architects Marcel Breuer, Pier Luigi Nervi, and Bernard Zehrfuss, with art work by Alexander Calder, Joan Miró, Henry Moore, Isamu Noguchi, Picasso, and others

**1961** First manned satellite put into orbit by USSR; US manned satellite followed in 1962

**1962** Telstar, American communications satellite

**1962–1966** Lincoln Center built in New York City: Library and Museum of Performing Arts, by Skidmore, Owings & Merrill; New York State Theater, by Philip Johnson; Metropolitan Opera House, by Wallace K. Harrison; Philharmonic Hall, by Max Abramowitz; Vivian Beaumont Theater, by Eero Saarinen; paintings by Marc Chagall, Jasper Johns, and others; sculptures by Alexander Calder, Henry Moore, and others

**1963** President John F. Kennedy assassinated

**1964** Bay of Tonkin Resolution

**1968** Martin Luther King assassinated

**1969** US astronauts on moon

**1974** Successful completion of American Skylab series photographing the solar system and surveying the resources of the earth

## Architects

**1867–1959** Frank Lloyd Wright
**1883–1969** Walter Gropius
**1887–1965** Le Corbusier
**1886–1969** Miës van der Rohe
**1891–** Pier Luigi Nervi
**1892–1970** Richard Neutra
**1895–** R. Buckminster Fuller
**1901–1974** Louis I. Kahn
**1902–** Marcel Breuer
**1906–** Philip Johnson
**1910–1961** Eero Saarinen
**1925–** Robert Venturi

## New York School
### First Generation: Abstract-Expressionist Painters

**1880–1966** Hans Hofmann
**1904–1948** Arshile Gorky
**1903–1974** Adolph Gottlieb
**1903–1970** Mark Rothko
**1904–** William de Kooning
**1904–** Clyfford Still
**1905–1970** Barnett Newman
**1910–1962** Franz Kline
**1912–1956** Jackson Pollock
**1912–1963** William Baziotes
**1913–1967** Ad Reinhardt
**1915–** Robert Motherwell

## First Generation: Sculptors

**1900–** Louise Nevelson
**1903–** Seymour Lipton
**1904–** Isamu Noguchi
**1906–1965** David Smith

## Second Generation: Neodada and Pop Artists

**1887–1968** Marcel Duchamp
**1923–** Roy Lichtenstein
**1924–** George Segal
**1925–** Robert Rauschenberg
**1927–** John Chamberlain
**1928–** Robert Indiana
**1929–** Claes Oldenberg
**1930–** Jasper Johns
**1930–** Marisol
**1930–** Andy Warhol
**1933–** James Rosenquist
**1935–** Jim Dine

## Second Generation: Color-Field and "Optical" Painters

**1912–1962** Morris Louis
**1922–** Jules Olitski
**1923–** Ellsworth Kelly
**1923–** Sam Francis
**1924–** Kenneth Noland
**1926–** Jack Youngerman
**1928–** Helen Frankenthaler
**1933–** Sam Gilliam
**1936–** Frank Stella

## Minimal and Conceptual Artists

**1912–** Tony Smith
**1914–** Bernard Rosenthal
**1928–** Donald Judd
**1928–** Sol LeWitt
**1928–1972** Robert Smithson
**1931–** Robert Morris
**1933–** Dan Flavin
**1935–** Carl André
**1936–1970** Eva Hesse
**1939–** Richard Serra
**1941–** Bruce Nauman
**1944–** Michael Heizer
**1945–** Joseph Kosuth

## The New Realists

**1927–** Philip Pearlstein
**1936–** Alex Katz
**1938–** Janet Fish
**1941–** Chuck Close
**1941–** John de Andrea
**1941–** Richard Estes

## Kinetic Artists

**1898–** Alexander Calder
**1912–** Nicolas Schöffer
**1922–** Howard Jones
**1925–** Jean Tinguely

hisses and screams. The picture of social organization is one of a steaming jungle populated by sweat-smeared human forms. In short, the acropolis seems to have given way to the apocalypse.

In the modern theater, the past is also intimately interwoven with the present. The bare medieval stage without curtain or proscenium arch has its counterpart in the modern arrangement of theater-in-the-round. Members of the cast or stagehands shift all props in full view of the audience or when the lights are out. Too, a nonindividuality bordering on medieval anonymity seems to be favored in reaction against Renaissance individualism and the star system. Several writers may collaborate on a sequence of scenes the end result of which can be distinguished only as a group effort. And in "total theater" the audience is invited to react in concert with the players. This parallels the medieval mind, since miracle plays were group productions, just as the cathedral sculptures emerged from schools of craftsmen and liturgical masses were written by several different composers. Not until the 15th century does one find an entire mass written by a single musician.

The explosive fragmentation in the arts that began with cubism has gone so far that artists no longer view life as a whole. The 18th century—which evolved the aristocratic palace and townhouse as a complete way of life, the rococo church as a *Gesamtkunstwerk* or "complete work of art," the cyclically complete multimovement, sonata-symphony form—was an age of enlightenment and reason in which society could perceive the world as a whole. Typical of the contemporary age is the tendency to capitalize on the fragments, to abstract one aspect of the visual, verbal, or musical activity so as to zero in on a single element. Some composers take their lead from the everyday experience of hearing sounds coming simultaneously from many sources, by, for example, exploiting the mixture of chance sounds that transpire from ten transistor radios, all tuned in at once to different stations, with the performers manipulating the controls to raise and lower the volume at will. Others select the element of silence and achieve a degree of musical abstraction from the absence of sound so that each listener can imagine what he wants to hear. Some contemporary canvases offer simply colors arranged on flat surfaces, which otherwise remain unarticulated by lines, geometrical shapes, or forms in the traditional sense. One sees paintings in which the total preoccupation has been with textures, also monochromatic color-field pictures painted all black or all red. Quite possibly the ultimate in abstraction has been achieved in a framed canvas presented with nothing at all on it. Here the viewer feels what the artist experiences before beginning a work, and the observer can paint his own picture in his imagination.

The philosophy of existentialism has caught up with painting as it has with the "theater of the absurd." Such neodada movements as pop art, which produce sculpture lipsticks two stories high and plastic hamburgers gigantic enough to fill a large room, tell of the essential absurdity of life. Just as in existentialism the act of living itself becomes the affirmation and meaning of life, so in one phase of contemporary art, the very act of painting becomes the work of art and its only meaning.

## THE NEW YORK SCHOOL

During the dark days of World War II, the United States continued to live up to her image as the melting pot. But this time it was a meeting and merging not so much of peoples as it was of personages and personalities. Prior to the American entry into the conflict, the great scientist Albert Einstein had come from Hitler's Germany, while Enrico Fermi arrived from Italy and Niels Bohr from Denmark. Together they succeeded in splitting the atom and ushering in the nuclear age. Formerly of the Bauhaus in Germany, the renowned international-style architects Walter Gropius and Miës van der Rohe began to teach and build in the United States, while Eliel Saarinen and his son Eero migrated from Finland to make their careers on the Eastern Seaboard. Such literary figures as Thomas Mann and Aldous Huxley found Southern California a congenial place to live and write. The composers Igor Stravinsky, Arnold Schoenberg, and Darius Milhaud were also working and teaching in California, while Paul Hindemith joined the faculty of Yale University. The outstanding nonobjective artist Piet Mondrian from Holland and the abstractionist Josef Albers, of the Bauhaus faculty, opened studios and began painting in New York. When the war clouds darkened and the Nazis occupied France, leading figures of the School of Paris also found in New York a sanctuary where they could live and work. These included the sculptor Jacques Lipschitz and such painters as Léger, Chagall, Dali, and Max Ernst. Already established in New York, since World War I, was the great French dadaist Marcel Duchamp. In the twenties and thirties aspiring young American artists and musicians had sailed for Paris in the wake of writers Gertrude Stein, Ernest Hemingway, and Henry Miller and composers Virgil Thomson and Aaron Copland. Now it was a reverse migration that changed the posture of the American artist toward his Continental colleagues. In the early forties he stood squarely in the center of things.

When such eminent minds combined forces with their American counterparts they acted as catalytic agents that catapulted the New York artists to the forefront. After 1945 and the war's end most of the Europeans returned to the Continent, but their mission had been accomplished. The School of Paris had lost its momentum, and most of the younger creative talents were to be found in New York. American ar-

398. New York City in the 1940s, looking north up University Place from Washington Square, toward East 8th, 9th, and 10th Streets, the neighborhood of the abstract expressionists.

tists were now free to effect their own creative synthesis of European styles in combination with their American heritage and personal idioms. For the first time in American history an international style was evolved on the American scene. New York (Fig. 398) became the cosmopolitan capital of art and music, the achievements of the New York School reverberated throughout the world, and abstract expressionism took its place in the history of art alongside impressionism, cubism, expressionism, and surrealism and became the true heir and logical successor to this great evolutionary sequence of stylistic developments.

While major architectural developments depended on the expansion of American commerce and industry, painting and poetry belonged to the dispossessed few. Theirs were the voices of angry young men who had been confronted with the specter of the Great Depression at the beginning of their careers and the horror of war as they reached maturity. At first they had been sustained as artists only through the grace of government-sponsored projects. To relieve mass unemployment, President Franklin D. Roosevelt's New Deal included artists and musicians among those aided by the Works Progress Ad-

399. ARSHILE GORKY. *Enigmatic Combat.* c. 1936–37. Oil on canvas, 2'11¾" × 4'. San Francisco Museum of Art (gift of Miss Jeanne Reynal).

ministration. These programs brought artists, writers, and composers together in group enterprises that afforded them modest incomes. As they worked together creating murals for public buildings, plays for regional theaters, and music for ballet productions and symphonic ensembles, American artists found themselves lifted out of their individual isolation and their alienation from society. They formed friendships, developed a sense of community, and discussed philosophies of life and art in a way that could be translated into action.

The Depression years had produced an atmosphere of radical politics among intellectuals and artists at a time when the basic structures of government and social institutions were scrutinized and questioned in the light of their apparent collapse. In this context art tended toward social realism and to become an instrument of political propaganda for the exposure of poverty, hypocrisy, and injustice. It was to the credit of the abstract expressionists, who were nurtured in this environment, that they sublimated their revolt and submitted it to an aesthetic radicalism whose purpose was to reexamine the basic assumptions and conventions of the American heritage. Although the dominant theme of American art in the 1930s had been social realism (Fig. 392), such artists as the sculptor David Smith and the painters Willem de Kooning and Arshile Gorky (Fig. 399) possessed the vision and the daring to explore the aesthetic and expressive potential of the more advanced vocabularies and syntax offered by cubism, expressionism, and surrealism.

**The First Generation: Abstract Expressionism**   The designation *New York School* was first coined to distinguish the younger generation of American painters and sculptors from the "School of Paris," itself an unofficial term signifying the entire spectrum of artistic genius whose residence and practice in Paris throughout the 19th century and the first four decades of the 20th had made the French capital not only a brilliant scene of ever-evolving aesthetic innovation, audacity, and success but also the very touchstone and symbol of achievement in high art. At first only the abstract expressionists were thought to constitute the New York School, but the meaning of the term has been widened to embrace all the styles whose development and acceptance have centered on New York since 1945.

Just as the School of Paris had embraced the Spaniards Picasso, Juan Gris, and Joan Miró, the Italians Modigliani and de Chirico, and the Russian Chagall, in addition to the Frenchmen Braque and Matisse, so the New York School, who developed the abstract-expressionist style, comprised a cosmopolitan group. The German master Hans Hofmann was already in his fifties when he established an art school on West 8th Street. The Dutchman Willem de

Kooning had moved to New York in the late 1920s, as had Mark Rothko from Russia by way of Portland, Oregon, and Arshile Gorky from Armenia. Jackson Pollock had been born in Wyoming and raised in California and Franz Kline in the coalmining country of Pennsylvania, while Robert Motherwell hailed from San Francisco, Clyfford Still from Spokane, Washington, and the sculptor David Smith from Indiana. Barnett Newman was the native New Yorker in the group. Once WPA projects fell casualty to the war, the artists all found themselves living on the ragged edge of poverty, even desperation, in the bare lofts and coldwater flats of the Greenwich Village section of lower Manhattan off Washington Square (Fig. 398). Theirs was not the prosperous, glittering New York of Wall Street, Madison Avenue, and the art galleries of the establishment on 57th Street. Alienation from American society, which they saw as a machine for brutality, was one of the common bonds linking their attitudes and giving them shape.

The focal point of these "loft rats" was The Club, located at 35 East 8th Street, a local version of a Paris café where those who painted by day could talk to each other by night. In their vigorous arguments the habitués often came to blows, but they all shared a messianic belief that art should be invested with powerful content and that the most powerful means for giving expression to that content lay in the reductive possibilities of abstraction. In 1943 Newman, Rothko, and Adolph Gottlieb—three member painters of the group—published a statement in the *New York Times* declaring that "there is no such thing as a good painting about nothing. . . . the subject is crucial and only that subject matter is valid which is tragic and timeless." At the same time, they asserted that the "impact of elemental truth" called for the "simple expression of the complex thought, and the importance of the large shape because it has the impact of the unequivocal."

Of an evening at The Club, Hans Hofmann could be heard discoursing on the doctrine of abstraction. A naturalist or painter of physical life, he declared, could never become the creator of pictorial life. "You must give the most with the least," he taught, and "a work of art can never be the imitation of life but only . . . the generation of life." On a Friday night the avant-garde composer John Cage might be giving "A Lecture on Nothing," or sit before a keyboard for four and a half minutes of silence. W. H. Auden, the British-born poet who had settled in New York in 1939, would drop in to discuss his *Age of Anxiety* or give voice to some of the pessimistic existentialist reflections that occupied him in those days. The Welshman Dylan Thomas came to read his lyric poems, and the restless Allen Ginsberg, poetic spokesman of the "beat" generation, would appear from time to time. There he read his poem *Howl*, a paean of defeat, a hell of despair. But like a Jackson Pollock web of interpenetrating lines (Pl. 70, p. 407), *Howl* weaves a tapestry of images that captures the spirit of the seething metropolis:

> I saw the best minds of my generation destroyed by madness, starving hysterical naked, . . .
> who poverty and tatters and hollow-eyed and high sat up smoking in the supernatural darkness of cold-water flats floating across the tops of cities contemplating jazz, . . .
> who were expelled from the academies for crazy & publishing obscene odes on the windows of the skull, . . .
> . . . wine drunkenness over the roof tops, storefront boroughs of teahead joyride neon blinking traffic light, sun and moon and tree vibrations in the roaring winter dusks of Brooklyn, ashcan rantings and kind king light of mind, . . .
> who sank all night in submarine light of Bickford's floated out and sat through the stale beer afternoon in desolate Fugazzi's, listening to the crack of doom on the hydrogen jukebox,
> who talked continuously seventy hours from park to pad to bar to Bellevue to museum to the Brooklyn Bridge,
> a lost battalion of platonic conversationalists jumping down the stoops off fire escapes off windowsills off Empire State out of the moon. . . .*

The artists of the New York School did not think of themselves as a group with common ideals. The most that can be said for the unity of the school was that its members shared a range of attitudes, derived principally from the despair and anxiety of the times, from the opportunity for professional activity and cooperation afforded by the WPA, from the breakthrough in aesthetic form achieved by the cubists in their experiments with abstraction, and from the liberation of the subconscious attained among the surrealists using Freudian methods of analysis. They all insisted on spontaneity, intensity of feeling, and a vast range of individual choices, materials, and situations, but in practice, after all the talking, the goal of these American artists became the realization of an entirely new pictorial style, one synthesized from cubism and surrealism and fully equal to these in ambition and accomplishment. Within this spectrum each retained his individuality, each availed himself of an infinite set of options, each strained after his own direction, and each sought the intuition of himself. As the critic Harold Rosenberg noted, each was "fatally aware that only what he constructs for himself will ever be real to him." Or, as William Baziotes said, "[my paintings] are my mirrors. They tell me what I am like at the moment." For the New York School as for the existentialist thinkers, painting was being in nonbeing. Jean Paul Sartre articulated this view

when he observed that "man first of all exists, encounters himself, surges up in the world—and defines himself afterwards."

Cubism taught the American artists the analytical processes of abstracting from natural phenomena for the purpose of creating new forms and relationships whose integrity corresponds much less to the actual appearance of subject matter than to the artist's sense of the need for pictorial effect. Cubist layouts and designs—structured in gridlike formations so as to articulate the painting across its surface and acknowledge the shape of the canvas, rather than simulate the deep space and fully rounded forms present in nature—endowed the New Yorkers with profound respect for those irreducible physical elements of pictorial art: the limitations of the visual field as defined by the edges of the painting support and the two-dimensionality of the painting surface. As Hans Hofmann put it, "The essence of pictorial space is flatness."

Surrealism had an even more powerful effect on the New York group, for it reinforced their commitment to content in art, content meaning not the literal illustration of actual tragedies in the lives of men and nations but an all-informing, transcendental assertion of the elemental, the profound, and the universal in human emotions. But Freud, the great mentor of the European surrealists, proved alien and overly intellectualized for the Americans' purposes and sensibilities, and they thus turned to Jung and his theories of archetypes and the collective unconscious. Their need then was for the signs and symbols, the pictorial equivalents of the myths of universal experience. Surrealism pointed the way to their discovery in the subconscious, the long-buried memory residue of the innocent and unsullied primitive in modern man, the source of the free, the instinctual, and the fantastic in human imagination. Surrealism also indicated a technique for liberating the images trapped in the subconscious and making them available to the conscious mind of the artist for use as the vehicles of his expressive intent. Deriving it from Freud's method of free association, the surrealists developed "psychic automatism," which allowed the artist's hand to move spontaneously and at random, laying down on paper or canvas lines and patterns in no way formed by reason or logic. Once psychic automatism had released a free flow of creativity, the artist could work over and realize from the doodling it produced designs and configurations of a more controlled sort.

Such a methodology gave precedence to process over conception, which reversed the order of values present in abstract art, based as it is on an intellectually derived notion of form. The imagery the abstract expressionists sought was not so much the literal representation of Freudian dreams but rather an ambiguous and sexually evocative biomorphism akin to the swelling and contracting contours in the vo-

---

cabulary of forms devised by Arp and Miró (Fig. 384). Then, having accepted automatism as basic to the creative enterprise, the abstract expressionists converted it from the surrealist process of generating images to the process of painting itself, a way of preserving freshness, of cultivating accidental dribbles and splashes for the evidence they offered of spontaneity and creative vigor. Thus, in artistic creation the abstract expressionists found a metaphor for the myth of universal genesis.

In the life and work of Jackson Pollock come together all the elements of the heroic and mythic associated with the first generation or abstract-expressionist group of post-1945 New York artists. Born in the Far West and maturing in the East, Pollock suffered the agonies of poverty, alienation, world holocaust, public indifference, and alchoholism, yet survived to give effect to a new and monumentally valid revisualization of high art as it had evolved in European civilization—only to die violently in an automobile accident at the age of 44. Gifted with powerful graphic abilities and potent with large emotions, Pollock struggled with the conflict, brutishness, passion, and chaos of his nature and experience until he wrested from them an order so transcendent that in his best works it possesses the harmony and balance of the genuine classic.

In earlier paintings Pollock expressed raw feeling through totemic images of primeval generation rendered with the whiplash calligraphy of an electrically charged line (Fig. 400). Using a highly liquefied medium and the surrealist method of automatic creation, Pollock made a momentous breakthrough, out of the thickly applied, turgid, impastoed facture of such works as *Pasiphaë*, into the drip technique that permitted him to develop his nervous, meandering line as a brilliant arabesque of poured pigment spun out in an allover web of open, transparent skeins and nets (Pl. 70, p. 407). To achieve this effect, the artist further modified his technique by abandoning the easel and laying an uncut length of raw, unprimed duck on the floor (or material stained a single, uniform color), where he had access to it from above and all sides, moving as rhythmically as a dancer to fling, drip, and dribble the fluid medium in large and graceful arcs over the vast area of the canvas (Fig. 401). In this way Pollock could work on a scale that for sheer size was virtually unprecedented in the history of modern abstract art. The technique also permitted him to give equal emphasis to all passages of the picture, which brought to an ultimate realization the tendency first felt in 19th-century impressionism

402. CLAUDE MONET. *Water Lilies.* c. 1920. Oil on canvas, 6'6½" × 19'7½". Museum of Modern Art, New York (Mrs. Simon Guggenheim Fund).

to orient a composition not toward a specific climax within a hierarchy of images but in favor of a single characteristic image made to articulate and embrace the whole of the visual field as a densely packed continuum (Fig. 402). Here, the unity resides in the consistency of Pollock's inflection of his calligraphy and in the perpetual energy and movement of the lines, which weave into such a labyrinthine complexity that the eye gives up following along endless convolutions and accepts the indivisibility of the total configuration. Thus, Pollock attained an altogether new and holistic image, one consisting entirely of line and movement, since the lines do not define shapes and forms, and without these the distinction between figure and ground, an age-old issue in artists' concern for the composition of pictorial space, has been eliminated. Or, should the viewer choose to read the skeins as standing forward and separate from a background, the uniform color and value of the support permit it to suggest a very near plane like that at the back of a bas-relief or the kind of infinite or atmospheric space preferred by the surrealists for the environment of their "dreamscapes." Also synthesized are drawing and painting—those fraternal but traditionally opposed elements of pictorial expression—for now line and color have become one and the same.

Having placed his canvas on the floor and then adopted such unorthodox means as sticks and trowels dipped into buckets of commercial house paint, all to effect not only greater freedom of gesture but also greater control over it, as well as over the space of the painting surface spread before him, Pollock exercised an ultimate act of free choice and control when he fixed the composition finally by cutting it from the total canvas for mounting on a stretcher.

The new spaceless space invented by Pollock has been called purely "optical," a term that contrasts it to conventional "pictorial" space in which the artist has provided imagery containing certain indications of planes that could be perceived as located at a sequence of points receding into the distance. These allow the eye to move through and beyond the picture plane and to return to it. Pollock's drip paintings, however, offer no such visual clues and thus hold the eye at the painting's frontal plane, where it remains fascinated in the perpetuum mobile of lyric linearity. At the same time, works of such scale create an environment and so involve the viewer that they enter his space; thus, by association they take account of three-dimensionality.

Synthesizing so many disparate and fundamentally opposite elements—cubism and surrealism, form and content, reason and emotion, control and freedom, line and color, drawing and painting, figure and ground, abstraction and expression—and doing it on such a heroic scale and without identifiable subject matter of any sort, Pollock accomplished an equilibrium so rare and exquisite that even he could not sustain the delicate poise for long. Eventually he chose to develop individually certain selected aspects of the totality present in his masterpieces, just as his followers carried modern art forward to new advances in aesthetic vision by basing their work on one feature or another of the complete statement made by Pollock in his most fertile and triumphant period, from 1948 through 1950.

Fundamental as color was to many of the group and despite the greatness of their achievement in color, black runs like a leitmotif through much abstract-expressionist painting. Scientifically, black is the total absorption or absence of light, which is the medium of color. Thus, by reducing pigmentation to basic simplicity, black could be seen as a contribution to the quality of abstraction and as an acceleration of the painting process. For others, black played a symbolic role for moods of renunciation, grief, or despair. In the work of Franz Kline black used exclusively with white—like drawings enlarged to the scale of paintings—meant the value contrasts characteristic of the urban scene, whose great bristling structures he was happy to celebrate. *Pennsylvania* (Fig. 403) grows mysteriously in swift, sooty, gestural strokes like the structural stresses of opposing forces in the skeletons of iron bridges, railway trestles, and locomotive engines of the artist's coal-country origins. The image thus created is that of nostalgic, self-revealing memory.

Pollock and Kline are often regarded as the exemplars of "gestural abstraction" within the New York group, while painters like Mark Rothko and Barnett Newman appear as "chromatic abstractionists." A comparison of the Pollock and Kline works with Rothko's *Green and Maroon* in Plate 71 (p. 408) or with Newman's *Vir Heroicus Sublimis* (Pl. 72, p. 409) provides evidence of the reason for the distinction. While Kline's *Pennsylvania* is coherent as a monochrome reproduction, as would be, though slightly less so, Pollock's *Lucifer* (Pl. 70), the Rothko painting could survive in black-and-white reproduction as little more than a gray, somewhat mottled rectangular shape. It also reveals why the popular term *action painting* cannot be accepted as a synonym for abstract expressionism, since vigorous and muscular movement had nothing whatever to do with the subtle and sensitive processes employed by such artists as Rothko and Newman, who were nonetheless members in full standing of the abstract-expressionist group. Their work also provides a striking illustration of the nature and power of the holistic image, one of such simple

monumentality that it quite candidly recapitulates the flatness and shape of the painting support.

Rothko refined the image characteristic of his work as two or three vaporous rectangles floating in a generalized, atmospheric space. The rectangles are painted in close-valued, luminous hues and brushed on with such delicacy that light seems to radiate from within the amorphous films of color. It is the painterly edges and the sheer harmonies of the color keys that set off the vibrations and cause the shapes to appear pneumatic and buoyant within a light- and color-suffused space. In their grandeur and harmony, Rothko's paintings have been taken as objects of contemplation, even of a religious nature.

Perhaps even more than Rothko, Newman worked toward radical simplicity as the most powerful means of creating dramatic impact (Pl. 72). He arrived at a reductive abstraction in which the main pictorial elements consist of a great expanse of pure, eye-dazzling color punctuated by one or more narrow bands whose verticality echoes the shape of the canvas at its lateral edges. (In the art of such colorists as Rothko and Newman, even black functions as color.) Because the image this creates is single, fills the entire picture space, and derives its character from the shape of the canvas—rather than from designed or representational forms and some relationship among them within the pictorial field—Newman's imagery, like Pollock's, has been called "allover composition" and his method of composing "nonrelational." The "zips," as Newman termed his bands, serve to "cut" the great field of absolute color and shock it into waves of visual energy that roll back and

403. FRANZ KLINE. *Pennsylvania.* 1954. Oil on canvas, 3'11" × 5'3". Courtesy Pace Gallery, New York.

forth between bands and edges. This makes dynamic what otherwise might seem a totally static image. The zips can also be read as abstract figures standing out against a field of color; in this way, a third dimension enters the viewer's experience of an irreducibly flat composition. The title *Vir Heroicus Sublimis* ("Sublime

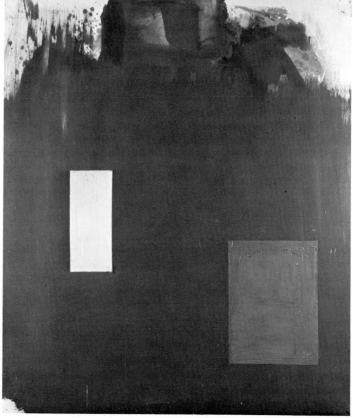

above: 404. PABLO PICASSO. *Woman in the Garden.* 1929–30. Bronze, after welded iron; 6'10$\frac{3}{4}$'' high. Collection the artist's estate.

Was Now") suggests something of the metaphysical content of abstract expressionism and the degree of romantic *hubris* that inspired the New York painters to create an art capable of challenging all of history. While they would not have wished to illustrate classical subject matter, the first-generation artists took as content for their work the classical values of Western humanism and attempted to sustain these in a time of universal inhumanity.

David Smith, quite probably the greatest sculptor in the history of American art, not only was subject to the same forces influencing the abstract-expressionist painters, he also associated intimately with these contemporaries and shared their goal of realizing new forms and a new style through a synthesis of abstraction and expression. A descendant of a blacksmith who had pioneered in Decatur, Indiana, Smith added to this experience of metalwork that obtained on jobs in automobile and locomotive factories where he assembled and welded metal parts. He began his artistic life as a student of painting at New York's Art Students League but switched in the early thirties to sculpture after seeing reproductions of sculptures made by Picasso and Julio González using what then constituted a radically new technique for art—metal pieces and parts joined by welding into cubist *assemblage* (Fig. 404). Throughout his career Smith felt a great fascination for the intrinsic quality of steel: "The metal possesses little art history. What associations it has are those of this century: power, structure, movement, progress, suspension, destruction, brutality." Thus, Smith worked in the medium of constructed sculpture rather than in the traditonal ones of carved stone and cast bronze. To have room for a machine-shop-studio large enough to permit the construction of works on an architectural scale and ample environment for their display, Smith moved to a farm at Bolton Landing in upstate New York. There, he could achieve not only the epic scale of the *Cubi* works (Fig. 405) but also the perspective to conceptualize them within a series of related materials and forms. Some of the constructions retain the rough blackness of iron, others have been painted bright hues, while in the *Cubi* series Smith scored the stainless-steel surfaces of the geometric volumes to make them flash, dazzle, and all but dissolve in refracted sunlight. The sense of lightness this creates seems a contradiction of the heavy, solid appearance of the monumental forms, the mass of them raised aloft by cylinders and balanced there in dynamic majesty.

A master draftsman, who all his life drew from the model, Smith designed sculptures with such strong silhouettes and transparent interiors that they seem like "drawings-in-space"; in scale and proportion, they often relate to the human figure. The frontal views he designed also give many of the works a strong pictorial character. Smith possessed something of the surrealists' automatism in his astonishing facil-

ity for devising new forms. These frequently included standard industrial units or "found" objects from junkyards, which Smith transformed into aesthetic significance by making them integral with the whole of his design. His iron and steel constructions, like those in the *Cubi* series, create open and closed spaces that interpenetrate with their environment, giving effect to space, movement, and color as they stand silhouetted against trees, buildings, or sky.

Like most American artists, Smith saw in geometry not a restrictive canon but a flexible means of ordering. Like his contemporaries, the abstract-expressionist painters, he also sought to illuminate his works with moral conviction. In the late thirties Smith forged a series of "medals of dishonor" whose expressionistic images indicated the unfairness and hypocrisy of modern life. Seeing symbol in structure, Smith wrote: "When one chooses a couple of old iron rings from the hub of a wagon, they are circles, they are suns; they all have the same radius; they all perform the same Euclidean relationships."

Success eventually came to the "loft rats," but after so much poverty, despair, and struggle, it seemed not a harbinger of the good life but the end of an epoch and the death of its heroes. Gorky committed suicide in 1948, and Pollock perished in an automobile accident in 1956, as did David Smith in 1965. Kline's untimely demise occurred in 1962 at the age of 51, and Rothko hanged himself in his studio in 1970. It was the years 1947–53 that saw the movement experience its most intense activity and dialogue and achieve the highest quality in innovation as well as in production. As late as 1951, however, the artists' state was so desperate for the want of recognition that a group calling themselves "the irascible eight," which included Pollock, Kline, Rothko, Newman, de Kooning, Hofmann, Motherwell, Gottlieb, and Reinhardt, picketed the Metropolitan Museum to demand the establishment of a department of American art. In the same year, the Museum of Modern Art responded to the occasion and gave the movement the imprimatur of an exhibition entitled "Abstract Painting and Sculpture in America." Then in 1958–59 the "heroic generation" realized something of an apotheosis when the museum circulated throughout Europe a comprehensive show of their work under the title "The New American Painting." This made abstract expressionism into an international style that transformed the character and appearance of new painting virtually all over the world.

In *Memoria in Aeternum* (Fig. 406) Hans Hofmann, the old master of the style who survived many of his younger colleagues, paid tribute to the movement. Executed shortly after Kline's death, it is a melancholy picture of stark black-and-white contrasts, but one revealing the artist's astonishingly vigorous "push-pull" dynamic by which he caused painterly planes to achieve daring architectonic structure.

**407.** Robert Rauschenberg. *Monogram.* 1959. Construction, 4 × 6 × 6'. Courtesy Leo Castelli Gallery, New York.

**The Second Generation: After Abstract Expressionism**
Abstract expressionism made a compound of cubism and surrealism, and it proved so unstable that following a brief synthesis the two elements separated anew to follow different paths of development in the work of the New York School's "second generation." These found the painterliness of action painting deficient in clear structure and the emotions of abstract expressionism in general too personal to satisfy the objectives of universal sublimity. Rejecting the movement's strong rhetoric, they also discarded its concern for myth, symbol, and metaphor. Some even challenged the viability of abstraction as a vehicle for the communication of anything. This was to be a "cool" generation, one unafraid of and altogether ironic, analytical, and even amused toward the here and now of the palpable realities of the American scene. As Robert Rauschenberg disarmingly remarked, he just wants to live in the world, not reform it.

Out of the dissolution of abstract expressionism emerged two trends, one generally called *pop art* and the other known by a number of terms, among which *post-painterly abstraction* seems descriptive enough to do no harm to the other labels frequently substituted. Pop art took from abstract expressionism its tactile surfaces, involvement with the urban scene, and implicit romanticism. The new abstraction carried forward into still greater reductive advances the formal possibilities of allover and nonrelational compositions and the chromaticism of Rothko and Newman. Common to the whole of the new generation was the older artists' taste for large-scale works. But whatever their respective picking and choosing among the

qualities of abstract expressionism, the younger artists were one in desiring a more objective, detached, and clearly articulated art.

*Pop Art*   In some respects, pop art arrived as a neo-dada manifestation to declare art to be art as a result, not of its inherent value, but of the context selected for it by the artist. It did this using the original dada's vocabulary of the banal and the commonplace, the assemblages of debris from attics and junkyards (see p. 374). Missing, however, has been the bitterness present in the older fare, for pop or neodadaism continues to be nurtured by a joyous acceptance of modern materialism and the inundations from mass media. While dada was a desperately serious movement, the new art revels in nonsense for its own sake and laughs with the world, not at it.

In Rauschenberg's *Monogram* (Fig. 407) it is apparent that pop art has allowed no boundary to separate art from life. Here is a hybrid form, an assemblage or "combine painting" in which the artist has incorporated objects of such palpability—a stuffed angora ram encircled by an automobile tire—that they spill out to challenge the ambiguous spaces of abstract expressionism and literally close the gap between art and life. Completing the three-dimensional collage are photographs, cutout letters, and colors applied with the painterly abandon inherited from the first generation. The real irony at the heart of pop works like *Monogram* is that however vulgar, commercial, debased, and nostalgic the contents, they have been composed, interpreted, and transformed by the means and standards of a high pictorial tradi-

**Plate 70.** Jackson Pollock. *Lucifer.* 1947. Oil, enamel, and aluminum paint on canvas; 3'5" × 6'9".
Collection Mr. and Mrs. Harry W. Anderson, Atherton, Calif. (See p. 401.)

**Plate 71.** Mark Rothko. *Green and Maroon.* 1953. Oil on canvas, $7'6\frac{3}{4}''\times4'6\frac{1}{2}''$. Phillips Collection, Washington, D.C. (See p. 403.)

above: **Plate 72.** Barnett Newman. *Vir Heroicus Sublimis ("Sublime Was Now").* 1950, 1951. Oil on canvas, 7'11¾" × 17'9¼". Museum of Modern Art, New York (gift of Mr. and Mrs. Ben Heller, 1969). (See p. 403.)

left: **Plate 73.** John Chamberlain. *Silverheels.* 1963. Welded auto metal, 46 × 41 × 36". Collection Mr. and Mrs. Leo Castelli, New York. (See p. 411.)

**Plate 74.** JASPER JOHNS. *0 through 9.* 1960. Oil on canvas, 6′ × 4′6″. Private collection. (See p. 411.)

right: 415. ALEXANDER CALDER. *Mobile.* 1963. Sheet steel, height 27'. Connecticut Bank and Trust Company, Hartford.

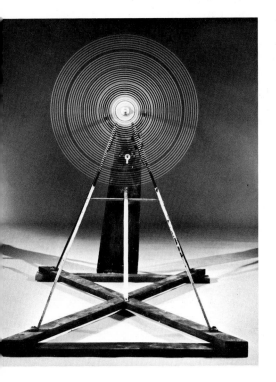

above: 414. MARCEL DUCHAMP. *Revolving Glass.* 1920. Motorized optical device: five painted glass plates, wood and metal braces, turning on a metal axis, electrically operated. 3'11½" × 6'½". Yale University Art Gallery, New Haven, Conn. (gift of Collection Société Anonyme).

Instead of seeing is believing, with op art seeing is deceiving. Like the impressionists, optical artists are concerned primarily with the work of art as an act of the eye. But unlike the impressionists, they avoid all association with the outside world and concentrate on the way the eye and brain respond to optical data. By activating the responsive eye, by the impact on perception of color patterns, optical art has produced effects of constant motion and ceaseless change that constitute a new way of seeing.

The *minimalist* point of departure can be found in David Smith's late *Cubi* series (Fig. 405), but unlike Smith, the minimalists deemphasize personal involvement, expressive content, and hand welding in favor of fabricated impersonality. They also prefer "primary structures" (Figs. 412, 413)—basic geometric volumes so simple as to be redundant—over the planes typical of cubist-derived sculpture (Figs. 374–

376). Materials tend to be the industrial ones of galvanized iron, aluminum, stainless steel, laminated wood, fiber glass, and plastics. The minimalists also employ industrial methods, drawing up plans and specifications and making a small model in painted wood. This then is turned over to an industrial shop for final execution. Like architects, they project their schemes on a huge scale for siting in public places and must await patrons with the capital to finance such enterprises. Before Tony Smith could arrange for *Smoke* to be constructed in steel, he had it built in plywood for exhibition in a court at New York's Metropolitan Museum (Fig. 412). Here the spectator is overwhelmed as he wanders in and out and through the work's huge arched forms and elemental shapes.

The minimalists shun the conception of sculpture as an isolated object. Their productions do not sit on pedestals, rather they rest on the floor, stand against a wall, are suspended from the ceiling, or occupy a whole room. Better yet, they take to the out-of-doors, like Bernard Rosenthal's dramatically poised cube *Alamo* (Fig. 413), where they merge with the surrounding architectonic space and become part of the total environment.

*Kinetic Art*   Many artists of the sixties and seventies have dematerialized their creations so that motion and colored light become the substance of the work of art. In this, sophisticated engineering and computer technology come into play. Leading the way earlier in the century were Marcel Duchamp with his primitive motorized works (Fig. 414) and Alexander Calder with his mobiles animated by air currents (Fig. 415).

above: 416. NICOLAS SCHÖFFER. *Prime Multiple with Lux II.* 1960. Copper-coated steel. Courtesy Galerie Denise René, Paris.

left: 417. LEN LYE. *Fountain II.* 1963. Steel rods and base, height 7'5½". Tel Aviv Museum.

right: 418. HOWARD JONES. *Skylight Two* (two stages). 1966. Aluminum with programmed lights, 4' square. Minneapolis Institute of Art (gift of Mr. and Mrs. Bruce B. Dayton).

Now with advancing electronic technology, light, action, and sound can be combined in time-space creations that are variously referred to as *kinetic, serially programmed,* or *luminist art.*

Nicolas Schöffer uses cybernetics and computers to program his creations in motion and light (Fig. 416) and employs such terms as "spatiodynamics" and "luminiodynamics" to discuss their alliance with science and engineering. Others construct with gleaming metallic rods that whirl in fountainlike patterns whose oscillations set up strange sound effects (Fig. 417). Electromagnets can be programmed to sustain metal objects in a perpetual pattern of attraction and repulsion. Howard Jones combines metal panels of high sheen with computer-programmed lights in a way to yield illusions of spatial depth and mercurially shifting time-light resonances (Fig. 418). The artist working in this type of serialization can depend on chance or computerization. The technology of such systems reflects the rigors of an orga-

nized, automated, industrial society existing in an electronic time-space continuum.

*Conceptual Art*    Art as process, art as problem solving, art as kinetics, art as technology, art as an event or happening, art as the monumentalization of the minimal—all have tended to reduce and dematerialize, even to devisualize, the aesthetic experience to the point where, for some, all that remains is the idea the artist has conceived for his work, often referred to as a "piece." Sculptor Sol LeWitt has called the *idea* "the machine that makes the work." As if to demonstrate this, LeWitt drew up specifications for a metal cube or box and arranged for it to be fabricated, "containing an object that is important but not valuable." He then buried the form in the ground in Holland. As it disappeared, the process was documented photographically in a sequence of stills (Fig. 419). This record alone should be sufficient to generate discussion concerning whether the scheme or any aspect of it might constitute an essential experience in art—the physical cube, the presence of something in it, the act of burial, the image record made by the medium of photography, or the residual event lingering in the memory of observers. The baffling banality of it all should suggest that significance of any kind would need to be sought elsewhere—in the artist's guiding conception—for once the idea of a cube has been established, the object itself is scarcely worth viewing, and might as well be buried, given the fact of the form's being so universal, everyone in the world already knows what it looks like.

But in the realm of art one must always be prepared to look a second time, for only careful consideration can bring about the heightened experience that is art. A second glance might reveal that a cube is one of the purest of abstract forms, the physical analogue of a Platonic idea, a thing of wonder and transcendency. It is also, as the artist implies, a box to receive and contain something important, however invaluable. Next, burial is a ritual that mankind has enacted throughout time immemorial, an act of reverence for the mysterious energies that create life and the equally mysterious forces that take it away. In addition, the attempt to record the event suggests a desire on the part of the artist to communicate with his viewers, if not to provide them with a collectable and preservable form. Too, by communicating so much mystery, the artist has posed more questions than answers—mainly about the nature of an art that his consciousness and sensibility permit him to offer to the civilization he partakes of. Possibly what he has done is make a witty postulation that in a depersonalized and highly abstracted industrial society—glutted with things, products, and media-generated images—art may have nothing whatever to do with sensuous form and composition or even with objects. Interring the artist's product shocks society's age-old obsession with the objectness of art, with its value as property. LeWitt's act somewhat parallels that of Watteau in the 18th century, when this innovative artist saluted the new intimate style of the rococo by depicting in *Gersaint's Signboard* (Pl. 39, p. 267) the packing away of the image of Louis XIV, the chief sponsor of the

old grandiose and ostentatious baroque style. In the case of LeWitt, one might assume, at the least, that the artist has made an effort to engage in the sort of vital inquiry that is at the very heart of the aesthetic experience.

In a seminally provocative book, *Beyond Modern Sculpture* (1968), Jack Burnham sees in art like LeWitt's cube piece evidence of modern society passing into a new form of civilization. There, sculptors will cease to concern themselves with the physical elements of scale, volume, and mass, and even with expressiveness, until through dematerialization sculpture has evolved into forms still unimagined but related to the patterns of organization and informational systems destined to control and automate an increasingly technological culture. LeWitt himself has written that he aims "not to instruct the viewer, but to give him information. Whether the viewer understands this information is incidental to the artist. . . . He would follow his predetermined premise to its conclusion, avoiding subjectivity. Chance, taste, or unconsciously remembered forms would play no part in the outcome. The serial artist does not attempt to produce a beautiful or mysterious object but functions merely as a clerk cataloguing the results of his premise."

Thus, certain conceptualists do not offer objects for purchase and possession by collectors but idea projects to be financed by patrons. There is whimsy in Robert Barry's proposal to create *Something which can never be any specific thing*. Many such enterprises remain in their verbal state, which hardly seems a defeat for an art whose primary value resides in its conception. Joseph Kosuth, in his art system called *Art as Idea as Idea*, relies entirely upon language and

**419.** Sol LeWitt. *Buried Cube.* 1968. a. The Visser family, on whose ground the cube is buried; b. Dick V.D. Net, who made the cube; c. The artist; d. The shovel; e. The artist shoveling; f. The hole; g. The cube in the hole; h. The cube being covered with earth; i. The hole filled in.

**left: 420.** Joseph Kosuth. *Art as Idea as Idea.* 1967. Enlargement of dictionary definition, 5' square. Courtesy the artist.

**below: 421.** William M. Harnett. *Old
Models.* 1892. Oil on canvas, 4'6" × 2'4".
Museum of Fine arts, Boston (Charles Henry
Hayden Fund).

**right: 422.** Philip Pearlstein. *Couple on Old
Indian Rug.* 1971. Oil on canvas, 6 × 5'. Col-
lection Mr. and Mrs. Henry Buchbinder,
Chicago.

presents wall-size photographic enlargements of dictionary entries defining abstract words (Fig. 420).
    The riddles, conundrums, wit, and irony, the re-
morseless verbalization and intellectuality of conceptual art are a legacy from Duchamp, the dadaists, and
the Zen preoccupations of John Cage. Conceptual art,
however, differs from its sources by referring largely
to itself rather than to an audience or theater situation. Often using his own body and physical actions,
the conceptual artist is too concerned for the expansion of his own consciousness in relation to art and
language to allow for the involvement of spectators
in the creation of his piece.
    In 1913, Duchamp enlarged the possibilities for
art virtually into infinity when he anticipated the war
of attrition between art and nonart: "Can one make
works which are not works of 'art'?" What he questioned was whether *anything* made by man—idea,
phrase, or object—is *not* art. Conceptual art has pro-

duced body works, earth works, mere labels, and works consisting of such curious materials as grease, cheesecloth, vinyl, plastic, cornflakes, ice blocks, or dirt whose removal from galleries—by scrubbing, sweeping, wadding up, chipping, or shoveling—results in either destruction or total mutation. All that remains of the piece is a memory experience and a documentary record in the form of videotape or photographic stills. Antiform, anti-illusion, antipermanence, anticommercial, and antistyle—conceptual art is cerebration that creates an event of artistic import involving ideas and materials in a space-time continuum. And the ultimate irony may be that anything as intensely deliberated as a conceptualized event inevitably will bear the hallmarks of heightened sensibility and human genius, which set the experience apart and give it the selectiveness and distinction that are the very nature of aesthetic integrity.

*The New Realism*    The power of art to survive even its own dissolution into ephemera has been reasserted by a group of artists working in the modes of high art to render visible phenomena with a factuality and specificity that only the camera could rival. Indeed, despite its total devaluation by the avant-garde during the long hegemony of postwar reductive abstraction, realist easel painting—the oldest and grandest tradition in American art (Fig. 421)—survived well enough for the style to have produced an "old master," just at the moment when conceptualization had taken art so far out the only way for it to reenter the realm of visual experience was to turn back to subject matter, representation, and the object quality of a well-crafted product. Only a tough-minded, thoroughly self-aware, and secure artist could have justified persisting in a figurative style so universally deplored that for long it seemed suitable mainly for the purveyors of kitsch. Philip Pearlstein is such an artist (Fig. 422), and he reasons his own case thus: "I have made a contribution to humanism in 20th-century painting—I rescued the human figure from its tormented, agonized condition given it by the expressionistic artists, and the cubist dissectors and distorters of the figure, and at the other extreme I have rescued it from the pornographers, and their easy exploitation of the figure for its sexual implications. I have presented the figure for itself, allowed it its own dignity as a form among other forms in nature."

In his unblinking, up-close presentation of human flesh as it actually is—not the cosmetic counterfeits traditionally offered by both romantic and academic image-makers—Pearlstein seems a literalist of the most blatant sort. But the viewer capable of assimilating the candor of this imagery may well succeed in granting to the human body its "dignity as a form among other forms in nature." The artist advances this cause by adopting a keen but dispassionate attitude toward his subject—the studio model—and by cropping faces and heads so as to depersonalize the body. Simultaneously, however, Pearlstein is a creature of his own time, and his interest in aesthetic form appears no less committed than that of his abstractionist contemporaries. Like Noland and Stella, Pearlstein is a cool rationalist who reacted against the reckless fervor and formlessness of the gestural painters. Too, each painting represents both an intricate problem in composition and the resolution the artist has been able to bring to it. Although depicting rounded forms in volumetric space, Pearlstein slants his view down so as to bring images and background planes forward to define a shallow space aligned generally with the picture plane. Colorism also plays an important role, for Pearlstein has rendered the cascading volumes of flesh by means of rich and complex blends of hues applied in a wide range of light and dark values.

The *photo* or *super realism* of Richard Estes is so emphatic that, more than actual quotidian reality, it resembles the glossiness and intense coloration of imagery rendered in Ektachrome transparency by a camera equipped with a powerful lens (Pl. 82, p. 430). Here, physical matter as subject, the cult of things as content, and as form the product of the artists' highly skilled professionalism have replaced the preoccupations of the abstract expressionists and the conceptualists with process, subjectivity, and the metaphysics of creativity. While continuing pop art's involvement with mass culture, Estes has supplanted the older movement's humor and messiness with sober, amoral objectivity and assured craftsmanship. The high-keyed, synthetic colors echo the brilliance pioneered in the formalist abstractions of the "second generation" New York painters. Clarity of focus on objects both near and far serves not only to unite figure and ground into the planar relationships suitable for modernist painting but also to spread interest equally all over the picture surface. This flattens space while creating a collective vision that parallels the collective tendencies and the relativistic values of modern society. This is an art hedonist in content and puritan in form. By concentrating on popular subject matter and crisp definition of form, the photo realists may succeed where all other styles have failed—and close the credibility gap between high, advanced art and the expectations of the public at large.

If the new realism can be accepted as the avant-garde movement of the early seventies, then the position of realistic painting in relation to abstraction has completely reversed the hierarchies that prevailed in American culture until about thirty years ago. At that time, the establishment style had long been academic realism, and abstract art was obliged to struggle against ridicule, contempt, and, worse, indifference. Now, abstraction is the instituted academy, with its establishmentarian position assailed by the latest reversal in taste. Nothing could be more natural in an age of unremitting irony.

# RECENT MUSICAL DEVELOPMENTS

Modern science has provided composers and audiences with a whole new world of sound. Instead of vibrations resulting from strings or columns of air as with traditional instruments, sound waves can now be produced by electronic oscillations. With the invention and development of electronically generated sound, the use and alteration of everyday sound data by tape recorder, the random choices of musical happenings, the management of mathematical-musical formulas via the computer, and the psychedelic manifestations in mixed media, there is a whole host of novel possibilities. However, just because a composer is of the experimental persuasion does not necessarily place him in the front of the procession, for experiments can lead to blind alleys and dead ends just as easily as to significant breakthroughs. And if such experiments do succeed in making major breakthroughs, the mere manipulation of new materials and ideas is not sufficient in itself to become the stuff of new art forms. For that it takes the appearance and efforts of a master composer, one able to control the new resources and shape them into the forms of a new creative synthesis. So whether a composer moves in the direction of rigidly controlled serialism, orients himself toward electronic computerization, or adopts the tried-and-true traditions of selective eclecticism, only time can tell which road leads to the future. Historical experience reveals that these seemingly new phenomena are actually variants and extensions of age-old principles and basic human urges. Viewed in this objective light, the events of the last quarter of the 20th century will in all likelihood exhibit about the same mixture of old, new, and experimental elements, of conservative, liberal, and progressive directions, of past, present, and future trends as those to be encountered at any historical cross section of time.

*Concrete music* is the term used to identify one aspect of contemporary composition. It involves using the tape recorder to capture everyday sounds and manipulate them on magnetic tape. The procedure might be compared with the way Robert Rauschenberg puts together one of his assemblages (Fig. 407). The artist selects some random objects—coke bottles, a birdcage, bedsprings, old newspaper clippings—and then combines them into a three-dimensional collage, painting some sections, leaving others as they are. The composer of *concrete music* finds sounds and noises all around him—the clanking of trash cans, the whine of jet engines, the roar of city traffic, the sirens of fire trucks. Once recorded, these environmental sounds can be edited, the sequence controlled, and the tape run at varying speeds, spliced or scrambled, and played backwards. The material can also be filtered by eliminating overtones, with feedback added or subtracted, and certain sounds may be isolated, fragmented, and broken down into separate components. The possibilities are far-ranging.

Another and more sophisticated approach is found in sounds artificially generated by means of the synthesizer used in combination with a computer. By converting sound waves, with their elements of pitch, dynamics, duration, and tone color, into digits or a number series, the synthesizer-computer can then be programmed to produce a tape capable of being played back on a tape recorder. There are also portable synthesizers suitable for use in live performance.

Composers who have mastered the techniques of computer sound generation can now dispense with conventional instruments and live musicians, if they wish, and use tapes or disks to distribute their works directly to the listener. The process of producing a musical work on tape is analogous to that of the graphic arts, in which the artist creates a master plate of an etching or lithograph from which subsequently prints can be made. Many composers from Gluck to Stravinsky have protested bitterly against singers, instrumentalists, and conductors who take liberties with their scores in live performances. Thus, in one instance the composer runs the risk of having his purposes altered by the interpreter, but in the other he loses the spontaneity of a live performance and the creative insights that a skilled and responsible performer can bring to music. Some composers have found a middle ground by combining electronically produced material with live musical situations. It is also possible to write a symphony in which electronic sound becomes one of the sections of the symphony orchestra, or compose a concerto for synthesizer or tape recorder and orchestra. Whatever the case, it should be stressed that the medium is not the music. Computer-synthesizers, to be sure, are far more complex than pianos, violins, or even the symphony orchestra. But ultimately they are only instruments, the means to an end. The electronically minded composer can work in any style he may desire. History, however, establishes that each breakthrough must evolve its own vocabularies and exploit areas idiomatic and unique to the properties of the particular medium. Eventually the composer must summon the whole of his creative imagination in order to produce a valid tonal continuum interesting and significant enough to establish contact with the listener.

Whether the musical process is improvisatory, as with concrete music and chance happenings, or rationally controlled, as with computerization, ample precedents in the musical past can be cited. Random fancy is apparently as old as music itself. If the 20th-century composer seems to stress chance, the procedure is not essentially different from the vocal improvisations worked in medieval times on old Gregorian tunes, an organist inventing variants on Protestant hymns, Bach writing out his free toccatas and fantasies, or a virtuoso instrumentalist ad-libbing cadenzas in a classical concerto. Freedom and strictness are neither mutually nor musically exclusive, and the wise composer maintains both options separately or in combination. The work of Karlheinz Stockhausen and John Cage, both prominent figures on the international musical scene, reveal some of the possibilities of this mode of music making.

When today's mathematically minded composer turns to the computer, the process may differ in kind but not in spirit from certain musical methods of the past. The mathematical basis for music, for instance, has been known ever since Pythagoras discovered the ratios of the musical intervals in the late 6th century B.C. (see p. 34). Some medieval composers accelerated or slowed down the note values of melodies and thereby expanded or contracted the rhythmic ratios of their isorhythmic motets. In his thirty variations on a theme, the famous *"Goldberg" Variations,* Bach in every third variation (the third, sixth, ninth, etc.) devised a series of canons from the unison to the ninth. In the earlier 20th century Schoenberg and Berg employed rigorous serial techniques with the tone rows and their segments appearing straightforward, in inversion, in retrograde, and in retrograde inversion (see pp. 370, 371). The musical thought of Milton Babbitt ilustrates this approach, while a string quartet by Elliott Carter exemplifies the continuity of the classical tradition.

**Karlheinz Stockhausen**　Now perhaps the outstanding representative of electronic composition, Karlheinz Stockhausen is one of a group associated with the Studio for Electronic Music, a subsidiary of the West German Radio at Cologne. Chance elements in his music are controlled so as to bring new forms into being—forms that grow out of the musical material, shapes that the composer holds to be both necessary and inevitable. Stockhausen began by working with "sine-wave tones," pure sounds stripped of their overtones, and then synthesizing them into a new and inventive sound spectrum. This implies the rearrangement and alteration of fundamental acoustical elements for the purpose of forming new textures and densities that become the building blocks of sound structures. This early phase of Stockhausen's work may be heard in *Study I* and *Study II* that date from 1953.

In *Gesang der Jünglinge* ("Song of the Boys in the Fiery Furnace") of 1956 Stockhausen intended to bring the human voice into a working relationship with electronic sounds. He chose the text from Chapter 3 of the *Book of Daniel.* The story, dating from the Babylonian captivity, is that of the men cast into the fiery furnace by Nebuchadnezzar whose golden statue they refused to worship. The materials are the vowels and consonants sung and spoken by a boy soprano, then pulverized into Webernlike pointillistic sounds and superimposed on electronically generated sound mixtures of varying density. The vocal fragments seem to float in and out, creating an effect that is airy, spacious, and transparent. Occasionally the listener hears intelligible words, but more often the vocal part comes across as pure sound. The work was conceived and recorded before stereophonic sound became widely available. Thus, Stockhausen prepared it to be heard in a large round room where five speakers could throw the tonal materials back and forth and around the listener, so as to envelop and surround him with sound waves moving through space.

Despite his invention of ingenious notational symbols for scoring electronic sounds, Stockhausen, in his more recent work, has parted company with a written score in favor of composing directly on tape. The genesis of such a composition is to delimit the time dimension arbitrarily to, say, 20 or 40 minutes and do perhaps a dozen "takes." Then the composer, like a film director, edits and chooses what will eventually become the final version. For this style he has evolved a complicated technique in which he may use players to produce short motifs, often in the extreme registers of their instruments. Also, in the manner of the theater of the absurd, the composer can call on them to improvise a sequence of grunts and groans, shrieks and squawks, hisses and sighs. Each instrumentalist has a contact microphone connected with a central control panel. Here sits Stockhausen, like the conductor of old; but instead of a baton, he has a complex of electronic devices called "sine-wave generators," "potentiometers," and "ring modulators." In a series of takes he develops the final composition. Developing, according to Stockhausen, means that the sounds are "spread, condensed, extended, shortened, differently colored, more or less articulated, transposed, modulated, multiplied, synchronized."

This approach is illustrated in *Opus 1970.* Each of the four players is provided with a previously prepared tape consisting of various fragments of Beethoven's piano sonatas, symphonies, the violin concerto, and some vocal music. The tapes play continuously, but the player may turn the loudspeakers up or down at will. All the while Stockhausen sits at his controls filtering, altering, changing the speed, blending the timbres, so as to achieve the effects and shapes he desires. The listener's impression is that of an electronic soundscape in which Beethoven's music is atomized, reassembled, and cubistically combined into a sequence of tantalizing, wispy fragments. Occasionally the synthesizer may pick up a Beethovenian theme or line and carry on an ingenious dialogue with it. Stockhausen says his intention is not to interpret, but "to hear familiar, old, performed musical material with new ears, to penetrate and transform it with a musical consciousness of today." To some, the result may sound like confusion confounded, a mixture of serenity and hysteria. For others it may accomplish what the composer hoped it would—that is, put Beethoven's music in a new relationship with the contemporary scene. In all events, it must be conceded that Stockhausen is a major musical mind, a composer of invention and ingenuity, a craftsman who manipulates his materials with a sure hand.

**John Cage**    From the thirties through the seventies, John Cage has invariably proved a provocative, often articulate spokesman for avant-garde experimental developments. Nowadays he is most closely identified with the kind of chance techniques and musical happenings commonly referred to as *aleatory music.* The word "aleatory" derives from the Latin *alea,* meaning "dice," and John Cage believes in rolling the musical dice, tossing tonal coins, and accepting whatever comes up at random in the world of sound. His announced objective is to bring about a "revolution in the nature of musical experience." It could be said that the concern of earlier Western music with the nature and reconciliation of the opposites of dissonance and consonance eventually led to the present complete emancipation of dissonance. Should this be true, Cage shares with other contemporary composers the problem of synthesizing musical sounds and noise. An early 20th-century composer much admired by Cage is Erik Satie (see p. 380), who once declared himself ambitious to invent a music that would be like the furniture—a music partaking of the noises of the environment, one capable of softening the sounds of knives and forks at the dinner table and of filling the awkward silences in conversation.

Cage's revolt is against the extreme ordering and ultracontrolled conditions of such music as twelve-tone serialism, in which a precise reason exists for the placement of each note. So he conceives his own music as an experimental activity that creates conditions in which nothing is foreseen. He would free sounds from any preordained formal continuity. Composer-critic Virgil Thompson finds in Cage a "healthy lawlessness," and he hears Cage's music as a "collage of noises" that produces a "homogenized chaos" carrying "no program, no plot, no reminders of the history of beauty, and no personal statement."

According to Cage, music should give people a feeling that they are doing something rather than having something done to them. Listeners, he believes, should experience involvement, and the music should afford them "the opportunity to have experiences they would not otherwise have had."

A recent phase of his work (1967–69) is heard in *HPSCHD* (computerese for "harpsichord," since the computer was not programmed to accommodate words of more than 6 letters). He and his co-composer Lejaren Hiller "scored" the work for from 1 to 7 harpsichordists playing simultaneously and at random various compositions or fragments (chosen individually by each harpsichordist) from the music of Bach, Mozart, and Beethoven, as well as from jazz and blues. They play against a background of from 1 to 51 computer-generated sound tapes superimposed on each other in random montage structures. When first presented at the University of Illinois, the performance, complete with a light show that included 64 projectors, lasted well over 4 hours. It is now available in condensed form as a publication and recording, the latter timed for a little over 20 minutes. The 51 sound tapes were programmed to produce a composite of tones and silences based on a series of equal-tempered scales consisting of from 5 to 56 tones in the octave. The sequences then appear as an intermixture of "successive events, melodic 'goals' (without cadence) and types (diatonic, chromatic, chordal arpeggiation), volume, and dynamics. . . ."

The hi-fi operator and the listener are also invited to get into the act as the composers provide a computer printout for playback control. At five-second intervals, the operator can change the volume and alternate the treble and bass controls. He also is directed to switch the stereo channels from left to right as well as to combine both together. The home listener's stereo set thus becomes integral with the composition.

Cage's pieces avoid the conventional sense of a beginning or an end. At a given point one begins to hear sounds, and after a while one does not. By avoiding repetition, Cage causes his works to seem endlessly repetitious, so that some listeners may agree with Virgil Thompson that there is no need for playing any of Cage's recordings for longer than five minutes, ". . . since we know that it will not be going any deeper into an emotion already depicted as static. Nor will it be following nature's way by developing an organic structure." In coming to terms with the realities of musical experience, Cage's chance happenings and aleatory ramblings are essentially negated the moment they appear as recordings. He declares, with justification, that a composition played for a second time is something quite other than it was, and that a "recording of such a work has no more value than a postcard; it provides a knowledge of something that happened, whereas the action was a non-knowledge of something that had not yet happened." At one of his lectures Cage summarized himself as follows: "I have nothing to say and I am saying it, and that is poetry."

**Milton Babbitt**    Milton Babbitt's taking-off point was Schoenberg's twelve-tone method, but he extends serialism to include rhythm, dynamics, tone color, and speed, as well as pitch, harmony, and counterpoint. The computer is a natural instrument for Babbitt. He thinks with it and through it. With the computer, sounds can be superimposed; retrograde progressions become available by reversing the numbers; and all manner of speed changes, including

**423.** Milton Babbitt at the RCA Mark II Electronic Sound Synthesizer, Columbia-Princeton Electronic Music Center.

rhythmic augmentation, diminution, and fluctuations of tempo can be accurately programmed. The serialization of rhythm, for instance, involves ordering durational values in a graduated scale. Various rhythmic patterns and variants can then be programmed by multiplying or fractionalizing a proportional mathematical series. It could be a simple arithmetical progression such as 1, 2, 3, 4, 5, 6; or something more complex like 1, 2, 3, 5, 8, 13. Dynamic values—levels of soft and loud, fade-outs and fade-ins—may also be rotated in series.

The computer (Fig. 423), in contrast to the limitations of conventional musical instruments, has the capability to control a limitless supply of musical and nonmusical sounds. With so vast a range of sonorities available to it, the computer can be programmed to perform as a composing machine. As such it can construct works based on self-generated numbers, or become the partner of a human composer.

Babbitt's *Vision and Prayer* (1961) for soprano and synthesizer merges the nonelectronic and electronic worlds of sound with a soprano singing live along with a tape produced by the computer (in this case the RCA Mark II Electronic Sound Synthesizer that fills an entire room at the Columbia-Princeton Electronic Music Center). The text by Dylan Thomas is intoned by the soprano in wide-skipping intervals, while the computer's tape deals with the tone quality and the structure of the poem.

It is not surprising that Babbitt was attracted to a poem like Dylan Thomas' *Vision and Prayer*. It is a well-known anthology piece, a sonorous vision that reads with a sense of verbal grandeur. Yet it is a serial poem, the length of the lines predetermined by the number of syllables that, according to the series, it

must possess. The number series 1 to 9 yields on the printed page two visual designs, each with seventeen lines. The first design (for the first six stanzas) proceeds on the basis of one syllable for the first line, two for the second, three for the third, and so on up to nine syllables for the ninth line. The series then moves in retrograde. The tenth line has eight syllables, the eleventh has seven, and so on until at the seventeenth line one arrives again at a one-syllable word. This progression—1, 2, 3, 4, 5, 6, 7, 8, 9, 8, 7, 6, 5, 4, 3, 2, 1—yields a diamond-shaped stanza. For the second set of six stanzas, the syllables per line follow the progression 9, 8, 7, 6, 5, 4, 3, 2, 1, 2, 3, 4, 5, 6, 7, 8, 9, which produces on the page two triangles linked at their common apex (line 9). The first and last stanzas follow:

> Who
> Are you
> Who is born
> In the next room
> So loud to my own
> That I can hear the womb
> Opening and the dark run
> Over the ghost and the dropped son
> Behind the wall thin as a wren's bone?
> In the birth bloody room unknown
> To the burn and turn of time
> And the heart print of man
> Bows no baptism
> But dark alone
> Blessing on
> The wild
> Child.

. . . . . . . .

> I turn the corner of prayer and burn
> In a blessing of the sudden
> Sun. In the name of the damned
> I would turn back and run
> To the hidden land
> But the loud sun
> Christens down
> The sky.
> I
> Am found.
> O let him
> Scald me and drown
> Me in his world's wound.
> His lightning answers my
> Cry. My voice burns in his hand.
> Now I am lost in the blinding
> One. The sun roars at the prayer's end.*

Babbitt also produces purely computerized works as in his *Ensembles for Synthesizer* (1964), a work on which he has commented thus:

---

* From *The Poems of Dylan Thomas*, copyright 1946 by New Directions Publishing Corporation, reprinted by permission of New Directions Publishing Corporation.

The title *Ensembles* refers to the multiple characteristics of the work. In both its customary meaning and its more general one signifying "collections," the term refers more immediately to the different pitch, rhythmic, registral, textural, and timbral "ensembles" associated with each of the many so delineated sections of the composition, no two of which are identical, and no one of which is more than a few seconds duration in this ten-minute work.... Also, in its meaning of "set" the word "ensemble" relevantly suggests the, I trust, familiar principles of tonal and temporal organizations which are employed in this as in other of my compositions.

Babbitt's aesthetic stance rests upon an appeal to intellectual rigor as the basis for the putting together (i.e., the composing) of a piece of music. It is an uncompromising view that makes no concession to immediate popular understanding. As he himself has said, "the composer's first obligation is to his art, to the evolution of music and the advancement of musical concepts."

**Elliott Carter**    Igor Stravinsky once remarked that a new work by Elliott Carter was an event awaited in the musical world by all concerned with the serious music of the present time. Carter's *String Quartet No. 1* (1951) received first prize in the prestigious *Concours International de Quatuor* of 1953 in Liège, Belgium. His *String Quartet No. 2* (1959) has won several awards—the Pulitzer Prize for Music (1960), the New York Music Critics Circle Award (1960), and the International Rostrum of Composers Award (UNESCO) in Paris (1961). His superb *Double Concerto for Piano, Harpsichord, and Small Orchestra* was hailed by Stravinsky as a masterpiece. It is worth adding that the acclaim and the awards have been richly deserved.

Nurtured on traditional techniques as well as on Schoenberg's twelve-tone method, Carter also found inspiration in the idealism of Charles Ives, the old master of American music whom he knew as mentor, friend, and neighbor. Carter has said that for him music must have "an audible order that can be distinguished, remembered, and followed." He also points out that his compositions are no longer built on themes or tone rows. Instead, the building blocks of his musical structures can just as well be "tone color, a chord, or a texture."

"I like music to be beautiful, ordered, and expressive of the more important aspects of life," Carter has observed. "The idea of my music, if it can be considered apart from its expressive and communicative character (which I doubt), could be said to be a constantly evolving series of shapes, like the patterns of choreography." And indeed it is to Carter's remarkable rhythmic invention and unique command of the time experience that the listener must look for his initial contact with the composer's work. "Metrical modulation," as Carter calls it, is central to his thought. This is a rhythmic phenomenon in which tempos fluctuate in the different instrumental parts, and the rhythmic and metrical values are lengthened and shortened in a kind of neomedieval version of mensuration or isorhythmic construction. In earlier times, however, such rhythmic complexities involved simple augmentation and diminution, as when, for example, the basic unit is in quarter notes and the variants appear in halves or eighths. Carter's technique, however, is much more subtle and involves exact metronomic timing, with the proportions—to cite the case of the Adagio of his *Cello Concerto*—set at seven to six as the eighth notes broaden from seventy per minute to sixty. Constant variety rather than repetition thus prevails in a kind of tidal motion of ebbs and flows, with constantly changing pulsations brought about by the overlapping of speeds in the various parts. Carter has said that he thinks of a work as "... one large motion including many inner ones. The motion is often circular, in that there is a recall or return of the beginning. Within this, events emerge and disappear, usually affording hints or pretexts for succeeding ones."

"I regard my scores as scenarios—auditory scenario—for performers to act out with their instruments, dramatizing the players as individuals and as participants in the ensemble," says Elliott Carter in his comments on the *String Quartet No. 2*. "To me the special teamwork of ensemble playing is very wonderful and moving, and this feeling is always an important consideration in my chamber music." In this quartet Carter sets himself the problem of how a player can remain an individual while forming part of a group—essentially the basic aspect of the individual in society. A string quartet, the composer points out, has four instruments all very much alike in sound, "so in my Second Quartet, I had the idea of composing a piece for string quartet which would be, so to speak, a 'non-string quartet,' one in which the instruments were separate in sound and character. This involved composing parts that were much more highly differentiated in pitch, rhythm, and tessatura than those of the Double Concerto because of the similarity in timbres." Each instrument, he says, maintains its own character "in a special set of melodic and harmonic intervals and of rhythms that result in four different patterns of slow and fast tempi with associated types of expression." To emphasize the distinction of the parts, the composer suggests that the players "be more widely spaced than usual on the stage so that each is clearly separated from the others." This, he feels, makes not only for a more spacious play of sound, but allows the four semi-independent parts to interact dramatically while maintaining their separate identities in a four-way "conversation and argumentation."

Each instrument is thus typecast, "for each fairly consistently invents its own material out of its own special attitude and its own repertory of musical speeds and intervals." The first violin, the composer says, "should exhibit the greatest variety of character, sometimes playing with insistent rigidity (where indicated) but more often in bravura style." It also has its intervallic idioms. While all instruments use major and minor seconds, the first violin plays mainly in minor thirds, perfect fifths, major ninths, and major tenths. "Throughout the entire Quartet," Carter continues, "the second violin acts as a moderating influence, using its pizzicato and arco notes to mark regular time, its half, or double—always at the same speed." The second fiddle therefore becomes the "square" of the group contributing an attitude of "regularity and steadiness." A marked preference for major thirds, sixths, and sevenths is noted. The viola is "entrusted with the most expressive passages featuring glissandos and portamentos," while using the more pungent augmented fourths, minor sevenths, and minor ninths. The composer conceives of the role of the cello as a "firmer, less fickle counterpart of the first violin."

While the *Second Quartet* seems as closely knit and continuous as a single movement, it nevertheless has clearly defined sections. Between the introduction and conclusion, the score distinguishes four movements punctuated by three cadenzas that act as dividers as well as devices for bringing about various instrumental confrontations and oppositions. In the introduction the instruments present themselves as personalities through the rhythms and motifs that define their individual roles and characters. The first violin then takes over the leadership in the opening Allegro fantastico by initiating the ideas and their manner of development in a "whimsical and ornate part," which is imitated by the other three, each according to his own individuality. As an interlude, the viola plays an "expressive, almost lamenting, cadenza to be confronted with explosions of what may be anger or ridicule by the other three. . . ." In the Presto scherzando the second violin takes over with characteristically square and regular rhythms. Carter comments that the second fiddle here has a "laconic, orderly character, which is sometimes humorous."

As a bridge to the third movement, the cello asserts itself in an impetuous, virtuoso cadenza with a style that approximates that of the first violin, playing, as the composer observes, while "its romantic free way is confronted by the others' insistence on strict time. . . ." The viola leads in the Andante espressivo. Then the first violin takes off in a rhapsodic cadenza, only to be faced with the stony silence of the other instruments. To show their impatience, they commence the final Allegro before the cadenza is over. Cooperation and ensemble team work supercede the previous individual leadership as the drive toward a dramatic climax gets underway. Partly led by the cello, which at one point persuades the others to join

in one of its characteristic accelerations, the fourth movement stresses a "championship" rather than a "discipleship" pattern. The conclusion is a counterpart of the introduction, returning the four instruments to the "state of individualization of the first part of the work."

Carter's *Second Quartet* might be described as a string-quartet player's quartet. Condensed and concentrated, it is concerned with what the composer terms "behavioral patterns" of time continuities, intervallic changes, and motivic lines in an "everchanging series of motives and figures having certain internal relationships with each other." Carter here reveals an enormous erudition in building up his structure in rhythmic layers with the role of the tempo being modified at each different level. As such, this masterly quartet is a reflection of the thought and meticulous craftsmanship of a major musical mind—a model for the reconciliation of the opposites of individualism and group action, of improvisatory freedom under thoughtful formal controls.

In conclusion, this review of avant-garde developments should be qualified by recalling that at the present stage of expanded historical horizons, contemporary music in the larger context is what contemporary audiences choose to listen to. Concert programs as well as recording collections reveal that Bach, Beethoven, and other classic masters enjoy a greater following on the current scene than do Karlheinz Stockhausen, John Cage, Milton Babbitt, and Elliott Carter. The approach to recent developments in music leads in many directions. It is possible to feel secure in savoring tried-and-true classics. But modern listeners, like contemporary composers, can find adventure in exploring novel ideas and unfamiliar pathways.

## THE NEW ARCHITECTURE

The strident arguments between the pure functionalism of the international style and the more humanistic orientation of Frank Lloyd Wright's organic structures have become muted in architectural developments since 1945. While Corbusier's "machines for living" still hum and whir (Pl. 69, p. 390) and Wright's more personal designs for living continue to grow (Figs. 395, 396), both sides have had to give ground when confronted in the new environment with the complex problems of increasing urbanization and megalopolis.

Today's architect has once again become the partner of the painter, sculptor, and mosaicist. From the bleak utilitarianism of the early international style, architecture has turned once more to the principle of ornamentation—not, however, extraneous embellishment or mere architectural embroidery, but the inclusion of sculptures and murals as integral parts of the larger architectonic statement. Well-placed sculptural groups, frescoes, or mosaics as points of interest can always give definition to exteriors and interiors; serve as symbols of human involvement or images of social activities; and an unexpected turn here or twist there can create an element of fantasy, whimsy, warmth, and delight.

The continuity of the international tradition, appropriately modified, can be seen on the New York skyline in two striking examples—Lever House (Fig. 424) and the Seagram Building (Fig. 425). Here, the architects have offset the pronounced verticality of early skyscrapers by limiting the number of stories, setting the structures back from the street, and adding to them a horizontal base that becomes the pedestal on which the buildings are balanced. Lever House is cantilevered outward beyond its structural supports to allow the great rise of gleaming translucent glass wall to reflect the city and sky with mirrorlike brightness. By omitting the ground floor and reducing the supporting steel shafts to a minimum, the architects created a small public garden and an open passageway at the street level.

The Seagram Building has been called by its designers, Miës van der Rohe and Philip Johnson, the "Tower of Light" (Fig. 425). Open at the ground level, the building is supported by stilts whose functionalism is offset by outdoor pools and gardens sunk into a pink granite platform. The tower of smoky-amber glass is cantilevered over bronze-colored steel piers to impart a light airiness to the soaring mass. With

a taste for the structurally spare, Miës went beyond mere practicality and delighted in the proportions of his buildings and reveled in the beauty of their materials. While baser metals would have been equally functional, Miës showed extreme sensitivity to the qualities and potentialities of his chosen materials. In the Seagram Building the bronze finish of the rising lines is alternately smooth and textured to provide an interesting contrapuntal pattern.

Le Corbusier, who was also a painter of note, allowed more color, poetry, and freedom to enter the designs of his later architecture. His pilgrimage church of Notre-Dame-du-Haut at Ronchamp (Fig. 426), high up in the Vosges Mountains of southeastern France, is a delightful fantasy of free sculpturesque forms in ferroconcrete and stained glass. A prowlike roof harkens back to the early Christian meaning of the word *nave,* which signified a "ship" steering its way through the stormy seas of life toward a haven of refuge.

The grandeur of the exterior of Ronchamp has the power to rival the splendid natural setting, but the interior offers the intimacy of human scale (Fig. 427). Years before, Le Corbusier and his associates had devised a proportional system based on 7½ feet, the approximate height attainable by an average man when standing with an arm raised. Using this dimension as a basic unit of measure, the architect felt confident of achieving in his structures a scale suitable to the human being's sense of himself.

right: **Plate 75.** JOSEF ALBERS. *Homage to the Square, Early Diary.* 1955. Oil on Masonite, 15″ square. Nebraska Art Association, Lincoln (Thomas C. Woods Fund). (See p. 412.)

below: **Plate 76.** JOSEF ALBERS. *Homage to the Square: Ascending.* 1953. Oil on composition board, 43½″ square. Whitney Museum of American Art, New York. (See p. 412.)

**above left: Plate 77.** Henri
Matisse. *The Snail.* 1953. Gouache
on cut-and-pasted paper, 9'4'' ×
9'5''. Tate Gallery, London (courtesy of the Trustees). (See p. 412.)

**above right: Plate 78.** Kenneth
Noland. *Blue Minor.* 1968.
Acrylic on canvas, 3'1½'' × 7'9''.
Collection Mr. and Mrs. Robert
Kardon, Gladwyne, Pa. (See
p. 412.)

**right: Plate 79.** Frank Stella.
*Sinjerli Variation IV.* 1968. Fluor-
escent acrylic on canvas, dia-
meter 10'. Collection Mr. and
Mrs. Burton Tremaine, Meriden,
Conn. (See p. 412.)

right: **Plate 80.** HELEN FRANKENTHALER. *Formation.* 1963. Acrylic on canvas, 6'4" × 5'5". Collection Alexis Gregory, New York. (See p. 413.)

**Plate 81.** LARRY POONS. *Han-San Cadence.* 1963. Acrylic and fabric dye on canvas, 6' × 11'2''. Collection Des Moines Art Center, Iowa (Coffin Fine Arts Trust Fund). (See p. 414.)

**Plate 82.** RICHARD ESTES. *Storefront.* 1972. Oil on canvas, $32\frac{1}{8}$ × $44\frac{1}{8}$''. Collection Frances and Sydney Lewis, Richmond, Va. (See p. 419.)

On the interior, the south wall may well be one of the great surfaces in the history of architecture (Fig. 427). The pitch, curve, and massiveness of the wall suggest living strength and vitality, but its fine, expressive beauty derives from the inspired subtlety with which the apertures have been coordinated through their differences not only in scale, proportion, color, and decoration but also in the angles of their reveals or niches. Here and there on the stained glass have been painted those ancient praises of the Virgin: *Je vous salue Marie, pleine de grâce* ("Hail Mary, full of grace"). At Ronchamp, Le Corbusier achieved an interior whose richness and complexity are functionally appropriate to the enactment of the rites of holy mystery.

In the closing years of his notable career, Frank Lloyd Wright finally received a commission to construct a building in his country's largest city—the Solomon R. Guggenheim Museum, a gallery for abstract art (Fig. 428). For Wright a museum should never be a group of boxlike compartments but a continuous flow of floor space in which the eye encounters no obstruction. To achieve this ideal, he designed a single, round room of reinforced concrete nearly 100 feet in diameter, with a hollow cylindrical center core surmounted by a wire-glass dome 92 feet above ground (Fig. 429). Spiraling upward around the room, traversing a distance of a quarter of a mile, is an open 6-story cantilevered ramp rising at a 3 percent grade and broadening from a width of 17 feet at its lowest level to almost 35 feet at the top. Throngs of spectators can be accommodated without congestion as they move easily up or down the ramp. The visitor can take the elevator to the top level and wind downward at leisure, or he can start at the bottom and walk up. He can inspect part of the exhibit at close range and at eye level or view three levels simultaneously across the open room.

Pier Luigi Nervi and Eero Saarinen, in their imaginative solutions to the problems of contemporary building, have achieved a working synthesis by providing for the functional needs of the many without sacrificing beauty of design and style. Nervi's Palazzetto dello Sport is, as the title suggests, a sports palace erected in Rome for the 1960 Olympic games (Figs. 430, 431). The **Y**-shaped ferroconcrete columns are like caryatids in their suggestion of human forms whose outstretched arms seem to converge in a concerted muscular effort to support the spreading shell.

The new technology has greatly expanded the possibilities inherent in dome construction. Buckminster Fuller's geodesic domes span large light-filled spaces with airiness and strength. "Bucky's biggest bubble," as his friends dubbed the project for the United States Pavilion at the Montreal Exposition of 1967, is a three-quarter sphere that measures 250 feet in diameter and 200 feet in height and encloses almost

**above: 429.** FRANK LLOYD WRIGHT. Interior, Solomon R. Guggenheim Museum. 1957–59. Ramp over $\frac{1}{4}$ mile long.

**right: 430.** PIER LUIGI NERVI. Palazzetto dello Sport, Rome. 1960.

**below right: 431.** Interior, Palazzetto dello Sport.

**below: 432.** R. BUCKMINSTER FULLER. United States Pavilion at Expo 67, Montreal. Geodesic dome constructed of steel pipes and transparent acrylic, diameter 250'.

forms. Embellishing this are plugs of lead that fill the tie-holes left when the forms were removed. Kahn designed the structure to function but also to "have the sense of man," a human quality. In the Salk Institute at La Jolla he provided an environment to "engage the full sentient capacities of the men who are its occupants."

In revolt against the entire myth and tradition of the hero-architect and of his work as a monument standing sublimely aloof from all that surrounds it is Kahn's former student Robert Venturi, of the Philadelphia firm of Venturi & Rauch, along with his wife, planner Denise Scott Brown (Fig. 439). The title of Venturi's book—*Complexity and Contradiction in Architecture* (1966)—and those of two studies—*Learning from Las Vegas* and *Learning from Levittown*—suggest the challenge that these new architect-designers have put to modernist dogma. Noting that environment, more than monuments, is the reality of human experience, the Venturis declare that "the world can't wait for the architect to build his utopia, and the architect's concern ought not to be with what it ought to be but with what it is—and with how to help improve it now. This is a humbler role for architects than the modern movement has wanted to accept." Thus, the Venturis have sought out the urban environment on its own terms, because it is there, and because it is there, they have studied the highway strip and the subdivision, to see why and how these ubiquitous and despised features of the modern scene may have the vigor to make chaos work.

With insight and analysis, the Venturis have reasoned back through the history of style and symbolism so as to come forward with a concept of a new architecture capable of responding to the speed and mobility of a society caught in the never-ending cycle of changing life styles. Admirers of pop art, the Venturis accept the premise of the commonplace and of the cheap, expedient, and practical ways that mass culture has of serving its needs. But like the pop artists, they possess the education, wit, and irony to deal in paradox and perversity. They point out that having renounced decoration, modernist architects manipulate structural forms until the entire building takes on the quality of decorative sculpture. Using the theory of the building as a symbol, they cite the building on the highway in the shape of a duck (the sales outlet for a duck farm)—and say they design "ducks" and "decorated sheds." The Venturis even think Main Street "is almost all right." The dictum of Miës van der Rohe (Fig. 425) was: "Less is more." The Venturis turn this inside out and assert that "more is not less."

Taking the label meant as an insult from an outraged modernist, the Venturis call their work "dumb and ordinary," all the while they are filtering the ordinary through their taste and erudition until it becomes the extraordinary. A case in point is Guild

below: 437. Louis I. Kahn. Salk Institute of Biological Studies, La Jolla, Calif. 1968.

bottom: 438. Plan and section of Salk Institute of Biological Studies.

**439.** Venturi & Rauch, with Cope & Lippincott, associate architects, and the assistance of Gerod Clark. Guild House, Philadelphia. 1965.

House (Fig. 439), an apartment building sponsored by the Society of Friends to house elderly tenants who wanted to remain in the old neighborhood, a lower-middle-class district of Philadelphia. With utmost candor, it recalls "traditional Philadelphia row houses, or even tenement backs of Edwardian apartment houses." But all sorts of mannered elements—from the emphatic façade, through the notched shadow of the recessed entrance, the extreme left and right alignment of trimless, slightly overscaled but "standard" double-hung windows, the single, central arch form in an otherwise rectilinear design, the narrow white band running horizontally at the next-to-top story, the colorism of the materials, to the pop sign mounted like a movie marquee and the rooftop flourish in the purely decorative and nonfunctional wire sculpture formed like a television antenna—give it away that here a highly personal, idiosyncratic intelligence has been at work—to make the educated viewer feel compelled to look again, to discover why the commonplace seems so uncommon. This is contradictory and complex, like life, and in a time when construction costs make the dumb and ordinary inevitable, it may prove a valid response to the complex and contradictory needs of modern life.

## IDEAS: EXISTENTIALISM

The 20th century has witnessed vast advances in scientific knowledge, the development of nuclear energy, the expansion of electronic communications, the convenience of jet transportation, the computerization of knowledge, the exploitation of the wealth of nations, the exploration of the moon and planets, and

significant breakthroughs in the ways man perceives his world through art, music, poetry, and literature. At the same time the same century has seen carnage on the unparalleled scale of two world wars plus the Korean and Indo-China conflicts, attempted genocide of massive proportions, an ever-widening gulf between the benefits of wealth for some and the deprivations of poverty for others, and confrontation with the possibility of the imminent obliteration of the human race.

The bomb, in fact, has confronted everyone with a doomsday frame of mind, and it haunts present-day life and art like a specter at the feast. The potential obliteration of the planet has torn asunder the sense of vital continuity and futurity, whether this may be sought in the biosphere by living on through one's children, or theologically by belief in a life after death, or through nature, which will go on into eons of geological time, or in creativity by which one's work can influence unborn generations to come. The possibility of a sudden end to the human species has led to a psychological disorientation that makes the past seem obsolete if not abhorrent for the very reason of its having produced this impass, which renders the present futile and meaningless and any future ridiculous and fanciful. Certainly such an attitude is reflected in the arts, where the critical measurement of contemporary works by past standards of classical craftsmanship and excellence has broken down, and where traditional forms have fragmented and fallen into disintegration. Artists may now feel that they are creating only for the moment rather than for the future, and a neodadaist sense of absurdity and futility pervades many of their works. Ultimately, if nothing is going to last, why bother to write it down, paint it, or compose it? Why not just consider art as a strategy of the imagination, as the inspiration or fantasy of a pipe dream. What else is a happening except something that is immediately experienced, then ceases to exist?

Yet such a confrontation with extinction can be the greatest challenge to the affirmation of life. As expressed in the pursuit of knowledge and the enjoyment of the arts, living on the brink has the effect of making each moment count. None is more aware of this challenge than the artist. Whether poet, painter or composer, the will to create works that reveal the myriad possibilities in human attitudes, insights, and lifestyles is irresistible.

Of all recent philosophies, *existentialism* perhaps comes closest to comprehending the overall current artistic situation. The rational man of Aristotle and Descartes declared: "I think therefore I am." A more emotional and romantic counterpart might say: "I feel therefore I am." All existential man can do is utter: "I exist therefore I am." Getting down to bare essentials, deeds, actions, and attitudes are the affirmation of his being. Existentialism spreads a large ideational umbrella over the broadest range of choices, possibilities, and contingencies. It can include pessimism and optimism, tragedy and comedy, despair and hope, skepticism and faith, destruction and construction, the absurd and the serious, the trivial and the sublime, negation and affirmation, rejection and conviction, together with all degrees in between. In music existentialism allows the improvisatory happenings of a John Cage to coexist alongside the mathematical computerization of Milton Babbitt's programmed compositions. Existential thought also allowed the abstract expressionists to develop individual styles within the field of abstraction. Theirs was a solemn style involving deep commitment to the image of order through sweeping statements of epical scope. The philosophy also makes room for the reduction to absurdity of neodadaism and pop art, as well as the surrealistic assemblages of miscellaneous objects found in the works of Robert Rauschenberg.

Existentialism is essentially the ultimate humanism. For one must constantly ask: What does it mean to exist? What is human existence like? How does it feel to be human? In this world of infinite possibilities, any choice or action is of necessity not derived from, directed toward, or done for the sake of anything else. Everything can be, but nothing has to be, or must be. With existentialism all art might be said to approach the condition of still-life painting—everything is, nothing is becoming, nor does it have any need to become.

In the world of Jean Paul Sartre existence precedes essence. First man must exist, project his image, define himself, and draw his portrait through the actions he takes and the works of art he creates. Man is condemned to be free, and the only limit to his freedom is freedom itself. One of the corollaries of Sartre's thought is the essential absurdity of life. As the notion of the absurd appears in existentialist art and drama, it takes on a very grim coloration. There is nothing lighthearted about it. Samuel Beckett's 1953 play *Waiting for Godot* (a paraphrase of the existentialist philosopher Martin Heidegger's dictum "waiting for God") unfolds in a series of inconsequential episodes that reveal the endless tedium and futility of life. As Macbeth says when tragedy closes in on him,

> Tomorrow, and tomorrow, and tomorrow,
> Creeps in this petty pace from day to day,
> To the last syllable of recorded time;
> And all our yesterdays have lighted fools
> The way to dusty death. Out, out, brief candle!
> Life's but a walking shadow; a poor player,
> That struts and frets his hour upon the stage,
> And then is heard no more: it is a tale
> Told by an idiot, full of sound and fury,
> Signifying nothing.

For Sartre death is the ultimate absurdity. He would agree with Leonardo da Vinci who observed

that when he thought he was learning to live, he was only learning to die. Paradoxically, one cannot know life until confronted with death, or experience affirmation until one encounters negation. All life, human or otherwise, has a death sentence hanging over it. There can be no sunshine without shadow, no light without darkness. In life there is always the imminent presence of death, in victory the specter of defeat, and every joy is haunted by sadness.

Further along the line of recent thought, existentialism and its more systematic companion *phenomenology* have faced up to the full implications of the objective knowledge produced by modern science. Astronomers have revealed that the multiverse surrounding the earth was produced by one or more cosmic explosions, which yielded the solar system as a mere byproduct. Any order that is perceived becomes not a part of things out there but a mental construct that an individual mind may impose upon it. Biochemists have affirmed that life is also the result of one or more biological accidents. In a cogent and challenging book entitled *Chance and Necessity* (1970) the Nobel-Prize-winning biochemist Jacques Monod points out that eons ago quite by chance certain proteins and nucleic acids somehow combined to create metabolism and the reproduction of cells. As he remarks, "We would like to think ourselves necessary, inevitable, ordained from all eternity. All religions, nearly all philosophies, and even a part of science testify to the unwearying, heroic effort of mankind desperately denying his own contingency."

Man, then, faces an environment that is oblivious to his hopes and fears, blind to his arts, deaf to his poetry and music. He is at last alone in the immensity of a multiverse that is neither hostile nor benevolent but totally indifferent. Gone with the existentialist winds are the gods and original sin, gone are the heroes and villains, gone is the tribal fiction of a chosen people, gone are the determinisms of heredity and environment, and equally gone are the preconceptions of the past. Suddenly all taboos, religious beliefs, moral codes, traditional folkways have been swept away. Despite all the mythical, religious, philosophical ideologies that have arisen over the ages to affirm the existence of some cosmic eternal laws; despite the myriad social structures that have developed from Cro-Magnon times to the present; despite man's prodigious proliferation of knowledge in all fields over the past centuries; despite all histories that unfold according to some evolutionary, necessary, and propitious plan that affirms the ascent of man—all that the sum total of human knowledge and experience can show is that man faces an endless abyss, utter solitude, and complete isolation.

So man must now look himself directly in the eye and freely make his own decisions and assume the responsibility for his own heritage. He alone controls the meaning and values he accepts or rejects. He is, in fact, right back to primeval chaos. Indeed, the great illusion is that he ever left it. Faced with an infinity of choices, he can create a new set of values, a new humanism, new expressions in the arts—new because these values are not categorical imperatives imposed from on high, valid for all time and eternity, but because they are man's and man's alone, a new covenant in a new world in which he chooses to live, move, and have his being. Man is alone, he simply *is*. But being can mean that man can choose to be a creative animal. The spiritual kingdom, the creative power, and the full glory are now within man himself.

To the existentialist world view, all works of art are creative acts in the face of nothingness. The artist can do something or nothing, become god or beast, Prometheus or Lucifer. Mythology becomes fact insofar as metaphor and fiction are products of men's imagination and fact for the reason that men have believed in them, acted upon them, written, built, carved, and composed because of them.

What is relevant for the contemporary audience as well as for the modern artist is the great growth of knowledge about past and present, plus the easy accessibility to the vast body of literature, art, and music across the ages. So with the multiplicity of media at his command, with the tremendous extension in the span of human experience, with so many levels of taste, with the multinational and international frames of reference, the artist and his audience have an unlimited number of choices. These range from the traditional to the experimental, from the manipulation of mathematical formulas to chance and random happenings, from logical and cyclical wholes (as in classical symphonies and dramas) to fragmented reflections of a broken and distorted world, from the historical repertory in recorded and live performances to acoustical jungles and electronic collages, from the revival of ancient media such as frescoes and mosaics to exploring Plexiglas and plastic fantasies, from static sculptures that rest securely on pedestals to mobiles and kinetic art in mechanical motion, from works limited to a single medium to multimedia mixtures of all the arts. So when it comes to doing one's own thing, the bewildering problem is that there are so many possible things to do.

All art past and present becomes contemporary by virtue of its living presence in the here and now. In the larger picture, 20th-century art is not only abstraction. Cubism and expressionism, aleatory and computerized music, soaring structures of steel and glass are but a few within the wide range of choices. For all the arts of man, over all ages of time, all reaches of space are now contemporary art. The Parthenon, Chartres Cathedral, the Sistine Chapel, quite as much as the Guggenheim Museum, Lincoln Center, and the Trans World Flight Center, the paintings of Giotto, Rembrandt, and Picasso, the music of Bach, Wagner, and Stravinsky—all exist in the expanded present. Ultimately it is up to the contemporary reader, viewer, and listener to choose whether he wants to read Plato or Sartre, to look at Praxiteles' statues or at those of David Smith, to listen to Gregorian chant or to Babbitt's computerized compositions. The outlines of the past, present, and future have become blurred, just as in cubist and abstract-expressionist painting spatiality has flattened out. In modern literature, music, and films time is experienced in a flowing continuum as in dreams, with flashes backward and forward. Foreground, middle ground, background; beginning, middle, end; past, present, future—are all telescoped together. The new is also the old, and the old ever new.

All man has at his command are the spark of life and a moment in time. When man chooses the creative life, his creativity can bring forth new forces and forms. From the void of the mind and the range of experience, the artist catches a glimpse of order, even if that order seems to be contrived or controlled chaos as some contemporary works of art might appear. Whether the artist goes to nature for his inspiration, to classical ruins, to the supermarket, or to the junkyard, it has always been the age-old prerogative of the artist to find poetry where no one has perceived it before.

So, in effect, man has arrived simultaneously at the brink of a fathomless future and right back to primeval chaos, when, as the Book of Genesis records, "... the earth was without form, and void; and darkness was on the face of the deep." Looking out over the vast panorama of human experience the wise words of the sage of Ecclesiastes also come to mind: "The thing that hath been, it is that which shall be; and that which is done is that which shall be done: and there is nothing new under the sun."

Now that humanity can rekindle the fires of faith and reassert creative forces, the arts become focal points in the act of reaffirmation. In the brave new world that stretches ahead, visual artists have found scope for their pictorial projections, modern architects regard the needs of the pluralistic society as a renewed challenge to their powers, writers have discovered many new avenues for communication in the new media, and contemporary composers have reveled in the possibilities of novel sound.

This, then, is the exciting and exhilarating challenge of our time. For man can pursue the trivialities or sublimities of life, leap into the gaping abyss, wallow in the primordial ooze, or else create some mode of order in a world of arts and ideas. As the philosopher Nietzsche said in *So Spake Zarathustra*, you must have chaos in you to give birth to a dancing star. "I say unto you: you still have chaos in yourselves." So it becomes possible to foresee a shining creative future, a whole galaxy of dancing stars. Because when we look at the world around us, the supply of chaos seems truly inexhaustible.

# Glossary

Within the definitions *italics* have been used to indicate terms that themselves are defined in the glossary and, in a few instances, to distinguish terms that fundamentally belong to languages other than English.

**abacus** (ahb'-ah-kus) In an *architectural column*, the uppermost member of the *capital*; the slab upon which rests the *architrave*.

**abstract** See *abstraction*.

**abstraction** In the *visual arts*, the essential rather than the particular, in certain instances even the *ideal*. The process of subordinating the real appearance of *forms* in nature to an *aesthetic* concept of form composed of *shapes, lines, colors, values*, etc. Also, the process of analyzing, simplifying, and distilling the essence from nature and sense experience. The opposite of *concretion*. See *nonrepresentational* art.

**academy** Derived from the name of the grove, the Akademeia, where Plato held his philosophical seminars. In modern history, from the French Académie des Beaux-Arts, the term has often been applied to conservative and traditional *forms*. It came to signify the *cultural* and artistic establishment exercising teaching and standard-maintaining responsibilities.

**a cappella** (ah kah-pehl'-lah) Italian for "in the *chapel* style"; that is, human *voices* without *instrumental accompaniment*.

**accompaniment** The music supporting a soloist or group of performers; music subordinate to the *melody*.

**accompany** See *accompaniment*.

**acoustics** That having to do with the nature and character of sound.

**acrylic, acrylic resin** A clear plastic used as a *vehicle* in paints and as a *casting* material in *sculpture*.

**action theater** A contemporary phenomenon in which *plays*, happenings, and other types of performance are strongly committed to broad moral and social issues with the overt purpose of effecting a change for the better in society at large. The actors may actually confront the audience directly, even move among its members, so as to engage them in dialogue and debate.

**adagio** (ah-dah'-zh-yoh) Italian for "slow"; in musical *composition* an instruction to the performer.

**aerial perspective** See *perspective*.

**aesthetic** Having to do with the pleasurable and beautiful as opposed to the useful, practical, scientific, etc. The distinctive vocabulary of a given *style*. An aesthetic response is the perception and enjoyment of a work of art.

**aesthetics** A branch of philosophy having to do with the nature of beauty and art and their relation to man.

**agitato** (ah-gee-tah'-toh) Italian for "agitated" or "restless."

**agora** (ah'-gho-rah) In ancient Greek cities, could assemble and hold meetings.

**air** A simple *song*, not to be confused with *aria*.

**aisle** In *basilican architecture*, the longitudinal *spaces* situated parallel to the *nave* and *formed* by *walls, arcades*, and *colonnades*.

**aleatory music** From the Latin for "gamble," a music that is uncontrolled or left to chance. Whatever the elements introduced by the *composer*, their disposition is left to the performer or to circumstance.

**allegory** *Expression* by means of *symbols* so as to make a more effective generalization or moral commentary about human experience than could be achieved by direct or literal means.

**allegro** (ah-leh'-groh) Italian for "fast," "brisk," or "merry."

**altar** Originally a stone slab or table where offerings were made or victims sacrificed; in the Christian era, a raised *structure* in a church at which the sacrament of the Holy Eucharist is consecrated; a center of worship and ritual.

**altarpiece** A painted or *sculptured panel* placed above and behind an *altar* as an object capable of inspiring religious devotion.

**alto** The lowest *range* of the female *voice*; also known as *contralto*. Too, the *line* in musical writing corresponding to the alto range. In addition, an *instrument* with this range.

**ambulatory** A covered passage for walking, found around the *apse* or *choir* of a church, in a *cloister*, or along the *peristyle* of an ancient Greek temple.

**analogous forms** *Forms* that relate to each other *compositionally* because of their *size, shape, color, texture*, etc.

**andante** (ahn-dahn'-teh) Italian for "moderately slow."

**anthem** An inspirational *song*, usually nationalistic; a *choral* selection performed as part of a sacred service.

**anthropomorphic** Human characteristics attributed to nonhuman things.

**antiphony** Music in which two or more groups—*voices* or *instruments*—alternate with one another.

**apotheosis** Deification, or the realization of a divine status.

**apse** (aap'-ss) A large nichelike *space*—usually semicircular in *shape* and *domed* or *vaulted*—projecting from and extending the interior space of such *architectural forms* as Roman and Christian *basilicas*. Most often found at the eastern end of a church *nave* and serving to house the high *altar*.

**apsidal** (aap-sigh'-dahl) See *apse*.

**arcade** A series of *arches supported* by *piers* or *columns*; passageways with arched roofs.

**arch** See Fig. 83.

**architectonic** Overall *design* and *composition*, that which is *structural*.

**architectural** See *architecture* and *structure*.

**architecture** The science and art of building for human use, including *design*, construction, and decorative treatment.

**architrave** (ahr'-kuh-trayv) In *post-and-lintel* architecture, the *lintel* or lowest division of the *entablature* that rests directly upon the *capitals* of columns.

**archivolt** (ahr'-chuh-vohlt) The *molding* that frames an *arch*.

**area** Extent, *range*, or scope, having the character of *space*, whether two- or three-dimensional.

**aria** (ah'-ree-ah) A fairly complex *song* for solo singer and *instrumental accompaniment* occurring normally in *cantatas, oratorios*, and *operas*.

**arpeggio** (ahr-pehj'-gee-oh) The *notes* of a *chord played* successively rather than simultaneously, in either ascending or descending *order* and throughout one or more *octaves*.

**assemblage** (ah-sehm'-bledge; also aa-sahmh-blahj') The technique of creating three-dimensional works of art by combining a variety of elements—such as *found objects*—into a *compositional* whole.

**atmospheric perspective** See *perspective*.

**atonality** The character of music in which no particular *pitch* serves as the *tonic* or *key note*.

**augmentation** In music, a technique for slowing down a phrase or *theme* by increasing (usually doubling) its *note values*.

**avant-garde** (ah-vahn-gahrd') French meaning "advanced guard"; a term used to designate innovators whose experimental art challenges the *values* of the *cultural* establishment or even those of the immediately preceeding avant-garde *styles*.

**axis** An imaginary *line* passing through a figure, building, or groups of *forms* about which component elements are organized, their direction and focus actually establishing the axis.

**background** In the *pictorial* arts, that part of the *composition* which appears to be behind *forms represented* as close to the viewer; the most distant of the three zones conceived in *linear perspective* to exist in deep *space*, beyond the *foreground* and *middle ground*. See *perspective, relief*.

**balance** In *composition*, the equilibrium of opposing or self-completing forces.

**ballad** A narrative *song* usually set to relatively simple music.

**ballet** Highly *stylized dancing* for *aesthetic* or theatrical, rather than social, purposes, in which often are involved elements of *plot* or narrative, costumes, scenery, and musical *accompaniment*.

**band** A music *ensemble* consisting of *woodwind, brass*, and *percussion instruments*, but no *strings*.

**bar** See *measure*.

**baritone** The male vocal *range* between the high of the *tenor* and the low of the *bass*.

**barrel vault** See Fig. 83.

**basilica** A rectangular-*plan* building, with an *apse* at one or both ends, originating in Roman *secular architecture* as a hall and early adopted as the *form* most suited to the needs of Christian architecture.

**basilican** See *basilica*.

**bas-relief** (bah ruh-leef') See *relief*.

**bass** The lowest *range* of the male *voice*. Also, the lowest vocal or *instrumental line* in musical writing. Too, an instrument with the range to play these *notes*. The notes to the music for this range appear on a *staff* identified by a *bass clef* (𝄢).

**basso**  Italian for *bass*.

**basso continuo**  See *continuo*.

**bay**  In *basilican architecture*, the *space* defined at four corners by the principal upright *structural* members, with the character of the space usually established by the need to sustain aloft the great weight of a *vault*.

**beat**  In music, the unit for measuring time.

**binder**  (bighn'-dehr)  See *painting, vehicle.*

**biomorphic**  In the *visual* or *plastic arts, imagery* derived from, but not necessarily an imitation of, the *forms* of living things.

**brass instruments**  The trumpet, French horn, trombone, and tuba, all of which have metal mouthpieces for blowing and a tube *shape* that flares into an opening like a bell.

**buttress**  A *support*, usually an exterior projection of *masonry* or wood, for a *wall, arch*, or *vault*, that opposes the lateral *thrust* of these *structural* elements.

**cadence**  A point of rest, pause, or conclusion in a musical *composition*; a strong, regular *rhythm* as in a march.

**cadenza**  In music for solo *voice* or *instrument* a free or florid passage inserted by the *composer* or *improvised* by the performer, usually toward the end of an *aria* or *movement*, whose purpose is to display the performer's technical brilliance.

**canon**  A body of principles, rules, standards, or norms; a criterion for establishing *measure, scale*, and *proportion*. In music, a type of strict *imitative counterpoint*, wherein the *melody* stated by one *voice* is imitated in its entirety by a second voice, which enters before the previous one has concluded.

**cantata**  (kahn-tah'-tah)  Italian for music that is "sung," as opposed to music that is *played*, which in Italian goes by the term *sonata*. In the 17th-century sense of Bach, Scarlatti, and Handel, a multimovement *composition* for solo *voices, chorus*, and *orchestra* consisting of *recitatives* and *arias* for performance in church or chamber. Briefer than *oratorio* but, like oratorio, differs from *opera* in being mainly nontheatrical.

**cantilever**  In *architecture*, a *lintel* or beam that extends beyond its *supports*.

**cantus firmus**  (kahn'-toos feer' moos)  Latin for "fixed song," a preexistent *melody* that medieval and Renaissance *composers* used as the basis for *polyphonic* pieces in which they added new melodies above and/or below the cantus firmus.

**canvas**  A fabric woven of cotton or linen and used as the *support* for *painting*. Also called *duck*, especially when made of cotton.

**capital**  The upper member of a *column*, serving as transition from shaft to *lintel* or *architrave*.

**caricature**  An amusing distortion or exaggeration of something so familiar it would be recognized even in the distortion.

**cartoon**  A full-*scale*, preparatory *drawing* for a *pictorial composition*, usually a large one such as a *wall painting* or a tapestry. Also a humorous drawing or *caricature*.

**casein**  (kay-seen')  Made of milk protein, a *binder* for paint.

**cast**  The molded replica made by the *casting* process.

**casting**  A process using plaster, clay, wax, or metal that, in a liquid form, is poured into a mold. When the liquid has solidified, the mold is removed, leaving a replica of the original work of art from which the mold was taken.

**catharsis**  The purgation or purification of the emotions through the experience of art, the result of which is spiritual release and renewal.

**cathedra**  An episcopal throne, or throne for a bishop; also known for its Latin name *sedes* or "see."

**cathedral**  The official church of a bishop containing his *cathedra* or throne; a church that traditionally has been given *monumental* and magnificent *architectural form*.

**cella**  An enclosed windowless chamber, the essential feature of a *classical* temple, in which the *cult* statue usually stood.

**central plan**  In *architecture*, an organization in which *spaces* and *structural* elements are *ordered* round a central point.

**chamber music**  Music for small groups.

**chanson de geste**  (shahnh-sohnh' duh jhehst')  French for "song of heroic deeds"; an *epic* poem written in Old French during the 11th to 13th centuries and designed to be performed by *minstrels* and *jongleurs*.

**chant**  In *liturgical* music, a single *melody* for *voice* or *chorus* that is *monophonic*, un*accompanied*, and in free *rhythm*.

**chapel**  A small church or compartment within a church, castle, or palace containing an *altar* consecrated for ritual use.

**choir**  An organized group of singers or *instrumentalists* of the same class. A division of angels. In *basilican-plan* church *architecture*, the complex at the east end beyond the *crossing*, which could include *apse, ambulatory*, and radiating *chapels*.

**choral**  That having to do with *chorus*.

**chorale**  From the German for *choral song* or *hymn*, a term for the type of devotional *tune* introduced in the 16th century by Martin Luther. The term can also serve as a synonym for *choir* or *chorus*.

**chord**  Any combination of three or more *tones* or *pitches* sounded simultaneously.

**chordal**  See *chord*.

**chorus**  In ancient Greek drama, a group of singers and dancers commenting on the main action. In modern times, a *choir* or group of singers organized to perform in *concert* with one another. Music *composed* for such a group.

**chroma**  In *color*, the purity of a *hue*; synonymous with *intensity* and *saturation*.

**chromatic**  From *chroma*; in the *visual arts*, that which has a full or broad *range* of color.

**chromatic scale**  In Western music, the full set of *tones* or *pitches* available in an *octave*, or all the piano's white and black *notes* for an octave. The opposite of the *diatonic scale*, whose pitches would be sounded by the piano's white notes within an octave.

**civilization**  A *culture* in an advanced state of self-realization, thought to be characterized by marked efficiency and achievement in such realms as art, science, and letters, as well as in personal security and dignity.

**classical**  All that relates to the *civilizations* of Greece and Rome, and subsequent *stylistic* imitations of Western antiquity. Classical can also mean established excellence, whatever the period, *style*, or *form*.

**clearstory**  A row of windows in the upper part of a *wall*; also, in church *architecture*, the upper portion of the interior walls pierced by windows for the admission of light.

**clef**  French for "key"; in musical *composition*, a sign placed at the beginning of a *staff* to determine the placement of *notes*. See *bass, treble*.

**cloister**  A *monastic* establishment; more particularly, a covered passage, usually *arcaded*, at the side of or surrounding a courtyard within a complex of monastic buildings.

**coda**  Italian for "tail"; in music the term characterizes the terminal section of a *movement* or *composition* that uses previously heard *thematic* material in a sort of summing-up conclusion.

**collage**  (kohl-lahzh')  From *papiers collés*, the French for "pasted papers"; a *composition* deriving from cubism and made by pasting together on a flat *surface* such originally unrelated materials as bits of newspaper, wallpaper, cloth, cigarette packages, and printed photographs.

**colonnade**  A row of *columns* usually spanned or connected by *lintels*.

**colonnette**  A small *column*, performing a decorative as well as a *structural* function.

**color**  A perceived quality in direct light or in objects reflecting light that varies with the wavelength of the light energy, the brilliance of the light source, and the degree to which objects reflect or absorb the light energy falling on them. In paint, color is the light-reflecting and -absorbing characteristic, which is a function of the *pigment* giving the paint its primary visual identity.

**column**  A cylindrical post or *support* which often has three distinct parts: base, shaft, and *capital*.

**comedy**  A light and amusing *play* or other literary work whose purpose is to arouse laughter in the beholder.

**comic**  See *comedy*.

**complementary colors**  Two contrasting *hues* that are found opposite each other on a color wheel, which hues neutralize one another when combined (such as red and green) and mutually intensify when placed adjacent to one other.

**compose**  See *composition*.

**composer**  The writer of music or of musical *composition*.

**composition**  An organization or arrangement imposed upon the component elements within an individual work of art.

**compound pier**  In *architecture*, a *pier* with *columns* and *pilasters* bundled or clustered together, with each component usually responding to a member in the *ribs* and *vaults*.

**compression**  In *architecture*, stress that results from two forces moving toward each other, as in dead weight or squeezing.

**concert** In music, artists performing together for an audience, or a single artist performing for an audience (a situation also known as a *recital*). Unison, agreement, or *harmony* among two or more factors.

**concerting style** In music, a *style* that developed in 16th-century Venice by pitting *choirs*, *ensembles*, or soloists against one another in a variety of contrasting manners—slow *tempo* versus fast, *polyphony* versus *homophony*, soft versus loud, etc.

**concertino** (kahn-chair-teen'-oh) A small or solo *ensemble* within a *concerto grosso*. Also a short *concerto*.

**concerto** (kahn-chair'-toh) A multi*movement instrumental composition* featuring a soloist (violin, piano, cello, etc.) pitted against a full *orchestra*.

**concerto grosso** (kahn-chair'-toh grow' soh) A multi*movement instrumental composition* in which a small solo *ensemble* (the *concertino*) is contrasted to the full *orchestra*.

**concretion** Having to do with the physical actuality of things, in all their particular and peculiar details. For the realist artist, the process of *rendering* the *surface* appearance of *forms* in nature, or *representing* them as palpable and precisely as the eye would perceive them. The opposite of *abstraction*.

**connoisseurship** A discriminating knowledge of the qualities of art works and their *styles*.

**consonance** In *tonal harmony*, two or more *pitches* that when sounded simultaneously do not create *tension*. Since consonance occurs in an established tonal system when only the tones of that system are used, it creates the effect of stability and repose. The opposite is *dissonance*.

**construct** See *construction*.

**construction** In *sculpture*, the process of making a *form* by assembling and joining a wide variety of materials, such as wood, cardboard, plastic, paper, and metal. See *assemblage*.

**content** See *expressive content*.

**continuo** A *contrapuntal* concept favored by baroque *composers* in which a continuous *line* of *bass chords* underlies the upper parts of a *composition* and is sufficiently distinguishable from them to set up a polarization between the continuo and the *melody* above. Also known as "basso continuo," "continuous bass," "figured bass," and "thorough bass."

**contour** In the *pictorial arts*, an outline that forms the boundary of one *shape* and defines it in relation to other shapes and is *expressively* handled so as to suggest fullness and recession of *forms* and varieties in *texture*, such as those in body *structure* and soft tissue. Contrasts with simple outline, which is no more than the boundary of a form defining a *silhouette*.

**contralto** See *alto*.

**contrapuntal** The adjectival *form* of *counterpoint*.

**contrapposto** The disposition of the human figure in which one part is turned in a direction opposite that of the other (usually hips and legs one way, shoulder and chest

another); a counterpositioning of the body about its central *axis*.

**conventions** A formula, rule, or practice developed by the artist to create a usage or *mode* that is individual to the artist, yet communicable to the *culture* he partakes of. Conventions exist in both *form* and *subject matter*, and they constitute the vocabulary and syntax of the artist's language. Conventions can simplify certain *pictorial* problems, as when a single tree serves to *symbolize* and substitute for an entire forest.

**cool color** A *hue* generally in the blue, green, and violet section of the *spectrum*. Psychologically, cool colors tend to be calming and unemphatic; optically they often appear to recede.

**Corinthian** The most elaborate of the three *classical orders* of temple *architecture*, characterized by slender fluted *columns* topped by highly carved, ornate *capitals* whose decorative *forms* derive from the acanthus leaf.

**cornice** Any horizontal *architectural* member projecting from the top of a *wall*; in *classical* architecture the crowning member of the *entablature*.

**counterpoint** The combination of two or more independent *melodic lines* into a single musical fabric; in other words, *polyphony*.

**crescendo** (kreh-shehn'-doh) A continuous increase in loudness.

**crossing** In a *cruciform* church, the *space formed* by the intersection of *nave* and *transept*.

**cross vault** See Fig. 83.

**cruciform** Arranged or *shaped* like a cross.

**crypt** A *vaulted* chamber, wholly or partly underground, that usually houses a *chapel* and is found in a church under the *choir*.

**cult** A system of religious belief and its adherents.

**culture** The *values* and the system of their interrelationships that inform a society, motivate its behavior, and cause it to be functional to the general satisfaction of its members and to have a distinctive quality and character.

**dance** A *rhythmic* and patterned succession of bodily movements, usually performed to music.

**design** A comprehensive scheme, plan, or conception. In *painting*, the pattern organization of a *composition*, usually seen in the arrangement of *lines* or the light-and-dark elements, rather than in *color*.

**develop** See *development*.

**development** In music, the process of manipulating *themes* and *motifs* so as to expand them into larger sections of music, as in the second section of a *sonata-form movement*.

**diatonic scale** (digh-uh-tahn'-ick) In Western music, the seven *tones* or *pitches* corresponding to the piano's white *notes* in an *octave*. The opposite of *chromatic scale*.

**diminuendo** (dee-meen-oo-ehn'-doh) In music, gradually getting softer.

**diminution** In music, a technique for speeding up a phrase or *theme* by decreasing (usually halving) its *note values*.

**dissonance** In *tonal harmony*, *intervals* or *chords* that sound discordant and create the effect of instability and *tension*. The oppo-

site of *consonance*.

**divertimento** (dee-vair-tee-mehn'-toh) An *instrumental composition* originating in the 18th century for use at festive occasions, outdoor performances, or nocturnal gatherings. Such works contain from two to six or more *movements* consisting of marches, *dances*, spritely *allegros*, and at least one *andante*.

**dome** A hemispherical *vault*; theoretically, an *arch* rotated on its vertical *axis*. See Fig. 83.

**dominant** The fifth *note* of a *diatonic scale*; a *chord* built on the dominant.

**Doric** The oldest of the *classical styles* of temple *architecture*, characterized by simple, sturdy *columns* that rise without a base to an unornamented, cushionlike *capital*.

**dramatis personae** (drah-mah'-tehs pair-soh'-nigh) Actors or characters in a drama.

**drawing** A process of visualization by which an artist, using such *media* as pencil, chalk, or watercolor, delineates *shapes* and *forms* on a *surface*, typically paper or *canvas*.

**duck** See *canvas*.

**duplum** (doo'-pluhm) In the music of medieval *organum*, the second *voice part* counting up from the *tenor* or *cantus firmus*.

**dynamics** In music, the relationship of loud to soft, and the nature of change from one level of *intensity* to another.

**earth work** In the *visual arts* of the contemporary period, an intervention in open nature by the artist for no purpose other than the enactment of his own ideas of art.

**elevation** An *architectural drawing* of the side of a building without *perspective* distortion.

**empirical** Based on experiments, observation, and practical experience without regard to science and theory.

**empiricism** See *empirical*.

**encaustic** A paint *medium* in which the *vehicle* is wax.

**engaged column** A *columnlike form* projecting from a *wall* and articulating it visually.

**ensemble** In music, a group of two or more performers engaged in the same musical enterprise.

**entablature** In architecture, that portion of a building between the *capitals* of the *columns* and the roof, including in *classical* architecture the *architrave*, *frieze*, *cornices*, and *pediment*.

**epic** A long narrative poem in heightened *style* about the deeds and adventures of a hero. Also, simply heroic.

**ethos** (ee'-thahs) Greek meaning "custom" or "character." In art, that which gives a work tone or character and distinguishes it from other works. Also understood to mean the *ideal* or an ethical character. In music, the Greeks associated this with the lyre.

**Evangelist** One of the authors of the four *Gospels* in the Bible: Matthew, Mark, Luke, and John. Respectively, their *symbols* are an angel, a lion, an ox, and an eagle, all derived from Revelations 4:6–10.

**exposition** The presentation of musical materials to be *developed* later; the opening section of a *sonata-form movement* or a *fugue*.

**expression** Having to do with those factors

of *form* and *subject* that together give the work of art its *content* and meaning.

**expressive, expressiveness**  See *expression.*

**expressive content**  The fusion of *form* and *subject* that gives art its meaning and significance.

**façade**  Usually the front of a building; also, the other sides when they are emphasized *architecturally.*

**facture**  The way of making something or the way something has been made; in *painting,* the characteristic of the *medium*—its *texture,* opacity, etc.—as it has been applied.

**ferroconcrete**  A building material composed of concrete with rods or webs of steel imbedded in it. Also known as *reinforced concrete.*

**figuration**  In the *visual arts,* the representation of *forms* and objects seen in nature, however *abstracted* and *schematized* the representations may be. That having to do with the human figure.

**figurative**  See *figuration.*

**figure-ground**  In the *pictorial* arts, the relationship between *imagery* and the *plane, background,* or generalized *space* against which the *images* are seen. Modern *abstract* artists tend to regard figure and ground as a relationship between positive and negative *volumes.* An issue or problem in the *aesthetics* of *form,* it has proved fundamental to the pictorial arts of the modern period.

**finale**  The final *movement* of a large *instrumental composition;* in opera, the *ensemble* terminating an act.

**flat**  A symbol (♭) signifying that the *note* it precedes should be lowered to a *pitch* by one half-step.

**flying buttress**  A *masonry* strut or segment of an *arch* that carries the *thrust* of a *vault* to a *buttress* positioned away from the main portion of the building; an important *structural* element in the *architecture* of Gothic *cathedrals.*

**foreground**  In the *pictorial* arts, that part of the *composition* which appears to be closest to the viewer. See *middle ground* and *background.*

**foreshortening**  The effect of three-dimensionality made in two dimensions by basing *representation* on the principle of continuous diminution in size along the entire length of a *form* whose bulk is intended to be seen as receding in *space.*

**form**  In the *visual arts,* a *shape* or *mass,* or, more comprehensively, the total configuration of shapes, *structure,* and *expressiveness.* In music, the large-*scale* organization, structure, or *design* of a piece; the *ordering* in time of a *composition's* component sections. To give shape to something or achieve *style* in it.

**formal**  See *form* and *style.*

**format**  In the *pictorial* arts, the *shape* (usually rectangular) of the *support* at its edges; also the encompassing *volume* of *space* in relation to which a *sculpture* or building seems to have its *formal* order.

**forte** (for'-teh)  Italian meaning "loud."

**fortissimo** (for-tees'-ee-moh)  Italian meaning "very loud."

**found object**  An object discovered and se-

lected by an artist and exhibited without alteration as an *aesthetic* object, or incorporated without alteration into a more complex *composition* intended to create an aesthetic experience.

**fresco**  A process of *painting* on plaster, either wet or dry, wherein the *pigments* are mixed with water and become integral with the plaster; a *medium* perfected during the Italian Renaissance.

**frieze**  The central portion of the *entablature* between the *architrave* and the *cornice;* any horizontal decorative or *sculptural* band.

**fugal**  See *fugue.*

**fugue** (fewg)  A *polyphonic* composition characterized primarily by the *imitative* treatment of a single *theme* or *subject,* or subject complex.

**gallery**  A long and narrow room or passage, such as that in the *nave walls* above the *aisles* of a *basilican-plan* church.

**genre** (zhahnh'-ruh)  In the *pictorial* arts and *sculpture,* the casual *representation* of everyday life and surroundings. Also, a type, *style,* or category of art.

**geodesic**  *Architectural structure* based on light, straight elements suspended together in a state of *tension.* Used mainly in the *design* and construction of *domes.*

**Gesamtkunstwerk** (guh-zahmt'-koonst-vairk)  German for a "complete," "total," or "consummate work of art"; a term coined in the late 19th century by Richard Wagner to characterize his *music dramas,* in which he brought about an alliance of all the arts—music, literature, theater, and the *visual arts*—to realize a program of ideas.

**glaze**  In *oil painting,* a transparent film of paint laid over dried underpainting; in ceramics, a thin vitreous coating fused to a clay body by firing in a kiln.

**gloriole**  A ring of light, like a large halo, surrounding a figure.

**Gospels**  Ascribed to Matthew, Mark, Luke, and John, the four Biblical accounts of the birth, life, death, and resurrection of Jesus Christ. See *Evangelists.*

**gouache** (goo-ahsh')  Watercolor made opaque by the addition of chalk.

**graphic**  Demonstration and description by visual means.

**graphic arts**  Vaguely related to the *linear* element, a term that identifies the *visual arts* of *drawing,* printmaking, typographic *design,* advertising design, and the technology of printing.

**Greek cross**  A cross in which all arms are the same length.

**Gregorian chant**  *Liturgical* music named for Pope Gregory I (590–604), who codified the divers *chants* prevalent in his time into a single body of music. Also known as *plainsong,* these chants are *monophonic,* unaccompanied *melodies* in free *rhythm* sung partly by soloists and partly by *choir.*

**groin**  See Fig. 83.

**groin vault**  See Fig. 83.

**ground**  A coating, such as *priming* or *sizing,* applied to a *support* to prepare the *surface* for *painting;* also *background.*

**ground bass**  See *ostinato.*

**ground plane**  In the *pictorial* arts, the *surface*

represented as that on which figures seem to stand.

**harmonics**  High-*pitched,* ethereal *tones* produced by touching the string of an *instrument* lightly with the finger so that it vibrates in segments rather than as a whole. See *overtone.*

**harmony**  The vertical or *chordal* structure of musical *composition;* the study of all relationships that can exist between simultaneously sounding *pitches* and the progressions of chords.

**hierarchy**  Any system of persons or things which has higher and lower ranks.

**holistic**  An entity in which significance derives from the *organic* and irreducible relationship between the parts and the whole they make—in which the total configuration is what counts.

**homophonic**  See *homophony.*

**homophony** (hoh-mah'-foh-nee)  Music in which a principal *melody* is supported by *accompaniment* in a *chordal* or harmonic *style.*

**horizon line**  A real or implied *line* across the *picture plane* parallel with its top and bottom edges, which, like the horizon in nature, tends to fix the viewer's eye level, and toward which in *linear perspective* all receding parallel lines seem to converge.

**hubris**  Arrogance, as in a prideful act designed to supplant God with self.

**hue**  The property of *color* that distinguishes one color from another as red, green, violet, etc. See *saturation, value.*

**hymn**  A religious *song* meant to give praise and adoration.

**icon** (eye'-kahn)  Greek for *image,* used to identify *panel paintings* made under Greek Orthodox influence that *represent* the image of a holy person—Christ, Mary, or a saint; such works often imbued with sanctity.

**iconography** (eye'-kah-nah'-grah-fee)  In the *pictorial arts* and *sculpture,* the meaning of the *images* and *symbols* depicted; *subject* matter.

**ideal**  The *representation* of objects, individuals, and events according to a *stylized,* perfected, preconceived model; a kind of *aesthetic* distortion of perceived reality.

**idealize**  See *ideal.*

**idol**  A *representation* or *symbol* of a deity used as an object of worship.

**illusion**  See *illusionism.*

**illusionism**  The endeavor of the artist to *represent* as completely as his *formal* means permit the visual phenomena of a palpably real world, even if imaginary, as in a scene of muscular and voluptuous bodies floating high in the sky.

**image**  A *representation* of an object, an individual, or event. An image may also be an evocation of a state of being in representational or *nonrepresentational* art.

**imagery**  In the *visual arts,* the particular *subjects* and objects chosen by an artist for depiction in a work, or, in the instance of totally *abstract* or *nonrepresentational* art, the particular *forms* and *shapes* with which the artist has *composed* a work.

**imitation**  In musical *composition,* the successive restatement of a *theme* or *motif* in different *voice parts* of a *contrapuntal* complex.

A *canon* is an example of strict imitation; modified forms occur by *inversion, augmentation,* and *diminution.*

**imitative** See *imitation.*

**impasto** (ehm-pah'-stoh) Paint laid on in richly *textured* quantities.

**improvisation** On the spur of the moment, spontaneous musical *composition* at the *instrument.* Also, in the performance of music, adding to the basic composition such decorative embellishments as *chords* and new *melodies;* a major aspect of *jazz* and baroque music.

**incising** Cutting into a *surface* with a sharp instrument.

**instrument** In music, a mechanism capable of generating the vibrations of musical sound. See *string instruments, woodwind instruments, brass instruments,* and *percussion instruments.*

**instrumental** See *instrument.*

**instrumentation** The practice by *composers* of organizing all *instrumental* possibilities for *expressive* purposes. It may also refer to the types and numbers of instruments used in a *composition.*

**intensity** In the *visual arts,* the relative purity or brilliance of a *hue.* In music, the relative softness or loudness of a *tone.*

**interval** In music, the distance between two *notes* as determined by *pitch.* A *melodic* interval occurs when two notes are sounded successively; an *harmonic* interval occurs when two notes sound simultaneously. In the *visual arts,* the distance—real, represented, or implied—between things, such as measurable extent from *foreground* to *middle ground* to *background* or from one *form* to another on the same *plane.*

**intervallic** See *interval.*

**intrinsic** Belonging to a thing by its very nature.

**inversion** In musical *composition,* a means of *imitation* by which the original ascending (or descending) *voice* is imitated by a descending (or ascending) voice at an equivalent *intervallic* distance.

**Ionic** One of the Greek *classical styles* of temple *architecture,* which developed in Ionia in Asia Minor and is distinguished by slender, fluted *columns* and *capitals* decorated with volutes and scrolls.

**isocephaly** (eye'-soh-seh'-fah-lee) In *pictorial composition,* figures arranged so that all heads align at the same level.

**isorhythmic** *Polyphonal* music in which the *forms* are compounded of sections unified by an identity of *rhythmic* relationships but not necessarily of *melodic* patterns.

**jamb** The upright piece forming the side of a doorway or window frame; on the portals of Romanesque and Gothic church *architecture* the locus of *figural* sculpture.

**jazz** An American music, originating in the Black community early in the 20th century, in which *players improvise* on a *melodic theme, expressing* it in a highly personal way with *syncopated rhythms* and *contrapuntal ensemble playing.*

**jongleur** See *minstrel.*

**katharsis** See *catharsis.*

**key** The *pitch* of the *tonic* or *tonal* center within the *tonality* established by the *composer* for a particular piece of music. It is the sum of all the musical relationships that can be perceived by constant comparison with a given pitch level. Also, a mechanism by which an *instrument* (piano, organ, clarinet, valve horn, etc.) can be caused to sound.

**keyboard** The arrangement of *keys* on such *instruments* as the piano, the spinet, and the organ; therefore, "keyboard instruments."

**keystone** See Fig. 83.

**laendler** (lehnd'-lehr) An Austrian peasant *dance* similar in its triple *meter* to a slow *waltz;* popular in the 19th century.

**landscape** In the *pictorial* arts, the *representation* of scenery in nature.

**Latin cross** A cross in which the vertical member is longer than the horizontal member, through whose midpoint it passes.

**leading tone** In music, the seventh degree of a *major* or *minor scale;* it pulls toward or "leads" to the *tonic* a half-step above.

**legato** (leh-gah'-toh) Italian for "tied"; in music, the performance of *notes* in a smooth, continuous line; the opposite of *staccato.*

**leitmotif** (light'-moh-teef) German for "leading motif"; a *melodic theme* introduced by Richard Wagner into *orchestral* writing to characterize an individual, an idea, an inanimate object, etc., and *developed* to reflect transformations in the person, idea, or thing, recalling the past, prophesying the future, or explaining the present.

**lento** Italian for "slow."

**libretto** (lee-breh'-toh) (pl. **libretti**) Italian for "little book"; the text, words, or "book" of an *opera, oratorio,* or other musico-dramatic work.

**line** A mark left in its path by a moving point, or anything, such as an edge, a boundary, or a horizon, that suggests such a mark; a succession of *notes* or ideas, as in a *melodic* line or a line of thought. The *linear* might be considered one-dimensional, as opposed to the *spatial,* which is either two- or three-dimensional.

**linear** See *line.*

**linear perspective** See *perspective.*

**lintel** In *architecture,* a *structural* member that spans an opening between posts or *columns.* See *post-and-lintel* and Fig. 83.

**liturgical** That having to do with *liturgy.*

**liturgy** A rite or body of rites prescribed for religious worship.

**local color** The identifying *color* of an object when it is perceived without shadows under a standard light source.

**lyric** Of or relating to the lyre, such as a *song* to be performed to lyre *accompaniment.* In a modern sense, that which is intensely personal, ecstatic, and exuberant, even poetic. Also (in the plural) words or verses written to be set to music. The lyric theater is that involving words and music, such as *opera* and musical *comedy.*

**madrigal** In the early 14th century, a *secular* two- or three-*voice song* with a fixed *form:* two or three *strophes* set to the same music plus a concluding two-line *ritornello* with different music. The upper voices are usually in a florid *style,* with the lower *notes* written for longer *values.* In the 16th century, a *secular* four- or five-voice *composition* based on love poetry or *lyrics,* with no set form but highly *imitative* and often *homophonic* in passages.

**major** A type of *diatonic scale* in which half-tones or semitones occur between the third and fourth and seventh and eighth degrees of the scale (as opposed to the natural *minor,* in which the semitones occur between the second and third and fifth and sixth degrees). A *key* or *tonality* based on such a scale.

**masonry** In *architecture,* stone or brickwork.

**mass** In the *visual arts,* the actual or implied physical bulk, weight, and density of three-dimensional *forms* occupying real or suggested *spatial* depth. Also, the term for the principal solemn *rite* of the Roman Catholic Church, traditionally containing both sung and spoken parts.

**measure** A standard of comparison; a means; in musical *composition,* a regular division of time, set off on the *staff* by vertical *bars.* In *rhythm* and *metrics,* "measured" means slow and stately.

**medium** (pl. **media**) In general, the process employed by the artist; in a more strict sense the binding substance or *binder* used to hold pigments together, such as linseed oil for *oil paint.* See *vehicle.*

**melisma** (meh-liz'-muh) An extended sequence of *notes* sung to one syllable of text.

**melismatic** See *melisma.*

**melodic** See *melody.*

**melody** Single *tones* organized successively to create a musical line.

**mensuration** Taking the *measure* of things.

**meter** In music and poetry, the scheme of accented and unaccented *beats.*

**metrical, metrics** See *meter.*

**mezzo** Italian for "half," "middle," or "medium"; thus, *mezzoforte* means "medium loud" and *mezzo-soprano* means "middle soprano" or a female *voice* with a *range* between *soprano* and *contralto.*

**middle ground** In the *pictorial arts,* that part of the *composition* which appears to exist between the *foreground* and the *background;* the intermediate of the three zones of recession in *linear perspective.*

**minor** In music, a type of *diatonic scale* in which the *interval* between the first and third *notes* or *pitches* contains three semitones (as opposed to four in a *major scale*). A *key* or *tonality* based on such a scale.

**minstrel** In the 12th and 13th centuries, a professional singing actor or mime in the service of a castle or wandering from town to town and from castle to castle. Also known as *jongleur,* and in an expanded meaning refers to troubadours, trouvères, and Minnesingers.

**minuet** In the 17th century, at the court of Louis IV, an elegant *dance* of peasant origin in triple *meter* and moderate *tempo.* In the 18th century, incorporated as a *movement* (with an overall ABA *form*) into most multimovement *instrumental compositions.*

**mobile** A *constructed sculpture* whose components have been articulated to move by force of wind or motor.

**mode** A particular *form, style,* or manner. In music, the *ordering* of *pitches* into a *scale* pattern, *major* or *minor;* also, a pattern of *rhythm.*

**model** See *modeling.*

**modeling** The *shaping* of three-dimensional *forms* in a soft material such as clay; also, the *representation* on a flat *surface* of three-dimensional forms by means of variations in the use of *color* properties.

**molto** Italian for "much," meaning "very."

**monastery** A dwelling place where monks live in a community for spiritual purposes.

**monastic** That having to do with monks and *monasteries.*

**monochrome** A single *color* or the *value* variations of a single *hue.*

**monophonic** See *monophony.*

**monophony** (moh'-nah-phoh-nee) Music in which one *voice* or a group of voices sings the same *melody.*

**montage** (mohnn-tahzh') In the *visual arts,* a *composition* formed of pictures or portions of pictures previously photographed, painted, or drawn.

**monumental** A work of art or *architecture* that is grand, noble, timeless, and essentially simple in *composition* and execution, whatever its actual *size.*

**motet** A *polyphonic choral composition* with a sacred Latin text that, like its *secular* counterpart, the *madrigal,* had a long and complicated history throughout the Middle Ages and Renaissance. It developed in the 13th century when words *(mots)* were added to the *duplum* (which became known as the "motetus") of the *melismatic organum.*

**motif** In music, a *melodic* or *rhythmic* fragment or *theme* capable of being developed into different and larger contexts. In the *visual arts,* the *subject* or idea of an art work, such as *still life* or *landscape,* or an individual feature of a subject or *form,* usually one that recurs or predominates in the *composition.*

**motive** See *motif.*

**movement** A self-contained section of a larger piece of musical *composition,* such as a *symphony.*

**multiple** An art work realized by a duplication process, such as printmaking and *casting.*

**mural** A *painting* on a *wall,* usually large in *size.*

**mystical** Having a spiritual meaning or reality that can be known only by intuition, insight, or similar subjective experience.

**myth** A legend or story that seems to express the world view of a people or explain a practice.

**narthex** The porch or vestibule of a church.

**natural** In musical *composition,* a sign (♮) meaning that, for the *note* to which it is attached, any previous indications of *sharp* (♯) or *flat* (♭) should be canceled.

**nave** The great central *space* in a church; in *basilican plans* the space extending from the entrance to the *apse,* or to the *crossing* or *choir,* and usually flanked by *aisles.*

**nonobjective** A synonym for *nonrepresentational* art, but not a very workable one, since totally *abstract* art cannot be proved to be any less "objective" than any other kind of art.

**nonrepresentational** In the *visual arts,* works so transcendent in their *abstraction* as to make no reference whatever to the world of persons, places, and the objects associated with them; art from which all identifiable *subject matter* has been eliminated.

**notation** The system and process for writing out music in characters and *symbols* so that it can be read for performance.

**note** A musical sound of a certain *pitch* and duration; the sign in written music for such a sound; a *key* on an *instrument* such as the piano or organ that when pressed makes a specific musical sound.

**obbligato** (oh-blee-gah'-toh) Italian for "obliged," meaning, in music, *parts* that must not be omitted; also, a decorative *line* of music meant to be heard as a foil to the main *melody.*

**octave** The *interval* from one *note* to the next of the same *pitch* name (as from C to C), either higher or lower, which is a span of eight *diatonic* notes.

**oeuvre** (uhv) French for "work"; the whole of an artist's production, his lifework.

**oil painting** The process of *painting* with a *medium* formed of ground *colors* held together with a *binder* of oil, usually linseed.

**opera** A *composition* in which vocal and *instrumental* music merge with a whole *range* of stagecraft to create total theater. In opera, music serves as the principal dramatic agent. Also the plural form of *opus.*

**opus** Latin for "work"; in music a term used with a number to distinguish a particular *composition* or group of compositions within the chronology of the *composer's* total *oeuvre.*

**oratorio** A semidramatic musical *composition* for soloists, *chorus,* and *orchestra,* usually based on a religious text and performed without staging in churches and *concert* halls.

**orchestra** In Greek theaters, the circular *space* before the *proscenium* used by the *chorus.* Also a group of *instrumentalists,* including *string players,* joined together to perform *ensemble* music.

**orchestration** The art and technique of arranging or *scoring* a musical *composition* for performance by the *instruments* of an *orchestra* or band.

**order** In *classical architecture,* a *style* represented by a characteristic *design* of the *column* and its *entablature;* see *Doric, Ionic,* and *Corinthian.* Also the arrangement imposed upon all elements within a *composition;* in addition, a harmonious arrangement. To arrange or organize something, give it order.

**organic** That which is living, such as plants; that which is integral to the whole; a system in which all parts are coordinated with one another.

**organum** From the 9th through the 13th centuries, the earliest *form* of *polyphonal* music, in which one or more *lines* of *melody* sound simultaneously along with the *plainsong* of *Gregorian chant.* In *parallel organum* (9th–10th centuries) an added *voice* runs exactly parallel and below the Gregorian melody. In free organum (c. 1050–1150) the main melody occurs in the lower voice while the upper voice moves in a combination of parallel and contrary motion. In *melismatic* organum (c. 1150–1250) a few *notes* of the main chant or melody are prolonged and sustained in the lower voice while the upper voice moves freely through a melismatic melody with numerous notes occurring for each note in the main chant. Two-part organum is known as organum *duplum;* three-part organum as organum *triplum.*

**ostinato** (aws-stee-nah'-toh) Italian for "obstinate," which in musical *composition* is the persistent repetition over and again, usually in the *bass,* of a clearly defined musical figure or phrase, while other *parts* or *voices* change around and above it. Sometimes called *basso ostinato* or *ground bass.*

**overture** *Instrumental* music written usually to precede an *opera, oratorio,* or *ballet.* It may be an entity unto itself or directly related to the music that follows. Also, a *concert piece* in one *movement,* often with an extramusical reference.

**painting** Traditionally, *painting* has been thought of as an art *form* in which *colors* are applied through a liquid *medium* to a flat, that is two-dimensional, *surface,* called a *ground* or *support.* A dry powder called *pigment* is the coloring agent in painter's *colors,* and, depending on the binding agent or *binder* used, pigments can produce such media of painting as *oil, tempera, watercolor, fresco, encaustic, casein,* and *acrylic resin.* These can be worked on such grounds or supports as paper, *canvas,* wood *panel,* and plaster. If the support has been given a preparatory coating, by *priming* and *sizing,* the surface thus *formed* is considered to be the *ground,* which intervenes between the painting and its support.

**painterly** *Painting* in which the buttery substance of the *medium* and the gestural aspect of paint application constitute a principal aspect of the art's quality.

**palette** A tray or shaped *planar surface* on which a painter mixes his *colors;* also the characteristic *range* and combination of colors typical of a painter or a *style* of *painting.*

**panel** Any rigid, flat *support* for *painting,* such as wood, usually prepared with a *ground.* Any flat, slablike *surface,* usually rectangular in shape.

**pantheon** All the gods of a people; a temple dedicated to them; a public building containing tombs or memorials of the illustrious dead.

**papiers collés** (pahp-yay' cawl-lay') See *collage.*

**parallel organum** See *organum.*

**part** In musical *composition,* the writing for a single *instrument* or *voice* or a group of them; also, a section of a composition.

**pathos** Greek meaning the experience of emotion, grief, or passion. In art, an element that evokes pity or sympathy. Also that which deals with personal and transitory experience or emotions, as opposed to those which are universally significant.

**pediment** In *architecture*, the triangular *space* or gable at the end of a building, *formed* in the *entablature* by the sloping roof and the *cornice.*

**percussion instruments** Drums, celesta, chimes, triangle, tambourine, castanets, gongs, cymbals, glockenspiel, etc., all of which must be struck or shaken to make a musical sound.

**performing arts** The arts that have their full existence only in time and that to realize full existence must be *played*: music, *dance,* and drama.

**peristyle** A *colonnade* surrounding a temple or court.

**perspective** A *pictorial* technique for simulating on a *flat,* two-dimensional *surface,* or in a shallow *space,* the three-dimensional characteristics of *volumetric forms* and deep space. During the Renaissance in Italy, a quasi-mathematical scheme called *linear perspective* developed from the fact that parallel lines going in one direction away from the viewer must be seen as converging toward a single point on the horizon known as a *vanishing point.* Placed, in this system, at *intervals* along the assumed and converging parallels, objects are scaled in their *sizes* to diminish in relation to their distance from the *picture plane.* In northern Europe, at about the same time, painters developed a perspective system known long before to the Romans and the Chinese. Called *atmospheric* or *aerial perspective,* the system effected blurred outlines, loss of detail, alteration of *hues* toward the *cool colors,* and the diminution of color *saturation* and *value* contrast—all in proportion to the distance of the object from the viewer. See *foreshortening.*

**phenomenology** The study of the progressive development of the human mind, from a philosophical point of view; the description of the actual physical appearance of things as these can be perceived by the senses.

**piano** Italian for "soft"; *pianissimo* means "very soft"; *pianississimo,* "extremely soft."

**pictorial** That having to do with the *flat* arts of *painting* and *drawing* and, to a certain extent, with the art of *bas-relief,* in that its three-dimensional *subject matter* and *imagery* are *composed* in relation to a flat rear *plane* that physically is parallel to and only slightly behind what would be a *picture plane* and whose edges constitute a frame or *format* of specific *shape* like that of a picture. Picture or pictorial *space* is that of the *support,* which is a flat *surface* defined by a specific shape, usually rectangular. To achieve here, at the picture plane on the support, the appearance of deep space, the artist must employ such *illusionistic* devices as *modeling, foreshortening,* and *perspective* so that, in a *still life* or *landscape,* for instance, objects and *forms* seem to rest firmly on a *ground plane* at *intervals* beginning in the foreground and moving through the *middle ground* to the *background* and beyond.

**picture plane** An imaginary vertical *plane* assumed to be at the front *surface* of a *painting.*

**pier** (peer) A *mass* of *masonry* rising vertically to *support* an *arch, vault,* or other roofing member.

**pietà** (pee-ay-tah') A devotional *image* of the sorrowing Virgin holding the dead Christ.

**pigment** Finely powdered coloring matter mixed or ground with various *vehicles* to *form* paint, crayons, etc.; also a term used loosely to mean *color* or paint.

**pilaster** (pigh'-lass-tehr) In *architecture,* a shallow, *flat,* vertical member projecting from a *wall surface* and, like a *column,* articulated as a base, shaft, and *capital.* Usually more decorative than *structural.*

**pillar** Any vertical architectural member—*pier, column,* or *pilaster.*

**pitch** A musical *tone,* or its relative highness or lowness as fixed by the frequency of the vibrations occurring per second within it.

**pizzicato** (pits-ee-kah'-toh) Italian for "plucked"; in musical *composition* an instruction to the performer to pluck the *strings* of an *instrument* instead of bowing.

**plainsong** From early medieval Christian worship, a type of sacred music or *liturgical chant, monophonic* in *style* and set to a Latin text. See *Gregorian chant.*

**plan** An *architectural drawing* that reveals in two dimensions the arrangement and distribution of interior *spaces* and *walls,* as well as door and window openings, of a building.

**planar** See *plane.*

**plane** A *surface* that is defined and measurable in two dimensions.

**plastic** That which is capable of receiving physical *form;* therefore, the *visual arts.* More narrowly, that which is pliant and malleable enough to be *modeled;* therefore, the material of *sculpture.*

**plasticity** The three-dimensional quality of a *form,* its roundness and apparent solidity; the capability of material for being *shaped, modeled,* and manipulated.

**play** A literary text consisting of dialogue *composed* to be acted out in dramatic *form* for the benefit of an audience. To give effect to and bring to life in time any one of the *performing arts.*

**player** One who *plays;* a performer.

**plot** In literature, the plan or scheme of the story and its unfolding action.

**poco** Italian for "little."

**podium** A platform, base, or pedestal for a building or a monument.

**polychrome** Several *colors* rather than one (monochrome).

**polyphony** (pah-lif'-ah-nee) "Many-voiced" music; musical *composition* in which two or more *melodic lines* are heard simultaneously. *Counterpoint* is the technique used for composing polyphonal music.

**post-and-lintel** In *architecture,* a *structural* system employing two uprights or posts to *support* a member, the *lintel* or beam, that spans the *space* between the uprights.

**prelude** A musical *composition* designed to introduce the main body of a work, such as an *opera;* a separate *concert* piece for piano or *orchestra,* usually based on a single *theme.*

**presto** Italian for "fast."

**primary colors** *Colors* that in various combi-

nations are capable of creating any other color or *hue.* In artists' *pigments* these are red, yellow, and blue; in natural or "white" light, they are red, green, and blue. See *color, complementary colors.*

**prime** To prepare a *canvas* or *panel* for *painting* by giving it a *ground* of white paint or one made with a gluey or resinous substance called *size.*

**program music** *Instrumental* music based on a story or an extra-musical idea, in which occurs the conscious imitation of bird calls, bells, thunderstorms, hunting scenes, etc., all in a sequence of episodes designed to make narrative or dramatic sense.

**proportion** The relation, or ratio, of one part to another and of each part to the whole with regard to *size,* height, width, length, or depth.

**proscenium** (proh-shee'-nee-uhm) From the Greek meaning "before the *skene*"; the proscenium *arch* is that which is set before the stage *space* and enframes it in traditional theaters.

**prosody** The art of setting words to music. Also, a particular system or *style* of versification.

**psalter** (sahl'-tehr) A book of the psalms (hymns) found in the Bible.

**range** The extent and limitation of a *series,* such as the *notes* that a human *voice* is capable of singing, or a sequence or *values* from light to dark.

**recital** See *concert.*

**recitative** (rehss-ih-tah-teev') In *opera, oratorio,* and *cantata,* a *form* of declamation that, although highly *stylized* and set to music, follows the *pitch* and *rhythms* of speech more than a *melodic* line. Recitative tends to serve a narrative function and often leads into an *aria* or connects arias and *ensembles.*

**register** A *range* (upper, middle, lower) within the capacity of the *voice,* human or *instrumental.*

**reinforced concrete** See *ferroconcrete.*

**relief** A *plane* that exists three-dimensionally as a projection from a *background.* Also, *sculpture* that is not freestanding but projects from a *surface* of which it is a part. When the projection is relatively slight, it is called *bas-relief* ("low relief"); when pronounced, the term is "high relief."

**reliquary** A small box, casket, or shrine for keeping sacred relics, usually made and decorated of precious materials.

**render** To reproduce or *represent* by *graphic* means.

**represent** See *representation.*

**representation** The depiction or illustration by the *graphic* means of the *visual arts* (lines, values, colors, etc.) of *forms* and *images* in such a way that the eye would perceive a correspondence between them and their sources in the real world of *empirical* experience.

**representative style** A type of *word painting* by which the descriptive *imagery* of the text is reflected in the *shape* and turn of the *melodic lines.*

**requiem** (reek'-wee-ehm) A *mass* for the dead.

**rhythm** In the *visual arts,* the regular repetition of a *form*. That aspect of music having to do with the relative duration of *notes* in time.

**rhythmic** See *rhythm*.

**rib** In *architecture*, a slender *arched support* that in a *vault* system typically projects from the *surface* along the *groins* where semicircular vaults intersect each other. Ribs both reinforce the vaults and articulate them *aesthetically*.

**ribbed groin vault** A *groin vault* reinforced with *ribs*.

**ritardando** In music, the gradual slowing of *tempo*.

**ritornel, ritornello** Italian for "refrain"; a recurrent passage in a *concerto, rondo, operatic* scene, etc.

**rondo** A musical *form* in which one main *theme* recurs to alternate with other themes, making a *structure* that can be diagrammed as ABACADA.

**sanctuary** A consecrated, sacred, or holy place; in Christian *architecture*, that part of the building where the *altar* is placed; also a refuge.

**sarcophagus** (sahr-kahf'-ah-guhs) A stone coffin.

**satire** Greek for "satyr *play*"; a witty exposure of vice and folly, the purpose of which is to effect moral reform.

**saturation** The purity, vividness, or *intensity* of a *color*.

**scabellum** Latin for "cymbals."

**scale** Relative or proportional *size*. In music, a succession of *pitches* or *tones* that together, in either ascending or descending *order*, make an *octave*.

**schematize** The process of reducing the identifying characteristics of a *form*—the human head, a plant, a building, etc.—to its diagrammatic essentials; a process of *abstraction*.

**scherzo** (skair'-tzoh) Italian for "joke"; in *sonatas, symphonies,* and quartets, a *movement* substituted for the *minuet* and, like the minuet, *composed* in ¾ *meter* but at a faster *tempo*. Normally, the scherzo is linked with a trio in a sequence of scherzo, trio, and scherzo repeat.

**score** The written version of music, with all *parts* indicated both separately and in relation to one another. To prepare music in written *form*.

**sculptural** That which is *plastic* or has to do with *sculpture*.

**sculpture** A type of three-dimensional art in which *form* is created by subtractive or additive methods. In subtractive sculpture the form is found by removing (as in carving) material from a block or *mass*. In additive sculpture, the form is built up by *modeling* in clay, by *constructing* with materials as a carpenter or welder might, or by *assembling* such preexistent forms as *found objects*. Whatever the method, the final form can be *cast* in a material, such as bronze, that modifies from a liquid state to a hard and permanent one. Sculpture can be freestanding or *relief*.

**section** An *architectural drawing* showing the side of a building without *perspective* distortion.

**secular** Not religious, but relating to the worldly or temporal.

**sedes** See *cathedra*.

**sequence** In musical *composition* the repetition of a *melody* or *motif* at different *pitch* levels.

**serenade** See *divertimento*.

**shade, shaded** See *shading, value*.

**shading** The property of *color* that makes it seem light or dark. See *value*.

**shape** A two-dimensional *area* or *plane* with distinguishable boundaries, such as a square or a circle, which can be *formed* whenever a *line* turns or meets, as in an S-shape or a T-shape.

**sharp** A sign (♯) in musical *composition* instructing the performer to raise the *note* it precedes one half-step higher.

**silhouette** A *form* as defined by its outline.

**size** The physical magnitude of objects, *forms*, elements, and quantities. See *scale*; also *prime*.

**skene** (skay'-nuh) In the theaters of ancient Greece, which were open-air, the small building that provided for performances both a stage and a background. It is the root word for "scene" and "scenery."

**sonata** (soh-nah'-tah) Italian for "sounded"; in musical *composition*, a work composed in three or four *movements*.

**sonata form** See pp. 309, 310.

**song** A literary text set to music for *vocal* performance, with or without *instrumental accompaniment*.

**soprano** The highest *range* of the female *voice*, or an *instrument* with this range. Also, the *line* in musical writing corresponding to the soprano range.

**space** A *volume* available for occupation by a *form*; an extent, measurable or infinite, that can be understood as an *area* or a distance, one capable of being used both negatively and positively.

**spacing** See *space*.

**spatial, spatiality** That having to do with *space*.

**spectrum** The full array of rainbow *colors* that appear when white light (sunlight) has been refracted into its component wavelengths by means of a transparent substance, such as a prism.

**springing** See Fig. 83.

**staccato** (stah-kah'-toh) Italian for "detached"; in musical *composition* an instruction to perform *notes* in a short and detached manner. The opposite of *legato*.

**staff** The five horizontal *lines* and four intervening *spaces* on which musical *notation* can be written out. See *clef, bass, treble*.

**stereotype** Something conforming to a fixed or general pattern.

**still life** In the *pictorial* arts, an arrangement of inanimate objects—fruit, flowers, pottery, etc.—taken as the *subject* or *motif* of a work of art.

**stoa** (stoh'-ah) In the *agoras* of ancient Greece, a building of one or two stories in the *form* of a *colonnade* or roofed portico providing *space* for a walkway and shops, offices, and storerooms.

**stretcher** A wooden or metal framework upon which a painter's *canvas* can be stretched.

**string intruments** The violin, viola, violoncello (or cello), and double bass, all of which are equipped with strings capable of generating musical sound when either stroked with a bow or plucked.

**string quartet** An *ensemble* of two violins, viola, and cello; a *composition* in *sonata form* written for such an ensemble.

**structural** See *structure*.

**structure** The *compositional* relationships in a work of art; a building or other constructed *architectural* unity; the operative framework that *supports* a building.

**style** *Form* and *style*, "formal analysis" and "stylistic analysis"—these terms serve interchangeably in any discussion of the way artists work or the way their art works once it has been accomplished. Professor Meyer Schapiro, an authority on the subject, has defined style as ". . . the constant form, qualities, and expression in the art of an individual or group." Both form and style are concerned with those quantitative and measurable aspects of art that caused the elements, principles, and materials to come together as a *composition*; but they are equally concerned with the *expressive* effect all this has and the way the expressiveness has been effected. Form and style signify a sensitive, knowing, trained, and controlled *shaping* and *ordering* of ideas, feelings, elements, and materials. The artist who has achieved form and style has attained mastery and individuality in all that constitutes his art. Style can be the identifying characteristic of the work of a single artist, of a group of artists, or of an entire society.

**stylize** To simplify or generalize *forms* found in nature for the purpose of increasing their *aesthetic* and *expressive* effect.

**subject** In the *visual arts*, the identifiable objects, incidents, and situations represented. See *iconography*. In music, the *theme* or *melody* used as the basic element in the *structure* of a *composition*, as in a *fugue*.

**subject matter** See *subject*.

**suite** (sweet) In music, a collection of miscellaneous *movements* without specific relationships in *key* or musical material. The music usually is *dancelike*, since suites before 1750 consisted almost invariably of four principal dance movements: the allemande, the courante, the sarabande, and the gigue. Often, simply excerpts from *scores* for *ballet* and *opera*.

**support** In the *pictorial* arts, the physical material serving as a base for and sustaining a two-dimensional work of art, such as paper in the instance of *drawings* and prints, and *canvas* and board *panels* in *painting*. In *architecture*, a sustaining *structural* member.

**surface** The two-dimensional exterior *plane* of a *form* or object.

**symbol** A *form, image*, sign, or *subject* standing for something else; in the *visual arts*, often a visible suggestion of something invisible.

**symbolize** See *symbol*.

**symmetry** An arrangement or balanced *design* in which similar or identical elements have been organized in comparable *order* on either side of an *axis*.

**symphonic poem**  *Program music* in one long *movement*.

**symphony**  A musical *composition* in *sonata form* written for full *orchestra*.

**syncopation**  Stressing a *beat* that normally should remain weak or unaccented.

**synoptic** (sighn-ahp'-tick)  Affording a general, comprehensive, broad, or common view.

**synthesis**  The deduction of independent factors or entities into a compound that becomes a new, more complex whole.

**tabernacle**  A receptacle for a holy or precious object; a container placed on the *altar* of a Catholic church to house the consecrated elements of the Eucharist.

**taste**  The evidence of preference having to do with enjoyment and appreciation.

**tempera**  A *painting* technique using as a *medium pigment* mixed with egg yolk, glue, or *casein*.

**tempo**  In music, the pace or rate of speed at which the *notes* progress.

**tenor**  The highest *range* of the male *voice*, or an *instrument* with this range. Also, the *line* in musical writing corresponding to the tenor range.

**tensile**  In *architecture, structure* that is capable of sustaining *tension*.

**tension**  Balance among opposing forces; a state of unrest. In *architecture*, stress from two forces moving in opposite directions, like the pulling and stretching imposed on bridge cables.

**terra-cotta**  Italian meaning "baked earth"; baked clay used in ceramics, *sculpture,* and *architectural* decoration; also a reddish-brown *color* similar to the color of baked clay.

**texture**  In the *visual* or *plastic arts*, the tactile quality of a *surface* or the *representation* of that surface. In music, the relationship of the *melodic* elements and the elements that *accompany* them, and the particular blend of sound these create.

**thematic**  See *theme.*

**theme**  In music, a short *melodic* statement or an entire self-contained melody; *subject matter* to be treated *compositionally* through *development, imitation,* contrast, *variation,* expansion, juxtaposition, etc.

**through-composed**  An *opera* with the whole of its text set to music; music that varies according to the needs of the text, instead of following a preconceived pattern of repeats and contrasts.

**thrust**  A strong continued pressure, as in the force moving sideways from one part of a *structure* against another.

**timbre** (tam'-behr)  *Tone color,* or the particular quality of sound produced by a *voice* or an *instrument.*

**toccata** (toh-kah'-tah)  Italian for "touched"; music composed for the touch system of *keyboard instruments,* typically written in a free *style* with running passages, *chords,* and sometime *imitative* sections.

**tonal**  See *tone* and *tonality.*

**tonality**  See *key.*

**tone**  In music, a *note*; that is, a sound of definite *pitch* and duration. In the *visual arts,* a general coloristic quality, as this might be expressed in a degree of *saturation* and *value.*

**tone poem**  See *symphonic poem.*

**tonic**  The *key note* of a *tonality,* which is the first and principal note of the key, serving for music *composed* in the key as a place of rest, a home base, a point of departure and return.

**tragedy**  A serious drama or other literary work in which conflict between a protagonist and a superior force (often fate) concludes in calamity for the protagonist, whose sorrow excites pity and terror in the beholder and produces *catharsis.*

**transept**  In a *cruciform* church, the whole arm set at right angles to the *nave,* which makes the *crossing.*

**treble**  In music, the higher *voices,* both human and *instrumental,* the *notes* to whose music appear on a *staff* identified by a treble *clef* (𝄞).

**triad**  In music, the simultaneous sounding of three *notes* to make a *chord* of only three *pitches* built up in thirds from the root note.

**triforium**  In church *architecture,* an *arcaded* area in the *nave* wall system that lies below the *clearstory* and above the *gallery,* if there is one, and the nave arcade. It can be open like a gallery or be sealed (blind).

**triplum**  In the music of medieval *organum,* the third *voice* part counting upward from the *tenor* or *cantus firmus.*

**trompe-l'oeil** (trohmp-luh'-yuh)  French for "fool the eye"; a type of *representation* in *painting* in which the *illusion* of *form, space,* light, and *texture* has been so cunningly contrived as to convince the observer that what he perceives is the actual *subject matter* and not a two-dimensional equivalent.

**trumeau** (troo'-moh)  A post or pillar placed in the center of a *portal* to help *support* the *lintel* above, especially in medieval *architecture.*

**tune**  A *song* or *melody*; a musical *key*; the correct *pitch* or *tonality.*

**tunnel vault**  See *barrel vault.*

**tympanum** (tihm'-pah-nuhm)  In medieval *architecture,* the *surface* enclosed by a *lintel* and an *arch* over a doorway; in *classical* architecture, the recessed face of a *pediment.*

**unity**  The quality of similarity, shared identity, or consistency to be found among parts of a *composition*; a logical connection between separate elements in a work of art; the opposite of *variety.*

**value**  The property of *color* that makes it seem light or dark; *shading.* In music, the duration of a *note.* In general, the relative worth accorded to an idea, a concept, or an object.

**vanishing point**  In *linear perspective,* that point on the horizon toward which parallel *lines* appear to converge and at which they seem to vanish.

**variations**  A section of music that follows a *theme* section and alters it in some respects while duplicating the theme in others, as in theme-and-variation *compositions.*

**variety**  Contrast and difference, the lack of sameness among separate elements in a *composition*; the opposite of *unity.*

**vault**  A *masonry* or concrete roof constructed on the principles of an *arch.* See Fig. 83.

**vehicle**  The liquid in which *pigments* are dispersed to make paint. See *binder, medium.*

**verisimilitude**  The appearance of being true to the reality of the tangibly present world; in the *visual arts,* a kind of naturalism or realism. See *illusionism, representation, trompe-l'oeil.*

**visual arts**  Those arts that appeal to the optical sense—*painting, sculpture, drawing, printmaking, architecture,* etc.

**vivace** (vee-vah'-cheh)  Italian for "lively" or "vivacious."

**voice**  The sound made by the human throat or by a musical *instrument*; the *part* in music written for that sound.

**void**  A hollow or empty *space.*

**volume**  Any three-dimensional quantity that is bounded or enclosed, whether solid or void.

**volumetric**  See *volume.*

**votive**  From the Latin for "vow," an offering made to God or in His name in petition, in fulfillment of a vow, or in gratitude or devotion.

**voussoir** (voo'-swahr)  See Fig. 83.

**wall**  In *architecture,* a *plane*like upright *structure* and *surface* capable of serving as a *support,* barrier, or enclosure.

**waltz**  A *dance* in moderate ¾ time that developed from the Austrian *laendler* in the early 19th century.

**warm colors**  *Hues* in the red, yellow, orange, and sometimes violet sections of the *spectrum.* Psychologically, warm colors tend to excite and stimulate; optically, they appear to advance.

**wind instruments**  See *woodwind* and *brass instruments.*

**woodwind instruments**  The flute, oboe, English horn, clarinet, bass clarinet, bassoon, contrabassoon, and saxophone, all of which are pipes with holes in the side and can produce musical sound when blowing causes their columns of air to vibrate. Several of the woodwinds have mouthpieces fitted with reeds.

**word painting**  See *representative style.*

# Index

References are to page numbers, except for black-and-white and color illustrations, which are also identified by figure and plate numbers. Works have been listed under the names of their creators—composers, painters, poets, sculptors, etc. Architectural works and the paintings, sculptures, mosaics, etc., associated with them—in other words, the visual arts not collected into museums—have additionally been listed under the cities where they can now be found. The purpose of this feature is to serve the reader who may have the opportunity to travel and wish to use *Arts & Ideas* as a handbook-guide to the monuments it discusses. The Table of Contents should be consulted for further guidance to passages on periods, styles, media, and ideas. Unless repeated in the text, the events, births, and deaths cited in the Chronologies at the opening of chapters have not been indexed. Also excluded from the Index are the definitions provided in the Glossary, which commences on page 439.

baroque, 280–282, 283; and the Enlightenment, 294–295

Rauschenberg, Robert, 406, 420, 437; *Monogram*, 406 (Fig. 407), 411

Ravel, Maurice, 367; *L'Enfant et les Sortilèges*, 380

Ravenna, Italy, 77, 93–95, 97, 98, 110, 155; and authoritarianism, 95–96; 5th–6th century, 77–88; in mosaic, 79 (Fig. 89), 82, 83 (Fig. 95); music of, 93–94; mysticism of, 96–97; Arian Baptistry, *Baptism of Christ and Procession of Twelve Apostles*, 85 (Fig. 99); San Vitale, 83–85 (Figs. 97, 98), 86 (Fig. 102), 87–88, 95–96, Byzantine capital of, 88 (Fig. 105), music of, 94–95, *Emperor Justinian and Courtiers*, 87 (Fig. 104), 89, 97; Sant' Apollinare Nuovo, 73, 79–83 (Figs. 89, 90), 84, 85, 94, 96, *Good Shepherd Separating the Sheep from the Goats*, 82, 91 (Pl. 9), *Last Supper*, 82 (Fig. 94), *Procession of Virgin Martyrs*, 82–83 (Fig. 95), Mausoleum of Galla Placidia, 78 (Fig. 88), 79, 86

realism, Hellenistic, 58–60; in literature, 349, 352; 19th-century, 336, 351, 360; 20th-century, 419

recitative, 255, 279, 288, 350

Reinhardt, Ad, 405, 412

relativism, 392–394

relief sculpture. *See* high relief, low relief, frieze

Rembrandt van Rijn, 228, 257, 258, 260–264, 270, 282, 315, 438; *vs.* Vermeer, 268; *Christ Healing the Sick*, 262 (Fig. 279); *Dr. Tulp's Anatomy Lesson*, 261 (Fig. 278); self-portraits, 262–263 (Figs. 280–283); *Portrait of Jan Uytenbogaert, Receiver General*, 259 (Fig. 277); *Night Watch*, 250 (Pl. 37), 261–262

Renaissance, term explained, 181; dying of, 218; early Italian, 149–163; Florentine, 164–184, 188, 220, 369; and mannerism, 219; revival of, 330; Roman, 185–201; style of, 205, 241, 331; Venetian, 202–217

Renoir, Pierre Auguste, *Le Moulin de la Galette*, 353 (Pl. 49), 355

Renwick, James, 331; Grace Church, 332 (Fig, 343); St. Patrick's Cathedral, 332

requiem mass, 157–158. *See also* Berlioz

revolutions, American, 330; February 1848, 313, 331, 349; French, 285, 292, 294, 296, 303–304, 309, 317, 330, 331; July 1830, 313, 317, 322, 330, 331

Rheims, France, 127, 132, 137, 141; cathedral of, 136, 323

Rigaud, Hyacinthe, *Louis XIV*, 242 (Fig. 262)

rococo, the, 9, 249 (Pl. 34), 267–268 (Pls. 39, 40), 283, 285–288 (Figs. 303–308), 289 (Figs. 309, 310), 291, 294, 295, 296, 312, 397, 417

Rodin, Auguste, 336, 344, 346, 351, 359; *The Bronze Age*, 344, 345 (Fig. 355); *Gates of Hell*, 344, 345 (Fig. 356); *Hand of God*, 344, 345 (Fig. 358); *The Thinker*, 344; *Three Shades*, 344, 345 (Fig. 357)

Rolland, Romain, 11, 309, 310; *Jean Christophe*, 394

Romano, Giulio, 219; Palazzo del Tè, 207 (Fig. 222)

romanticism, 285, 336, 406; *See also* Chapter 19

Rome, Italy, 9, 61, 93, 97, 98, 127, 149, 163, 203, 222, 228, 252, 270, 283, 295, 296–297, 303, 308, 380; early 16th-century, 185–188; 5th-century, 78–79; late 16th- and early 17th-century, 224–225; legendary foundation of, 254; music at, 198, 199, 215, "new," 93, 94; 2nd-century, 62–71; Ara Pacis Augustae, *Imperial Procession*, 61 (Fig. 66); Arch of Septimus Severus, 300, 312; Arch of Titus, 62; Basilica Ulpia, 65–66 (Figs. 72, 73), 67, 71, 75; Baths of Caracalla, 68 (Figs. 77, 78), 71; Baths of Diocletian, 68; Baths of Titus, 186; Baths of Trajan, 67, 71; Castel Sant' Angelo (Hadrian's tomb), 77 (Fig. 87), 84, 224; Il Gesù (G. Vignola and G. della Porta), 225–227 (Figs. 240–242); San Carlo alle Quattro Fontane (Boromini), 227–228 (Figs. 243–245); San Pietro in Montorio, Bramante, Tempietto, 199–200 (Fig. 209); San Pietro in Vincoli, 189. *See also* Michelangelo, *Moses* and Tomb of Julius II; Sant' Ignazio, 225; Santa Maria del Popolo, 185, Caravaggio, *Conversion of St. Paul*, 228–229 (Fig. 246); Colosseum, 68–69 (Fig. 79), 71, 73, 75; Column of Trajan, 64, 65 (Fig. 72), 71–73 (Figs. 84, 85); Forum of Trajan, 10, 63–67 (Figs. 68, 69, 71), 71, 75; Palazzetto dello Sport (Nervi), 432 (Figs. 430, 431); Pantheon, 42 (Pl. 7), 69–70 (Figs. 81, 82), 85, 86, 165, 197, 200, 201, 299, 303; Pons Aelius, 77 (Fig. 87); St. Peter's Basilica, 70, 80, 185 (Fig. 193), 188–189, 197–198 (Figs. 206–208), 199, 225, 226, 233, 274, apse and dome, 197–198 (Fig. 208), Old St. Peter's, 80–81 (Figs. 91, 92), Bernini's Piazza, 185 (Fig. 193), 229; Temple of Vesta, 8; Vatican, The, 191 (Fig. 201), 194, 297, 308, Sistine Chapel, 438, Michelangelo's ceiling frescoes, 186, 188, 191–194 (Figs. 201–205), 196 (Pl. 25), 197, 221, 225 (Fig. 239), music in, 187, 239; Stanza della segnatura, Raphael, *School of Athens*, 194, 196 (Pl. 26), 197

Ronchamp, France, Notre-Dame-du-Haut (Le Corbusier), 426, 430 (Figs. 426, 427)

Roosevelt, Franklin D., New Deal, 398–399

Rosenberg, Harold, 400

Rosenthal, Bernard, *Alamo*, 414 (Fig. 413), 415

Rothko, Mark, 399, 403, 405, 406, 412; *Green and Maroon*, 403, 408 (Pl. 71)

Rouault, Georges, *Guerre*, 383; *Miserere*, 383; *This Will Be the Last Time, Little Father*, 383 (Fig. 390)

Rouen, France, 127, 131; cathedral of, 136, 341, 413; Gothic house, 146 (Fig. 155)

Rousseau, Jean Jacques, 255, 285, 288, 291, 295, 332; *Le Devin du Village*, 332

Rubens, Peter Paul, 210, 220, 223, 228, 251–252, 268, 287, 288, 291, 315, 316; *vs.* Poussin, 253–254, 257; ceiling painting for Whitehall Banqueting House, 272; *Garden of Love*, 249 (Pl. 34), 251, 287; *Henry IV Receiving Portrait of Maria de' Medici*, 251 (Fig. 271); *Rape of Daughters of Leucippus*, 252 (Fig. 272)

rubricator, defined, 106

Rude, François, 313, 317–318, 323, 331; *Departure of the Volunteers of 1792*, 300, 317–318 (Fig. 334); *Joan of Arc Listening to the Voices*, 318 (Fig. 335)

Ruisdael, Jakob van, *The Jewish Graveyard*, 264–265 (Fig. 286); *Quay at Amsterdam*, 258, 259 (Fig. 276), 264

Saarinen, Eero, 397, 432; Gateway Arch, 433, 434 (Fig. 436); Trans World Flight Center, 433 (Figs. 434, 435), 438

St. Ambrose, 94

*St. Anne with Virgin*, 138 (Fig. 152)

St. Anthony, 110, 222

St. Augustine, 97, 110, 160; *Confessions*, 94; in El Greco painting, 236 (Fig. 257), 237

St. Benedict, 98, 162

St. Bernard, 145

St. Denis. *See* Paris

St. Francis, 149, 150–154, 157–164; frescoes of life, 151–154 (Figs. 158–161), 161–162; poetry of, 182; *Canticle of the Sun*, 156–159, 160; Basilica of. *See* Assisi

St. Ignatius Loyola. *See* Loyola

St. John, 103–104, 105, 108, 111, 112, 212, 239

St. John the Baptist, 105, 222, 369; in mosaic, 85 (Fig. 99); in sculpture, 90 (Fig. 108)

St. John Chrysostom, 94, 97

St. John of the Cross. *See* John of the Cross

St. John the Evangelist, 222

St. Louis, Missouri, Gateway Arch (Saarinen), 433, 434 (Fig. 436); Wainwright Building (Sullivan), 386 (Fig. 394)

St. Mark, 203. *See also* Venice

St. Martin-in-the-Fields. *See* London

St. Mary-le-Bow. *See* London

St. Omer, Evangeliary of, 92 (Pl. 12), 106

St. Paul, 93, 105, 110; in Caravaggio's painting, 228, 229 (Fig. 246). *See also* London

St. Peter, 79, 105, 112, 123, 173, 212. *See also* Rome

St. Sernin. *See* Toulouse

St. Trophîme. *See* Arles

SS. Sergius and Bacchus. *See* Istanbul

Saint-Saëns, Camille, *Danse Macabre*, 328

Salamanca, Spain, Casa de las Conchas (Gomez de Mora), 235 (Fig. 254); Church of San Esteban, Churriguera altarpiece, 235 (Fig. 255), La Clérica (Gomez de Mora), 235 (Fig. 254)

Salisbury, England, Cathedral, 148 (Fig. 157)

San Carlo alle Quattro Fontane. *See* Rome

San Marco Monastery. *See* Florence

San Vitale. *See* Ravenna

Sansovino, Andrea, 185, 217

Sansovino, Jacopo, 205, 206, 207, 233; Library of St. Mark's, 203 (Fig. 214), 205

Sant' Ambrogio. *See* Milan

Sant' Apollinare in Classe. *See* Classe

Sant' Apollinare Nuovo. *See* Ravenna

Sant' Ignazio. *See* Rome

Santa Croce. *See* Florence

Santa Maria del Carmine. *See* Florence

Santa Maria della Salute. *See* Venice

Sartre, Jean Paul, 400, 437; *The Flies*, 382, 438

Satie, Erik, 422; *Desiccated Embryos*, 380; *Mercury*, 381

Savonarola, Girolamo, 200, 201, 203

Scamozzi, Vincenzo, *Procuratie Nuove*, 207 (Fig. 221)

Scheidt, Samuel, *Tablatura Nova*, 270

Schoenburg, Arnold, 361, 367, 369, 370–371, 394, 397, 421, 422, 424; *Die Glückliche Hand* and *Pierrot Lunaire*, 369

Schöffer, Nicolas, *Prime Multiple with Lux II*, 416 (Fig. 416)

Schola Cantorum, 107

scholasticism, 161; Aristotelian, 224; Gothic, 145, 146–148

Scholia enchiriaduo, 110, 187

Schönbrunn Palace. *See* Vienna

Schopenhauer, Arthur, *World as Will and Idea*, 335

Schumann, Robert, 325, 326, 327

Schutz, Heinrich, 223

science, 351–352

Scopas (?), School of, *Dionisian Procession*, 30 (Fig. 44)

Scott, Walter, 313, 321, 325, 329; *Rob Roy* and *Waverly*, 329

scriptorium, defined, 106

*sedes*, defined, 90 (Fig. 108)

sequence, musical, 157–158

Seneca, 74, 296, 311

serialism, 412–413, 416, 417; musical, 413, 420, 421, 422–423

Sérusier, Paul, *Landscape: The Bois d'Amour (The Talisman)*, 343, 357 (Pl. 54)

Seurat, Georges, 379; *Sunday Afternoon on the Island of La Grande Jatte*, 341, 355 (Pl. 51)

Severini, Gino, *Armoured Train*, 372 (Fig. 377)

Shahn, Ben, *Miners' Wives*, 383–384 (Fig. 392)

Shakespeare, William, 291, 295, 306, 325, 329; *Hamlet*, 313, 323; *Macbeth*, 323, 324, 395, 437; *The Merchant of Venice*, 34

Shelley, Percy B., 310, 311, 316; *Hellas*, 43

Sicily, Palace of the Norman Kings, 114, 115 (Fig. 128)

Siena, Italy, 149, 154, 155, 203

Sinfonia, 215, 216

*Singspiel*, 291

Sistine Chapel. *See* Rome

Sistine Chapel Choir, 186, 198, 225

Sixtus IV, Pope, 186, 191, 198

skene, defined, 30

skolion, defined, 56

Smith, David, 399, 405, 412, 438; *Cubi* series, 404 (Fig. 405), 415

Smith, Tony, *Smoke*, 414 (Fig. 412), 415

social realism, 364, 383–385, 397

Society of Jesus, 10, 224, 225, 229, 233, 240–241, 282, 283

Socrates, 12, 13, 33, 34, 36, 38, 39, 43, 55, 56, 57, 60, 97, 181, 310

solmization, Guido's system of, 107–108

sonata, 309, 397

*Song of Roland*, 118–119, 120, 122–124

Sophists, 13

Sophocles, 13, 15, 30, 35, 36, 43; *Antigone*, 29, 381, 395; *Elektra*, 369; *Oedipus Rex*, 30, 32, 39, 381

Sosus, *Unswept Dining Room Floor*, 53 (Fig. 56)

Souillac, France, Church of Notre Dame, *Isaiah*, 111 (Fig. 124)

Southey, Robert, *Thalabor the Destroyer*, 334

space, cubists and, 369–370; deep, 207; early Christian concept of, 97, 139; Renaissance, 173; 20th-century view of, 393, 394, 400, 402, 412, 413; Venetian, 217

space-time, 364, 393, 394

Spain, 222, 223, 225; influence of, 224

Spinoza, Baruch, 258, 271

Spohr, Ludwig, *Faust*, 292, 326

Spontini, Gasparo, 297, 309; *La Vestale*, 308–309, 312

Squarcialupi, Antonio, 165, 180, 183, 200

squinch, defined, 86 (Fig. 101)

*Stabat Mater Dolorosa*. *See* Jacopone da Todi

stained glass, 395; of Chartres, 129, 131–132, 134, 135, 138–141 (Figs. 153, 154), 143 (Pl. 17), 148; making of, 139; of Ste. Clotilde, 323; of Notre-

Index  **453**